Yearbook on

International

Communist Affairs

1978

Yearbook on

International

Communist Affairs

1978

EDITOR: Richard F. Staar

Associate Area Editors:

Eastern Europe and the Soviet Union	Milorad M. Drachkovitch
Western Europe	Dennis L. Bark
Asia and the Pacific	Ramon H. Myers
The Americas	William E. Ratliff
Middle East and Africa	Lewis H. Gann
International Communist Front Organizations	Witold S. Sworakowski

HOOVER INSTITUTION PRESS
STANFORD UNIVERSITY, STANFORD, CALIFORNIA

Hoover Institution Publication 195

CONTENTS

Asia and the Pacific

The Americas

Middle East and Africa

International Communist Front Organizations (Paul F. Magnelia)

PREFACE

"Indispensable" is a word to be used rarely and carefully. But one would be absolutely accurate in saying that the *1978 Yearbook on International Communist Affairs* truly is indispensable for all who seek to understand the modern world, whether they are political scientists, those involved in the making of public opinion, or statesmen and diplomats directly concerned with the conduct of foreign affairs.

Like its eleven predecessors (though the 1978 volume seems to be even more comprehensive and informative), it covers every aspect of world politics for those interested in the power and progress of the various communist movements—and how can anyone seriously concerned with the fate of our planet fail to be so concerned?

The mere scope of this array of profiles, written by specialists, is unique and covers the entire world from the Politburo in Moscow to full details on the illegal pro-Soviet "Communist Party of Yugoslavia," from the Standing Committee in Peking to factions in the 350-member-strong (and split) Communist Party of New Zealand. The clarity, detail, and essential documentation, are equally impressive.

Moreover, though dealing in principle with the communist element everywhere, the contributors in every case give a general political and national background of the countries they consider in a way rarely to be found in so concentrated and generally useful and instructive form.

Thus, I am sure I can speak for all who feel called upon to study the USSR, or China, or the communist movement in the world at large, in saying that this is a reference work without which they would be severely handicapped. With the best will in the world, how can we keep up with the progress of a movement which is admittedly the main opponent of Western attitudes in all its various—and often mutually hostile—manifestations, in Thailand, or Colombia, in Poland or Cambodia. Yet, even as to the last named, it should surely be evident by now that the West's interests, even its whole future, may be involved in an understanding of the politics of an otherwise obscure Asian land.

Thus we have a series of expert, yet easily assimilated, essays and summaries—a concentrated wealth of information to be found, I believe, nowhere else. For many years, one of the great gaps in public understanding of the world was absence of information—in particular, information about the communist countries and the communist movements outside them. Misunderstandings arose, to put it mildly. Whatever else may be said about the Vietnam war, one thing is quite clear: those in charge of the American war effort did not understand the motivations of the Politburo in Hanoi. They were unaware that it did not accept the language of escalation and the signals and responses our side thought automatic for any rational political leadership. To put it another way, our representatives were unable, for lack of the imaginative and intellectual effort they did not realize was required, to see 'the other side of the hill.'

The massive information given in this *Yearbook* will not in itself correct such cultural insularity, but it will go a long way in that direction. Delusions common for years among politicians, journalists, and others concerned with molding policy or opinion, could not have arisen if they had briefed themselves adequately on the mere *facts* registered so fully in these pages.

In the current state of international affairs, there are those who speak of the crux in international relations in the epoch before us as being no longer centered on the issues between the West and the

USSR. Some talk, instead, of a "North-South" division having replaced the "East-West" relationship as crucial. But how can this be, when the USSR is the single power in open rivalry with the West, which matches, or overmatches, the West in armaments, and looms large and continual on the West's frontier? And, moreover, how is this possible when all the problems arising in other, supposedly more crucial, spheres are invariably complicated, or exacerbated, or even created, precisely by the presence of the USSR, either in the form of puppet Cuban mercenaries, or in the blue-ocean navy offshore, or in political or other forms of intervention through trained agents or intermediaries?

Views which ignore the importance of such matters should at least be modified by a careful consideration of the facts recorded here—of the intricate interlocking of Soviet-sponsored political and other movements throughout the world. Indeed, given the decline of the effect of the Soviet myth in many Western circles, and given also the various splits in the communist movements, one of the most striking lessons of a true examination of world communism is how widely Soviet infallibility is still accepted, from the Communist Party of Chile to the Communist Party of South Africa. Need one add that a careful consideration is needed of the extent to which the so-called Eurocommunist parties, while criticizing some specific Soviet actions unpopular with their own electorates, still support the USSR against the West? The vital facts are here; indeed there is hardly a page in this book which is not relevant to some extent to the great issues before us. The Hoover Institution, and Richard Staar in particular, are to be congratulated on making available to scholars and statesmen alike such a mass of information which is not merely relevant, but crucial, to international understanding and the avoidance of international illusion.

Palo Alto, California   Robert Conquest

INTRODUCTION

The purpose of the *1978 Yearbook on International Communist Affairs*, the twelfth consecutive volume in this series, is to provide basic data and preliminary evaluations concerning organizational and personnel changes, attitudes toward domestic and foreign policies, and activities of communist parties and international front organizations throughout the world. Much of the information comes from primary source materials in the native languages. Profiles on each party include founding date, legal or proscribed status, membership, electoral and parliamentary (if any) strength, leadership, auxiliary organizations, domestic activities, ideological orientation, views on international issues, attitude toward the Sino-Soviet dispute, and principal news media. Identity as a Marxist-Leninist party remains the criterion for inclusion and, hence, pro-Soviet, pro-Chinese, Castroite, Trotskyist, as well as other rival communist movements, are treated whenever applicable.

Excluded from the *Yearbook* are Marxist liberation movements and Marxist ruling parties that specifically disclaim being communist. The Frente de Libertação de Moçambique (FRELIMO), for example, has transformed itself into a political party and governs the People's Republic of Mozambique. It has announced a Marxist program and is organized on the basis of "democratic centralism," but is not, properly speaking, a communist party. The Movimento Popular de Libertação de Angola (MPLA) also reorganized itself into the Popular Movement Workers' Party and rules most of the People's Republic of Angola; it derives support from Soviet advisers and Cuban armed forces in a continuing struggle against opposition. The Partido Africano de Indêpendencia de Guiné e Cabo Verde (PAIGC) is the ruling party of Guinea-Bissau. MPLA and PAIGC both share FRELIMO's general orientation; they also have been excluded.

The ruling movement in the Congo People's Republic, the Parti Congolais du Travail, claims to be Marxist-Leninist; its leaders state that they are communists committed to "scientific socialism." But the party is not regarded as an orthodox Marxist-Leninist movement by its peers. The president of the Congo People's Republic has stated that, while Marx's writings remain valid, they must be adapted to local conditons. The ruling Somali Revolutionary Socialist Party, while likewise committed to establishment of "scientific socialism," is in a similar category. The same applies to the National Front in the People's Democratic Republic of Yemen and the Party of the People's Revolution in the People's Republic of Benin (previously known as Dahomey).

Leftist organizations of an oppositional type, such as the Mouvement National pour l'indépendance de Malagasy (Monima), the Eritrean Liberation Front, as well as the so-called national liberation movements in Bahrain, former Spanish Sahara (Polisario), Rhodesia (ZANU and ZAPU), and South-West Africa (SWAPO) are not discussed. Omitted also because of insufficient data are groups such as the communist parties of the Faroe Islands, Hong Kong, Jamaica, Lesotho, the Maghreb, Malta, Nigeria (the Socialist Workers' and Farmers' Party), Pakistan, and Saudi Arabia, even though their Marxist-Leninist orthodoxy may not be in dispute. The following is a brief summary of *Yearbook* highlights for 1977.

Membership. Among the communist movements in ninety-eight countries, only sixteen of which are in power, fewer than one-third (twenty-eight) operate as secret organizations and are proscribed by the authorities. Membership is estimated or claimed to be in excess of 70 million. Most of the 5.5

million growth during the past year can be accounted for by the Chinese who announced that their party had increased by 5 million to 35 million or exactly one-half of the world's total.

In geographic terms, the East European ruling movements grew by approximately 500,000 over the past year, most of which growth accrued to the 16.2 million-member Soviet party. The movements throughout Western Europe made no appreciable gains. Almost two-thirds of their total reported membership was in the Italian party.[1] The difficulty in establishing accurate figures can be seen from the British example. The movement claims 26,000 members, yet a former communist alleges that the true figure is only 4,000. The same allegation is made regarding the movement in France which boasts 632,814 but, in fact, supposedly has only 386,000 members.[2]

Apart from the ruling communist parties on the China Mainland, North Korea, Vietnam, Cambodia, Mongolia, and Laos, the remaining fifteen Asian movements total fewer than 650,000 members. Those in Burma, Malaysia, the Philippines (pro-Chinese only), and Thailand belong to the insurgent category, for which an estimate of hard-core membership is all but impossible.

The total in both Americas remained about the same despite revised estimates lower for Argentina and Canada, but higher for Mexico. The largest movement, including almost two-thirds of the total membership in the twenty-seven Western Hemisphere parties, is the ruling one in Cuba. The CPUSA claims 18,000 members, an increase of 3,000 over last year; but this figure is probably inflated, although perhaps not as much as in Great Britain or France as mentioned above.

The seventeen movements throughout Africa and the Middle East boast approximately 16,000 adherents, a decline of almost 4,000 in the course of one year. According to a communist source, only four of these are recognized as active in the forty states of Black Africa below the Sahara: the Communist Party of South Africa, the African Party of Independence in Senegal (PAI), the Workers' and Farmers' Socialist Party in Nigeria, and the Communist Party of Lesotho.[3] In fact, the first of these movements mainly operates in exile; the remaining three are devoid of significance.

Much more successful in terms of size and propaganda activity are the international front organizations. Eight of the twelve on which data could be found claim a membership of over one-half billion, or more than seven times the total for all communists throughout the world. Probably only a small fraction of the non-party members should be counted as genuine adherents to the international communist movement.

USSR and Eastern Europe. Three events dominated the internal political life of the Soviet Union. Politburo member and titular chief of state, Nikolai V. Podgorny, was eliminated from the leadership on 16 June 1977, and later replaced in the USSR presidency by Leonid I. Brezhnev. Election of seventy-six-year-old Vasily V. Kuznetsov as first deputy chairman (vice-president) indicated that Brezhnev was unwilling to promote a younger and more prominent individual who could become a political rival. On 7 October the Supreme Soviet unanimously ratified a new constitution replacing the 1936 one, which had been called Stalin's. The new Brezhnev constitution does not make any real change in the political machinery of the system, although it codifies in explicit terms the role of the communist party as "the leading and guiding force in Soviet society." These two developments were followed by celebration of the October Revolution's sixtieth anniversary which confirmed the dominant role of General Secretary Brezhnev.

Related campaigns dominated the Soviet political scene throughout the year. Massive efforts to re-indoctrinate both the party and society with Marxist-Leninist ideology as well as systematic

---

[1]*Za rubezhom,* no. 41, Moscow, 1977, p. 11. The 1,850,000 total for Italy allegedly is the count after an exchange of communist party identification cards.

[2]Sid French, quoted by Pat Jordan, "The British Communist Party in Crisis," *Intercontinental Press,* London, 12 December 1977, p. 1373; Jean Montaldo, *Les Finances du P.C.F.,* Paris: Albin Michel, 1977, p. 236; cited from book review in *Free Trade Union News,* XXXII, no. 12, December 1977, p. 10.

[3]Khristo Mashkov, "The Revolutionary Process in Tropical and Southern Africa," *Policheska prosveta,* no. 8, Sofia, August, 1977, pp. 102-09.

propaganda/repression campaigns against dissidents represented two sides of the same coin. The fight against human rights' activists, particularly monitoring groups to observe implementation of the Helsinki accords being reviewed at the conference in Belgrade during the latter part of 1977 and into early 1978, continued unabated. There were frequent arrests, commitments to psychiatric institutions, treason charges, and sentences to jail or internal exile. Repressive measures hit Jews applying for emigration, the predominantly Russian civil liberties' groups, and various ethnic and religious activists. The problem of dissent took on special meaning in view of the human rights policies of the new administration in Washington, D.C. The two most publicized events of the year included the reply on 17 February by President Carter to a letter from Andrei Sakharov and reception at the White House on 1 March of former political prisoner Vladimir Bukovsky.

Adding to Soviet problems was the mediocre performance of the economy. A disappointing grain harvest brought in only 195 in comparison with 224 million tons for the previous year. Scarcities continued to plague the construction, consumers' goods, metal-working, coal, and forestry industries and created even greater problems. All of this culminated in lowering goals for the current five-year-plan, 1976-1980. Steel output should level off for the first time in three decades, and the target for heavy industry is an increase of 4.5 percent and for the consumer sector only 3.7 percent.[4]

Party and government activities in the international arena were extensive, marked by rigidity in ideology but flexibility in practice. Although the new phenomenon of Eurocommunism occasionally received doctrinal criticism and official spokesmen insisted on "proletarian internationalism," i.e., Soviet leadership of the international communist movement, USSR leaders appeared careful enough not to push their relations with Italian, French, and Spanish communists to the breaking point. Representatives of these three parties attended the sixtieth anniversary celebration of the Bolshevik revolution in the Kremlin, attesting in this way their alignment with Moscow. However the Spanish leader Santiago Carrillo was not permitted to speak, and French leader Georges Marchais failed to attend.

There were no indications that Moscow had changed its thesis about the correlation of world forces having tilted irreversibly in its favor. Editor of *World Marxist Review,* Konstantin Zarodov, whose radical views in 1975 had elicited Brezhnev's approval, surfaced again as spokesman for the tough line.[5] His theme of the Bolshevik revolution as model for all others received official sanction the following month. Politburo member and KGB chief Yuri A. Andropov stressed the importance of revolutionary violence on the 100th anniversary of Cheka founder Feliks Dzerzhinsky's birth.

This world outlook and considerations of prestige as a superpower undoubtedly explain continuing efforts to strengthen the Soviet military arsenal as well as to engage by proxy in politico-military intervention, especially throughout Africa. Such a stance does not exclude diplomatic moves of a different kind, explainable in terms of Lenin's legacy and extolled by Brezhnev at the twenty-fifth party congress as the "USSR's peace policy." Consequently, normal and friendly relations with bourgeois governments are encouraged, as exemplified by Brezhnev's state visit in June to France.

Over-all relations with the United States fluctuated; open and occasionally acerbic verbal disagreements, especially about human rights, were balanced by a readiness to make limited agreements. U.S. Secretary of State Cyrus Vance brought Moscow new and unexpected SALT II proposals in March which were bluntly rejected. Compounded by the Carter administration's human rights policy, this seemed to represent a serious blow to detente between the superpowers. During the next several months, despite verbal skirmishes at the Belgrade conference, the two sides again moved toward accommodation. In a press conference, President Carter stated that "on SALT, a comprehensive test ban, the Indian Ocean, and many other items, we have had a very constructive relationship with the Soviet Union."[6]

---

[4]Announced by Gosplan Chairman N.K. Baibakov, according to the *New York Times* (18 December 1977).

[5]*Pravda,* Moscow, 26 August 1977.

[6]Cited in the *New York Times* (16 December 1977).

The so-called constructive relationship could not have pertained to developments in late 1977 and early 1978. Doubling the size of Soviet and Cuban military missions, delivery by air and sea of arms to Ethiopia, accelerated tests of a major new long-range submarine-launched missile, as well as the public accusation by a former defense secretary[7] that withheld evidence proved repeated violation of SALT I accords by the Soviet Union, all raised the specter of a grave threat to United States' security.

In relations with other governments, the ledger of USSR transactions had both credit and debit entries. It is a fact that strengthening the new "Marxist-Leninist" regimes in Angola and Mozambique has opened politico-strategic perspectives with regard to Rhodesia and the Republic of South Africa. However, the earlier ploy of simultaneously offering friendship and aid to Somalia as well as to Ethiopia resulted in bitter estrangement of the former and uncertainty regarding the latter. The proximity of views between Egypt and the Sudan, cemented by anti-communism, and the spectacular rapprochement between Egypt and Israel appeared to push the Soviets into exclusive reliance upon the radical Arab camp: Algeria, Iraq, Libya, South Yemen, and the Palestine Liberation Organization. These developments shattered the USSR objective of becoming the sole protector of a unified "anti-imperialist" Arab world.

Likewise, relations with China did not improve after Mao's death. The Soviet position in India appeared less favorable than under Indira Gandhi's rule which also complicated the standing of local pro-Moscow communists. The unresolved problem of the Southern Kurile Islands, among others, affected negotiations with the Japanese government. It contributed to continuing unfriendly relations with the major Eurocommunist movement outside of Western Europe, namely, the Communist Party of Japan.

Conditions within East-Central Europe, whose stability is guaranteed by the presence of thirty-two Soviet divisions stationed in Czechoslovakia, East Germany, Hungary, and Poland presented many similarities. On the other hand, the ruling communist party in each individual country displayed its own distinctive features.[8]

All party-states in the region were forced to cope with the same kinds of problems. Mounting economic difficulties, some of their own making, others reflecting the broader problems of the world economic order, included: unsatisfactory foreign trade balances, rapidly growing indebtedness toward the West, and necessary yet politically sensitive revision of the retail price structure. Satisfaction of energy requirements for all East European client states became jeopardized by the poor performance of the Soviet economy. Another problem involved the Belgrade conference to appraise fulfilment of the Helsinki accords, which gave human and civil rights activists in the Soviet bloc an opportunity to reaffirm their belief in these rights and to point out violations. Czechoslovakia became the focal point, due to its "Charter 77" movement,[9] harsh repressive measures against it, and the solidarity shown abroad.

Finally the controversy over Eurocommunism between Moscow and the largest West European parties attracted much attention throughout East-Central Europe, especially in Hungary and Poland. To cope with this problem, bloc secretaries for ideology and foreign policy met at Sofia during 2-3 March 1977 and called for intensification of the ideological struggle against capitalism. They also condemned the so-called imperialist propaganda campaign, Eurocommunism being allegedly one of its fabrications. At the end of June, a much larger conference took place at Prague, sponsored by *World Marxist Review* and attended by representatives of seventy-five communist movements. It reached similar conclusions, but reactions to Eurocommunism continued to vary considerably from party to party.

As in the recent past, with the exception of those in Albania and Yugoslavia, all ruling

---

[7]Melvin R. Laird, "Arms Control: The Russians are Cheating!," *The Reader's Digest*, no. 12, December 1977, pp. 97-101.

[8]R.F. Staar, "Soviet-East European Relations," *Current History*, LXXIV, no. 436, April 1978; lead article.

[9]Signed by about 700 Czechoslovaks. A new statement denouncing violation of human and civil rights is being planned for January 1978 (*New York Times*, 19 December 1977).

movements in the region were firmly aligned with inter-party and foreign policies of the Soviet Union. Bulgarian, Czechoslovak and East German[10] leaderships remained unconditionally loyal. Poland was above all preoccupied with its domestic economic crisis, and U.S. President Carter promised $200 million in credits for grain purchases during his 30 December 1977 visit to Warsaw. Hungary pursued a policy of moderation but showed concern about unfavorable developments in its New Economic Mechanism. Romania experienced labor unrest, centered on a prolonged and widespread miners' strike. Flamboyantly staged celebrations on Tito's eighty-fifth birthday in May, as well as a visit to three continents (including the USSR, North Korea, and Mainland China during August-September) emphasized his unique role for Yugoslavia's domestic cohesion and external nonalignment. Albania continued in its anachronistic isolation, openly criticizing the policies of Mainland China and verging on a break in relations with its only ally.[11]

Western Europe. Over the past several years, two principal themes increasingly have tended to dominate the domestic and foreign policy positions of local communist parties: "Unity of the Left" and detente or peaceful coexistence between communist-ruled and other states. These themes continued to receive attention from most of Western Europe's twenty-four communist movements. Both, however, were overshadowed by the constant discussion of Eurocommunism throughout 1977 and into 1978.

This is defined as a specific form of revisionist communism, currently strong in Western Europe. Three general characteristics are commonly ascribed to the term: (1) independence from Moscow, (2) commitment to the parliamentary system and bourgeois-type civil liberties, and (3) the practice of inner-party democracy.[12] However, not one of these points has been endorsed unanimously by all of Western Europe's communist parties. Some of these movements (those of Austria, Cyprus, Denmark, the Federal Republic of Germany, Finland, Iceland, Ireland, the Netherlands, Norway, Portugal, and West Berlin) either openly reject the term "Eurocommunism," as does the Communist Party of the Soviet Union, or take no clear position on its meaning.

What emerges clearly in 1978 is that Eurocommunism, as well as the activities of individual West European communist parties, presents a major challenge to the West. While the movements in France, Italy, and Spain have received the greatest public attention, activities of most parties (especially those in Britain, Sweden, and the liberal faction of the CP in Finland) continue to focus ultimately on gaining power by means of establishing credible reputations as legitimate participants in the democratic electoral process, the primary objective behind the "Unity of the Left" slogan.

The questions at issue prompted a former secretary of state, in his first major foreign policy address since leaving office, to analyze this challenge as follows:[13]

> To be sure, the French, Spanish and Italian communist parties have all recently declared their resolve "to work within the pluralism of political and social forces and to respect guarantees and develop all individual and collective freedoms." Enrico Berlinguer and Georges Marchais pledged their devotion to national independence and political pluralism at a conference of communist parties in East Berlin in June 1976. But can we take these declarations at face value? After all, Marchais has listed Bulgaria, Poland, and East Germany as countries having a "pluralistic" party system.

---

[10]See, however, the article in *Der Spiegel,* XXXII, no. 1, Hamburg, 2 January 1978, pp. 19-24, which suggests the existence of a revisionist movement which may even exist in the top East German leadership. There is some question about the authenticity of the information on which the article is based (*Washington Post,* 3 January 1978).

[11]See Louis Zanga, "Das aussenpolitische Modell Albaniens," *Osteuropa,* XXVII, no. 9, Aachen, September 1977, pp. 767-80; Nicholas Pano, "Albania in the 1970s," *Problems of Communism,* XXVI, no. 6, November-December 1977, pp. 33-43.

[12]*The Guardian,* London, 20 November 1977.

[13]Henry A. Kissinger, *Communist Parties in Western Europe: Challenge to the West,* Stanford, California: Hoover Institution Press, 1977, p. 6; address at a conference on Italy and Eurocommunism, co-sponsored by the Hoover Institution and the American Enterprise Institute in June 1977 at Washington, D.C.
See also Jean-Francois Revel, "The Myths of Eurocommunism," *Foreign Affairs,* LVI, no. 2, New York, January 1978, pp. 295-305.

Another major concern expressed by the same speaker was that "there are now many people on both sides of the Atlantic who have permitted themselves to be convinced that European communism is only social democracy with a Leninist face."

In early 1978, with legalization of the movement in Spain the previous year, a total of sixteen among Western Europe's twenty-four parties are now represented in their respective parliaments. (Austria, Faroe Islands, the Federal Republic of Germany, Great Britain, Ireland, Malta, Turkey, and West Berlin have no communists in their legislatures.) Three party members hold cabinet or sub-cabinet positions in Finland. During 1977 national elections were held in seven West European countries. In four of these (Belgium, Denmark, the Netherlands, Norway), the communist vote declined slightly. In Greece, two parties won 11 (previously 8) of the 300 seats in parliament; the Spanish communists captured 9 percent of the vote which gave them 20 out of 350 seats. In Ireland, the party received only a negligible vote.

Communist representation continues to be largest in Italy, where the party has slightly more than one-third of the seats in parliament. The next highest percentage (over 25) is in San Marino, followed by Iceland and Finland (each with 18), Portugal and France (about 15), and Luxembourg (almost 8.5 percent). None of the remaining nine parties held even 6 percent of their respective parliamentary seats (see checklist).

These statistics do not illustrate the dramatic growth of influence exercised by Western Europe's three major communist movements, especially since mid-1976. Italian, French, and Spanish parties all have endorsed Eurocommunism as a vehicle, allegedly independent of Moscow, for achievement of power. During the latter part of 1977, attention shifted to the French movement. Its official line appeared in an article by Jean Kanapa, who received an important platform in the Council on Foreign Relations's prestigious quarterly. He wrote that[14]

> In order to pull out of her crisis, France must start on the right path toward democratic changes in her structures and in her objectives in every area. It is this uninterrupted extension of democracy which will lead the country to socialism, a socialism which must be authentically democratic.

Although other communist assertions about protecting individual liberty, pluralism, and private property were strikingly similar to those made by communist leaders in Bulgaria, especially Czechoslovakia, East Germany, Hungary, and Poland between 1944 and 1947, they seemingly had no effect on the March 1977 municipal elections throughout France. The leftist coalition (communist, socialist, and left radical) won 51 percent of the vote. As a result, it now controls local government in 157 of the 221 cities and towns with more than 30,000 population. This represents 71 compared to only 44 percent (or 97 cities) previously. Growth in communist membership reportedly has been equally striking. During the two calendar years 1976 and 1977, the party claimed an increase from 491,000 to an even 600,000 members.[15]

While events in Italy were not as dramatic, the movement there, with more than a third of the seats in parliament, exercises a crucial impact on the political situation. Its influence at municipal, province, and national levels is growing. As the most powerful in Western Europe, the Italian communists stand to benefit or lose from any increase or decline in the strengths of their sister parties in France and Spain. They again are demanding an emergency government that would include themselves, Christian Democrats, Republicans, Socialists, Liberals, and Social Democrats.[16]

The Spanish movement has emerged as the foremost champion of Eurocommunism, with the spring 1977 publication of Santiago Carrillo's book *Eurocomunismo y estado*. Throughout the year,

---

[14]Jean Kanapa, "A 'New Policy' of the French Communists?," *Foreign Affairs,* LV, no. 2, New York, January 1977, p. 282.

[15]"Eurocommunism: The Long, Long March away from Stalin," *The Economist,* London, 5 November 1977. However, see note 2 and what it documents.

[16]The *New York Times* (19 December 1977).

the author underscored his party's commitment to democratic processes. He emphasized that advocates of Eurocommunism agreed on the need to work for socialism by respecting human rights and freedoms, by accepting the multi-party system and parliamentary elections. In his book he assailed the Soviet Union for ignoring the fact that "the international communist movement is not a church, that Moscow is not Rome, that we do not accept the existence of a holy office . . . which can excommunicate or bless us." However, in the same volume, Carillo's vision of the future includes disappearance of "private enterprise" which will be replaced with "national planification."[17]

At a meeting held in Madrid during early March 1977 (attended by Enrico Berlinguer, Georges Marchais, and Carrillo), the three leaders reaffirmed their commitment to a multi-party system, democratic freedoms and independence, and the necessity for adapting communist tenets to the conditions of one's own country. During the following several months, Soviet newspapers and journals[18] denounced Carrillo for trying to split the international communist movement and accused him of playing into the hands of "reactionary imperialist forces." All forms of Eurocommunism were denounced as the creation of "bourgeois political theorists" who desired West European communists to cease being communists. Although King Juan Carlos received Carrillo in private audience early in December, the two largest socialist trade unions agreed to merge later that month as a counterweight against the communist-led Workers' Commissions.[19]

While the three above-mentioned movements remained the strongest proponents of Eurocommunism, others (Belgian, the British at their December 1977 congress, Portuguese, Swedish, and Swiss) indicated that they were sympathetic toward the electoral coalition in France, which really involves united front tactics.

However, the French party unexpectedly undertook to revise its Common Program with the socialists during the summer. As a consequence of the attempt to expand proposed nationalization from nine to fifteen major companies and from 1,100 to 1,450 subsidiaries, a major rift developed among the three coalition partners. Neither the socialists nor the left radicals agreed to the proposed changes. They also opposed newly raised communist proposals, e.g., changes in the minimum wage law, tax legislation, and wage differential limitations.

The role communists would play in a new socialist-led government received major public attention, including which ministerial posts they might occupy and the question of veto power over decisions. Nationalization assumed added importance, because trade union influence on management of industries could enable communists to control the nationalized sector through their domination of the largest French trade union (Confederation Generale du Travail).

Negotiations on a revised Common Program broke off in September 1977, and it remains uncertain how the leftist coalition will contest the 12 and 19 March 1978 legislative elections. A leftist victory is now less probable than it appeared to be only a few months ago. It is possible, however, that the coalition will re-group around a simple electoral agreement for mutual second ballot withdrawal.

The dilemma that confronts French voters is that, if the coalition wins in 1978, it will introduce fundamental changes and probably create economic problems of such magnitude that instability almost certainly will follow. Public expenditures forecast by the communists would require an annual growth rate of 13 percent, and they propose that each percentage point increase in the GNP should be accompanied by a 14 percent growth in imports. If these proposals are carried out "there

---

[17]Santiago Carrillo, *Eurocommunismo y estado*, Barcelona: Editorial Critica, 1977, pp. 218; Hugh Thomas, "Senor Carrillo's Schism," *Encounter,* XLIX, no. 10, October 1977, p. 65.

[18]M. Suslov, "Marxism-Leninism and World Revolutionary Renewal," *Kommunist,* no. 14, Moscow, September 1977, pp. 13-28.

[19]The new General Union of Workers, resulting from a merger between the Socialist Workers' Party-controlled union bearing the same name and the Syndical Workers' Union, will have about 1 million members compared with 1.1 million in the Workers' Commissions (*New York Times,* 19 December 1977).

would be a staggering deficit in the French international balance of trade, collapse of the franc, and runaway inflation. The French economy would quite literally collapse under the strain."[20]

Activities of communist movements elsewhere in Western Europe did not attract as much attention, but their views were influenced by developments in France, Italy, and Spain. Portuguese leader Alvaro Cunhal resigned his parliamentary seat to devote full time to party work. He emphasized the need to develop a new image of moderation on the assumption that economic difficulties would force the socialists to turn to other political groups for support. Despite collapse of the government, this had not occurred prior to the end of 1977.

In Great Britain and Ireland, the communist parties themselves did not warrant serious attention. In parliamentary elections, the Irish communists won no seats. Several prominent members, who resigned during the year, are now organized into a Eurocommunist group called the Irish Marxist Society. In Britain a potentially more serious split developed on the basis of a new policy platform entitled "The British Road to Socialism." The first change in the party program since 1968, it endorsed support for a left-wing Labour government pledged to the destruction of "monopoly capitalism." The statement was judged too moderate by some members, and in July 1977 they formed the New Communist Party which is pro-Soviet in orientation. It does not approve of Eurocommunism and opposes dropping references to "dictatorship of the proletariat," as in France.[21]

In the Nordic countries of Finland, Iceland, Norway, and Sweden, the activities of local parties produced only two significant changes. During 1977, the Finnish communists regained what they had enjoyed two years before, becoming the only West European movement with three members in the cabinet or at sub-cabinet level (Agriculture, Labor, and deputy minister of Educaton). A split occurred in the Swedish movement which resulted in formation of a new Communist Workers' Party with about 4,500 members. It is anti-Eurocommunist.

In the Federal Republic of Germany (FRG) and West Berlin, traditional pro-Soviet positions were maintained by the largest among the communist groups. The chairman of the West German party expressly rejected Eurocommunism as an attempt by FRG socialists to divide the movement. While the Moscow-oriented communists did not encourage terrorist activities, the FRG experienced a rash of assassination, kidnapping, bombing, and bank robbery during the entire year committed by extremist left-wing groups. Links have been uncovered between the Red Army faction, previously known as the Baader-Meinhof gang, in West Germany and the Communist Frontline in Italy.[22]

Toward the end of the year, the 300 communists in the 23.4 square mile republic of San Marino were invited to form a government and report back to the captains regent on its composition by 29 December 1977. Although they hold only sixteen of the sixty seats in parliament, the twenty-five Christian Democrats had lost support of the nine socialists. The communists came within one vote of a majority and, thus, failed.[23] At year's end, the socialists were given a chance to form a coalition, with parliamentary elections probably scheduled for March 1978.

Asia and the Pacific. This area saw communist movements engaged in consolidation and retrenchment. In many cases, this meant a decline in membership and influence. For others, it brought reappraisal and reassessment of policies and activities. The majority of the parties concluded their meetings with strong calls for unity and demands that members study doctrine more seriously and apply the proper tactics.

---

[20]Xavier Marchetti, "The French Left and the March Election," *The Washington Review of Strategic and International Studies,* I, no. 1, January 1978, p. 47. The author is a former assistant to Georges Pompidou.

Actually, the French CP has advocated a reorientation in foreign trade which would ameliorate the balance of payments' problem in contradiction to the above.

[21]Pat Jordan, op. cit., pp. 1370-76, provides a detailed analysis of this development (see note 2). One should add that the communist party, though numerically tiny, holds important trade union posts and has some influence in the Labour Party.

[22]*New York Times* (28 December 1977).

[23]Ibid. (25 and 31 December 1977).

In Japan the party had lost more than half of its seats (down to 17 out of 511) in the lower house of the Diet after the December 1976 national elections. This trend continued, with a drop from 20 to 16 seats in the upper house, where only half, or 126, were up for election in July 1977. The electoral fiasco was due probably to intransigence by the USSR on the fishery and northern territory issues, even though the Japanese communists called for the return of the latter and projected a Eurocommunist "image." It was not surprising, then, that the fourteenth party congress in mid-October placed emphasis on how to improve education of party members and how to increase the movement's size to its former half-million all time record.

That same month in Sri Lanka, both the pro-Moscow communist movement and the (Marxist) Lanka Sama Samaja party lost all seats they had held previously in the 151-seat parliament, 6 and 19, respectively. Both had withdrawn from the coalition led by Mrs. Bandaranaike, and the communists attempted to exploit popular dissatisfaction with the prime minister's administration shortly before the general election. The result meant a weakening of Soviet influence in Sri Lanka.[24]

In mid-March 1977 the Communist Party of India saw its strength reduced from 23 to 7 (4 in Kerala and 3 in Tamil Nadu) in the 525-seat lower house of parliament. At this time, CP Chairman S.A. Dange had stated that Mrs. Gandhi "remains the symbol of democratic and progressive policies."[25] The policy of avoiding confrontation with the neutral (neither pro-Soviet nor pro-Peking) CPI-Marxist and other left-wing parties did not help. The CPI(M) won 22 seats in the national parliament and achieved a clear majority (178 from 294) of seats in the assembly for West Bengal. This led to an editorial which stated that, "the CPI has forfeited its claim to be the country's chief communist party, and it is the CPI(M) which has assumed that role."[26] Dange resigned at year's end.

The eleventh Chinese party congress in August 1977 unanimously denounced the Gang of Four faction and stressed the importance of modernizing the country. Chairman Hua Kuo-feng confirmed the USSR as the main enemy and endorsed Mao's theory of the three worlds: the two "hegemonic" superpowers comprising the First; the developed states of Western Europe, Japan, Australia, and Canada, the Second; which should be allied with the progressive Third World of developing states against the First. China was described as both a Third World and a socialist country. Only Albania, North Korea, Romania, and Vietnam were classified in the latter category, which means that they can have party relations with Peking. Warsaw Pact members, apart from Romania, as well as Cuba and Mongolia are considered dominated by the USSR, but "revisionist" Yugoslavia was praised for resisting Soviet influence.[27] Tito, of course, had scheduled a visit to Peking which took place the following month.

There was an atmosphere of purge in the aftermath of the December 1976 fourth party congress in Vietnam. Cadres were forced to spend considerable time studying the proceedings, a number of middle and lower echelon members were expelled, and the leadership also ordered that discipline be tightened. Full-scale battles with warplanes and artillery took place as late as the end of December 1977 along the Cambodian border, apparently over territory occupied by the North Vietnamese during their final assault against the South. Cambodia severed its diplomatic relations with Vietnam, giving the latter's diplomats until 7 January 1978 to leave the country.[28]

Toward the end of December, Cambodia was launching raids across the border into Thailand, at least twenty-nine occurring in one week alone. On the domestic front, refugees brought reports of a

---

[24]See Don Wimalasiri Subasinghe, "Political Alliances in the Anti-Imperialist Struggle," *World Marxist Review,* XX, no. 7, July 1977, pp. 86-95.

[25]*Illustrated Weekly,* Bombay, 13-19 March 1977. Dange resigned as party leader on 30 December because of ill health. Although seventy-eight, he remains a member of the national council (*New York Times,* 1 January 1978).

[26]*Times of India,* Bombay, 23 June 1977. CPI(M) won 49 of the 60 seats in the Tripura assembly, the second state to elect a communist government (AP dispatch, New Delhi, 3 January 1978).

[27]*New China News Agency* (12 August 1977).

[28]Phnom Penh radio, 31 December 1977; as reported by the *New York Times* (1 January 1978).

CHECKLIST OF COMMUNIST PARTIES AND FRONTS

Eastern Europe and the Soviet Union (9)

Area	Population (est)	Communist party membership	Percent of vote; seats in legislature	Status	Sino-Soviet dispute
*Albania	2,530,000	101,500 (1976)	99.9 (1974); all 250 Democratic Front	In power	Anti-Soviet
Bulgaria	8,864,000	789,796	99.9 (1976); 272 of 400 Fatherland Front	In power	Pro-Moscow
Czechoslovakia	15,049,000	1,382,860 (1976)	99.9 (1976); all 200 National Front	In power	Pro-Moscow
East Germany (GDR)	16,786,000	2,077,262	99.9 (1976); 127 of 500 National Front	In power	Pro-Moscow
Hungary	10,695,000	765,566	99.6 (1975); all 352 Patriotic People's Front	In power	Pro-Moscow
Poland	35,000,000	2,573,000	99.4 (1976); 262 of 460 Front of National Unity	In power	Pro-Moscow
*Romania	21,559,400	2,700,000	99.9 (1975); all 349 Front of Socialist Unity	In power	Neutral
USSR	260,178,000	16,203,446	99.9 (1974); all 1,517 CPSU-approved	In power	– –
Yugoslavia	21,770,000	1,537,000	– – (1974); all 200 Socialist Alliance	In power	Independent
Total	392,431,400	28,130,430			

Western Europe (24)

Area	Population (est)	Communist party membership	Percent of vote; seats in legislature	Status	Sino-Soviet dispute
*Austria	7,520,000	20,000 est.	1.2 (1975); none	Legal	Pro-Moscow
*Belgium	10,000,000	11,000 est.	2.7 (1977); 2 of 212	Legal	Pro-Moscow
Cyprus	640,000	11,000 est.	30.0 (1976); 9 of 35 Greek Cypriot seats	Legal	Pro-Moscow
*Denmark	5,090,000	8,000 est.	3.7 (1977); 7 of 179	Legal	Pro-Moscow
*Faroe Islands	42,000	insignificant	-- (1975); none	Allowed	Split
*Finland	4,746,000	48,000	19.0 (1975); 36 of 200	Legal	Pro-Moscow
*France	53,352,000	600,000 claim	21.3 (1973); 73 of 490	Legal	Pro-Moscow
*Germany (FRG)	61,520,000	40,000 est.	0.3 (1976); none	Legal	Pro-Moscow
West Berlin	2,100,000	7,500	1.9 (1975); none	Legal	Pro-Moscow
*Great Britain	56,000,000	25,293 claim	0.5 (1974); none	Legal	Split
*Greece	9,150,000	27,500 est.	9.3 (1977); 11 of 300	Legal	Split (3)
*Iceland	223,000	2,500 est.	18.3 (1974); 11 of 60	Legal	Independent
Ireland	3,199,000	500 est.	-- (1977); none	Legal	Pro-Moscow
*Italy	58,000,000	1,800,000 claim	34.4 (1976); 228 of 630	Legal	Pro-Moscow
*Luxembourg	356,400	600 est.	9.0 (1974); 5 of 59	Legal	Pro-Moscow
*Malta	322,000	100	-- (1976); none	Legal	Pro-Moscow
*Netherlands	13,869,000	14,500	1.7 (1977); 2 of 150	Legal	Independent
*Norway	4,050,000	1,500 est.	4.2 (1977); 2 of 155 coalition of 3 (incl. CP)	Legal	Pro-Moscow
*Portugal	9,634,000	115,000	14.6 (1976); 40 of 263	Legal	Pro-Moscow
*San Marino	20,000	300	23.7 (1974); 16 of 60	Legal	Pro-Moscow
*Spain	36,542,000	200,000 claim	9.2 (1977); 20 of 350	Legal	Pro-Moscow
*Sweden	8,250,000	17,500 est.	5.0 (1976); 17 of 349	Legal	Split
*Switzerland	6,421,000	5,000 est.	2.5 (1975); 5 of 200	Legal	Pro-Moscow
Turkey	42,518,000	26,000 claim	-- (1977)	Proscribed	Pro-Moscow
Total	393,564,400	3,215,793			

Asia and the Pacific (21)

Area	Population (est.)	Communist party membership	Percent of vote; seats in legislature	Status	Sino-Soviet dispute
*Australia	13,861,000	1,500 est.	— (1977); none	Legal	Split (3)
*Bangladesh	78,000,000	2,500 est.	— (1973)	Proscribed	Split
*Burma	31,700,000	10,000 est.	— (1974)	Proscribed	Pro-Peking
*Cambodia	8,060,000	10,000 est.	100.0 (1976); all 250	In power	Pro-Peking
China	950,000,000	35,000,000 claim	No elections scheduled	In power	—
*Hong Kong	4,563,000	2,000		Legal	Pro-Peking
*India	649,354,000	90,000 CPI est. 120,000 CPI (M) (1974)	2.8 (1977); 7 of 244 4.3 (1977); 22 of 244	Legal	Pro-Moscow Neutral
*Indonesia	139,075,000	1,000 est.	— (1971)	Proscribed	Split
*Japan	113,000,000	370,000 est.	10.4 (1976); 17 of 511	Legal	Independent
*Korea (DPRK)	17,500,000	1,800,000 claim	100.0 (1977); all 579	In power	Neutral
*Laos	3,400,000	15,000 est.	No elections scheduled	In power	Neutral
*Malaysia	12,736,000	2,750,000 insurgents	— (1974)	Proscribed	Pro-Peking
Mongolia	1,561,000	67,000 claim	99.9 (1973); all 336	In power	Pro-Moscow
Nepal	13,199,000	6,500 est.	— (1959)	Proscribed	Split
*New Zealand	3,100,000	500 est.	0.2 (1975); none	Legal	Split
Pakistan	75,657,000	1,500 est.	— (1977)	Proscribed	Pro-Moscow (mostly)
*Philippines	40,000,000	2,000 insurgents	Elections suspended	Proscribed	Split
Singapore	2,400,000	400 est.	— (1972)	Proscribed	Pro-Peking
*Sri Lanka	14,349,000	5,000 SLCP est. 1,000 LSSP est.	1.9 (1977); none 3.9 (1977); none	Legal Legal	Pro-Moscow Pro-Peking
*Thailand	44,790,000	unknown	— (1976)	Proscribed	Pro-Peking
*Vietnam	51,152,000	1,533,500 claim	99.0 (1976); all 492	In power	Neutral
Total	2,267,457,000	39,042,150			

The Americas (27)

Area	Population (est.)	Communist party membership	Percent of vote; seats in legislature	Status	Sino-Soviet dispute
*Argentina	26,224,000	65,000 est.	No elections scheduled	Legal	Pro-Moscow
*Bolivia	5,500,500	500 est.	Elections scheduled 1978	Proscribed	Split
Brazil	110,000,000	4,500 est.	— (1974)	Proscribed	Split
*Canada	23,437,000	2,000 est.	— (1974); none	Legal	Split
*Chile	10,742,000	unknown	Elections promised	Proscribed	Pro-Moscow
*Colombia	24,880,000	12,000 est.	— (1974); 2 of 311	Legal	Split
Costa Rica	2,100,000	1,000 est.	2.3 (1974); 2 of 57	Legal	Pro-Moscow
Cuba	9,700,000	204,000 est.	(1976); 441 of 481	In power	Pro-Moscow
*Dominican Republic	5,051,000	1,000 est.	— (1974); none	Legal	Factions
Ecuador	7,680,000	800 est.	Elections scheduled 1978	Legal	Split
El Salvador	4,310,000	150 est.	— (1976)	Proscribed	Pro-Moscow
*Guadeloupe	329,000	3,000 est.	— (1976); 7 of 36	Legal	Pro-Moscow
Guatemala	6,183,000	750 est.	— (1974)	Proscribed	Pro-Moscow
Guyana	850,000	unknown	3.6 (1973); 14 of 53	Legal	Pro-Moscow
*Haiti	5,000,000	unknown	— (1973)	Proscribed	Pro-Moscow
*Honduras	2,912,000	650	Elections scheduled 1979/80	Proscribed	Split
Jamaica	2,130,000	200 est.	— (1976); none	Allowed	Pro-Moscow
Martinique	327,000	1,000 est.	— (1976); 3 of 36	Legal	Pro-Moscow
Mexico	64,487,000	60,000 est.	— (1976); none	Legal	Pro-Moscow
Nicaragua	2,224,000	160 est.	— (1974)	Proscribed	Split
Panama	1,750,000	425	— (1972); none	Allowed	Pro-Moscow
Paraguay	2,700,000	3,500 est.	— (1973)	Proscribed	Split
*Peru	16,579,000	3,200	Elections scheduled 1978	Legal	Split
Puerto Rico	3,200,000	125 est.	— (1976); none	Legal	Pro-Moscow
*United States	217,799,000	18,000 claimed	0.2 (1976); none	Legal	Pro-Moscow
*Uruguay	2,800,000	6,000 est.	Elections scheduled 1980	Proscribed	Pro-Moscow
*Venezuela	12,500,000	10,000 est.	9.0 (1973); 11 of 195	Legal	Factions
Total	571,394,500	397,960			

Middle East and Africa (17)

Area	Population (est.)	Communist party membership	Percent of vote; seats in legislature	Status	Sino-Soviet dispute
Egypt	39,396,000	1,000 est.	—— (1976); 2 of 350	Proscribed	Pro-Moscow
Iran	35,000,000	1,500 est.	—— (1975)	Proscribed	Pro-Moscow
Iraq	10,000,000	2,000 est.	No elections since 1958	Allowed	Pro-Moscow
Israel	3,628,000	1,500 est.	4.6 (1977); 5 of 120	Legal	Pro-Moscow
Jordan	2,899,000	500 est.	No elections since 1967	Proscribed	Pro-Moscow
Lebanon	2,500,000	2,500 est.	—— (1972); none	Legal	Pro-Moscow
Lesotho	1,098,000				
The Maghreb					
Algeria	18,120,000	400 est.	—— (1976)	Proscribed	Pro-Moscow
Morocco	18,644,000	400 est.	—— (1977); none	Allowed	Pro-Moscow
Tunisia	5,936,000	100 est.	—— (1974)	Proscribed	Pro-Moscow
Nigeria	66,555,000	unknown	—— (1976); no parties	Banned	Pro-Moscow
*Reunion	504,000	2,000 est.	40 (1973); none in Paris	Legal	Independent
Saudi Arabia	7,746,000	negligible	No elections scheduled	Proscribed	Pro-Moscow
Senegal	5,301,000	unknown	—— (1973); none	Legal	Pro-Moscow
South Africa	27,188,000	unknown	—— (1977)	Proscribed	Pro-Moscow
Sudan	16,740,000	unknown	—— (1974); no parties	Proscribed	Pro-Moscow
Syria	8,000,000	4,000 est.	—— (1977); 6 of 195	Allowed	Pro-Moscow
Total	269,255,000	15,900			

Note: *Based on fraternal greetings sent to the 11th communist party congress in Peking (12–18 August 1977), these 52 countries either have pro-Chinese splinter groups or ruling movements that are at least neutral in the Sino-Soviet dispute. Many of them include more than one organization. Not listed above are CP (M/L) organizations claimed by the Chinese to operate in Macao, South Korea, and Surinam.

International Communist Front Organizations (12)

	Claimed Membership	Headquarters
	Claimed Membership[a]	
Afro-Asian People's Solidarity Organization	No data[a]	Cairo
Afro-Asian Writers' Permanent Bureau	No data	Cairo
Christian Peace Conference	(Members claimed in 48 countries)	Prague
International Association of Democratic Lawyers	25,000	Brussels
International Federation of Resistance Fighters	3,000,000[b]	Vienna
International Organization of Journalists	150,000	Prague
International Union of Students	ca. 10,000,000[c]	Prague
Women's International Democratic Federation	over 200,000,000[d]	East Berlin
World Federation of Democratic Youth	ca. 150,000,000[e]	Budapest
World Federation of Scientific Workers	300,000[f]	London
World Federation of Trade Unions	ca. 150,000,000[g]	Prague
World Peace Council	(Affiliates in 120 countries)	Helsinki

Sources: Official figures on CP membership claimed during 1977 by party newspapers or journals; est(imates) are from Central Intelligence Agency, *National Basic Intelligence Factbook* (Washington, D.C., January 1978), passim; and *International Front Organizations* (London, April 1977), passim, for the fronts above.

Notes: [a] AAPSO-affiliated committees exist in most countries of Asia and Africa.
  [b] Forty "national" organizations exist in 20 countries of Europe plus Israel.
  [c] The bulk of membership comes from communist-ruled states.
  [d] Figures for 1966; none issued since then.
  [e] Most members live in CP-ruled countries; others generally represent small groups attached to local communist parties.
  [f] Bulk of membership is from communist-ruled states.
  [g] Some 90 percent live in CP-ruled states, including 107 million from the USSR. Communist China is not a member.

purge begun already in the spring of 1977. It may be a sign of depletion of communist ranks that women are being named province and district chiefs. During a four-hour speech in September, party leader Pol Pot stated that between 1 and 2 percent of the population (up to 120,000) comprised "reactionary elements" still opposed to his regime[29] and, thus, presumably slated for extermination.

The movements in other Asian countries remained splintered and their memberships small; leadership energy was dissipated in factional conflict. No decisive changes in either membership size or political influence seem to have occurred. New Zealand's left-wing Marxists continue to publish their irregular bulletins and news sheets. The party remains split; membership in the two largest factions totals at the most 350. The party also is divided in Australia, with pro-Soviet, independent and pro-Chinese groups adding up to about 1,500 members. Some of them, however, hold important posts in trade unions and reportedly organized several work stoppages during the year. National elections in December 1977 consolidated the Liberal Party's power, and communists were unable to exploit a national unemployment level of 6 percent.

In the Asian countries where communist parties are banned, government crackdowns on underground political activities have temporarily paralyzed the communist organizational apparatus. Revival may depend upon future economic instability.

Toward the end of 1976 several top commanders of the National People's Army, the military arm of the pro-Chinese communist party in the Philippines, were captured by regime troops. José Sison, leader of this Chinese faction, was caught in November 1977.[30] The pro-Soviet group has adopted a line of critical acceptance of the Marcos government. In Singapore, early in 1977, the Lee Kuan Yew government arrested several professional lawyers and journalists alleged to be pro-communist.

The Indonesian regime put on trial several communist leaders. It constantly stressed the necessity for vigilance against the latent danger of subversive activities, although some 10,000 political prisoners were released in a December 1977 amnesty.[31] The two splinter movements in Malaysia continued guerrilla warfare along the Thai border, with attacks launched from bases mainly in Thailand. A combined Malaysian-Thai government force destroyed some of these base areas during the spring months of 1977 and routed the pro-Chinese guerrillas. Communist rebels in Thailand received a thirty-fifth anniversary greeting from Peking, praising them for "encircling the cities so as to seize political power," the first such message in five years.[32]

No major shake-ups took place at the highest party levels in Asia, except for India, mentioned above. In some cases, individual leaders asserted their dominant roles by presenting major speeches at party congresses or traveling to friendly countries. For example. Premier Pol Pot (concurrently general secretary of the Khmer communist movement) stated before leaving for Peking early in September 1977 that the party did exist and exercised full power throughout Cambodia. The top leadership in Vietnam still appears to be united.

Restoration of Teng Hsiao-p'ing to the Chinese politburo undoubtedly strengthens what had been a weak coalition between the military (Yeh Chien-ying) and civilian bureaucrats (Hua Kuo-feng). This new alliance now seeks to consolidate its power at province and district levels. On the international scene, Burmese President Ne Win traveled to Peking twice during the second half of 1977. A purge from his ruling Socialist Program party of pro-Soviet elements in September and the

---

[29]*The Washington Post,* 3, 14, 22 December 1977. All diplomats in the Cambodian embassy at Moscow suddenly left in mid-summer without explanation.

[30]Moscow radio (29 November 1977) claimed that Peking supplies the New Peoples' Army with arms, ammunition, communications equipment, propaganda literature, and trains its commanders.

[31]Some 20,000 others will be released during the next two years. The *New York Times* (21 December 1977) also cites Admiral Sudomo, chief of the Security and Order Command, to the effect that 500,000 communists had been killed after the 1965 coup attempt.

[32]*The Washington Post* (3 December 1977).

forthcoming visit to Rangoon by Teng Hsiao p'ing[33] in January 1978 may result in an end to Chinese military supplies for an estimated 7,000 Burma communist party insurgents.

An important development occurred in Indo-China: Laos and Vietnam signed a treaty in July 1977 at Vientiane, specifying various types of cooperation and mutual aid. The agreement reportedly permits stationing of Vietnamese military units on Laotian territory, with the latter henceforth a de facto province controlled by Hanoi.

In the Asian countries ruled by communist parties, 1977 was a poor year economically. North Korea's balance of payments with the outside world continued to deteriorate.[34] That government still has not repaid long-standing loans from "friendly" countries and is apparently finding it difficult to obtain additional credits abroad. Economic growth in the People's Republic of China continued at a slower rate than during the recent past. The mid-year wheat harvest suffered from drought.[35] Industrial production still lags because of widespread reorganization and change.

The harvest in Vietnam was particularly poor. China, which usually exports rice to that country when shortages arise, sent very little in 1977. Rationing of rice, edible oils, and cloth is now reported to be as severe as during the height of the Vietnamese war. The Hanoi regime continues its policy of relocating large numbers of people from Ho Chi Minh City (Saigon) to carry out its plan of establishing huge agro-farms, on each of which several tens of thousands of persons will live and work. Little is known about the selection process for urban households forced to resettle and take up farming. In the Mongolian People's Republic, bad weather and organizational difficulties reduced herds. The twenty-three million head of livestock probably have declined in numbers, because severe cold and winds struck the country early in 1977. Lower exports to the USSR over the past few years may indicate other difficulties.

The Americas. Most pro-Soviet communist parties throughout Latin America, except for Cuba, continued to pursue non-armed broad front forms of struggle against governments in power. The Dominican Communist Party became legalized, and political reforms underway in Mexico should provide for communist participation in the electoral process during the years ahead. While nonviolent policies at times included varying degrees of "critical support" for existing regimes (Argentina, Dominican Republic, Ecuador, Guyana, Peru) or active and significant involvement in legislatures (Guadeloupe and Martinique), they also meant active opposition to most governments in power. Opposition ranged from calls for overthrow of regimes (Chile, Haiti, Paraguay)[36] to some form of electoral competition (Bolivia, Costa Rica, Guyana, Mexico, U.S.A., Venezuela). Communists and the Socialist Workers' party remained active in civil rights and other movements throughout the United States.

The once-powerful communist party in Chile maintained a low domestic profile; exiled leaders attempted to create a broad "anti-fascist" front with members of the former Popular Unity alliance as well as Christian Democrats. After failing to form a leftist front in preparation for 1978 elections, the Communist Party of Venezuela (PCV) nominated its own presidential candidate. The Movement

---

[33]*Far Eastern Economic Review,* Hong Kong, 16 December 1977, p. 7. It should be noted that Teng has many bitter, long-time enemies who will oppose him from many sides within China itself.

[34]An alleged plot against Kim Il-song and his son, the heir apparent Kim Chong-il, has resulted in a purge of military and political leaders. Those affected include the Russian educated party secretary for ideology, Yang Hyong-Sop, and the director of the armed forces political administration, Yi Yong-Mu (Seoul radio, 22 November, 7 December 1977). On the government side, a new premier (Yi Chong-oh) and younger ministers for metal industry as well as electric power were appointed to prepare for the new, 1978-1984, seven-year plan (Tokyo radio, 15 December 1977).

[35]The end of the year Hsinhua reported a harvest equal to 1976, when a shortage resulted in substantial grain purchases abroad and a 14 percent higher industrial output value. However, no specific figures were given for performance by individual sectors of the economy (*Wall Street Journal,* 28 December 1977).

[36] For a survey of Latin American military regimes, see the *New York Times* (25 November 1977) which also provides dates on forthcoming national elections.

Toward Socialism, a PCV splinter which is larger than the parent group, selected its own candidate. It obviously hopes to become the third most important party on the political scene and has won the backing of the Communist Vanguard, another small PCV splinter. The Communist Party of Cuba introduced a new economic management system, dubbed by some foreign observers "state capitalism with a tropical flavor," and generally has sought to institutionalize the domestic revolutionary process.

A meeting of communists from the Caribbean region convened at Havana immediately following the 1977 May First celebrations. Party members from Cuba, the Dominican Republic, Guadeloupe, Guyana, Haiti, Martinique, and Puerto Rico were there. Earlier, on 1 February, it was announced that the first gathering in some time of representatives from "Marxist-Leninist" communist movements had taken place in Albania. Delegations came from Argentina, Bolivia, Brazil, Colombia, Chile, Ecuador, and Uruguay; all proclaimed (anti-Chinese) opposition to both superpowers and support for revolutionary change. On 17 April at Rome, eleven European and Latin American "Marxist-Leninist" parties voiced their support for the Albanian rather than the Chinese line about the relative danger of the USSR and the United States.

Guerrilla movements remained at a low ebb in the southern cone of Latin America, while an upsurge occurred in Nicaragua and Guatemala, and a slight increase in Venezuela and Mexico, and activity continued in Colombia. Both once-powerful guerrilla organizations of Argentina, the People's Revolutionary Army (ERP) and the Peronist Montoneros, were virtually eliminated. However, the latter established an office in European exile.

Cuba's limited support of foreign guerrilla warfare in Latin America[37] sharply contrasted with its growing involvement throughout Africa. Military support to the MPLA government in Angola increased as 1977 progressed, and military/technical/medical forces from Cuba were deployed in fourteen other countries as well.[38] Although Cuba continues to court U.S. businessmen, signs of a rapprochement with Washington, D.C., had all but disappeared by early 1978, at least in part because of intensified Cuban activities in Africa.

Africa and the Middle East. Communist strategy calls for a series of "national democratic" revolutions, to be achieved in cooperation with progressive elements of the bourgeoisie in the Third World, and "national revolution" is seen as a stepping stone toward seizure of power. Tactics are based on a variety of expedients: cooperation with incumbent governments (not necessarily leftist), support from local non-communist political groups and, above all, communist participation in wider "fronts" or movements that will ultimately adopt a Marxist-Leninist platform. Communist parties of the orthodox variety, on the other hand, play as yet only a negligible role on the continent of Africa.

Moscow's diplomacy continued its activist course, but suffered a serious blow when Somalia abrogated its friendship treaty with the USSR and broke off relations with Cuba over the conflict in Ethiopia. The Soviet Union had thrown its support behind the so-called revolutionary regime in Addis Ababa,[39] but Ethiopia appears to be threatened with possible breakup of its empire. The USSR

---

[37]It should be noted, however, that a returning Jamaican youth construction brigade decided to organize itself into a movement along Marxist-Leninist lines, as a result of indoctrination while in Cuba. The new league has declared that it will "foster and encourage the growth and development of the socialist process in Jamaica, following the works expounded by V. I. Lenin in establishing the first socialist state in the Soviet Union" (*The Daily Gleaner*, Jamaica, as cited by the *Christian Science Monitor*, 30 November 1977).

[38]According to a classified National Security Council study, these included the following: Angola (23,000), Ethiopia (550), Uganda (25), Sierra Leone (125), Tanzania (350 to 500), Mozambique (650 to 750), Madagascar (30), Libya (100 to 125), Guinea (300 to 500), Guinea-Bissau (100 to 200), Equatorial Guinea (300 to 400), Congo (400 to 500), Cape Verde (10 to 15), Benin (10 to 20), and Algeria (35) (*Washington Post*, 18 November 1977).

[39]A United Front of five Marxist-Leninist organizations has been established as a first step toward establishing a proletarian party in Ethiopia, according to Moscow radio (18 October 1977). During the last month of the year, Soviet advisors increased from 100 to 500 and Cubans from 400 to 800 in Ethiopia (*New York Times*, 29 December 1977).

position in Africa is strongest in Angola, whose ruling movement (MPLA) reorganized itself into a new Popular Movement Workers' Party at a congress in early December 1977. The Soviet Union sent Politburo member Andrei P. Kirilenko as its representative. Yet guerrilla warfare continued throughout much of the Angolan hinterland.

FRELIMO, the ruling movement in Mozambique and a sister party of the MPLA, is likewise determined to transform itself from a "popular front" into a Marxist-Leninist group. Mozambique, however, remains closely tied to the Republic of South Africa's economy; its links with Cuba and the USSR remained more tenuous[40] than those of Angola. MPLA and FRELIMO both claim to operate along Marxist-Leninist lines, but neither is yet regarded as an orthodox communist movement by the ruling parties of the Soviet bloc.

The Sudanese Communist Party, once the largest in Africa, remains banned and powerless. The movement in South Africa, though claiming responsibility for much of the rioting[41] that had disturbed the country during 1977, fundamentally is a party of exiles. It operates in alliance with various "liberation movements" including SWAPO in South-West Africa and ZAPU in Rhodesia. All of these groups, though strongly anti-Western, are too complex and heterogeneous in their composition to be categorized simply as Marxist-Leninist.

The communists throughout North Africa and the Middle East exercise limited influence, except in Syria and Iraq,[42] where local movements operate as junior partners in alliance with the ruling Ba'ath parties. Syria's incursion into Lebanon, however, led to severe disagreements. Iraq strongly disapproved of this move, which had serious consequences for local communists. The movements of the Maghreb, Egypt, and Iran remain unimportant. Ironically, the most freely active party in the Middle East is found in Israel,[43] where members are allowed to operate without government interference and where they draw considerable support from Arab nationalists not otherwise wedded to Marxism-Leninism.

Fronts. International communist front organizations predominantly continued to support the foreign interests and policies of the Soviet Union. Indeed, on no issue did the fronts openly criticize the USSR. There were, however, a number of dissenting voices within certain of the organizations. These internal differences could be noted especially in the World Federation of Trade Unions, where the Italian delegation[44] on several occasions spoke up in opposition to what it called "inadequate attention paid to the problems of the socialist states," i.e., the communist-ruled countries in Eastern Europe.

Interwoven with their basic effort to expand membership and influence by attracting collaboration of nonpolitical organizations through the use of such slogans as "defend detente, disarmament, and peace," were general denunciations by the fronts of the governments in Chile, Israel, and South Africa as well as the United States specifically for its emphasis on human rights and proposed development of a neutron bomb. Consistent adherence over the years to the Soviet line was reflected also in stability of leadership, which has changed little during the past decade. The only

[40]Mozambique leaders appear to be concerned about the large Soviet and Cuban forces in Angola which seems to be turning them toward the West for diplomatic and economic support (*Washington Post,* 15 December 1977).

[41]According to the Institute of Race Relations at Johannesburg, only 714 individuals have been detained without trial and another 160 remain free but are restricted by "banning orders" which silence them. (Ibid., 29 November 1977.)

[42]The parties in Syria, Jordan, and Iraq have come out with statements attacking Egyptian President Anwar Sadat for his attempts to "impose U.S.-Israeli dominance in the Middle East" (Moscow radio, 4 December 1977; *Pravda,* 6 December 1977). In actual fact, the CP Lebanon may be more influential domestically than the CP Syria.

[43]Leaders of the Israeli and Turkish communist parties agreed that their relations should be based on "proletarian internationalism," i.e., following the Soviet line (Moscow radio, 28 November 1977).

[44]It is possible that the Italian CGIL may withdraw from membership because of failure to agree on documents for the ninth WFTU congress, to be held at Prague during 16-23 April 1978 (*L'Unita,* Rome, 28 September 1977).

exceptions in 1977 were the "election" of Miroslav Stepan as new president of the International Union of Students[45] and the death of Pierre Cot, who headed the International Association of Democratic Lawyers.

In reviewing activities of the fronts, one has the impression that some are aging, which may affect their vitality. Certain international issues, especially the question of apartheid in South Africa, still arouse a considerable degree of moral fervor in the West, a sense of commitment that communists attempt to channel for their own purposes. But in many cases, mundane issues of the day are perhaps insufficiently emotive to attract a following and the attention required to sustain such mass organizations.[46]

*   *   *

Staff members and several of the associate editors were responsible for some of the writing, research, and most of the data-collecting effort that produced this *Yearbook*. Profiles were contributed by a total of sixty-two outside scholars, many of whom prepared more than one. Names and affiliations appear at the end of individual essays. Mrs. Ica Juilland and Mrs. Dorothy Grouse Fontana assisted in the processing and filing of research material as well as in assembling some of the data. Much of the final typing was done by Mrs. Margit Grigory, who also handled correspondence with contributors. Special appreciation is due the curators and their staffs as well as members of the Readers' Services department at the Hoover Institution for their response to emergency requests and for the bibliography. We are indebted particularly to the copy editor, Mr. Jesse M. Phillips, for putting the manuscript in its final form.

Sources are cited throughout the text, with news agencies normally identified by generally accepted initials. Abbreviations are also used for the following widely quoted publications:

FBIS   *Foreign Broadcast Information Service*
NYT   *New York Times*
WMR   *World Marxist Review*
IB   *Information Bulletin* (of the WMR)
YICA   *Yearbook on International Communist Affairs*

January 1978   Richard F. Staar

---

[45]The IUS and the World Federation of Democratic Youth will hold the eleventh world youth festival in Havana from 28 July through 5 August 1978.

[46]This may be one reason for announcement of a "new Programme" by the World Peace Council (Moscow radio, 8 December 1977; Tass dispatch from Delhi).

EASTERN EUROPE AND THE SOVIET UNION

Albania

The Albanian Communist Party was founded on 8 November 1941. At its First Congress, November 1948, the name was changed to the Albanian Party of Labor (Partia e Punës e Shqipërisë; APL). As the only legal political party in Albania, the APL exercises a monopoly of power. Party members hold key posts in the government and the mass organizations. All 250 seats in the national legislature, the People's Assembly, are held by members of the Democratic Front (DF), the party-controlled mass organization to which all Albanian voters belong.

At the Seventh APL Congress (1-7 November 1976), it was announced that there were 101,500 party members. Of these, 88,000 were full members and 13,500 candidate members. In 1976, 37.5 percent of APL members were reportedly laborers, 29.0 percent peasants, and 33.5 percent white-collar workers. Women in 1976 comprised 27 percent of the party's membership (*Zëri i popullit,* 2, 8 November 1976). Approximately 4 percent of the Albanian population are party members.

The population of Albania in mid-1977 was approximately 2,530,000 (Tirana radio, 30 June). According to 1975 census data, peasants comprise 49.4 percent of the population, laborers 36.2 percent, and white-collar workers 14.4 percent. Approximately 42 percent of the population is under the age of fifteen (*Zëri i popullit*, 28 May, 8 June 1975).

Leadership and Organization. There were no significant top-echelon changes in the APL leadership during 1977. The composition of the Politburo and Central Committee elected at the Seventh Congress (see *YICA, 1977,* pp.1-2) does not appear to have been altered.

In the only noteworthy leadership change, Politburo candidate member Simon Stefani replaced Qirjako Mihali, also a Politburo candidate member, as first secretary of the Tirana district party organization (*Zëri i popullit,* 29 November). Stefani was appointed to the secretariat of the Tirana district party organization in October 1976 after having served as first secretary of the Përmet district party organization since 1972. Mihali, who had served in the Tirana post since October 1976, was named a deputy prime minister. (Ibid., 27 November.)

APL First Secretary Enver Hoxha, who remains the dominant personality in the ruling elite, turned sixty-nine in October. He maintained a well-publicized, active schedule throughout the year. In addition to appearances at numerous functions in Tirana, he toured the Vlorë district in March and attended the Congress of the Union of Albanian Labor Youth in Elbasan in September. (Ibid., 22-24 March, 30 September). If Hoxha has indeed experienced the poor health attributed to him in recent years (see, e.g. *YICA, 1977,* p. 1), he seems to have made a strong recovery. Prime Minister Mehmet Shehu, the second-ranking member of the regime, who also reportedly has been ailing, likewise made a number of public appearances outside Tirana during the year (e.g., *Zëri i popullit,*

30 April, 21 June, 27 September). The public activities of the Albanian leaders were apparently intended to allay rumors and doubts about their health and to inspire support for their policies in the wake of Tirana's worsening relations with China and the leadership purges of the mid-1970s.

Although the Albanian regime has not officially revealed the fates of the major victims of the 1973-76 purges (see *YICA, 1977*, p. 3), it appears they all have been expelled from the party and tried on various charges, including treason, and that "several" have been executed (*Zëri i popullit*, 20 February). It has also been reported that "thousands" of civil servants and officials, including prominent party members removed from their positions in the massive purge of the bureaucracy initiated by Hoxha have been imprisoned or sent to corrective labor camps (*Washington Post*, 9 September).

Despite the extensive leadership changes at both the national and district levels in recent years, there apparently is still some opposition to Hoxha's hard-line policies within the ranks of the APL (e.g., *Zëri i popullit*, 24 July; *Rruga e partisë*, September). Consequently, the campaign to rid the APL of its "unworthy elements" is likely to continue for the foreseeable future.

Auxiliary and Mass Organizations. The congress of the Albanian Trade Unions (ATU) met at Korçë on 20-23 June. Politburo member Rita Marko was reelected ATU president (*Zëri i popullit*, 24 June). It was reported that the current membership of the organization was "in excess of 500,000" (ibid., 21 June). Marko's report to the congress dealt mainly with economic matters. It stressed the "heavy responsibility" of the working class for the success of the current five-year plan and exhorted ATU members to become more actively involved in the political life of the nation (ibid).

On 26-29 September the congress of the Union of Albanian Labor Youth (UALY) met at Elbasan. Lumturi Rexha, who had been named UALY first secretary in 1976, was confirmed in this position at the congress. (Ibid., 29 September.) In 1977 there were approximately 370,000 UALY members in 18,000 basic organizations. UALY members reportedly comprised 63 percent of those admitted to the APL between 1972 and 1976 (ibid., 27 September). As a consequence of the purge of UALY leadership at the national and district levels during 1973-74, there were few changes in the top echelons of the organization at either level during 1977 (ibid., 29 September; *Zëri i rinisë*, Tirana, 30 July-20 August).

In her report ot the congress, Rexha strongly endorsed Hoxha's domestic and foreign policies and attacked the position, which had considerable support within the UALY leadership during the early 1970s, that the organization should enjoy a greater degree of autonomy from the party (*Zëri i popullit*, 27 September). The resolution adopted by the congress stated UALY's "main task" was to "educate the nation's youth in the ideology of Marxism-Leninism and in the teachings of the Party and Comrade Enver Hoxha" (*Zëri i rinisë*, 5 October).

A highlight of the congress was the appearance of Hoxha. In an emotional speech, the APL first secretary defended his domestic and foreign policies of recent years and expressed his confidence in the ability of the younger generation of Albanians to preserve the "Marxist-Leninist purity" which he asserted has been characteristic of the APL since its founding (*Zëri i popullit*, 30 September).

To commemorate the thirty-fifth anniversary of the establishment of the Democratic Front (DF), Hoxha on 16 September authorized publication in the Albanian press of his reminiscences concerning the formation of the organization (ibid., 16 September). Hoxha's partisan account of this episode stressed the role of the DF, under the tutelage of the APL, in fostering patriotism and national unity during World War II and in the subsequent crises that have confronted Albania. By implication, the Albanian leader was appealing for popular support in what he viewed as another time of trial for his regime.

In his address to the March plenum of the Albanian League of Writers and Artists (ALWA), APL Politburo member Ramiz Alia, a leading party spokesman on ideology and culture, emphasized the need to "intensify the two-front war against bourgeois and revisionist influences in literature and the arts." Only in this manner, he asserted, could "ideological correctness" in Albanian culture be preserved and "superpower dominance" in this area be avoided (*Nëntori,* Tirana, May). The reports presented to the plenum by Alia and ALWA leaders suggested that the cultural crackdown instituted in 1973 has been successful, and that the party has reestablished its control over the nation's writers and artists (ibid.).

Party Internal Affairs. There were two plenary sessions of the APL Central Committee in 1977. The items considered at these meetings reflected the major concerns of the Albanian leadership during the year. The Second Plenum (28-29 June) dealt with economic issues. Hoxha presented a detailed, critical report on the performance of the economy during the first half of 1977 and outlined the measures he believed necessary to ensure that the economic goals for the year would be realized (see below) (*Zëri i popullit,* 30 June, 2 July). At its Third Plenum, 17-18 November, the Central Committee discussed the deepening Sino-Albanian ideological rift. Hoxha presented a lengthy analysis of "modern revisionist tendencies within the world Communist movement" and condemned such ideological "heresies" as social democracy, Yugoslav and Soviet revisionism, Eurocommunism, and "the so-called three world theory." Ramiz Alia presented a report on the necessity of "strengthening the work of the party for the education of Communists and cadres." (Ibid., 19, 20 November.) The proceedings of the Third Plenum suggested that the Albanians were preparing for an ideological break with the Chinese (see below).

Domestic Attitudes and Activities. *Political Developments.* With the promulgation of the new constitution in December 1976, Albania became known as the People's Socialist Republic of Albania (Republika Popullore Socialiste e Shqipërisë; PSRA).

In June 1977 the People's Assembly approved a new penal code designed to bring the nation's criminal law into conformity with the constitution. According to a government spokesman, the new penal code, along with the constitution, is intended to "safeguard the independence of Albania" and the "foundations of the Socialist order." Accordingly, there is heavy emphasis in the code on the definition of political, economic, and social crimes. For example, the scope of the crime of treason has been expanded to include: organizing armed uprisings and "military putsches" to overthrow the government or party leadership, accepting the surrender or permitting foreign occupation of the country, and granting economic concessions to or obtaining credits from capitalist or revisionist countries. The penal code also outlaws "activities that might incite hatreds or quarrels between nations or peoples" and the preparation, dissemination, or possession of materials of this nature. It further protects national minorities and women from all forms of discrimination and sanctions the punishment of persons who "violate" the provisions of state economic plans and directives (*Zëri i popullit,* 15, 16 June).

According to official data, all of the nation's 1,354,992 eligible voters participated in the 3 April elections for district, city, and local people's councils and for local judicial officials. Only sixty-nine votes were cast against the DF candidates for the people's councils and twenty-nine against its judicial candidates. An additional sixty-three ballots were declared invalid. (Ibid., 5 April.) The regime claimed that the near unanimous endorsement of the unopposed DF candidates testified to the "boundless love of the Albanian people for the party and for the beloved leader of the party and people, Comrade Enver Hoxha" and constituted a mandate to "continue to the end the fight against American imperialism, Soviet social-imperialism, and revisionism" (ibid., 6 April).

The changes in the composition of the Albanian cabinet during 1977 reflected the continuing concern of the party leadership over the unsatisfactory performance of the economy. In February Kristaq Dollaku replaced Myqerem Fuga as minister of light and food industry (ibid., 12 February).

Fuga had headed this ministry since December 1972 . Dollaku, a Central Committee member since 1966, in recent years had served as first secretary of the Berat and Korcë district party organizations and during the 1960s was a deputy minister of industry and mining.

In November the Ministry of Trade was split into two components, the Ministry of Domestic Trade and the Ministry of Foreign Trade. The incumbent trade minister, Nedin Hoxha, became minister of foreign trade and his former deputy, Viktor Nushi, minister of domestic trade. At this time Qirjako Mihali was appointed a deputy prime minister. (Ibid., 27 November.) These cabinet changes were made at the November session of the People's Assembly, which was devoted to the question of the "further development of the light and food industries." It was evident from the debate in the People's Assembly, as in press commentaries on this issue, that the consumer sector of the Albanian economy is not growing rapidly enough to satisfy the rising expectations of the Albanian masses (e.g., ibid., 30 July, 5 October, 1 December).

The Ideological and Cultural Revolution. February 1977 marked the tenth anniversary of Hoxha's inauguration of the "intensive phase" of the Ideological and Cultural Revolution. Although party spokesmen expressed general satisfaction with the progress that had been made in achieving the aims of the cultural revolution, they acknowledged that considerable effort was still required to eliminate "alien" influences and attitudes, especially in the private lives of party members and large segments of the Albanian population (e.g., ibid., 10 April, 8 May). The APL leadership seemed especially concerned that both party and non-party members tended to take an active interest in carrying out party directives regarding ideological issues only when the party launched special campaigns to achieve its revolutionary objectives (ibid., 12 April, 28 June).

According to Albanian press accounts, the nation's youth was not yet entirely reconciled to following the party line regarding clothing and hair styles, while some older-generation Albanians, both in the rural areas and in such cities as Tirana, Durrës, and Fier, had not freed themselves of the "religious mentality and outlook" (ibid., 16 March, 14 May). It was also appreciated that greater efforts needed to be made to fully emancipate the nation's women so that more of them might be added to the labor force and exposed to political education in order to be better mobilized to serve the various needs of the state (*Rruga e partisë,* March). The regime was further concerned about "increasing manifestations" of violence and "excessive displays of emotions" at athletic events. This latter development was attributed to "harmful external influences" which had presumably penetrated the country by means of foreign telecasts (*Zëri i popullit*, 13 November).

Although the APL initiated massive anti-bureaucratic campaigns in 1966 and 1975, "bureaucratism" has apparently not yet been eliminated. The nation's civil servants and office workers continue to be taken to task for engaging in "excessive paperwork" and for being arrogant and nonaccountable to the masses. Some high-and middle-rank party and state cadres transferred from Tirana to outlying regions continued to use their influence in efforts to rescind or delay their transfers (ibid., 28 June, 24 July).

The "national aktiv" on education held in March emphasized the crucial role of the school system in the ultimate success of the revolution. After noting the progress in purging "liberalism" and other anti-Socialist influences from the schools since 1973, this session stressed the need for new textbooks and learning materials grounded in Marxist-Leninist principles and for better integrating the three components of the school system—academic study, productive work, and physical and military training—in the educational process (ibid., 19 March). Despite the successful party reassertion of control over the school system, the Albanian leadership continues to be unhappy about the number of school dropouts, especially among those students who believe they are destined for factory or farm work (ibid., 14 December).

Following the conclusion of a national seminar on the topic of the "class struggle" in late June, a series of scientific sessions devoted to this theme were organized for party cadres in most districts of the country. The purpose of these meetings was to explain the "correct" stand of the APL on the major issues confronting the world Communist movement as the ideological conflict between the Albanian and Chinese parties began to intensify (e.g., Tirana radio, 16 July; *Zëri i popullit*, 9 December).

The Economy. The Sixth Five-Year Plan appears to have gotten off to a poor start. Neither the industrial nor the agricultural goals for 1976 were realized and it is unlikely either of these sectors will fulfill its 1977 targets. The regime was quite disappointed that worker productivity was not growing at the desired rate, especially since increased productivity is to account for 50 percent of the planned rise in industrial output and 80 percent of that in agriculture. Also of concern to the APL leadership is the reluctance of workers and managers to institute work norms in those sectors of the economy in which they are not currently found (*Zëri i popullit*, 13, 20 May).

It is also recognized that significant improvements must be made in the quality of production both in agriculture and industry. There were repeated complaints throughout the year about the poor quality of shoes, clothing, glassware, household goods, television sets, and other Albanian-manufactured consumer goods. In addition, the "continuing problems" which have plagued the wholesale and retail distribution systems in recent years resulted in shortages of consumer goods in various regions of the country (*Rruga e partisë*, August; *Zëri i popullit*, 30 July, 5 October, 1 December). As previously noted, the Albanian leadership made several cabinet changes during the year in an effort to correct the problems that have plagued the consumer sector of the economy.

A summer-long drought which continued into the fall may have adversely affected agricultural production. This situation also had a serious impact in the generation of electricity from the country's thermal power plants, which were forced to increase their output to compensate for the decline in hydroelectric output. This development created a heavy demand for oil, a commodity the regime is trying to conserve, and led to demands that Albania rely more heavily on solid energy fuels for heating and thermal power generation. (Ibid., 23 July, 7 October, 12 November.)

The APL leadership up to this point has blamed the economic difficulties during the current Five-Year Plan on deposed State Planning Commission Chairman Abdyl Këllezi and his associates, the former minister of heavy industry and mining and the former trade minister. (*Probleme ekonomike*, Tirana, April-June). The economic difficulties seemed to be of sufficient seriousness to serve as a restraining influence on Tirana as its relations with Peking worsened.

It was revealed that women comprise 47 percent of the labor force. Women made up 53 percent of the labor force in agriculture, 65 percent in light industry, and 70 percent in the health sector (*Zëri i popullit*, 8 March). On the occasion of the twentieth anniversary of the founding of Tirana State University, it was reported that the institution had graduated approximately 21,000 students. Since 1957 the university's student body had grown from 3,613 to 11,095 and its faculty members from 200 to 600. In 1977 the university was comprised of seven colleges, which provided instruction in forty-one specialties (*Ylli*, Tirana, September, *Zëri i popullit*, 1 November).

International Views and Policies. The PSRA during 1977 established diplomatic relations with Upper Volta, Portugal, Togo, and Bangladesh, and at the year's end had diplomatic ties with eighty-one countries.

Aside from the worsening relations with China and expanding ties with Greece, there were no significant changes in Albania's foreign policy stands or attitudes. In his address to the UN General Assembly, Foreign Minister Nesti Nase reaffirmed the Albanian position that the U.S. and the Soviet Union constitute the greatest threats to world peace and the independence and sovereignty of all peoples and countries. He left no doubt that Tirana had no intention of changing its basic foreign policy line, which he alleged enjoyed "broad support." On this point he asserted: "No one should cherish illusions that 'Albania is an isolated country,' that it cannot live without foreign aid or that it will be compelled to stretch a begging hand to anybody" (*Zëri i popullit,* 7 October). Nase concluded by vowing that "Albania will stand free, independent, and firm as a rock" irrespective of any challenges it may face "from whatever source." His sentiments were echoed by Mehmet Shehu and Hysni Kapo, the second- and third-ranking members of the Albanian ruling elite, in important addresses (ibid., 8, 30 November).

Albanian-Chinese Relations. Sino-Albanian party relations began to deteriorate seriously immediately following the APL congress in November 1976. Hoxha and his associates had become distressed about developments in China following the death of Mao Tse-tung in September 1976, when Hua Kuo-feng aligned himself with the "pragmatists" and moved against the "radicals" headed by the Gang of Four. Hoxha viewed this Chinese move to the right as a potential threat to his domestic position, since it could have led to demands that he pattern his policies more closely after those of the Chinese and, perhaps, that he rehabilitate some of the victims of his purges of the mid-1970s whose views were in some respects similar to those of the new Chinese leadership. The Albanians also seem to have been disappointed by the amount of aid China has pledged to furnish for the Sixth Five-Year Plan. In addition to these practical concerns, the Albanian leadership does appear to have been genuinely disturbed by China's seeming loss of interest in the anti-Soviet Marxist-Leninist movement, its rapprochement with the United States and Western Europe, and its growing support of non-Marxist Third World nationalist rulers and leaders. Tirana viewed these latter developments as a "betrayal" of the cause of world revolution (e.g., ibid., 8 February, 7 July, 30 November; *Rruga e partisë,* June).

In December 1976 the Albanians, using pro-Tirana Marxist-Leninist parties as proxies, initiated their ideological polemics with Peking. For the most part, Tirana's allies recited the APL's litany of charges against the Chinese (e.g., *Zëri i popullit,* 5 January and 1, 8, 16 February). Although Peking did not attempt to hide the fact that ideological differences had arisen, it expressed the desire to maintain friendly ties with the PSRA (*NYT,* 10 April). Indeed, Sino-Albanian state relations remained outwardly correct throughout the year. The Albanian press also provided fairly extensive coverage of economic and social developments in China (e.g., *Zëri i popullit,* 2 February, 29 March, 13 April).

The Albanian leadership, however, was becoming increasingly agitated as Hua routed the "radicals"; paved the way for the rehabilitation of Tirana's bête noire, Teng Hsiao-p'ing; built up a strong pro-Chinese faction in the Marxist-Leninist movement; and continued to pursue better relations with Third World countries, Western Europe, the U.S., and even Tito's Yugoslavia.

Frustrated by its inability to influence Hua to change his course, the Albanian leadership authorized the publication of a lengthy editorial entitled "The Theory and Practice of Revolution" in the 7 July issue of *Zëri i popullit.* In addition to reiterating the Albanian list of grievances against Peking, this statement branded Mao's "three world theory" as an "anti-Leninist" and "pseudo-imperialist concept." Mao in 1974 had formulated this doctrine according to which he divided the world into three categories of nations—superpowers, developed countries, and developing nations. In criticizing Mao's doctrine a leading Albanian party theoretician observed that "true Marxist-Leninists do not divide the world on the basis of blocs, but on that of socioeconomic systems" (*Rruga e partisë,* June). The APL at this point escalated its dispute with China not only by condemning the "three world theory," but also by distributing foreign-language translations of the *Zëri i popullit* editorial to journalists in Peking, Belgrade, Athens, and other capitals where the PSRA maintained diplomatic missions (*Christian Science Monitor,* 11 July).

Tirana followed its initial frontal attack on China with the publication on 14 August of the text of a 1965 conversation between Enver Hoxha and Chou En-lai (*Zëri i popullit,* 14 August). By publicizing this exchange of views between Hoxha and the late Chinese prime minister, the Albanians sought to establish that it was Peking which had abandoned the principles that had forged the Sino-Albanian alliance during the 1960s. A similar motivation was behind the APL leadership's decision to publish in early September—while Tito was visiting Peking—a 1963 *Zëri i popullit* editorial denouncing the Soviet-Yugoslav rapprochement. (Ibid., 2 September.)

During November the Albanians further escalated their polemics with Peking when the three leading members of the ruling elite—Hoxha, Shehu, and Hysni Kapo—all strongly condemned the "three world theory" and the policies of the new Chinese regime. In his address commemorating the sixtieth anniversary of the Bolshevik Revolution, Kapo maintained that to "defend the 'three world theory' is to serve as an advocate of imperialism, headed by the United States, as well as of the international bourgeoisie." (Ibid., 8 November.) In his report to the November APL plenum, Hoxha included the so-called "three world theory" in his list of "modern revisionist tendencies" that had "contaminated" the world Communist movement (ibid., 20 November). Mehmet Shehu characterized the "three world theory" as a "fruit of the revisionist anti-Marxist jungle," and admonished the Chinese that, so far as Tirana was concerned, "to make common cause with and to become ideologically reconciled with the Yugoslav leadership is to say you are not a Marxist but a revisionist" (ibid., 30 November).

Since they followed a lengthy Chinese defense of the "three world theory" (see *Peking Review,* 4 November), the strong statements by the Albanian leaders reflected Tirana's determination to persist in its ideological quarrel with Peking. Although it seemed in late 1977 that an ideological break between Albania and China was in the offing, a rupture in Sino-Albanian diplomatic and economic relations appeared less likely. While the Chinese have significantly reduced their level of economic support for the current Albanian Five-Year Plan from the $485 million the PSRA reportedly received between 1971-75 (*International Currency Review,* London, March), the Albanian leaders do not seem eager to exacerbate the nation's economic problems by abruptly terminating Chinese assistance programs (e.g., *Zëri i popullit,* 4 November). A diplomatic break with China would underscore Albania's isolation and could have a negative impact on the morale of the people (BBC, London, 9 November).

Albanian-Soviet Relations. The Soviet Union sought to lure Albania back into its fold as Sino-Albanian relations worsened. Moscow reminded the Albanians of the generous aid the USSR had provided them during the 1950s and expressed a willingness to resume economic relations (Moscow radio, 12, 18 April). Moscow also enthusiastically endorsed Tirana's attacks on the "three world theory" (ibid., 17 July).

Since the APL leaders have taken the Chinese to task for discarding the "Marxist-Leninist position" that both "American imperialism" and "Soviet modern revisionism and social-imperialism" pose equal dangers to the world revolutionary movement, it was not surprising that Tirana rejected all Soviet conciliatory overtures and continued to bitterly criticize the USSR (e.g., *Zëri i popullit,* 14 January, 14 July, 13 December). In their major commentary on the new Soviet constitution, the Albanians charged that it "codified the modern revisionist ideology of a superpower" and "sanctioned the restoration of capitalism" (ibid., 1 November).

Relations with Eastern Europe. Albania's changing relationship with China had a significant impact on its policies and attitudes toward the East European Communist party states as well as Greece. Albania somewhat muted her ideological polemics with the CMEA member-states (e.g., ibid., 21, 27 July, 5 October). This development stemmed from Tirana's recognition that it would probably need to increase its trade with these countries, which between 1971 and 1975 provided approximately 27 percent of Albania's imports and accounted for 49 percent of its exports (*International Currency Review,* March), in the event of an economic break with China.

After nearly a year and a half of steady decline, the volume of Albanian-Yugoslav trade was projected to rise by $20 million during 1977 and expected to total $35 million at year's end (Tanjug, Belgrade, 27 October). This development also appears to have been related to Tirana's growing difficulties with Peking. Although the APL leadership has rebuked China for strengthening its ties with Belgrade (e.g., *Zëri i popullit,* 30 November) and continues to criticize the Yugoslav self-management system (*Rruga e partisë,* September), the Yugoslavs have ignored the Albanian attacks. Belgrade, however, is apparently becoming increasingly apprehensive over the growth of national consciousness among the Albanians of the Kosovo autonomous province (*Chicago Daily News,* 12 October).

In the mid 1970s, as their ties with both China and Yugoslavia cooled, the Albanians expressed interest in improving their relationship with Greece. Cultural exchanges between the two nations were expanded during 1977 (*Zëri i popullit,* 18 May, 19 October; *Shqipëria e re,* July). In July Albania and Greece signed a civil air transport agreement which will give the Albanians their only air service provided by a non-Communist airline (*Zëri i popullit,* 16 July). Both Athens and Tirana reportedly favor the further development of relations, especially in the area of culture and trade (*Washington Post,* 24 September). Since Greece, unlike Yugoslavia, is not a Communist-ruled state, relations between Tirana and Athens are not complicated by the ideological disagreements that have plagued the Yugoslav-Albanian relationship since the end of World War II. As a consequence of Tirana's improving relations with Athens, Albanian-Turkish relations have noticeably deteriorated (*Zëri i popullit,* 31 March).

Relations with Western Europe and the United States. In respect to Western Europe, Tirana seemed mainly interested in promoting cultural activities in those countries with which it maintains diplomatic relations. A major concern of the Albanian regime was to dispel the view both at home and abroad that the PSRA is an isolated country. In addition to increasing the activities of the Albanian friendship societies abroad, Tirana has begun to make available, in greater numbers than previously, translations of Albanian literary works as well as books with political and social themes (see *Ylli,* July; *Shqipëria e re,* January, May, July). The Albanians continued to participate in international trade fairs and displayed an interest in expanding commerce with Western Europe (*Shqipëria e re,* September, October). From 1970 to 1975, non-Socialist countries accounted for about 20 percent of Albania's imports and 27 percent of its exports (*International Currency Review,* March). Among the West European countries, Albania was most critical of Germany, Great Britain, and Spain (*Zëri i popullit,* 20 July, 6 October).

There was no change in Tirana's attitude toward the United States. If anything, Tirana's conflict with Peking has reinforced the conviction of the APL leadership that the United States has been "the greatest oppressor of the peoples of the world since the end of World War II." The Albanians further maintain that since both the United States and the USSR today pose the greatest threats to world peace and the success of the world Communist movement, the APL and all "true Marxist-Leninists" must continue to oppose their "hegemonistic policies." (Ibid., 16 January, 6 October, 30 November.) Tirana was also harshly critical of President Carter for allegedly ignoring the economic plight of the American masses while pursuing "aggression" and "expansionism" abroad (ibid., 21 October).

International Activities and Contacts. The APL has actively sought to gain the backing of the anti-Soviet Marxist-Leninist parties in its ideological quarrel with China. Tirana's staunchest supporters in this dispute include the established Marxist-Leninist parties in Italy, West Germany, Spain, Portugal, Great Britain, Greece, Argentina, Brazil, Chile, Ecuador, Bolivia, Colombia, Uruguay,

Japan, and India. These parties at various times during the year endorsed the Albanian line on the issues that divided Peking and Tirana (e.g., *Rruga e partisë*, February, May; *Zëri i popullit*, 4 November). Although they have been active in their defense of Hoxha and his policies, the pro-Albanian Marxist-Leninists have only a limited following. Their position was further weakened as Peking moved to strengthen its own support among the Marxist-Leninists (*Peking Review*, 21 January, 4 February, 8 April). Alarmed by Chinese moves to create a pro-Peking faction within the Marxist-Leninist camp, the Albanians called for the holding of multilateral meetings to develop common policies and "reestablish" unity among the Marxist-Leninists (*Rruga e partisë*, March). The Chinese, however, ignored these overtures and appear to have thwarted Albanian efforts to gain control of the anti-Soviet faction of the Communist movement.

Insofar as the pro-Albanian Marxist-Leninists are concerned, Enver Hoxha is now the leader of world Communism. In February Spanish Marxist-Leninist leader Raul Marco declared: "Support of and solidarity with socialist Albania and with the heroic Albanian Party of Labor headed by Enver Hoxha has now become the indelible line that distinguishes true Communists from false Communists and opportunists." (Ibid., March.)

The proceedings of the APL Seventh Congress and several of Hoxha's major ideological pronouncements have been translated into such languages as English, French, Spanish, Italian, German, Greek, Portuguese, and Japanese to popularize the Albanian line among the Marxist-Leninists and their sympathizers (*Shqipëria e re*, February, April; *Zëri i popullit*, 11 December). Although the regime has sought to create the impression that the APL enjoys a large following and "great prestige" within world Communism (e.g. *Ylli*, June), it appears that some Albanians were impressed with neither the quantity nor the quality of the party's support (*Rruga e partisë*, June).

Only two Communist party states, Vietnam and Laos, sent delegations to the Albanian Trade Union Congress (*Zëri i popullit*, 21 June) and only one, Vietnam, to the Congress of the Union of Albanian Labor Youth (ibid., 27 September).

Publications. The APL daily newspaper (with a claimed circulation of 108,000) is *Zëri i popullit*. The party's monthly theoretical journal is *Rruga e partisë*. Another major publication is *Bashkimi*, the daily organ of the DF (claimed average circulation of 45,000). The newspapers of the Union of Albanian Labor Youth, *Seri i rinisë*, and the Albanian Trade Unions, *Puna*, are published twice weekly. The official news agency is the Albanian Telegraphic Agency (ATA).

Western Illinois University   Nicholas C. Pano

Bulgaria

The Bulgarian Communist Party (Bulgarska komunisticheska partiya; BCP) traces its origins from the Bulgarian Social Democratic Party, founded in 1891, but its separate existence dates from 1903, resulting from the split between "broad" and "narrow" Socialists. The latter assumed the official name of BCP in 1919, when the party also became a charter member of the Communist International. For tactical reasons the BCP changed its name to "Workers Party" in 1927 and to "Bulgarian Workers Party (Communist)" in 1934, but reverted to the BCP name in 1948, after it had consolidated its rule. Its best-known leader was Georgi Dimitrov, secretary general of the Comintern under Stalin and Bulgarian head of state until his death in 1949.

The BCP assumed power as a result of the unexpected declaration of war on Bulgaria by the USSR and the entry of the Red Army in September 1944, at a time when the pro-Western Muraviev government had broken with the Axis and was arranging an armistice with the Western powers. In the ensuing confusion, the Communist-inspired "Fatherland Front" (FF) coalition, which had refused to join the Muraviev government, staged a coup d'état with the secret support of Muraviev's minister of war and installed itself in power. It took the BCP several years to consolidate its rule by force and violence, disregarding formal pledges and international agreements. Even the former FF allies, combining forces with the "United Opposition," were subdued in a memorable struggle inside and outside parliament, culminating in the mock trial and hanging of their leader, the Agrarian Nikola Petkov in 1948. Ever since, the BCP has maintained its monopoly of power, although nominally an Agrarian party (Bulgarski zemedelski naroden suyuz; BZNS) of sympathizers is allowed to coexist, yet not to compete for power. Since the purge within its own ranks, including the hanging of Traycho Kostov as Titoist in 1949, the BCP has become one of the most obedient pro-Soviet allies as well as one of the most oppressive Communist parties domestically. The present leader, Todor Zhivkov, became party secretary in 1954 and has maintained his power ever since.

The BCP's Eleventh Congress, in 1976, reported a membership of 789,795. This is an increase of over 90,000 (nearly 13 percent) in five years. Party members comprise about 9 percent of the total population of some 8,800,000. Every eighth adult Bulgarian (above eighteen) is a member.

The Congress gave the proportion of workers in the membership as 41.1 percent (a slow increase over 1971), white-collar workers 35.6 percent (a faster growth), and peasants 23.1 percent (a further decline), reflecting the continued bureaucratization and industrialization. The share of women members was reported on the increase (27.5 percent), but it is still too low in view of the preponderance of women in the sex distribution of the population.

As in other Communist states, the BCP holds a majority in the government, including the National Assembly, and in all mass organizations.

Leadership and Organization. The BCP closely follows the Soviet pattern in its organizational and power structure. First secretary Zhivkov, sixty-seven, is also head of state, as chairman of the State Council. Zhivkov has asserted his top position to a point of becoming the object of public adulation, having succeeded so far in eliminating every potential or actual competitor. The most recent purge involved Boris Velchev, Politburo member and Central Committee secretary as well as one of Zhivkov's closest collaborators, who was dropped unexpectedly from both the Politburo and the Central Committee in May 1977. His ouster was followed by major changes in the central party apparatus which were announced at the 19 December Plenum of the Central Committee. At that occasion the Politburo was expanded from eight to eleven members; the number of Central Committee secretaries was increased from four to seven, while nineteen new full Central Committee members were elected (see Radio Free Europe Research, *Bulgaria, Background Report 23*, 1 February 1978). The previous eight Politburo members were: Tsola Dragoycheva, Grisha Filipov, Pencho Kubadinski, Aleksandur Lilov, Ivan Mikhaylov, Stanko Todorov (also premier), Tano Tsolov, and Zhivkov. The three new members are: Dobri Dzhurov (minister of National Defense since March 1962), Petur Mladenov (minister of Foreign Affairs), and Ognyan Doynov, a deputy premier and a rising star of Bulgarian politics. The number of Politburo candidate members was reduced from six to four. The four previous secretaries of the Central Committee (Grisha Filipov, Aleksandur Lilov, Ivan Prunov, Ognyan Doynov) were joined by Dimitur Stanishev, Petur Dyulgerov, and Georgi Atanasov. With 19 December additions, the Central Committee presently has 171 members; there are 107 candidate members.

The unexpected ouster of Velchev, sixty-two, who had been for fifteen years a Politburo member and Central Committee secretary, is attributed to a struggle for power. Speculations have it that Velchev was paying for serious shortcomings in party organization and for striving toward more independence from Moscow, taking advantage of the impact of Eurocommunism (see RFE Research, *Bulgaria: Situation Report*, 16 May), but the most likely reason seems to be personal ambition. It is clear that as long as Zhivkov has the confidence of the Kremlin, his position is safe and the storm around Velchev's elimination was bound to subside. The 19 December Plenum was a case in point, because all the persons promoted to top leadership positions are considered as either Zhivkov's protégés or loyalists.

Mass Organizations. All mass organizations are "transmission belts" of the BCP, functioning under its leadership or control and following its ideology and policies. The Fatherland Front, the largest "non-partisan mass organization," reported over four million members at its Eighth Congress, in June 1977, and includes as its collective members the Agrarian party (120,000), the trade unions (2.5 milion) and the Bulgarian Komsomol (1.4 million), among others. All BCP members are also individual members of the FF.

Party Internal Affairs. The purge of Velchev also brought the removal of his followers. The shakeup in June of the Yambol provincial party committee, in the presence of Zhivkov, where its first secretary — a Velchev appointee — was dismissed for serious violations of party rules as well as for "political shortsightedness" and fostering a climate of dissent, indicated that major disagreements in the top party leadership must have taken place. Changes in the Central Committee's Organization Department pointed to the policy of cleansing key party bodies from Velchev's influence (RFE Research, *Bulgaria: Situation Report*, 15 June). During the last months of the year important personnel reshuffles took place in ministries, Central Committee departments, and provincial party committees. The 19 December changes at the highest level meant, besides the consolidation of Zhivkov's leadership, an overall rejuvenation of key political personnel (Doynov is forty-three, and Mladenov forty-two), with an average age of Politburo members dropping from sixty-three to fifty-nine (RFE Research, *Bulgaria: Background Report 23*, 1 February 1978).

Among other party actions, one may point to a statement of the Central Committee (Radio Sofia, 26 May) concerning serious violations of state planning and fiscal discipline, singling out "Communists who through negligence, arbitrariness, or abuse of their official positions cause violation, squandering of state property, and disregard of the public interests." The Central Committee later on gave a final warning to the first secretaries of the Tolbukhin and Silistra district committees for reporting false data, wasting fodder and the like (see also *Trud.* Sofia, 27 July).

Domestic Attitudes and Activities. The year has registered little new or extraordinary in the various fields of domestic life. The FF's congress (14-16 June) displayed the usual exhortations for involving the popular masses in building an advanced Socialist society, with also the familiar criticism of ideological and behavioral shortcomings. The congress of the Bulgarian Komsomol (9-11 May) also repeated familiar themes: promising full loyalty and dedication to the party and the Soviet Union, and also denouncing apathy and disdain for physical work (40 percent of the graduates of vocational schools were reported not working in their trade), and complaining that many young people still resisted membership in the organization, despite the known pressures and rewards (*Narodna mladezh,* 10 May).

The Komsomol daily, *Narodna mladezh,* witnessed changes in its editorial staff, including the editor in chief, most likely because of open dissatisfaction with his occasionally provocative coverage of social events. The new rubric of "discussions" seemingly went too far in the 20 January issue when the dialogue between writer Radoy Ralin and cartoonist Boris Dimovski contained many implied criticisms of government policies. Also *Rabotnichesko delo* was not immune from criticism: a special decree of the Politburo called for improvements in a range of topics—from increasing the paper's role in the building of Socialism to popularizing the country's ties with the Soviet Union (*RD,* 28 January).

The Third Congress of Bulgarian Culture, 18-20 May, called for strict and comprehensive management and control of all cultural activities. The major report was made by the chairman of the Committee on Arts and Culture, Zhivkov's daughter Lydmila, who found fault with the "ideological and artistic mediocrity" of artists and writers while at the same time speaking of a current "golden age" of Bulgarian culture. She also called for a "total offensive against bourgeois ideology" (*Narodna kultura,* 19 May). Zhivkova's assertiveness was expressed anew in the removal of her predecessor, Pavel Matev, from the Art and Culture Department of the Central Committee and his replacement by her protégé, Lyubomir Pavlov. Also her own husband, Ivan Slavkov, was elevated to the post of director of Bulgarian Television and Radio.

Members of the armed forces were also reminded repeatedly about the role of ideology and discipline, especially during a conference of party secretaries of military units in April: the minister of defense stressed the unquestionable primacy of party over army, while the conference called for "vigilance and aggressiveness in the struggle against bourgeois propaganda and imperialism's slanderous campaign against the USSR and the socialist countries" (*Narodna armiya,* 22, 23 April).

The economy, which was to continue its appreciable growth under the current five-year plan (1976-80), revealed a more or less familiar pattern during the first year of the plan, despite promises and exhortations for a more "intensive" and cost-conscious development than in the past. The plan report for 1976 (*RD,* 3 February) showed a general underfulfillment of scaled-down goals, although overall growth remainted quantitatively high. Thus, national income increased 7 instead of the planned 9 percent, with labor productivity accounting for all of the increase. While total investment exceeded the target, the share devoted to modernization, reconstruction, and expansion of the existing stock fell well below the goal (54 as against 75 percent). The favored industrial sector (accounting for 54 percent of the national income and, in its power, metallurgical, engineering, and chemical branches alone, for half of industrial production) was reported as having fulfilled its plan, but actual fulfillment (8.0 percent) was below the target (9.2 percent). Among the priority branches, the chemical industry showed the poorest results (5.1 percent increases as against 13.4 percent target), but also metallurgy, engineering, and construction missed their goals. The lower-priority consumer goods (light and food) industries also failed their aggregate goal of 9.0 percent growth (the separate results given were 5.3 and 7.7 percent, respectively). The traditionally fluctuating agricultural sector registered an increase in output of 3.1 percent, thus missing again its 5.0 percent target; still, one should consider the results as relatively good. Preliminary estimates for 1977 reported another near-record crop of wheat but a backslide for barley (*Kooperativno selo*, 16 August). Livestock results were mixed to poor (milk production declined, as did the size of sheep herds). The increasingly critical agricultural performance spurred special decrees aimed at assuring a timely harvest, the full utilization of all available resources, and agricultural self-sufficiency (*RD*, 26 May, 20 October); this indicated anticipated problems, due partly to poor weather conditions but also to the perennial shortcomings in farm organization and incentives. The decrees called among other things for mobilization of all available labor, including students and other non-farmers, and promised premiums in kind and cash for overfulfillment of the assigned tasks.

The country's foreign trade suffered a relative decline, with total trade turnover registering an increase of only 8.4 percent. Trade with the Socialist countries, planned to increase over 20.0 percent, realized only a 12.5 percent growth, and trade with the non-Socialist world declined, since Bulgarian imports had to be curtailed drastically (by 15.3 percent) due to the severe deficits of the past. The shares of the Socialist countries and (separately) the Soviet Union in total trade were 80 and 54 percent, respectively, reversing recent trends of a growing Western share. Additional difficulties were higher prices of badly needed raw and other materials which the country imported from East and West. (Ibid., 14 April.)

As to living standards, real per capita income was reportedly increased by 4.4 percent (as against a 4.8 target); public consumption also missed its goal (6.7 as against an 8.2 target); and services to the population showed a drastic underfulfillment (3.7 percent increase as against a target of 11.2 percent.) The average monthly per capita wage was given by Todorov (ibid.) as 149 leva (U.S. $156 at the artifical official exchange rate). Cooperative farmers, whose incomes are still lagging, were to receive higher old-age pensions as well as disability supplements. It might be added that average farmers' pensions in 1977 were about 30 leva, whereas those of workers and employees were about 65 leva (*Durzhaven vestnik*, no. 2, 7 January).

A new system of labor remuneration was outlined (ibid., no. 19, 8 March). It tries once more to relate pay to productivity, simplify the wage rate schedule (ranging between 80 and 244 leva), and cover collective farmers as well, but its complicated provisions have given rise to numerous comments about its practical application. (See discussion in Radio Free Europe, Research, *Bulgaria: Situation Report*, 1 June.) The new system was also on the agenda of the trade unions at their congress in April, but generated only cursory references about the need for its further clarification. The congress reported a large increase in membership (by over one million) due to the recent inclusion of cooperative farmers in union membership (*Trud*, 5-7 April).

The admittedly over-swollen administrative-managerial apparatus (accounting for 13.5 percent of the total labor force, about twice as large as in the other Socialist countries (see *Otechestven front*, 20 April) was trimmed further in 1977, as a result of the decisions of the July 1976 plenum of the BCP. The goal was an overall reduction of 30 to 40 percent. Reported cuts in some regions have affected thus far slightly over 10 percent of administrative personnel, who have been either dismissed or transferred, usually to lower-paid jobs (*RD*, 14 April.)

The National Assembly, convened in April for a two-day session, heard a report by Premier Todorov. Among other matters, it voted a "Law on National Assembly Deputies and People's Councilors," which aimed to broaden their rights but in fact made minor changes, more in form than in substance (ibid).

International Views and Policies. The year 1977 witnessed the continuation of the usual pro-Soviet line in official pronouncements and policy acts. A communiqué following the official visit to

Moscow of the Bulgarian party-state delegation, led by Zhivkov in June, summed it up: "The Bulgarian People's Republic once more confirmed its full support of the foreign policy of the Communist Party and of the Soviet Union. It supports all Soviet initiatives on the international scene." (*RD*, 5 June). The speech by the Bulgarian foreign minister before the U.N. General Assembly on 30 September (ibid., 1 October) and the report by Premier Todorov before the National Assembly (ibid., 14 April) covered in greater detail the gamut of international problems and relations, fully echoing the Soviet views.

Within the Communist movement, the BCP stood firmly behind the Soviet interpretation of "proletarian internationalism" and the need for "international unity and solidarity of Communist and all progressive forces." The most outspoken criticism was reserved for China's "hostile activity of the renegades of the revolution—the Maoists" (Zhivkov, in *RD*, 26 October), while "Eurocommunism" was attacked only obliquely, except for castigating Santiago Carrillo (ibid., 9 July).

Relations with the Soviet Union continued on the road to an "even closer integration in all spheres of life." The six-day official visit to the USSR (30 May-4 June) gave occasion to reaffirm this special "sacred friendship." Zhivkov, who was amply decorated, gave a glowing eulogy to Brezhnev on his return, stating in his speech that Bulgaria's development was possible "only if it followed the line of consistent integration and drawing closer together first of all with the stronghold of the fraternal Socialist community, the great Soviet Union." (Ibid., 5, 10 June.)

The 1977 trade protocol with the USSR called for an 11 percent increase over 1976. The USSR is to supply Bulgaria with most of its needed oil, coal, natural gas, iron ore, and electric power, along with various iron and steel products. Bulgaria is to export agricultural and industrial goods and invest in the development of Soviet resources at a higher rate than before especially in gas, chemical, paper and cellulose, and ferrous metallurgy projects on Soviet territory, to be repaid by future Soviet deliveries. (Ibid, 13 January, and communiqué of Zhivkov's visit in June.)

This growing integration was publicly denounced by the Paris correspondent of the Bulgarian Television and Radio, Vladimir Kostov, a former party official, and given as a reason for his requesting political asylum in France, in July. Kostov was "convinced that the Bulgarian policy of integration with the Soviet Union gravely threatens Bulgarian national independence and restricts the Bulgarian national spirit" (*AFP*, 13 July). In a subsequent "open letter" (*Le Monde*, 15 July) he expressed fear that Bulgaria might soon be officially incorporated in the USSR, and laid the blame on the Soviet leaders and indirectly on their Bulgarian agent, Todor Zhivkov, as the "cult for him and his family" had been inspired in Moscow. He also requested that the plan on Soviet-Bulgarian integration, approved at the BCP's July 1973 plenum, finally be made public, so that the Bulgarian people could realize the impending limitation on their national sovereignty, in violation also of the Bulgarian constitution. These accusations, which generated strong Bulgarian reactions and for a while strained official relations with France, had no visible domestic effect.

The Bulgarian regime outdid itself in eulogizing the Soviet bond on the occasion of the sixtieth anniversary of the October Revolution (see Zhivkov's speech in Moscow, *RD*, 3 November).

The Macedonian issue caused the usual flare-up of polemics with Yugoslavia on two occasions, with regard to Bulgaria's role in the liberation of Yugoslavia at the end of World War II (*Novo Vreme*, February), and in connection with an article in the *Frankfurter Allgemeine Zeitung*, with dateline Skoplje, allegedly inspired by Yugoslav sources and suggesting concessions by Bulgaria on the Macedonian issue, which Sofia resented (*RD*, 10 May).

Relations with many Middle Eastern countries were further strengthened by Zhivkov's visit to Libya and Todorov's visits to Iraq and Iran (all in December 1976). As a supporter of the anti-Israeli line, Bulgaria nurtures active ties with the Arab world and also considers economic exchanges beneficial. During his visit, Zhivkov signed several documents with Libya, including a five-year trade agreement; Bulgaria is to participate in the construction of several industrial and agricultural projects, while Libya is likely to continue to deliver oil. Similar arrangements exist with Iraq. As to Iran, Bulgaria obtained renewed credits for $150 million, seemingly for enlarging its capacity to produce some agricultural foods needed by Iran.

As a result of the heavy trade and payments deficits vis-à-vis the industrial West, estimated at up to $3 billion, Bulgaria restricted its imports, whose value in 1976 fell by 15.3 percent below 1975, while its exports increased by 13.4 percent (*RD,* 3 February). This development confirmed the difficulties which the country is experiencing. It cannot balance its trade with the West, from which it hopes to obtain modern equipment and occasional grains. Thus its modernization is retarded, and at the same time its trade with the Soviet Union and the Soviet bloc has slowed, while the need for energy and raw materials for its industrial plant, in order to step up its exports, becomes greater. In order to encourage tourism, quite important as an earner of hard currency, the government abolished the recently enacted compulsory minimum exchange of foreign currency (*Otechestven front,* 23 April).

Paying lip service to the Helsinki accords, the government permitted more travel to the West and some reunification of families, but rejected as interference in its domestic affairs most of the demands for freedom of information or for the observance of human rights and liberties.

Publications. The daily official organ of the BCP is *Rabotnichesko delo* (Workers' Cause), the monthly is *Partien zhivot* (Party Life), and the theoretical journal is *Novo vreme* (New Times). Other mass party publications are *Politicheska prosveta* (Political Education) and *Ikonomicheski zhivot* (Economic Life). The official news agency is Bulgarska telegrafna agentsiya (BTA).

University of Vermont   L. A. D. Dellin

Czechoslovakia

The Communist Party of Czechoslovakia (Komunistická strana Československa; KSČ) was founded at a merger congress of radical left parties and splinter groups in Prague in November 1921. The so-called Marxist left of the Czechoslovak Social Democracy constituted the core of the KSČ; it had seceded from the mother party in 1920. Shortly after the merger, the KSČ became a member of the Communist International.

In contrast to other ruling Communist parties in Central and Eastern Europe, the KSČ did not gain control gradually but seized power by a coup d'état in February 1948, bringing to a sudden end a pluralist system of long tradition. Formally another three political parties continued to exist in Czechoslovakia, but these are included in the National Front of the Working People, an indissoluble coalition which presents a single ballot at the elections and the statutes of which guarantee to the KSČ a two-thirds majority in all legislative and administrative organs. The president of the republic, Gustav Husák, and the federal prime minister, Lubomír Štrougal, are both members of the KSČ.

Since October 1968 Czechoslovakia, which until then had been a centralist state, has existed as a federation of two ethnic units: the Czech Socialist Republic and the Slovak Socialist Republic. This constitutional reform is all that is left of an ambitious program introduced by a liberal party leadership, with Alexander Dubček as first secretary, in January 1968, but prevented from implementation by a Soviet-sponsored military intervention of five countries of the Warsaw Pact, in August of the same year. The federalist polity, however, has no counterpart in the structure of the KSČ. While Slovak members are organized in the Communist Party of Slovakia (Komunistická strana Slovenska; KSS), an autonomous body within the national party organization, there is no corresponding section for the two Czech provinces, Bohemia and Moravia. This anomaly, often referred to as "asymmetric dualism," has been characteristic of the KSČ since the 1930s; an attempt at its correction in 1968 was abandoned after the Soviet intervention.

The KSČ is one of the largest Communist parties of the world; considered per capita of the population, it is by far the largest of all. According to the most recent official statistics, released in June 1976, it had 1,382,860 members and candidates, in 43,506 party organizations. Almost two-thirds of the membership are of worker origin. Czechoslovak population passed the 15 million mark in 1977 and reached the figure of 15,049,000 (ČETEKA, 16 March); this means that 9.16 percent of all inhabitants of Czechoslovakia are KSČ members or candidates to membership.

Organization and Leadership. Two supreme organs govern the KSČ: the Central Committee and the Presidium. The party held its latest congress, the fifteenth, in April 1976. (The congress was actually the sixteenth in sequence if we consider the emergency congress called by the Dubcek leadership during the Soviet-led invasion in August 1968, the legitimacy of which, however, the present group in control does not recognize.) The next ordinary congress is due in 1981.

The Central Committee includes 121 members and 52 candidates. The Presidium is composed of 12 members and 2 candidates. The Secretariat, headed by Secretary General Husák, comprises six secretaries and two secretariat members. The first secretary of the Communist Party of Slovakia is Jozef Lenárt. The present party line is one of unreserved obedience to the Soviet Union in all internal and external matters. It was imposed upon the KSČ in the spring of 1969, under Soviet threat, while the majority of the members still supported the reformist, more independent course of Alexander Dubček.

Party Internal Affairs. There were no major changes in the internal affairs of the KSČ during 1977. The legitimacy of the present leadership appears to be still a major problem. The conflict about the most suitable course has become less salient since the 1968 intervention, but it has not been eliminated. The so-called normalization which the military occupation of Czechoslovakia should have brought about, and which is understood by the Soviet sponsors largely as a return to the pre-1968 conditions, has been very slow in coming. The opposition against the actual policies is still very strong both among the party membership and the population at large. It flared up in 1977 in a public dissident action which involved all elements of Czechoslovak society (see "Domestic Affairs"). In connection with this action and the sharp countermeasures by the regime, which somehow lacked consistency, it was inferred by a number of observers that there may have been disagreement at the highest power levels about the issue. It was found striking that at the Central Committee meeting which convened at the very height of the regime's campaign against the dissidents, 17 March, no mention was made of this subject. Presidium member Vasil Bil'ák, on another occasion, felt it necessary to deny explicitly "the speculations in the West about some sort of disunity in the leadership of the KSČ" (Radio Prague, 7 February).

Domestic Affairs. A major topic which since January 1977 was part of the domestic scene and on several occasions during the year commanded the attention of world public opinion was a protest by a large number of Czech and Slovak intellectuals, artists, and politicians against the violations and the curtailments of human and civil rights in Czechoslovakia. This published protest became known as "Charter 77."

Based on the principles enunciated in the 1975 Final Act of the European Conference on Security and Cooperation in Helsinki, of which Czechoslovakia is signatory, the authors of the Charter charged that the present Czechoslovak government did not abide by these principles. The Charter made reference to the Czechoslovak Law No. 120, of 13 October 1976, implementing the International Covenants on Civil and Political Rights and on Economic, Social and Cultural Rights, and pointed out that these rights were not respected in Czechoslovakia: the right of free expression was impaired by the existence of the regime's monopoly of the mass media; free circulation of information among nations was impeded by postal censorship; the right of the free exercise of religion was infringed upon by disqualifying the believers from the access to education and professional careers; freedom of travel was restricted by political criteria (*Frankfurter Allgemeine Zeitung,* 7 January).

At the moment of its publication, 257 signatures were appended to the "Charter 77." By the end of the year, some 700 more persons had signed the document. The supporters came from all walks of life: writers, journalists, artists, former politicians, scientists, civil servants, teachers, economic and business executives, military personnel, farmers, and industrial workers. The original text of the Charter was subsequently completed by a number of separate documents dealing with complaints about the violation of the Helsinki agreement and of the pertinent Czechoslovak legislation in specific areas. The remarkable feature of the Charter initiative was that it received endorsement from party members, past and present, as well as from non-Communists. This new coalition of dissidents could hardly be seen as a good omen for the leadership in power.

The regime immediately recognized the potential dangers of the Charter movement. Police harassment of the spokesmen began on the publication of the document and was gradually escalated into a mass campaign of defamation in the official media using distortions and fabricated evidence typical of the peak of the Stalinist era. Simultaneously a number of known dissidents were arrested, among them playwright Václav Havel and journalist Jiří Lederer. Other prominent Charter supporters were put under house arrest, such as the former minister of foreign affairs, Jiří Hájek. The forceful reaction of the regime reached its climax in March, after the sponsors of the Charter approached some Western political representatives during their visit to Czechoslovakia. One of the authors of the manifesto, Professor Jan Patočka died in a Prague hospital on 13 March, of cerebral hemmorrhage, following intense police interrogation (Reuters, Prague, 13 March). Patočka's funeral turned into another manifestation of public dissent, despite police measures restricting participation (*Frankfurter Allgemeine Zeitung,* 17 March). Since then, the regime seemed to opt for the so-called political solution of the problem, previously advocated by some party media (*Rudé právo,* 12 February). This "political solution" consisted of economic and administrative pressures put on the signatories and the sponsors, such as dismissal from employment, loss of apartment lease or of driver's license, and so on. Military persons, for example Lieutenant General Vilém Sacher, former party member and decorated World War II hero, were stripped of their rank and forbidden to wear Soviet and Czechoslovak orders. (*Unità,* Rome, 8 April.) Several Charter spokesmen were given the option between reduction to the status of outcasts at home and emigration to the West. Some yielded to the pressure—former secretary of the party Central Committee Zdeněk Mlynář and historian Jaroslav Krejčí—but many refused to leave the country. (Reuters, Prague, 27 January; AFP, Vienna, 28 April.) In September, the regional court in Ústi nad Labem, in northern Bohemia, condemned each of two defendants to several years in prison for having distributed "subversive literature," which included the text of the Charter (AFP/UPI, Prague, 29 September). About three weeks later, four persons who had been arrested immediately after the publication of the Charter in January received similar sentences at a trial held in Prague (*NYT*, 23 October). Although the regime had insisted that mere signature on the Charter would not be subject to court action, the circumstance that all defendants were either authors or supporters of the Charter suggested that the actual purpose of the trials was to deter the sympathizers with the manifesto, whose number continued to grow.

In July the government approved new directives relative to the status of former Czechoslovak citizens living in the West who had left the country after the Communist takeover in 1948 or after the Soviet-led invasion in 1968. These regulations indicated concern in the party about the neutralization of another source of tension and dissent. The onetime political refugees were invited to "regularize" ex post facto their legal situation vis-à-vis the Czechoslovak state (Radio Hvězda, 30 June). Observers believe that the regime expected the regulation of the status of some 250,000 to 300,000 people who had fled the country since 1948 would provide evidence of its abiding by the stipulations of the Helsinki covenants (*Christian Science Monitor*, 14 July).

Culture, Education, Youth, and Religion. The public action of the dissidents associated with the Charter 77 affected the life of Czechoslovak cultural organizations, either because a number of their members and leaders joined the movement or because the regime used them as spokesmen against it. Thus the congresses of the Union of Czech Writers and of the Union of Slovak Writers, in Prague 1-2 March and Bratislava 2 March, voiced a condemnation of the manifesto. Both congresses, which prepared the way for a National Writers Congress, also stressed the importance of an unqualified commitment to Socialism on the part of writers. (*Rudé právo*, 2 March; *Pravda*, Bratislava, 3 March.) The Czech state minister of culture took a similar stance in his New Year's talk on television (*Rudé právo*, 1 January). On the other hand, the 1977 Workers' Winter Festival showed a more balanced view of art insofar as it presented movies from many countries, inspired by varied "Weltanschauungen" (*Záběr*, no. 2, 14 February). Later in the year, the party's interest in "ideological purity" came to the fore in connection with the admission procedures to Czech and Slovak universities. The importance of class criteria in the selection process was restated by the Slovak minister of education (*Pravda*, Bratislava, 24 June). At the congress of the Socialist Youth Union of Czechoslovakia, in Prague 29 September-2 October, party secretary general Husák warned the youth and students of the "great lie of anti-Communism" and stressed the need for the young people to "strengthen their socialist ideological formation" (Radio Prague, 29 September).

One of the sources of apprehension within the party seemed to be the continuing influence of religious beliefs among the students. The Slovak organ of the Socialist Youth Union complained at the start of the year that "religion still remains the most widespread nonscientific ideology in Czechoslovak society" (*Smena*, 12 January). A call for the intensification of atheistic propaganda was heard on several occasions from party spokesmen. Official relations between the state and the churches were also marked by the controversy with the Charter dissenters; the regime secured a condemnation of the manifesto from church authorities, without even providing the text of the document to be condemned. Nevertheless, there was a visible effort to improve the formal aspect of these relations. In 1977 the seat of the Prague cardinal of the Catholic Church was filled by the apostolic administrator, Bishop František Tomášek, who received his purple hat in Rome, 27 June. Gustav Husák officially congratulated Tomášek on his promotion (CETEKA, 14 July), which was interpreted by some observers as a sign of the betterment of the climate between Prague and the Vatican, troubled by unresolved questions of incumbency of several episcopal seats in Czechoslovakia (DPA, Prague, 16 July).

Economy. In addition to the chronic problems identified by the regime's experts and the media as slow progress in vital investment projects—for example, superhighways (*Silniční obzor*, no. 1,

January), housing (*Plánované hospodářství,* no. 1, January), energy (*Tribuna,* 23 February)—or as alarming proportions of theft and damage to public property (*Pravda,* Bratislava, 4 August), the economy faced two major challenges. One was the unsatisfactory foreign trade balance, especially with the areas of hard currency; the deficit reached 4.5 billion Kčs, a record figure in the entire postwar period (*Statistické Přehledy,* no. 4, April). The disproportions in the supply of and demand for consumer goods forced a rather unpopular revision of retail prices. Although some non-food items became cheaper, the prices of a number of basic groceries rose sharply—above all, coffee and chocolate—and also the prices of woolen and cotton textiles increased (ČETEKA, 22 July). The semiannual report on the 1977 economic plan revealed that the main targets had been reached, although shortcomings of various kinds occurred (Czechoslovak Television, 20 July).

Foreign Affairs. The regime's campaign against the Charter 77 deeply affected its foreign relations. The Charter found sympathetic echo not only in the West but also among non-conformist circles in other Communist countries of the Soviet bloc, in the USSR, and in Yugoslavia (see "International Communist Movement").

Charter sponsor Jiří Hájek sent a memorandum to the Dutch minister of foreign affairs on the occasion of the latter's official visit in Czechoslovakia, informing him of the purpose of the Charter. The minister subsequently received another author of the manifesto, Jan Patočka, in a private audience. This was held by the Communist hosts to be "an insult to the Czechoslovak people, in contrast with all the international standards of conduct and decency" (*Rudé právo,* 5 March).

Czechoslovak-Austrian relations became strained because of the sympathetic attitude of the federal chancellor Bruno Kreisky toward the Charterists. The media of the regime combined criticism of his stand with supposedly more popular attacks on the Austrian government for having allowed the traditional Pentecost rally of the organizations of the expelled German ethnic minority, the Sudeten Germans, to be held in Vienna (ČETEKA, 17 April).

Communist spokesmen and media also scored the U.S. president Carter and his adviser Zbigniew Brzezinski as alleged "instigators and accomplices of the odious Charter business" (*Rolnícke noviny,* Bratislava, 8 March; Radio Prague, in English, 21 July). In this context the Charter was presented as a U.S. maneuver with the intention to torpedo the follow-up of the Helsinki conference, scheduled for the fall in Belgrade. Czechoslovakia participated in the preparatory talks of this meeting, held during the summer (Radio Hvězda, 3 August). Another subject of the dispute between Czechoslovakia and the United States was the still unresolved problem of the return of the Czechoslovak gold reserves, deposited in the U.S. during the Second World War, in exchange for the compensation of U.S. citizens for their former assets expropriated by the Communist authorities. The issue continued to be blocked in the U.S. Congress although on the part of the Czechoslovak negotiators an offer had been made which compared favorably with the agreements already concluded with other Communist countries (ČETEKA, 30 June; *NYT,* 10 April).

An important diplomatic event was the renewal of the representation of Czechoslovakia in Spain and of the Spanish representation in Prague, interrupted since the end of the Spanish Civil War in 1938 (Radio Prague in English, 9 February).

President of the republic Gustav Husák paid an official visit to Iraq in May (*Rudé právo,* 30 May). Shortly afterward the minister of foreign affairs visited Greece and signed an international agreement on road transport and transit traffic (Radio Hvězda, 6 June). In July, a delegation of the Provisional Government of Socialist Ethiopia arrived in Prague for deliberations with the Czechoslovak representatives (ibid., 10 July). The ostentatious moral support lent to left radical regimes of the developing countries by the Czechoslovak government did not prevent the party and the public representatives from celebrating with great pomp the visit of the Iranian shah, Muhammad Reza Pahlevi and his wife (Radio Prague, in English, 27 August). The ruling couple received honorary doctorates in the humanities from Charles University, although the shah passes in the radical circles of the developing countries as the personification of political and social reaction.

Among the most significant official contacts with Communist countries was the accreditation in Peking of the new Czechoslovak ambassador to the People's Republic of China (Hsinhua, 2 February).

In September, a Czechoslovak governmental and party delegation led by Husák visited Hungary for discussions on questions of cooperation and cultural exchange between the two countries (ČETEKA, Budapest, 16 September). In October, a high-level Czechoslovak delegation, headed by Husák, arrived in East Berlin to sign a new Treaty of Friendship, Cooperation and Mutual Assistance with the German Democratic Republic. (Radio Hvězda, 3 October.)

International Communist Movement. The KSČ, which since the Soviet-sponsored military intervention in 1968 has been both the object and the source of crises and disagreements in the world Communist movement, supplied a new topic of controversy by its approach to the Charter 77 action. Virtually all Western Communist parties condemned the punitive measures against the Charter supporters, but not even all ruling parties in Central and Eastern Europe shared the KSČ view of the issue.

An indirect sign of a more tolerant view of the dissident initiative on the part of other ruling Communist parties was given when the Charter 77 was greeted with declarations of solidarity by similar groups in Communist countries. On 9 January about thirty Hungarian artists and scholars sent a statement of sympathy to Pavel Kohout (DPA, Paris, 19 January). On 29 January Soviet physicist Andrei Sakharov and sixty other personalities expressed their support of the Charter cause (AFP, Paris, 1 March). In Yugoslavia, ninety-two intellectuals sent a message of encouragement to the Charter leaders Hájek, Havel, and Patočka (AFP, Paris, 1 March). When Patočka died, twenty-three members of the Polish Workers' Defense Committee in Warsaw expressed their condolence to Jiři Hájek (UPI, Warsaw, 14 March). The respective Communist governments did not take any action against these sympathizers, and either minimized the significance of the gestures or passed them in silence. The invectives against the Charterists by KSČ Presidium member Antonin Kapek during his visit in Moscow and the trip to Prague in March of the Soviet federal minister of interior made some observers speculate about possible Soviet pressure put on the Czechoslovak government for harsher measures against the dissidents. There was no evidence in support of these speculations, however (AFP, Prague, 4 March). On the other hand, it was reported that at the meeting of the secretaries of the central committees of the East European Communist parties in Sofia, 2-3 March, the way in which the Charter affair had been handled by Czechoslovak authorities was criticized, reportedly because of its inflexibility and inconsistency (*Le Monde*, Paris, 19 March).

Among the West European Communist parties, the criticism by the Italian party leaders was the most outspoken. Italian Communists not only rejected the official Czechoslovak thesis about the Charter being a "reactionary maneuver with the purpose of discrediting the cause of Socialism," but also denounced on several occasions the methods used against the promoters of the manifesto (*Unità,* Rome, 13 January, 1 July; *Rinascità,* Rome, 13 January). As the regime's pressure against the Charterists escalated, the Italian Communists offered one of the victims, Milan Huebl, an important position in their press and publication network (*NYT*, 8 May). French party chief Georges Marchais declared that the repression of the Charter 77 had harmed Socialist ideals and was disquietingly reminiscent of the methods used in the Stalinist past (*L'Humanité,* Paris, 26 January). The British party's daily *Morning Star* (19 January) condemned in sharp terms the arrests made in connection with the Charter. The British Communist press also reported that Japanese party chairman Kenji Miyamoto had suggested investigation of the case by a delegation of his party. However, as the Czechoslovak party leadership was not willing to permit this delegation to contact the sponsors of the Charter directly, the initiative did not materialize (ibid., 31 January).

On 17 March eleven former members of the Central Committee of the KSČ (Hájek, Jodl, Kaderka, Kadlec, Kriegel, Mlynář, Šimon, Špacek, Vodsloh and Zelenková) appealed to all European Communist parties for help in inducing the Czechoslovak government and party to abide by the conclusions which in matters of "comradely discussion" and differences of opinion among Communists had been reached at the conference of Communist and workers' parties in East Berlin in June 1976 (Reuter, Prague, 17 March). Although only West European parties acknowledged receipt of the appeal, it drew considerable attention in all Communist circles.

Acting as if relations with the major European parties were not enough strained on account of the Charter dispute, some leading officials of the KSČ made gestures and statements which aggravated the situation. Presidium member Vasil Bil'ák, known as an inveterate pro-Soviet hard-liner, on several occasions attacked West European Communists, especially the French, Italian, and Spanish, for espousing the theories and tactics known as "Eurocommunism." Bil'ák aired his displeasure at the Sofia meeting in March, and at the same month's session of the Central Committee of the KSČ (*Le Monde,* 1 April). In May, he expressed his views of "Eurocommunism" in an article prepared for the Soviet review *Voprosy Istorii.* His analysis was probably stimulated by the publication in April the book *Eurocommunism and the State,* by the secretary general of the Spanish party, Santiago Carrillo. In his article Bil'ák claimed that Eurocommunism was a "bourgeois device to divert attention from genuine Socialism," invented after the "failure of the gimmick of so-called Socialism with human face"—an obvious allusion to the brief democratization period in Czechoslovakia in 1968. He repeated these statements on the occasion of interparty talks with the Austrian party in June. At a press conference with Austrian journalists, Bil'ák concentrated his attacks upon the Italian party (*Volkstimme,* Vienna, 18 June). Soon afterward he again assailed Eurocommunism in his welcoming address at the congress of the Union of Czechoslovak Journalists in Prague (*Rudé právo,* 18 June), labeling Eurocommunism as having "traitorous content" and being an "anti-Soviet instrument." His invectives were followed by a series of endorsements in the KSC daily press (*Rudé právo,* 25, 28 June) and theoretical periodicals (*Tribuna,* 29 June). These elicited energetic rebuke from the spokesmen of the Italian and the Yugoslav parties (*Unità,* Rome, 19 June; *Politika.* Belgrade, 17 May).

Publications. The official organ of the KSC is the daily *Rudé právo* published in Prague in the Czech language. The daily newspaper of the Communist Party of Slovakia is *Pravda,* appearing in Bratislava. Problems of theory and general party policy are treated in the weekly *Tribuna* published by the KSC in Czech. Another party weekly, *Tvorba,* deals especially with international affairs. The biweekly *Zivot strany* is devoted to the questions of the organization and the administration of the party. Problems of Communist economic and social theory are discussed by the monthly review *Nová mysl,* which occasionally also prints articles on historical and philosophical subjects. The Slovak counterpart of *Tribuna* is *Predvoj.* The Central Trade Union Council of Czechoslovakia publishes the daily *Práce,* which has a Slovak counterpart *Práca.* The press organ of the Socialist Youth Union is the daily *Mladá fronta,* apearing in Prague; the Slovak-language journal of the SYU is *Smena.* Czechoslovakia has an official press agency called *Ceskoslovenská tisková kancelár,* abbreviated as CETEKA or CTK.

University of Pittsburgh   Zdenek Suda

Germany:
German Democratic Republic

About a month after the hostilities of World War II had stopped in Europe and the Allied military occupation zones had become operational in Germany, the Soviet Military Administration (SMA) issued its Order No. 2 on 10 June 1945 which gave permission for the founding or reactivation of "anti-fascist" political parties in its zone. This early action by the SMA is an indication of the steps the Soviet Union had carefully planned in order to influence political developments. The Communist Party of Germany (Kommunistische Partei Deutschlands; KPD), an underground organization during the Third Reich, was first to be reactivated. The Social Democratic Party (Sozialdemokratische Partei Deutschlands; SPD) followed shortly thereafter. The Christian Democratic Union of Germany (CDU) and the Liberal Party of Germany (LDPD) were new political creations and also received permission to organize.

Despite substantial material support by the SMA, which regarded the KPD as its indigenous instrument to implement Soviet policies, the Communists failed to gain the confidence of the population—in all probability because of the brutal behavior of the Red Army in the Soviet Zone and the experience of the people with totalitarianism of the Nazi brand. In order to eliminate the competition of the Social Democrats, the SMA forced the merger of the KPD and SPD by "founding" a new party, the Socialist Unity Party of Germany (Sozialistische Einheitspartei Deutschlands; SED) at a "unity party congress" (21-22 April 1946) attended by delegates representing 680,000 Social Democrats and 620,000 Communists, who decided "unanimously" to combine their two parties. Many Social Democrats resisted the merger and continued to work underground. Many were imprisoned and some killed. The SPD could hold a plebiscite only in the Berlin sectors, where 82 percent of its members rejected the merger. Walter Ulbricht, Moscow's most trusted agent and SED deputy chairman, stated at the congress that from then on there were only Socialists, replacing the terms Social Democrats and Communists. Thirty years later, SED chief Erich Honecker recognized only the existence of Communists in the German Democratic Republic (Deutsche Demokratische Republik; DDR; English, GDR). He also declared that from the beginning the SED considered itself "a part of the international Communist movement" (*Die Welt,* Hamburg, 22 April 1976). As early as July 1948, with the help of the SMA, the Communists had gained control of the party apparatus and changed the SED into a "party of new type," modeled after the Communist Party of the Soviet Union (CPSU).

On 7 October 1949, a "German People's Congress" unanimously approved a proposal to create the GDR. This was about a month after the establishment of the Federal Republic of Germany (FRG) in the three Western occupation zones. Three days later, the SMA transferred its administrative functions to the GDR government, and on 15 October the Soviet Union extended diplomatic recognition to the GDR, the "first German socialist state." The SED leadership was in control from the inception of the GDR.

Moscow believed that its occupation zone could be the nucleus for a reunited Germany under Soviet control. This explains a number of developments different from those in other areas under Soviet domination. For example, the first constitution of the GDR consciously resembled certain aspects of the Weimar constitution, including a federal system and a multi-party arrangement, although the SED assumed control of the non-Communist parties, which together with the mass organizations formed the "National Front." The federal system was eventually replaced by a highly centralized order. In 1968 the GDR received a "new Socialist constitution." In September 1974, a number of significant amendments and additions were unanimously adopted by the People's Chamber. For example, in line with the changed overall policy, any reference to the "German Nation" and to "German Reunification" was left out.

The SED initiated quite early a program of socialization of the entire economy, including agriculture. The traditional professional civil service was eliminated, as were the free trade unions. Terror and various methods of mass intimidation succeeded in creating the political, economic, and social structure of a "people's democracy." About three million persons fled to the West before the Berlin Wall and massive border fortifications made *Republikflucht* highly dangerous.

Soviet economic exploitation of the Soviet Occupation Zone and later the GDR required an effective system of controls. Only Moscow-loyal SED functionaries were permitted to hold any significant office. The progressive economic and military integration of the GDR with the Soviet Union and the other Communist-ruled countries of Eastern Europe are other means of achieving and maintaining control. In September 1950 the GDR joined the Council for Mutual Economic Assistance (CMEA). The remilitarization of the GDR started as early as 3 July 1948 when the SMA authorized the formation of armed and garrisoned units of the People's Police, designated in 1952 as the National Armed Forces. After the GDR became a member of the Warsaw Pact, its military forces were renamed the National People's Army (NVA).

The SED in 1977 officially had 2,077,262 members and candidates (*Die Welt,* Hamburg, 10 October). The population of the GDR is 16,786,000. Every eighth person is a member of the party.

Government and Party Structure. The decision-making institutions in the GDR are the SED Politburo and Central Committee. These leading organs also select the key personnel within the party and government bureaucracy. Erich Honecker, secretary general since 1971, also heads the State Council.

The State Council and the Council of Ministers are appointed by the People's Chamber (for a detailed discussion of the governmental institutions see *YICA, 1977,* p. 26). In October 1976, Honecker became chairman of the State Council, which, like the Soviet Presidium, manages the business of the People's Chamber between its infrequent sessions. He also is chairman of the National Defense Council, a government organ with unlimited powers in case of emergency situations resulting from domestic or external causes. Honecker, by combining the three most significant power positions in his own person, has followed the example of Walter Ulbricht.

The present People's Chamber's 500 members were elected on 17 October 1976. The National Front (the SED-controlled alliance with the four "block parties"), the trade unions, and the "mass organizations," such as the Free German Youth (Freie Deutsche Jugend; FDJ), provided a single list of candidates which received 99.86 percent of the valid votes.

The formerly "bourgeois" parties—the [East] CDU, the LDPD, the Democratic Peasant Party of Germany (DBD), and the National-Democratic Party of Germany (NDPD)—exist to draw specific segments of the population to support the SED program and to integrate them politically and socially into the Socialist society. The LDPD at its 1977 congress (Weimar, 2-4 March), attended by about 1,000 delegates, completely endorsed the program adopted at the Ninth SED Congress (1976). The LDPD in 1948 had 183,000 members and at present has about 75,000 (*Rheinischer Merkur,* Cologne, 11 March 1977). Its congress hailed "Socialism as the expression of humanism of the twentieth century." The NDPD at its 1977 congress (East Berlin, 21-23 April) declared that "the members of the NDPD accept without reservation the increased leading role of the working class and its Marxist-Leninist party, the SED" (Bundesminister fuer innerdeutsche Beziehungen, *Informationen,* Bonn, no. 10, p. 9). The DBD congress (Schwerin, 18-20 May) drew 1,140 delegates. The chairman told them that their "highest duty" was to "continue to stand in the first rows at the realization of the great objectives adopted by the Ninth Party Congress of the SED" (ibid., no. 11, p. 12). The party has 92,000 members.

As for the SED, no changes in the composition of its Politburo and Secretariat were announced in 1977. (For names see *YICA, 1976,* p. 27.)

Mass Organizations. The mass organizations assist the SED in its work and control functions. They also provide the party with a mass basis for political indoctrination and pre-military training. They serve as recruiting ground for future party functionaries, and in the case of the Free German Youth, the most important of them, as supplier of new members also. It was reported that as part of the "Party Initiative of the FDJ" on the occasion of the Ninth SED Party Congress (1976), 109,935 of the best FDJ members asked for acceptance in the SED (*Junge Welt,* East Berlin, 31 May 1977). FDJ members in June 1976 numbered 2,157,734 (ibid.). The FDJ first secretary is Egon Krenz, a candidate member of the SED Politburo. The FDJ supervises the Ernst Thälmann Pioneers, the Communist children's organization, with close to two million members.

In 1977 the Free German Trade Union Federation (FDGB) held its Ninth Congress (East Berlin, 16-19 May). The 3,009 delegates represented 8,373,000 members; also attending were seventy-seven trade union delegations from seventy-one countries, including representation from the German Communist Party in the FRG. SED-Politburo member Harry Tisch was reelected chairman. Some 350,000 meetings within the trade unions, started in November 1976, elected the workers' representatives. Women make up 51 percent of the FDGB membership and hold 40 percent of the union jobs (*Informationen,* no. 11, p. 14; Press Department of the Ministry of Foreign Affairs, *Foreign Affairs Bulletin,* East Berlin, 13 July, p. 154). The congress pledged the FDGB's friendship with the Soviet Union, endorsed proletarian internationalism and social patriotism, and stressed the working people's "profound confidence" in the policy of the SED (ibid.).

Another mass organization, the Culture League (Kulturbund) also had a congress (East Berlin, 22-24 September), with 580 delegates. The main topic was "Life-Style and Culture in the Developed Socialist Society" (*Die Welt,* 23 September). The league has some 205,000 members, in 1,828 local groups; the first secretary is Dr. Karl-Heinz Schulmeister (*Informationen,* no. 17, p. 8).

The pre-military training of the majority of the youth in GDR is provided by the Society for Sport and Technique (GST). Its congress (Karl-Marx-Stadt, 17-19 June) had about 1,200 delegates and 300 guests from the "Socialist countries." Lieutenant General Günter Teller was reelected chairman of the GST Central Executive Committee. Resolutions pledged the strengthening of the GDR's defense capability and the combat readiness and ability of the working people (Voice of the GDR, East Berlin, domestic service, 17 June; ADN, international service, 19 June). (For other mass organizations see *YICA, 1976,* p. 26.)

Party Internal Affairs. The first party elections in the SED basic organizations since the Ninth Congress (1976) constituted a high point in the party's 1977 activities. Elections were held from 1 March to 30 April in some 85,600 party groups, 20,790 departmental organizations, and 51,560 basic organizations. The election meetings, attended by 90.3 percent of the membership, reviewed the implementation of decisions of the Ninth Party Congress and set out new tasks (ADN, international service, 11 March). At the lower levels, 366,633 members were elected into leadership positions; 51.6 percent of them were workers (*Informationen,* no. 11, p. 3).

The SED Central Committee reported one significant personnel change. The former director of the sector of the Central Committee dealing with church matters, Willi Barth, retired for reasons of age; he was replaced by Rudi Bellman (ibid., no. 9, p. 13).

The SED Politburo on 18 May called upon the party membership to intensify political work among the masses. Members were advised not to avoid the "dialogue with the people," and SED propagandists were ordered to pursue their ideological controversy with the opponents aggressively. The Politburo recognized that there is a critical attitude among the people concerning the armament build-up of the Socialist countries. Also the attempts of the opponents to assume the role of the "improvers of Socialism" are being discussed amongst the population and must be dealt with offensively (*Die Welt,* 23 June). A two-day conference on "Further Tasks of the Political Work among the Masses by the SED" was organized (East Berlin, late May) by the Central Committee to instruct about 900 party officials, propagandists, social scientists, journalists, cultural workers, and functionaries of social organizations (*Informationen,* no. 12, p. 3).

· SED chief Honecker received the highest national award, the Karl-Marx-Order, on the occasion of his sixty-fifth birthday; also he was honored by the Supreme Soviet of the USSR with the Order of the October Revolution. Various others received the Karl-Marx-Order, including Honecker's wife on her fiftieth birthday for her work as minister of education.

Domestic Affairs. *Legal Reforms.* The People's Chamber unanimously approved on 7 April 1977 a number of new laws intended to "give further substance to the Socialist legal system and its humanistic content." One such law linked the work of the public prosecutor's office with the social bodies in enforcing Socialist legality and ensuring order and security. Others dealt with prison sentences and the reintegration of convicted persons into society. (*Foreign Affairs Bulletin,* 22 April, p. 89). The changes of the criminal laws provided for more severe penalties for political offenses such as "anti-state incitement" and "trade with human beings" (assistance given to persons attempting to leave the GDR illegally). Life sentences can be given in severe cases of this latter offense. New also is the concept of "public malignment of the state, its institutions, organs, or social organizations (*Informationen,* no. 8, pp. 4-5).

On 1 January 1978 the new Labor Code (Arbeitsgesetzbuch, AGB) will come into force. It was approved unanimously by the People's Chamber on 16 June 1977. (Ibid., no. 15, pp. 6-8.) The Labor Code should be understood as a directive to the ministers, the factory managers, and all work collectives to give full support to raising the quality and efficiency of work in accordance with the standards of the Ninth Congress and to fully utilize scientific-technical progress ("Voice of the GDR," domestic service, 13 June). Erich Honecker called it the "Magna Charta of Work." It does not include the right to strike (*Die Welt,* 18 June).

Effective 1 May 1977, about 1.2 million workers had their work week shortened from forty-two to forty hours. The same applied to about 300,000 working mothers with at least two children below the age of sixteen. About 600,000 shift workers had the weekly work time reduced from forty-three and three fourths to forty-two hours (*Die Wirtschaft,* East Berlin, no. 8).

Youth Indoctrination. Prior to the commencement of the 1977/78 school year, teachers' conferences were held in all the 218 districts. The teachers were told that all students should be given more convincing instruction about the content and aims of the SED program. Also the "irreconcilability of the two social systems" was to be emphasized. (There are about 200,000 teachers for the 2,595,000 children of school age.) (*Informationen,* no. 18, p. 7.) In the GDR, political-ideological instruction begins with the start of a child's education. The teachers must instill "a hatred of everything which endangers life within Socialism. This hatred of the imperialist policy of the Bonn state [FRG] must be in the nature of a principle . . ." (*Deutsche Lehrerzeitung,* as noted in *Die Welt,* 18 December 1976).

In 1977 the so-called Youth Consecration (*Jugendweihe*) was given to 283,500 students of the fourteen-year-old or eighth grade group (*Deutsche Lehrerzeitung*, no. 13, 1 April). In East Berlin alone, 18,000 boys and girls pledged their "allegiance to Socialism" (*BZ am Abend*, East Berlin, 12 February). The Committee of Anti-Fascist Resistance Fighters of the GDR assisted in the ideological preparation of the youths (*Berliner Zeitung*, East Berlin, 11 January).

GDR Anniversaries. Celebrations in 1977 marked the twenty-fifth anniversary of the para-military GST and the thirtieth of the German Democratic Women's League. The FDJ Central Committee organized a meeting in East Berlin to mark the seventieth anniversary of the Socialist Youth International.

On 7 October, the annual "National Day," the founding of the GDR was celebrated throughout East Germany with award ceremonies, inaugurals of new economic projects, meetings of German-Soviet friendship societies, and public festivals. A military parade, including the display of heavy weapons and Soviet-made rockets, took place in East Berlin in violation of the special status of Greater Berlin (*Die Welt*, 8 October).

State-Church Relations. The 1977 documentation of Amnesty International draws attention to the difficult situation of the church in East Germany. The self-immolation of Pastor Oskar Brüsewitz in 1976 gave evidence of the tensions between the atheist state and the various churches in spite of the existing co-existence agreement. (Ibid., 11 October.)

East Berlin bishop Albrecht Schönherr, chairman of the Synod of Evangelical Churches, asserted that the data provided by state authorities, which claimed that only about 10 percent of the GDR population are Christians, was much too low (ibid., 10 March). In May, at a meeting of the synod in Goerlitz, Bishop Schönherr criticized the manner in which the SED implements its role of leadership, noting that the self-interpretation of the Protestant Church Federation as a "church under Socialism" represented a "formula of co-existence" despite existing disagreements in ideas and basic views. He also referred to the many cases in which parents were warned by teachers against allowing their children to receive Christian instruction. He emphasized that young Christians in the GDR stand little chance of reaching important positions regardless of their skills. (Ibid., 16 May.) The continuous decrease in the number of Protestant pastors is a matter of great concern to the churches in the GDR (ibid., 20 June).

Catholic bishop Hugo Aufderbeck in 1973 characterized his church in the GDR as a small body of about 1.3 million Catholics in the Diaspora, facing a powerful and atheistic *Weltanschauung*. This situation has not changed. Of greatest importance for the church is the training of new priests. More than half of the present 1,303 active priests have gone through the philosophical-theological faculty at Erfurt, the only educational institution for Catholic priests, and the seminaries at Neuzelle/Oder and Huysburg b.Halberstad (*Rheinischer Merkur*, 21 January 1977). At present, there are 120 theology students at Erfurt (*Informationen*, no. 13, pp. 12-13).

On the other hand, the SED manages to mobilize a number of Catholics for the party's political objectives. For example, a group of "Catholic figures," not further identified, welcomed the convening of the World Conference of Religious Representatives to be held in June 1977 in Moscow. The group declared:

> In the GDR we feel sheltered because [the state] guarantees the dignity of man, his basic rights and freedoms. Equal rights guarantees for us Catholics an unrestricted service to our neighbor and to the whole society .... Satisfied that our state is doing everything in its power to implement the principles of the Helskinki final document, we call for full observance of the principles by all other signatories states as well. (*Neue Zeit*, East Berlin, 24 March 1977, p. 2.)

The Jews in the GDR number about 750. Four hundred of them live in East Berlin. In 1962, the Jewish community of East Germany totaled 1,800. (At the time of Hitler's rise to power, in the area of East Berlin alone there were 160,000 Jews.) The Jews in the GDR have been without a rabbi since 1969. Services are conducted by lay members. The 6,000-strong Jewish community in West Berlin helps out, and cantors from the West provide funeral services (*NYT,* 17 April 1977). Helmut Aris, chairman of the Association of Jewish Congregations in the GDR, speaks for those among the East German Jews who reject Zionism and Israel's actions. "The members of our eight congregations are proud to have made their contribution toward the building of Socialism in the GDR" (ADN, international service, 6 January).

Military Affairs. The GDR budget for 1977 foresees an expenditure for the military of 7.87 billion marks (6.5 percent of the entire budget) and 3.2 billion marks for "public security," including the security of the state borders. Together this amounts to 11.07 billion marks, representing an increase over 1976 of 800 million marks or 7.7 percent. GDR military expenditures have increased since 1969 by 61.1 percent; the outlay per capita of the population went up from 372 to 602 marks in 1976. The high cost is due at least in part to the fact that the GDR has no noteworthy armament industry and depends almost exclusively on Soviet imports (*Die Welt,* 17 December 1976).

The estimated strength of the different components of the NVA is: army, 98,000; air force and air defense units, 28,000; naval forces, 17,000; border troops, 46,000; total, 189,000. The NVA has about 2,000 tanks, predominantly T54/55 and T62; 850 artillery pieces; 450 antiaircraft guns; 330 combat planes, mostly MIG 21 but also some MIG 17 and 19; and a limited number of tactical rockets which also can be armed with nuclear warheads. The NVA is considered the best of the Warsaw Pact armed forces, after that of the Soviet Union (*Rheinischer Merkur,* 21 January). The NVA naval forces are subordinated to the Soviet Naval Command, located at Königsberg (*Die Welt,* 30 March). Substantial tactical support comes from the Armed Factory Units (*Betriebskampfgruppen*), which have about 500,000 men. Many of them are reservists of the regular forces. "Civilian border troops' helpers" provide support to the regular border troops (*Die Welt,* 2 December 1976).

The GDR Civil Defense, formerly under the Interior Ministry, now belongs to the Ministry of National Defense. The former Garrisoned Air Raid Battalions (*Kasernierte Luftschutzbataillone*), with about 15,000 men, are now the Civil Defense Action Forces (*Einsatzkraefte*). These troops together with special installations and armament institutions are part of civil defense (*Informationen,* 1977, no. 9, p. 7). The defense minister, Army General Heinz Hoffmann, regards civil defense as a "fundamental requirement for securing the viability" of the GDR (*Neues Deutschland,* 14/15 May).

Political reliability is a determining factor to be noted when evaluating the NVA. No army in Europe has had as many deserters as that of East Germany. Nevertheless, this fact may not now be relevant, since the NVA has developed a system, modeled after the Soviet armed forces, for the penetration and control of every unit. Three separate commands parallel each with independent report channels: the SED, the Political Main Administration, and the Ministry of State Security (*Die Welt,* 15 October). Also the continuous political indoctrination and education to hate the "imperialist class enemy" is supposed to improve the reliability of the troops (see Eric Waldman, "The Military Policies of an Archetypical Soviet Satellite, the German Democratic Republic," *Canadian Defense Quarterly,* Toronto, no. 4, Spring 1976, pp. 46-52). An additional source of strength, according to the defense minister, is the "close alliance with the glorious Soviet Army" and the fraternal armies of the Socialist countries (*Krasnaiya Zvezda,* Moscow, 1 March 1977).

Security Matters. The SED regime, faced by the problem that thousands of GDR inhabitants would like to leave either legally or by escaping across the formidable fortifications along the border facing West Germany took further steps to discourage and prevent exodus during 1977. Prison sentences of persons apprehended when attempting to leave the country and of those who assisted them were made stiffer (*Die Welt,* 16 June). The number of applicants who wish to emigrate is estimated to be close to 200,000. In their appeals they refer to the GDR constitution, the U.N.

Declaration of Human Rights, and the Final Act of Helsinki. The GDR counters their efforts by posting police around the Office of the Permanent Representation of the FRG in East Berlin, dismissing these people from their jobs, and intimidating them by various other means. (Ibid., 12 January, 25 April.) The Foreign Office declares that there is no universal freedom to emigrate under existing international law and that therefore the GDR citizen has no personal right to emigrate (ibid., 18 December 1976). And finally, the physical obstacles, the fortified and well-guarded borders were further perfected in 1977. NVA engineers closed the last gaps of the 840-mile long border with metal fences and added automatic firing devices of a new type, "New Barrier 501," to the about 40,000 shrapnel mines of the SM-70 type. It is estimated that 1.2 million mines have been placed along the demarcation line. Also a new type of control tower has made its appearance (*Washington Post,* 25 April 1977; *Die Welt,* 24 February, 6, 15 August; Hamburg radio, 1522 GMT 11 August). The cost per mile of the border fortification is estimated by the U.S. Army officers at about $650,000 (*Washington Post,* 25 April).

In spite of the reduced chances to cross the fortified border, 493 persons managed to escape during the first eight months of 1977 (*Die Welt,* 8 September). Since 1961, at least 101 persons have been killed while attempting to escape. Numerous individuals were injured and arrested by the East German border troops. According to the SED, the military measures along the border with the FRG are necessary in the interest of maintaining peace in Europe (*Einheit,* 8 February).

The system of close surveillance of every inhabitant of the GDR has also improved. Everyone has had to fill out a long questionnaire which provides a complete personal background and also information about relatives, including their membership in party and mass organizations. Also relatives who have moved into "capitalist" countries had to be enumerated. (Ibid., 4 January.) Each person in the GDR has an identity number which facilitates the storage of personal data through electronic data processing (East Berlin, domestic service, 20 February).

It has been reported that since the signing of the Basic Treaty with the FRG in 1972, the GDR has drastically increased its secret control apparatus. More than 250,000 agents (one out of every 67 GDR residents) work for the State Security Service. About 150,000 "house stewards" in apartment houses report on any unusual occurrences or visitors. In enterprises, schools, hospitals, and public offices about 800,000 secret informers keep the rest of their co-workers under observation (*Die Welt,* 21 July). These figures do not include the "scouts of peace" (*Kundschafter fuer den Frieden*) of the Ministry of Security who carry on their work abroad. During 1977, West German counterintelligence apprehended several of these agents, some of whom had attained highly sensitive positions within the government and industry.

The political protest in East Berlin's Alexanderplatz on 7 October during the GDR's anniversary celebration showed that spontaneous outbursts cannot be prevented. Some 1,000 young people demonstrated and chanted "Russians out" and smashed windows (*Christian Science Monitor,* 11 October). Reportedly, two policemen and one girl lost their lives, while about 700 youths were arrested (*Die Welt,* 13 October). The authorities blamed the disturbances on rowdies (ADN, international service, 8 October).

The regime, assured of the Soviet leadership's complete support against dissidents, uses at least three methods to silence the opposition. One method is isolation, as in the case of Professor Robert Havemann, who lives in East Berlin under house arrest and under constant surveillance (*Sunday Times,* London, 13 February). His daughter, a student of psychology, was expelled from the University of Jena (*Der Spiegel,* Hamburg, 14 February). His lawyer was expelled from the lawyers' association (*Die Welt,* 2 March). A second method is forced exile. After being blacklisted and denied jobs, these people eventually ask permission to leave. More than twenty East German artists have been affected in this manner during the last year and a half, among them authors and poets, musicians, and theater personalities (*Washington Post,* 6 September). And finally, a third method is to arrest dissidents and charge them with various "political crimes." The oustanding example is the arrest of Rudolf Bahro, an economist and political scientist, who published a book in West Germany highly critical of the SED state. He describes the present party organization as a structure which actively produces wrong images of the actual requirements of society (*Die Welt*, 26 August). The official SED organ (*Neues Deutschland*, 25 August) reported that Bahro was arested on 23 August as an alleged spy, the first East German dissident to be so charged. Although the majority of the approximately thirty cultural figures who have left the GDR are not of Jewish origin, subtle anti-Semitic overtones are noticeable. A Communist party member in Dresden reported that officials had commented in closed sessions that "the ringleaders among the opposing intellectuals are Jews" (*NYT*, 14 August).

Political Prisoners. West German authorities estimate that about 7,000 political prisoners are held in GDR penal institutions. At least 4,000 of them are serving terms of two to ten years for "flight from the republic," a crime which includes attempted escape or aiding others to escape (*US News and World Report*, 17 January 1977). Amnesty International reports that political prisoners are kept together with criminals of all kinds (*Die Welt*, 11 October). As in previous years, the FRG government bought the freedom of a number of political prisoners detained in the GDR. In 1976, about 1,300 prisoners were freed in this manner at a cost of about $50 million (131 million marks) (ibid., *Die Zeit*, Hamburg, 25 March). This trade in human lives had a slow start in 1977. Until the end of May, the freedom of only 50 prisoners could be bought. In June, 86 prisoners arrived in the FRG and in September an additional 144 (*Die Welt*, 25 June, 20 September).

For the first time a case became known where a prisoner's freedom was bought by private persons. A twenty-five year-old student of medicine was released from prison after his parents paid over $100,000 (250,000 marks). He had been sentenced to four and one-half years for assisting in the crime of *Republikflucht*. (Ibid., 26 August.)

Eleven East German political prisoners were released in exchange for Chilean Communist leader Jorge Montes, following the example set by Moscow in the exchange of Vladimir Bukovsky for Luis Corvalán. (Ibid., 20 June).

The Economy. The Report of the Central Statistical Board of the GDR on the 1976 economic plan stated that the national income, the closest equivalent to the gross national product in the West, grew by 3.7 percent, as compared with a rather low target of 5.3 percent. The main reasons for the poor results were the rising costs of imports and the severe summer drought. Agriculture fell 9.8 percent below the 1975 levels (*Foreign Affairs Bulletin*, 17, no. 4, 4 February). The foreign trade balance for 1976 registered a record deficit of $2.68 billion, 50 percent above the 1975 deficit (*NYT*, 5 July 1977). The import of raw materials has been the greatest economic problem for the GDR ever since Moscow boosted prices to East Germany and other CMEA members. Oil prices, for example, were doubled within three years (*Die Welt*, 23 June). Moreover, Soviet supplies of raw materials became inadequate to meet requirements, and East Berlin had to turn to Western resources. In addition to the trade deficit of 430 million rubles with the Soviet Union, the GDR's largest trading partner, indebtedness to the West grew to $5 billion (from $4.5 billion) in loans and credits, plus $1.15 billion owed to the FRG (one-third in government-sponsored credits on which no interest is paid) (*Informationen*, no. 9, p. 7; *NYT*, 5 July). Before the end of 1977, the GDR had already borrowed $470 million. The sum does not contain the additional $150 million of credit for the Foreign Trade Bank in East Berlin which in October was still in negotiation (*Die Welt*, 8 October).

On 17 December 1976 *Neues Deutschland* published excerpts of the Five Year Plan for 1976-80 and the Economic Plan for 1977. One indication of the implementation of the 1977 economic plan was given by SED chief Honecker in his report to the Central Committee meeting of 17-18 March.

He stated that "the dynamic growth of achievements was continued in 1977, thus the growth rate in the production of goods amounted to 5.6 percent in the sphere of the industrial ministries at the end of February" (ADN, international service, 1704 GMT in German, 17 March). He did not mention the other fields of production, such as agriculture, which reduced the overall 1976 growth rate considerably. Other reports gave industrial growth at 4.8 percent, as compared with the planned 5.1 percent (Deutsches Institut fuer Wissenschaftforschung, Berlin, as reported in *Die Welt*, 11 August). *Neues Deutschland* reported on 15 July the results of the first half of the 1977 Economic Plan. It asserted that all targets had been met or were surpassed. However, comparison with the growth rate of 1976 and the planned objectives for 1977 show that important targets were not reached. For example, the projected growth rate was 5.5 percent, but only 4.5 percent was achieved in the first half year (*Informationen*, no. 16, pp. 8-10). East Berlin expected a better harvest in 1977 than in the two previous years, but the GDR is not self-sufficient despite increased acreage. It buys normally two to four million tons of grain from the Soviet Union. The FRG since 1971 has delivered annually about 20,000 tons of fish meal and 500,000 tons of other fodder rich in albumen. To increase agricultural production, the industrialization of agriculture has been intensified and more Agricultural Production Associations (Landwirtschaftliche Produktionsgenossenschaften; LPG) are being combined (*Die Welt*, 9 August).

The part women play in the GDR economy is impressive: women comprise 49.8 percent of the working population and 45 percent of the working force in industry; 86.8 percent of the women able to work are either employed or studying (*Die Welt*, 24 January; 9 March).

Trade with the Soviet Union during the first half of 1977 increased by 16.5 percent, as compared with the same period in 1976. Imports from the Soviet Union went up by 23.1 percent and reached 1,820.4 million rubles. Exports to the Soviet Union increased by 9.5 percent and had a value of 1,519.9 million rubles. The trade deficit for the first half of 1977 amounted to 304 million rubles, or 200 million more than during the same period in 1976 (*Informationen*, no. 19, p. 8).

Erich Honecker is fully aware of the economic problems faced by the GDR. Under the current Five-Year Plan the GDR has imported 14.5 billion tons of petroleum from the West. In 1972, the price of each ton was 58.73 Valuta Marks; in 1976 it went up to 212.94 Valuta Marks. Hence one of the objectives is to get foreign currency in every way possible. The establishment of so-called "intershops" proved to be a valuable source for hard currency and they provided higher profit margins than those of the general foreign trade (*Der Spiegel*, 21 March). These intershops sell merchandise only for foreign currency and have high-quality goods which normally are not available in the regular stores. The inhabitants of the GDR are permitted to obtain foreign currency from abroad which enables them to buy in the intershops. Since 1974, any East German is allowed to own up to $200 in West German funds. It is estimated that the annual business amounts to 700 to 800 million marks in hard currency (*Die Welt*, 6 September).

East Germans complain that a two-class system has developed, because those without foreign currency cannot buy in the intershops. A factory team of East Berliners demanded that 20 percent of their pay should be in West German marks. The demand was rejected, and the dissatisfaction remains unsolved (*NYT*, 2 October). As a result of the pressure to increase exports, consumer goods production suffers, with the result that private consumption in the GDR is a third lower than in the FRG (*Die Welt*, 9 June).

Prices remained stable in the GDR as a result of massive price support by the government in the amount of 13.5 billion marks. However, increased prices for luxury items, appliances, and cars were to bring in more than 30 billion marks. (Ibid., 3 February.) In May, Honecker warned for the first time that price increases might also be necessary in the GDR and stated that "the capitalist crisis also affects us" (ibid., 20 May).

Contrary to the Communist opposition to the building of nuclear power plants in the Western industrial countries, the GDR and the other Soviet bloc nations have placed increased emphasis on nuclear power. East Germany at present generates 950 megawatts from such plants and expects to increase this source of energy (*Horizont,* East Berlin, no. 12, 1977; *NYT,* 25 March). For the GDR this is most important because by the end of 1977 the bituminous coal mines will be exhausted and closed. East Germany has rich deposits of brown coal which supply 70 percent of the energy needs (*Die Welt,* 23 August).

The GDR has been trying to improve its trade relations with the United States. A trade agreement between the two countries was signed on 16 June (*NYT,* 27 June). According to East German statistics, trade with the U.S. in 1976 amounted to $936 million, as compared with about half that amount in 1975 (ibid., 5 July).

Foreign Affairs. *Relations with the Federal Republic of Germany.* GDR Deputy Foreign Minister Kurt Nier noted on 14 August 1977 the issues of importance, as viewed by East Berlin, which are to be considered in the discussions by the permanent representative of the GDR in the FRG, Dr. Michael Kohl, and the FRG minister of state in the Federal Chancellery, Hans-Jürgen Wischnewski, as follows:

> The policy of detente and the further normalization of the relations between the GDR and the FRG have, as far as the GDR is concerned, the highest priority in these talks. Issues such as the acceptance of sovereignty and the sovereign equality of states, the observance of the border between the GDR and FRG as state border between two sovereign states independent from each other, the non-interference in domestic affairs, as well as the question of citizenship and a series of other problems are part [of the objectives of these talks]. (*Informationen, no 17, p. 4.)*

The official SED organ *Neues Deutschland* (22/23 January) rejected categorically FRG Chancellor Helmut Schmidt's concept of "special relations" between the two German states, characterizing it as "infamous fiction" along with his "phantom" idea of "one German Nation" which has long ceased to exist. The paper continued:

> ... there exist on German soil two sovereign German states which are independent of each other and have different political and social systems. This state of affairs also suggests conclusions for the FRG which must be drawn without reserve. There is no alternative.

SED chief Honecker in his widely publicized interview with the West German newspaper *Saarbrueckner Zeitung* on 17 February emphasized East Berlin's insistence that the FRG recognize GDR citizenship, without which a "general freedom of travel" to Western countries was absolutely out of the question (*Foreign Affairs Bulletin,* 17, no. 7, 8 March, p. 50). The FRG Supreme Court has ruled that there is only one citizenship according to West Germany's Basic Law. East Berlin wishes to end the situation that permits any East German who can manage to enter the FRG to claim his rights as West German citizen (*Christian Science Monitor,* 9 February).

Honecker pointed at the refusal of Bonn to recognize the "state borders" and the "GDR citizenship" as the real cause of the poor relations between the two states, and added that if the "old revanchistic laws of the FRG" were the reason for its not recognizing these basic demands, then the laws must be changed (*Die Welt,* 28 September).

Throughout the year, so-called preliminary talks between East and West German representatives took place without finding mutual agreements on the pending issues. The demands by the Christian Democrats that economic pressures be used by the FRG have been rejected by the Socialist-liberal coalition government in Bonn. Also Erich Honecker is of the opinion that the economic relations between the two German states should develop independently from the political situation. The reason for his view is obvious, considering the benefits which the GDR derives from the economic relations. According to a calculation prepared by the Christian Democrats, financial contributions by Bonn to East Berlin amounted in 1976 to 656 million marks. This amount does not include the financial advantage of the interest-free FRG credit of 850 million marks and a number of rather high monetary gains from trade within the European Common Market and FRG-insured private credits (*Deutschland-Union-Dienst*, Bonn, 31, no. 78, 25 April).

A number of serious aggravations had a direct impact on relations. Because of the great numerical increase of visitors from West Germany and West Berlin, the East German authorities continued with the implementation of their policy of "ideological delimitation." Between 1 December 1976 and the end of August 1977, a total of 1,182 West Berliners were prevented from entering the GDR (*Informationen,* no. 19, p. 2). Some citizens from the FRG had the same experience. For example, about 170 persons who intended to visit the Leipzig Spring Fair did not receive permission to do so (ibid., no 6, p. 6).

The new $4 fee on cars going to East Berlin in addition to the $2 visa fee and the required conversion of $2.60 into East German currency, introduced in February, serves two purposes. It discourages some visitors, and it brings in greatly needed hard currency (*NYT,* 26 February). The GDR also requested from the West Berlin Senate about six million marks for the visits of 852,000 West Berliners into East Berlin between 20 February and 10 June (*Die Welt,* 24 June).

When GDR police blocked the Office of the Permanent Representation of the FRG in East Berlin to prevent East Germans from inquiring about legal emigration, Bonn protested against this action. At the same time, a campaign against receiving visitors from the West and against wishes to emigrate was conducted in factory and mass organizations. (Ibid., 12 January.)

The replacement of signs with the designation "Magistrate of Greater Berlin" by new ones reading "Magistrate of Berlin, Capital of the GDR" reflected the SED's effort to remove any indication of the Four Powers status of all of Berlin (ibid., 21 May). Yet with regard to West Berlin the SED regime repeatedly demanded complete observance of the Quadripartite Agreement and accused the FRG of violating its provisions. In response to the London declaration of the Western powers concerning their "common rights in all of Berlin," *Neues Deutschland* (12 May) published a speech by Honecker stating: "Berlin is the capital of the German Democratic Republic and West Berlin a special territory which as a result of the Four Power Agreement of 3 September 1971 received a chance for the future." His rejection of the existence of a German citizenship is of great significance for West Berlin. West Berliners would no longer have German citizenship but a newly created one for West Berlin, a step which would further support the Soviet and East German assertion that West Berlin is an "independent political entity" (*Die Welt,* 24 February).

Trade between GDR and FRG showed a much lower increase than in former years. During the first half of 1977, trade increased by 4.2 percent as compared to the average annual increase from 1969 to 1976 of 14.5 percent. Total trade for this period came to 4.04 billion marks. After the Soviet Union, the FRG remained the second-largest trading partner, with half of the entire Western trade of the GDR. (*Ibid.,* 9, 16 March.)

Relations with the Soviet Bloc. Honecker in his report to the SED Central Committee on 17-18 March described in the following way the relations between the GDR and the USSR:

The most important event this year is the 60th anniversary of the great October Socialist Revolution. The working people of our country are preparing to celebrate it as befits the occasion.

Sixty years after the October Revolution the Soviet Union is . . . again pointing the way to the future by establishing the material-technological basis of communism . . . .

The true position of the Communist party is evident from its attitude toward the Soviet Union . . . . [our] party works untiringly to ensure that friendship for the Soviet Union [will] always be a matter close to the hearts of the citizens of the German Democratic Republic and that the process of the convergence of our peoples and states will make further headway . . . . In the field of foreign policy the strengthening of our eternal alliance with the Soviet Union and the other Socialist countries will have priority also in the future. (*Foreign Affairs Bulletin,* 17, no. 10, 5 April, pp. 73-75.)

Honecker maintained a close personal contact with the secretary general of the CPSU, Leonid Brezhnev. The two leaders met on 19 July in the Crimea during Honecker's vacation in the Soviet Union. Their discussion centered on economic and scientific-technological cooperation and on the program for productional specialization and cooperation for the period 1980 to 1990. (Ibid., 17, no. 22, 8 August, pp. 169-70.) The GDR's celebration of the anniversary of the October Revolution involved more than 600 events and 100,000 participants (*Die Welt,* 24 October).

The GDR minister of foreign affairs, Oskar Fischer, visited Moscow on 7-9 April and met with Soviet Foreign Minister Gromyko to discuss common objectives (*Foreign Affairs Bulletin, 17,* no. 12, 22 April, p. 92).

A military delegation of the USSR led by Marshal of the Soviet Union D. F. Ustinov, CPSU Politburo member and minister of defense, paid an official visit to the GDR on 11-15 April. They conferred with minister of national defense, General Hoffmann, and other members of the NVA. Both sides reaffirmed their cooperation in military matters (ibid., no. 13, 4 May, pp. 98-99).

Long-range Soviet influence is also assured as a result of the thousands of students from the GDR who attend institutions of higher learning in the Soviet Union, the number in 1977 being reported as more than 4,000 (*Informationen,* no. 16, p. 7).

During 1977 the GDR concluded treaties of friendship, cooperation, and mutual assistance with the following Socialist countries: Hungarian People's Republic (24 March), Mongolian People's Republic (10 May), Polish People's Republic (28 May), People's Republic of Bulgaria (14 September), and Czechoslovak Socialist Republic (3 October). Honecker's visit to Yugoslavia (12-15 January) continued East Berlin's efforts to improve Yugoslavia's relations with the Soviet bloc (see below). Fidel Castro headed a Cuban party and government delegation in the GDR (1-3 April). On 8 August, Honecker discussed bilateral relations with the Cuban defense minister, Army General Raúl Castro.

The GDR participated in the conference of deputy foreign ministers of the Soviet bloc countries in Moscow (5-7 April) and the conference of foreign ministers of the Warsaw Pact countries, also in Moscow, which commenced on 25 May (*Die Welt,* 26 May). The Central Committee secretaries of their parties met in Warsaw in May and discussed improvements in inter-party relations on the basis of democratic centralism (*Leipziger Volkszeitung,* 14/15 May). Of particular significance was the thirty-first session of the CMEA in Warsaw (21-23 June). Its Executive Committee had met before in Moscow on 12 April.

A two-day meeting (26-27 May) of generals and officers of the military-political academies of the Soviet Army and the People's Armies of Bulgaria, Poland, and Czechoslovakia and of educational establishments and troop formations of the NVA and GDR border troops was held at the Friedrich Engels Military Academy in Dresden. The conference focused on the "reinforcement of the military fighting community of Socialism and class education in the armed forces" ("Voice of the GDR," domestic service, 27 May).

Following the lead of the CPSU, the SED strongly condemned the civil rights movement in Czechoslovakia, known as "Charta 77," and referred to its supporters as a small group of reactionaries and participants in the counterrevolution of 1968, working for anti-Communist and Zionist centers (*Der Morgen,* East Berlin, 17 January). The SED is also strongly opposed to Eurocommunism.

Other International Positions. The GDR, having securely established itself in the international community, appeared to be more active in 1977 in pursuing its foreign policy objectives. Diplomatic relations with Spain were resumed (4 April) and were established with Jamaica (21 March), Botswana (13 May), and the new state of Djibouti (30 June). The GDR took an active part in the United Nations and its Specialized Agencies and was elected into the Executive Committee of the World Health Organization in Geneva on 11 May. East Berlin went on record for its support of the Soviet proposal to call a world disarmament conference (23 March), and addressed the Commission on Human Rights in Geneva about "Violation of Human Rights in Chile" (9 March) and the U.N. Special Committee against Apartheid in South Africa (21 March).

Mutual visits of government officials took place between the GDR and Austria, Belgium, Canada, Finland, France, Great Britain and Northern Ireland, India, Malaysia, Netherlands, Norway, San Marino, the United States, Vietnam, and various countries in the Middle East and Africa. Consular agreements were signed with Mexico and with some African states. Trade agreements were signed with India (7 March) and Bangladesh (7 July).

The GDR showed a marked interest in improving relations with the United States. East Germany has made a number of humanitarian and economic gestures, including the granting of permission for sixty persons to emigrate and join relatives in the U.S. East Berlin is intensely interested in increasing trade with the U.S. (*Washington Post,* 24 May). The GDR also has proposed a resumption of negotiations on a consular agreement. However, two important issues remain unresolved. The East Germans have not been willing to make restitution to U.S. citizens who lost property during World War II in the territory now under the control of East Berlin. The second point is the question of GDR citizenship, which the United States is not ready to accept because of American solidarity with the West German position that there is only one German citizenship. (Ibid., 27 May.)

The GDR continued to maintain a close relationship with the left-wing regimes in the Middle East, such as Iraq, Syria, and South Yemen. Government and party delegations paid mutual visits and signed various cultural, scientific-technological and economic agreements. The Institute for Local Politics in Weimar provided a four-week course for thirty Iraqi functionaries of central and local state organs (*Neues Deutschland,* 14 January).

GDR support of "anti-imperialist" and "anti-colonial" movements in Latin America, Asia, and Africa continued throughout 1977, with the main effort in Africa. As early as November 1976 there were reports concerning East German military involvement in the black continent. NVA instructors have been reported in at least twelve African countries and in the People's Republic of South Yemen (see *Die Welt,* 10 November 1976). The GDR engagement in Africa proceeds in at least two phases. The first is a political-diplomatic approach. The second consists of military aid to utilize African countries for the implementation of Soviet foreign policy objectives. The luncheon given on 23 May by GDR minister of foreign affairs, Oskar Fischer, for the ambassadors of the Organization of African Unity countries accredited in the GDR, during the "week of solidarity with the peoples of Africa in their struggle for national and social liberation," was an instance of the political-diplomatic phase. Fischer attacked in his speech the "last bastions of racism and colonialism" in Africa, "the regimes in Pretoria and Salisbury." He also stated that the GDR "insists on the immediate withdrawal of South Africa from illegally occupied Namibia and on the unconditional transfer of all power to the people of Zimbabwe." He told the African diplomats that experience has shown that the Socialist countries are the unselfish friends and allies of the African peoples (*Foreign Affairs Bulletin,* 17, no. 17, 10 June, p. 136). Attacks against the "Apartheid regime in South Africa," calling it a threat to peace and security, were made in the U.N. Security Council (14 January, 29 March) (ibid., no 12, 15 March, 22 April, pp. 62, 93-94). The GDR's permanent representative at the United Nations and leader of the East German delegation at the U. N. World Conference for Action against Apartheid, in Lagos, stated that "coercive measures against the apartheid regime, in accordance with Chapter VII of the United Nations Charter—an effective arms embargo, sanctions and termination of any kind of investment—are urgently necessary" (ibid., no. 24, 5 September, p. 187).

The many mutual visits between GDR party and government officials and African political and government leaders also belong to the political-diplomatic offensive. Some of these visits were connected with the signing of economic, cultural, and technological cooperation agreements. Potential trouble areas received special attention. The African tour of the twenty-five man party and government delegation of the GDR was an outstanding example. Between 17 and 25 June, the delegation visited Angola, the People's Republic of Congo, Nigeria, and Zambia. The GDR delegation also met during this tour leaders of the Zimbabwe African People's Union (ZAPU) and representatives of the African National Congress (ANC) of South Africa. (Ibid., no. 21, 22 July, pp. 163-65.) SED Politburo member Werner Lamberz declared while in Nigeria that East Germany will consider sending troops to Southern Africa if a request is made by "appropriate authorities" (*AFP*, Paris, 23 June).

The growing activities of the GDR in Africa may be seen as carrying out policies for the Soviets where an increased Russian presence might be sensitive or unwelcomed. The GDR had for most of the postwar years no international image and thus it is less suspected of imperialist designs than the Soviet Union. It has become, after Cuba and the USSR, the third most influential Communist power in Africa. In Mozambique, the GDR has the largest embassy staff of any Eastern bloc country, including the USSR. Its presence has substantially increased in Ethiopia. Support of the left-wing liberation movements and left-wing African states has taken the form of small arms supply, military advisers, and internal security training. GDR military advisers and technicians in sub-Sahara Africa, estimated in 1973 as about 100, are now believed to number between 300 and 400 (*NYT*, 23 August).

The GDR's only known setback suffered in Africa occurred in May 1977 when the government of Zaire expelled the East German diplomats and suspended diplomatic relations with East Berlin. The GDR was accused of having supplied anti-government rebels in the Shaba province with arms. The official GDR news agency, ADN, rejected this accusation and claimed that the Zaire government was the victim of propaganda lies spread by those who intend to divert attention from the "racist regimes in Southern Africa." (*Informationen*, no. 10, p. 5).

The SED regime continued to seek to improve relations of the Soviet bloc with Yugoslavia. At the conclusion of Honecker's visit (12-15 January), his and Tito's statement emphasized that full agreement was reached on all major issues and that the already well-developed bilateral relations would be deepened (*Neues Deutschland*, 18 January). Honecker bestowed on President Tito the highest East German decoration, the Karl-Marx-Order.

The fact that the GDR takes the same position as the Soviet Union with regard to China and Albania did not deter East Berlin from signing a trade and payment agreement for 1977 with Peking (3 May) and a trade agreement for the period 1976-1980 with Tirana (10 February).

International Party Contacts. Aside from the consultative meeting of representatives of Communist and workers' parties in Prague on 28 April, no significant international conference of the Communist organizations took place in 1977. The SED had to rely on bilateral contacts in order to maintain liaison with fraternal Communist parties in the "capitalist" area. Party leaders and delegations from Austria, Denmark, Italy, Portugal, Sweden, Uruguay, and the FRG visited the GDR. SED functionaries and delegations made return visits to parties in Austria, Italy, and the FRG. Exchange visits also took place with the Iraqi Communist Party. A delegation of the MAPU workers' and peasants' party from Chile was received by Honecker. The visit of the secretary general of the Communist Party of Chile, Luis Corvalán, at the end of January was the occasion of solidarity demonstrations. An SED delegation attended the Eighteenth Congress of the Communist Party in Mexico (24 May). Werner Lamberz led a party delegation to the Third Congress of FRELIMO in Mozambique.

Publications. Erich Honecker in an address to the congress of the GDR Organization of Journalists (23 June) asserted that as a result of the removal of the "shackles of capitalist manipulation of opinion," freedom of the press has become a reality in the GDR (*Informationen*, no. 14, p. 4). The Berliner Verlag is the largest opinion factory of the SED. Practically all important newspapers, including *Neues Deutschland*, and all periodicals with national circulation, are printed there in editions of several millions. All publications are under the direction, control, and evaluation of the Agitation and Propaganda Department of the Central Committee of the SED. (For a listing of SED newspapers see *YICA, 1977*, pp. 43-44.)

Radio and TV are similarly utilized for propaganda purposes. East German TV relies 35 to 40 percent on foreign productions, mostly of Soviet origin (*National Zeitung*, 14/15 May).

University of Calgary   Eric Waldman

Hungary

Hungarian Communists formed a party in November 1918. Soon proscribed, the party functioned as a minute and faction-ridden movement in domestic illegality and in exile. With the Soviet occupation at the end of World War II the Hungarian Communist party emerged as a partner in the coalition government, exercised an influence disproportionate to its modest electoral support, and gained effective control of the country in 1947. In 1948 it absorbed left-wing social democrats into the newly-named Hungarian Workers' Party. On 1 November 1956, during the popular revolt that momentarily restored a multiparty government, the name was changed to Hungarian Socialist Workers' Party (Magyar Szocialista Munkáspárt; HSWP).

The HSWP rules unchallenged as the sole political party, firmly aligned with the USSR. Its exclusive status is confirmed in the revised state constitution of 1972: "The Marxist-Leninist party of the working class is the leading force in society." Coordination of formal political activities, such as elections, is the function of the Patriotic People's Front (PPF).

In the 1971-75 Parliament, 71 percent of the deputies were party members. About 47 percent of municipal and local council members belong to the HSWP, as do about 90 percent of those of officer rank in the police forces. Party membership on 31 December 1976 stood at 765,566. The population of Hungary is 10,664,000. At the time of the HSWP's Eleventh Congress (March 1975), physical workers comprised 45.5 percent of the membership, "immediate supervisors of production" 6.1 percent, intellectual workers 40 percent, and dependents and others 8.4 percent.

The broadest umbrella organization for political mobilization, the agent of the party's "alliance policy," is the PPF. It works through some 4,000 committees with 112,400 members. A related agency is the National Peace Council, with international responsibilities. Trade unions, directed by the National Council of Trade Unions (NCTU), comprise close to four million organized workers. The Communist Youth League (Kommunista Ifjusági Szövetség; KISZ) has more than 800,000 members, in 25,600 basic organizations. Thirty-one percent of working youths, 56 percent of secondary school students, and 96 percent of postsecondary students belong to the KISZ. Other active mobilizing agents are the National Council of Hungarian Women and the Hungarian-Soviet Friendship Society.

Leadership and Organization. Ultimate political power in the HSWP, and therefore in Hungary, remains in the hands of the first secretary, János Kádár. The 65-year-old Kádár has been party leader longer than any of his counterparts in the Soviet bloc. He holds no state office. Current Politburo members are Kádár, György Aczél, Antal Apró, Valéria Benke, Béla Biszku (party building), Jenö Fock, Sándor Gáspár, István Huszár, György Lázár, Pál Losonczi, László Maróthy, Dezsö Nemes, Károly Németh (economic policy), Miklós Ovári (agitprop, cultural policy), and István Sarlós. In addition to Kádár, the Central Committee Secretariat includes Biszku, Sándor Borbély, András Gyénes, Imre Györi, Németh, and Ovári. János Brutyó is chairman of the Central Control Committee, and Árpád Pullai of the youth committee. Pál Romány (also minister of agriculture) is chairman of the Central Committee's cooperative policy collective.

Losonczi is chairman of the Presidential Council and therefore head of state. Lázár is prime minister, and Aczél and Huszár are deputy premiers. Apró is chairman of the National Assembly. Gáspár is secretary general of the NCTU, Maróthy of the KISZ, and Sarlós of the PPF.

The Central Committee elected at the party's 11th Congress has 125 members. County party committees, together with the Budapest Party Committee, number 24. There are also 97 district party committees, 104 city and Budapest district party committees, 1,033 plant and office party committees, and 24,450 primary party organizations. The leaders in the latter organizations number 106,692. Of these primary organizations, 7,066 are active in industry and construction, 4,215 in agriculture, 1,473 in transportation, and 1,216 in commerce. As reported in 1973, the party retains full appointing authority over 90,000 posts and a generally respected advisory right over a further 350,000 leading positions (*Pártélet,* January 1974).

At its 14 April 1977 meeting the Central Committee approved the appointment of István Katona (born 1928) as head of the Central Committee's bureau. He was replaced as editor in chief of the party daily *Népszabadság* by the Muscovite veteran and Politburo member Dezsö Nemes (born 1908), formerly rector of the Party Academy and editor of the same paper from 1957 to 1961. The appointment of the ideologically orthodox Nemes should guarantee the party daily's perfect adhesion to the official pro-Soviet line amid the uncertainties of détente. József Szabó was promoted from deputy rector to head the Party Academy. In keeping with the established policy of switching leading members between state and party positions, minister of labor László Karakas was moved to head the Central Committee's financial and administrative department, and was himself replaced by Ferenc Trethon. Antal Kovács, a Central Committee member and first secretary of the Vas county party committee, was appointed head of the industrial, agricultural, and communications department, replacing Borbély, who had been elevated to the Secretariat in October 1976.

Party Internal Affairs. The party card exchange requested by the 11th Congress was implemented during 1976. In the exchange 20,760 members, 2.7 percent of the total, were released from the party, and 40 percent of the basic organizations were affected by this attrition. More than half resigned their membership voluntarily, and allegedly only 34 of these did so for political reasons. Of those who were expelled, 64 appealed the ruling. An additional one percent of the membership was put on probation for 6-12 months, and this has since led to numerous new expulsions and some 600 resignations. The expulsions and resignations were largely balanced by the intake of 27,620 new members, with the result that overall membership declined by only 381. The party stressed that departure from its ranks carried no further negative consequences.

In his report to the Central Committee on 22 June 1977, Borbély affirmed that the card exchange had in no way transgressed the authority of party organizations or the rights of individual members. Some 150,000 activists had conducted "comradely interviews" with the entire membership, and the process had not only weeded out unsuitable members but provided a survey of opinion within the party. Among the issues raised was the need to make leaders more answerable for their actions, and Borbély recognized that more suitable positions would have to be found for incompetent leaders, while the dictatorial and the corrupt would have to be disciplined. He claimed that the card exchange reflected a spirit of democratic debate which was healthy as long as members recognized that they were bound to accept and implement the ultimate decision of the majority, i.e., follow the Leninist principle of democratic centralism. As evidence of the growing responsibility of membership it was noted that 85 percent of members were charged with accountable party tasks.

Borbély noted further that party recruitment must follow the prescription of the 11th Congress by increasing the proportion of physical workers, particularly from the large industrial plants, though in order to preserve the distinction between the vanguard party and the working masses, the emphasis must be on quality. Candidates must be exemplary in their ideological conviction and in their public and private life. Casual and careerist members are not acceptable, and for this reason the party adheres to the principle that competent non-members can hold all offices outside of the party itself.

Borbély, dealing with suggestions and complaints, dismissed the view, advanced by the party committees of Budapest and two counties, that members elected to party bodies did not receive adequate moral and material reward. Another recommendation, endorsed by all of the county party committees, called for greater recognition of those who had joined the party in 1944-45. Borbély admitted that pre-1944 members did receive special benefits, and argued that this was warranted by their struggles in conditions of illegality, but said that to favor similarly the 10 percent of members who joined immediately upon liberation and worked in less difficult circumstances would be inappropriate. He received more favorably the complaint that intellectuals and white-collar workers were often the subject of discrimination and urged that mechanical application of the recruitment guidelines against these groups be avoided.

The Central Committee resolution on the lessons of the card exchange recommended, inter alia, that party members be given more opportunities to express their views and that the basic organizations devote greater attention to matters of immediate public concern (*Pártélet,* July). A round-table discussion in August on admission policy produced confirmation of the inappropriateness of "quotas" favoring industrial workers and indicated that, at least in student circles, candidates for party membership were regarded by others as careerists (*Népszabadság,* 27 August).

Domestic Attitudes and Activities. Economic problems remained at the forefront of official and public concern in 1977. Addressing a national agitprop conference on economic propaganda in March, Györi observed that changes in the world economy had caught Hungary unprepared, and that the system of economic regulators had proved to be less than adequate in simulating appropriate enterprise responses. At the same time, public opinion surveys showed that most Hungarians are dissatisfied with the standard of living and believe that improvement is feasible. The regime's task therefore was to explain that while the Socialist state "regulates price changes by systematic and purposeful planning . . . our party and state authorities have no absolute freedom in the shaping of prices." Györi stressed the need to improve the quality and not the quantity of economic information for the population. (*Társadalmi Szemle,* May.)

Official statistics indicated that wages have kept pace with the aggregate consumer price index, but the prices of certain essential items, notably food products, have risen disproportionately. The steady rise in the standard of living has virtually stopped: in 1976 real wages grew by 0.5 percent and real incomes by 1.0 percent. On 10 January 1977 increases of up to 35 percent on important food industry products were imposed to reflect reduced agricultural output in 1976 as well as the rise in the world price of coffee, a favorite Hungarian beverage that is still subsidized by the state. Wage and salary increases were approved by the Council of Ministers on 19 May for 1.2 million workers, of whom 1 million were manual workers, partly to provide an incentive for second and third shifts in industry.

The housing shortage is slowly being alleviated, the number of people per 100 rooms having fallen from 236 in 1960 to 157 in 1976. Demand, particularly in Budapest, still far outstrips new construction. The government provides special credit facilities to encourage cooperative housing projects. At the beginning of 1977 there were over 600,000 private cars in Hungary, reflecting a current rate of increase of some 80,000 a year. All cars have to be imported, and there are long waiting lists, delays in delivery, and shortages of spare parts. Most private cars are imported from the Soviet Union, Poland, East Germany, Czechoslovakia, and Romania.

In presenting the new budget to the National Assembly on 16 December 1976, Finance Minister Lajos Faluvégi reported that the 1976 plan had not been fulfilled. Shortfalls occurred in agricultural output (due mainly to bad weather), in certain industrial sectors, in national and per capita real income, and in exports. The economic plan for 1977 projected increases in the national income of 6.0 to 6.5 percent, in industrial production of 6.0 percent, in agricultural production of 7 to 8 percent (over 1975), in per capita real income of 3.5 to 4.0 percent, in personal consumption of 3.7 to 4.0 percent, and in consumer price levels (maximum) of 3.8 to 4.0 percent. Investments were expected to rise by 45 percent over 1976 levels, principally in export-oriented industries. The state budget for 1977 was to have a small deficit. Price supports and other subsidies account for 32.6 percent of the budget, and interest and repayment of foreign debts for 7.2 percent. (*Magyar Hirlap,* 17 December 1976.)

The guiding principles for economic policy approved by the Central Committee at its 20 October meeting did not depart significantly from previous official pronouncements, but they imparted a sense of heightened urgency inspired by the deepening economic crisis. The communiqué noted that the terms of trade had deteriorated and that qualitative standards in both Socialist and capitalist markets had increased. Hungary's economy was in a state of intensive development and, given the stable labor pool, production increases could only be achieved by improvement in labor productivity. The guidelines called therefore for transformation and simplification of the state's subsidy and profit-regulation system, including the curtailment of unjustified subsidies; better harmony between the domestic price system and world market prices; greater differentiation of enterprise and personal income according to performance; and the selective development of industrial branches. (*Népszabadság,* 22 October.) Whether these guidelines will promote a reinvigoration of the more competitive, market-oriented aspects of the New Economic Mechanism remains to be seen.

The number of private artisans, badly needed particularly in the consumer service sector, has been declining steadily over the past fifteen years. Deterrents include complex regulations, high taxation, erratic supply of materials, and inadequate social services. Official endorsement is tempered by a certain fear of entrepreneurial excess and self-enrichment, but limited tax concessions were instituted in 1977 to stimulate activity in the areas of greatest need, and in fact the number of artisans began to rise once again the the first half of 1977. (*Népszabadság,* 5 March; *Magyar Nemzet,* 8 October.) On 27 May the Presidential Council issued a decree regulating artisans and shopkeepers in the private sector. It imposes stiffer professional qualifications but also relaxes certain restrictions, notably on subcontracting. (*Népszabadság,* 28 May.)

The weight of agriculture in the national economy has shifted markedly over the last few years. In 1975 it accounted for 22.75 percent of the labor force and 15 percent of national income, down from 39.27 percent and 29 percent in 1960. Agriculture nevertheless remains a key sector not only in terms of domestic consumption but also because food and livestock account for over one-fifth of all exports, and more than half of exports to the West.

The consolidation of agricultural production by the merger of cooperative farms is coming to an end. In mid-1976 there were 1,462 agricultural producers' cooperatives (compared with 2,300 in 1972), covering 67 percent of all arable land and with a membership of one million, 42 percent of whom were pensioners. Instead of more mergers, the party now favors the formation of agro-industrial complexes linking cooperative and state farms and food industry enterprises. Many of the earlier mergers, encompassing several villages, were attributable to the zeal of local party and state officials and did not result in real economies of scale.

The Third National Congress of Agricultural Cooperatives, 14-15 December 1976, was attended by Kádár and Németh. Kádár noted with satisfaction that the Socialist brigade movement was spreading in agriculture and that nearly 10 percent of cooperative members belonged to the HSWP. He reiterated the party's favorable disposition toward private plots and ancillary farms; its opposition to the cooperatives' diversification into ancillary nonagricultural activities—a phenomenon of the early years of the New Economic Mechanism; and the shift in emphasis from mergers to agro-industrial complexes, a new stage in the development of Socialist agriculture. (Ibid., 15 December.) The 1967 law on agricultural cooperatives has been amended to accommodate changes in their scale and style of work. The amendments, inter alia, regularize the status of private plot farming; provide for new levels of self-management with delegate meetings and working collectives as well as the annual membership meeting; relax rules for entry and departure from the cooperative and abolish arbitrary exclusion; and expand the role of regional associations, in part to "assert the national economic interest." (*Magyar Közlöny,* 12 March.) Since 1976, employees of the agricultural producers' cooperatives—numbering more than 130,000—have been allowed to join the Union of Agricultural and Forestry Workers; to date only one-third have taken this step. The cooperatives tend to prefer that employees become members to preserve their own form of democracy and autonomy.

In addition to the agricultural producers' cooperatives, there are 134 state farms encompassing 12.6 percent of arable land and accounting for 14 percent of gross agricultural output. They benefit from heavy subsidies which allow for a higher level of specialist and manual labor and technical aid than that enjoyed by the cooperatives.

The Central Committee's plenum of 1 December 1976 declared that "support of the private plot and ancillary farms must continue in order to exploit their production potential." (*Népszabadság,* 3 December 1976.) Small-scale producers account for 18 percent of arable land (including 800,000 private plots within the cooperatives) but provide a far higher proportion of net agricultural output. Over 1.5 million families are involved in some minor agricultural production, mostly on a part-time basis, and three-quarters of them are not professional farmers. To stimulate this sector the government is providing new tax concessions, subsidies, and technical assistance, including for the first time some provision for the rental of small agricultural machinery.

Due largely to unfavorable weather conditions agricultural production in 1976 fell below the 1975 level. The consequent decline in retained earnings has made the cooperatives reluctant to invest. To achieve the high 1977 production targets, the regime has issued urgent appeals to farmers to meet their social responsibilities and purchase sufficient fertilizer even at some financial sacrifice. Shortages of machinery and spare parts also have a negative effect on the farmers' morale.

The importance of foreign trade in Hungary's economy is underscored by the fact that it accounts for 40 to 50 percent of the national income. In recent years trade with the Soviet Union, Hungary's principal supplier of energy and raw materials, has expanded to over 36 percent of total trade. Trade with the rest of Comecon has declined somewhat to 28 percent, while with the developed Western countries it has risen to 23 percent. The most important Western trade partners are

West Germany and Austria. Energy and raw materials account for 55 to 60 percent of imports, and finished products for 65 to 70 percent of exports.

Global recession, the increase in energy costs, Hungary's desire to modernize her industries with Western technology, the limited competitiveness of her industrial products on Western markets, and EEC restrictions on agricultural imports have in the aggregate had an unfavorable effect on Hungary's balance of trade. The terms of trade within Comecon have changed to Hungary's disadvantage with the disproportionate increase in energy prices, and a heavy deficit has also been accumulated in trade with the non-Socialist sector. Between 1970 and 1976 the aggregate of trade deficit with the West and of gross credits (excluding repayments) raised on Western money markets has been estimated at $2.2 billion.

Preliminary statistics for the first half of 1977 indicate further deterioration in Hungary's balance of trade in both the ruble and dollar sectors, most seriously in the latter. Imports were running according to plan, but exports were lagging badly. The largest single deficit was with the Soviet Union. (*Világgazdaság,* 7 July.) Prices of several major imports, ranging from lead to coffee, rose sharply, while the price of certain exports such as rolled steel and wheat fell. The Soviet-Hungarian trade agreement for 1977 was signed 1 November 1976 in Moscow. Fifty percent of Hungary's designated exports are machinery and equipment; other major items are pharmaceuticals and textiles. The major imports are oil (whose price is still below world market levels but catching up by means of a moving three-year average of world prices), natural gas, coal, coke, and electrical power.

Reservations about Comecon were voiced by one of the principal architects of the New Economic Mechanism, Rezsö Nyers. His particular concern was about the "national economic effects" of Hungary's contribution to joint Comecon investments (amounting to over 10 percent of national industrial investments) in Soviet natural resource development projects. Their impact cannot be accurately measured because of the inadequacies of Comecon's price, foreign exchange, and credit systems. National and international interests must be harmonized in determining the limits of such investments, but the Comecon mechanism is inadequate for this purpose. (*Gazdasági Szemle,* April.) At the 31st Comecon Council session, held in Warsaw in June, energy and raw material supply was a major topic, and Prime Minister Lázár indicated that in a conservation measure Hungary would gradually shift away from high-energy consuming industries. He was the only participant to argue for convertibility and more rational pricing in intra-Comecon trade.

A new ministry of finance decree allows for joint enterprises with foreign partners in production as well as in trade and services. It simplifies the taxation of joint stock enterprises and provides, with ministerial permission, for majority control by the foreign partner in joint financial and service activities. (*Magyar Közlöny,* 6 May.) Hungary claims to have the largest number (but not value) of cooperative ventures with Western partners among the Socialist states. Another new decree specifies terms under which foreign banks can open branches in Hungary. These facilities are only to serve cooperation ventures and export-import financing. (*Magyar Közlöny,* 24 January.) Three Western banks, an American, an Austrian, and an Italian, now have permanent branches in Budapest.

Some concern has been expressed regarding reliance on the West for the modernization of agriculture, but the responsible minister, Pál Romány, has declared that "no enterprise should fear for Hungary's Socialist integrity just because it has relations with an enterprise in one of the capitalist states." (*Magyar Hirlap,* 7 January.) American technology and know-how have had significant application in Hungarian agriculture, including closed production systems, high-yield seeds, the manufacture under license of Raba-Steiger heavy tractors, and most recently a license agreement with the International Harvester Company.

Trade negotiations with Italy have not resolved the problem of Italy's quota restrictions and the

EEC's restrictions on Hungarian cattle and beef exports, both of which have reduced the volume of Italian-Hungarian trade. Hungary has 40 bilateral cooperation agreements with Italian enterprises, and another 50 are under negotiation.

At the meeting of the Hungarian-Yugoslav Economic Cooperation Committee, held in Budapest 24-27 June, two agreements were signed. The first provides for a more flexible clearing system allowing for payment in any convertible currency instead of only U.S. dollars. The second is a 20-year natural gas agreement for the export of Hungarian natural gas to Yugoslavia, to be compensated by an extra allocation of Soviet gas originally earmarked for Yugoslavia, and for a Yugoslav loan to finance the construction of a natural gas pipeline through Hungary which will eventually carry Soviet gas to Yugoslavia. (*Világgazdaság,* 29 June.) The opening of the Adria oil pipeline, designed to carry Middle Eastern and North African crude from the Yugoslav coast to Hungary and Czechoslovakia, has been delayed until 1978.

Tourism, a major hard currency earner, expanded rapidly between 1966 and 1975 but has been declining since then. Price inflation in the tourist industry and a shortage of hotel space are cited as negative factors. The requirement that Western tourists purchase Hungarian currency before entry has been lifted effective 1 January 1978.

The New Economic Mechanism and the attendant alliance policy, with its stress on Socialist democracy, may be under pressure in the current difficult economic circumstances, but the party has issued reassurances that democratization will not be reversed: "Not less, but more democracy is required, so that the masses can be brought to consider as their own the nation's struggle, to realize its aims, and to overcome its difficulties. It is true that discipline is not possible without disciplined work, but Socialist democracy and Socialist discipline are not contradictory terms. . . . Socialist work discipline requires that leaders and political activists make their decisions after consulting the workers and asking for their advice. . . . There are still a large number of people who try to sidestep this question." Democracy was said to be needed to safeguard the party line from rightist and pseudo-leftist errors. (*Társadalmi Szemle,* April.)

NCTU Secretary General Sándor Gáspar has been tirelessly reiterating the theme espoused by the HSWP's Eleventh Congress that the trade union movement must "exploit the potential for enterprise democracy." The exercise of "direct democracy" by conferences of shop stewards, introduced on an experimental basis in 50 enterprises in late 1975, is to be extended to all other enterprises. The allocation of retained profits, hitherto determined by management, the party organization, and trade union bodies, will now also come before the shop stewards, who will discuss proposals with the workers. (*Népszava,* 28 November 1976.) The Council of Ministers and the NCTU passed a resolution in April providing for a joint meeting of the enterprise trade union council, the trade union committee, and the shop stewards' committee, with concurring and advisory rights over the collective contract, distribution of certain funds, wage rates, and enterprise plans. (*Népszava,* 1 May.) The party expects, of course, that the extension of enterprise democracy will stimulate productivity. At the same time, enterprise managers are exhorted to overcome their bureaucratic caution and show greater willingness to take risks. (*Népszabadság,* 4 March.)

The hiring freeze on administrative workers, imposed 1 January 1976, has reduced the overall complement and is now being rationalized. A new regulation, effective 1 January 1977, precludes increase in the complement but does allow for replacement in certain sectors, while other organizations are required to further reduce their white-collar complement by 5 percent. The measures are designed to steer young job-seekers to less desirable blue-collar employment, where shortages are endemic. Part of the problem is that between 1970 and 1976 the number of pupils entering schools for skilled workers declined by 25 percent.

For years Hungary had one of the lowest birth rates in the world, and concern about economic consequences led to the introduction in 1967 of a child-care scheme providing extended leave for mothers. This has had a favorable demographic effect, raising the birth rate to over 18 per thousand, although it momentarily also aggravated the shortage of manpower (*Népszabadság*, 25 December 1976). Pensioners account for 17.6 percent of the population, a proportion that has been rising steadily over recent years. The retirement age for workers and employees is 60 for men and 55 for women; for agricultural cooperative workers it is being gradually lowered to reach the same level by 1980. All this places a heavy burden on the economy, although there are wide discrepancies in pension income and the majority of pensioners live at a bare subsistence level. (*Magyar Hirlap*, 27 February 1977).

Official reports deprecate the incidence of anti-state activity in Hungary. This accounted for 0.5 percent of all crimes in 1975; 214 adults and 28 juveniles were sentenced, mostly for "minor incitement." In 1976, 0.2 percent of crimes were "offenses against the state, peace, or humanity." (*Magyar Nemzet*, 26 February.) Known cases in past years include leftist intellectuals such as Miklós Haraszti and several priests. The latest amnesty law allowed persons who left illegally to return to Hungary by 31 December 1976. Some 500 individuals availed themselves of the offer, while 8 percent of the applications were refused.

The National Assembly on 17 March approved a law inviting citizens to submit reports on matters of public interest, suggestions, and complaints, and providing for procedures to process such submissions. The purpose of the measure is to enhance Socialist democracy by ensuring the security of public property and the purity of public life. Anonymous complaints will also be investigated if the situation warrants it. The new law provides a comprehensive framework for dealing with the numerous collective and individual grievances through official channels. (*Magyar Közlöny*, 30 March.)

The HSWP has been persisting in its effort to demonstrate to the world at large its tolerance of organized religion. The head of the State Office of Church Affairs, Imre Miklós, has written that "it would be a mistake to minimize the role played by religious belief in the private life of the individual, in interpersonal relations, and in the service of moral norms." The churches and their adherents can help national goals by offering "constructive criticism" through the PPF. A state agreement with the Vatican allows members of the Bishops' Conference to make "ad limina" visits to Rome, and Cardinal Lékai led eleven bishops on such a visit in April 1977. Kádár's audience with Pope Paul on 9 June served to symbolize the normalization of church-state relations. The HSWP leader stated afterward that in Hungary the state does not interfere in the life of religious organizations or with the free practice of religion (*Népszabadság*, 10 June). Hungary's chief rabbi, László Salgó, speaking for an active community of some 100,000 Jews, was also impelled to proclaim that Hungarians enjoyed complete religious freedom. Billy Graham's visit in September further displayed an official tolerance that may be aimed in part at the Belgrade review of the Helsinki Final Act.

Although the churches survive, their difficulties and the limits of tolerance receive less airing. Party members and their families are forbidden to practice or show ideological tolerance for religion. KISZ members are similarly discouraged from religious practice and are instructed in atheism. A more general discrimination prevails against religious practitioners in education and employment, and they are excluded from high office. Eight church-administered high schools remain in existence, but most of the religious orders have been proscribed since 1950, and the teaching of catechism is limited to a restricted number of children, in the churches, twice a week. State-church negotiations are proceeding on minor issues, but Miklos has taken pains to dampen speculation that the amelioration in church-state relations might amount to a "historic change." Ideological convergence is impossible and secularization is in the ascendant. (*Magyar Hirlap*, 20 August.)

The political socialization of young people remains a prominent but frustrating objective of the regime. Implementation of the youth law of 1971 requires that "youth parliaments" be organized every second year with the aid of the KISZ and the trade unions in places of work and educational institutions. The second series of youth parliaments, held in 1976-77, prompted a general criticism of redundancy and futility. The assemblies generate many proposals to little effect, and their primary purpose is to politicize young people. Since 1973 the approximately 4,000 youth clubs have been required to seek an official license, but this rule has been unevenly applied. A national conference of youth club directors on 27 October 1976 discussed the modalities of state support, which consists of technical aid and "program parcels" with a heavy political content. Central direction and the training of club leaders aim at a greater emphasis on indoctrination at the expense of entertainment, which in turn is what most members seek.

Cultural policy is liberal by East European standards, which is to say that most of the censorship is self-imposed. The minister of culture, Imre Pozsgay, affirmed in an interview that his ministry relies on ideological and intellectual persuasion rather than on "administrative methods" to apply the official guidelines, although this sometimes results in sharp arguments with the leaders of cultural organizations. (*Valóság,* August.) Public criticism of the selectiveness and caution exercised by the Committee for Film Imports in bringing Western films to Hungary, and of the low quality of the two-thirds of films shown that came from the Socialist countries, was aired in a radio debate (Radio Budapest, 3 March.) A documentary film on the pentathlon champion András Balczó—who has abruptly retired, denounced the corruption of the sport establishment, and professed religious beliefs—aroused widespread interest and controversy. A conference of the heads of the Socialist writers' unions was held in Budapest 19-21 April in preparation for the international writers' conference scheduled for June in Bulgaria, the theme of which was the responsibility of the writer in the context of the "Helsinki spirit." The participants were warned to gird for the conflicting views of non-Socialist delegates.

The twentieth anniversary of the Workers' Militia, established in the wake of the 1956 revolution, was celebrated in February. The volunteer paramilitary force is generally hailed as an important defender of the "Socialist order" and is occasionally mobilized to cope with natural disasters. Some 80 percent of its members belong to the HSWP, and every membership application must be approved by a basic party unit. Most young members come from the young guard units of the KISZ. In 1977 courses were instituted for professional militia commanders.

International Policies and Activities. Hungary's foreign and inter-party policies remain firmly aligned with those of the Soviet Union, but in all the controversial spheres, such as Eurocommunism, the Kádár regime has professed a finely calculated moderation. In the course of a visit to Vienna in December 1976 Kádár disagreed with the equation of Eurocommunism with anti-Sovietism, a charge made by the Bulgarian leader Todor Zhivkov in *Problems of Peace and Socialism* (December). In a subsequent article Kádár elaborated on his moderate line, confirming the "special significance" of the Sovet party's theoretical and practical experience but, allowing for national circumstances, not requiring its "mechanical application" or the curtailment of a sister party's independence. Stating that Socialism could conceivably be developed by way of a multi-party system, he noted that in the Hungarian one-party system the party must give consideration to various group and individual interests—it cannot build a Socialist society alone, but must seek allies and appeal to the masses. (*Béke és Szocializmus,* January 1977.)

On the whole, the HSWP has avoided polemics in its treatment of Eurocommunism (apart from a sharp exchange in articles by Dezsö Nemes and the French Communist Jean Kanapa in 1976), but Eurocommunism is deprecated as a creation of bourgeois propaganda not representing a Socialist alternative or the views of the West European parties (*Társadalmi Szemle,* February), and the pluralization and fragmentation of Communism is seen as an imperialist strategy (*Népszabadság,* 8 February). At the same time, the West European Communists are warned not to criticize or undervalue the experience of the single-party Socialist states or to generalize the superiority of pluralistic Socialism (*Külpolitika,* no. 4).

East European party secretaries in charge of ideology and foreign policy met for one of their periodic conferences at Sofia on 2-3 March. The HSWP delegation was led by Óvári and included Gyénes and Györi. According to their report, the conference affirmed that the ideological struggle between capitalism and Socialism had become accentuated and that Communist propaganda would have to be intensified to counter the current "imperialist propaganda campaign," encompassing the Eurocommunist fabrication (*Pártélet,* April). The conference was scheduled to coincide with the meeting of Berlinguer, Marchais, and Carrillo in Madrid, but the fears that their meeting would produce an anti-Soviet stand proved unwarranted. According to one report on the Sofia conference, the Hungarians adopted a moderate line against urgings, notably from the Bulgarians, that Eurocommunist deviationism be publicly condemned, and even the Soviet delegate, Ponomarev, advised that apparent diversity had its uses (*Il Giornale,* 12 April).

A certain hardening of positions materialized after the Soviet denunciation of Carrillo's book on Eurocommunism. At the ideological conference in Prague on 28 June-1 July, of representatives of 67 parties, Györi hailed proletarian internationalism and excoriated imperialist attempts to disrupt the unity of the Socialist countries, the Western Communist parties, and the "revolutionary liberation forces" of the Third World (*Népszava,* 29 June). At his press conference in Rome Kádár had allowed that what mattered was to achieve Socialism "with or without the dictatorship of the proletariat, with pluralistic Socialism or any other kind of Socialism" (*Népzabadság.* 10 June). In a subsequent interview he shaded his opinion by stressing that it was not "Eurocommunism" if parties sought their own path to Socialism as long as they bore in mind the experiences of the international workers' movement and showed faith in the solidarity of all European Communist parties (ibid., 3 July). Meanwhile, the head of the Central Committee's foreign affairs department, János Berecz, finally criticized Carrillo by name for his "unfounded" attacks on the Socialist systems of the Soviet bloc (ibid., 24 June).

The HSWP has shown cautious sympathy particularly for the Italian party's attempts to find its own road to power. A collection of Berlinguer's speeches on the "historic compromise" was published in translation at the beginning of the year. After visiting Tito, the Italian secretary general met with Kádár 30 September-3 October. The communiqué issuing from the talks called for "free and frank negotiations, internationalist solidarity, and voluntary cooperation among Communist and workers' parties, with full respect for the complete independence of each party." It also referred to the need for links between the Communists and other "progressive" forces. (MTI, 3 October.) In his meetings with the leaders of various other Communist parties Kádár has avoided taking extreme positions on the Eurocommunist issue by invoking the agreement of the June 1976 East Berlin conference of European parties and laying nuanced emphasis on its provisions for party autonomy and proletarian internationalism. Kádár has thus emerged as a symbol of moderation in the schismatic debate.

Notwithstanding such displays of pragmatism and moderation, the HSWP and its leader profess unstinting loyalty to the Soviet Union. On 2 June, Soviet academician Nikolai Blokhin visited Budapest and presented Kádár with the International Lenin Peace Prize for the Consolidation of Friendship among Peoples. In July Kádár paid his annual visit to Brezhnev in the Crimea and reportedly agreed on the need to reinforce the solidarity of the movement. The pattern of frequent lower-level Soviet-Hungarian visits remains unchanged. In May the Hungarian defense minister led a delegation to the Soviet Union at the invitation of his Soviet counterpart.

On the domestic front pro-Soviet manifestations were only intensified as the 60th anniversary of the Bolshevik Revolution approached. A work competition in celebration of that anniversary by the Csepel metallurgical works was formally acknowledged by Brezhnev, who is an honorary member of the Csepel workers' collective. The eighth national conference of the Hungarian-Soviet Friendship Society, held 30-31 October 1976 in the Parliament building, was attended by over 600 delegates. It was reported that since the last such meeting, in November 1971, the number of active member groups had tripled (to 1,297), that attendance at Russian-language courses had risen "spectacularly," that the twinning of Hungarian and Soviet cities and counties was progressing, and that in general the "overwhelming majority of our people understands, approves, and supports the policy of our party in drawing closer the ties of friendship between the Hungarian and Soviet peoples." The dominant themes of the conference were the need for more personal and cultural interaction and the benefits of the existing close relationship.

Kádár and Lázár led a party and government delegation to the German Democratic Republic 22-26 March. A new 25-year agreement on friendship, cooperation, and mutual assistance was signed despite the fact that a similar 20-year agreement was signed in 1967. The latest accord omits earlier references, notably to a German peace treaty, which might have implied that the German question was not definitively settled. Peaceful coexistence and the inviolability of frontiers are endorsed; relations with West Berlin are to be conducted on the principle that it is not part of the Federal Republic of Germany and cannot be governed by the latter. The communiqué issuing from the meeting expressed full identity of views and joint determination to "take a stand against imperialist forces and against the anti-Communist and anti-Soviet slander campaign that is trying to divide the forces that are working on behalf of the Communist movement, anti-imperialism, peace, and social progress." Kádár dismissed East European dissidents as a "small number of groups" who were trying to hinder the march of Socialism and draw attention away from the crisis of capitalism, and who encouraged "provocations" against the GDR. Hungary has a trade deficit with the GDR, and an agreement was signed to expand economic cooperation and specialization. A *Gästarbeiter* agreement with the GDR has been in force for ten years, and since 1967 some 33,000 young Hungarians have worked in that country on three-year stints. In recent times the recruitment of volunteers for the program has become more difficult.

Czechoslovakia's foreign minister paid an official visit to Budapest 7-9 March. The joint communiqué voiced "commitment to reject, in harmony with the spirit and letter of the Helsinki Final Act, any attempt at interference in the internal affairs of their countries." The visits of Czechoslovak party leader Gustav Husák (14-16 September) and the Polish party's Edward Gierek (5-6 October) produced routine statements of friendship and expanded collaboration.

Relations with Romania remain less cordial than with the other East European party-states, partly because of the Romanian regime's voluntaristic tendencies in foreign policy but more specifically because of its discriminatory policies against the two-million-strong Hungarian minority. An occasional Hungarian article has reflected on the difficulty of solving nationality problems even under Socialism and criticized Romanian historians' praise of the World War I peace settlement for neglecting to note its anti-Bolshevik character and the oppression of minorities by the bourgeois-nationalist regime (*Magyar Hirlap,* 31 October, and *Elet és irodalom,* 6 November 1976). Prime Minister Lázár visited Bucharest 20-21 December 1976 for discussions on economic cooperation, cultural relations, the situation of the Hungarian minority, and the easing of travel restrictions. One of the agreements concluded was for joint exploitation of hydrocarbon deposits in the border area. Kádár met Romanian party leader Nicolae Ceauşescu at Debrecen, Hungary, and Oradea, Romania, 15 and 16 June. Agreements were signed on postal and telecommunications cooperation, border trade, and the establishment of consulates-general. The official communiqué noted that the "just solution in the spirit of Marxism-Leninism of the ethnic minorities issue and securing equal rights and many-sided development of the ethnic minorities are a minor element of Socialist construction in the two countries, and of deepening Hungarian-Romanian friendly relations." It referred to international norms for the protection of minority rights, which is the exclusive responsibility of each country, and stressed that the ethnic minorities should serve as a link in Hungarian-Romanian rapprochement. (MTI, 17 June.)

Notably friendly relations prevail between Hungary and Yugoslavia. Foreign minister and vice-premier Miloš Minić visited Budapest 31 January-2 February for discussions on the upcoming Belgrade conference. "Close or identical" views were expressed on international questions, and bilateral relations were considered to be developing positively. The ethnic minorities of the two countries were once again hailed as helpful bridges in the forging of good relations, and educational and cultural assistance to them will be promoted further. Stane Dolanc, secretary of the Yugoslav party presidium's Executive Committee, visited Budapest 12-14 May for talks with Kádár and Biszku. Dolanc noted upon his return that relations were good even though differences existed in domestic and foreign policies due to the fact that Yugoslavia was non-aligned while Hungary was a member of the Warsaw Pact; he and the Hungarians had agreed that "every party and every working class had the right to choose its own path to Socialist construction." (Tanjug, 15 May.) Kádár met Tito 22-24 September at a hunting lodge near the Hungarian border, their ninth meeting since 1962. The communiqué reflected the mutual respect of the two leaders.

Reports to the Central Committee and articles in the party press expressed regret that since the death of Mao Tse-tung China has continued to pursue "great power and nationalistic" policies and to prepare for war against the Soviet Union despite the willingness of the Socialist countries to improve relations.

Apart from his unhappy appearance at the United Nations accompanying Khrushchev in 1960 and attendance at the Helsinki conference in 1975, Kádár has foregone travel to Western countries, but in 1976-77 he spearheaded a flurry of diplomatic activity that has raised Hungary's profile in the West. His first official visit to a Western state was to Austria 6-7 December 1976. Agreement was reached on the expansion of the prevailing cordial relations, and particularly of economic cooperation. In these and other Hungarian-Western talks it was emphasized that political détente arising from the European security conference and its reviews must lead to military détente, notably through the mutual force reduction negotiations in Vienna (at which Hungary is only an observer). Reflecting on the "good atmosphere" of the talks, Kádár said of Chancellor Bruno Kreisky: "Everyone knows that he is a Social Democrat and that I am a Communist, but we respect each other's ideological positions." In answer to a question from the press, he said that Soviet forces would remain in Hungary until the "general situation of world politics" changed. Kreisky for his part reported that Kádár had shown a "relatively relaxed" attitude on the question of freer East-West human contacts. (Radio Free Europe Research, 14 December.) Austrian President Rudolf Kirchschläger received a warm reception in Budapest 24-27 May. His Hungarian counterpart, Pál Losonczi, indicated that negotiations would begin on the long-standing Austrian request for elimination of visas for travel between the two countries. Hungary's trade deficit with Austria, her second most important Western trading parter, and the consequences of the abolition of industrial tariffs between the EEC and EFTA (of which Austria is a member) were also discussed.

Kádár's visit to Italy 7-9 June was his first to a NATO country. Apart from official talks, he also met with an Italian Communist party delegation at the Hungarian Embassy, and was received in private audience by the pope. At a press conference he concurred with Pope Paul that the interview marked the completion of the normalization of state-church relations, observing that both church and state would endure for generations. Hungary had no human rights problems, he claimed: "We are not afraid of the views of the people." (*Népszabadság*, 10 June.)

On 4-7 July Kádár made an official visit to the German Federal Republic. A cultural cooperation agreement was signed, and Chancellor Helmut Schmidt praised Kádár and his domestic policies.

Finland's President Urho Kekkonen paid a visit to Hungary 17-20 November 1976. Hungarian-Finnish cooperation, said Kádár, is a good example of the peaceful coexistence between countries with different social systems advocated by the Helsinki Final Act. Several economic, cultural, and consular agreements are in force between Hungary and Finland, and relations are genuinely cordial. Customs duties on bilateral trade were eliminated in 1977.

Foreign Minister Frigyes Puja visited Turkey 10-14 January and raised a minor controversy with the suggestion that Balkan multilateral cooperation should not exclude proximate countries such as Hungary. On his visit to Greece 16-19 March Puja reiterated Hungary's request that the barter system of clearing bilateral trade be replaced by a free currency system. A consular convention and agreements on road transport and cultural exchanges were signed, and the official communiqué expressed the wish for a final solution to the Cyprus problem guaranteeing the republic's independence and territorial integrity. The latter position was also expressed on the occasion of the visit of a Greek Communist party delegation to Hungary 1-4 February. Puja also visited Great Britain 27 February-2 March for "cordial and constructive" talks on détente and bilateral trade and cultural relations, and similar questions were discussed by Prime Minister Lázár in Norway 2-4 May. Lázár visited Iraq, an important buyer of Hungarian products and supplier of crude oil, on 1-3 October. The official communiqué stressed the common struggle against imperialism and Hungary's endorsement of the Arab position regarding the Middle East problem.

The Kádár regime has for years pursued the goal of normalizing relations with the United States, principally to gain most-favored-nation trading status. The Jackson amendment has been the enduring obstacle. Hungary has an interest in expanding trade to gain access to American technology. In September the Hungarian National Bank opened a branch in New York and negotiated a seven-year $200 million credit with a group of U.S. and Canadian banks; in November the Hungarian Chamber of Commerce organized a series of "economic days" in major American cities. Meanwhile, official permission for the visit of U.S. evangelist Billy Graham, 4-9 September, was designed to demonstrate the regime's liberal attitude, and Graham duly reported positively on religious freedom, including that of the Jews, who, he said, were allowed to emigrate. In November the Carter administration indicated that in the light of "substantial improvement" in U.S.-Hungarian relations the 977-year old Crown of St. Stephen and other royal jewels, in U.S. safekeeping since the last days of World War II, would finally be returned to Hungary.

The official Hungarian position on the review of the Helsinki Final Act has been to minimize opposition to Socialism in Eastern Europe and to claim that the Socialist countries have a better record on the "free flow of people and ideas" than the West. At the same time, it is emphasized that differences in social system mean that it will take decades to fully implement the accord. (*Népszabadság*, 18 February.) To demonstrate Hungary's openness to debate, the third television program in the "International Studio" series presented on 22 February a discussion between American, Soviet, and Japanese journalists on international affairs, and viewers were treated to conflicting opinions on the arms race and the implementation of the Final Act.

President Carter's human rights campaign has been sharply condemned for creating an atmosphere unpropitious for successful conduct of the talks on strategic arms limitation and on force reductions in Europe. (Ibid., 20 March.) Hungary and other Socialist states were, according to repeated official assertions, heading for Belgrade with a constructive and positive program of implementation. At the opening session of the conference, Foreign Minister Puja retaliated against the American stress on human rights by complaining of discriminative trade and visa restrictions on the part of the West (Reuter, 8 October).

The Charter 77 proclamation of the Czech dissidents drew a statement of support from 34 Hungarian intellectuals. The message, sent to Pavel Kohout on 9 January, read in part: "We declare our solidarity with the signers of Charter 77 and we condemn the repressive measures used against them. We are convinced that the defense of human and civil rights is a common concern of all of Eastern Europe." The signatories include a number of intellectuals already in disgrace for earlier acts of dissent: the philosophers György Márkus, János Kis, Mihály Vajda, Ágnes Heller, and Vilmos Sós, who were expelled from the party for neo-leftist views or for protesting the 1968 invasion of Czechoslovakia, and the writer Miklós Haraszti, who was briefly jailed in 1974 for his provocative novel on the distress of Hungarian industrial workers. Other signatories include the popular writers Sándor Csoóri and Miklós Mészoly, and Ferenc Donáth, a veteran of the prewar Communist party who was imprisoned from 1958 to 1963 for his association with Imre Nagy and the 1956 revolution. In a Radio Vienna interview on 20 January, one of the signatories, the philosopher Ferenc Fehér, pointed out that the letter was a simple act of solidarity that did not represent any organized movement and had no bearing on the situation in Hungary. The letter provoked no immediate official reaction or reprisals, although it has been rumored that some of the signatories may be induced to leave the country. (*Washington Post,* 14 September.)

The third "mother-tongue conference" was held in Budapest 8-13 August under the auspices of the World Federation of Hungarians, whose task it is to forge cultural links with the approximately 1.5 million ethnic Hungarians living outside Eastern Europe. For the first time, representatives of Hungarian ethnic groups in Slovakia, Yugoslavia, and the sub-Carpathian region of the Soviet Union were in attendance. In his summing up speech, State Secretary for Education János Gosztonyi drew a distinction between the émigrés in the world at large and the minorities in the neighboring countries, and he expressed regret at the absence of representatives from the Hungarian community in Romania.

Publications. The HSWP's principal daily newspaper is *Népszabadság* (People's Freedom), edited by Dezsö Nemes, with a circulation of 750,000. The theoretical monthly *Társadalmi Szemle* (Social Review) has a circulation of 40,700. The monthly organizational journal *Pártélet* (Party Life) has a circulation of 130,000. Other major newspapers are *Magyar Hirlap,* the "government" daily; *Magyar Nemzet,* published under the auspices of the Patriotic People's Front; and *Népszava,* the organ of the trade unions. The official news agency is Magyar Távirati Iroda (Hungarian Telegraphic Agency; MTI).

University of Toronto   Bennett Kovrig

Poland

Since December 1948 the Communist movement in Poland has carried the name Polish United Workers' Party (Polska Zjednoczona Partia Robotnicza; PUWP). Its history goes back to December 1918 and the establishment of the Communist Workers' Party of Poland, which became the Communist Party of Poland in 1925. During the interwar years the movement operated underground with a limited membership and little public support. It was dissolved by the Comintern in 1938, after most of its leaders had already disappeared in the Soviet purges.

In January 1942 the movement was revived by the Comintern as the Polish Workers' Party. Following the advance of the Red Army, the party seized power in Poland and consolidated control through gradual elimination of potential competitors. In December 1948 the Communists forced a merger with the Polish Socialist Party to form the Polish United Workers' Party. Ever since, the PUWP has maintained a dominant position in Polish politics, using the Front of National Unity (FNU)—a formal coalition of social, political, and economic groups—as an instrument for electoral and governmental control. The FNU has been headed since February 1976 by PUWP Politburo member Henryk Jabłonski. No institutional opposition, in the sense of organized groups capable of competing for power with the Front of National Unity, has been allowed to exist. Two other political organizations operate in Poland, the Democratic Party and the United Peasant Party, but are restricted to essentially supportive functions. In 1976 a constitutional amendment gave legal recognition to the leading role of the PUWP in political and economic life.

Since the last parliamentary (Sejm) elections in March 1976, the ruling party has had 262 out of 460 available seats, with 112 held by the United Peasant Party and 39 by the Democratic Party. The remaining 49 seats have been filled with non-party deputies, including 13 from various Catholic groups (five PAX, five Znak, two Christian Social Association, one Caritas).

The PUWP has 2,573,000 members, in a population of 35 million (*Nowe drogi*, June 1977, p. 9). The UPP has about 420,000 and the DP about 95,000.

Organization and Leadership. The PUWP's primary, occupationally centered organizations (currently about 72,000 civilian and 3,500 in the armed forces) are administratively subordinated to the territorially based communal and town committees (2,300); these, in turn, report to provincial organs (49) which are controlled by the Central Committee (figures in *Nowe drogi*, June 1977, p. 6). The distribution of power is based on the principle of democratic centralism: each organizational unit elects its executive organs, which conduct party work in their spheres of competence and are accountable to the unit membership, while decisions taken by higher organs are binding on lower ones.

The highest authority is the congress, which meets at least once every five years (most recently on 8-12 December 1975). It elects the Central Committee and Central Party Control Commission. The Central Committee (141 full and 110 candidate members) directs and controls all party activities between congresses. To perform this task effectively it elects from among its members the Politburo and the Secretariat. The Politburo acts as the main policy-making body between Central Committee plenary meetings (plenums). The Secretariat is the executive organ of the Central Committee and is charged with supervision over party work. The Party Control Commission watches over internal discipline and also serves as an appellate office from decisions made by lower units. Corresponding structures are maintained at lower organizational levels.

The party leader has been first secretary Edward Gierek, since December 1970, when he replaced Władysław Gomułka.

The Politburo consists of fourteen full members: Edward Babiuch,* Edward Gierek,* Zdzisław Grudzien, Henryk Jabłonski, Mieczysław Jagielski, Piotr Jaroszewicz, Wojciech Jaruzelski, Stanisław Kania,* Józef Kępa, Stanisław Kowalczyk, Władysław Kruczek, Stefan Olszowski,* Jan Szydlak, Józef Tejchma. The three candidate members are Kazimierz Barcikowski, Jerzy Lukaszewicz,* and Tadeusz Wrzaszczyk. The Secretariat includes ten secretaries: the five marked above by an asterisk (*) and Ryszard Frelek, Alojzy Karkoszka, Józef Pinkowski, Andrzej Werblan, Zdzisław Żandarowski. The two Secretariat members are Zdisław Kurowski and Zbigniew Zielienski (elected in April, see below). The chairman of the Party Control Commission is Stefan Misiaszek.

Political and administrative work of the PUWP is carried out by full-time, paid party employees (the apparatus). The exact size of this group remains obscure. Estimates, which must rely on sporadic and far from complete official and semiofficial reports, place their number at about 20,000 with the great majority (more than 64 percent) employed by regional and local organs (ibid., p. 13). As the hard core of the organizational structure, the apparatus members provide the main source of recruitment to top leadership positions and play a major role in the formulation and implementation of party policies. They are assisted by 445,000 party activists (ibid., January 1976, p. 40) who participate in organizational work mainly on an elective basis.

The PUWP's attitude toward society goes back to the Leninist concept of a revolutionary party acting as vanguard of the proletariat. Its contemporary expression is more practical and involves the directed coordination of all organized political and social activities, in order to achieve a centrally planned program of economic development.

A crucial feature of this directing role has been the PUWP's operational control over state institutions and public organizations. The most important government functions remain in the hands of party leaders. By the end of 1977, Central Committee members occupied eight out of seventeen positions on the Council of State, including that of the chairman, who is the titular head of state (Jabłonski). They also held the office of the prime minister (Jaroszewicz); eight out of ten deputies to the prime minister, five of whom are Politburo members (Jagielski, Kępa, Szydlak, Tejchma, Wrzaszczyk); and twenty-two out of thirty-one ministerial posts. (C.I.A. Reference Aid, Chiefs of State and Cabinet Members of Foreign Countries, August 1977, pp. 54-55, lists all incumbents.)

A similar pattern of supervisory controls extends to public mass organizations. Foremost among them are the twenty-three trade unions, with a total membership of more than 12.5 million. Their activities are coordinated by the Central Council of Trade Unions (chairman, Politburo member Kruczek), which serves as policy organ for the entire movement. Its work ranges from supervision of safety standards to administration of social programs, and it has an advisory role in the formulation of government economic policies, but its most important task is to secure cooperation between workers and management to achieve economic targets. Official duties of the unions and the 7,600 local Conferences of Workers' Self-Management are restricted to cooperation with appropriate governmental bodies in preparing and implementing labor legislation.

The party's three youth organizations are the Union of Polish Socialist Youth (about 2,200,000 members) headed by Central Committee member Krzysztof Trebaczkiewicz; the Socialist Union of Polish Students (250,000), under Central Committee candidate member Stanisław Gabrielski; and the Union of Polish Scouts (3,000,000), under Central Committee member Jerzy Wojciechowski. All three are united in the Federation of Socialist Unions of Polish Youth, headed since April 1977 by Trebaczkiewicz, who replaced Secretariat member Kurowski (Warsaw radio, 27 April).

Among other mass organizations, the most important politically are the Union of Fighters for Freedom and Democracy (ZBoWiD), a veterans' group (500,000); the League of Women, active in propagating a proper model of family life (445,000); the Volunteer Citizens' Militia Reserve (ORMO), a para-police force frequently used in quelling dissent and disturbances (322,000); and the League for Defense of the Country (LOK), a civil defense organization (1,847,000). All are headed by members of the party's Central Committee.

Internal Party Affairs. The PUWP Central Committee met four times during 1977, with economic issues clearly dominant: agricultural problems and how to cope with shortages of food and meat (January), the ideological approach to reinforcing socialist consciousness and patriotism (April), the continuing housing shortage (June), and improvement in management of the economy (October).

Only two changes were made in the PUWP leadership, and they did not seem to reflect any serious internal problems. Jan Szydlak was relieved in January as party secretary in connection with his appointment as deputy prime minister in December 1976. Zielinski became a member of the Secretariat in April but also continued as head of the Heavy Industry, Transportation and Construction Department in the Central Committee.

Efforts to improve the proletarian character of PUWP social composition intensified. In May the percentage of workers in the party rose to 44.7 (1,150,000), the highest since 1955; white-collar members comprised 39.6 percent (1,018,000), peasants 8.7 percent (225,000), and others 7.0 percent (180,000) (*Nowe drogi*, June, p. 9).

The Central Committee announced that the second national PUWP conference would be held in January 1978 to review social, political, and economic developments since the Seventh Congress.

Domestic Policies. The main emphasis of PUWP domestic activity in 1977 was on ways to secure a continuing program of economic development without provoking social protest or political disruption. The 1976 attempt to impose restrictive economic measures (see *YICA, 1977*, pp. 57-59) failed under the pressure of massive workers' opposition. It also led to resurgence of political dissent which, having been triggered by punitive measures against selected groups of workers, developed into a movement of criticism against the government and its methods. PUWP policies in 1977 were aimed at economic and political stabilization and the regaining of social support for the party and its leadership.

The Economy. Coming on the heels of two successive years of economic difficulty and the related increase in social tension, the PUWP was forced to adopt a series of measures aimed at a growth in production and improvement of supplies. Officially described as a new "economic maneuver," these initiatives marked a shift in emphasis from heavy industry to investments in consumer goods, food production, and services (Gierek's speech at the "Ursus" tractor factory on 3 February, in *Contemporary Poland*, no. 4, March).

Highest priority was placed on agricultural development, with special attention to stimulating productivity on privately owned farms, which comprise about 71 percent of the arable land and provide more than half of the entire agricultural output and most of the meat (e.g., 67 percent of all pork). The PUWP proposed a comprehensive program of benefits for individual farmers, tied to indices of production and deliveries to the state. Announced at the Central Committee plenum in January, it encouraged more efficient farmers to expand their holdings by making it easier to purchase land and equipment. It also included a retirement plan with pensions based on production records and sales to the state. Further, the party recognized the legality of private farm ownership by accepting inheritance, providing that the owners delivered their produce to the state on a contractual basis for a certain period of time and maintained their farms in good working condition.

Similar measures to encourage expansion of private enterprise were extended to crafts and services (at the beginning of 1977, there were about 190,000 small private businesses, employing 373,000 persons). Scheduled for gradual implementation during 1977, they included increased profits by lowering tax rates, a guarantee of greater access to tools and machinery (previously restricted to the socialized sector), and permission to calculate prices under guidance and approval of state authorities.

At the June plenum the Central Committee adopted a new housing policy which envisages a long-term plan for constructing about 7.3 million dwellings by 1990, with more than 1.5 million to be built during 1976-80. At the same time the party acknowledged the persistent housing shortage, both in private and public sectors (more than 850,000 persons were registered on various waiting lists for cooperative housing), as well as difficulties in fulfilling planned construction targets (in the first three months of 1977, only 11.3 percent of the annual plan had been achieved). No decision, however, was made on methods of improving the situation. New proposals are to be presented at the PUWP national conference in January 1978.

In industrial development, the rate of investment declined during the first six months of 1977 from 32 percent to about 30 percent of national income. Several new projects were canceled or postponed, including a $1 billion truck plant by General Motors. Average employment went up by 0.5 percent (in comparison with the first half of 1976), to 11,800,000 while the increase in real wages amounted to only 2.4 percent. During the same time, industrial production grew by 9 percent, which could be misleading since the increase was calculated in 1977 prices without taking into consideration significant price changes resulting from inflation.

Despite these stabilization efforts, economic difficulties continued throughout 1977 and in some areas, notably agriculture and food supplies, were intensified. Particularly dangerous was a further decline in meat procurement, off during the first six months by more than 8 percent in comparison with the previous year, which had also dropped by some 10 percent from 1975. Additional imports of about 150,000 tons of meat and lard in the first six months of 1977 did not bring market supplies to their 1976 levels, which were down some 26,000 tons or 3 percent from 1975.

Owing to bad weather during the late summer harvest, preliminary estimates indicated that, as a result of excessive rains and floods, which inundated some 350,000 acres of arable land, lower harvests than in 1976 of the four main cereal crops (wheat, rye, barley, and oats) were expected in more than half of the provinces. During 1976 they had dropped by about 3.4 percent from the preceding year. Further imports of food and grain appeared all but inevitable.

This was a serious development for a country with estimated debts to the West reaching at least $10 billion and a debt service rate of about 25 percent (*Washington Post*, 30 October). To make matters worse, export difficulties continued unabated, accounting for only 13 percent of overall national income, instead of a planned 14.8 percent during the first six months. Already at the end of the previous year, Soviet economic aid had helped to prevent a serious economic crisis. An agreement negotiated in November 1976 included a low-interest loan of $1.3 billion, together with deliveries of food, other consumer goods, and raw materials. In the long run, however, Soviet aid should have little if any effect on the adverse balance of payments, which may make it more difficult to obtain credits from the West.

The gravity of the situation was fully recognized at the October plenum. Yet no new decisions were taken. Instead the party leadership postponed action until the national conference in January 1978, appealing in the meantime for full and correct implementation of previous policies and calling for more efficient economic management.

Political Dissent. The year 1977 marked a significant expansion in the active, semi-organized opposition against party and government policies. Although generated by protests over government repression against the workers, which followed the June 1976 strikes, this movement of criticism rapidly extended beyond any specific demands for leniency. Responding to a growing restlessness, produced by long-existing tension in public life, it developed a momentum of its own and crystallized around current issues.

The movement of political dissent did not constitute any discernible social or ideological entity. It embraced rather a wide variety of separate centers, each different from the other, with their own internal characteristics and specific patterns of activity.

They included the Committee for Defense of Workers (Komitet Obrony Robotnikow; KOR), a left-wing Socialist group organized in September 1976 by fourteen prominent intellectuals for providing legal and financial aid to imprisoned workers' families as well as campaigning for their release; the Movement for Defense of Human and Civil Rights (Ruch Obrony Praw Czlowieka i Obywatela; ROPCO), formed in March 1977 in support of the more general issue of human and democratic rights but without any clearly defined ideological preference; and the Polish Agreement on Independence (Polskie Prozumienie Niepodlegosciowe: PPN), unifying several political and ideological currents on the basis of a clearly patriotic platform which calls for gradual transformation of Poland into a fully independent, democratically organized state.

Several other groups also made their appearance in 1977. Among them were an *ad hoc* group to monitor implementation of the Helsinki agreements, the Polish branch of Amnesty International, and (in May) a Student Solidarity Committee (Studencki Komitet Solidarnosci; SKS), established in Krakow as an alternative to the official Socialist Union of Polish Students.

Some of these organizations insist on open, semi-institutionalized dissent against party policies within the limits of existing law. Thus ROPCO had established six offices by the end of October and planned to open branches in each of the forty-nine provinces, while KOR set up an Intervention Bureau in May to collect and publicize information on official violations of human rights. Others (such as the PPN) preferred clandestine activity in the style of traditional underground movements reminiscent of nineteenth-century Polish resistance against tsarist Russia. All claim considerable support from the public at large (KOR and ROPCO claim more than 1,000 active supporters each). They publish several typed or mimeographed but regularly appearing periodicals such as KOR's *Biuletyn informacyjny* and *Robotnik* (first appeared in September), ROPCO's *Opinia*, the less clearly identified *U progu*, and the samizdat-type literary review, *Zapis*.

Their activities, and particularly the work of KOR on behalf of imprisoned workers, received a significant response both at home and abroad. Especially important is the ability of KOR to collect substantial funds for assistance to needy workers. By September, more than three million zlotys had been spent in financial and medical help for several hundred worker families. Another indication of widespread public support for dissident activities was a series of letters and petitions addressed to the authorities and demanding an investigation of police brutality: a letter signed by 172 intellectuals to .the Sejm in January (*L'Unità*, Rome, 9 January; *Sunday Telegraph*, London, 9 January), a letter from about 750 Warsaw students (*London Times*, 12 April), and more than 2,000 individual letters of protest from around the country (*L'Unità*, 25 March).

To contain social and political ferment, the government used a variety of different tactics ranging from benevolent measures of appeasement to physical harassment of KOR members, police intimidation, and attempts at professional ostracism. Most of the imprisoned workers were freed early in January and a conditional pardon for those who "showed repentance" was declared the following month (Gierek's letter to Radom workers as reported by PAP, 3 February). At the same time, however, a press campaign of vilification against dissenters intensified (e.g., *Trybuna ludu*, 18 January and 28 March; *Zolnierz wolnosci*, 2-3 April). The Central Committee plenum in mid-April called attention of the party and government to a continuing persistence of politically "alarming phenomena which must be counteracted with determination" (Warsaw radio, Gierek's speech, 14 April; also his speech to secretaries of PUWP local organizations, 25 April). This was accompanied with new harassment of KOR members (in late April seven were arrested and held for several days).

In May a student and KOR supporter, Stanisław Pyjas, was found dead in rather obscure circumstances. This provoked a peaceful student demonstration in Krakow and an almost total boycott of the traditional student festival. A protest by KOR leaders against the lack of an official investigation into the death led to the arrest of several prominent representatives of the dissident organization. The government's attempt to silence its critics led to counteraction by KOR: ten members and sympathizers went on a hunger strike in a Warsaw church to gain the release of those arrested as well as five still imprisoned workers. In turn, this brought a renewed press campaign replete with accusations of dissidents' collaboration with foreign espionage agencies (*Polityka*, 28 May; *Zycie Warszawy*, 1 June). Finally, a general amnesty in July freed all arrested dissidents and workers, and their cases were officially closed.

Insofar as this action represented an attempt by the government to satisfy dissident demands and calm the political tension, it failed to end the momentum of opposition activities. The success in obtaining release of the workers appeared rather to the dissidents as an indication of their growing strength and brought further expansion of their work. Hence KOR changed its name in September to the Committee for Social Self-Defense "KOR" (Komitet Samoobrony Spolecznej "KOR") and adopted the goal of establishing itself as an institutionalized opposition for defense of human rights (interview with a KOR leader, Jacek Kuron, *Dagens Hyheter*, Stockholm, 9 September).

In October, ROPCO revealed that a series of local strikes had taken place in several Silesian mines as a protest against inadequate food supplies. No punitive action followed.

In other developments, two feature films attacked the recent history and morality of Communist rule ("The Marble Man" by Andrzej Wajda and "The Protective Colors" by Krzysztof Zanussi), despite frequent and outspoken criticism in the official party organs.

Relations with the Catholic Church. The most important political development in this area was the rapprochement between the Church and dissidents. In late 1976 the Church officially protested against mistreatment of workers by the government. Catholic priests were also among founders of principal opposition organizations. On their part, dissidents openly proclaimed their appreciation of Church support and called for more cooperation. This, at least, was the message in a book by a KOR leader which, while published abroad, was circulated and discussed in Poland (Adam Michnik, *Kosciol, lewica, dialog*. Paris, Instytut Literacki, 1977).

Church criticism of government policies intensified during the spring. At the end of April and the beginning of May, Primate Stefan Wyszyński delivered a series of speeches on human rights. Following the death of Pyjas, special requiem services were held at churches in Krakow and Warsaw. Catholic activists took part in the hunger strike at Warsaw which, significantly, was held in a church building.

On 9 June, Corpus Christi holiday, Cardinals Karol Wojtyla and Wyszyński delivered sermons critical of governmental policies toward human rights and condemned biased press accounts about student and dissident movements. On 19 September a pastoral letter read in all Polish churches again attacked the media, accusing them of promoting "godless ideology" and "total dictatorship" (*Washington Post*, 19 September). Two weeks later, on 1 October, another pastoral letter from the primate strongly criticized the government's human rights and economic policies, stressing the need for "compassion and concern for the nation in the spirit of Christian charity" (Vatican City radio, 2 October).

Aside from the hardening of its political opposition to these policies, Church leaders were active in promoting several special issues of considerable importance in the continuing adversary relationship. They included demands for construction of new churches, stress on the right to provide religious education in schools, criticism of discrimination against practicing Catholics in professional advancement, and strong attacks on the government's educational policies.

Response to Church criticism was both conciliatory and antagonistic. The state (after twenty years) permitted completion of a church building in Nowa Huta, the largest "Socialist town" in Poland, with more than 100,000 inhabitants. In October additional construction permits were granted for eighteen new churches in Warsaw and its suburbs. And in the same month, Primate Wyszyński met for the first time since 1970 with Gierek to discuss questions of "great importance to both nation and church and the unity of all Poles in the task of shaping the welfare of Poland" (*Christian Science Monitor*, 31 October). On the other hand, several steps were taken to weaken the political and social influence of lay Catholic organizations and to separate them from the episcopate. On 21 January, the government suspended distribution of funds to the Clubs of Catholic Intelligentsia, which are close to the episcopate (there are five such clubs, with a membership of several thousands), and transferred them to a newly formed splinter group, called Polish Club of Catholic Intelligentsia and more in tune with official policies. Combined with earlier efforts to dismember the parliamentary Znak group, manipulation of financial resources may lead to imposition of centralized state control over the lay Catholic movement in general.

In other developments, noteworthy was the visit of Archbishop Luigi Poggi, envoy for contact between Rome and Warsaw, who spent two weeks in Poland during March. He held discussions with

Cardinal Wyszyński and top governmental officials, notably the head of the Office of Religious Affairs (Central Committee member Kazimierz Kakol).

In October, Cardinal Wojtyla traveled to Rome to attend the World Synod of Bishops. Primate Wyszyński was at the Vatican when party leader Gierek had an audience with Pope Paul VI on 2 December.

International Policies. In its attitude toward the West, Poland maintained a strongly cooperative posture in an effort to expand economic contacts. Several important visits were exchanged during 1977. They included visits by Premier Jaroszewicz to the Netherlands (March) and to Norway (May) as well as Gierek's trips to India (January), France (September), and Italy (December). Iran's Shah Reza Pahlevi paid an official visit to Poland in August. In each case, credits and industrial cooperation were main topics of discussions. The tour of Poland by Belgium's King Baudouin and Queen Fabiola, in October, was primarily ceremonial.

The Federal Republic of Germany continued as a primary area for Poland's diplomatic activity and as its most important trade partner. Throughout the year, numerous official exchanges were held between the two countries, including an inaugural meeting of Forum Poland-FRG in June, to be continued as annual symposia. Willy Brandt, chairman of the Social-Democratic Party, visited Poland that same month; Politburo member Babiuch traveled to West Germany in May. There were also several meetings of the Polish-West German educational commission charged with review and coordination of the treatment of Polish-German relations in school programs. During August, Poland received a two billion DM credit from a consortium of West German banks, the largest ever received from the FRG. In November Chancellor Helmut Schmidt visited Warsaw. His talks with the Poles produced mutual assurances for extended economic and political cooperation between the two countries.

Economic problems also dominated Polish-American relations. In early December U.S. Secretary of Commerce Juanita Kreps took part in a session of the joint U.S.-Polish Trade Council in Warsaw. On 29-31 December President Carter came to Poland for talks with the Polish leaders. At the news conference in Warsaw, President Carter announced that the U.S. would provide credits to Poland for $200 million worth of grain. Mrs. Carter and Zbigniew Brzezinski, White House national security advisor, met with Cardinal Wyszyński.

Poland ratified (February) the UN human rights declaration. From early October through December, the Polish delegation actively participated in the Belgrade conference on European security and cooperation.

In relations with other Communist-ruled countries, the most important were extensive contacts with Soviet party and state officials. Several Politburo members traveled to Moscow: Olszowski for economic consultations and Szydlak on preparations for the sixtieth anniversary of the October Revolution (both in March), Babiuch on party work and ideological questions (April), and Jaruzelski on coordination of defense policies in September. Gierek visited the USSR twice: for a short holiday in July, and with Premier Jaroszewicz to take part in the sixtieth anniversary during November.

Further expansion took place in economic cooperation between Moscow and Warsaw. Already involved with building the Orenburg gas pipeline, through which Poland is to receive 2.8 billion cubic meters of gas per annum for twenty years, work commenced in 1977 on construction of the Novopolotsk oil pipeline. After completion, one million tons of petroleum per annum for a decade will be forthcoming. By the end of the current five-year plan, trade between the two countries should total 28 billion rubles, about 70 percent more than during 1970-75. Poland's exports concentrate on shipbuilding for the Soviet Union (by 1980, about seventy-five vessels with a total displacement of 900,000 tons should be delivered to the USSR), machinery, and coal. Imports will consist primarily of raw materials and energy resources.

The long-term outline of Polish policies toward the Soviet Union appeared in a special article by Gierek (*Pravda*, 30 September), where he promised intensified "efforts toward deepening of the relations uniting both states [and] toward strengthening of fraternal ties between the PUWP and the CPSU."

Among bilateral contacts, the most important were Gierek's visits to the German Democratic Republic (a new twenty-five-year friendship treaty was signed on 28 May) and to Czechoslovakia in July. The more important visitors to Poland were the GDR's Erich Honecker (February), Czechoslovakia's Gustav Husák (March) and Romania's Nicolae Ceauşescu (May). While the first two came for working sessions, the last was a ceremonial visit during which the Romanian leader openly proclaimed "rigorous observance of the right of each party to work out its own political line, corresponding to the concrete social and national conditions in which it operates" (*Trybuna ludu*, 20 May).

Polish representatives also took part in several multilateral Communist meetings, including conferences on ideological problems at Sofia (March) and Prague (April). A conference on party organizational matters was held at Warsaw in April.

Poland entered the ideological controversy about the book by Santiago Carrillo, *Eurocommunism and the State*. Two official party organs (*Trybuna ludu*, 3 August, and *Nowe drogi*, August) attacked Carrillo's views in the name of proletarian internationalism and condemned his "separatist deviations."

Publications. The official organ of the PUWP is the daily *Trybuna ludu*; it also has daily newspapers in all forty-nine provinces. The monthly theoretical journal is *Nowe drogi*. The monthly *Zycie partii* and the biweekly *Zagadnienia i materialy* are for party activists. The biweekly *Chlopska droga* is for rural readers and the monthly *Ideologia i polityka* for the general public. The most important weekly, *Polityka*, is closely linked to the party without, however, any official identification.

University of South Carolina   Jan B. de Weydenthal

Romania

The Communist Party of Romania (Partidul Comunist român; CPR) was founded on 8 May 1921. Throughout most of the interwar period the CPR was outlawed. Factionalized and controlled by the Soviet-dominated Communist International, it had little popular support. The Soviet occupation of Romania in 1944 ensured the emergence of a people's republic headed by the party, which was renamed the Romanian Workers' Party (Partidul Muncitoresc Romîn) in 1948. Under the leadership of Gheorghe Gheorghiu-Dej, the party gradually initiated, in the 1960s, a more nationalistic internal course and a more autonomous foreign policy. This orientation has been continued by Nicolae Ceauşescu who succeeded Dej upon the latter's death in 1965. In that same year the Ninth Congress of the CPR proclaimed Romania a Socialist republic and the party reverted to its original name. Since 1948 the CPR has been the only party in Romania.

As of September 1977, party membership was 2.7 million (up from 2.5 million as of 31 December 1975), of which 51 percent were workers, 19 percent were peasants, 22 percent were intellectuals and white collar personnel, and 8 percent were in other categories. Women constituted 26 percent of party membership. (*Scînteia,* 24 September.) The CPR's ethnic composition approximated that of the country as a whole—88.1 percent Romanian, 7.9 percent Hungarian, 1.6 percent German, and 2.4 percent other nationalities. Total population as of 5 January 1977 was 21,559,416 (ibid., 4 January).

Organization and Leadership. The CPR is organized into basic units—at the various local working places—and into organizations at the communal, town, municipal, county, and national levels. In 1977 there were 59,000 basic party units (*Scînteia,* 24 September). Every five years the thirty-nine county organizations elect deputies to a national party congress which, according to party statutes, is the supreme authority of the CPR. In practice, congresses (the most recent was in 1974) have merely ratified personnel and policy decisions made by other party bodies: the Central Committee, the Secretariat, the Political Executive Committee, and the Permanent Bureau. These, in turn, have been dominated increasingly by the CPR secretary general, Nicolae Ceauşescu, whose "personality cult" was undiminished in 1977. In addition to his party positions, Ceauşescu holds many others including president of the republic and supreme commander.

Unlike most other Communist parties, the CPR does not have a Politburo. Decision-making power is centered in two bodies: the Political Executive Committee (PEC) and the Permanent Bureau. Since its creation in 1965, the PEC (twenty-three full and fifteen candidate members) has had wide-ranging power to decide party and state matters, while the Permanent Bureau, created in 1974, seemed to specialize in economic and trade matters. In January 1977 the PEC increased the Permanent Bureau from five to nine members, giving that body an expanded role in policymaking. The new members are: Cornel Burtică, Gheorghe Radulescu, Illie Verdeţ, and Ceauşescu's wife, Elena. The latter appointment continues the secretary general's policy of bringing family and relatives into leading party bodies.

At the same time the PEC decided to enlarge the Secretariat from ten to eleven members, with the addition of Ion Stanescu, and to give two of the secretaries, Stanescu and Burtică, the additional responsibility of being deputy prime ministers. Thus, in addition to its purview over policy and personnel, the Secretariat will now monitor more closely the administration of party decisions by the government. The PEC also decided to shift six county party first secretaries into government positions. (Ibid., 26, 27 January.)

The increasing power of Ceauşescu and his hand-picked people in the leading party bodies has tended to diminish the role of the Central Committee (205 full and 156 candidate members), which is charged with the direction of the party between congresses. It still meets in plenary sessions several times a year to approve important programs, but with little apparent debate.

Supplementing the work of the ongoing bodies is the National Conference of the CPR which meets two or three years after a party congress to review the progress made in implementing the congress's decisions and to set policy guidelines for the next several years. The most recent conference was held 7-9 December 1977.

Mass and Auxiliary Organizations. In 1977 the CPR gave major attention to mass organizations dealing with the working class. This was, in part, a response to the emergence of popular and workers' unrest,but it also was in keeping with the desire to mobilize the society through party-dominated mass organizations and ad hoc bodies. There were three firsts: a National Conference on Workers' Control Councils (*Scînteia,* 18-19 February), a National Congress of the Councils of Working People (ibid., 12-15 July), and a Peasantry Congress (ibid., 19 April). The various councils are enterprise-based worker/management bodies, headed by party people, charged with supervising and improving enterprise activity in meeting economic plan goals. In his speech to the Congress of the Councils of Working People, Ceauşescu announced that another mass organization would be created: the National Council of Working People, to be composed of 300 workers, representatives of mass organizations and leaders from the party-state apparat. The new body is charged with the vague responsibility of providing leadership for the working people's councils. All of this was part of the CPR's renewed ideological emphasis on "workers' democracy."

Other activities of note included the holding of the twice-postponed National Conference of the Romanian Writers' Union, at which Foreign Minister George Macovescu assumed the additional duties of union chairman (ibid., 27 May), and the holding of local elections on 20 November supervised by the Socialist Unity Front. Ceauşescu's son, Nicu, was elected a secretary of the Union of Communist Youth.

National Party Conference. The most important party event in 1977 was the convening of the CPR's National Conference, 7-9 December. Although the conference was confronted with an unprecedented year of internal unrest, it essentially approved ongoing domestic and foreign policies (*Scînteia*, 8-10 December).

In his opening address to the conference (ibid., 8 December), Ceauşescu gave primary attention to economic matters, noting that the key element of the 1976-80 plan—industrial production—had been "overfulfilled" in the first two years of the plan, with an average annual growth rate of 11.6 percent as opposed to the planned 10 percent. Agricultural output had increased at a rate of almost 9 percent, light industry at 11.8 percent, and the food industry at 10.6 percent during 1976-77. While there were areas of weak or lower than planned growth, such as in investments, foreign trade exports, and certain agricultural and industrial sectors, Ceauşescu indicated that the remaining three years would see all aspects of the plan fulfilled. He called for greater attention to the qualitative factors affecting growth: research, efficiency, productivity, and conservation of resources. Projecting economic guidelines for 1981-85, Ceauşescu reaffirmed the CPR's domestic priority of rapid industrialization, with only a slight reduction of the current one-third reinvestment rate of national income, so that during the next five-year plan "Romania will leave the stage of a developing country . . . and will pass to the stage of a country of average development."

While Ceauşescu did not shift to "consumerism" as an answer to popular discontent, he did indicate that there would be improvements in housing, food supplies, and salaries, and that starting in 1978 the work week would be cut from forty-eight to forty-four hours. Attention was also given to a "new revolutionary workers' democracy" which, he said, would be implemented by expanding the power of the various workers' organizations and by ensuring "the direct presence of workers . . . in central and local leadership bodies." The details, however, remained vague, as did Ceauşescu's plan to decentralize the judicial and penal systems by turning less serious criminals over to working people's bodies for sentencing involving work rather than jail. He made it very clear, though, that "socialist democracy" does not supplant the "leading role of the party" in all areas of society.

Although the CPR had given a major focus during 1977 to ideological mobilization and the improvement of party cadres, Ceauşescu's report spent little time on these matters. Ceauşescu, at the conference, seemed to back away from what had looked like the beginnings of a major shake-up of the party. Beginning with the party-state reshuffles in January and continuing with Ceauşescu's sweeping criticism of party cadres' deficiencies in implementing decisions, which he had voiced at the March (ibid., 7 April), September (ibid., 10, 24 September), and October (ibid., 27-28 October) meetings of the Central Committee, there seemed to be a campaign afoot to rearrange again the leadership and middle levels of the party. That did not materialize and Ceauşescu even adopted a more pragmatic than ideological tone in his address.

Many of the issues discussed at the conference had been approved previously by a joint meeting of the Central Committee and the Supreme Council on Socioeconomic Development (ibid., 30 June). That joint plenum *inter alia* had authorized what was to be a highly unpopular revision of the pension law and had accepted Ceauşescu's proposals to decentralize the judicial and censorship systems. Instead of one censorship body, each media unit's leadership, augmented by other party and mass representatives, will now decide whether a particular work is appropriate in the light of party ideology. But Ceauşescu made it clear that "there is no question of abolishing control; what we are doing away with is a certain kind of control of a bureaucratic character."

Domestic Events and Policies. While development and modernization remained the predominant internal focus of the regime, the pursuit of such goals was made more difficult in 1977 as a result of a major earthquake and varieties of popular discontent. The CPR was confronted with the task of rectifying the enormous damage caused by an earthquake on 4 March. Ceauşescu rushed back from a tour of Africa, called the PEC into daily sessions, and personally directed the recovery effort. Officially it was stated that 1,570 people had died and 11,300 were injured; the economic loss was put at over $2 billion. This figure included the destruction of thousands of homes and apartments, hundreds of industrial and agricultural units, several towns, and the center of Bucharest itself. In reporting on the destruction, Ceauşescu went out of his way to indicate that the plan would be fulfilled on schedule and that economic priorities would be maintained. (*Scînteia*, 10-11, 29 March.) The vast majority of the population made contributions of money or overtime work and joined with the army in cleanup operations.

Yet that national unity was to be short-lived. A small political dissident movement, which had emerged in February, continued to attract adherents, eventually numbering over a hundred. Led by the Romanian author Paul Goma, the movement was organized around an "open letter" to the Belgrade follow-up meeting of the Conference on Security and Cooperation in Europe. The dissenters, originally no more than nine, appealed for help regarding what they perceived as human-rights violations in Romania which contravened the CSCE's 1975 Final Act (*NYT*, 15 February). The regime responded with a mixture of coercion and conciliation. While Ceauşescu called the dissenters "traitors" (ibid., 18 February), the regime offered many of them passports and encouraged their emigration. In April a tougher line was adopted, with the harassment and arrest of those who continued to dissent, including a small group of Romanian Baptists. Through expatration and judicial trials, the small movement was soon decimated. Goma himself emigrated in November to Paris. Although many of the dissidents were sincere in their protest, some simply used it as a vehicle for obtaining passports to the West.

Political dissent was followed by manifestations of popular unrest. The over-booking of a concert in the Bucharest stadium on 13 June led ticketholders without seats to storm the stadium, rip down political propaganda, and clash with police in what was the first known riot in Communist Romania. In early August a large-scale, organized strike and demonstrations broke out among Romanian miners in the Jiu Valley. The miners were protesting changes in the pension law which they viewed as regressive: raising the time requirements for eligibility, reducing the government's share of contributions, and basing pensions on any five-year period during the last ten years of work, a time when miners are usually working aboveground and making less. The protest over the pension changes, however, soon turned into a generalized demonstration over poor living and working conditions. When Ceauşescu's emissaries were unable to placate the miners, Ceausescu himself visited the valley on 3 August. He was informed by the miners of "some shortcomings in the organization of work, some abuses in the application of laws, and some deficiencies in the leadership of the mines," and he called upon local party officials to rectify "abuses" (ibid., 4 August). Following this visit, certain concessions were made to the miners: secondary aspects of the pension law were revised, miners received an additional wage increase over that announced earlier for all workers, and the administration of the mines was reorganized. But these initial concessions were followed by sanctions: protest leaders were transferred to other jobs, miners' wages were docked for nonfulfillment of production goals, and military/security personnel were sent into the valley. (*NYT,* 27 November.) The net effect of these measures was to contain the protest. A return visit by Ceaușescu on 9-10 November indicated that the situation had calmed down, but the miners remained restive over the crackdown. The replacement of the minister of mines with Vasile Patilineț, a former party secretary in charge of security affairs, did not bode well for harmony between the miners and the regime.

For the CPR—long accustomed to a pliant population which had gone along with forced industrialization and a low standard of living—1977 may have been a turning point. The year's events demonstrated that the population's tolerance for bureaucratic inefficiency, authoritarianism, and party policy priorities was beginning to erode. While this development did not threaten Ceaușescu's political position or policy priorities, it will be more difficult to mobilize the society for industrialization at the expense of consumer gratification. Nationalistic appeals, such as surrounded the centenary of Romanian state independence on 9 May, will be less productive than in the past in terms of generating support for the party. It was symptomatic of these difficulties that Ceaușescu's amnesty of 28,500 prisoners at the time of the centenary led to an upsurge of crime in Bucharest and elsewhere (Reuters, Bucharest, 23 December).

International Events and Policies. The unique foreign policy position of Romania was reaffirmed in 1977. Although a member of the Council for Mutual Economic Assistance (CMEA) and the Warsaw Pact, Romania has long deviated from many Soviet-East European bloc positions. This was manifested again in 1977 in Romania's approach to the Middle East, Eurocommunism, the People's Republic of China, the Third World, and the West. At the same time, though, the CPR was careful to keep its deviation within limits so as not to jeopardize its remaining economic and political linkages to the Soviet Union and the other East European Socialist states. But, generally, the objective continued to be that of balancing its bloc relationship with positive relations toward the West, Third World, and other independent Communist states and parties as a basis for achieving a meaningful political autonomy.

The first half of 1977 saw a continuation of Romania's bettering of relations with the Soviet bloc—a course that became more noticeable after Brezhnev's visit to Bucharest in 1976. In the aftermath of the earthquake, Ceaușescu praised the Soviet Union for its aid and noted that Soviet-Romanian relations had "greatly developed" (*Scînteia,* 29 March). Mikhail Zimianin, Communist Party of the Soviet Union secretary in charge of ideology, visited Bucharest in June for the signing of an agreement on ideological cooperation between the two parties during 1977-1980; on that occasion both sides noted "satisfaction with the increasing development of relations of close friendship and fruitful cooperation between the CPR and CPSU" (Radio Bucharest, 1 June). Continuing this spirit, Ceaușescu visited several bloc states with which Romania's relations had, at times, been strained: Poland, 17-19 May; East Germany, 8-10 June; and Hungary, 15-16 June. In addition, visits were made to Romania by East German party leader Honecker, 4-6 February, and Czech party head Husák, 22-24 June.

In the second half of 1977, however, the CPR was confronted by a renewal of Soviet attempts to dominate European Communist parties—as exemplified by the Soviet attack on the Spanish Communist Party's leader, Santiago Carrillo, and his book *Eurocommunism and the State.* Unlike most other East European parties, the CPR proclaimed its support for the Eurocommunists by reasserting its well-known principles of party autonomy and the right to choose Socialist forms in keeping with national particularities, principles it believes were validated at the 1976 Berlin Conference of Communist and Workers' Parties (ibid., 5, 19 July). In the midst of the Soviet and Spanish clash, Carrillo made a publicized visit to Ceaușescu's vacation villa—in an obvious show of Romanian support for Eurocommunism's right to an independent existence. This right was also proclaimed in an article by party ideologist Valter Roman; the article called the first 1956 Hungarian revolt "justified" as a response to the excesses of Stalinism, and once again (but for the first time in several years) condemned the invasion of Czechoslovakia in 1968 (*Anale de Istorie,* May-June 1977).

The polemic over the Eurocommunist question conjoined with Romanian involvement in the Middle East, the People's Republic of China, and the Belgrade CSCE cast something of a pall over the newly refurbished Soviet-Romanian relations. This was symbolized by Ceauşescu's brief trip (in contrast to other East European party leaders) to Moscow on the occasion of the sixtieth anniversary of the Bolshevik revolution.

Romania, the only Warsaw Pact state with political ties to both the Arab world and Israel, renewed its intermediary role between the two sides. Ceauşescu visited Egyptian president Sadat, 11-13 May; Israeli premier Begin traveled to Bucharest, 26-30 August; and Sadat returned Ceauşescu's visit, 29-31 October. In the wake of Sadat's dramatic journey to Israel, Ceauşescu was credited by Begin with having been helpful in facilitating the dramatic breakthrough (*NYT,* 27 November). And Ceauşescu praised Sadat's initiative, a development which went against Soviet Middle East policies (*Scînteia,* 8 December). Concomitantly, Romania and China were exchanging a continuous stream of delegations, with Ceauşescu and Hua Kuo-feng pledging to put relations "onto a superior stage" (Radio Bucharest, 14 November)—this at a time when Romania's closest Socialist supporter, Yugoslavia, was undertaking a rapprochement with Peking. Romanian deviation also manifested itself at the Belgrade CSCE, where Bucharest often sided with the neutralist/nonaligned states, especially in the area of military security. Some of its Belgrade proposals contravened both NATO and Warsaw Pact interests, such as that requiring advance warning of naval and air maneuvers.

As a "socialist, developing European" state, Romania continued to pursue political and economic relations with the Third World and Western states. Having already been admitted to the "Group of 77" and given permanent "guest" status at nonaligned meetings, the Romanians sought to expand their trade and economic interactions with the Third World. The CPR hope was that Romanian trade turnover with the less-developed states, which stood at 15.5 percent in 1975, could reach 30 percent by 1980 and thereby lessen dependence on CMEA for raw material imports and manufactured exports. CMEA trade accounted for 37.5 percent of turnover in 1975 and that with the West 38.1 percent (*Anuarul Statistic al RSR,* 1976).

Major cooperative endeavors were concluded with companies in France, Britain, and West Germany. And Romania became the first Communist country to invest in an American enterprise: $58 million in Occidental Petroleum's Island Creek Coal Company in return for one-third of the high grade coking coal therefrom (*NYT,* 13 May). Nevertheless, Romania's interactions with the West, especially the United States, lacked the momentum of previous years. Bucharest still remained heavily indebted to the West from annual trade deficits. Political relations with the United States cooled a bit as a result of President Carter's "human rights" emphasis in foreign policy, which the Romanians saw as a display of superpower intervention in the internal affairs of other states (*Scînteia,* 20 December). Despite such difficulties, the U.S. Congress followed Carter's recommendation and renewed for one year Romania's most-favored-nation status and Romanian officials visited the United States seeking to expand economic ties.

Ceauşescu took the opportunity of the National Conference to recapitulate Romania's independent foreign policy positions. He expressed renewed apprehensions at the motivations of the big powers: "we are witnessing a forceful intensification of the struggle for a new redivision of the world into zones of influence and of the struggle by various states and groups of states to secure new positions of dominance" (ibid., 8 December). Thus, as 1977 ended, the CPR gave every indication of continuing its quest for autonomy in a world dominated by others.

Publications. *Scînteia* is the official daily of the CPR Central Committee. Agerpres is the Romanian news agency.

Council on Foreign Relations
   International Affairs Fellow, 1977-78
Washington, D.C.
   and
Muskingum College
New Concord, Ohio

Robert L. Farlow

Union of Soviet Socialist Republics

The Communist Party of the Soviet Union (Kommunisticheskaia Partiia Sovetskogo Soiuza; CPSU) traces its origins to the founding of the Russian Social Democratic Labor Party in 1898. The party split into Bolshevik ("majority") and Menshevik ("minority") factions at the Second Congress, held at Brussels and London in 1903. The Bolshevik faction led by Vladimir I. Lenin was actually a minority after 1904. Unable to regain policy-making dominance, it broke away from the Mensheviks in 1912 at the Prague conference to form a separate party. In March 1918, after seizing power, this party was renamed the "All-Russian Communist Party (Bolsheviks)." After the "Union of Soviet Socialist Republics" became the name of the country in 1924, the party's designation was changed in 1925 to "All-Union Communist Party (Bolsheviks)." The present CPSU name was adopted in 1952. The CPSU is the only legal political party in the USSR.

Party Secretary Mikhail A. Suslov reported in November 1977 that the CPSU had a total membership of 16,203,446 (*NYT,* 7 November). This represents an increase of 3.25 percent over the reported membership of 15,694,187 as of 1 January 1976 and continues the recent trend toward stabilization of party size. Between 1961 and 1966, the average annual increase in CPSU membership was 6.0 percent; between 1966 and 1971, 3.16 percent; between 1971 and 1973, 1.28 percent; and between 1973 and 1976, 1.96 percent. Since 1975 the average annual increment has been less than 1.80 percent. Notably, the percentage of increase in party membership during the years 1976 and 1977 was slightly less than the average annual increase for the years 1973-75, when an exchange of party cards was conducted and 347,000 members failed to receive new cards. It appears that, with the exception of the years 1971-73, admission to the party is now subject to more stringent quantitative limitations than at any other time in recent decades.

Workers reportedly account for 41.6 percent of the CPSU membership, collective farmers 13.9 percent, engineers and technicians about 20 percent, and other white-collar employees and servicemen about 24.5 percent; 24.7 percent of the members are women, as against 20.9 perent in 1967; 2.7 million members, or 16.6 percent of the total, are under the age of 30. The most recent data on educational levels show that 24.3 percent of members have a higher education and 41 percent have an incomplete higher or secondary education. The present CPSU membership is 6.26 percent of total USSR population of 258,900,000 (Tass, 22 July). At the beginning of 1977, CPSU membership reportedly constituted approximately 9.2 percent of the adult population (Tass, 14 January). The Great Russians are still disproportionately represented in the party membership, accounting for more than 60 percent of the total, while approximately 16 percent of the members are Ukrainian and more than 3.5 percent Belorussian. Other nationalities, who make up nearly one-fourth of the USSR's population, account for only about 20 percent of the party membership.

A February article in *Kommunist* stressed that the CPSU while "remaining essentially a party of the working class, has become a party of the whole people" (No. 4, 1977). However, according to this same source, 58 percent of those joining the party are workers, but among those who joined the party since 1971 only 11 percent are peasants. About 80 percent of new party members were said to be "employed in the sphere of material production." Every fourth Soviet engineer, technician, agronomist, and teacher, every fifth or sixth physician, and half of the candidates in science were reported to be party members.

The most recent quadrennial elections for the Supreme Soviet, the country's nominal legislature, were held in June 1974. The Supreme Soviet has 1,517 members and is divded into two chambers—the Soviet of the Union, in which each deputy represents approximately 300,000 persons, and the Soviet of the Nationalities, in which deputies represent the republics, regions, and national areas of the USSR. All candidates on the single slate supported by the CPSU were elected in the June 1974 balloting, with a total of 578,414 negative votes against nearly 161 million for the official slate (*Izvestiia,* 19 June). The Supreme Soviet includes 1,096 party-member deputies, who make up 72.2 percent of the total number.

In the Supreme Soviets of the Union Republics elected in June 1975, CPSU full and candidate members constituted 67.5 percent of the membership. In local governing bodies elected then, 968,000 (43.8 percent) were CPSU members.

Organization and Leadership. The structure of the CPSU parallels the administrative organization of the Soviet state. There are 390,000 primary party organizations. Above this lowest level are 2,857 rural *raion* committees, 815 city committees, 10 *okrug* (area) committees, 148 *oblast'* (district) committees, 6 *krai* (territorial) committees, and 14 union-republic committees. There is no separate subsidiary organization for the Russian republic (RSFSR), the largest constituent unit of the union. At the top, the All-Union Congress is, according to party rules, the supreme policy-making body. The Congress elects the Central Committee and the Central Auditing Commission. The Twenty-fourth Congress, in 1971, set the maximal interval between congresses at five years. Between congresses, the highest representative organ is the Central Committee. At this level, power is concentrated in the Politburo, the Secretariat, and the various departments of the Central Committee.

There were two plenums of the Central Committee during 1977. The first, in May, featured a report by General Secretary Leonid I. Brezhnev on the draft constitution of the USSR and made two important changes in the top-level leadership of the CPSU.

Nikolai V. Podgorny, the Soviet head of state (chairman of the Presidium of the Supreme Soviet, commonly referred to as the president of the USSR), was dropped from the Politburo in a move that surprised both Russian and Western observers (*NYT,* 25 May). Podgorny's ouster was a prelude to the Supreme Soviet session of 16 June at which he was replaced in the Soviet presidency by Brezhnev.

The Central Committee also confirmed the demotion of Konstantin F. Katushev by removing him from the post of party secretary responsible for relations with ruling Communist parties (*Pravda,* 25 May). In March, Katushev had been appointed a deputy prime minister, with responsibility for economic relations with the other member countries of the Council for Mutual Economic Assistance

(CMEA), Katushev was replaced in the Secretariat by Konstantin V. Rusakov, a close associate of Brezhnev.

The October plenum approved the draft of the new USSR constitution (ibid, 4 October), which was formally ratified by the Supreme Soviet on 7 October. Konstantin V. Chernenko, party secretary and head of the General Department of the Central Committee, was promoted to candidate member of the Politburo, as was Vasily V. Kuznetsov, deputy foreign minister (*NYT*, 3 October). Kuznetsov's party promotion prepared the way for his subsequent election to the newly-created post of first deputy chairman of the Presidium of the Supreme Soviet, or "assistant vice-president" of the USSR.

The October plenum also raised four candidate members of the Central Committee to full membership: Vasily P. Demidenko, first secretary of the North Kazakhstan *oblast'*; Nikolai K. Kirichenko, first secretary of the Crimea *oblast'*; Piotr S. Pleshakov. minister of the Soviet radio industry; and Alexandra M. Fominykh, a collective farmer (*Pravda,* 3 October). While most Central Committee members are drawn from the inner core of the country's political elite, Fominykh is an example of the token representation accorded to both women and ordinary workers.

The demotion of Podgorny left the Politburo with only fourteen members, and there was some surprise that a replacement was not named at the October plenum. Podgorny is Ukrainian and his ouster means that the non-Russian nationalities are even more underrepresented in the party's most powerful unit. Great Russians outnumber non-Russians by ten to four among the voting membership.

The present compositon of the Politburo is shown in the accompanying list.

Politburo

Members:

Brezhnev, Leonid I.	General Secretary, CPSU Central Committee and Chairman, Presidium of the USSR Supreme Soviet
Kosygin, Aleksei N.	Chairman, USSR Council of Ministers
Suslov, Mikhail A.	Secretary, CPSU Central Committee
Kirilenko, Andrei P.	Secretary, CPSU Central Committee
Pel'she, Arvid I.	Chairman, Party Control Commission
Mazurov, Kiril T.	First Deputy Chairman, USSR Council of Ministers
Grishin, Victor V.	First Secretary, Moscow City Party Committee
Kunaev, Dinmukhamed A.	First Secretary, Kazakh Central Committee
Shcherbitsky, Vladimir V.	First Secretary, Ukrainian Central Committee
Kulakov, Fedor D.	Secretary, CPSU Central Committee
Andropov, Yuri V.	Chairman, Committee of State Security (KGB)

Gromyko, Andrei A.	Minister of Foreign Affairs, USSR Council of Ministers
Romanov, Grigori V.	First Secretary, Leningrad *oblast'* Party Committee
Ustinov, Dimitri F.	Minister of Defense, USSR Council of Minsters

Candidate Members:

Demichev, Piotr N.	Minister of Culture, USSR Council of Ministers
Rashidov, Sharaf R.	First Secretary, Uzbek Central Committee
Masherov, Piotr M.	First Secretary, Belorussian Central Committee
Solomentsev, Mikhail S.	Chairman, RSFSR Council of Ministers
Ponomarev, Boris N.	Secretary, CPSU Central Committee
Aliev, Geidar A.	First Secretary, Azerbaidzhan Central Committee
Chernenko, Konstantin U.	Secretary, CPSU Central Committee
Kuznetsov, Vasily V.	Deputy Minister of Foreign Affairs, USSR Council of Ministers, and First Deputy Chairman, Presidium of the USSR Supreme Soviet

The present Central Committee Secretariat is composed of twelve men. Their names and Secretariat functions are: Brezhnev (general secretary), Kirilenko (organizational affairs), Suslov (ideology), Kulakov (agriculture), Ustinov (armed forces), Ponomarev (non-ruling Communist parties), Vladimir I. Dolgikh (heavy industry), Ivan V. Kapitonov (cadres), Konstantin V. Chernenko (General Department, Central Committee), Mikhail V. Zimianin (culture), Yakov P. Ryabov (defense industry), Konstantin V. Rusakov (ruling Communist parties). Ustinov's position in the Secretariat appears to be *pro forma;* his former responsibilities for the defense industry have been assumed by Ryabov, who was appointed to the Secretariat in October 1976 (Radio Liberty, 9 February 1977). Ryabov advanced to the Secretariat from the position of first secretary of the Sverdlovsk *obkom* party committee.

Republic first secretaries are: Karen S. Demichyan (Armenia), Geidar A. Aliev (Azerbaidzhan), Piotr M. Masherov (Belorussia), Ivan G. Kebin (Estonia), Eduard A. Shevardnadze (Georgia), Dinmukhamed A. Kunaev (Kazakhstan), Turdakun V. Usbaliev (Kirghizia), August E. Voss (Latvia), Piatras P. Griskiavicus (Lithuania), Ivan I. Bodiul (Moldavia), Dzhabar R. Rasulov (Tadzhikistan), Mukhamednazar G. Gapurov (Turkmenia), Vladimir V. Shcherbitsky (Ukraine), Sharaf R. Rashidov (Uzbekistan).

Auxiliary and Mass Organizations. The most important of the many "voluntary" organizations allied with the CPSU is the Communist Youth League (Kommunisticheskii Soyuz Molodezhi; Komsomol). The eighth plenum of the Central Committee of the Komsomol, meeting in Moscow in May, named Boris Pastukhov, 44, as first secretary of the Komsomol Central Committee to replace Yevgeny M. Tyazhelnikov, who had been named to fill the vacancy as head of the Propaganda

Department of the CPSU Central Committee (Tass, 27 May). Pastukhov had been a secretary of the Komsomol Central Committee since 1964. At the beginning of 1977, the Komsomol had more than 35 million members.

Other large mass organizations include the All-Union Central Council of Trade Unions (AUCCTU), with 107 million members; the Soviet Voluntary Society for the Promotion of the Army, Aviation and Navy (DOSAAF), whose 70 million members seek to "instill patriotism and pride" in the armed forces; the Union of Soviet Societies for Friendship and Cultural Relations with Foreign Countries; and the Soviet Committee of Women.

Party and Government Affairs. Much activity in both party and government ranks during 1977 was devoted to preparations for the sixtieth anniversary of the October Revolution. A major effort was made to fulfill quantitative goals for the first two years of the Five-Year Plan before 7 November, regardless of the economic costs involved (Radio Liberty, 22 April). Party slogans put forward during the year, pointing toward the celebration, emphasized the central themes of material and cultural progress and the claim that the Soviet people are united on a monolithic basis behind the leadership of the CPSU. The thesis on the "party and state of all the people" was given a new form in the May Day slogans, with an unprecedented reference to "socialist democracy," which was said to guarantee "the harmonious combination of the interests of society, the collective, and the individual" (*Izvestiia,* 17 April). Evidently in response to the pressures of the human rights movement, the decree of the CPSU Central Committee on the sixtieth anniversary advanced the slogan "Socialism is the society of real humanism" (*Kommunist,* no. 2).

For General Secretary Brezhnev, the capstone of the jubilee was the adoption of the new USSR constitution, which was ratified unanimously by the Supreme Soviet on 7 October (*Izvestiia,* 8 October). The project for a new constitution to replace the one drafted under Stalin in 1936 had been launched by Nikita Khrushchev in 1959. After his assumption of the top party post in 1964, Brezhnev made completion of the constitutional reform one of his main priorities. However, domestic political obstacles made this a protracted process and as late as the twenty-fifth CPSU congress, in 1976, Brezhnev's opponents had forced another somewhat embarrassing postponement. Ratification of the long-delayed document prior to the sixtieth anniversary celebration was a signal public-relations triumph for Brezhnev and was widely acknowledged as an impressive indicator of his consolidation of personal power. The party leader's identification with the latest legal charter of the regime was so pronounced that Western observers in late 1977 were referring to it as the "Brezhnev constitution," an appelation reminiscent of the usual descriptions of the 1936 document as the "Stalin constitution."

At the Central Committee meeting in May, Brezhnev pointed to three major reasons for constitutional change: the development of the "state of the entire people"; the dramatic change in the world correlation of forces; and the entry into the stage of "communist construction." Brezhnev argued that a new constitutional framework was necessary to reflect these important developments (Tass, 24 May). His speech indicated that the most important provisions of the new constitution were those pertaining to the "further expansion and deepening of socialist democracy," the further development of the "principles of the formation and activites of the soviets of all levels as the political base of the socialist state," the "further consolidation of socialist legality and law and order," and the "solution of questions of national-state organization" related to the multinational union (*Pravda* and *Izvestiia,* 25 May).

For all of the fanfare associated with adoption of the new constitution, there was considerable doubt among Western observers that it would lead to any significant changes in the actual operation of the Soviet political system. Article 1 describes the USSR as a "socialist state of the whole people," a formula already employed under Khrushchev, and one which is patently contradictory in terms of original Marxism. Notably, this article recognizes the intelligentsia as one of the groups represented by the Soviet state, an indication of the acceptance of the contemporary class structure of Soviet society. The strong thread of anti-utopianism that has characterized Soviet political thought in the 1970s finds some expression in Articles 12 and 13. Article 12 guarantees the right of ownership of houses and other personal property and assures the continuation of private plots for the collective farmers. Article 13 enshrines the principle: "From each according to his ability, to each according to his work."

The constitution provides for an apparent formal extension of the role of the soviets. Article 106 specifies that the Supreme Soviet of the USSR "shall be the highest organ of state power," and Article 2 declares that "all other state organs shall be under the control of and accountable to the soviets." However, these provisions are more than balanced by the inclusion of a stronger statement on the leading role of the party than any contained in the 1936 constitution. According to Article 6, "the Communist party of the Soviet Union is the leading and guiding force of Soviet society and the nucleus of its political system. The party defines the long-term development of society and outlines domestic and foreign policy."

The rights of nationalities are given somewhat less emphasis than in the former constitution, an unsurprising development in view of the regime's general commitment to the *sliianie* (amalgamation) approach to nationalities questions. The right of secession for the union-republics is retained in Article 71, but this is surely no more meaningful for Soviet practice than the similar 1936 provision. Rights of the individual are given considerably less attention than in the old constitution. Moreover, Article 50 conditions the rights of citizens by "due account for the needs of society" and Article 59 provides that "the exercise of rights and freedoms shall be inseparable from the performance by citizens of their duties." Article 59 also obliges citizens to "respect the rules of socialist behavior," a category that is no doubt purposefully left undefined. In this general area, one interesting provision is contained in Article 56: "The privacy of citizens, of correspondence, telephone conversations and telegraphic messages shall be protected by law."

Of some practical importance is Article 118, which sets up the organization of the Supreme Soviet and provides for the new office of first deputy chairman of the Presidium. This provision was included to accommodate Brezhnev's need for a deputy so that he could simultaneously exercise the roles of chief of state and head of the party. Indeed, if the new constitution has any major practical significance, it apparently lies in the projected increased role for the party in the operation of the various levels of the soviets, although it is difficult to see how the party's role in this realm could be expanded very much. In any case, the new constitution does not grant a real parliamentary role to the soviets, and the Supreme Soviet is expected to be restricted to its current function of ratifying government decrees and decisions of party bodies.

Brezhnev's success in the constitutional project was but the latest in a series of notable events since 1975 that have indicated his steadily increasing hegemony over the Soviet political system. At the 25th CPSU congress in February 1976, Brezhnev was the clearly dominant figure, and he was lauded by several union-republic party chieftains in terms surpassing any homage paid to Khrushchev at the peak of his power. Later in 1976 he was named a marshal of the Soviet Union, assumed leadership of the Defense Council, and had a public dedication of a bust of himself, the first living person to be so honored since Stalin. On the occasion of his 70th birthday he was hailed as the *vozhd* (leader) (*Pravda,* 19 December), the first usage of this term since the heyday of Stalin's "cult of personality." Events during the course of 1977 indicated that there was pehaps more political substance behind the encomiums than most Western observers had realized.

Changes in top personnel during 1977 were all to Brezhnev's political advantage. The most spectacular change was, of course, the ouster of President Podgorny from both his government position and his seat on the Politburo. Podgorny was apparently taken by surprise when the Central

Committee ousted him on 24 May, reportedly by unanimous vote, from his seat on the Politburo. The circumstances were also particularly humiliating since the way was not prepared, as is often the case with ousted officials holding both party and government posts, by earlier removal from his governmental position. There was speculation that Podgorny had differed with Brezhnev over the latter's proposed assumption of the presidency and had refused to give up the position voluntarily (*NYT,* 24 May). At the same meeting of the Central Committee, a resolution was passed unanimously calling for the general secretary "from now on" to hold also the rank of chief of state. Reportedly, it was introduced by B.V. Kachura, first secretary of the Donetsk *oblast'* party committee (*Die Presse,* Vienna, 28-29 May). If true, this was an important milestone in the career of the fast-rising Kachura, a protégé of Ukrainian party chief Shcherbitsky, who personally installed him as head of the Donetsk party organization in January 1976 (*Pravda ukrainy,* 7, 11 January 1976). It is, of course, not surprising that a prominent official in the Ukrainian party would be called upon to seal the political fate of the Ukrainian Podgorny. Also significant for the assessment of rising political fortunes in the upper party elite is the report that it was Politburo member Grigori V. Romanov who made the specific motion for Podgorny's ouster.

After the loss of his Politburo membership, it was a foregone conclusion that Podgorny would also be deprived of the USSR presidency. This was made official on 17 June, when Brezhnev was voted into the chief of state position by the Supreme Soviet. On his assumption of the presidency, Brezhnev declared that it was an act of "deep political meaning" that recognized the party's dominant role in the Soviet Union. He also acknowledged that the presidency strengthened his diplomatic hand by giving him parallel protocol status with non-Communist heads of state. Brezhnev implied that Podgorny had not been sufficiently cooperative as president. (*NYT,* 18 June.)

Podgorny was Brezhnev's chief competitor for power in the later years of the Khrushchev era. Coming to Moscow from the post of party boss in the Ukraine in 1963, he replaced the stricken Frol Kozlov as a major figure in the succession sweepstakes as Khrushchev's political power rapidly eroded. Brezhnev won that battle and Podgorny's thrust for political primacy was definitely thwarted when he was kicked upstairs to the presidency in 1965. There were periodic reports of policy disagreements between the two men, but Podgorny seemed reconciled to a secondary role. He was publicly linked with Brezhnev and Kosygin in the *troika* of "collective leadership," and in 1971 at the 24th Party Congress was ranked ahead of Kosygin in official announcements.

Aside from the matter of Brezhnev's personal convenience, the significance of his assumption of the top state post seemed to lie in the clear indication of his hegemony over the party and in the continuing pattern of his slow but steady success in removal of major political figures not under his personal patronage. Kosygin seemed to be the logical next candidate on any Brezhnev "hit list," but the premier's age and poor health made it appear that he would soon leave the leadership ranks in any case. The purging of a member of the erstwhile "collective leadership" may have created a precedent that could come back to haunt Brezhnev later.

The ouster of the Ukrainian Podgorny left all three major party and government posts in the hands of Great Russians, leading to speculation that when Kosygin steps down his replacement as premier might be First Deputy Premier Kiril T. Mazurov, a Belorussian, or Ukrainian party first secretary Shcherbitsky, who has governmental experience, having served two terms as the Ukraine's prime minister. If the general secretaryship and the presidency are to be combined on a continuing basis, then presumably an additional barrier has been added to the already obvious obstacles faced by any non-Russian candidate for the first position in the party.

The May Central Committee plenum also named a close Brezhnev associate, Konstantin V. Rusakov, 68, to the post of party secretary responsible for relations with ruling Communist parties (*Pravda,* 25 May), replacing Konstantin F. Katushev, 50. This move was prefigured by the earlier appointment of Katushev as a deputy premier and as USSR delegate to the CMEA (Tass, 15, 17

March). This change probably can be attributed mostly to Brezhnev's understandable motivation in placing protégés in key party and governmental positions. However, Katushev's demotion adds another name to the list of young Soviet politicians who have come "too far, too fast" and have made themselves obvious candidates for a political knockdown. The ouster of Katushev from the Secretariat should end Western speculation about him as a possible successor to Brezhnev. Although political comebacks are not unknown in the Soviet Union, as Brezhnev's career amply illustrates, Katushev seemed to have been sidetracked for the foreseeable future. It is well known that he made many enemies as a ruthless party boss in Gorky during the 1960s; hence there may have been reasons of intra-party politics for his demotion, in addition to Brezhnev's personal political interests.

The October plenum of the Central Committee named Konstantin V. Chernenko, 65, and Vasily V. Kuznetsov, 76, as candidate members of the Central Committee (*Pravda,* 3 October). Again aging officials who pose no threat to Brezhnev's political domination were promoted to positions of high responsibility. Kuznetsov's subsequent election as first deputy chairman of the Soviet Presidium (*Izvestiia,* 8 October) showed once again that Brezhnev had learned well the lesson contained in the coup that brought him to power in 1964—the danger of building up a potential successor. Prior to Kuznetsov's election, several prominent officials figured in speculation among Western observers of the Moscow scene about the position—Kirilenko, Gromyko, Shcherbitsky, and Romanov. The Leningrad party chieftain was the favorite among those who considered the new post as a likely training ground for the future party leader (ABC News, 2 October). This speculation was proved groundless with Kuznetsov's election. Clearly, the first deputy chairmanship will not be a position of real political power; the Supreme Soviet will have no more powerful role than previously; and Brezhnev is most unlikely to encourage a potential successor.

Brezhnev's methodical political maneuvering has created a situation where there is no obvious or entirely satisfactory candidate to succeed him, and this was an important ingredient in his dominant role at the end of 1977. His continuation in power for an indefinite period no doubt appeared preferable to most members of the party hierarchy when compared with any possible alternative. Moreover, while Brezhnev's health is a matter of some concern, he has displayed no inclination toward voluntary retirement, something which would be unprecedented in the history of CPSU leadership. Among possible successors, Kirilenko and Suslov are both too old to be considered. Shcherbitsky apparently possesses more of the needed qualities of leadership than any other candidate and was about the right age, 59, at the end of 1977, but the fact that he is an ethnic Ukrainian in a party dominated by Great Russians is a negative factor. Romanov, aged 55, is a possibility if he can survive the perils that have often plagued prominent Leningraders; but, at the end of 1977, he still lacked the breadth of experience expected in the top party post. It was duly noted by Western Kremlinologists that party secretary Fedor D. Kulakov, 59, was given precedence at the October Supreme Soviet session right behind Kosygin and Suslov, and he is widely regarded as the likely interim successor to Brezhnev if an early change becomes necessary; however, his background has been almost entirely in agriculture, and he presumably lacks the power base required for the acquisition and maintenance of supreme power in the system. In view of Brezhnev's age, there is likely to be a cautious but intense jockeying for position among these and other possible contenders for the succession during 1978.

Although it clearly is in accord with Brezhnev's political interests, the tendency toward gerontocratic politics must be largely attributed to much broader systemic factors. A generation of party activists, whose members entered politics during the Stalin era and witnessed the horrors of the purges, achieved predominance during the Brezhnev era, coincident with the maturation of the super-bureaucratized Soviet system, with all its resistance to change and its propensity for avoiding even "normal" attrition in the upper ranks. Firmly entrenched in power, these aging bureaucrats stand as a barrier against advancement of younger cadres. At the end of 1977, the average age of full

Politburo members was nearly 67; forced retirement of the 74-year-old Podgorny reduced the average only slightly. Candidate members of the Politburo had an average age of 64 and members of the Secretariat, 65. The average age of full members of the Central Committee was almost 62.

Among full members of the Politburo, only Romanov, 55, and Kulakov and Shcherbitsky, both 59, were under the age of 60. Assuming continuation of the present membership, in February 1978 Geidar A. Aliev, 54, will be the only candidate member under 60. Newcomer Yakov P. Ryabov is the only Secretariat member under 50, and Vladimir I. Dolgikh, 53, is the only other member under 60. Recent moves made necessary by the age and health of certain leading officials indicate a tendency for the aging hierarchs to make patchwork substitutions from their own restricted ranks. When Kosygin, 73, became seriously ill in 1976, Nikolai A. Tikhonov, then 71, was appointed as a first deputy premier to assist him. Chernenko, nearly 66, reportedly began to assume some of the organizational responsibilities of the 71-year-old party secretary Kirilenko during 1977. And party secretary Mikhail V. Zimianin, 63, a protégé of Suslov, was also reported to be taking over much of the workload of the veteran party ideologist.

The severe clogging of the upper echelons by veteran *aparatchiks* means that when personnel changes are inevitably made, they will be massive. Instead of a regular, measured renewal of the upper ranks, there will be a wholesale turnover within a relatively short period of time, perhaps quantitatively comparable to Stalin's purge of the leadership between 1934 and 1939. The present dominant elites may be reluctant to yield power, but the actuarial tables soon will override the "protective association" mentality and politics of the old bureaucrats. The transitional period may be difficult and there are no clear indications as to what policy changes, if any, a younger leadership might bring. Further changes in the full membership of the Politburo, including retirement of some of the more venerable members and expansion of the currently under-strength ruling body, are likely soon, perhaps as early as the first Central Committee plenum of 1978. Such a reshuffle would provides important clues to the eventual succession to Brezhnev, the adaptability of the leadership in coping with the generational problem, and the likely course of future policy.

A matter of some importance for the coming political transition is the apparent decline of ideological fervor within Communist ranks and the evidence of political apathy among the masses. Prominent party officials have frankly acknowledged the decline in ideological commitment and have issued repeated calls in recent years for major efforts to correct this deficiency. Since 1970, in the pages of theoretical journals, party ideologues have carried out without much fanfare a substantial reworking of Marxism-Leninism, involving a revision of the utopian elements of Communist theory to justify the long-run continuation of existing social and political relationships in the USSR. This is reflected in the revisionist passages of the new constitution. At the same time, massive campaigns have been carried out for the re-ideologizing of both party and society through political indoctrination to spur the stagnant system and reassure the dominant elites against external and internal threats to their legitimacy. This activity continued undiminished during 1977. In February a Central Committee resolution called for improvement in the work of verbal political agitation at all levels (*Pravda,* 25 February), and later *Pravda* issued a call for more efficient political propaganda throughout the society (1 June). Far more important than the rhetoric was a seemingly long-overdue practical move in this area. In May, Komsomol first secretary Yevgeny M. Tyazhelnikov, 49, was appointed head of the Propaganda Department of the Central Committee, after a seven-year vacancy in that position (Radio Liberty, 29 May).

Some important personnel changes occurred during 1977 in the Ukraine, where party boss Shcherbitsky continued his implacable drive to render party and governmental organizations more reliable and efficient. In February Ivan P. Kochevykh was appointed deputy chairman of the Ukrainian Council of Ministers (Kiev domestic service, 10 February, in *FBIS,* 14 February) and on 30 June, Nikolai K. Kirichenko, 54, replaced Pavel P. Kozyr, 63, as first secretary of the Odessa *oblast'* party committee (Radio Liberty, 14 July). Further changes in the Ukraine seemed probable after the Ukrainian party Central Committee issued a statement in July denouncing the republic's ministers of the coal industry, light industry, and heavy industry for inefficiency (Kiev domestic service, 29 July, in *FBIS*, 2 August).

Konstantin E. Fomichenko was elected second secretary of the Kirghiz party Central Committee in July, replacing Yuri N. Pugachev, who had been switched to the second secretary's post in the Azerbaidzhan Central Committee in April (Radio Liberty, 20 July). Prior to this appointment, Fomichenko had served for several years as head of a sector in the Organizational Party Work Department of the CPSU Central Committee.

Domestic Policies. The USSR continued to struggle with seemingly intractable economic problems during 1977. Some successes on the economic front were reported, but these were overshadowed by the continuing bleak picture in the areas of labor productivity, fulfillment of construction demands, and satisfaction of consumer interests. Notable reforms were announced in the system of distribution of consumer goods, and concessions were made to demands for improved material conditions for workers, with announcement of wage increments accompanying a renewed emphasis upon incentives. Major efforts were devoted to the aim of fulfillment of the goals for the first two years of the Tenth Five-Year Plan prior to the sixtieth anniversary celebration in November, a politically inspired initiative that conflicted with the professed economic goal of greater cost effectiveness.

The annual government report on plan fulfillment, released by the Central Statistical Administration on 23 January, showed an increase of 5 percent in national income in the year 1976. Industrial output reportedly increased 4.8 percent, with a 5.5 percent rise in capital goods and only 3.0 percent in consumer goods. However, increased labor productivity accounted for only 80 percent of the increment in national income, against a planned 85-90 percent. Per capita real incomes reportedly rose by 3.7 percent, with workers' and employees' wages increasing by 3.6 percent and remuneration of collective farmers by 6.0 percent.

In view of the anticipated approaching energy crunch in the USSR, it was particularly significant that the power and electrification, oil, oil-refining and petrochemical, and coal industries all barely met their quotas for planned sale of output. Production in the meat and dairy industry was only 93 percent of the 1975 figure, reflecting the wholesale slaughtering of cattle due to 1975's poor grain harvest. However, the 1976 grain harvest was a record 224 million tons, compared with an average annual yield of 181.6 million tons for the years 1971-75.

Certain consumer-goods sectors fared poorly in production records, notably milk, sugar, vegetable oil, clothing and footwear, radios, and television sets. Among the union republics, Kazakhstan, Moldavia, Tadzhikistan, and Turkmenia had the worst records of productivity. Labor productivity in Turkmenia was reportedly only 99.1 percent of the level achieved in 1975 (*Pravda*, 23 January).

Despite the record grain production in 1976, a Central Committee public "letter" to agricultural personnel in January noted that "despite the tremendous efforts, the influence of the bad weather was not fully overcome in a number of places and the final results in agricultural production proved to be lower than envisaged by plans and pledges" (ibid., 8 January). Also in January, a special report to the collegium of the RSFSR Ministry of Agriculture pointed out that "farms still have considerable unutilized reserves; crop losses continue to be high. Expenditure of labor on the production of produce is declining slowly. The capacity of new livestock farming complexes is not being exploited adequately" (Moscow domestic service, 21 January, in *FBIS*, 24 January). The usual proclamations demanding exceptional efforts to get the harvest in on time were issued and, as usual, Soviet agriculture muddled through with no fundamental reforms. In early October, Western estimates placed the 1977 grain harvest at 215 million tons, and on 6 October, the U.S. Department of

Agriculture raised the annual ceiling on exports of corn and wheat to the USSR from 8 to 15 million tons (*Washington Post,* 7 October).

Addressing the Supreme Soviet on 14 December, Nikolai K. Baibakov, the economic planning chief, painted an unsatisfactory picture of Soviet economic performance in 1977 and announced a low rate of growth for 1978. A revised figure for the 1977 grain harvest of 195.5 compared poorly with last year's 224 million metric tons. The low economic goals for 1978 included a leveling of steel output (breaking a pattern of the last thirty years), reductions in the field of energy, and an overall planned growth of 4.5 compared with the 1977 plan of 5.6 percent. The targets of the 1976-1980 five-year plan consequently will be affected (*NYT; Wall Street Journal,* 15 December).

A joint decree issued by the CPSU Central Committee, the USSR Council of Ministers, the AUCCTU, and the Komsomol Central Committee on 10 January set the themes for the year's economic activity, calling for enhanced "socialist competition" in industry and agriculture and lauding workers in various areas for the adoption of increased "socialist pledges" and augmented plans for the sixtieth anniversary year (Moscow domestic service, 10 January, in *FBIS,* 14 January). The call for greater emphasis upon "socialist competition" was stressed by Viktor V. Grishin, Politburo member and first secretary of the Moscow *gorkom,* at a large rally of workers in Moscow on 13 January and was repeated frequently by party and government spokesmen throughout the year. Grishin was also sharply critical of deficiencies in the Moscow area in labor productivity and discipline, cadre turnover, and adaptation of technology (*Moskovskaia pravda,* 13 January, in *FBIS,* 26 January).

Planning for the 1977 year continued the major thrust of the overall Tenth Five-Year Plan toward the setting of more modest and more realistic goals than had been common previously; this seemed to render feasible the goal of fulfillment of the second year of the plan prior to the October Revolution anniversary. Of particular note were the planned reductions in the rates of growth for gas and electric power, automobiles, and tractors, and an absolute decline in the planned fish catch. One exception to the general trend was a 50 percent jump in the target for granulated sugar (*Vestnik statistiki,* no. 7). However, despite the tendency toward more reasonable goal-setting, results by mid-year were not encouraging.

The mid-year economic report, released on 22 July, claimed that Soviet industry had overfulfilled the plan for the first six months "for the marketing of products and production of the majority of products" (Tass, 22 July). The overall increment in production over the corresponding period in 1976 was 5.7 percent, as against the planned 5.6 percent, and was well below the figure for 1975, 7.5 percent. Labor productivity was up only 4.2 percent, against the planned growth rate of 4.8 percent; three-fourths of the increment in production was said to be obtained through higher labor productivity. Turkmenistan again declined in labor productivity; slight gains were recorded in the Kirgiz, Tadzhik, Uzbek, and Kazakh Republics.

Substantial shortcomings were noted in capital construction. The plan for the commissioning of fixed assets and state capital investments and the plan for contract work were underfulfilled (*Pravda* and *Izvestiia,* 23 July). Only three of nine major construction industries met their targets in the first half of 1977. Meat production was up but still about 11 percent behind the pre-drought figures of 1975 (*Christian Science Monitor,* 25 July).

An August editorial in *Sovetskaia Rossiia* pointed out specific major deficiencies in the Russian republic's plan fulfillment. Serious shortfalls were reported in labor productivity, the threshing of grain, and capital construction. The editorial attributed construction failures in the RSFSR to "shortcomings in the planning and organization of capital construction" and the "dissipation of resources and manpower over numerous projects to the detriment of the most important construction sites." (*FBIS* 18 August.)

While party and government stepped up the drive for "socialist competition," special attention was also given during the year to material incentives. A joint decree of the CPSU Central Committee, the USSR Council of Ministers, and the AUCCTU on 27 December 1976 implemented pay increases for 31 million workers mandated by the 25th CPSU congress. Wages of these workers were scheduled to rise an average of 18 percent by 1980. The largest increases went to education, health, social service, cultural, and shop employees. The raises were to be introduced gradually, beginning for workers in the far north and east in early 1977 and reaching all those involved by 1980 (*NYT,* 28 December). At the same time, it was announced that incentive bonuses would be added to salaries and wages and that a widespread system of rewards would be introduced for "extending various public services and improving their quality" (Moscow domestic service, 27 December, in *FBIS,* 28 December).

The strong commitment to material incentives was reemphasized in a featured article in *Izvestiia* (23 June) on "Work Quality and Labor Payment." "It is very important to give rewards and incentives for good work," the article maintained, "and to strive for payment to grow in the wake of labor productivity." While there was no doubt about the Soviet resolve to push labor productivity through material incentives, Western observers were somewhat skeptical about the likely results. Very little has been done to improve the quality of consumer products, and as a result Soviet citizens have accumulated huge savings in recent years while restricting their expenditures on the inferior goods offered. If higher wages cannot be readily translated into a real improvement in living standards, then prospects for economic gains through monetary incentives may be dubious.

Possibly greater economic importance should be attributed to the government's encouragement of private-plot farming. In early 1977, Brezhnev described the private plots as a "reserve of no small importance" in food supplies. During the year, the government carried out a campaign to aid the private plots, including special encouragement for poultry, pig, and rabbit breeding, new supplies of herbicides and pesticides, increased availability of feed and mineral fertilizer, and more irrigation pumps and hoses. Private-plot farmers also received help in grinding grain into meal and in canning (*NYT,* 10 July). Inclusion of private-plot farming as a "right" in the new constitution was an expectedly popular move among Soviet farmers.

The Central Committee and Council of Ministers in a joint resolution on 19 July promised improvements for consumers in one of the most depressing aspects of Soviet life, shopping in state stores. The resolution noted "serious shortcomings in the work of organizations and enterprises dealing with trade" and set out as priorities the construction of efficient supermarkets and department stores, better storage and transportation facilities for agricultural products, and improved manners and performance on the part of sales and service workers (*Pravda,* 19 July; *Washington Post,* 20 July).

One major impediment to improved economic efficiency that has been rather frankly acknowledged in recent years is official corruption. Notable revelations of corruption had touched Latvia, Azerbaidzhan, Georgia, and the Ukraine in 1976. There were two spectacular cases during 1977. In March, Piotr M. Masherov, Belorussian party first secretary, roundly denounced widespread falsification of agricultural statistics in a speech in Minsk (*Christian Science Monitor,* 10 March). The speech followed the dismissal and arrest of sixty party and government officials charged with falsification of documents and defrauding the government. According to Masherov, those arrested included his own party vice-chairman, three district secretaries from Minsk, and the manager of a local collective. Thirty-six officials of the Belorussian Ministry of Agriculture were degraded for lack of state and party discipline and for "tolerating these criminal manipulations." An even larger scandal developed in Azerbaidzhan, where some 300 officials were tried in Baku in March for what was described as "enormous corruption" (*Jyllands-Posten,* Copenhagen, 27 March).

Dissent. Although troublesome, official corruption could not begin to compare with dissident activity as a source of concern for the Kremlin leaders. Activists for national and human rights in the USSR have been quite limited in their numbers and have never been able to form a cohesive front uniting all shades and elements of opposition to the regime. However, a measure of continuity has been provided by the immunity to arrest of Andrei Sakharov, the movement's chief spokesman, apprently because of his international reputation. Moreover, despite a steady succession of measures of exile and imprisonment against dissidents in recent years, the movement has been able to replenish its thin ranks, a phenomenon which continued in 1977 under new threats from the regime. (See *YICA, 1976,* pp. 75-77, and *1977,* pp. 80-83.)

The Helsinki Accords of 1975 provided new opportunities for dissidents to spotlight abuses, as did U.S. president Carter's outspoken defense of human rights. However, these opportunities for arousing world opinion also brought additional dangers for the dissidents, as the USSR leadership employed new strategies during 1977 aiming at the criminalization of dissent and the breaking of communication linkages between dissidents and the West. In the process, new tensions appeared in U.S.-Soviet relations and the Soviet leaders adopted a tough stance toward alleged American interference in the USSR's internal affairs.

Some hopes had been raised in the West for at least slight modification of the anti-dissident campaign when Eduard Fedotov, a religious activist who had been confined in a psychiatric institution, and three other dissidents were released from custody in November 1976 (AP, 22 November). Greater Soviet flexibility also seemed to be indicated, in December, by the exchange of prominent civil-rights activist Vladimir Bukovsky for Chilean Communist leader Luis Corvalán. The exchange, believed to be the first involving political prisoners, had been proposed by Andrei Sakharov (*NYT,* 18, 19 December). However, the detention of Vladimir Borisov, a thirty-three-year-old electrical engineer, who was confined in a Leningrad psychiatric institution on 25 December, showed that there had been no real change in policy, and in the first week of the new year the regime began the next phase in its program of repression.

Yuri Orlov, leader of the group set up in 1976 to monitor the Helsinki Accords, was seized on the street while on his way to a news conference with Western reporters on 5 January, and was questioned by police for seven hours. The apartments of three other members of the monitoring group, Aleksandr Ginzburg, Lyudmila Alekseyeva, and Lidiya Voronina, were also searched by police officers (*NYT,* 6 January). This action was the prelude to the arrests of Orlov and Ginzburg a month later. In the second week of January, two prominent Soviet dissenters, Roy Medvedev and Valentin Turchin, president of the Moscow branch of Amnesty International, issued an implicit appeal to Western Communist and Socialist parties to defend the monitoring group. In their appeal, read to Western newsmen over the telephone, the two dissident leaders contended that the moves against the Moscow group and similar ones against human rights activists in Kiev suggested the preparation of "further repressions." This forecast proved to be quite accurate; subsequent actions by the regime included the "voluntary" exile of Dr. Turchin in October (see below). Medvedev and Turchin stressed the new approach of the KGB, the attempted criminalization of the activities of dissidents. They said that the authorities had planted foreign currency in the homes they searched and had issued "slanderous" charges against the monitoring group through the official press agency Tass.

Early in the year, the Soviet television network featured a documentary "exposing anti-Soviet political subversion by Zionists." According to Tass (22 January), the documentary showed that "so-called prisoners of Zion" in the USSR were actually "common criminals" and revealed how "Zionists use misinformation to block businesslike and cultural cooperation between the USSR and USA." In an apparent slap at West European Communist parties which had sympathized with Soviet human rights activists, the Central Committee issued a resolution on 31 January which coupled the reassertion of "proletarian internationalism" and the "dictatorship of the proletariat" with a counterattack against the claims of internal dissenters and émigrés. According to the statement, the Soviet system has provided its people with "unprecedented freedom and democracy, impossible in any capitalist country" (*Pravda,* 1 February; *Christian Science Monitor,* 2 February).

Western reporters in Moscow had served as the major conduit for information from the dissidents to the outside world about Soviet internal repression; on 4 February, Soviet authorities took an important step aimed toward the breaking of this communications link. Associated Press correspondent George A. Krimsky, who had been reporting on the activities of dissidents, was ordered to leave the USSR within a week (*NYT,* 5 February). Yuri Orlov was arrested on 10 February (ibid., 11 February). Aleksandr Ginzburg was also arrested a week earlier, as were Mikola Rudenko and Oleksa Tikhy, two members of the monitoring group in Kiev. Lyudmila Alekseyeva was also given "permission" to emigrate in early February. These actions were followed by an article in *Pravda* (12 February) which defended Soviet actions against dissidents and denounced them as "pawns of the West."

In the midst of this accelerating campaign against dissidents, Andrei Sakharov addressed a letter to U. S. president Carter appealing for American support in the context of the Helsinki Accords. Sakharov named fifteen human rights activists who had been victims of repression and needed support. Sakharov also called attention to repression in Yugoslavia, Czechoslovakia, and Poland, and to persecution on religious grounds within the USSR. He charged that terror against dissidents even extended to murder, citing the specific case of the poet and translator Konstantin Bogatyryov. Sakharov also claimed that an explosion in the Moscow subway in early January had been designed to discredit the human rights movement, and compared it to the Reichstag fire of 1933 and the killing of Kirov in 1934. The text of the letter was released on 28 January; on the same day, four prominent dissidents issued an appeal to Pope Paul VI and six Western heads of state and/or chiefs of government, including Carter, on behalf of Sakharov, who was said to be threatened with criminal prosecution. The appeal was signed by Lidiya Chukovskaya, Vladimir Voinovich, Lev Kopelev, and Vladimir Kornilov. (*NYT,* 29 January.)

Carter's response to Sakharov, a warm expression of support, was delivered on 17 February in circumstances which seemed to leave little doubt about the intentions of the U. S. administration. Sakharov was escorted to the American Embassy in Moscow, past the police guards who usually prevent Soviet citizens from entering, and was presented with Carter's reply. In his letter to Sakharov, the U. S. president said that "human rights is a central concern of my administration." Carter further spelled out his conception of the American role in defense of human rights:

> You may rest assured that the American people and our government will continue our firm commitment to promote respect for human rights not only in our own country but also abroad. We shall use our good offices to seek the release of prisoners of conscience, and we will continue our efforts to shape a world responsive to human aspirations in which nations of differing cultures and histories can live side by side in peace and justice. I am always glad to hear from you and I wish you well. (Ibid., 18 February.)

Sakharov called the letter "a great honor for me and a support for the whole movement for human rights in the USSR and in the countries of Eastern Europe." He promptly sent off a new letter to Carter, calling attention to the illness of Sergei A. Kovalev, a prominent dissident serving a seven-year term in a labor camp for "anti-Soviet activity," and to the arrests of the four members of the monitoring group noted above (*Washington Post* and *NYT,* 18 February).

Carter added to the effect of his letter to Sakharov by meeting with exiled dissident leader

Vladimir Bukovsky at the White House on 1 March (*NYT*, 2 March). On the same day, the six remaining members of the original group set up to monitor the Helsinki Accords, plus two new members, met in Orlov's Moscow apartment and declared that they would not be intimidated by the official campaign to discredit their activities (ibid., 2 March). On 8 March ten demonstrators in Moscow's Red Square displayed a banner supporting the right to emigrate. They were arrested by security police. This was the first such demonstration in Red Square since the Soviet intervention in Czechoslovakia in 1968. (Ibid., 9 March.)

The Soviet response to this combination of external and internal pressure was a further hardening of official attitudes and actions. On 28 February two Jewish activists were seized by police at the entrance of the American Embassy in Moscow over the protests of an embassy official who had come to escort them inside. The police explained that the two men, Veniamin Fein and Iosif Begun, were "dangerous criminals." They were released six hours later and an embassy spokesman said that a formal protest had been filed "at an appropriate level." (Ibid., 2 March.)

Although the intensification of the anti-dissident campaign had begun well before the Carter letter to Sakharov, the Soviet authorities seemed eager to convey the impression of a direct linkage between overt U.S. support for dissidents and repressive moves against them. Five days after Carter received Bukovsky at the White House, *Izvestiia* published a letter from Sanya Lipavsky, a doctor and former member of the Jewish emigration movement, who charged certain American diplomats and journalists, as well as certain Jewish dissidents, notably Anatoli Shcharansky, with working for U.S. intelligence and for anti-Soviet organizations in the West (*Izvestiia*, 5 March). The charges posed a severe threat to dissidents, since there was a clear warning that their activities might lead to charges of treason. Some Western observers noted an element of anti-Semitism in the denunciation by *Izvestiia*; not only was there a direct attack upon Soviet Jewish activists but the two diplomats named, Joseph Presel and Melvin Levitsky, were also Jewish (Radio Liberty, 12 July).

An article in *Pravda* (13 March) said that Carter's position on human rights might affect the mood of the upcoming negotiations on strategic arms limitations, and on 21 March, Brezhnev accused the U.S. of "interfering in the internal affairs of the Soviet Union." Speaking at a Soviet trade union congress, Brezhnev said: "Washington's claims to teach others how to live cannot be accepted by any sovereign state." (*Pravda*, 13 March; Tass, 21 March; *NYT*, 14, 22 March.)

When U.S. Secretary of State Cyrus Vance arrived in Moscow for talks concerning limitation of strategic arms on 28 March, the political atmosphere was decidedly cool. Prior to his departure on 30 March, the Soviets flatly rejected the American proposals on grounds of their one-sidedness (*NYT*, 31 March). However, the Kremlin did nothing to dispel the view that open American support for human rights activists in the USSR had been partly responsible for failure of the negotiations.

The growing chill in U.S.-Soviet relations did not deter American leaders from further overt manifestations of support for human rights activists. In April, Vance's Law Day speech outlined a formal U.S. policy on human rights. (Ibid., 1 May.) In May, Carter's address at the University of Notre Dame reaffirmed his commitment to human rights as an essential element of U.S. foreign policy (ibid., 23 May). The only concession by the American administration amid the growing superpower tensions was repeated assurances by Carter, Vance, and other officials that the USSR had not been singled out for criticism.

Additional confrontations exacerbated Soviet-American tensions in June and July. In early June, Shcharansky was charged with treason. In mid-June, just a few days before the convening of the Belgrade conference to review compliance with the Helsinki Accords, *Los Angeles Times* correspondent Robert C. Toth was detained for lengthy interrogation by the KGB about articles he had written and about his relationship with Shcharansky. Toth was picked up by the KGB moments after he had been handed an article on parapsychology by a Soviet scientist. The formal basis for his detention seemed to be the presumption that he might have received Soviet official secret "scientific" information. (Ibid., 15 June.) Toth was prevented from leaving for his new assignment for several days. Then after strong official U.S. protests he was allowed to leave the country.

In July, U.S. Ambassador Malcolm Toon was denied permission to broadcast a traditional Fourth of July address over Soviet television because his speech contained a reference to the U.S. policy on human rights (*Washington Post,* 5 July). Also in early July, Ambassador Toon was summoned by Brezhnev for a harsh lecture on the Soviet view of alleged American intervention in Soviet internal affairs. Brezhnev informed Toon that a "number of aspects" of President Carter's policy on human rights did "not accord with the aim of a constructive development" of U.S.-Soviet relations (Tass, 5 July). Adding more fuel to the continuing controversy, a week later the official Soviet news agency released a statement accusing Toth of working for unspecified "American special agencies" (ibid., 12 July). This presumably was a riposte to Carter's earlier disclaimer that Shcharansky had had any connection with the CIA.

The direct confrontations with the U.S. in June and July appeared to be closely related to the convening of the Belgrade conference in June. Indeed, many observers among the ranks of both Soviet dissidents and Western analysts believed that the widespread roundup and prosecution of human rights activists had as a major purpose the silencing of dissidence to the fullest extent possible before the final Belgrade conclave in October, so as to convince outsiders that such protests were no longer sufficient to justify international concern. In any case, by October the Soviet authorities had gone very far in undermining the organizational base of the domestic protest movement. In the process, the Soviet leadership had succeeded in conveying the impression that external pressures were likely to worsen the situation of the dissidents, and had shown that the U.S. was extremely limited in its ability to effect any liberalization in Soviet domestic policies.

Prior to the open denunciation of the U.S. in Brezhnev's 21 March speech, the authorities had shown an inclination to make some concessions that did not contradict the general policy of attempting to destroy the dissidents' organizational network and communications channels. In February, the ailing Sergei Kovalev was transferred from a labor camp to a prison hospital, and Vladimir Borisov, a major subject of activists' concern at the beginning of the year, was released from a mental asylum. In March, the government released a jailed Jewish physician, Mikhail Shtern (*NYT,* 21 March). Thereafter, the Soviet leadership displayed scant inclinations toward leniency, although a few additional activists seeking political asylum were allowed to leave the USSR.

Three human rights activists in Georgia were arrested in April: Zviad Gamsakhurdia, a member of both Amnesty International and the Helsinki Accords monitoring group; Viktor Rtskhiladze, a former official of the Georgian Ministry of Culture; and Merab Kostova, a member of the Georgian Action Group for the Defense of Human Rights (*Christian Science Monitor,* 27 April). Rtskhiladze, a member of the monitoring group, was arrested on 7 April and released the same evening (Reuters, 11 April), but the other two remained in detention, presumably awaiting trial. By mid-summer, no formal charges had been filed, but fellow dissidents expected indictments on charges of spreading anti-Soviet propaganda—an offense punishable by a maximum of seven years in prison and five years of internal exile.

Yuri Orlov's wife was informed by the KGB on 27 June that he faced charges of slandering the Soviet system (Reuters, 5 July). On 4 July it was unofficially disclosed that Aleksandr Ginzburg was being charged with anti-Soviet agitation and propaganda (*NYT,* 28 June). Orlov faced a possible sentence of ten years' imprisonment and five years of internal exile; Ginzburg could receive a maximum sentence of "deprivation of freedom" for three years.

The two Ukrainian members of the monitoring group arrested in February received lengthy sentences in late June: Mykola Rudenko to seven years' and Oleksa Tikhy to ten years' imprisonment. Both men were also sentenced to five years of internal exile. Their trial was held in Druzhkovka, a small town about sixty-five miles from Donetsk, making it difficult for relatives and supporters from the Kiev area to get there. (Ibid., 2 July.)

After a lull of several weeks in overt acts of suppression of dissidence, Soviet authorities arrested two more associates of the monitoring group in late August. Feliks Serebrov, a member of the group's committee working on the abuse of psychiatry in the USSR, was arrested in Moscow on 22 August on charges of using incorrectly documented working-papers. Viktoras Petkus, a religious activist and member of the Lithuanian branch of the monitoring group, was arrested in Vilnius on 24 August (Radio Liberty, 25 August). The arrest of Petkus was the first such action taken against a member of the Lithuanian branch of the group since its formation in November 1976. Like the earlier actions against Georgians and Ukrainians, the detention of Petkus showed that the KGB maintains its special interest in the prevention of linkage between predominantly Russian civil liberties groups and national and religious rights activists.

The arrest of Serebrov occurred on the eve of the World Psychiatric Association's meeting in Honolulu. Members of the "Commission for the Investigation of the Use of Psychiatry for Political Ends" (the dissident group, founded in 1976, of which Serebrov is a member) sent an appeal for the Association to "come out in defense of Feliks Serebrov." A separate, broader appeal was filed by thirty-four dissidents, including Andrei Sakharov, calling upon the Association to condemn the use of psychiatry in the USSR as an "instrument to suppress civil rights." (Ibid., 31 August.) The Association narrowly approved, by a vote of ninety to eighty-eight, a resolution condemning "the systematic abuse of psychiatry for political purposes in the USSR" over the vehement protests of the chief Soviet delegate, Dr. Eduard Babayan, who termed the accusations "slander" (ibid., 1 September).

Another victim of the campaign against dissent was added in October when Valentin Turchin founder of the unofficial Moscow chapter of Amnesty International, left the USSR for exile in the West. Turchin, 46, subsequently assumed a teaching position at Columbia University. He was replaced as leader of the Moscow group by a prominent writer, Georgi Vladimov, who had resigned from the Soviet Writers Union a few days prior to Turchin's departure. (*Washington Post,* 15 October.)

Soviet police kept twenty Jews under house arrest during the Supreme Soviet session in October to prevent them from protesting against not being allowed to emigrate (*NYT,* 6 October). Meanwhile, the Kremlin continued to have troubles with other minority groups. Police and army troops reportedly broke up a major student demonstration in Estonia in December 1976. In October 1977 anti-Soviet rioting hit Lithuania. Thousands of Lithuanians shouted anti-Soviet and nationalist slogans at a soccer match and then went on a rampage through the streets of Vilnius (*Washington Post,* 31 October).

At year's end, the protest movement remained alive in the USSR, having once again demonstrated its capacity for renewal. However, the movement remained restricted to a handful of intellectuals. It had failed to put down roots among the masses, as perhaps was inevitable, given the official control of media and the apolitical inertia of much of the Soviet population. The movement's principal effectiveness was in its ability to embarrass the regime virtually at will by disclosures shocking to Western public opinion. Success in this activity had been heavily dependent upon ties with Western newsmen in Moscow; during 1977 the Soviet authorities made it clear that mutual access by the Western press and Soviet dissidents would henceforth require payment of a heavy price by both parties.

Some dissidents feared that Brezhnev would be succeeded by a neo-Stalinist on the right and that internal bureaucratic pressures within the unrepresentative, self-perpetuating Soviet political elite would bring harsher policies in the future. Most dissidents welcomed the Carter approach and saw continued U.S. support for the movement as the best lever for the mitigation of oppression by the Soviet regime. One notable exception was Roy Medvedev, who believed that the quiet diplomacy of Henry Kissinger had produced better results. Many Western observers agreed with Medvedev, but others pointed out that Kissinger's major achievement in this area had been a limited increase in Jewish emigration, with no advancement whatever in civil liberties within the USSR. The more subdued American tone at the second Belgrade conference in October (see below) indicated that the Carter administration might be coming around to Medvedev's view, with a less demonstrative stance on human rights as a probability for the future.

International Views and Policies. Soviet activity in the international arena during 1977 featured a belligerent defense of the USSR's record on fulfillment of the Helsinki Accords, a very tough approach to strategic arms limitations negotiations, and an attempt to convey the impression of a linkage between progress on SALT and American restraint on the issues of human rights within the USSR and the monitoring of compliance with the agreements signed at Helsinki in 1975. The USSR received an unexpected bonanza when the new U.S. administration invited the Soviets to reenter the tangled diplomacy of the Middle East, an area from which the major Arab states had largely excluded them. Elsewhere, the USSR made new overtures to India, maintained somewhat tense relations with Japan, and launched a major diplomatic offensive for increased influence in Africa, particularly in the Horn area, with mixed results.

The Soviet leadership continued to face the problem of fissures in the world Communist movement, and the independent-minded West European Communists seemed to be increasingly obstreperous. Relations with China continued to follow a rocky path; overtures to the new Chinese leadership in late 1976 failed to evoke a positive response, and China continued to treat the USSR as the most dangerous superpower. Nevertheless, the USSR persisted in its hard-line approach to problems of the Communist movement; Soviet spokesmen repeatedly and emphatically asserted the line of "proletarian internationalism" and reaffirmed the USSR's leadership of world revolutionary forces.

The general picture that emerged was one of a rationally cautious but genuinely confident Soviet leadership, emboldened by the favorable tilt in the world "correlation of forces" to press its advantages everywhere, as it proceeded relentlessly toward the goal of attaining recognition as the number one superpower. With its military might steadily growing and with the Soviet social system under increasing critical scrutiny by both bourgeois and Communist leaders abroad, the USSR seemed disinclined to yield any vestige of its system of monolithic internal control or its newly found material power in the interest of an improved image among outside elements resistant to the sweep of Soviet power.

The inflexibility of Soviet attitudes was evident at the first round of the Belgrade conference of thirty-five countries to review fulfillment of the Helsinki Accords in June. In their desire to legitimize Soviet dominance over Eastern Europe through the apparent guaranteeing of the status quo in the region by the Western powers, the Soviets had agreed to the "Basket Three" provisions on emigration, exchange of information, and other matters. On paper, the provisions had not appeared overly unfavorable for Soviet control interests as of 1975, and the trade of "normalization" in East Europe for the somewhat ambiguous provisions of "Basket Three" seemed a fair exchange for the Soviet side. Events in 1976, however, indicated that the Soviet moves at Helsinki had backfired badly. The West had not really contested the status quo in Eastern Europe, and the apparent legitimation of Soviet dominance in that region attraced little attention in the West in the aftermath of Helsinki. On the other hand, Soviet dissidents seized upon the provisions related to human rights, formed the monitoring group, and issued a barrage of complaints directed to the Western powers concerning alleged violations of the pact. When U.S. President Carter mounted his human rights campaign, the Soviet miscalculation became even more evident and the USSR was clearly placed on the defensive. Compounding the Soviet problem was the widespread adverse reaction in the West, causing leaders of several West European Communist parties to question the Soviet record on human rights and publicly dissociate themselves from the worst excesses of repression within the USSR.

The June session in Belgrade, designed merely to set the agenda for the October meeting, quickly degenerated into an unrestrained wrangling of charge and counter-charge. The U.S. delegation presented a detailed account of Soviet human rights violations since December 1976. The Soviet representatives countered with a lengthy catalogue of alleged American violations of human rights, emphasizing unemployment and racial discrimination. Further, the Soviet delegation called attention to the provisions in the USSR constitution making the exercise of certain rights contingent upon conformity with the "strengthening of the socialist system."

When the second session convened, it appeared that a reprise of the June encounter was in the making. In the opening week of the three-month session, U.S., European and some neutral delegates attacked Communist failures to live up to pledges on human rights made at Helsinki in 1975. Soviet delegates rejected the charges as interference in the USSR's internal affairs. Chief delegate Yuri Vorontsov said that détente could be improved by concentrating on military issues, such as a treaty banning first use of atomic weapons or an agreement not to enlarge military alliances. The USSR evidently wanted a general discussion of all major point of the Accords, so that human rights violations could be glossed over more easily. Western delegates argued that the Soviet proposals were issues for other forums. (AP, 10 October.)

The conference atmosphere began to change in the second week. Chief U.S. delegate Arthur Goldberg had told Vorontsov on 8 October that he intended to conduct a point-by-point discussion of the Accords, starting with a "full review" of human rights violations in Soviet bloc countries. But indicative of a more cautious U.S. approach was Goldberg's added comment that the review would be conducted "without rancor or polemics." In the following week the U.S. went further, quietly agreeing to exercise restraint in reviewing the human rights record of the USSR and the East European Communist regimes in order not to "get too far in front of the allies." (Ibid., 19 October.)

Other NATO members were said to fear that a volley of specific charges would be counter-productive and lead to a total impasse in the talks. But the U.S. had strong reasons of its own for proceeding with caution, and there were indications that a milder approach was already in formation at the session's beginning, notably the fact that the U.S. delegation directly criticized the USSR only once during the first two weeks, accusing the Soviets of tampering with mail from the West. The Carter administration had evidently been convinced that there was indeed a linkage between the human rights issue and progress on strategic arms limitations. Moreover, the U.S. was reportedly also concerned about the possible negative effects upon Soviet cooperation in regard to a Middle East peace settlement.

In November the USSR launched a counteroffensive at the Belgrade conference against its Western critics and it appeared that the parley might be heading toward a breakdown, despite the earlier indications of some moderation of the American stance. Following a speech by U.S. delegate Goldberg in support of proposals that would strengthen the humanitarian provisions of the Helsinki agreement, Soviet delegate Vorontsov described the speech, which had raised the issue of imprisonment of dissidents in the USSR, as "crude, provocative, and hypocritical." Vorontsov charged that economic and social injustice was widespread in the U.S. and that the U.S. was guilty of "hundreds of thousands of violations" of the Helsinki Declaration. Therefore, the Soviet delegate added, the U.S. had no moral right to criticize the human rights record of other countries (*Washington Post,* 12 November).

Talks on strategic arms limitations between the U.S. and the USSR proceeded intermittently throughout the year, with no progress reported until September, when both sides saw some prospect for a breakthrough. Negotiations were marked by a notable increase in Soviet intransigence during the first half of the year and by an apparent unsureness on the part of the fledgling U.S. administration during the same period. Negotiations were sometimes clouded by the side issue of human rights, but neither side was really deflected from the substantive matters and the overriding concern with the strategic balance. Differing perceptions of the strategic balance and the effect of new weapons upon that balance were clearly the main factors inhibiting new agreements.

The CIA's 1977 estimate of Soviet strategic objectives reportedly concurred for the first time in the conclusion widely held by Western analysts that the USSR's objective is military superiority, not parity (*NYT,* 26 December 1976). Georgi A. Arbatov, director of the Institute of the U.S.A. and Canada, responded to reports of the CIA evaluation in an article in February. Arbatov maintained that the Soviet arms buildup is aimed at the achievement of military parity with the West, not superiority (*Pravda,* 5 February). Arbatov's claim was inconsistent with a number of authoritative statements by Soviet spokesmen over the previous three years, notably an article by Foreign Secretary Andrei A. Gromyko in *Kommunist,* (September 1975), in which he spoke of a "visibly increased preponderance" over "imperialist" opponents that would permit the socialist camp to "lay down the direction of international politics" (see *YICA, 1977,* p. 88).

The major specific stumbling blocks to agreement continued to be the difficult questions concerning inclusion or exclusion of the projected American B-1 bomber and cruise missile, and the Soviet Backfire bomber. When the U.S. secretary of state arrived in Moscow for a round of negotiations on 28 March, relations were soured by President Carter's human rights stance and the indignant Soviet response to it. The Soviets rejected Vance's proposals for a new agreement *in toto* as "too one-sided," apparently without seriously advancing counterproposals (*NYT,* 1 April). Criticism followed in the American press over the alleged inflexibility of the Carter administration, and some analysts contrasted Vance's failure with former secretary Henry Kissinger's apparent sure-handedness. Some commentators considered such criticisms unfair, noting that Kissinger's relationship with the Soviets had required years to build up and that agreements negotiated by him had been frequently brought into question on grounds of inordinate concessions. Some observers saw in the U.S. negotiating position at Moscow the hand of national security adviser Zbigniew K. Brzezinski, long regarded by the Soviets as one of the leading American "hawks." Largely overlooked was the fact that the breakdown in the Moscow talks resulted directly from a Soviet display of inflexibility.

President Carter maintained a public posture of confidence. On the day of Vance's departure from Moscow, Carter said at a White House press conference that he was not discouraged by the negative outcome, and vowed to continue to press for an agreement. However, he warned that he would be forced to consider an acceleration in U.S. weapons development if progress on arms limitations was not forthcoming in the near future. (Ibid., 1 April.) Nevertheless, the impression persisted among many observers of the Washington scene that the Carter administration was having some difficulty in setting foreign policy priorities and in deciding upon appropriate strategies. Criticisms along this line were apparently taken to heart by the U.S. administration; in July, Carter approved the formation by the State Department of an inter-agency committee to coordinate policies toward the USSR, Marshall Shulman, adviser on Soviet affairs to Secretary Vance, and George Vest, assistant secretary of state for European affairs, were appointed co-chairmen of the committee. (Ibid., 19 July.)

The Soviet leadership went to some lengths to place full blame for failure of the Moscow talks on the U.S. In featured articles in *Pravda* and *Izvestiia* four days after Vance's departure, party and government spokesmen said that the USSR expected the U.S. to take the initiative in correcting damaged relations resulting from the American position in the Moscow talks (*Pravda* and *Izvestiia,* 3 April).

Later in the year, a report surfaced in the West that the Soviet leadership's blunt rejection of Vance's SALT II proposals was partly due to Brezhnev's reaction to a remark attributed to President Carter. The president was said to have told a congressional breakfast shortly before Vance's Moscow trip that "Some people get upset every time Brezhnev sneezes." According to the report, a special Politburo meeting was held during Vance's visit and Brezhnev bitterly related the incident while the group was considering the options of a point-by-point reply to the U.S. proposals or an outright rejection; supposedly the Politburo members' indignation over the reported slighting remark led them to adopt the latter course. (*Newsweek,* 31 October.) Whatever the validity of this report, it was clear that the well-known extraordinary sensitivity of the Soviet leaders on matters of prestige did not alter their basic strategy. That strategy was dictated by the USSR's upsurge toward superiority in virtually every category of armaments and the Soviet leaders' unwillingness to sacrifice any advantages attained by them in the world "correlation of forces."

One obstacle to a settlement was seemingly removed by President Carter's mid-year decision to scrap plans for production of the B-1 bomber (*NYT,* 2 July). However, his decision at the same time to proceed with development of the cruise missile drew vehement attacks in the Soviet press. *Pravda* (3 July) said that the U.S. was beginning a new round of the arms race and called the decision on the cruise missile a policy "dangerous to mankind." *Izvestiia* (6 July) claimed that the decision violated an understanding reached by Brezhnev and former President Richard Nixon.

Secretary Vance had conferred with Soviet ambassador Anatoli Dobrynin in April on resumption of strategic arms limitation talks (*NYT,* 8 April) and in May, SALT II negotiations were resumed in Geneva. Meanwhile, two new problems added to the complexity of the issues. The U.S. administration and Congress were actively considering production of a neutron bomb, which would kill personnel but not destroy buildings (*Washington Post,* 7 July). It was not certain that the USSR had no plans to develop such a bomb, but Soviet spokesmen predictably denounced the neutron bomb as an inhuman weapon. U.S. officials were increasingly concerned about Soviet development of a "killer" satellite which had the potential of wiping out an essential component of the U.S. early warning system. It was reliably reported that the USSR had conducted three successful tests during 1977 (ABC News, 28 October), and the U.S. wanted a ban on this weapon included in any new agreement.

Two unrelated matters further irritated relations while the U.S. was trying to get the stalled strategic arms talks back on track. On 9 April President Carter ordered the Coast Guard to seize the Soviet fishing trawler *Taras Shevchenko* for violating the newly imposed 200-mile fishing zone limit (*NYT,* 10 April). Three days later, Carter met with Ambassador Dobrynin at the White House to discuss Soviet violations of the new fishing restrictions and issues of strategic arms limitations (*Washington Post,* 13 April). Carter had earlier rejected three requests from the Coast Guard for seizures of Soviet trawlers after the new regulations went into effect on 10 March; evidently the U.S. president was playing a bit of the "linkage" game himself. The State Department announced on 16 April that three Soviet trade unionists had been denied permission to attend the International Long-shoremen's convention in Seattle; this move reportedly was due to AFL-CIO pressure (*NYT,* 17 April). Soviet delegates filed a bitter protest over this incident at the Belgrade conference.

By September, relations had simmered down to the point where progress toward a new accord on arms seemed possible. Reported narrowing of differences between the two sides seemed to reflect at least partial acceptance by the U.S. of the necessity of informal linkage between SALT II and other issues. In late September, Gromyko met twice with Vance at the U.N. and both side indicated that some progress toward agreement had been made. Arms negotiator Paul Warnke was dispatched to Geneva by the U.S. to discuss the fundamental issues of SALT II, plus the demilitarization of the Indian Ocean and a total ban on nuclear tests.

Gromyko made a surprise move in a UN speech on 27 September, offering to join with the U.S. and Britain in a suspension of all underground nuclear weapons tests for an indefinite period. American officials noted approvingly that the USSR was no longer conditioning such offers upon the compliance of France and China, and saw the offer as a serious positive step by the Soviets.

However, while taking this conciliatory approach, Gromyko had sharply criticized the U.S. on two fronts. He suggested that "those who clamor for 'human rights' could best apply their efforts" in Southern Africa. Further, Gromyko questioned how the U.S. could call for "drastic reductions" in armaments while authorizing "merciless types of weapons such as the neutron bomb." (AP, 27 September.)

Gromyko journeyed to Washington on 27 September for a talk with Carter and other top U.S. officials regarding SALT II. Afterward, Carter declared that he was "encouraged" by the "cooperative attitude of the Soviets," but Gromyko cautioned that there were "remaining issues" before an agreement could be "finalized" (*NYT*, 28, 29 September).

A significant development in the apparent U.S. acceptance of the politics of linkage occurred during the same week when the U.S. and USSR issued a joint statement calling for a comprehensive peace settlement in the Middle East and the convening of a Geneva conference "not later than December 1977." To the dismay of Israel, the statement urged that an agreement should insure "the legitimate rights of the Palestinian people." (Ibid., 2 October.)

When SALT I interim agreement expired at the beginning of October, the U.S. had already unilaterally announced its intention of continuing to abide by the agreement's provisions. The USSR added its concurrence, and in mid-October President Carter announced at a press conference that the U.S. was making progress in the SALT II talks.

Brezhnev sounded a sanguine note about the negotiations on 21 October. "Recently there has been a definite turn for the better in these negotiations,"" he said. "We would like to bring these negotiations to a successful conclusion without any undue delays. With a realistic and businesslike approach by the Americans, this is quite attainable." (Tass, 21 October.) On the same day, in a speech in Des Moines, Carter said that agreement on a new strategic arms limitation treaty would be reached "within a few weeks." Six days later he tempered his enthusiasm, saying that it might be many weeks before there could be a final agreement. (*NYT*, 22, 28 October.)

The Carter administration had apparently limited its negotiating options by the decision to scrap the B-1 bomber, although U.S. military planners hoped to provide a suitable substitute by a modification of the swing-wing FB-111 H, using the B-1's engines and electronic gear. Any agreement by the Soviets seemed contingent upon limitation of the range of the cruise missile, if not its banning altogether. If the U.S. accepted limitations upon the cruise missile, it would be imperative to obtain a sharply limited ceiling on the mammoth Soviet SS-X-18 silo-killing rockets— the primary strategic component in potential Soviet military superiority. Accordingly, limitations on the SS-X-18 would provide the crucial test of Soviet claims about their desire for strategic parity.

In other arms limitation matters, the USSR displayed some flexibility. On 2 November Brezhnev dropped the earlier Soviet insistence that any halt to nuclear explosions exclude blasts for peaceful purposes (*NYT*, 3 November), and in late November the USSR agreed to a week of talks in Moscow in mid-December on limiting Soviet and American sales of conventional arms (*NYT*, 24 November).

The apparent improvement in U.S.-Soviet relations evidenced by the SALT II negotiations received a stiff test with the revelation on 29 October of a bizarre episode involving a U.S. diplomat. After a semi-official Soviet news agency released an article charging that Constantine Warvariv, deputy chief of the U.S. delegation to a UNESCO environmental conference in Tbilisi, had been a collaborator with the Nazis in the Ukraine in 1941-43 (*Novosti*, 29 October), the U.S. embassy in Moscow revealed an earlier protest about an alleged crude attempt to blackmail Warvariv: two KGB agents were said to have broken into his hotel room in Tbilisi on 16 October, produced a file of forged documents concerning his wartime role, and threatened him with exposure unless he cooperated with Soviet intelligence.

The embassy's protest note formally demanded that the Ministry of Foreign Affairs "ensure that those Soviet individuals involved be speedily brought to account" and "take immediate measures to prevent the repetition of such outrageous incidents" (AP, 29 October). In view of the public accusation after the private U.S. protest, it seemed quite likely that, while the incident may have originated in a standard KGB counterintelligence operation, the Soviet authorities were using it as a means for continuation of the campaign of intimidation against U.S. diplomats related to human rights issues. The fact that U.S. officials released the story only after Soviet pressure compelled them to do so seemed to underscore the lengths to which the U.S. would go to maintain the fragile framework of detente. Accordingly, the episode seemed likely to strengthen the hand of Soviet leadership circles supporting a hard line toward the U.S.

That approach, much in evidence throughout 1977, had already produced an unexpected pay-off in the Middle East. The U.S. invitation to the Soviets to join in the peacemaking efforts, culminating in the joint statement of early fall, dazed the Israelis and left some veteran Western diplomats dumbfounded, since the Arabs themselves had largely excluded the USSR from influence in the area. Clearly, the U.S. policy of "even-handed" diplomacy in the Middle East had raised such expectations that a settlement satisfactory to the Arab forces seemed unlikely through U.S. efforts alone, particularly in view of the intransigent attitude of the new Begin government in Israel. But the sequence of events suggested strongly that the Soviets had convinced the Americans of a necessary linkage between Middle East and SALT II bargaining. In any case, the American initiative gave the Soviets a new opening for influence in the area, in the aftermath of near-catastrophic Soviet policy failures dating back to 1971. How well the Soviets could exploit the opening still depended upon factors beyond U.S. control. The first few weeks following the joint U.S.-USSR statement saw a further deterioration in Soviet relations with Egypt and the Sudan.

The Soviets had been trying desperately to refurbish their tattered position in the Middle East by a flurry of diplomatic activity and by continued support for radical Arab "confrontation" forces. In December 1976 Libyan leader Qaddafi had been invited to Moscow, where he conferred with Brezhnev (Izvestiia, 7 December). The visit was followed by renewed assertions of Soviet support in Qaddafi's quarrel with Egyptian president Anwar Sadat. When border fighting broke out between Egypt and Libya in the summer of 1977, a strong Soviet statement blamed the clash upon Sadat and the Egyptians (Pravda, 26 July). Worried by the Syrian turn against the Palestine Liberation Organization (PLO) forces in 1976, the Soviet leadership welcomed Syrian president Asad to Moscow for two days of talks in April (Izvestiia, 19 April), but evidently failed to turn Asad back toward his formerly largely pro-Soviet stance; he continued to follow a rather independent course. But a radical change in Egyptian-Israeli relations in November gave a new impetus for closer Syrian ties with Moscow (see below).

The USSR reaffirmed its support for PLO leader Yasir Arafat on his visit to Moscow, 29-31 August. In so doing, the Soviets held to their revolutionary stance on liberation movements in line with the doctrine of "proletarian internationalism," while at the same time serving notice of their unwillingness to support the even more radical "rejectionist" PLO factions, who consider Arafat too moderate. The communiqué referred to conversations "in an atmosphere of friendship and mutual understanding," and denounced the "continuing attempts of Israel and its protectors to block the resolution of questions of a Middle East settlement on a just basis and to delay the resumption of the Geneva conference" (Pravda, 1 September; Izvestiia, 2 September).

The USSR continued its policy of leaning toward the leftist states of Iraq and Libya, which received additional large arms supplies from the Soviets during 1977, while leaving the door open for an unlikely reconciliation with Syria. At the same time the Soviet leadership gave some reassurance to moderate Arab elements by refusing to back "rejectionist" PLO factions and by the continued assertion of its desire for a full-scale peace settlement in the Middle East. However, USSR relations with Egypt and Sudan appeared beyond repair.

A joint front against Soviet influence seemed to be firmly established following an unprecedented joint session of the Egyptian and Sudanese parliaments in Cairo on 24 October. Egyptian President Sadat announced that he and Sudanese President Ja'far Numairi had evolved a joint strategy to protect their region from any attempt at domination and aggression. This was understood to be a warning to the Soviet-backed governments of Libya and Ethiopia (*Washington Post,* 25 October).

Sadat dealt the Soviets another blow on the day following the joint parliamentary session when he declared a ten-year moratorium on repayment of Egypt's military debts to Moscow, beginning in 1978. Sadat also halted all Egyptian cotton shipments to the USSR. The actions followed repeated public appeals to Moscow for rescheduling of Egypt's civilian debts, estimated at $500 million, and for a ten-year grace period on military debts, believed to total about $4 billion. According to Sadat, the USSR was "still imposing an embargo on arms and spare parts and [had] even canceled some old contracts" (AP, 27 October).

Following Sadat's visit to Israel in November and his call for an Arab-Israeli peace conference in Cairo, the USSR quickly aligned itself with Syria's position vis-à-vis the Sadat initiatives. Rejecting an invitation to attend the Cairo talks, the Soviet leadership welcomed Syrian Foreign Minister Abdel Halin Khaddam to Moscow. The official communiqué on the visit stated that Syria and the USSR expressed "their mutual determination to seek an all-embracing Middle East settlement excluding the possibility of separate deals" (Tass, 30 November). Representatives of Syria, Libya, South Yemen, Iraq, Algeria, and the PLO met in Tripoli in early December and, with Iraq holding out for an even harder line, announced a "freeze" in their relations with Egypt. The Egyptians responded by severing diplomatic relations with the five "rejectionist" Arab states and on 7 December closed the consulates and cultural centers of the USSR and four Eastern European countries outside Cairo. The Egyptian government charged that Communist agents were trying to foment opposition to President Sadat's peace initiatives with Israel (Associated Press, 7 December).

Often stymied in its attempts to influence developments in the Eastern Mediterranean in recent years, the USSR had made special efforts to secure footholds in the Arabian peninsula and in the Horn of Africa, with the People's Democratic Republic of Yemen and the regime of Mohammed Siad-Barre in Somalia as particular targets. By 1977, however, Saudi Arabia had made great inroads in its attempts to detach the PDRY from Soviet influence and appeared to be gaining influence with Siad-Barre and the Somalis. The USSR had also been trying to bring the new Ethiopian regime within its orbit, but the growing territorial conflict between Somalia and Ethiopia made the Soviet balancing act in the Horn area increasingly difficult. The coup d'état led by Colonel Mariam Mengistu in Ethiopia in February brought matters to a head, and an early Soviet decision to take sides openly in the Somali-Ethiopian conflict followed.

USSR President Podgorny was dispatched to Africa in March on a mission that included stops in Tanzania, Zambia, Mozambique, and Somalia (*Izvestiia,* 4 April). Podgorny avoided Ethiopia, but Cuban Premier Fidel Castro, on an African tour at the same time, went there and immediately afterward to Moscow, where Brezhnev greeted him at the airport one day after Podgorny's return (*Pravda,* 5 April). Castro reportedly had also arranged a secret meeting between the leaders of Ethiopia and Somalia in Aden, in an unsuccessful attempt to resolve their differences (*NYT,* 14 November). Subsequently, Mengistu moved unreservedly into the Soviet camp. In May he went to Moscow and signed a declaration and protocol of friendship and aid (*Pravda,* 7 May).

Tensions continued to rise in the Horn area, not only between Somalia and Ethiopia but also on the Sudan-Ethiopia border. Sudan expelled the Soviet military mission from Khartoum, and the USSR came down squarely on the side of Ethiopia. An official statement in *Pravda* (7 June) "strongly condemned" those "preparing aggression against Ethiopia" and spoke of their "heavy responsibility before the peoples of Africa and the whole world."

The Soviets subsequently stepped up shipments of arms to Ethiopia, including tanks and jet fighters, at the same time cutting supplies to Somalia, which had been an ally of the USSR since

1969. Nevertheless, Somali guerrillas in late October held control of all but two key towns in the Ogaden region, which comprises about a third of Ethiopia. Despite successes by the guerrillas, long-range prospects looked bleak for Somalia,which had failed to find alternative sources of arms in the West, having been turned down by the U.S., Britain, and France. On 21 October, Siad-Barre warned the USSR that unless it halted military aid to Ethiopia its relations with Somalia would be in "great jeopardy" (AP, 23 October). On 13 November Somalia renounced the 1974 treaty of friendship and cooperation with the USSR and ordered all Soviet advisers to leave the country. Siad-Barre made good on this threat in November when he closed Soviet bases in Somalia and broke diplomatic relations with Cuba. All Soviet advisors were ordered to leave the country within one week (*NYT*, 14 November).

Podgorny's trip spotlighted Moscow's continuing interest in southern Africa, and throughout 1977 the USSR sought to consolidate its bridgehead of influence in this region. In February, the CPSU sent a delegation to Tanzania for ceremonies in Dar es Salaam on the occasion of the amalgamation of the Tanganyika African National Union and Afro-Shinazi parties into a single revolutionary party (*Pravda,* 12 February). Also in February, a CPSU delegation attended the congress of the Front for the Liberation of Mozambique (ibid). In March the USSR and Mozambique signed a twenty-year treaty of friendship and collaboration.

A similar treaty signed with Angola in 1976 was ratified by the Angolan Council of the Revolution on 25 February (AFP, Paris, 26 February, in *FBIS,* 28 February). The USSR had played a major supportive role, in collaboration with its Cuban ally, in the victory of the Popular Movement for the Liberation of Angola (MPLA) in 1975-76, and the MPLA appeared to be the keystone of the Soviet presence in southern Africa. In May, however, an unsuccessful coup attempt by a pro-Soviet faction in Angola clouded USSR-Angolan relations and raised some doubts about MPLA leader Neto's future reliability. Meanwhile the USSR continued to proffer encouragement and material support to all regimes and guerrilla factions opposed to the white-dominated governments in southern Africa and appeared to maintain a close coordination of its liberationist policies throughout the continent with those of Cuba's Fidel Castro.

Soviet policy in Africa clearly reflected long-range strategic interests. Control of the gateway to the Red Sea and of the southern third of the African continent by forces favorable to the USSR would place the West, particularly the U.S., in an untenable strategic position, possibly threatening supplies of oil to the Western countries. Strategic calculations concerning the world "correlation of forces" also dovetail neatly with the recent Soviet reversion to an emphasis upon the "two camps" doctrine in the classification of world political forces and with the slogan of "proletarian internationalism," which has formed the ideological watchword for Soviet international policy since mid-1975. "Proletarian internationalism" is generally understood to mean the solidarity of the world revolutionary movement, the absence of any distinction between particular party and national interests and those of international Communism and, at least implicitly, the primacy of the CPSU and the USSR in the world movement. Further, Soviet theoreticians have recently put forward the proposition that the present period is favorable for revolutionary development due to the weakening of imperialism, that the unfavorable position of the imperialists is primarily due to the change in the world "correlation of forces" in favor of the Socialist camp and that the major factor in the increased strength of the Socialist camp is the rising power of the USSR. The USSR is thus viewed by Soviet theoreticians as being objectively the center of the world revolutionary forces.

Such conceptions have aroused frictions within the world Communist movement, particularly in CPSU relations with West European Communist parties. The French and Italian parties, in their drives for electoral success and access to governmental power, continued in 1977 their "Eurocommunist" approach, featuring rejection of Soviet primacy and the dictatorship of the proletariat, and ostensible commitment to democratic freedoms. In regard to the Spanish party, whose secretary general Santiago Carrillo has been the most vehement opponent of the conception of the USSR as the "center" of the world movement, the CPSU sought to encourage factional interests favorable to the Soviet approach. In March, the Soviet leadership welcomed to Moscow with much fanfare the octogenarian president of the Spanish Communist Party, Dolores Ibarruri. Conversations were held between Ibarruri and Andrei Kirilenko, Ponomarev, and the deputy chief of the Central Committee's International Department, Vadim Zagladin (Tass, 24 March). The communiqué said that "the representatives of the Communist parties of the Soviet Union and Spain spoke in favor of the development of their internationalist, equal and voluntary cooperation on the basis of the great ideals of Marx, Engels, and Lenin" (Moscow domestic service, 24 March, in *FBIS,* 25 March). The troublesome Carrillo was pointedly ignored, with no references to him in the Soviet press during the Ibarruri visit. In April, the CPSU Central Committee sent a warm message of congratulations to the Central Committee of the Spanish party on the occasion of its legalization (Tass, 12 April). Again, the Soviets avoided any reference to their critic Carrillo. During his attendance at the 60th anniversary celebration of the October Revolution in Moscow, Carrillo was not given opportunity to address a formal meeting, despite his readiness to do so.

There were two exceptions to the general hard line on "proletarian internationalism." The Soviet delegation to the Fifth Congress of the Socialist Unity Party of West Berlin (SEW) in April emphasized the contribution of normalization of the West Berlin situation to détente vis-à-vis Western Europe. Chief USSR delegate Ivan V. Kapitonov, CPSU Central Committee secretary for cadres, said that the four-power agreement on West Berlin "promotes the deepening of the processes of the relaxation of tensions in the European continent." (Ibid., 16 April, in *FBIS,* 18 April.) However, Kapitonov inserted one reference relevant to "proletarian internationalism" in his otherwise low-key speech: "The Great October Revolution became the most important event of the Twentieth century which changes basically the process of development for the whole of humanity" (ADN, East Berlin, 16 April, in *FBIS,* 18 April).

The second concerned Yugoslavia, which reportedly had forced the Soviet leadership to downgrade emphasis upon "proletarian internationalism" at the June 1976 conference of European parties in East Berlin. Further, the Yugoslavs have exhibited concern about the possibility of Soviet intervention in their country when President Tito leaves the political scene. Apparently eager to mollify the uneasy Yugoslav Communists, Soviet leaders welcomed Tito to Moscow for a state visit in August. Brezhnev's speech at a dinner honoring Tito emphasized "peace and international cooperation" and "strict observance of the principles of independence and equality among Communist parties and regimes. Tito's reply pointedly concentrated upon the "wealth of forms and paths for bringing about the revolutionary transformation of the contemporary world" and the need for respect for the "principles of independence and equality of revolutionary movements" and "noninterference in one another's internal affairs." (*Izvestiia,* 18 August.)

Although the Soviet leaders demonstrated again, as they had in 1976, a willingness to make tactical concessions on occasion in the interest of particular immediate policy objectives, they left no doubt about their commitment to "proletarian internationalism" as the guiding principle of world policy, and with regularity throughout the year sounded the call for militancy by the "Socialist camp" under Soviet leadership. Bulgaria, the USSR's staunchest ally in Eastern Europe, was clearly speaking for Moscow when its ruling party attacked the West European revisionists on 26 January, warning against the "infiltration of nationalist elements using Eurocommunism as a disguise" (*Christian Science Monitor,* 2 February). Five days later, the CPSU Central Committee, in its resolution on the 60th anniversary of the October Revolution, strongly reaffirmed "proletarian internationalism" and the "dictatorship of the proletariat," and hailed the Soviet bloc as the "most dynamic force in the world" (*Pravda,* 1 February).

A conference on "proletarian internationalism" was held in Tashkent in April, attended by "leading Soviet scientists and party workers" and representatives of several parties from Europe,

Asia, Africa, and Latin America. The importance of the conference and its theme was demonstrated by the presence of General Secretary Brezhnev, who delivered a speech on the "theory and policy of proletarian internationalism in the present-day stage of the world revolutionary process" (Tanyug, Belgrade, 16 April, in *FBIS*, 19 April).

The importance attached by the leadership to the current line on world policy was emphasized by the selection of Mikhail V. Zimianin, alternate Politburo member, as the principal speaker at the Lenin anniversary celebration in April. Zimianin is a protégé of Politburo member Mikhail A. Suslov, recognized as the principal advocate of "proletarian internationalism" within Soviet leadership ranks. As expected, Zimianin stressed the importance of "proletarian internationalism" and the central role of the USSR in the world revolutionary movement. He denounced China for "continuing attempts . . . to whip up international tension and to form the most reactionary forces into a bloc" and the "whipping up of anti-Soviet propaganda." Echoing Gromyko's September 1975 *Kommunist* article, Zimianin claimed that "world socialism reliably holds the foreign political initiative." Reaffirming the official adherence to "two camps" doctrine, Zimianin emphasized the importance of the contemporary struggle between Socialist and bourgeois ideologies (Moscow domestic service, 22 April, in *FBIS*, 25 April).

Konstantin Zarodov, editor of the journal *Problemy mira i sotsializma* (Problems of Peace and Socialism), emerged again as a key spokesman in the ideological offensive of "proletarian internationalism" with an important *Pravda* article in August. Zarodov had been singled out by Brezhnev for special praise following his August 1975 *Pravda* article criticizing parliamentary methods and calling for direct revolutionary action among the masses (see *YICA, 1976*, p. 66). In the 1977 article Zarodov pointed to the Bolshevik revolution as a model for all others. The article bristled with "two camps" rhetoric as Zarodov evoked the memory of Lenin to implicitly denounce opponents of "proletarian internationalism" within the world Communist movement for "opportunist emasculation" and "reformist vulgarization" (*Pravda,* 26 August). In his major speech at ceremonies commemorating the 100th anniversary of the birth of Cheka founder Feliks Dzerzhinsky in September, KGB chief Yuri V. Andropov seemed to echo Zarodov's much publicized August 1975 article by his marked emphasis, unusual even for a Dzerzhinsky fete, upon the importance of revolutionary violence (ibid., 10 September).

The Chinese Communists could hardly criticize Soviet encouragement of revolutionary violence, but they continued to denounce "proletarian internationalism" as a cover for Soviet "social imperialism." Moreover, there were practical reasons for continuing Chinese acrimony toward the USSR, in particular the simmering border disputes since the open fighting on the Ussuri River in 1969. In late 1976 the Soviet leadership made overtures to the new Chinese leadership concerning the possibility of mending relations between the two Communist powers. Soviet anti-Chinese rhetoric was toned down considerably, and chief Soviet negotiator (and deputy foreign minister) Leonid Ilichev, after an absence of eighteen months, was sent back to Peking to resume negotiations. On 22 January Ilichev met with the Chinese foreign minister, Huang Hua, in what was described as a "courtesy call" and in February it was reported that Soviet and Chinese negotiating teams had been meeting regularly twice a week (AFP, 9 February, in *FBIS*, 10 February). It was also reported that Ilichev had recently presented new proposals on the borders issue. These proposals evidently elicited no favorable response. Thereafter, the Soviet leadership resumed the polemic against China, notably in Zimianin's Lenin anniversary speech, indicating that Moscow had largely written off any hopes of compromise with Peking. However, in his 60th anniversary speech on 2 November, Brehnev warned that Western countries should not expect the Sino-Soviet split to last forever (*Pravda,* 3 November). At the same time his renewed criticism of the Chinese leadership prompted the Chinese ambassador to stalk out of the Kremlin Palace of Congresses (AP, 3 November).

On the Chinese side there appeared to be no change in the anti-Soviet position of the leadership, with bitter attacks upon the USSR continuing even during the peak efforts of Ilichev's negotiating mission. At the time of the 60th anniversary celebration, a Peking editorial accused the CPSU of having turned "fascist" and said that the USSR had become "one of the biggest international exploiters and oppressors in the present era" (*Daily Telegraph,* London, 8 November). Soviet-Chinese competition for influence in the world revolutionary movement, especially in Africa, continued unabated. However, the Chinese foreign minister attended the Russian National Day reception on 7 November for the first time in years and the USSR and the PRC reportedly concluded an agreement on the navigation of border rivers in early autumn.

Alongside the hard-line revolutionary stance of "proletarian internationalism" the USSR continued to play the game of traditional great power diplomacy vis-à-vis major non-Communist regimes, emphasizing detente and "peaceful coexistence," a duality of tactics reminiscent of the Chicherin period of Soviet diplomacy in the 1920s. In late June, Brezhnev made a state visit to France, conferred with French President Valéry Giscard d'Estaing, and signed a number of routine documents of no particular importance (*NYT,* 28, 29 June). The main significance of the visit seemed to lie in the demonstration of normal Soviet relations with the Giscard government. The Soviet attitude remained unclear toward the sudden change (announced in September) by the French Communists vis-à-vis their Socialist partners, a change threatening the earlier "unity of the left" in France.

Soviet relations with Britain appeared to be improved following British Foreign Secretary David Owen's visit to Moscow in October. Owen met with Brezhnev and signed a treaty on the prevention of accidental nuclear war. The meeting followed a luncheon with the Soviet foreign minister, Gromyko, at which Owen expressed hopes for the further development of détente and for an increase in British-Soviet trade (AP, 11 October).

The USSR sought to reassure its relations with India in the aftermath of the fall of Indira Gandhi by an official visit of Gromyko to New Delhi in April (Tass, 25 April). A Soviet press release just prior to Gromyko's trip said that "certain quarters in India are trying to cast a shadow on Soviet-Indian relations," and condemned "provocative reports" according to which the new Soviet-Indian treaty of peace, friendship, and cooperation "has detrimental effects for India" (Tass, 24 April). Indian Prime Minister Morarji Desai, along with his foreign minister, returned Gromyko's visit in October, when the Indian leader journeyed to Moscow for six days of talks with Soviet leaders. At the end of the visit, Desai stated that there had been no shift in the policy either of New Delhi or of Moscow since the Janata Party came to power in March (*FEER,* 11 November).

A Soviet-Japanese agreement on fishing in the northwestern Pacific, setting terms and procedures for Japanese fishing within the 200-mile zone off the shores of the USSR during 1977, was signed in Moscow in May (Tass, 27 May). However, demands for the return of the four Kurile Islands occupied by the USSR since World War II continued to be an irritant in relations. Particularly upsetting for Moscow was the Japan Communist Party's continued support for these demands. *Pravda* (12 June) attacked the Japanese Communists for "adapting themselves to chauvinistic, nationalistic attitudes and fostering hostile feelings in Japan toward the Soviet Union." The article maintained the adamant Soviet rejection of Japan's claim to the Kuriles, "known to be an inseparable part of the Soviet Union's territory."

There were some indications of dissatisfaction in Japan over the alleged one-sidedness of the fishing agreement and further irritation was added by Soviet arrests of Japanese fishermen later in the year. On the Soviet side, there was apparent distress over the reluctance of Japanese financial interests to invest in Siberian ventures.

Soviet interests in Southeast Asia received a sharp jolt in midsummer when Cambodia recalled all of its diplomatic representatives in Moscow. Late in the year, Soviet officials expressed uncertainty concerning possible resumption of diplomatic relations (Associated Press, 2 December).

Publications. The Main CPSU organs are the daily newspaper *Pravda* (circulation more than eleven million, the theoretical and ideological journal *Kommunist* (appearing seventeen times a year, circulation more than one million, and the twice-monthly *Partiinaia zhizn'*, a journal for internal party affairs and organizational matters (circulation more than 1.16 million). *Kommunist vooruzhennikh sil* is the party theoretical journal for the armed forces and *Agitator* is the journal for party propagandists, both appearing twice a month. The Komsomol has a newspaper, *Komsomolskaia pravda* (six days a week); a monthly theoretical journal, *Molodoi kommunist;* and a monthly literary journal, *Molodaia gvardia.* Each USSR republic prints similar party newspapers in local languages, and usually also in Russian. Specialized publications issued under supervision of the CPSU Central Committee include the newspapers *Sovetskaia rossiia, Selskaia zhizn', Sotzialisticheskaia industria, Sovetskaia kultura,* and *Ekonomicheskaia gazeta,* and the journal *Politicheskoye samoobrazovaniie.*

University of New Orleans   R. Judson Mitchell

Yugoslavia

Yugoslav Communists date the beginning of their party back to April 1919 when a "unification congress" in Belgrade established a Socialist Workers' Party of Yugoslavia (Communists), including both Communist and non-Communist elements. This party was disbanded in June 1920, and a Communist Party of Yugoslavia (CPY) was formed. At its Sixth Congress, in November 1952, the name was changed to the League of Communists of Yugoslavia (Savez komunista Jugoslavije; LCY). The LCY is the only political party in the Socialist Federative Republic of Yugoslavia (SFRY) and exercises power through its leading role in the Socialist Alliance of the Working People of Yugoslavia (Socijalistički savez radnog naroda Jugoslavije; SAWPY), a front organization that includes all the mass political organizations as well as individuals representing various social groups.

In November 1977 the LCY claimed a membership of 1,537,000. Only 454,000 (28.9 percent) were blue-collar workers (*Borba*, 16 November). According to an official estimate, in August 1977 Yugoslavia had 21,770,000 inhabitants (*Nedeljne novosti*, Belgrade, 28 August), which means that 7.2 percent were LCY members. There were 42,000 basic party organizations (*Dnevnik*, Ljubljana, 9 November).

Leadership and Organization. The supreme bodies of the LCY are the 166-member Central Committee and its 48-member Presidium (47 plus Tito, LCY president for life). At the Tenth Congress in May 1974, the Presidium elected the 12-member Executive Committee. (For names and offices see *YICA, 1975,* pp. 112-14; *1976,* pp. 91-92.) There are central committees also for the LCY's six republic and two autonomous provincial branches.

Following the death of Džemal Bijedić, Yugoslavia's prime minister, who perished in a plane crash on 18 January 1977, his place both as prime minister and Presidium member was taken by Veselin Djuranović. Until 15 March, Djuranović, 52, was president of the Presidium of the Montenegrin Central Committee and as such an *ex officio* member of the LCY Presidium. His place in Montenegro was taken by Vojo Srzentić, 43, who thus also became a member of the Presidium. A vacant place remained in the Presidium after SAWPY Chairman Dušan Petrović died of a heart attack on 21 July.

In June Western news reports from Belgrade, quoting Yugoslav "party sources," said that President Tito might reduce the size of both the Presidium and the Executive Committee. A new, streamlined policy-making body (a seven-member Politburo) was said to have been planned and the following names were mentioned: Tito, Edvard Kardelj, Dr. Vladimir Bakarić, Petar Stambolić, Kiro Gligorov, Stane Dolanc, and a representative of the army (probably General Nikola Ljubičić). The first four are members both of the collective state leadership called the Presidency of the SFRY and of the Central Committee Presidium (*The Times*, London, 2 June; *The Guardian*, London, 2 June; *Süddeutsche Zeitung*, Munich, 1 June; *Frankfurter Allgemeine Zeitung*, 2 June).

In November a member of the LCY Executive Committee in charge of party organization, Jure Bilić, confirmed the planned reshuffle of the top party bodies. He stated that the Executive Committee would be abolished and replaced by several secretaries responsible to the Presidium, and one of them would be an executive secretary. Stressing that the final decision would be made at the LCY congress in 1978, Bilić said the 48-member Presidium would probably be more than halved, and would be composed of 3 representatives from each of Yugoslavia's 6 constituent republics and 2 each from the autonomous provinces of Vojvodina and Kosovo. The 166-member Central Committee would be retained as supreme body between the party congresses. The presidency of the SFRY, which includes the president and 8 senior leaders from each republic and province, would remain unchanged (*Financial Times*, London, 17 November).

Party Internal Affairs. *Tito's Birthday Anniversary.* The only session of the LCY Central Committee in 1977 was convoked for 24 May on the occasion of Tito's eighty-fifth birthday, which was celebrated the next day. Tito was decorated for the third time with the order of the National Hero of Yugoslavia "for extraordinary merits," and for his "visionary and creative contributions" (*Borba*, 25 May).

The eulogies spoken and written during the months preceding Tito's birthday this year went beyond anything that has appeared in the past. Yugoslav information media were full of panegyrics by the country's state, party, and military leaders describing Tito as one of the greatest personalities in modern history. The exuberance of the encomia did not, however, conceal the fears, widespread in Yugoslavia as well as abroad, of what may happen to the country and the party when he disappears from political life. Echoing these persistent preoccupations, Tito stated at a banquet honoring the Yugoslav military that the army is the best guarantee for unity in Yugoslavia and the maintenance of Socialism after he leaves the scene (*NYT*, 23 December).

Top Party Meetings. The LCY Presidium held seven sessions during 1977. The twenty-sixth (31 January) discussed preparations for the 1978 congress and elected a Preparatory Committee of 28 members, headed by Stane Dolanc; a report dealing with the international activities of the Presidium was approved; Milan Rakas, a Central Committee member, was appointed new editor in chief of the LCY weekly *Komunist*. The twenty-seventh (2 March) discussed problems of the country's "self-protection," following a report by General Ivan Kukoč, a member of the Executive Committee; a 111-member committee for the preparations of the celebrations of Tito's birthday and the fortieth anniversary of his being the head of the CPY/LCY was formed. The twenty-eighth (8 April) meeting discussed agricultural problems and heard a report by Milutin Baltić, head of Croatia's trade union organization; Ali Shukri, a member of the Executive Committee in charge of party cadres, talked about the party work in rural areas. The twenty-ninth (17 May) considered ideological-political aspects of the Socialist transformation of education. The thirtieth (13 June) was concerned with the foundations of the political system of Socialist self-management democracy; a major report was submitted by Edvard Kardelj, who said that neither the multiparty system nor the one-party system was good—the only system that guarantees working people full human rights and freedom is Yugoslavia's system of "self-management pluralism," a new term coined by Kardelj. He stressed the leading role of the party even though he admitted that neither the state nor a single Communist party could bring happiness to man—"only man himself can create his own happiness." His report was a summary of ideas presented in his new book (which became later a Yugoslav best-seller), *Roads of Development of the Socialist Self-Management Political System.* The thirty-first session (6 October) heard and approved Tito's report on his visits to the Soviet Union, North Korea, and China. The thirty-second (23 December) discussed political-ideological problems and socioeconomic developments.

LCY Organization in the Army. On 30 March the fifth regular electoral conference of the LCY organization in the Yugoslav People's Army took place in Belgrade. These gatherings are held every second year and the last was held in February 1975. Stane Dolanc and Jure Bilić were present, and Tito sent a letter of greetings urging party members in the army to continue to implement "Marx's concept of an armed people" (*Borba*, 31 March). The main report was submitted by General Dane Petkovski, a Macedonian, and was followed by speeches from General Džemil Šarac, a Moslem, secretary of the Committee of the LCY Conference in the Yugoslav army; General Nikola Ljubičić, a Serb, minister of defense; General Stane Potočar, a Slovene, chief of staff; and General Milan Krdzić, a Serb, also a secretary of the Committee. The Yugoslav army, the only institution in Yugoslavia not conducted under the self-management system, comprises 250,000 officers, non-commissioned officers, soldiers, and civilian employees. General Šarac told the conference that there were 90,000 party members in the army, in 2,100 basic party organizations. He also said that more than 13,000 members of the armed forces work in various civil, political and self-managing organizations over the country. According to Šarac, 98.5 percent of the officers and more than 90 percent of the NCOs were members of the LCY, as were about 24,000 ordinary soldiers. (Ibid.) The delegates elected a new sixty-member Committee of the Conference of the LCY Organization in the Army—two more than previously. Of these, only eighteen were incumbents, so forty-two newcomers were elected. The secretary of the committee is again General Sarac. (Ibid.)

The army organization of the LCY performs its role in the following ways: (1) by carrying out ideological-political activities, (2) by promoting the Socialist consciousness of members of the army and engaging them in efforts to apply LCY policies, and (3) by encouraging each to make a critical self-analysis of his practice and achievements (*Review of International Affairs*, Belgrade, nos. 656/657, 5-20 August).

Domestic Affairs. *Presidency of the SFRY Meetings.* Between 10 January and 28 December the Presidency of the SFRY held twenty-six sessions, in most cases discussing and approving various foreign political issues, such as the visits of President Tito abroad.

Socialist Alliance (SAWPY) Activities. The highest organ of the SAWPY, its Federal Conference, held two plenary sessions during the year. The first met on 26 January and the main report was delivered by Dušan Petrović, the president of the Presidium of the FC. Petrović dealt with the problems of the country's defense and the role to be played by the SAWPY in this respect. Petrović, who died in July, indirectly accused the Soviet Union and its allies of trying to undermine Yugoslavia's independence and internal security. He also denounced some "former Cominformists" and the followers of Aleksandar Ranković (purged in July 1966), as well as Milovan Djilas and the *Praxis* group, for trying to harm Yugoslavia's self-management system. Petrović said that "various Stalinist and neo-Stalinist forces have been exerting continuous pressure upon the international workers' movement in general and upon Socialist and self-managing Yugoslavia in particular." Some unnamed "neighboring countries" were blamed for exerting "pressure upon our nationalities," while "hostile elements among our exiles" were said to have intensified their actions against Yugoslavia (*Borba*, 27 January).

The second plenary session of the SAWPY's FC, on 14 December, concentrated on the situafion in the Socialist sector of agriculture. The official report insisted that private peasants had to be permitted voluntarily to decide whether to join agricultural cooperatives or not. The same report made known that in Yugoslavia there were 28,000 villages, and that annually between 700,000 and 900,000 hectares of arable land remained untilled. (Ibid., 15 December.)

The executive organ of SAWPY's FC, its Presidium, met seven times in 1977. Its 18 January session passed two resolutions: one dealing with the SAWPY tasks in implementation of the Helsinki agreements, and the other promising full support and aid to the people of South Africa (ibid., 30 January). The meeting of 25 April approved a report regarding SAWPY activities in furthering the system of delegations at all levels (ibid., 26 April). The next, on 2 June, discussed the role of the SAWPY in the development of Socialist self-managing democracy and of collaboration with political parties and movements on the African continent (ibid., 3 June). The Presidium's session of 23 June handled the problem of the country's political-economic stability (ibid., 24 June).

The economically and politically delicate problem of manpower export was discussed at the 20 September Presidium meeting. According to official Yugoslav data, in Western Europe in 1977 there were "more than 800,000 of our workers, some of whom have been there 'temporarily' for more than ten years." (Ibid., 12 November.) The most important task to be carried out was how to employ these workers returning home from abroad. A great number of the Yugoslavs employed in Western countries think that by working abroad the Yugoslav workers "help the strengthening of the capitalist system" (*NIN*, Belgrade, 9 October). A report, delivered at the meeting, stressed the danger of the "hostile exiles" trying to influence Yugoslav workers abroad. It mentioned both the "fascist-terroristic" and the "Cominformist" exiles as enemies (*Borba*, 21 September).

The Presidium's session on 22 November discussed the performance of the information media. The main report criticized "many quasi-liberalistic views" in the Yugoslav press. It asserted that the press must be "creative rather than apologetic and oppositional," and that "freedom of political action in Yugoslavia cannot be given to the counterrevolutionary forces trying to impose their forms of government, i.e., the exploitation, the subjugation of our country or its destruction. . . . Freedom cannot have any supra-class character." (Ibid., 23 November.) A four-point resolution, adopted at the session, stated that all information media have to establish their "operational tasks" designed to implement party decisions (ibid., 26 November).

Finally, the Presidium on 13 December discussed the perspectives for the economic and social developments of the country in 1978 and the SAWPY's tasks in these developments. In the chair was Marin Cetinić, who became acting president of the Presidium after Dušan Petrović's death.

Edvard Kardelj and Self-Managing Pluralism. On 11 November, in Zagreb, Kardelj addressed a conference of the Croatian Socialist Alliance attended by delegates from all six republics of the country and its two autonomous provinces. In a long and significant speech Kardelj emphasized the necessity to change the organizational forms and the work methods of the essential political entities ("the subjective factors of Socialism") in the country. He endorsed Lenin's views about the insufficiency of the spontaneous activity of the working class that could result only in an empirical trade unionism. He assailed three enemies of the Yugoslav system: (1) the liberalistic tendency with its catchword "freedom," (2) the ultra-left tendency which "stresses primarily the decision making by meetings of workers . . . and which has an almost hostile attitude toward the role of subjective forces of Socialism in the entire system and in particular toward the social role of the League of Communists," (3) a "technocratic tendency," i.e., the subordination of political bodies to the "managerial technocratic interests," which, if successful, would make the LCY "the policeman of the technocratic structure."

After stating that Yugoslavia has abandoned the system of parliamentarianism in all its aspects, including one-party rule, and has replaced it with a new system of delegates as a direct expression of the self-managing organized working people, Kardelj discussed the still unresolved problems of the political functioning of that new system of total "collectiveness." He admitted the failure of the communes, which contrary to expectation have become "bureaucratic organizations." He also warned about the danger for the LCY of isolating itself from the masses, and for the SAWPY in persisting in "deeply anchored forum-like work," i.e., adopting resolutions without caring whether or not they will be implemented. As a way out, Kardelj stated that "we must do our utmost to insure the leading political-ideological role of the LCY" as "an integral part of the self-management democratic system." No less important, in his opinion, was the need for the SAWPY to assume a better-defined role as the "link" between the self-management delegates system and the LCY. As he envisioned the indispensable restructuring, the SAWPY—as the most massive "front" organization, opening the doors to everybody who adheres to the working class positions—would be the bridge between the workers' delegates, coping with the economic problems through the multiple organisms defined in the new Yugoslav constitution, and the LCY, remaining the political backbone of the entire system (*Borba*, 12, 13 November).

Kardelj's own description of the present uncertainties and functioning difficulties of the Yugoslav system, as well as his vague remedies to resolve them, demonstrated how complicated it has become to harmonize a self-management system being developed from below and a party machinery centralistically administered from above.

Nationalism in Serbia. Following strong party attacks against him, Dragan Jeremić, 52, a noted Serbian writer and critic, resigned as president of the Writers' Union of Serbia (*Politika*, 7 September). Jeremić, the editor in chief of Belgrade's most prominent literary journal, was accused of propagating nationalism by having published a poem by a Serbian poet and former partisan fighter, Tanasije Mladenović, 64, which lamented the sad fate that has overtaken Serbia (*Književne novine*, 1 April). In attacking Jeremić *Politika* suggested that the most important reason for Jeremić's condemnation was the fact that two Serbian-language newspapers published in the United States reproduced Mladenović's poem.

On 3 October, the LCY weekly *Komunist* attacked Serbia's most prominent author, Dobrica Ćosić, 55, for his speech delivered on 29 March in the Serbian Academy of Sciences, which had accepted him as a member. Ćosić was expelled from the Serbian Central Committee in May 1968, allegedly for what was termed his "Serbian nationalism." In fact he was being punished together with another Serbian intellectual, Professor Jovan Marjanović, for having protested against anti-Serbian excesses in Croatia, which in December 1971 led to major purges of "Croatian nationalists." *Komunist* repeated its anti-Ćosić attacks two months later (5 December), accusing him of "abusing the freedom of thought" and of falsifying facts by having deplored Serbia's "sad situation" in Yugoslavia. In his 29 March speech Ćosić deplored the fact that, in a short historical period of time, the Serbian people had "suffered from successive waves of genocide perpetrated by the Austro-Hungarians, fascists, and Ustashis" and been brought "to the verge of biological extinction."

The 1977 assaults against "Serbian nationalism" differed from those in the past by creating the impression that they had assumed this time a different nature. In the past "Serbian nationalists" were attacked for supporting the Yugoslav "unitarian state" rather than for trying to create a separate Serbian state. This has now changed.

Arrests and Amnesty. On 23 November the Yugoslav information media reported that Mileta Perović, 54, a pro-Soviet Cominformist leader living in the West (see *YICA, 1977,* pp. 111-20) had been arrested in Yugoslavia and would be brought to trial "for various criminal acts against the people and the state" (*Večernje novosti,* 23 November). A few weeks later, on 16 December, Reuters and other European news agencies announced that Perović's closest political associate among the Cominformist exiles, Professor Bogdan Jovović, had also been arrested by Yugoslav police.

On the Day of the Republic, celebrated on 29 November, the Yugoslav government announced the amnesty of 724 prisoners, including 218 political ones. The most prominent among them were the writer Mihajlo Mihajlov, the Croat professor Marko Veselica, the former Serbian anti-Communist politician Djura Djurović, and the Slovene judge Franc Miklavčič. Among the pardoned was also the Cominformist leader Komnen Jovović, while two other Cominformists, Dušan Brkić and Milivoje Stevanović, had their terms reduced by three years each (*Politika,* 25 November).

Economy. Despite great efforts to improve the deteriorating economic situation in the country, the economic performance in 1977 was poorer than expected. As in the previous year, measures taken were chiefly designed to expedite institutional and structural changes in accordance both with the new Law on Associated Labor (see *YICA, 1977,* pp. 99-100) and the new five-year plan adopted in 1976. As early as February, several top Yugoslav officials expressed their deep concern about the country's economic development. At a session devoted to the economic development, the party Presidium's Executive Committee pointed out dangerous distortions in economic development (*Vjesnik,* 12 February). The EC secretary, Stane Dolanc, said in a speech in Ljubljana that all party members had to unite "all their forces in helping to solve the serious situation in which Yugoslavia's economy currently finds itself" (*Večernje novosti,* 20 February). Finally, Yugoslavia's deputy prime minister, Dr. Berislav Šefer, warned in an interview that the negative trends noted at the beginning of 1977, if not brought under control, might provoke "unfavorable economic, social, and political consequences" (*Borba,* 25 February).

In the first ten months of 1977 Yugoslavia's exports amounted to 71,616 million dinars (about U.S. $4,212; $1 = 17 dinars) and imports to 134,521 million dinars (about $7,913 million), which means that the trade deficit in the first ten months was 62,905 million dinars (about $3,000 million) (*Ekonomska politika,* 28 November). The deficit in the balance of payments amounted in 1977 to $1,500 million (*NIN,* 4 December). The foreign currency reserves amounted, according to an estimate, to $1,500 million. The largest share of the country's indebtedness abroad ($4,800 million) resulted from imports of goods on credit, of which sum $4,300 million were used for the purchase of equipment. Yugoslavia's foreign debts amounted at the beginning of 1977 to $7,000 million. (Ibid.)

The level of prices was rather high; in comparison to 1976 the living costs increased by 15.2 percent (*Vus,* 12 November). As far as the retail prices are concerned, the official data revealed that in the first ten months of 1977 (compared with the same period in 1976) these prices increased by 31.1 percent. Inflation amounted to 11.6 percent (ibid.).

It was the losses of 3,324 enterprises in Yugoslavia, amounting to 1,500 million dinars (about $88,235,000), in the first nine months of 1977, which contributed much to the deterioration of the economic situation in some parts of the country (*Politika,* 22 November). In the enterprises working at a loss, 787,000 workers were employed (ibid.), out of a total of 5,130,000 workers employed in the country's Socialist sector (*Vjesnik,* 6 December). Along with more than 800,000 workers abroad, there were in Yugoslavia itself "about 700,000 unemployed persons" (ibid.). The average monthly salary of Yugoslav workers in the first six months of 1977 amounted to 3,970 dinars (about $233), with the workers in Slovenia paid best (4,541 dinars, or $267), followed by Croatia (4,237 dinars, or $249), Serbia (3,881 dinars, or $228), Vojvodina (3,869 dinars, or $228), Bosnia-Hercegovina (3,661 dinars, or $215), Montenegro (3,522 dinars, or $207), Kosovo (3,318 dinars, or $195), and Macedonia (3,292 dinars, or $193) (*Vus,* 12 November).

Official figures published in August showed that Yugoslavia's harvest was good, totaling about 5,600,000 tons of wheat, which was 400,000 tons less than in 1976 and 700,000 less than in the record year of 1974. Per hectare yield was maintained at 1976 record level; despite the fact that wheat was sown on 1,609,000 hectares, 10 percent less than in 1976, the 1977 average yield of 35 quintals still equaled the per hectare yield of 1976, which was the biggest wheat crop in the history of Yugoslavia (*Vjesnik*, 14 August).

The maize yield amounted to about 10,000,000 tons (*Borba*, 24 November), which means that an average yield of about 45 quintals per hectare was achieved. Since the annual domestic consumption of maize in 1977 was around 8,500,000 tons, about 1,500,000 could be exported (*NIN*, 21 August).

Foreign Affairs. As so often in the past, Yugoslav foreign relations in 1977, on both state and party levels, were conducted essentially through Tito's extensive trips abroad, East as well as West.

Tito's Visits to USSR, North Korea, and China. Tito spent twenty-four days visiting the Soviet Union (16-24 August), North Korea (24-30 August), and China (30 August-8 September). Returning home, he made a stopover of three hours in Tehran, where he met the Shah. More than a half million people turned out to welcome him in Belgrade. The brief statement which he read devoted thirty lines to the visit to the Soviet Union, eighteen lines to North Korea, and thirty lines to China. Tito was at pains to treat the two superpowers equally, even to the extent of shading the truth slightly: he spoke of the welcome he had received "in all the three countries" where "many hundreds of thousands of people" had cheered him (*Borba*, 9 September). Thus was true of North Korea and China, but not of the Soviet Union.

On his trip to the USSR, Tito was accompanied by Stane Dolanc, secretary of the Executive Committee of the LCY's Central Committee Presidium; Aleksandar Grličkov, the Executive Committee member in charge of relations with foreign Communist parties; Miloš Minić, the country's foreign minister and Presidium member; Veljko Milatović, president of the Socialist Republic of Montenegro and Presidium member; Emil Ludviger, the Yugoslav government member in charge of foreign trade; and Jože Smole, Yugoslavia's ambassador to Moscow and a party Presidium member. The only non-party person in the delegation was Emil Ludviger, whose role in the Moscow meeting was, nevertheless, rather prominent, in view of Tito's efforts to increase Yugoslav-Soviet trade and get more credits from Moscow.

The joint communiqué published after Tito's four-day party-state visit to Moscow had the routine wording known from the communiqués following previous Brezhnev-Tito meetings. Still, the 19 August communiqué—especially the section dealing with bilateral Yugoslav-Soviet party relations—reflected the Yugoslav insistence on "freedom of choice of different ways of social development" (*Politika*, 20 August). In this connection, the Belgrade Declaration of 1955, the Moscow Declaration of 1956, the September 1971 joint statement, and the November 1976 joint communiqué were mentioned, even though Brezhnev had not said a word about any of them in his toast a couple of days earlier. On the other hand, a comparison of the November 1976 and August 1977 joint communiqués shows that the former was a much greater success for Tito than the latter. This is especially true concerning the disagreements between Moscow and Belgrade over the situation within the international Communist movement. In the 1977 communiqué the two sides were at pains to avoid mentioning the word "differences," while in November 1976 a whole paragraph was devoted to differences. The 1977 communiqué also did not mention two points which the Yugoslavs have always considered essential both for their relations with Moscow and for the situation within the international Communist movement: "The freedom to choose different ways of socialist development" and "the responsibility to one's own working class" (*YICA, 1976*, p. 105). These omissions were of special significance in the light of the polemics within the movement triggered by the 24 June *Novoe vremya* (Moscow) attack on Santiago Carrillo, which the Yugoslavs had followed with close critical attentiveness.

Another problem in the Soviet-Yugoslav relations discussed by Tito and Brezhnev was that of the economic relations between the two countries. One day before Tito's arrival a Belgrade paper said that the sum of $2,500 million as this year's trade volume between Yugoslavia and the USSR had been "conspicuously emphasized" by the Soviet information media, but asked whether "some unused possibilities" existed that might help solve "certain open problems concerning further boosting of the current bilateral economic relations" (*Politika*, 15 August). It is a well-known fact that Moscow has not been eager to expand the November 1972 credit arrangement, according to which Yugoslavia was promised a huge credit of $1,300 million for the period up to 1980, of which only two installments were made public: $540 million between 1973 and 1976, and $450 million between 1976 and 1980. The first installment is claimed by the Yugoslavs to have been almost exhausted, but under conditions that the Yugoslavs considered not very equitable, especially when it came to the prices of Soviet equipment, "which have notably changed over the past five years"—as Yugoslav Vice-Premier Berislav Šefer stated after his return from Moscow in July (Tanjug, in English, 21 July). It was, therefore, strange to read in the joint communiqué that "the proper offices in the two countries" were to "begin jointly drafting" a long-range economic program (*Politika*, 20 August). Such a program is believed to have been agreed upon in November 1972.

Tito and his entourage left Moscow on 19 August for a five-day rest at Lake Baikal before flying to Pyongyang. Heading the same party-government delegation that accompanied him to Moscow, Tito received a triumphal reception during his stay in North Korea. In a joint communiqué dated 29 August, the Yugoslav and North Korean presidents hailed their countries' struggle for independence and the "great successes" achieved by their parties. Tito condemned "imperialist quarters and the South Korean regime for their plan to create 'two Koreas' in an attempt to perpetuate the division of Korea," while Kim Il-song "greeted and expressed full solidarity with Yugoslavia in the struggle for the establishment of equal relations in the international field based on independence" and gave Yugoslavia credit "for its contribution to the active promotion of nonalignment" (*Borba*, 30 August).

The North Korean president, who visited Yugoslavia in June 1975, abundantly demonstrated his admiration for his visitor. Nonetheless, he avoided talking much about the international Communist movement—the pet topic of Tito—and placed the accent on the non-aligned movement, of which North Korea has been a full member since the Lima conference in August 1975. Tito and his colleagues were deeply impressed by the reception given them in Pyongyang, as he made clear in a toast on 25 August. In a special report from the North Korean capital, a Yugoslav paper enthusiastically recorded: "The capital of the DPRK received Tito in a manner reserved for guests who are highly respected and much loved" (*Vjesnik*, Zagreb, 26 August).

President Kim's expressions of admiration for Tito were obviously not without an element of self-interest. The Koreans reported on 28 August that Kim told a mass rally of more than 100,000 Pyongyang citizens that he had won President Tito's agreement in opposing the "two Koreas of the imperialists and colonialists and in supporting and encouraging the struggle for independence and peaceful unification" (KCNA, 28 August). There was in fact no question of "winning" Tito's support for North Korean views on this subject, for during Kim's June 1975 visit to Yugoslavia the joint communiqué recorded Tito's full support for his visitor's policies, including "the speedy withdrawal of all foreign troops—located in South Korea under the banner of the UN—whose presence constitutes a primary obstacle to the unification of the country" (*Borba*, 11 June 1975).

Tito and his delegation arrived in Peking on 30 August, and were there until 3 September, rounding out a ten-day visit with stopovers at Hangchow, Shanghai, and Urumchi, northwestern Sinkiang. No joint communiqué was published, because, according to Yugoslav reporters accompanying Tito, "it is not the custom in China to publish joint communiqués on such meetings" (Radio Belgrade, 3 September). They claimed, however, that even without such a document, it was "completely clear to all observers" that Tito's talk with Hua Kuo-feng had been "a historic dialogue." The two leaders were said to have agreed on almost all issues except for "certain differences in their approach to and understanding of the causes of détente and the problems of disarmament." (Ibid.)

Everywhere he went Tito was given an enthusiastic welcome by flower-waving and dancing youths, and by tens of thousands of citizens who lined the streets. According to a Belgrade daily, it was discovered that, in Chinese, "Ti-to" means "unyielding steel" (*Borba*, 27 August), which, strangely enough, appears to be very close to the Russian meaning of the name Stalin. In his toast at a banquet in Shanghai, Tito said his talks with Hua had been "very open, cordial, and fruitful," and expressed the hope that Chinese-Yugoslav relations—"primarily economic, scientific, and other kinds of cooperation"—would expand in the future (*Politika*, 6 September).

The fact that Stane Dolanc, secretary of the Executive Committee of the Presidium, and Aleksandar Grličkov, Executive Committee member in charge of relations with ruling Communist parties, were included in Tito's delegation created the impression that Tito and Hua would discuss interparty relations, which were unilaterally broken off by Mao in 1958. Nothing of the kind had happened, although almost to the last minute the Yugoslav information media continued to hope that relations between the two parties would be renewed. In his speech in Belgrade after the return from China, Tito did not mention ideological matters discussed previously by the Yugoslav information media. The only Chinese gestures concerning party links were that the Yugoslav president was addressed as "Comrade Tito" and that, during his visit to Mao's mausoleum, he was referred to first as "President of the League of Communists of Yugoslavia" and only secondly as "President of the Socialist Federative Republic of Yugoslavia" (*Politika*, 1 September). The Belgrade correspondent said that the use of the term "comrade" might seem at first glance a small matter, but "in view of Chinese precision it is a very important detail" (ibid.).

Yet, since Hua not only accorded Tito a triumphal reception but even claimed it was Mao Tsetung who had proposed such a treatment for the Yugoslav leader (*Borba*, 1 September), one cannot escape the conclusion that Tito scored a victory similar to that of May 1955 when Nikita Khrushchev came to Belgrade to apologize for Moscow's mistakes, especially in view of the fact that in 1958 the Chinese attacked the "Tito gang" as "anti-Marxist" supporters of "American imperialists" (*People's Daily*, Peking, 5 May 1958). Three weeks after his return from Peking, Tito revealed that Hua Kuo-feng had promised to visit Yugoslavia (*Borba*, 29 September).

Tito's Visits to France, Portugal, and Algeria. On 12-14 October, Tito paid an official visit to France at the invitation of France's President Valéry Giscard d'Estaing, who visited Yugoslavia in December 1976. Tito's last visit to France was in 1956. This time he was accompanied by Jakov Blazević, president of the Presidency of the Socialist Republic of Croatia; Milos Minić, foreign minister; Janko Smole, member of the government in charge of economic cooperation; and Radomir Radović, Yugoslavia's ambassador to France. The Yugoslav president was received with great pomp and even the French Communist party organ, *Humanité* (13 October), called Tito "a militant Communist" and criticized Stalin for expelling him and the Yugoslav party from the Cominform. Smole discussed with French officials chances for expanding and balancing trade between the two countries. Yugoslavia had a trade deficit of more than $235 million for the first eight months in 1977. French exports to Yugoslavia had increased by 61 percent, while Yugoslav exports to France grew by 41 percent (Tanjug in English, 13 October).

In a joint communiqué it was said that the two presidents discussed all important international problems as well as bilateral relations between the two countries (*Borba*, 15 October). While in Paris Tito also met with Jacques Chirac, mayor of Paris and leader of the Gaullist party.

After resting for two days in France, Tito paid an official visit to Portugal on 17-20 October. In a joint communiqué it was said that he discussed European and African problems during separate meetings with President Antonio Eanes and Premier Mario Soarés, who is also acting foreign minister. (Ibid, 21 October.) On 18 October Soarés and Minić signed an agreement on economic, scientific, and technological cooperation (*Politika*, 19 October).

On 20 and 21 October, Tito paid a "friendly visit" to Algeria, called "a short and working visit," with no joint communiqué issued. The main topic of the talks was the preparations for the next non-aligned conference in Havana (*Borba*, 22 October). In his conversations with Algerian President Houari Boumedienne, Tito is said to have also exchanged views on the Mediterranean problems and the leftist developments in West European countries. He also informed Boumedienne about his trips to the Soviet Union, North Korea, China, France, and Portugal.

Tito-Ceauşescu Meeting. Over the weekend 3-4 December, Tito and Romanian President Nicolae Ceauşescu met in the Romanian town of Drobeta-Turnu Severin at the Yugoslav-Romanian border to inaugurate the second stage of the common Iron Gates hydroelectric project on the Danube. The project is designed to permit steady passage of large ships throughout the year. Along with the bilateral relations which have been developing favorably for many years and a variety of other topics for a discussion, it seems that one of the real reasons for the meeting stemmed from Egyptian President Sadat's 19-21 November visit to Israel. Both Tito and Ceauşescu have special interest in the Middle East: the Yugoslav president as one of the non-aligned leaders, while the Romanian president was said to have done much to arrange Sadat's dramatic visit. Both Israeli Prime Minister Menahem Begin and the Egyptian president visited Romania before their meeting in Jerusalem. Tito, officially for reasons of health, canceled Sadat's projected subsequent visit to Yugoslavia on his way back from Bucharest. It was widely suggested that Tito might have learned about Sadat's plans to meet Begin and might have wanted to dissociate himself from an undertaking possibly offensive to some of Yugoslavia's other Arab allies. The Middle East did, indeed, figure both in the dinner toasts and the final communiqué. At the banquet, Tito stated that "Israel has the undubitable right to its existence," but he also called on Arab countries to mend their internal relations, describing them as "extremely unfavorable to date," and unify their positions on solving the Middle East dispute (*Politika*, 5 December).

In the joint 2,500-word communiqué it was said that Israel had to withdraw from Arab lands occupied in the 1967 war and that "recognition of the legitimate national rights of the Palestinian people, including the right to the formation of an independent state," was a part of "a just and lasting solution to the Middle East crisis." The communiqué also pledged "to continue consistent support for the affirmation of new democratic principles" in interparty relations, reaffirming the right of all parties "freely to choose the roads" for their respective revolutions to follow. Ceauşescu and Tito likewise called for an all-European conference to discuss broader economic and cultural cooperation in which UN agencies could play an important role (*Borba*, 5 December).

The United States. Tense and occasionally very unfriendly relations between the U.S. and Yugoslavia during the greater part of 1976 (see *YICA, 1977*, pp. 106-7) were replaced in 1977 by a high degree of official cordiality, especially on the American side. Shortly before meeting with Tito in Belgrade, on 21 May, U.S. Vice-President Mondale stated that relations between the two countries were "on the finest possible basis." He seemed, however, embarrassed when Tito in his presence politely but firmly declared—in reference to President Carter's human rights policy—that he would not be lectured on the subject of civil rights in Yugoslavia (*NYT*, 22 May).

The improvement of relations was particularly obvious when Edvard Kardelj paid an official visit to Washington between 28 September and 5 October, meeting President Carter, Vice-President Mondale, and other top American political personalities. Kardelj, who is considered to be the most probable successor to Tito, and is a member of the Presidency of the SFRY, was accompanied by Yugoslavia's foreign trade minister, Emil Ludviger, and deputy foreign minister, Dragan Bernardić. While in Washington Kardelj discussed political, military, and economic issues. During his talks with

President Carter on 30 September, Kardelj presented to him a written message from President Tito, as a reply to Carter's earlier message. The U.S. President stated that friendship with Yugoslavia was among basic principles of U.S. foreign policy and greeted "Yugoslavia's independent democratic road." He also welcomed Tito's acceptance of his invitation to visit the United States while Kardelj answered that Tito would come to Washington "in the beginning of next year" (*Borba*, 1 October).

Upon his return to Belgrade Kardelj said that during his Washington talks special emphasis was put on the policy of détente, disarmament, non-alignment, the Belgrade conference on European security, the Middle East, and the situation in Africa. He also stated that differences existing between the two countries should not be an obstacle to their further successful relations. Kardelj stressed especially the "extraordinary friendly welcome" he was accorded in the Congress and Senate. The American officials, he sid, "did not spare the words to convince us that the U.S. would continue to take energetic measures against all forces, including the terrorists, trying to hamper friendly relations between Yugoslavia and the United States" (*Komunist*, 10 October).

The official relationship notwithstanding, there were other voices in the United States highly critical of the Yugoslav policies and the American reaction to them. For example, a former U.S. ambassador to Yugoslavia, Laurence Silberman, who resigned his post in November 1976, wrote an article in the spring 1977 issue of the prominent Washington review *Foreign Policy*, in which he assailed both Tito's domestic and foreign political behavior. He denounced Yugoslav Communists for guarding jealously their political monopoly and dreading any real pluralism in Eastern Europe since its contagion would endanger their own dictatorial rule. Likewise, he found Yugoslavia, "an unstructured part of the worldwide Communist movement," to be "almost invariably on the opposite side of every issue in world politics that matters to the United States." He attacked especially Yugoslavia's leadership role in the evolution of the non-aligned countries toward the dictatorial left and increased hostility to the United States. By the end of the year, in a letter to the *New York Times* (14 November), Silberman contrasted the official U.S. warming toward Yugoslavia and the latter's "recent sending of U.S. arms to Ethiopia in blatant violation of solemn agreements with this country."

The Belgrade Conference on European Security and Cooperation. On 15 June the thirty-five countries that signed the Helsinki agreement on European security and cooperation in August 1975 began a follow-up conference in Belgrade with an appeal from Yugoslavia's foreign minister, Miloš Minić, to show a constructive and positive approach (*Borba*, 16 June). Minić expressed the view that détente could succeed only if it evolved in accordance with principles established by the Helsinki conference. He warned against "sinister forces which oppose détente and which resort to all sorts of means, from propaganda campaigns to various forms of pressure and acts of terrorism, in the attempt to undermine the relaxation of international tension and to thwart the efforts aimed at strengthening of confidence, security and international cooperation in Europe and the world." (Ibid.)

A day before, Tito urged the nations attending the Belgrade conference to assess compliance with the 1975 Helsinki accords, to hold "patient talks," and to "avoid confrontations" (*Politika*, 15 June). The confrontation, however, came in connection with human rights, over which Western and Eastern delegates clashed at the conference. The Yugoslav attitude was carefully presented by Milorad Pešić, the country's delegate at the conference. He stated that the approach to human rights must not amount to intervention in the internal affairs of other countries, but that national sovereignty should not be used to justify violations of human rights (*Borba*, 6 October).

The Balkans. During 1977 polemics between Yugoslav and Bulgarian information media continued. In an interview with the Greek ANA news agency, Yugoslav Foreign Minister Minić declared that Yugoslav-Bulgarian relations were not "very good" because of the Macedonian issue. He said "in question is the problem of the Macedonian national minority in Bulgaria and Bulgaria's attitude toward the Macedonian nation as a whole." (Ibid., 12 January.) A long article dealing with the "Roots of the

Greater Bulgarian Nationalism" was published in a LCY monthly (*Socijalizam*, Belgrade, no. 2, February 1977). A Bulgarian encyclopedia was attacked as "full of untruths and distortions" (Radio Zagreb, 25 June). In Geneva the Yugoslav and Bulgarian delegates clashed at a session of the UN Subcommission for the Struggle against Discrimination and the Protection of National Minorities (*Nova Makedonija*, Skopje, 3 September). A Bulgarian exhibition in the United States presenting a "distorted map" of Yugoslavia was sharply criticized (*Politika*, 10 September). The East German-Bulgarian Treaty of Friendship, Cooperation, and Mutual Assistance, signed in Sofia by Erich Honecker and Todor Zhivkov on 14 September, elicited negative comments in Yugoslavia (see below). From 4 to 24 November a series of eighteen installments appeared in a Belgrade daily (*Večernje novosti*) describing the alleged persecution of the Macedonians in Bulgaria. Conversely, the Bulgarian weekly *Pogled* (19 December) accused the same Belgrade paper of disseminating abroad "provocative" and "anti-Socialist" information about Bulgaria.

Everything, however, was not negative in the Yugoslav-Bulgarian relations. The trade between the two countries is expected to reach the $1,300-million mark (in both directions) between 1976 and 1980. Eleven Yugoslav and two Bulgarian banks formed a consortium for financing long-term cooperation between enterprises in the two countries, and "a tripartite agreement between Yugoslavia, Bulgaria, and Romania for the construction of a hydrotechnical complex on the Danube" was concluded. (*Večernje novosti*, 17 January).

With the improvement of Yugoslav-Chinese relations, those between Tirana and Belgrade deteriorated. During the past two years Tirana avoided any sharpening of the conflict fearing that anti-Yugoslav activities would strengthen pro-Moscow groups in Yugoslavia. The efforts made by Peking to improve its relations with Tito annoyed the Albanians to such an extent that they began open criticism of both the Chinese and the Yugoslavs. On 2 September the Albanian information media carried a lengthy article written by Albanian party First Secretary Enver Hoxha almost fourteen years ago. Hoxha's article was first published as an editorial in the Albanian party daily *Zeri i Popullit* on 13 September 1963 under the title "Khrushchev Kneeling before Tito." The article was distributed by the Albanian Embassy in Peking on 2 September 1977, at the moment Tito was accorded an overwhelming reception by Hua Kuo-feng.

The strongest anti-Yugoslav attack was made by Albania's Prime Minister Mehmet Shehu on 29 November, marking Yugoslavia's independence and liberation anniversaries. Shehu attacked Yugoslavia openly and China indirectly. In attacking Yugoslavia he appealed to the nationalistic feelings of the Albanian minority in Kosovo, while in connection with China he alluded to an alleged Chinese plot against the Albanian leadership. Shehu called Tito "the father of modern revisionism" because of which "all revisionists, from wherever they may be, pay great honors to him, welcome him in a pompous manner, and consider him to be their savior and god" (Radio Tirana, 29 November). Yugoslav reaction to the Albanian outbursts was muted.

East-Central Europe. With the sole exception of Bulgaria, Czechoslovakia was the Communist country against which the Yugoslavs polemicized the most during 1977. From the beginning of the Charter 77 affair the Yugoslav information media concentrated on straight reporting. They published both the official Czechoslovak commentaries and the criticisms leveled against Prague by the Italian, French, and British Communist organs; a hostile article in the Moscow *Izvestiia* was also reprinted. Although the commentators did their utmost to remain impartial, they did not hide the fact that Belgrade's sympathies were not necessarily with the official Czechoslovak party line (*NIN*, 23 January). A Zagreb daily distinguished between "good" and "bad" dissidents in Czechoslovakia (*Vjesnik*, 23 January). Since 1968 the Yugoslavs have regarded Czechoslovakia as a symbol of Soviet domination, and have frequently berated Prague's acceptance of proletarian internationalism, meaning Soviet domination (*NYT*, 2 February). The "intolerant attitude" of the Czechoslovak information media was strongly criticized in Belgrade (*Borba*, 5 February). The Czechoslovaks answered in the same tone (*Mlada Fronta*, 17 February), pointedly referring to a sharply worded reportage published in a Belgrade weekly (*Duga*, 5 February). The reportage was so biting that a LCY weekly (*Komunist*, 28 February) criticized it for giving what it called "an unacceptable picture of the current political climate in Czechoslovakia."

A group of ninety-two Serbian intellectuals sent a letter to the leaders of the Charter 77 group in Prague conveying to them their "full support." In the meantime a drama by a Macedonian author was banned in Bratislava (*Borba*, 8 March) while a Yugoslav army paper described some articles in the Czechoslovak and Bulgarian press about World War II as "manipulations with historical facts designed to justify momentary policy needs" (*Narodna armija*, 17 March). The Czechoslovak official attitude to Eurocommunism was reprimanded (*Politika*, 1 July) and Czechoslovak views of the Soviet constitution were criticized (ibid., 15 September). At the end of September the Yugoslavs defended China and Eurocommunism against Czechoslovak attacks (*NIN*, 25 September).

Between 26 and 28 October, Yugoslavia's premier, Veselin Djuranović, paid an official visit to Czechoslovakia. He met Czechoslovak Premier Lubomir Strougal and party leader Gustav Husák. In a joint communiqué it was stated that Yugoslavia and Czechoslovakia were to look for new ways to increase economic cooperation (Tanjug, 28 October). The trade between the two countries in the next five-year period is expected to amount to $4,300 million (*Borba*, 28 October).

Yugoslav-Polish relations were developing in 1977 almost without any disturbance, but with occasional mutual press criticism. The Yugoslav information media reported about the Polish regime's conflict with the "intellectual opposition" (*Vjesnik*, 19 January). In its 10 November issue a Belgrade daily (*Večernje novosti*) sharply attacked a report in the Polish weekly *Zycie Literackie* (23 October) in which the situation in Yugoslavia was described "in an extremely insipid manner." At the end of March the Polish deputy minister of defense paid an official visit to Belgrade and met with the Yugoslav defense minister (*Borba*, 30 March). A delegation of the Yugoslav parliamentarians paid a six-day visit to Warsaw (*Politika*, 19 June). Between 23 and 26 October Yugoslav Premier Djuranović paid an official visit to Poland. The central topic of his talks in Warsaw was the expansion of Polish-Yugoslav relations. In a joint communiqué both sides pledged to continue to develop their relations on the principles of independence and noninterference in internal affairs (Tanjug, 26 October). The trade between the two countries up to 1980 is envisaged to amount to $3,200 million; the 1977 Yugoslav deficit in trading with Poland was $45 million (*Vjesnik*, 23 October).

From 12 to 15 January, Erich Honecker, East Germany's Communist party chief and State Council chairman, paid an official visit to Yugoslavia. This was Honecker's first visit to Belgrade in his capacity of state and party leader. In a joint communiqué signed on 14 January the two governments pledged to respect the full independence of their countries in internal and foreign affairs. It also asserted respect by both countries for their various ways of Socialist development as "the firm and permanent basis for further improvement of mutually beneficial cooperation in all areas" (*Politika*, 15 January). Commenting on his talks with Honecker, Tito declared that such an agreement was made possible by the June 1976 meeting of Communist and workers' parties in East Berlin (ibid.). In September the Yugoslav information media criticized the East German-Bulgarian Treaty of Friendship providing for the right of either of the two countries to intervene if one of them required outside help to solve its "internal problems." Since East Germany and Bulgaria have no common frontier, the Yugoslavs were afraid that the armed forces of the one would have to pass through third countries in order to provide such "support" for the other (*Politika*, 23 September).

The 1975 trade exchange between the two countries totaled $390 million, with a balance of $33 million favorable to Yugoslavia (*Indeks*, Belgrade, February 1976). The trade agreement signed between Yugoslavia and East Germany in April 1976 provided for goods exchange totaling about $3,000 million over the next five-year period (Tanjug, 2 April 1976). On 4 February 1977 a protocol on amendments in the payments agreement between the two countries was signed in Belgrade providing for the value of trade to amount in 1977 to about $620 million (Tanjug, 4 February).

Non-alignment. The general Yugoslav attitude about non-alignment has been that the movement "must rid itself of, not create, the attributes of a closed group" because the non-aligned movement "is sufficiently strong not to be afraid of the theses about the Trojan Horse which might penetrate its ranks" (*Review of International Affairs*, Belgrade, no. 652, 20 June 1977). Explaining the differences between the terms "neutrality" and "non-alignment," the Yugoslav analysts admitted that "a certain degree of similarity and even identity (which is not absolute, of course) can be detected when comparing the aims of the non-aligned with those of the neutral countries in international life." They see neutrality as a "legal institution" while non-alignment "is first and foremost a political category." (Ibid., no. 653, 5 July.)

Throughout the year, however, Tito and many of his colleagues did not hide their pessimism concerning the future of non-alignment over the world. Tito's 1977 foreign trips were permeated with his concern about the unity and future of non-alignment. In a speech at Zagreb in September, Tito said that while a large number of countries had asked to be admitted to the non-aligned movement, "some of them did not meet the existing criteria for membership because of their connection with one power or another." He added, however, that "these obstacles will be removed one day, since we must be a little more flexible than we have been previously" (*Borba*, 28 September). He also said that conflicts among some non-aligned countries were being increasingly stimulated from the outside, and cited as examples conflicts between Ethiopia and Somalia, between Angola and some neighboring countries, as well as between some other African states. President Sadat's dramatic move to meet Israel's Premier Begin led Yugoslav information media to express misgivings as to what might happen to non-aligned countries as the consequence of the Egyptian-Israeli rapprochement.

Publications. The chief publications of the LCY are *Komunist* (weekly) and *Socijalizam* (monthly). The most important daily newspapers are *Borba* (with Belgrade and Zagreb editions), *Politika* (Belgrade), *Vjesnik* (Zagreb), *Nova Makedonija* (Skoplje), *Oslobodjenje* (Sarajevo), and *Delo* (Ljubljana). The most important weeklies are NIN (*Nedeljne informativne novine*) (Belgrade), *Vus* (*Vjesnik u srijedu*) (Zagreb), and *Ekonomska politika* (Belgrade). Tanjug is the official news agency.

Radio Free Europe   Slobodan Stanković
Munich

WESTERN EUROPE

Austria

The Communist Party of Austria (Kommunistische Partei Österreichs; KPÖ) founded 3 November 1918, has been a legal party throughout Austria's democratic history: 1918-33 and since 1945. It was represented in the Austrian parliament in 1945-59, and in the government, 1945-47. Memories of Soviet occupation of part of Austria, 1945-55, and of Soviet military intervention in neighboring Hungary and Czechoslovakia account for the party's increasing insignificance.

In a country of 7,520,000 inhabitants, the KPÖ has a slowly declining membership, consisting of at most 20,000 in 1977 (*Die Presse*, Vienna, 12 April). Its policy line closely follows that of the Soviet and East German parties.

Leadership and Organization. The party's leadership is elderly and stable. By occupation the four-teen members of the Politburo (these and other data are compiled from *Rundschreiben des ZK der KPÖ*, 1977), consist of a laborer, a craftsman, two journalists, and ten white-collar employees. Their median age is fifty-seven, their median length of service on the Central Committee seventeen years, and only four reside outside of Vienna. Similar are the characteristics of the forty-five members of the principal committees of the Central Committee (out of a total membership of ninety-eight). Among these are four journalists, seven craftsmen and skilled workers, and two laborers; the others are white-collar employees. Sixteen live outside Vienna, and the average age is also fifty-seven; only two are less than forty-three years old. Only three have academic degrees (one on the Politburo).

According to *Communists of the World* (Prague, 1976), over 50 percent of new members admitted in 1973 (their total number is not given) were less than thirty years old, 69 percent were "working people," and 43 percent women. The party's financial state is healthy, at least as long as it polls more than one percent of the national vote (1.2 percent in 1975), which entitles it to a public subsidy. Membership fees, donations, and this subsidy add up to about $2.5 million per year (*Die Presse*, 12 April).

Franz Muhri is the party chairman.

Party Internal Affairs. Much of the KPÖ's activity in 1977 was directed toward preparing for the Twenty-third Party Campaign, to be held 8-11 December. Meetings in late 1976 and early 1977 con-cerned themselves with a stepping up of all party activities, including a membership campaign, a press subscription campaign, and improvement of organization, the latter to include local leadership teams consisting of old and young members and personal discussion visits on the occasion of the collection of monthly membership dues. Further plans extended to celebrations, in the provincial capitals, of the sixtieth anniversary of the October Revolution, and a special effort to revise the class consciousness of youth in the face of contrary tendencies in schools and the media.

Domestic Attitudes and Activities. Although 1977 was not a key election year, Austria's easternmost and most heavily agrarian province, Burgenland, had a provincial election on 2 October, in which the governing Socialist Party expanded its majority. The KPÖ maintained its vote share of 1972 (0.4 percent) and once again went without a single seat (*Wiener Zeitung*, 1 October; *Arbeiter-Zeitung*, Vienna, 3 October). On 23 October, municipal elections were held in the same province. The KPÖ saved its 0.2 percent share of the vote, but its seats in local councils declined from two of 2,550 to none of 2,560 (*Wiener Zeitung*, 25 October).

Several municipal elections were held on 2 October. The KPÖ failed to obtain seats in Salzburg and Innsbruck, but it kept its single seat in the Lower Austrian city of Krems. Also in Lower Austria, in St. Pölten, KPÖ council representation was reduced from two seats to one on 13 March.

In industrial elections, the KPÖ sustained one spectacular defeat. A chemical plant in St. Pölten, held by the Soviet Usia organization till 1955, had had a Communist majority on its shop steward council ever since. On 21 April, the eight Communist seats were cut in half, and the Socialists obtained majority control of the council (*Arbeiter-Zeitung*, Vienna, 23 April).

The student election of 11-12 April brought modest gains to the Communists. They reentered student councils in Vienna and Salzburg with one seat each. They also placed one member on the sixty-five-member all-Austrian student parliament.

Austrian Communists could find some solace in the nationwide party-identification survey of the IMAS institute in Linz, in September. From 1975 to 1977, they had vacillated between 0.6 and 1.5 percent of respondents, the high figure stemming from February 1976. Their showing for September 1977 was also 1.5 percent. (*Kurier*, Vienna, 8 October.) The error margin of the sample does not, of course, enable the KPÖ to be particularly sanguine about this result.

In domestic politics, the KPÖ's main thrust was in the tax sector. The Socialist minister of finance had succeeded in obtaining the acquiescence of the Trade Union Congress (ÖGB) to his refusal to cut wage taxes. KPÖ chairman Muhri announced in a press conference on 10 February that Communists would collect signatures in Austria's industrial plants for a plan of "social tax reform." The Communist plan provides for a tax exemption on monthly wages up to $300, indexed against inflation. Fiscal losses were to be made up by tax increases on domestic and foreign capital. (*Die Presse*, 11 February.) In a speech in March, Muhri tied the inequities of Austria's tax system to the "social partnership" of the chambers of commerce, agriculture, and labor, and the Trade Union Congress. This system, Muhri said, is "used by bourgeois propaganda to conceal profound class contradictions between workers and employers and to divert the people's attention from the struggle for their vital intersts" (*New Age*, India, 27 March). In his yearly contribution to the *World Marxist Review*, (April, pp. 12-20) Muhri expanded on his attack on Austria's "social partnership," in which he blamed the governing Socialists for having adapted to their political competitors, the conservative People's Party:

> The Austrian Social-Democrat ideologists try to justify their "social partnership" policy by pleading that the workers and employers are "in the same boat." And from this they conclude that the class struggle, especially the political class struggle, has outlived its day, and even contradicts the principle of democracy. What we have is an attempt to paralyze the working class." (P. 19.)

In a press conference on 7 September, Muhri pointed to the new tax proposals of the government, with increased taxation of entrepreneurs, and claimed credit, on behalf of the KPÖ, for some of the proposed tax changes (*Wiener Zeitung*, 8 September).

The KPÖ voiced a few other domestic concerns during the year. When it was first alleged that the then minister of defense knew about arms sales to Syria (in contravention of the State Treaty), the party paper added allegations of arms shipments to Israel, South Africa, and Chile (*Volksstimme*, 21 January). Muhri also charged Austrian radio and television and the two major parties with joining the anti-Soviet campaign for "human rights activists" (ibid., 6 February). When Austria, ignoring Czecho-slovak protests, permitted Sudeten Germans to meet in Vienna, the government was roundly assailed by the KPÖ (*IB*, no. 12, 30 June).

In a eulogy prior to the anniversary of the October Revolution, a member of the KPÖ's Commission for Party History made these claims (*WMR*, September, pp. 135-36):

> The power and example of the Soviet Union have enabled the Austrian working class to achieve nationalization in industry on a scale unparalleled in any other capitalist country. . . .
> The social democrats' rightist policy is a major obstacle to the course we have chosen. . . . This reori-entation of the social democrats today [is] paradoxical indeed. When the young Soviet Union was locked in . . . battle with counter-revolution and intervention, Austria's social democrats recognized socialism in Russia and advanced socialist goals for their own country. . . . But now that socialism has become a reality and a force of global magnitude and that our country is in a position to go over to socialism without civil war, the social democrats . . . anathematize socialism.

International Views and Positions. Before the end of 1976, Muhri hailed the importance of the Warsaw Treaty countries' Bucharest declaration for the development of Austria's trade (Tass, 3 December). A bit later, at the seventeenth plenum of the KPÖ Central Committee, Muhri warned of the enemies of detente and a possible return to the cold war (*Pravda*, 26 February). A visit to Vienna by a member of the East German party's Politburo, 28 February-4 March, provided the forum for a strong statement on detente and for support of Soviet policy (*Volksstimme*, 5 March).

The party paper of 7 July published a careful critique of Eurocommunism. Three weeks later, however, it strongly attacked Chancellor Kreisky's discrimination between Moscow and the Eurocom-munists (ibid., 28 July).

There were greatly differing reports of a visit of Austrian psychiatrists to the Soviet Union. According to the KPÖ, all the patients in psychiatric clinics had been found genuinely ill by the Aus-trians (ibid., 30 August), contrary to the Amnesty International report that dissidents were being kept there. However, the doctors told *Die Presse* (31 August) that they had been interested only in Soviet psychiatry, that they had not looked for dissidents, and that they had nothing to say about their treat-ment.

A remarkable story, without follow-up that could be located, appeared in the *Arbeiter-Zeitung* (25 January) about "Charta 77":

> Monday [24 January] several members and sympathizers of the KPÖ, among them the writers Peter Turrini, Helmut Zenker, and Michael Scharang, and "Volksstimme" editor Lutz Holzinger, member of the KPÖ Central Committee, published a declaration regretting the silence of the KPÖ [on "Charta 77"]. The voices of the critics, they claim, have a fundamental right to "exist." The KPÖ should join the Communist parties of France and Italy in their criticism of the persecution.

International Activities and Party Contacts. The KPÖ's visiting year 1976 ended with the official visit to Vienna of the Hungarian party chief János Kádár, who met Muhri and other KPÖ leaders at the Hungarian Embassy (MTI Domestic Service, 7 December).

On 2 February 1977 Muhri visited East German party chief Erich Honecker in East Berlin. This visit was reciprocated by a five-day visit of an East German party delegation to Vienna (*Volksstimme*, 5 March). Anton Hofer, chief of Austria's Communist trade unionists, visited the Sixteenth Congress of Soviet trade unions in Moscow (Tass, 1 April). One of the candidate members of the Central Committee of the CPSU, Zagladin, came to Vienna in early June for party talks (Moscow Domestic Service, 5 June). Two weeks later, Vasil Bil'ák, one of the ranking Czechoslovak Communists, also visited Vienna (*Wiener Zeitung*, 16 June).

In July, Muhri visited Moscow (*Volkstimme*, 28 July). He reported on organizational work in Austria, mostly on preparation for the KPÖ's Twenty-third Congress. He had a conversation with Boris Ponomarev, secretary of the CPSU Central Committee.

Publications. The party continues to publish the daily *Volkstimme* and the theoretical monthly *Weg und Ziel. Die Presse* (12 April) noted a decline in the Austrian Communist press and the loss to the party of a few minor friendly publications.

Other Marxist Groups. The Communist League of Austria, the country's Maoist party, continued its newspaper *Klassenkampf.* At the end of 1976, the Communist League sent a message to the Chinese Communist Party, attacking the "Gang of Four" and extolling Chairman Hua (*Peking Review*, 10 December). On 25 March 1977 an Austria-China Friendship Association was founded in Salzburg (NCNA, 28 March).

Other Marxist groups did better than the Communist Student League (KSV) in the May student elections. This was true especially in the All-Austrian Student Parliament, in which the KSV won one seat, while the List of Communist University Students and the Group of Revolutionary Marxists won two seats each (*Wiener Zeitung*, 14 May).

The University of Alberta   F. C. Engelmann

Belgium

The Communist Party of Belgium (Parti Communiste de Belgique/Kommunistische Partij Van België; PCB/KPB), founded in 1921, is pro-Soviet in the Sino-Soviet dispute and has perhaps 11,000 members, in a population of almost ten million.

The marginal influence of the PCB/KPB in Belgian politics deteriorated in 1977 following losses in the October 1976 communal and April 1977 legislative elections. In April the party acquired 151,000 votes, or 2.7 percent of the total (1974: 170,000 votes; 3.2 percent), and lost two of its four seats in the 212-member Chamber of Representatives. It retained its single seat in the 181-member Senate (only 106 seats are elected). The party has insignificant representation in three of the nine provincial councils.

Electoral setbacks reflected a decline, particularly in the Walloon region, in party memberships. Memberships of the three competing Communist groups—the Marxist-Leninist Communist Party of Belgium, the Maoist-Stalinist AMADA/TPO, and the Trotskyist LRT/RAL (see below)—have increased. The latter two parties polled 40,000 votes (24,000 and 16,000, respectively) in the April elections, or about 26 percent of the PCB/KPB total.

The PCB/KPB does not have its own labor organization, but exercises influence in the two principal federations: the Walloon-dominated Belgian General Confederation of Workers (FGTB), tied with the Belgian Socialist Party (PSB/BSP), and the larger, Flemish-dominated Confederation of Christian Trade Unions (CSC), tenuously linked with the Christian Social Party (PSC/CVP). The PCB/KPB is also active in various front organizations.

Leadership and Organization. In January 1977 the PCB/KPB Central Committee reelected Louis Van Geyt as chairman and Claude Renard, Jef (Joseph) Turf, and the veteran Jean Terfve as vice-chairmen. There is a four-member National Secretariat (*Drapeau Rouge,* 31 January).

Reflecting the increasing regionalization of the country, the PCB/KPB has Flemish (Dutch-speaking), Walloon (French-speaking), and Brussels (bilingual) regional councils. PCB/KPB vice-chairmen Renard and Turf head, respectively, the Walloon and Flemish federations. The weakening of the Walloon federation and greater consolidation of the Flemish wing of the party have strengthened the hand of Turf, now considered the second-ranking person in the party. His book, *A Political Identity for Communists* (in Dutch), in November, projects a liberal, or Eurocommunist image. He was the subject of Belgian press speculation in July concerning a split in the party sparked by the Soviet attack on Eurocommunism . (See *Le Soir,* 17-18, 21 July; *Drapeau Rouge,* 19 July; *Special,* Brussels 27 July.)

The PCB/KPB's auxiliary organizations, limited to the Communist Youth of Belgium, the National Union of Communist Students, and the children's Union of Pioneers, are not mass organizations but serve primarily as party training and socialization outlets. More important outlets for influencing public opinion and political alignments are the strong Christian Workers' Movement (MOC), a united front of Christian workers and cooperative associations, which has been radicalized from within by the Communists and other leftists; the Belgian Union for the Defense of Peace; the International Committee for European Peace and Security, a Soviet front organization; and an active Belgian-Soviet Friendship Association.

Domestic Attitudes and Activities. In 1977 the PCB/KPB continued to pursue a general strategy of alliance with "progressive and democratic forces" (*Drapeau Rouge,* 19-20 February), aimed primarily at the Socialist Party and the left-wing of the Christian Socialists. In an address to the party's Brussels federation, Chairman Van Geyt said that "only joint efforts can bring success in coping with the crisis of the country" (Tass, 15 March).

Whatever hopes the PCB/KPB had for a joint progressive platform during the election campaign were dashed, however, when the PSB, after three years in opposition, joined the new government formed by Prime Minister Tindemans after the April 1977 election. Although formed with difffculty, the new, broader coalition—which included Tindemans' dominant PSC/CVP, People's Unity (VU, a Flemish nationalist party), and the French-speaking Democratic Front (FDF, of Brussels)—left the PCB/KPB more politically isolated than ever. During the campaign, the party did not formally oppose PSB's eventual participation in a new government, but expressed "regrets" that the Socialists, swayed by the right, were moving away from what had allegedly been an emerging unity of progressive forces (*Le Soir,* 19 March).

The PCB/KPB's own platform, based on tasks outlined at the Twenty-second Congress, held in April 1976, called for a "program of urgency" that included establishing "state control . . . over such key branches of the economy as power engineering and the granting of credits" (*WMR,* April 1977). Less radical social-reform measures were more frequently advocated, such as protecting employment (cutting the work week to thirty-six hours without wage reduction, lowering the pension age, subsidizing companies to retain or increase employment) and workers' wages (automatic indexing of taxes for low and medium incomes, revised price policy on consumer goods produced by monopolies), and preventing wastage of state funds (abolishing tax privileges for trusts, stronger punishment for company violations of tax laws) (ibid.).

The PCB/KPB's inlfuence in the two-million-strong trade union movement (two-thirds of Belgian labor is organized) has, on the other hand, increased. Due in part to the economic crisis and to effective Communist penetration, the CSC developed to the point where, in 1976, it broke its ties with the conservative PSC/CVP and adopted a more militant line (see *YICA, 1977,* pp. 124-126).

In the language dispute, the PCB/KPB supports the trend toward a Belgian federal state comprised of Flanders, Wallonia, and Brussels. Federalism, it claims, would broaden democracy, as elected assemblies and executive governments in the three regions would "bring the decision-making centers closer to the people directly concerned" (*WMR,* April). It criticized the traditional parties for having moved more slowly on this problem and asserted that the "big bourgeoisie" was "strongly opposed to the granting of genuine rights to Wallonia, Flanders, and Brussels" (ibid.).

International Views and Positions. While the PCB/KPB has, on the surface, remained an uncomplicated, loyalist (i.e., pro-Soviet) party, it has not refrained from criticism of features of the eastern Socialist regimes.

In 1977 its traditional reflex support of Soviet views was not infrequently accompanied by rejoinders that served to disassociate it from the Soviet, or eastern Socialist, model. For example, while hailing in an editorial (*Drapeau Rouge,* 31 January) the Socialist countries as the "principal artisans of détente in Europe," the PCB/KPB added that disrespect for "fundamental human rights," which it considered as being "inseparable from Socialism," provided "arms to the adversaries of peace." Citing concern for the members of the "Charta 77" movement in Czechoslovakia, the editorial held that "all states of Europe must honor their signature" of the Helsinki Final Declaration. In another editorial (ibid., 8 July), Jef Turf stated that the measures taken against dissidents in some eastern countries "helps the class enemy in its attempts to continue its domination over men's minds." (See *Drapeau rouge,* 19, 23 July; *Rode Vaan,* 2-9 November.)

At its Nineteenth Congress, in 1968, the PCB/KPB officially embarked upon an indigenous path to Socialism, drawing on its specific national conditions and historical features. This policy was reaffirmed by Van Geyt in his report to the Twenty-second Congress, in 1976. In addition to stressing a national, democratic way to Socialism, in which the previous democratic gains made by the working class were defended as progressive, the PCB/KPB also drew on the resolution of the 1976 Berlin Conference of European Communist and Workers' Parties to emphasize, in the words of Turf, the "indispensable autonomy of individual parties" under conditions of "mutual international solidarity" (*WMR,* September).

The PCB/KPB's attitude toward Eurocommunism in 1977 can in part be summarized by the words Van Geyt and Vice-chairman Renard used to describe the concept: "confused and ambiguous" (*Drapeau Rouge,* 25-26 June). After visits at the beginning of the year to the heads of the Italian and French Communist parties, Enrico Berlinguer and Georges Marchais, Van Geyt accorded an interview to *HEBDO 77* (Brussels, 1 March), published a day prior to the Eurocommunist Madrid summit. Asked whether the West European parties had a common strategy, he not only acknowledged a common "desire for an exchange of information," but "also common thinking regarding situations that present a number of aspects, both common and specific. For instance we are aware that the political changes that may happen in France and Italy will necessitate more active cooperation between the forces of labor and democracy throughout capitalistic Europe . . ." (in: *Joint Publications Research Service* [JPRS], Belgium, 29 August).

When the Communist Party of the Soviet Union (CPSU) strongly attacked Spanish party chief Carrillo's book, *Eurocommunism and the State,* in the June issue of *Novo Vreme* (New Times), the PCB/KPB guardedly came to Carrillo's defense (*Drapeau Rouge,* 24 June), as did the parties of Italy, France, Great Britain and Greece ("Interior") (*Le Monde,* 25 June; *Le Soir,* 15 July). The following day, however, in an obvious effort to play down the issue, Van Geyt and Renard backed off ("Our party is not worried about the accusations made by *Novo Vreme*") and denied any affinities with Eurocommunism: "It seems confused and ambiguous to us. This is why . . . we have not made it our own . . ." (*Drapeau Rouge,* 25-26 June). When these remarks created a stir in the Belgian press, in which doubts were raised about the party's proclaimed independence and commitment to democratic values, the PCB-KPB again retracted (ibid., 2-3 July) and printed parts of Van Geyt's *HEBDO 77* interview quoted above.

In the meantime, Jef Turf published a revealing editorial (ibid., 8 July) on Eurocommunism. On the one hand, he accused "Atlantic capital" of baptizing Eurocommunism for "the task of breaking up the international Communist movement." On the other, he recognized a convergence of interests peculiar "only" to Communists in the advanced capitalist countries, arising from the "concrete realities of each country."

In the 19 July issue of *Drapeau Rouge,* Turf and Van Geyt co-published an editorial emphasizing that the PCB/KPB was "in solidarity with the Communist parties of Western Europe in their fight for a democratic, pacific, and Socialist Europe." But Eurocommunism, "as it is manipulated by rightist forces, is an evident attempt to rupture the unity of the international communist movement. We repeat that we strongly oppose this attempt."

While refusing the Eurocommunist appellation for the PCB/KPB, Van Geyt recognized several days later the "common" elements in the programs of the West European Communist parties. These included the stands taken "for a peaceful and democratic way to Socialism, for the recognition of pluralism, for a program of combating the crisis through anti-monopolistic reforms (but not yet Socialism) to arrive at a phase of 'initial or antechamber socialism'." (Ibid., 22 July.)

International Activities and Party Contacts. Numerous high- and low-level bi-lateral party contacts took place during 1977. Of note were Van Geyt's trips to Rome (January), Paris (February), and Moscow (July). On the Moscow trip he was accompanied by Politburo member Augustin Duchateau. Both were received by and had meetings with the CPSU's Boris Ponomarev and Vadim Zagladin. A common text appeared in *Drapeau Rouge* and *Pravda* on 7 July that, inter alia, accused "reactionary NATO circles" of undermining detente by "agitating" on the human rights issue to the detriment of the other problems (see *FBIS,* 12 July; *JPRS*/Belgium, 23 August).

On 23 September Van Geyt was awarded the Soviet Order of Peoples' Friendship on his fiftieth birthday (*Pravda,* 24 September). Earlier, Terfve received the Soviet Order of the October Revolution on the occasion of his seventieth birthday (*Tass,* 27 January).

The BCP/KPB hosted a multilateral working conference of sixteen West European Communist parties in Brussels on 13-15 June. Devoted to a discussion of the economic crisis and ways to surmount it, the meeting was the first of its kind since the January 1974 Brussels meeting of twenty parties to discuss "The Present Crisis of Capitalism." The communiqué of the gathering noted the participants' desire to "develop their cooperation, in all forms."

In November the PCB/KPB sent a small, low-ranking delegation to Moscow for the sixtieth anniversary celebration of the October Revolution (Vice-chairman Renard and two Central Committee members). In addition, the current and past chairman of the Belgian Socialist Party also attended. On 7 November, Van Geyt sent a 300-word message to the CPSU praising the October Revolution as "an event unequaled in importance in the history of people" (*Drapeau Rouge,* 7 November).

Publications. The PCB/KPB's French daily, *Le Drapeau Rouge,* is the party's main organ. The Flemish weekly, *De Rode Vaan,* of which Jef Turf is political director, is of a higher literary standard. The party's monthly theoretical journal, *Cahiers Marxistes,* has a Flemish counterpart, *Vlaams Marxistisch Tijdschrif,* which now appears in Ghent three to four times annually. Local and provincial organizations publish some twenty newspapers, the majority consisting of six issues annually, which are distributed free.

The publications are in part financed by the Joseph Jacquemotte Fund and the more recent Masereel fund. In 1976, party activists collected some two million francs (U.S. $60,000) in a fund-raising campaign for the Communist press (Tass, 10 January).

Other Communits Groups. The Marxist-Leninist Communist Party of Belgium (Parti Communist Marxiste-Leninist de Belgique; PCMLB) split from the PCB/KPB in 1963 to become the first official Peking-line party in Western Europe. It held its Second Congress on 22-23 January 1977, in Brussels. In his report, First Secretary Fernand Lefebvre stated that the PCMLB's struggle was a "political struggle to lead the popular masses in a united front against the hegemonism of the two superpowers," of which "Soviet social-imperialism is the most dangerous" (*FBIS*, 1 February). Lefebvre headed a party delegation to China, 4-12 April. The party's organ in *Clarté et L'Exploité*.

To the left of PCMLB is the Antwerp-centered All Power to the Workers (Alle Macht Aan De Arbeiders/Tout le Pouvoir aux Ouvriers; AMADA/TPO), a disciplined, Maoist-Stalinist organization not recognized by China. After polling some 24,000 votes in the April elections, it announced its intention to create "a new Communist party" (*Le Soir*, 24 August).

The Trotskyist Revolutionary Workers League (Ligue Revolutionaire des Travailleurs/Revo-lutionaire Arbeiders Liga; LRT/RAL) represents the Belgian section of the Fourth International and appeals primarily to intellectuals, of whom the most prominent is Ernest Mandel. It publishes two weeklies, *La Gauche*, in French, and *Rood*, the Flemish counterpart.

Of the three groupings, LRT/RAL is the least politically significant and has the largest share of members in a combined total membership of about 3,500.

International Academy of Manternach   Peter Gyallay-Pap
Luxemburg

Cyprus

The original Communist party of Cyprus, secretly founded by Greek-trained Cypriots, held its first congress in August 1926 while the island was a British Crown Colony. Outlawed in 1933, it survived underground. In April 1941 it emerged as the Progressive Party of the Working People (Anorthotikon Komma Laou tis Kiprou; AKEL). It was proscribed by the British in 1955, along with all political organizations during the EOKA insurgency, but has had legal status since the proclamation of the republic in 1960.

As the oldest and best-organized political party in Cyprus, AKEL influences a following far larger than its estimated 11,000 members. Virtually all of its overt support comes from among the Greek

Cypriot majority, about 80 percent of the island's estimated 640,000 population. The proportion of party members to national adult populace probably ranks AKEL second only to its Italian counterpart among non-ruling Communist parties. Despite its overall potential, AKEL has played down its strength in parliamentary elections and has never held a cabinet portfolio.

Since July 1974 the socio-political setting in Cyprus has been a fragile calm after the Turkish invasion and subsequent occupation of some 40 percent of the island. The Turkish Cypriots theoretically hold a constitutional share of power in the government of the republic, but they have formed a "Turkish Federated State of Cyprus" and hold separate elections within their own community. On 5 September 1976 the republic held its first parliamentary elections since 1970. AKEL contested only its nine previously secured seats, winning all easily with the same incumbents and getting about 30 percent of the vote.

A three-party coalition composed of the Communists, the Socialists (EDEK), and the Democratic Front (a new center-right party) won thirty-four of thirty-five seats in the House of Representatives. The victory was a rousing endorsement for the government of the now-deceased President Makarios. (For the election results see *YICA, 1976*, pp. 127-128). AKEL general secretary Ezekias Papaioannou made these comments on the election:

> AKEL, which in the previous Parliament had nine seats, could have won more had it acted independently. It preferred, however, to restrict itself to nine in the interests of cooperation during the elections with the other democratic parties. This made possible the isolation and crushing defeat of the extreme right and fascist forces.
>
> The "Democratic Alarm" [the party of Makarios's rival, Glafkos Clerides] accounted for about 24 percent of the votes, but due to the "Majority" electoral system, and because of the overwhelming superiority of the three cooperating democratic parties, it was left with no seats.
>
> . . . The House of Representatives, now cleansed of avowedly rightist and pro-NATO elements, is more democratic (*WMR,* January 1977).

AKEL's reluctance to show its potential acknowledged two realities: (1) the fact that the 1959 Zurich and London Agreements—which gave Cyprus its original and unworkable form of independence—included a rationale for the three guarantor powers (the U.K., Greece, and Turkey) to intervene against an internal subversion of the republic, and (2) the probability that a legal push for power by AKEL would unite the nationalists and the rightists against the left. AKEL says it does not seek "partisan predominance" at the present time, nor does it care to "squabble over whether the island will become socialist or remain capitalist" (*Dhimokratia,* 26 September).

While AKEL continues to minimize its friction with the non-Communist Greek Cypriots, its one consistent tactic in recent years has been open endorsement of the domestic and foreign policies of the late Archbishop-President Makarios. AKEL supported Makarios for a third consecutive term in 1973 and as a result had a representative on the president's advisory body, the National Council. In an apparent effort not to embarrass Makarios, AKEL has until recently played down its differences with the Church of Cyprus, particularly as to redistribution of church-owned lands, which AKEL now wants given to the tenant farmers (Nicosia domestic service, 5 July). In Cyprus the autocephalous church has traditionally been influential in secular politics, and AKEL knows it cannot appeal to Greek Cypriots by attacking their Orthodox faith. After the death of Makarios, AKEL silently accepted the elevation of the Bishop of Pahos, Chrysotomos, to succeed him in the church. The Communists were resigned to the reality that they might never enjoy another close relationship with a Cypriot archbishop because the need for a prelate to become president would probably not arise again.

When a heart attack struck down President Makarios in August, the law of succession designated that the leader of the House of Representatives assume his office until the next election.

This created a vacancy in the House. A by-election for the remaining three years of this seat from the Nicosia constituency, held on 16 October, was won by the candidate of the Democratic Front, Georgios Ladas, with a convincing 20,000 votes. Ladas took part in the 1941 meeting which founded AKEL, and in his profession as a lawyer he has represented AKEL members from time to time. Ladas did not spout a leftist line during the campaign, but did enjoy the endorsement of the coalition which had swept to victory in the previous elections. Sources close to AKEL and EDEK, however, claimed that the high rate of abstentions, which exceeded 32 percent, was "due to the fact that the two leftist parties had given only half-hearted backing to Mr. Ladas' candidacy" (*Cyprus Mail,* 18 October). The final results gave the Democratic Front candidate 45,436 votes (64.3 percent) and his Democratic Rally opponent 25,225 (35.7 percent). Of the 105,391 registered voters, 71,476 (67.8 percent) cast their votes. The by-election indicated that the three-party coalition was still in control as the republic prepared for the 1978 presidential contest. Ladas chose to thank the "people and especially the refugees" for his victory, rather than give undue credit to the minimum support he received from the leftists. (Ibid., 19 October.)

Though AKEL is the only professed Marxist-Leninist party in Cyprus, there seems to be less and less competiton, with more convergence on current issues, from the active Socialist Party (EDEK), headed by a fifty-seven-year-old physician, Vassos Lyssarides. In the last elections, the Socialists increased their seats in the house from two to four, as a result of intentional support of the stronger Communist party. EDEK and AKEL have had differences, but as both are leftist parties their leaders seek to avoid open feuding. Papaioannou, seemingly speaking for both, made this observation on short-term political goals:

> AKEL and the left wing in general do not now seek to come to power, not out of fear, not due to an inferiority complex, nor to constitutional or other obstacles, but because they believe that the supreme interests of our liberation struggle dictate and command unity and the rallying together of the broadest patriotic democratic forces of the people irrespective of ideological or class differences and convictions (*Kharavyi,* 8 September).

Reportedly, Dr. Lyssarides commands a private band of heavily-armed fighters which has been in on much of the bloodletting in recent Cypriot life. AKEL has repeatedly called for "drastic measures" to disband illegal armed groups, but most of this ire is directed toward the regrouped EOKA-B terrorists. Supposedly EOKA-B was responsible for the attempt on the life of Lyssarides, in which his driver and party lieutenant was killed. After a parliamentary committee investigating the assassination reported that "certain members of the police did not carry out their duties as well as they should," Papaioannou "accused the Minister of Justice and Defence . . . of covering up coup elements and of persecuting the leftwing and demanded his removal from office" (*Cyprus Mail*, 17 June).

Leadership and Organization. The leading figures in AKEL are the general secretary, Ezekias Papaioannou, in office since 1949, and his deputy, Andreas Fantis. Both were reelected in April 1974 at the party's Thirteenth Congress. The congress, the party's supreme authority, is convened every four years.

The leadership structure follows the usual pattern of Communist party organization, from the primary party groups at members' places of work, through the elected town committees, and then up to the six provincial committees. It is estimated that 30 percent of the AKEL membership are under thirty years of age and that women make up about 24 percent. A Communist source gives the social composition as "workers 65.3 percent; peasants, 17.7 percent; artisans and small businessmen, 11.9 percent; professional and others 5.1 percent" (*Communists of the World and Their Parties,* Prague,

1976, p. 118). The party leadership is notable for stability and comparatively advanced age, mostly sixty and older. Kostas Partasidhis, fifty-eight, director of *Kharavyi* and *Dhimokratia,* died in August of natural causes. The Politburo assigned his newspaper duties to Yeoryios Savvidhis, chairman of the Central Control Committee and house member for Nicosia (*Kharavyi,* 28 August). (For names of leaders see *YICA, 1975,* p. 142.)

Auxiliary and Mass Organizations. The total membership for elements within the AKEL apparatus, including various front groups and allowing for overlapping memberships, is estimated at some 60,000. AKEL controls the largest labor organization, the Pan-Cypriot Workers' Confederation (PEO), which has about 45 percent of the 100,000 organized workers and is an affiliate of the Communist-front World Federation of Trade Unions. Andreas Ziartides, a labor leader for thirty-five years, was reelected as the PEO general secretary in April 1975, with Pavlos Dinglis as his deputy. Both are influential in party affairs. In February 1977, Ziartides and other Communists, for the first time ever, were official guests at the congress of the right-wing Cypriot labor federation, SEK. This gesture was interpreted by one political observer as

> a clear sign that the repugnant cold war period during which the two federations were fighting each other and were wasting their strength in destructive disputes has gone forever and that a new period of still greater cooperation between them has been ushered in   (*Ta Nea,* 18 February).

The AKEL-sponsored United Democratic Youth Organization (EDON) is headed by a thirty-year-old London-trained lawyer, Mikhail Papapetrou, elected in 1975. EDON claims to have over 10,000 members on the island and also has a branch in London. Through an active sports and social program, as well as a secondary school organization called PEOM, it extends its influence to more than three times its membership. EDON holds a seat on the executive committee of the Communist-front World Federation of Democratic Youth. The Pan-Cypriot Federation of Students and Young Professionals (POFNE) is composed of students and graduates of institutions of higher learning in the Soviet Union or other East European countries, who constitute about 8 percent of Cypriots studying abroad.

Other AKEL-dominated organizations include a farmers' union (EKA); the Confederation of Women's Organizations (POGO); the Pan-Cypriot Peace Council (PEI), a member of the Communist-front World Peace Council; and a number of friendship clubs with East European countries. The AKEL-sponsored Union of Greek Cypriots in England has about 1,200 members. Of the 40,000 Turkish Cypriots who reside in the United Kingdom, a few are open members of the Communist Party of Great Britain, and others are undoubtedly crypto-Communists.

While AKEL has claimed to have had "hundreds of Turkish Cypriot members in the past," many of these were supposedly murdered by the Turkish Resistance Organization (TMT) (*Kharavyi,* 12 December 1976). At present, Papaioannou claims that AKEL is in "contact with its Turkish Cypriot members and progressive Turkish Cypriots in general." He admitted this was not easy:

> Despite the fact that there are immense difficulties in keeping in touch with them, nevertheless, both they and AKEL find the means to hold regular contacts. We are briefed on the activities of progressive Turkish Cypriots in the occupied areas and we brief them on the policy and positions of the Cyprus government and our party. (Ibid.)

The Turkish Cypriot members of AKEL, who must be few in number, sent greetings to the celebration of the fiftieth anniversary of the Cypriot party, saying in part:

> Faithful to the ideal of the party, Marxism-Leninism and of proletarian internationalism, faithful to the heroic example of our comrades Kavazoglu and Misiaoulis, an immortal symbol of Greek-Turkish friend-

ship [who were murdered together in the early 1960s] we will intensify our struggle for an independent, unified and demilitarized Cyprus where Greeks and Turks will live fraternally and build a happy future for their common country (*Dhimokratia,* 13 December 1976).

Party Internal Affairs. AKEL's Central Committee and Central Auditing Commission meet in plenary session approximately every two months and also in "extraordinary" sessions as need arises. Each September, AKEL has a fund drive, traditionally for 25,000 Cypriot pounds, which there is usually no difficulty in raising. The Communists are also solidly based in two industrial enterprises, the Peoples' Spirits Manufacturing Co. Ltd. (LOEL), which also produces a selection of wines, and the Peoples' Coffee Grinding Co., Ltd. Both do a sizable business with the Eastern bloc countries.

Domestic Attitudes and Activities. AKEL's approach to the domestic issues facing Cyprus have been consistent over the past years. They exploit anti-colonialist sentiment by continual attacks on the 1959 Zurich-London Agreements which created the dyarchy government that failed to work. The presence of British troops in two sovereign bases has also been a fruitful target of Communist propaganda. Papaioannou has stressed that the people of Cyprus "will never recognize faits accomplis or accept the occupation of an inch of their territory, either by Turkey or any other foreign forces" (Nicosia domestic sevice, 22 May 1977). Also, he insists that the "partition of Cyprus" will never be accepted, and that "Cyprus should become an independent, sovereign, united and non-aligned federal state" (*IB,* 31 March).

Stating that the "primary duty of the Cypriot people now is the liberation of our island," Papaioannou outlined a "correct militant course to achieve this objective":

—A unified and incessant struggle
—All-sided strengthening of the resistance front
—Strengthening of our defense posture
—Further internationalization of the Cyprus question and the convening of an international conference
—Strengthening of international solidarity and the exercising of pressure on Turkey for the implementation of UN resolutions (*Dhimokratia*, 26 September).

Such a "single resistance front" for the liberation struggle would also make it easier to "decide on a joint candidate for February's presidential election and on the formation of a government of national unity." (Ibid.) Apparently the Communist leader does not regard the parliamentary election coalition formed in 1976 as a lasting arrangement, nor one that would meet all his standards of unity.

The "summit" meeting in the early part of 1977 between President Makarios and Turkish Cypriot leader Rauf Denktas gave AKEL reason to hope that a "new road" had been opened in the "Cypriot peoples' struggle" (*Kharavyi,* 20 February). The most substantial result of the two meetings was the reaching of agreement on the main trends of the conduct of the inter-communal talks which were to resume in Vienna on 31 March. The talks, held under the auspices of U.N. secretary general Kurt Waldheim, did not bear the fruit which the AKEL had hoped for. Accusing the Turkish Cypriots of demanding "the creation of two separate states that would be linked by a loose agreement," Papioannou said that the Communists will "undeviatingly insist on the line laid down by the National and Ministerial councils under President Makarios." (Ibid., 8 September.) This "line" was explained earlier to be "a federal republic with powers going to the central government which would safeguard the unity and cohesion of the Cyprus state" (ibid., 29 March).

Since the intercommunal talks did not resolve the governmental problem, AKEL returned to its plea for raising the discussion to an international level. This suggestion echoes earlier proposals by the Soviet Union, but these have received little support in diplomatic circles. The rationale for the conference is that it will "considerably strengthen our peoples' struggle." (Ibid., 8 September.) But expanding the Cyprus talks to include wider international participation would simply mean to include the Soviet Union in the discussion. Nevertheless, the AKEL leadership tries to fashion the conference as the "only safety valve of the solution to the entire Cyprus problem." (Ibid., 17 March.)

The economy of the Greek Cypriot-controlled south is recovering strongly from its nadir after the Turkish invasion. Still this does not satisfy Papaioannou, who said that it is unacceptable "that under the present conditions in our country there should be a few who make huge profits and live in luxury while the majority, the refugees and the working people, are deprived of the basic necessities of human life." (Ibid., 8 September.) This "terrible injustice and inequality" must be rectified along the lines of AKEL's "Second Emergency Economic Action Plan for 1977-78," which was issued as a document in July (Nicosia domestic service, 5 July). The plan proposes the strengthening of the economic front by "distributing the national income and financial burdens more fairly and solving the housing problem." To realize the targets of the plan, the document proposes: "a continued encouragement of private initiative, an end to loans from only capitalist credit organizations or countries and a turn toward those offering loans on terms truly beneficial to Cyprus." The plan also envisages: "nationalization of water resources, infrastructure projects, settlement of the question of debts and loan interests and nationalization of mining companies." At the same time, AKEL supports the increase of wages and salaries, completely free education, and "the formation of a special committee to examine and take additional measures for the control or even nationalization of banks and insurance companies." (Ibid.)

On other domestic issues, AKEL feels priority must be given to "the problems of refugees and of enslaved people, as well as to the problems of those who have suffered and of the relatives of missing people" (ibid., 8 September), and AKEL wants a purge and cleansing of the government machinery of those who took part in the 1974 coup. Papaioannou charged on the floor of the House that a serious domestic problem is posed by the revival of the EOKA-B organization, which has 3,000 weapons in its possession. He called on the minister of justice "to search for these arms and bring all those criminals to justice." (Ibid., 23 June.) Lastly, the AKEL leadership called for the ending "of all discrimination against democratic and leftist soldiers," because it is "essential that a feeling of trust be established among the members of the armed forces" (ibid., 30 March).

After the death of Makarios in August, the AKEL Politburo issued a statement stressing the great loss to the people and praising Makarios's prestige and "his personality as a leader extending far beyond the boundaries of Cyprus." The statement called upon "all political parties, all political factors, all professional and mass organizations, and all the people . . . to set aside political and other differences and place the interests of Cyprus above everything." AKEL promised to "devote all its power in this direction." (Ibid., 3 August.)

One disappointment for AKEL was the cancellation of village elections, scheduled for 20 February, which would have been the first village elections in over forty years. AKEL wanted to see them take place as proof of "the beginning of complete restoration of local self-government" (Tass, 23 December 1976). While AKEL had collaborated in the parliamentary elections, "there was no indication that a similar deal for the rural elections has been arranged" (*Cyprus Mail,* 23 December).

International Views and Policies. The line and tactics of AKEL's foreign policy were "decided by President Makarios," and while he was alive there was no change. Papaioannou in an important speech (*Kharavyi,* 8 September 1977), gave credit to this policy as saving the Republic of Cyprus:

> The orientation of our foreign policy cannot be other than that of a nonaligned bloc. Voices have been heard—and are still being heard—for abandoning our nonaligned foreign policy and for our induction into the NATO camp. If we exist today, as a state—even with 60 percent of the Cyprus territory—this is

due to our nonaligned foreign policy, which is respected not only by the nonaligned countries, but also by the Socialist states.

Had Cyprus belonged to NATO, he continued, it would have been "dissolved" as a state "a long time ago." He then launched into a severe attack on imperialist "intrigue":

> The Cypriot people's sufferings originate from NATO. It is NATO, and particularly its American section, that has been plotting and making plans from the first day of Cyprus' independence in order to undermine and dissolve the Cyprus state. Therefore we shall not be saved if we enter the wolf's den. NATO was, is, and will continue to be the evil genius not only of the Cypriot people, but also of every other people struggling for independence.

Therefore, he concluded, what is needed to achieve "a democratic and fair Cyprus solution" is greater stress on this foreign policy with "still closer ties with the nonaligned bloc, a still clearer anti-imperialist stand and course."

He took the opportunity of a party meeting in a village to laud the Soviet Union:

> The Soviet Union saved Cyprus from total enslavement in 1974 and stands firm by the side of the Cypriot people who struggle for their freedom, warning both Turkey and the imperialists in general that "the search for ways to settle the question must be conducted on the basis of unreserved respect for the independence, sovereignty and territorial integrity of the Republic of Cyprus and for its nonaligned policy." (Ibid., 17 March.)

He returned to his call for an "international conference within the U.N. framework, as the Soviet Union has proposed since August 1974," as the only way to insure "the strong and reliable international guarantees without which even the best constitutional solution of the Cyprus problem would not be of any big value" (ibid.). Referring to the danger of "self-styled mediators, who put the imperialist interests of their countries above everything," trying to impose their way (ibid., 8 September), he was surely referring in part to the February peace initiative attempted by U.S. president Carter through his emissary Clark Clifford. Papaioannou held that the record for the U.S. since January 1977 "confirms beyond any doubt the correctness of our assessment" that U.S. policy toward Cyprus is the "splitting of Cyprus between Greece and Turkey and turning it into an aircraft and missile base of NATO" (*I Simerini*, Nicosia, 13 September). AKEL saw the results of the Clifford mission as nothing more than the "hardening of Turkey's position on the Cyprus issue and the strengthening of Denktas's intransigence." Therefore, "such initiatives do not presage anything good for the Cypriot people and their cause, but constitute a dangerous NATOite trap." (*Kharavyi*, 16 September.)

Rather than look to support from the West, a statement by AKEL's Politburo seemed to indicate that the "international solidarity factor" was what the Communists felt was more important for gaining their goals:

> The support of the non-aligned countries, especially the meeting of foreign ministers and summit conference on the Cyprus question, is still another factor of pressure on Turkey and on imperialism in general . . . . The report from the European Council on Human Rights, the international conference on Cyprus in Frankfurt and the mounting international movement of solidarity in Cyprus, as also the fact that nearly all major international organizations have supported the UN resolutions on Cyprus and demanded their fulfillment, have proved instrumental too. (*IB*, 31 March.)

Papiaoannou noted that the 1976 Berlin conference of European Communist and workers' parties passed a resolution "firmly stating its support for a settlement of the Cyprus problem as demanded by its people and by the most consistent fighter for its interest, the working class party, AKEL" (*WMR*, January, p. 86). Further, the declaration of the summit conference of the Warsaw

Pact (Bucharest, November 1976) gave a "great and valuable reinforcement of the Cypriot people's struggle for a just, peaceful and democratic solution . . . that would be in the interest of all Cypriots" (*Kharavyi,* 3 December). Such a solution "would be fully in the spirit of the Helsinki Conference" (*WMR,* loc. cit.). Thus Papaioannou was able to pen this confident statement:

> Our people are waging their liberation battle under the slogan: "Cyprus will be saved! Imperialism will not pass." Thanks to the people's uncompromising struggle and unity and international solidarity and support, particularly on the part of the Soviet Union, this slogan will be carried out. (Ibid.)

This line is the same theme which has characterized AKEL foreign policy statements for the past three years. AKEL, as could be expected, is avowedly anti-China in its foreign policy and often speaks of how "the Maoists have betrayed the principles of Marxism-Leninism."

International Activities and Contacts. AKEL maintains extensive contacts with both ruling and non-ruling Communist parties, and with the various international Communist front organizations. For example, the secretary general of the World Peace Council, Romesh Chandra, visited Cyprus in November 1976 to state that "world public opinion was solidly behind Cyprus in its struggle for a just solution of its problems" (Nicosia domestic service, 29 November). Chandra is also president of the "International Solidarity Committee with Cyprus," which sponsored a world-wide conference in Frankfurt earlier in the year.

In December 1976, about the same time as AKEL was anticipating its fiftieth anniversary, the Soviet Union signed a five-year trade agreement with the Republic of Cyprus. The agreement was noted in Moscow as "just one of the many facts attesting to the effective solidarity of Soviet people with the Cypriots' struggle for Cyprus's independence, sovereignty and territorial integrity" (*Selskaya Zhizn,* 1 December). The Soviet civil airline, Aeroflot, signed an agreement to use the Larnaca airport in Cyprus "as a stopover for many of its flights to countries in the African continent and the Middle East" (*Apoyevmatini,* 28 December).

During 1977 AKEL officials made a number of contacts with sympathetic organizations. In January, AKEL sent a delegation to Aden at the invitation of the People's Democratic Republic of Yemen, to discuss the struggle of Palestinian people (Tass, 12 January). Papaioannou led a three-member delegation to Beirut in February to speak with Palestine Liberation Organization (PLO) leader Yassir Arafat and to pledge mutual support (Nicosia domestic service, 9 February). A second delegation visited Beirut later in the same month to celebrate the eighth anniversary of the founding of the Democratic Front for the Liberation of Palestine. The delegation held "important talks" on the "further development of fraternal relations between the two sides within the framework of the struggle against imperialism, Zionism, and reaction in the Middle East." (*Kharavyi,* 1 March.) Later an AKEL representative was invited to attend a session of the Palestine Nation Council which met in Cairo (ibid., 13 March). In April a delegation went to Baghdad for the thirtieth anniversary of the Ba'ath party (Nicosia domestic service, 13 April). AKEL met with leaders of the Communist Workers' Party of Egypt in Nicosia to hear, among other things, of "the persecution of Communists and patriots by the Egyptian government" (*Kharavyi,* 3 May). AKEL sent greetings to Colonel Qadhafi "on the occasion of the eighth anniversary of the Libyan anti-imperialist revolution " (ibid., 31 August). Toward the end of the year, a PLO delegation came to Nicosia to return the gesture AKEL had made earlier (ibid., 2 October).

Papaioannou made a spring tour to meet with leaders of Communist parties in France, Italy, Spain, Austria, and Czechoslovakia to "prepare the ground in support of the proposal for an international conference and the taking of concrete measures for the implementation of the U.N. resolutions on Cyprus" (Nicosia domestic service, 30 April). Later he went to Bulgaria and East Germany for "talks on the Cyprus problem and on other questions of joint interest" (ibid., 5 June).

Throughout, AKEL received delegations from Romania, Bulgaria, and Czechoslovakia. On the occasion of the anniversary of the Democratic People's Republic of Korea, Papaioannou sent a congratulatory cable (*Kharavyi*, 9 September).

Perhaps one of the more interesting trips by the AKEL leader was the one to Cuba in December 1976 (ibid., 15 December; Tass, 23 December).

Publications: The Communists in Cyprus have long enjoyed influential press channels. AKEL's central organ is the large-circulation daily *Kharavyi* (Dawn), but there are also sympathetic writers and editors on most of the island's periodicals. AKEL also publishes a weekly newspaper, *Dhimokratia* (Democracy), and a weekly magazine, *Neoi Kairoi* (New Times). Its *Theoritikos Dhimokratis* (Theoretical Democrat) is a scholarly journal. The PEO publishes a weekly newspaper, *Ergatiko Vima* (Workers Stride), and EDON a weekly called *Neolaia* (Youth). The Communist publications appear regularly but it would be difficult to find out the exact printing run of each. In London, a weekly called *Ta Vima* (The Stride) has been published by Greek Cypriot Communists for the past thirty-seven years.

Washington, D.C.   T. W. Adams

Denmark

The Communist Party of Denmark (Danmarks Kommunistiske Parti; DKP) sprang from the left-wing faction of the Social Democratic Party (SDP) in the turbulent aftermath of World War I. The DKP was organized on 9 November 1919, and except for the German occupation during World War II, it has always been a legal party.

The DKP draws most of its support from among urban industrial workers, together with some leftist intellectuals in Copenhagen and other urban centers. Membership has edged upward during the mid-1970s after a decade of stagnation and is now estimated between 7,500 and 8,500. The population of Denmark is about 5,090,000.

The continuing discontent of Danish wage-earners and taxpayers—first expressed by a high protest vote in the national election of 4 December 1973—has benefited the DKP and other leftist groups. A sudden parliamentary election on 15 February 1977 saw twelve parties vying for representation, and all but one of these parties gained entrance to the new parliament. Despite the continuing political turmoil, the governing Social Democrats significantly increased their mandates and continued to govern with shifting patterns of support from center and moderate-right parties. The DKP received 114,022 (3.7 percent) votes in the February elections, a loss of 0.5 percent from 1975, but the showing was sufficient to keep seven seats in the 179-member Folketing (Parliament). The DKP seems to have stabilized its electoral strength at around 4 percent during the past three elections, but this is a stronger performance than during the period 1953-73, when the DKP typically polled only 1 percent.

The DKP would appear to be the strongest of several Socialist parties to the left of the reformist governing Social Democrats. The Left Socialists (Venstresocialisterne; VS), who had fallen below the 2 percent threshold for parliamentary representation in the 1971 and 1973 elections, returned to parliament in 1975 and gained an additional seat in February 1977 for a total of five mandates (2.7 percent of the vote). The Socialist People's Party (Socialistisk Folkeparti; SF) received seven seats (3.9 percent of the vote), a loss of two seats from 1975. Intermittent intraparty strife in the SF during 1976 resulted in a large turnover of elected representatives, and internal disagreements (*inter alia*, about the extent of SF cooperation with the DKP and VS) have reappeared in the months since the disappointing electoral showing. On the whole, the 1977 parliamentary elections saw stagnation for the leftist parties, and frequent public opinion polls since February have not shown any significant changes.

Leadership and Organization. Supreme party authority is the DKP's triennial congress, which held its 25th meeting in September 1976. It discusses the report of the Central Committee, adopts the Party Program and Rules, and elects the leading party bodies, consisting of the Central Committee (41 members, 11 alternates), a five-member Control Commission, and two party auditors. The Central Committee elects the party chairman, the Executive Committee (15 members), and the Secretariat (5).

Ib Nørlund is acting DKP chairman and parliamentary leader, appointed to this position by the Central Committee on 26 November. He replaced the ailing Knud Jespersen, chairman since 1958, who died on 1 December. The Communist Party of the Soviet Union was represented at Jespersen's funeral by Latvian Party Secretary A.E. Voss. Meeting on 10 December, the DKP Central Committee chose DKP Parliamentarian Jørgen Jensen as its new chairman. Jensen, fifty-eight, is a veteran of many years of DKP activity and has been a member of the Central Committee since 1952. Trained as an automobile mechanic, Jensen is active in trade union affairs and is a member of the Danish Metalworkers' Union (Dansk Metalarbejderforbund) Executive Committee, despite the fact that the union is controlled by Social Democrats. He is also chairman of a union local in Lynby (a Copenhagen suburb). Poul Emanuel is party secretary.

The DKP is unique among the several Marxist parties in Denmark in that personality conflicts and policy differences, if any, are not discussed in public (since 1958). Party continuity has been typified not only by Jespersen's long chairmanship but by the reelection in February 1977 of the same seven parliamentary representatives as had sat in the previous session. It is felt that Jensen's election demonstrates the DKP's conservatism in internal affairs. Jensen is tried and true, but without the personal popularity that the late Knud Jespersen used to good avantage.

Not much is known about party finances other than that they seem to be adequate and that there are frequent collection campaigns for the party's daily newspaper, *Land og Folk*. Like all parties represented in the Folketing, the DKP receives a monthly subvention from the public treasury. It is currently D. Kr. 25,837 per month (equivalent to $51,720 per year).

The party's two main auxiliary organizations are the Communist Youth of Denmark (Danmarks Kommunistiske Ungdom; DKU) and the Communist Students of Denmark (Danmarks Kommunistiske Studenter; DKS). The autonomous Faroese Communist Party (FKP), which is active on the Faroe Islands, was formed in 1975 and is headed by Egon Thomsen. The FKP did not participate, however, in the 1977 parliamentary election. Neither is the DKP visibly active in Greenland, where one of the island's two parliamentary representatives (Lars Emil Johansen) has been affiliated with the SF parliamentary group.

Domestic Attitudes and Activities. During 1977 the Danish economy made only marginal progress against stagnation and the related problems of idle capacity, low rate of investment, and high unemployment. These issues remained the focus of the DKP's domestic policy comments. Attacks were directed against the Social Democratic minority government's efforts to reduce cost inflation through an incomes policy agreed to by the Social Democrats and four centrist and moderate-rightist parties in August 1976. Again in December 1976 the left-center coalition froze prices, rents, and income until the conclusion of the major collective bargaining negotiations in March. The DKP opposed these measures and continued their call for an attack against real estate speculation and monopolies as well as the removal of the Value Added Tax (VAT) from food, building materials, and medicines. Despite the setback at the February 1977 parliamentary elections, the DKP Central Committee reiterated these demands after their February meeting (*WMR,* March). The deadlocked collective bargaining negotiations, for which the deadline was 1 April, received considerable attention in the Communist press. The DKP's position was that there should be no state-imposed settlement, and that instead of the 2 percent wage guidelines specified by parliamentary action, workers should demand sizable wage increases, a 35-hour work week, and 35 days of paid vacation per year.

It is not unusual for the DKP to concentrate upon labor activities because the party has long been stronger in the trade union movement than in electoral politics. Although the national Trade Union Confederation (Landsorganisationen; LO) is firmly controlled by unionists loyal to the SDP, some Communists and other Marxist activists are prominent in union locals. Preben Møller Hansen, a member of the DKP Executive Committee, is head of the Seamen's Union, which was responsible for several strikes during the summer of 1977 against the private ferry companies which are vital for Danish internal communications. Another important instrument of the leftist trade unionists has been the Shop Stewards' Initiative Group (Formandsinitiativ), in which unionists sympathetic to the DKP compete with SF, VS, and other activists for control. The DKP generally takes a more moderate line and refused to support a "General Strike" scheduled for 7 January. Without DKP support and opposed by the SDP, the action was a fiasco. (*Intercontinental Press,* New York, 21 February; *Aktuelt* (SDP newspaper), 8 January.) The first half of 1977 nevertheless saw a continuation of wildcat strikes. The major conservative newspaper was idled for nearly six months by a typographer's strike, and when a special edition of *Berlingske Tidende* was printed in April, there was a violent physical confrontation on the streets (*Nordisk Kontakt,* No. 9). The DKP sought to defeat the central collective bargaining agreement with its income restrictions, but the agreement was enacted by the Folketing on 14 April after the employers' association rejected its terms (*Land og Folk,* 1 March; *Nordisk Kontakt,* No. 7).

April and May saw extensive student actions at all five Danish universities. Although the DKP was not prominent in these events, DKP parliamentarian Jørgen Jensen called the trouble an expression of sharpening social conflicts (*Nordisk Kontakt,* No. 10). Despite these statements, the DKP and the other left Socialist groups remained politically isolated. In late August the SDP government concluded a series of economic policy compromises with the major non-Socialist parties which will attempt economic stimulation without increasing inflationary pressures, and SF, VS, and DKP were without influence on these matters.

International Views and Positions. The 25th Congress and more recent statements by the DKP leadership reaffirmed the party's established international views. Primary attention is given to denouncing Danish participation in the EC, NATO, and other Western organizations. As the veteran DKP commentator on foreign affairs, Ib Nørlund put it, "by joining NATO and the Common Market, Denmark, a weaker partner, has shouldered an additional burden of the world capitalist crisis. In line with the supra-national policy of these blocs, the monopolies now attack the interests of the working class to rob it of gains. . . . The concessions won from the 'welfare state' are being whittled away." (*WMR,* December 1976.)

The Helsinki Accords are stressed by the DKP as the standards for continued détente in Europe, while much energy is used to fend off Western criticisms of civil liberty violations in the Soviet Union and other Warsaw bloc states. In line with the party's traditional anti-NATO policies, all defense expenditures are opposed by the DKP parliamentary group (*Nordisk Kontakt,* 1977, No. 7). Communist publications echo Soviet security concerns such as the growing West German role in NATO. In the Middle East, the DKP also reflects the Soviet position without noticeable deviation.

International Activities and Contacts. Danish Communists continue to participate in frequent contacts with their counterparts in other European Communist parties, and loyalty to the Soviet party remains the sine qua non of DKP international activity. The Berlin Conference of European Communist parties in June 1976 has become the symbol of DKP interparty standards (*Tiden,* 1976, No. 8). Bilateral visits during 1977 included a trip to Yugoslavia led by Ib Nørlund, who later made a positive factual report of the delegation's impressions (*Land og Folk,* 2 November). Trips to more familiar territory included East Germany in April, Poland in August, and Czechoslovakia in September. The official visit to Denmark by Vietnamese Premier Pham Van Dong in June also provided the occasion for contacts with the DKP leadership and with non-Communist Danes who had supported the Vietnamese Communist cause.

DKP admiration for their Soviet comrades was demonstrated on the occasion of the 60th anniversary of the Bolshevik Revolution. As Ib Nørlund expressed it, "the October Revolution stands out as a tower of inspiration and strength" (*WMR*, September).

Publications. *Land og Folk* (Nation and People), a daily newspaper, is the DKP central organ. Its circulation of some 10,000 increases on weekends to about 12-14,000. *Tiden-Verden Rund* (Time around the World) is the party's theoretical journal. The DKU publication is *Fremad* (Forward).

Other Marxist Groups. Mention has already been made of the two principal competitors with the DKP for left Socialist support. In domestic politics, both the VS and SF try to maintain their own profiles. Since 1958 the SF has been the most pragmatic of the various left socialist groups, and a consequence has been internal party splits and power struggles. Most severe have been the splits in 1967 (over support of SDP economic policy) and in 1976-77 over general party orientation. Although the SF is a unique Danish party, the party has had close ties to an analogous party in Norway (Sosialistisk Venstreparti) and expresses enthusiasm for the leading advocates of "Eurocommunism."

The VS is also a native party without institutional ties to foreign movements. It stresses the limitations of parliamentary action in its program, and has been vocal in its support for student activists and minority elements in the trade union movement. Although not uncritical of events in Communist countries, the VS, like the SF, directs most of its foreign policy criticism against the United States, NATO, and the EC.

In addition to these two small parties there are a myriad of "parties," cultural groups, and publications. The former Communist League of Marxist-Leninists (Kommunistforbund Marxist-Leninister), which has changed its name to the Communist Labor Party of Denmark (Kommunist Arbejderparti; KAP), is headed by Roskilde University lecturer Benito Scocozza. It maintains close ties with the Chinese Communist Party. The KAP's generally pro-Peking line on foreign policy contrasts with its active commitment to the student protest movement in Denmark. The Trotskyist Revolutionary Socialist League (Revolutionaere Socialisters Forbund; RSF) is critical of all foreign powers and domestic competitors.

Among the many non-DKP leftist publications are the SF's *Minavisen* (Mini-newspaper), the KAP's *Kommunist,* the RSF's *Klassekampen* (Class Struggle), and the independent radical Socialist *Politisk Revy*.

University of Massachusetts   Eric S. Einhorn
Amherst

Finland

Consistently attracting nearly a fifth of the electorate, the Communist Party of Finland (Suomen Kommunistinen Puolue; SKP) regained in 1977 the distinction of being the only European Communist party participating in a democratic parliamentary government. Given the strains facing any Finnish government, the SKP's distinction was perhaps a mixed pleasure. Nevertheless, the history of the Finnish Communist movement has been one of dramatic changes in fate reflecting the country's special history and geographic position. The SKP was established in Moscow on 29 August 1918 by "reds"—dissident Social Democrats—escaping from Finland's bloody civil war. Until 1930 the SKP operated through a variety of front organizations, but during the 1930s the party was forced underground by a government ban on its operations. It became legal in 1944, as stipulated by the Finnish-Soviet armistice. During the years of Soviet-Finnish armed conflict (1939-40 and 1941-44), Finnish Communists remained loyal to their country almost without exception.

The SKP draws most of its members from either the industrialized urban areas of southern Finland or the small farming communities of the northern and eastern districts, where a "northland" radical tradition thrives. SKP membership is estimated at 48,000, while the Finnish population totals 4,746,000.

The economic difficulties which had first appeared in 1974-75 (inflation, balance-of-payment difficulties, and rising unemployment) remained severe throughout 1977. The Communists participated in a left-center government led by Centrist Martti Miettunen between 30 November 1975 and 29 September 1976, but the coalition collapsed over economic crisis measures. The SKP participated through its traditional electoral and parliamentary front organization, the Finnish People's Democratic League (Suomen Kansan Demokraatinen Liitto; SKDL), but the SKP was divided internally over political and economic tactics. After months of attack upon the now-minority Miettunen government's economic stabilization measures, the SKP was persuaded to join, together with the larger Social Democratic party, a new left-center majority government under the leadership of the Social Democrat Kalevi Sorsa. With the formation of this five-party coalition on 15 May 1977, the SKP was included in Finland's sixtieth government in as many years of national independence.

Both before and after the cabinet changes of May, economic and labor issues dominated Finland's politics. As the deadline for the main collective bargaining agreement approached in April, debate focused on the wage-hour package recommended by the government's adviser Liinamaa. In an atmosphere of increasing strikes as Communists in the trade unions and in parliament opposed a settlement, the Social Democrats, who dominate the unions, finally accepted the compromise. Ironically, while these difficult wage negotiations were under way the Social Democratic leadership was investigating means of reestablishing a left-center majority government with the participation of the SKDL (SKP) (*Nordisk Kontakt*, 1977: no. 6).

Three communists hold posts in the fifteen-member cabinet of the Sorsa five-party coalition: the vice-minister of education, the traffic and agriculture minister, and the labor minister. The latter is Arvo Aalto, who has been secretary general of the SKP for nine years.

Leadership and Organization. Aarne Saarinen, age 64, a "liberal" Communist and popular former union leader, has been SKP chairman since 1966 and has supported SKDL participation in center-left governments. The 1975 party congress which reelected him also reelected the so-called Stalinist (hardline, particularly in parliamentary and cabinet issues) Taisto Sinisalo and liberal Olavi Hänninen as vice-chairmen, and liberal Arvo Aalto as secretary general. The relative strength of the two factions of the SKP has remained more or less constant since 1970: a ratio of liberals to Stalinists of 20-15 in the Central Committee, 9-6 in the Politburo, and 5-3 in the Secretariat. In the SKDL parliamentary front (containing mostly active Communists, but with non-Communists as well), the liberals dominate the parliamentary group 27-13 and the SKDL Executive Council by roughly the same ratio. There is, of course, some variation in these proportions depending on the actual issue. For the SKP the Central Committee is the highest decision-making body between the triennial congresses.

Party Internal Affairs. SKP Central Committee meetings in November 1976 and February 1977 reflected the desire of both party factions to lessen intraparty strife, which had become increasingly bitter during SKDL participation in the Miettunen government. In opposition, the SKP factions found it possible to agree in attacking the center government's economic policies (*Kansan Uutiset*, 20 February 1977). Speaking in March, Vice-Chairman Sinisalo explained that the unification process of the SKP "is based . . . on the principle that the elements for unified activity are being sought patiently [and] agreement is being reached . . . not in a dictatorial manner but according to joint decisions" (*Tiedonantaja*, 22 March). Chairman Saarinen defined proper party discipline as lower organs obeying the decisions of higher organs with the right of internal dissent and discussion through party channels (*Kansan Uutiset*, 27 February).

Intraparty détente has thus far survived the decision by the majority wing of the SKP to join the Social Democrats and the three center parties in the new coalition government. Sinisalo's faction opposed the coalition, but they were substantially outvoted in the SKDL group, 31-9 (*Nordisk Kontakt*, 1977, no. 10).

It is not easy to define the issues that split the two SKP factions. The division can be traced back at least to the ideological turmoil following the 1956 "de-Stalinization" congress of the Communist Party of the Soviet Union. Among the issues widening the split have been different reactions to the Warsaw Pact invasion of Czechoslovakia in 1968, domestic political tactics (especially the question of political collaboration with the Social Democrats), and interpretations of Moscow's preferences. Despite rising and falling tensions within the SKP, it is the only Nordic Communist party that has avoided a "liberal-conservative" split.

Domestic Attitudes and Activities. Economic affairs have preoccupied both SKP factions throughout 1977. A united Central Committee discussed Finland's economic, social, and political problems in a lengthy statement in November 1976. The Centrist government's restrictive measures seeking to curb inflation and balance of payments difficulties were denounced. Three general measures were advocated: (1) expansion of the state sector in industry and services, along with better parliamentary control of such activity, (2) nationalization of all banks and major financial institutions, and (3) dismantling of Finnish economic and trade ties with the West with increased economic and technological ties to the Soviet bloc (*WMR*, January 1977). Despite these statements, it was clear already in the fall of 1976 that a majority of the SKP, led by Chairman Saarinen, was ready to consider joint measures with the Social Democrats and other parties. Saarinen denounced bourgeois control of Finland and put much of the blame on "partly nonexistent and partly inadequate cooperation between workers' parties" (*Kansan Uutiset*, 18 November). Although the Central Committee repeated its long-term goals after its spring 1977 meeting, it was apparent in April that a majority of the SKP Politburo supported renewed cooperation with the Social Democrats even if it meant reentry into a government coalition in the midst of Finland's worst recession since World War II (ibid., 27 April; Finnish radio, domestic service, 13 April). After the formation of the new Social Democrat-led five-party government in May came the protracted negotiations within the government over a suitable economic package. The Finnish markka had already been devalued by 5.7 percent on 5 April by the Miettunen government. Finally, on 23 June 1977, the government presented a complex twenty-seven-point economic stimulation package, aimed primariy at increased exports and decreased unemployment—which had ranged around 155,000 (6 percent) during the early spring. The SKP majority accepted these measures and helped defend them from Conservative party attacks in parliament in October (*Nordisk Kontakt*, nos. 12, 13).

The events of 1977 demonstrate once again the gap between the SKP's dogmatic program and its pragmatic behavior. The SKP (majority wing) and SKDL are part of the modern political establishment in Finland. The current Sorsa government is the third left-center coalition in the past eleven years. Without SKP/SKDL, the Social Democrats have been unwilling to participate in close political cooperation with the center parties.

Nowhere are the Communists and Social Democrats bigger rivals than in the Finnish trade union movement. Typical of the intense competition between the two groups was the hotly contested Metalworkers Union election of November 1975. The Social Democrats kept control of this largest Finnish union, but with a reduced majority. As mentioned above, the difficult central collective bargaining agreement of April 1977 once again divided the SKP and Social Democrats. The wave of strikes that accompanied the negotiations brought a reprimand from Finnish President Urho Kekkonen when he addressed the Finnish Confederation of Trade Unions at their seventieth anniversary celebration on 16 April. Strikes, Kekkonen declared, were an obsolete weapon of economic competition. (Ibid., no. 8.) Both Communist and Social Democratic trade union leaders denounced his remarks.

The powerful role of President Kekkonen in Finnish politics has also affected the SKP. After more than twenty years of incumbency, Kekkonen is rather a unique institution in Finnish politics. The SKP/SKDL generally falls into line with most other factions in supporting Kekkonen's active foreign policy, which has satisfied the ever-vigilant Soviet neighbor for two decades. In domestic politics Kekkonen's proposals are received with respect but not always obedience by the SKP. Nevertheless, both SKP factions have joined with all of the other major political parties in supporting the reelection of Kekkonen in January 1978. Despite advanced age, he faces only token opposition. (Ibid., 11 March.)

After six months of government participation, therefore, the SKP has been able to accept, with predictable dissent from the "Stalinist" wing, the left-center program of modest economic stimulation aiming at a reduction of steadily rising unemployment. In early September, the markka was again devalued by 3 percent, but this was mainly a response to the much larger devaluation of the Swedish krona. Renewed government responsibility has not worsened relations between the two SKP wings. If the economic situation begins to improve in 1978, it is possible that the relative calm in Finnish domestic politics may be prolonged.

International Views and Positions. The intraparty schism in the SKP is least evident in foreign and international policy. The Helsinki accords of 1975 remain the keystone of SKP foreign policy views, along with the party's traditional opposition to NATO, the EC, and other ties with the Western community. Finland's special relationship with the Soviet Union is symbolized by the 1948 Treaty of Friendship, Cooperation, and Mutual Assistance (Finns frequently refer to the treaty by using the abbreviation YYA).

The most recent complete statement of SKP international views—"For Peace, Security, and Progress"—was adopted at the party's 1975 congress. The party welcomed the defeat of "U.S. imperialism" in Indochina and supported "national liberation" movements in other parts of the Third World. The SKP remained resolutely in the pro-Soviet camp—whether in advocacy of specific economic programs or general loyalty to the pro-Soviet international Communist movement. This position was reaffirmed by the SKP leadership at the June 1976 European Communist summit in East Berlin.

As mentioned above, foreign policy issues frequently are tied to domestic politics. Finland's loose ties with the EC and the Western economic system are denounced by the SKP as contributing to the country's economic woes. Closer economic collaboration with the Soviet Union and other Socialist countries is strongly and repeatedly advocated (*WMR*, January 1977). The minority "hard-line" wing of the SKP is frequently more aggressive in denouncing ties with Western states and more vocal in echoing Soviet foreign policy views. Vice-Chairman Sinisalo, for example, denounced domestic and foreign comments on Soviet treatment of "dissidents" on several occasions during 1977 (Tass, 8 February).

The basic principles of Finnish foreign policy, especially neutrality and good relations with the USSR, are not contested by any significant political group in Finland and are symbolized by the concentration of foreign policy power in President Kekkonen. Typically the USSR takes 20 percent of Finland's exports and provides 17 percent of imports (*Yearbook of Nordic Statistics*, 1976). The role of the SKP would appear to be that of a watchdog against alleged "right-wing" factions and a vocal critic of other Nordic states' foreign and security policies. Norway's NATO commitment was frequently the target of SKP and even presidential criticism during 1977 (*Kansan Uutiset*, 19 February, 2 April; *Suomen Kuvalehti*, 25 March).

International Party Contacts. The SKP maintains close relations with the Communist parties of both Western and Eastern Europe. The latter contacts are particularly intense, as demonstrated by visits to nearly all Eastern European countries during 1977.

Chairman Saarinen and Vice-Chairman Sinisalo met with Soviet Premier Kosygin in March and on several occasions during the year indicated that they do not have much sympathy with the concept of "Eurocommunism." Sinisalo's wing of the SKP was even more direct in its attack on "Eurocommunism" and particularly on the statements and writings of Spanish Communist Party Chairman Santiago Carrillo (*Tiedonantaja*, 29 June). *Pravda* (18 August) cited a speech by Saarinen which denounced public criticism of the Soviet Union by Western Communist parties.

The significance of the sixtieth anniversary of the October Revolution, which led to Lenin's decree of Finnish independence in December 1917, was stressed in all Communist publications (*WMR*, September).

Other Marxist Parties. The only noteworthy Marxist-Leninist group outside of the SKP is the pro-Chinese "Marxist-Leninist Groups of Finland," whose activities are regularly reported in the Chinese press. Despite visits to Peking and occasional demonstrations against "Soviet imperialism," the group remains practically without political significance.

Publications. The SKP/SKDL's *Kansan Uutiset* (People's News), published daily in Helsinki, is the principal organ of the liberal majority of the SKP (circulation 55,600). *Kommunisti* is the monthly theoretical journal. *Tiedonantaja* (Herald) and *Hämeen Yhteistyö* speak for the SKP's "Stalinist" faction. The weekly *Folktidningen* (People's News) is the Communist newspaper for Finland's small Swedish-speaking minority. The Finnish "Maoists" circulate several publications including *Lakakuu* (October) and *Punalippu* (Red Guard), which are perhaps the only violently anti-Soviet publications in the country.

University of Massachusetts   Eric S. Einhorn
Amherst

France

The French Communist Party (Parti communiste français; PCF) was founded in December 1920. Since the early 1960s it has pursued a policy of electoral alliances with the Socialist Party (Parti socialiste; PS) and various left-center forces. A "Common Program of Government," signed in 1972, until recently formed the basis of the "Union of the Left" alliance, which includes the PCF, the PS, and the Movement of Left Radicals (Mouvement des radicaux de gauche; MRG). While contributing to large parliamentary gains for the left as a whole, the alliance has benefited the PS far more than the PCF. Between 1973 and 1976 the latter's traditional electoral dominance on the French left was reversed, although its membership remains the largest and most militant of all French parties.

The PCF electorate today continues its post-1958 stagnation at about a fifth of the total vote, despite the Union of the Left alliance. The most recent legislative elections, March 1973, gave the PCF 21.3 percent (5,026,417 votes), compared with 20 percent in 1968, 22.5 percent in 1967, and 21.7 percent in 1962. In presidential elections, the PCF tactic in 1969 was, for the first time, to present a Communist candidate at the first ballot. Jacques Duclos's 21.5 percent total indicated that the party could muster its legislative electorate in a presidential election. In 1974 (as in 1965), the Union of the Left parties presented a joint first-ballot candidate, PS First Secretary François Mitterrand, who nearly won (49.3 percent) against Valéry Giscard d'Estaing. The full contrast between the PCF's electoral stagnation and the extraordinary gains of the PS, as well as the advantage which the latter has drawn from mutual second-ballot withdrawals, was revealed by the 1976 cantonal elections: whereas the PS (which received 18.9 percent in the 1973 legislative elections) won 25.6 percent on the first ballot and 30.8 percent on the second ballot, the PCF won 22.8 percent on the first and only 17.3 percent on the second.

The overall advance of the left was confirmed in the 13-21 March municipal elections. With steady across-the-board gains, at times fairly modest and generally less than 5 percent, the left alliance profited radically from the winner-take-all electoral system. It gained a total of 618 municipalities with more than 9,000 inhabitants and now controls the local government of 157 of France's 221 large cities (more than 30,000 inhabitants), as opposed to 97 before these elections. Yet the surprisingly strong first-ballot showing of united far left slates in 31 such large cities, receiving an average of 5.35 percent of the total vote, also revealed that supporters of the left were not entirely united behind the Common Program (see below).

The electoral system and the practice of united left slates on the first ballot make a comparison of PCF and PS results in the municipal elections rather difficult, and it is necessary to limit the present analysis to the 221 large cities. Previously holding the majority of government coalitions in fifty such cities, the PCF headed seventy-two winning left lists in March (losing none of the cities previously controlled), while PS-led municipal governments in large cities went from forty-seven to eighty-one (with a loss of three of those previously controlled). At this level, then, the Socialists continued to gain in relation to the PCF. The fact that nineteen out of thirty-nine Communist-led lists defeated incumbent center-right governments, roughly the same rate of success as that of Socialist-led lists in such cases (thirty-seven out of seventy-one), seemed to suggest that the PCF nevertheless had regained a certain electoral momentum. Yet a closer analysis comparing these results with the 1973 legislative elections does not support this conclusion. Such a comparative analysis shows that Socialist-led lists as a rule (in thirty-three out of forty-six cases) defeated incumbent center-right governments where the total left votes had been above 38.5 percent on the second ballot in 1973, while the same threshold for Communist-led lists was 47 percent of the 1973 vote (above which incumbent center-right governments were defeated in fifteen out of twenty-one cases). This difference of more than 8 percent marked a considerable decline of PCF strength vis-à-vis the PS in comparison with the 1973 elections, in which the normal first-ballot threshold of winning PS-led lists was 45 percent and that of PCF-led lists 49 percent. The relative success of the PCF in the municipal elections is thus to be explained in terms of the previous near-majority strength of the left in most of those areas where the Communists headed united slates. The pattern which emerges from these elections is one in which the PCF holds its own or even progresses in relation to the PS in its areas of preexisting strength, while losing ground to the latter elsewhere, PS growth hence being inversely proportional to PCF strength (cf. Frédéric Bon, "La Gauche éléctorale," *Esprit,* June 1977, pp. 103-10). At the same time, however, the PS previously ran twenty-six large cities and many smaller municipalities without PCF support (either by itself or on the basis of left-center alliances), whereas municipalities run by the PCF without Socialist support were much more rare (only ten large cities). In this respect the overall advance of united left municipal governments may prove a highly important means for the PCF to extend its influence and to build new areas of electoral strength through organizational efforts.

In the 490-seat National Assembly, the electoral agreement for mutual second-ballot withdrawals has benefited all three formations constituting the Union of the Left. In December 1977, the PCF had seventy-four seats (including one held by the Communist Party of Guadeloupe), as opposed to thirty-four in 1968, while the PS had ninety-three and the MRG thirteen. The Senate is presently in the process of being expanded to include 316 seats and as one third of the Senate was elected on September 25, 1977, the total number of seats was increased from 283 to 295. Since it is elected by indirect suffrage and municipal councilors consitute one of the electoral colleges, the success of the left in the municipal elections reflected itself in across-the-board gains in September, while the position of the PS within the left alliance was once again improved. The PCF advanced from twenty to twenty-three seats (including one held by the Communist Party of Guadeloupe), the PS from fifty-two to sixty-two and the MRG gained one more seat (sixteen Left-Radical senators constituted themselves as a subgroup of the "Democratic Left" coalition in the Senate after these elections).

The growth of the PCF's membership is in sharp contrast to its electoral frustration. After stagnating around 300,000 to 350,000 in the 1960s, the total number of members reached 491,000 in

1975 and 543,000 by the end of 1976. On 26 October 1977 the PCF's *L'Humanité* reported that the year's target of 600,000 members had been obtained. Georges Marchais said in early January that the total had reached 632,000 (*L'Humanité,* 9 January 1978). This indicates the party's recruitment drive was not seriously affected by the deterioration of PCF-PS relations in the summer and fall. For example, 9,300 new members were recruited at the two-day *L'Humanité* festival of 10-11 September alone, compared with the previous all-time record of 6,053 in 1976 (ibid., 14 September). The total figure of new members, however, is somewhat ambiguous in the sense that many who sign a membership form never get a party card or buy only a few of the monthly dues stamps. More important, the intensification of PCF recruitment has been to a great extent a process of increasing membership within the party's established sphere of influence, and mainly involves getting voters and and sympathizers to take out membership cards, which explains the discrepancy between the PCF's growing membership and its electoral stagnation. The nature and circumstances of the PCF's rapid membership expansion have serious implications whose significance cannot yet be fully determined. There are various signs (including numerous articles in the party press) that expansion has caused a variety of adjustment problems. Equally important, a very large proportion of party members have joined since 1972 and the central reference point of their political activism has been the Union of the Left and the government party role defined by the Common Program with the Socialists. This may at some point curtail the support for radical shifts by the PCF leadership, although the rank-and-file on the whole mobilized vigorously behind the leadership campaign against the Socialist Party in the fall.

As to the social composition of the PCF electorate and membership, certain considerable changes have taken place in recent years, though global statistics indicating their scope remain lacking. While PCF doctrine still insists upon the absolute priority of workers in all party activities, there has been for the past few years an attempt to shade the most dogmatic aspects of the party's traditional *ouvriériste* ideology in order to attract more electoral and organizational support from other classes and social groups. In 1966-67 the PCF claimed to be about 60 percent working class in its membership (including housewives of workers and retired workers) while André Vieuguet said at the 1976 Congress that the 1975 recruits were 45 percent workers and about 20 percent salaried employees. The percentage of women members has also increased in recent years. *L'Humanité* predicted on 19 September 1977 that the party would have 200,000 women members by October, roughly a third of the total membership (as opposed to 25.5 percent in 1966), and the present goal is to raise female membership to 40 percent.

The PCF electorate in 1973 was slightly over 50 percent working class (blue-collar workers make up about 32 percent of the total active work force; the PCF got 31 percent of the working-class vote in 1967 and 37 percent in 1973) and about 15 percent salaried employees. It is predominantly male (58 percent) and younger than any other large party electorate in France.

The setting for French Communist strategy, until the fall, continued to be a radical bipolarization of French party and electoral politics, and the potential majority strength of the left alliance. The March municipal elections confirmed both the possibility that the left could gain a majority of seats in the National Assembly in the 1978 legislative elections, and the Socialist Party intention to use its electoral superiority vis-à-vis the PCF to dominate a left-wing government. Within the framework of these prospects, the Union of the Left in the summer of 1977 undertook to "update" the Common Program. The Communists chose to confront the PS on policy, and, by implication, on the role the PCF would assume in a Socialist-led government. The PS and the MRG proved unwilling to concede to the PCF's demands on nationalizations, defense policy, social policy, and other issues. The negotiations on updating the Common Program then broke off in September. At this writing it is not certain how the left parties will contest the March 1978 elections, although, in any case, a left victory in 1978 is now much less certain than what recent electoral results would indicate. The left alliance could conceivably reunite around a Common Program, or the parties could return to a simple electoral agreement for mutual second-ballot withdrawals. No cooperation at all is a third possibility. The future of the bipolarization in French politics, the Communist-Socialist balance on the left, and the Communist strategy itself are suddenly thus all highly uncertain.

Leadership and Organization. The national leadership of the PCF was elected at the party's Twenty-second Congress, 4-8 February 1976, and no significant changes occured in 1977. The Central Committee numbers ninety-seven full and twenty-four candidate members. The Politburo's eighteen full members are: Gustave Ansart, Mireille Bertrand, Guy Besse, Jacques Chambaz, Jean Colpin, Etienne Fajon, Guy Hermier, Jean Kanapa, Henri Krasucki, Paul Laurent, Roland Leroy, Georges Marchais, René Piquet, Gaston Plissonier, Claude Poperen, Georges Séguy, André Vieuguet, and Madeleine Vincent; the three candidate members are: Charles Fiterman, Maxime Gremetz, and André Lajoinie. The Secretariat of the Central Committee consists of Colpin, Fiterman, Laurent, Leroy, Piquet, and Plissonier. Georges Marchais remained secretary general.

The cell structure of the PCF continued to show significant development along with the rise in membership. In January 1975 there were 21,340 cells in the ninety-seven federations, and Laurant gave the figure 26,099 in his 10 November Central Committee report (*L'Humanité,* 11 November). During the year the PCF continued its strong emphasis on increasing the number and relative percentage of work place cells as a means to foster membership recruitment and to reinforce the party's position vis-à-vis the Socialists, as well as to enhance its mobilization capacities for the prospect of a left government. The number of workplace cells has gone from 6,500 in 1975 to 8,000 in 1976, to 9,550 at the end of 1977. The 9,650 neighborhood cells and 5,450 rural cells of 1975 were cited as 10,600 and 5,930, respectively (ibid., rounded figures). Workplace cells constituted 20 percent of the total in 1945, 26 percent in 1970, and close to 40 percent in 1977.

Auxiliary and Mass Organizations. The Communist Youth Movement (Mouvement de la Jeunesse Communiste de France; MJCF) has made significant membership gains recently. With no more than 65,000 members in 1971 and 70,000 in 1975, the MJCF claimed a total membership of 110,000 at its national conference of 22-23 October 1977 (*L'Humanité,* 22 October). This conference was largely dedicated to a reconfirmation of the MJCF's fidelity to the line of the Twenty-second Congress, its support of the party leadership in the crisis of the left and a reorganization of the press of the MJCF (see below). Hermier is the Politburo member supervising the youth organizations, and the MJCF secretary general, Jean-Michel Catala, is also a member of the FCF Central Committee.

The Union of Communist Students (Union des Etudiants Communistes de France; UECF), part of the MJCF umbrella organization, is the PCF's organization among university students. It claimed 15,000 members in 1976 and is the dominant tendency of the National French Student Union (Union Nationale des Etudiants de France; UNEF), which has some 50,000 members. This organization is countered by another, Troskyist-led UNEF, claiming 26,000 members.

In keeping with the relative "feminization" of the PCF membership in recent years, the Union of French Women (Union des Femme Françaises; UFF) increased its membership from 100,000 in 1976 to 135,000 (*Le Monde,* 24 November) and continued its recent emphasis on women's rights issues.

The General Confederation of Labor (Confédération Générale du Travail; CGT) remains the major mass organization within the Communist sphere of influence and therefore continues to occupy a crucial position in the PCF's efforts to mobilize working-class support for its policies. Still by far the largest union organization in France (between 1.5 and 2.5 million members), the CGT is, according to the results of professional elections and mobilizing capacities, the dominant union in all three sectors of the French economy—private, nationalized, and public. In the public sector, however, this dominance is mitigated by the large impact of the autonomous Federation of National

Education (Fédération de l'Education Nationale; FEN), the union of teachers and professors, which is the third largest union after the CGT and the Socialist-oriented CFDT. Communist elements in the FEN comprise the second strongest of the five main tendencies.

The CGT's secretary general, Georges Séguy, as well as its second leading figure, Henri Krasucki, are both members of the PCF Politburo. But the trade union federation may no longer be as firmly under the control of its Communist-dominated leadership as used to be the case. A recent poll indicates that 40 to 50 percent of the members intend to vote for the Socialist Party, and the breakdown of the left alliance has caused public controversy in the union, the only labor federation to have endorsed formally the Common Program. In an unprecedented move, on 14 October, two members of the CGT Executive Committee (both also members of the PS) voted against a declaration which lined the CGT up with the PCF positions, and made their opposition public. The Communist leadership was forced to back down on this issue, and the Executive Committee adopted a new declaration on 18 October, reiterating the CGT's commitment to the Common Program, but being far more evasive on the issues separating the PCF and the PS (*Le Monde,* 20 October).

In rural areas, a Communist-influenced syndicate, the Movement for the Coordination and Defense of Agricultural Enterprises (Mouvement de Coordination et de Défense des Exploitations Agricoles; MODEF), occupies a rather distant second place, behind the autonomous FNSEA organization. Other Communist mass organizations such as the Peace Movement (Mouvement de la Paix), which had great importance during the Cold War, are of relatively little consequence today, though they are at times used as vehicles of symbolic gestures of international solidarity.

Party Internal Affairs. The year 1977 saw a continuation of two distinct, and at times contradictory, trends in the PCF's internal affairs. On the one hand, there is a trend toward consolidation and greater party unity around the domestic strategy of seeking political power within the framework of parliamentary democracy (though not necessarily in the Union of the Left alliance), and around its foreign policy correlate of a more critical distance vis-à-vis the Communist Party of the Soviet Union (CPSU). On the other hand, this new line has itself encouraged a limited trend toward greater diversity within the PCF. As a result of its outwardly "democratic image," the PCF leadership has in recent years been faced with demands for a certain liberalization in the party's internal affairs as well.

These demands for more internal democracy have created an atmosphere in which several leading PCF members have taken a number of individual public initiatives, at times even at odds with the party line. Communist historian Jean Ellenstein, who speaks for the current "democratic" evolution of the PCF in its most advanced form, had previously taken the lead in this respect and continued to do so. His articles in *Le Monde* of 30-31 December 1976 in effect provoked the party leadership to reveal that, contrary to all claims by Communist leaders since 1956, the French delegation to the Twentieth Congress of the CPSU had indeed been informed as to the content of Khrushchev's secret speech (*L'Humanité,* 13 January). The incident revealed the continued unease with which the PCF confronts its own Stalinist past. From the other side of the political spectrum, PCF "left-wing" philosopher Louis Althusser presented a critical analysis of the Twenty-second PCF Congress to the philosophy circle of the UECF at the Sorbonne in December 1976, despite the fact that the national UECF leadership had prohibited the meeting. He later published this work (*22e Congrès*) without the prior approval of the party leadership. Althusser also confronted members of the Central Committee in a public meeting on 30 March about the lack of internal party democracy, a concern which he shares with Ellenstein despite differences on most other issues. In response to Althusser's question, Lucien Sève noted that the question of party statutes was "open" and would be brought up at the next congress (*Le Monde,* 2 April). Laurent, secretary of the Central Committee in charge of organization, responded to the debate over party pluralism in an interview in *La Nouvelle*

Critique (April), arguing that democratic centralism was of crucial importance to the PCF's credibility as a revolutionary party and that it meant that the party could admit no factionalism.

In any case, certain kinds of debate within the PCF and open expressions of disagreement have continued, and can no longer be said to be strictly limited to party intellectuals. For example, Paul Chomat, secretary of the Loire federation, granted an unprecedented interview to the Trotskyist daily *Rouge* (10 May), saying that he considered this to be in line with the PCF's readiness to confront any and all political opinions (*Le Monde,* 11 May). Fiterman, on the other hand, declined a similar requests by *Rouge,* saying that any dialogue with the Trotskyists was totally inopportune (ibid., 14 May). The policy changes on the European Parliament and the nuclear strike force adopted by the PCF leadership in the spring also provoked some unrest among the rank and file, because they had not been discussed outside the top leadership and appeared to be motivated by electoralist considerations. Laurent defended the nature of these decisions, arguing that the democratically elected central leadership had to be capable of taking firm and clear positions on issues that arose, and went on to say that public expressions of internal differences were incompatible with democratic centralism (*France Nouvelle,* 6 June).

The breakdown of the Common Program renegotiation has thus far had a contradictory impact upon internal party affairs. There are signs that some elements in the rank and file are uneasy and even dismayed, something which even *L'Humanité* (12 October) reported, noting that many party members had yet to recognize the "right turn" of the Socialist Party. At the same time, the polemics between Communist and Socialist leaders have in certain respects served to reinforce party unity. At the militant level, many are satisfied to see the PCF return to a "harder" line, while, at the leadership level, a new consensus appears to have emerged on the policy of emphasizing the party over the left alliance.

An immense "educational" campaign was undertaken after September to mobilize the party behind the policy of attacking the Socialists. The very fact of its necessity, on the one hand, and the fact of its apparent success at this writing, on the other hand, testify to the continuing contradictory trends in recent party internal affairs.

Domestic Views and Activities. The general line of the PCF was given at the Twenty-second Congress in February 1976 (see *Cahiers du communisme,* February-March 1976 and *YICA, 1976,* for a general summary). Until the fall, the focus of the party's strategic outlook remained an electoral victory of the Union of the Left, which, as a government coalition, would implement the reforms of the Common Program and thereby create the conditions under which a transition to Socialism could begin. This transition is considered to depend upon the PCF's capacity to extend its influence as the political vanguard of the working class, and the party's role as a potential government partner is conceived of as a means to this end.

Forced to accept Socialist electoral superiority in the foreseeable future, the PCF has sought to mitigate its impact upon the relation of forces within the Union of the Left in a variety of ways. The recent recruitment drive, cell structure expansion, and reform of the party press organs (see below) are parts of this effort to enhance Communist influence. The PCF campaign around the issue of poverty in France, launched in November 1976 and culminating in a number of public mass meetings on the theme "Truth-Hope" in February, was one of several such mobilizations during the year, the purpose of which is to shift some of the focus away from the electoral level and to pose as the champion of the most disprivileged.

Within the Union of the Left itself, the attempt to mitigate the dominance of the PS has manifested itself in the PCF's willingness to broaden the alliance; e.g., to include dissident left-wing Gaullists and the Parti Socialiste Unifié (PSU) not only on the united left slates in the municipal elections. but also in the discussions on updating the Common Program. Whereas the left-wing Gaullists support some of the PCF's views on foreign policy and national defense, the PSU would clearly side with the Communists on issues of nationalizations and social reforms, both thereby providing a counterweight to the MRG's support of the Socialist party on most major issues. This tactic proved successful in negotiating united left lists for the municipal elections. In particular the PSU criticized PS unwillingness to draw up joint lists solely on the basis of the previous (1971) elections, when the Socialists were weaker. The tactic faltered when the PS and the MRG then refused to include in discussions of updating the Common Program any groups which had not originally signed it.

At the opening of the Central Committee's session on 31 March, shortly after the municipal elections, Marchais called for discussions to revise the Common Program, an idea which the MRG had previously endorsed. Although wary of a detailed or protracted negotiation, the PS bent to pressure from both its partners, and a summit meeting of left leaders on 17 May resulted in an agreement to form a fifteen-man working group, with equal representation. It still remained unclear whether the group would discuss only the technical aspects of the Common Program's application or whether it would negotiate the basic policy proposals of the 1972 text. The Communists were successful in expanding the discussions, which resulted in a shift away from electoral and parliamentary emphasis. It was thus through policy and program disagreements (which had never been formally discussed since the signing of the Common Program in 1972) that the electoral Union of the Left itself came to be called into question.

Differences between the PS and the PCF about how to indemnify shareholders in companies to be nationalized by a left government emerged following a colloqium on industrial policy organized by the PS in April, prior to any discussions on the updating of the Common Program. The Socialist leaders proposed that shareholders be given new shares in the same companies, yielding dividends and being freely exchanged on the stock market, but without voting power. The PCF attacked this proposal as a step away from genuine nationalizations, and proposed as an alternative that shareholders be issued state bonds, reimbursed through annual payments over a period of twenty years, but yielding no dividends. To this early controversy was added the PCF's estimated budget—of extraordinary proportions— for the Common Program, released by *L'Humanité* (10 May) just before a televised debate between Mitterrand and Prime Minister Barre. The Socialists disavowed the Communist calculations as unreasonably high. The episode as a whole severely embarrassed Mitterrand and the PS, adding to questions as to the workability of the alliance as a government coalition.

The controversy over indemnifying shareholders set the stage for the issue of nationalizations to emerge as a central difficulty in the formal negotiations to update the Common Program. The MRG from the beginning aimed to have the number of nationalizations proposed in the 1972 text reduced, and to eliminate the clause granting workers the right to petition the government for the nationalization of their company. The PCF on the contrary sought to expand the policy of nationalizations. In addition to the credit sector (banks and insurance companies) and the nine industrial groups included in the 1972 program, the PCF asked for nationalization of the French Petroleum Corporation, Peugeot-Citroën, and the four major industrial groups in the iron and steel industry. The PS opposed any such extension of the number of nationalizations and, more important, a fundamental difference between the PS and the PCF emerged on the subsidiaries of the companies to be nationalized. The original Socialist position was that only subsidiaries owned 100 percent by the parent corporation be nationalized, whereas the PCF demanded that the threshold for nationalization be 51 percent ownership.

A number of other disagreements arose through the discussions during the summer, notably on Communist proposals to make the increase of the minimum wage retroactive to the date of a new agreement, and to establish the goal of limiting wage differentials to a 1 to 5 ratio. The PS rejected both these measures as "unrealistic and dogmatic," proposing that the new minimum wage should go into effect as of April 1978 and that wage differentials conform to a 1 to 7 scale as an ultimate goal. National defense also emerged as a major issue separating the PS and the PCF. The Socialists originally criticized the PCF's controversial endorsement of the nuclear strike force in May 1977 as a unilateral breach of the Common Program (which called for giving up nuclear arms). The PS, which is itself moving to accept the *force de frappe,* later accused the Communists of seeking implicitly to undermine France's commitment to the Atlantic Alliance by allowing the nuclear force to become outmoded. The ambivalence of the PS on the security issue, which clearly weakened its bargaining position, was manifested in Mitterrand's suggestion that the "nuclear question" be submitted to the French people in a referendum, a proposal critized by the PCF as shirking a firm commitment by the left alliance. A tentative agreement on national defense was nevertheless reached within the fifteen-man working group on 28 July. It made no mention of a referendum or of the Communist proposal of an omni-directional, Gaullist-type defense strategy (*tous azimuts*). It called for maintenance and continued modernization of the nuclear force under exclusive French control (*Le Monde,* 10 August). Yet distrust persisted over this issue on both sides, and it proved to be a major issue again during the summit discussions in September.

Apart from the defense question, moreover, virtually all disagreements were simply set aside by the working group, to be resolved through a summit meeting of party leaders. On 29 July it was agreed that this summit should be held in September and that it should be prepared by the heads of the different party delegations in the working group. Because the PS refused to continue discussions on substantive matters, these preliminary contacts failed to materialize. In response to what appeared to the Communists as Socialist attempts to backslide, the PCF mobilized its rank and file in early September in an effort to exert "mass pressure" upon the PS. PCF-PS differences now became not only public but also more ideological. It became increasingly difficult for either party to make concessions without appearing weaker than the other. The first summit meeting, held on 14 September, was abruptly ended as the MRG delegation walked out in protest against the PCF's policy on nationalizations. The PCF then offered to continue negotiations with the PS alone, but the Socialists refused, not without expressing a certain dismay about the position adopted by the MRG. A new summit was scheduled, with both the PS and the PCF making certain conciliatory moves on the issue of nationalizations, and the MRG lining up behind the PS. The PS lowered the threshold for nationalization of subsidiaries to 98 percent ownership by the parent corporation, and added a number of "strategic" subsidiaries below this figure to the list of nationalizations it would consider acceptable. The PCF withdrew most of its nationalization proposals extending beyond the nine industrial groups in the 1972 program, and said that in the case of 279 subsidiaries owned more than 51 percent by these groups, majority state financial participation would be an acceptable substitute for outright nationalization.

However, the issue of nationalizations again could not be resolved at the second summit, begun on 21 September and suspended the following day. The PCF-PS disagreement finally came down to 400 small and medium-size companies, employing approximately 150,000 workers and representing slightly more than 0.5 percent of French industry. Given the large nationalizations already agreed upon, the nationalization issue at this point had become a pretext for the break. The real problem seemed to be the role which the Communists demanded in a possible left government, including an informal policy-veto power. In this context, the issue of nationalizations took on added importance to the PCF in that trade-union influence in choosing the management of nationalized industries would, given the CGT's strength, enable Communists to gain new and influential positions within the nationalized sector.

The PCF has called a national conference for January 1978, at which the leadership will evaluate the present crisis of the left and announce its policy for the March elections.

International Views and Policies. As always, it is necessary to distinguish two PCF foreign policies, that of a "government party" dealing with relations between nation-states and that of a Communist party dealing with other parties in the international movement.

The general framework for the PCF's international outlook as a potential partner in a left government was established at the Twenty-second Congress (see *Cahiers du communisme*, February-March 1976, and *YICA, 1977*). The PCF considers detente to be a victory for the Socialist bloc, which must be preserved. But it rejects the notion that detente implies accepting or maintaining the status quo in Western Europe, or the division of the world into zones of influence. The PCF proposes to resist U.S. and West German pressure further to consolidate the European community and Atlantic relations, both of which it considers dangerous to French national independence. The PCF is particularly vehement in its denunciation of President Giscard d'Estaing's renewal of an Atlanticist orientation in French policy, which Marchais characterized at the congress as a "criminal policy."

The PCF viewed French military involvement in Zaire as an outgrowth of this reorientation of French foreign policy, and launched a protest campaign against what it considered to be an "act of intimidation against the peoples of Africa who struggle for national independence and dignity" (*L'Humanité*, 13 April). In a similar vein, the PCF continued to criticize U.S. business interests in France, French cooperation with the International Energy Agency, widening of the French trade deficit with the U.S. and West Germany, "subordination" of the French franc to the dollar and the Deutschmark, and the "de facto reintegration of NATO." The PCF also made various protests against American refusals to grant landing rights to the Concorde and against the laxity of the French government on this issue. This campaign took an unexpected turn on 21 July: a French television studio was occupied by some hundred Communist workers from the aerospace industry, who demanded that a declaration denouncing the U.S. refusal be read. It appeared that this action either did not have the prior approval of the party leadership at all, or was provoked by a "hardline" group attempting to influence general party policy. In any case, approval of Concorde's landing rights was well received by *L'Humanité*, and the issue on the whole did not detract from a certain conciliatory attitude toward the U.S.A. and the Carter administration. Most notably, the party confirmed on 21 April that Kanapa had met with second-level American diplomats in Paris to discuss foreign policy (President Giscard d'Estaing was reported much displeased).

Within the framework of PCF's new emphasis on national independence, two major policy shifts occurred in 1977. First, Marchais announced on 17 April that the PCF would no longer oppose direct elections to the European Parliament, provided that the electoral law would limit the mandate of French representatives so as to protect the sovereignty of the National Assembly. Despite Communist arguments that if the electoral law did include such restrictions it would signify a victory for the PCF's position on national independence, this move did indeed mark a basic reversal and an apparent concession to the PS, though the Communist position still remains closer to that of the Gaullists. Second, at the 11 May Central Committee session, the PCF endorsed the French nuclear deterrent. The Socialists as well seem ready to drop the policy of giving up nuclear arms, but the Communists' overall notion of a totally independent, omni-directional defense strategy remains fundamentally different from that of the PS. The PCF, however, insists that its new defense policy is not incompatible with France's commitment to the Atlantic alliance, which the party is willing to honor until the military blocs are dismantled. (Ibid., 30 September.)

As the issue of French involvement in Zaire indicates, the PCF continued to agree in general with Soviet policy regarding trouble spots in world politics, such as the Middle East and Southern Africa. The major source of PCF-Soviet disagreements in foreign policy continued to be Soviet conciliation of conservative French governments and the West in general. The PCF took a particularly critical view of the privileged relations between Paris and Moscow, manifested by the

Giscard-Brezhnev summit in June and the following visits to Moscow by Prime Minister Barre and Defense Minister Bourges. *L'Humanité* (25 October) went so far as to suggest that the Soviet leadership was helping the French government to maintain the fiction of an independent French foreign policy, thereby improving its electoral chances. This critical attitude vis-à-vis the Soviet leadership also indicates the PCF's continued interest in Eurocommunism, consolidated by the Madrid summit meeting of Berlinguer, Carrillo, and Marchais on 2-3 March. In the joint press conference following these discussions and upon his return to France, Marchais for the first time publicly used the term "Eurocommunism," and he later defended the relevance of this concept against Soviet insinuations that it is an imperialist invention, arguing that "it is the invention of the Communist and workers' parties concerned" (ibid., 24 June). Though the PCF continues to reject the notion of a "new Communist center," contacts with the Southern European Communist parties were intensified this year, while the PCF's relations with the CPSU remain very restrained. Most notably, Marchais did not meet with Brezhnev during the latter's visit to France in June, explaining that "it is not obligatory for us to meet every time he comes to Paris" (ibid., 3 June). Apart from visits to Moscow by Krasucki in March and Séguy in September, both of whom went in the name of the CGT rather than the PCF, contacts between the PCF and the CPSU were limited generally to lower-level study delegations.

One source of this chill in PCF-CPSU relations continues to be the issue of civil and political rights in the Soviet Union and the Eastern bloc as a whole. The PCF's negative reaction to the exchange of the Chilean Communist leader Louis Corvalán for the Soviet dissident Vladimir Bukovsky in December 1976 set the stage for a new series of criticisms and provocations of the Soviet leadership by the French Communists. While welcoming the release of both men, the Politburo took the opportunity to reiterate its commitment to political freedoms and went on to characterize this exchange of political prisoners between a Socialist country and a fascist country as completely "inadmissable" (*Cahiers du communisme,* January). Marchais later responded to criticism by Corvalán in a *Pravda* article by saying that it was totally out of the question that the PCF would back down on its commitment to human rights everywhere. Marchais's discussion with Soviet dissident Andrei Amalrik on French television in February, the continued PCF contacts with Leonid Plyushch and *L'Humanité's* defense of the Czechoslovak dissidents who signed "Charter 77" (17 January) in turn drew further Soviet criticism, notably at the April meeting of the *Problems of Peace and Socialism* review in Prague. Some of this criticism has focused on Ellenstein's writings and statements on the nature of Soviet socialism, which the Soviets have used to criticize the present PCF line while attempting to avoid further deterioration of official party relations. *L'Humanité* (25 January) protested against these personal attacks on Ellenstein, just as it later defended Santiago Carrillo after Soviet attacks on his book *Eurocommunism and the State,* arguing, without endorsing the latter, that "anathematization" is no substitute for "in-depth analysis of complex problems" (24 June).

The recent deterioration of relations between the PCF and the Socialist Party has led to a shift in the Communists' attention. As a result, attacks on the Soviet leadership have been somewhat toned down. This does not, however, imply a reversal of the previous line, as indicated by *L'Humanité's* harsh criticism of the trial of four Czechoslovak dissidents in October and its protests against the denial by the Czechoslovak authorities of *L'Humanité's* request to send a reporter to the trial—"a refusal which deprives our readers of direct information on a trial putting into question the human rights for which we struggle" (16 October).

There has been much speculation about the role Soviets may have played in the breakdown of the French left alliance. The Soviet leadership may well be just as comfortable (if not more) dealing with the present French government as it would be dealing with a government headed by Mitterrand,

and a left government in France might provoke an undesirable upset of international relations, as well as a boost to the prestige of Eurocommunism. Naturally, the PCF has denied that it acted upon pressure from Moscow, and the almost complete absence of any contacts between the PCF and the CPSU at the leadership level in the months preceeding the break seems to support their argument. At the same time, however, the present crisis of the French left may provide the context for a certain rapprochement in PCF-CPSU relations. The choice of Paul Laurent, often seen as the second man in the leadership hierarchy, to head the PCF delegation to the sixtieth anniversary celebrations of the October Revolution, and the presence also of Kanapa, seem to indicate that the French Communists do not at this moment desire a further rift in their relations with Moscow. Marchais's absence from this delegation, partly due to domestic calculations, suggests that the PCF intends nonetheless to keep its distance.

International Activities and Contacts. In sharp contrast with the continued paucity of high-level official contacts with the CPSU (see above), there were numerous contacts between the PCF and its Southern European counterparts in 1977. Most notable among these was the 2-3 March summit meeting between Berlinguer, Carrillo and Marchais in Madrid. Both Berlinguer and Marchais resisted Carrillo's desire to elaborate a manifesto of shared principles, which would inevitably have involved staking out their differences with the CPSU. The joint declaration following these discussions was therefore limited to a brief statement of solidarity with the Spanish Communists and the struggle for democracy in Spain. At the summit, Marchais is said to have requested that the Portuguese Communist Party (PCP) be included in future consultations and the PCF's contacts with the more hard-line Portuguese Communists have remained much closer than those which the latter entertain with their Italian and Spanish comrades. A PCP delegation headed by Cunhal visited France on 12-15 April and held extensive discussions with Marchais and other top leaders of the PCF, the joint declaration reaffirming the ties of solidarity between the two parties. Above all, however, it was the apparent improvement of the PCF's relations with the Italian Communists (PCI) which characterized the year at this level. Shortly following the Madrid summit, Marchais again met with Berlinguer during his 19 April—3 May visit to Italy, and their discussions yielded a reaffirmation and updating of the joint declaration of 15 November 1975. In addition, French-Italian relations at the state level were for the first time discussed by the two parties, reflecting their hopes of becoming government partners in their respective countries. Following these discussions, Marchais said that the "cooperation between the PCI and the PCF is today at a level never before reached." A certain rapprochement was indeed confirmed by numerous organizational contacts at various levels throughout the year.

Contacts with the Communist parties in the people's democracies were primarily maintained through lower-level study delegations, though Kanapa also visited Bulgaria and Jacques Denis of the international section of the Secretariat visited Poland. Marchais spent his 1976 Christmas vacation in Cuba, as in 1975, holding several informal talks with Fidel Castro. Discussions with Pham Van Dong, premier of the Socialist Republic of Vietnam, during his visit to France in April, were attended by Marchais and most other top PCF leaders.

Publications. Consonant with the growth of the PCF's membership and organization, a number of changes occurred in the party press in 1977. Most notably, the format of the national daily *L'Humanité* was changed in January in both layout and content, more objective reportage of a greater amount of news being the stated goal in the latter respect. Roland Leroy remained director of *L'Humanité* and René Andrieu its editor in chief. Efforts to give the paper a new image have apparently paid off. Sales were up to 200,000 or more, and an independent media research group reported in July that average per day readership had gone from 660,000 in 1975 to 496,000 in 1976 and then back to 670,000 in 1977 (a 35 percent increase from 1976). Similarly, the popular weekend magazine *L'Humanité Dimanche* was reported to have increased its readership by 36 percent. The party's provincial newspapers include three dailies: *La Liberté* (Nord), *L'Echo du Centre*, and *La Marseillaise*. Plans to add a new regional daily in the fall, serving Lyons, Grenoble, and Saint-Etienne, were announced by Leroy on 26 March. In October 1976 the Paris federation began to publish a new weekly popular magazine, *Paris-Hebdo*, and in March-April 1977 the first issues of publications geared specifically to the police forces and the army appeared, *Police et Nation* and *Armée-Nation*. The regular party press also includes: the weekly *France Nouvelle;* the monthly theoretical journal, *Cahiers du Communisme;* a rural weekly, *La Terre;* an intellectual monthly, *La Nouvelle Critique;* a literary monthly, *Europe;* a philosophically oriented bimonthly, *La Pensée;* a bimonthly economic journal, *Economie et Politique;* a historical bimonthly, *Cahiers d'Histoire de l'Institut Maurice Thorez;* and a monthly review for teachers, *L'école et la Nation*. For intraparty communication, the Central Committee publishes *La Vie du Parti*. In the early 1970s there were approximately 5,000 cell newspapers or periodicals, about a tenth printed, the others mimeographed, and this figure has undoubtedly increased with the expansion of the party's cell structure in recent years. The press of the youth movement was reorganized at the national MJCF conference of 22-23 October: *Avant-Garde* (previously bimonthly) is to become a weekly, with the goal of reaching 150,000 young readers, and *Clarté* (previously also a bimonthly) becomes the monthly theoretical, ideological, political, and cultural review of the UECF. The major Communist publishing houses, Editions sociales and Editeurs français réunis, put out a considerable number and variety of books and pamphlets.

The Far Left. The Communist Party's response to the far left challenge which emerged in the aftermath of the 1968 May revolt has proven quite effective in recent years. The Union of the Left's electoral success has forced the far left to accept the position of an external opposition, whose policies are generally reactions to the left alliance. Most far left groups have thus abandoned imminent revolutionary strategies, and the Union of the Left has also imposed upon the far left a greater unity than before. The two major Trotskyist groups, the Revolutionary Communist League (Ligue Communiste Révolutionnaire; LCR) and the Workers Struggle (Lutte Ouvriére; LO), ran separate presidential candidates in 1974, receiving a combined total of 690,000 votes (roughly 3 percent). However, in the 1977 municipal elections they joined with the Maoist-oriented Communist Workers Organization (Organisation Communiste des Travailleurs; OCT) in united far left lists on the basis of a joint platform (reprinted in IPR [Fourth International/LCR in France], Brussels, no. 66, 27 January). Such joint efforts paid off and the far left received an average of 5.35 percent of the total vote in the thirty-one large cities where it ran lists, as opposed to the combined 1974 average of 2.14 percent in twenty-five of these cities. Moreover, these lists did consistently better in working-class districts than elsewhere, with a remarkably high 12 percent showing in Orleans (*Inprecor,* Argenteuil, n.s., no. 3, 31 March). The far left groups then supported the Union of the Left on the second ballot, except when its lists were headed by the MRG.

The far left groups all consider the Union of the Left to be an electoralist and class-collaborationist alliance of the reformist working-class parties with a part of the bourgeoisie (represented by the MRG). But fundamental differences separate the far left groups among themselves in their assessment of the significance of the Union of the Left and of how revolutionaries should relate to it. The most orthodox Trotskyists (notably the LO) and Maoists argue that a PS-PCF government would be qualitatively no different from a government of the right, and the LO supports the Union of the Left only in solidarity with the workers who still believe in the reformist parties. The Parti Socialiste Unifié (PSU), on the other hand, holds that the revolutionary struggle must be inserted within the framework of the Union of the Left and believes that mass mobilizations can pressure the PS and the PCF to break with their electoralism and class-collaborationism. The LCR and the OCT occupy an intermediary position in this regard, arguing that a defeat of the right is crucial today and that the formation of a left government would further the working-class struggle, but also that the far left must ultimately replace the reformist parties as the political vanguard of this struggle.

Given the pivotal role which the prospect of a left government has come to play in the strategic thinking of the entire far left, the PS-PCF split has caused considerable disarray. At the same time, this crisis may provide the possibility of the far left taking on a more prominent role. While still critical of the Union of the Left, certain far left groups, especially the PSU and the LCR, are urging the PS and the PCF to reform the alliance. The far left hopes to reimpose unity on the major parties from below through a broad debate/mobilization in the trade unions, thereby also to enhance its own influence. The LCR, the OCT, and the newly formed Communist Committees for Self-management (Comités Communistes pour l'Autogestion; CCA) have joined forces in this regard and have begun to prepare united slates for the legislative elections as well. The PSU stands aloof from this united far left effort, seeking instead to consolidate its relations with the ecology movement, while the LO seems to be preparing itself to run its own separate election campaign (*Le Monde,* 18 October).

Amherst College   Ronald Tiersky, with Jonas Pontusson

Germany: Federal Republic of Germany

The history of the Communist Party of Germany (Kommunistische Partei Deutschlands; KPD) commenced during World War I when a revolutionary group within the Social Democratic Party of Germany (Sozialdemokratische Partei Deutschlands; SPD) formed the Spartacist League in opposition to the SPD leaders' support of the war. On 31 December 1918 the Spartacists founded the KPD.

The economic depression that began in the late 1920s brought increasing strength to the Communists. In the November 1932 elections, the KPD received almost six million votes (out of about thirty-five million). Outlawed in 1933, the party continued its activities underground throughout the Third Reich (1933-45). In 1945, after the end of hostilities in Europe, the KPD was reconstituted in the four Allied Occupation Zones of Germany and the area of Greater Berlin, the occupation authorities having allowed the reestablishment or new formation of anti-Nazi political parties. When the KPD in the Soviet Occupied Zone failed to obtain support from the population despite substantial Soviet backing, Soviet authorities ordered the merger of the SPD with the smaller KPD in 1946. However, only in the Soviet Zone and the Soviet Sector of Berlin could this merger be enforced. Its product was the Socialist Unity Party of Germany (Sozialistische Einheitspartei Deutschlands; SED). In the remaining part of occupied Germany, the SPD membership rejected giving up their party's identity. In the Federal Republic of Germany (FRG), which emerged in 1949 from the three Western zones of occupation, the KPD received 5.7 percent of the votes in the first federal elections, entitling the Communists to fifteen seats in the Bundestag. In 1953, at the next elections, the KPD vote decreased to 2.2 percent, hence below the 5 percent required for representation in the legislature. On 17 August 1956 the KPD was outlawed as an unconstitutional party by the Federal Constitutional Court, which found its objectives and methods in violation of Article 21/2 of the Basic Law of the FRG.

The KPD operated as an underground organization after it was outlawed, and its chairman, Max Reimann, continued to direct the party's activities from East Berlin. The illegality resulted in a substantial decrease in membership. In 1965 the German Peace Union (Deutsche Friedensunion; DFU) was formed by Communists, former Socialists, and pacifists as a Communist front organization. The DFU participated in the federal elections that year and polled 1.3 percent of the vote. The DFU is still in existence, merged with the International of War Resisters (IDK) and the Association of War Service Resisters (VK), but has had only limited success in the Communist effort to organize "unity of action" activities in line with the World Peace Movement.

Since 1967, German Communists have been demanding that the outlawing of the KPD be annulled. Meanwhile another Communist party, the present DKP, was founded on 22 September 1968. Two reasons may be responsible for the annulment campaign: (1) to indicate that the DKP is not a successor organization, and thus to forestall prohibition of the DKP as an unconstitutional party, and (2) to utilize this topic as a means to unite "progressive forces" in the fight against the "undemocratic" practice of outlawing left-wing political parties.

At the time of the founding of the DKP, the underground KPD had an estimated membership of 7,000. Almost all of these were ordered to join the new DKP, and almost its entire leadership was comprised of KPD members. Even as late as 1971, 79 percent of the DKP functionaries at federal, Land, and district levels were former members of the KPD. Because of this identity of personalities and the same unconstitutional objectives of both parties, it is apparent that the DKP is a successor organization of the KPD and could be outlawed merely by a decree of the federal Interior Ministry (*Die Welt*, Hamburg, 12 October 1977; see also *YICA, 1975,* p. 174).

The DKP considers itself part of the Communist and anti-imperialist world movement and maintains close relations with fraternal parties throughout the world.

The accompanying tabulation from the annual report of the Federal Security Service (Bundesverfassungsschutz) provides an overview of the left-extremist organizations in the FRG in 1976. The DKP membership in 1977 was estimated at about 40,000 (reported at the Fourth Party Congress, March 1976, as 42, 453). The population of the FRG is 61,520,000 (*Die Welt,* 22 June 1977).

Type of Organization	Number of Organizations	Membership
Orthodox Communist:		
Basic organizations	2	47,500
Affiliated organizations	10	24,100
Organizations influenced by Communists	72	53,900[a]
Maoist:		
Basic organizations	12	6,000
Affiliated organizations	28	7,000
Organizations influenced by Maoists	7	3,000[a]

Type of Organization	Number of Organizations	Membership	
Trotskyist	10	1,200	
"New Left"	79	4,700	
Anarchist	23	400	
Total	243	90,900	56,900[a]
Deduction for membership in more than one organization		22,900	14,900
		68,000	42,000[a]
Total membership		110,000	

Source: Bundesminister des Innern, Bonn, *Verfassungsschutz 1976*, July 1977, p. 57.

Note: The membership of 110,000 for 1976 is 5,000 more than the membership given for 1975.

[a]Among them are also non-Communists.

Leadership and Organization. The outlawed KPD is still in existence and has about 6,000 members. Its importance to Moscow has decidely decreased as a result of the existence of the legal DKP (see *YICA, 1977,* p. 158). The DKP has difficulties maintaining its membership at the level of 40,000. The small response in the elections might be the reason for disinterest in the ranks of the party which in turn has resulted in loss of members (*Der Spiegel,* Hamburg, 13 June 1977).

Neither the organizational structure nor the party leadership has undergone any significant change since the DKP congress in 1976 (see *YICA, 1977,* p. 158). Max Reimann, formally chairman of the illegal KPD and later honorary president and member of the Presidium of the DKP, died in Düsseldorf on 18 January 1977 (*WMR,* March; *Die Welt,* 24 January; *Unsere Zeit,* 21 January).

The close cooperation of the DKP with the ruling SED in the German Democratic Republic (GDR) continued during 1977. The SED provided, as before, the major financial support and direct supervision of its activities including the political schooling of Communists from the FRG in SED party schools (*Deutscher Informationsdienst,* Bonn, 28, no. 1452/53, 2 March/1 April; hereafter cited as *DI*). In 1976 the DKP received more than DM 30 million from the GDR. This amount does not include SED financial support given to affiliated and Communist-influenced organizations (Bundesminister des Innern, Bonn, *Verfassungsschutz 1976,* p. 70; hereafter cited as *Verfassungsschutz 1976*).

The most important affiliated organizations of the DKP are, as before, the Socialist German Workers' Youth (SDAJ), Marxist Student Union-Spartakus (MSB-Spartakus), and Young Pioneers (JP), which were utilized for party activities, including election campaigns and "unity of action" undertakings.

The SDAJ, founded prior to the DKP on 4 May 1968, follows completely the policies of the senior party, in spite of its assertion of "independence." There have been no changes in structure or leadership since its congress in December 1976 (see *YICA, 1977,* p. 158). Of the 33,000 members, it is estimated that about 13,500 are actively engaged in the work of the SDAJ (Information zur Psychologischen Verteidigung, *Linksextremismus und Bundeswehr,* September 1977, p. x). The SDAJ is modeled after the Free German Youth (FDJ) of the GDR.

The Marxist Student Union-Spartakus was formed in May 1971. Its forerunner, Spartakus/Association of Marxist Students, has its origin in the orthodox Communist party of the predominantly anti-authoritarian Socialist German Student League (SDS) of the late 1960s. The MSB-Spartakus held its fifth federal congress on 8-9 October 1977 in Munich. Among the 700 participants were delegations from the other Communist and affiliated organizations, along with representatives of Communist youth and student organizations abroad. The reported membership of 5,800 represents an increase of 1,800 in the past two years. During the same period, MSB groups increased by 68 to a total of 210. Beate Landefeld was elected chairman by the congress (*DI,* 28, no. 1466, 29 October). Also in 1977, the MSB-Spartakus in coalition with the Socialist Student League (SHB), the former official SPD student organization, and in many instances with the Young Socialist University Groups (or "Jusos"), was able to control student governments in many institutions of higher learning. The MSB-Spartakus and the SHB together form the strongest faction in the student movement. (Ibid.) For example, in North Rhine-Westphalia, the left-extremist bloc of MSB-Spartakus, SHB, and the Liberal University League (LHV) controls the student government of twenty-five out of thirty-four institutions of higher learning (*Die Welt,* 22 April). The DKP maintains also its own DKP-University Groups, with a membership of about 3,500.

The Young Pioneers, for children, was founded by the DKP in 1974. In March 1977 this organization held its second federal conference, which was attended by 212 delegates, representing 232 JP groups. Some sixty delegations were present, including representatives of Pioneer organizations abroad. The conference's declaration on the U.N.'s "International Year of the Child, 1979" called upon all "democratic organizations" to assist in the elimination of the gross violations of the "UN Charter of the Child" in the FRG (*DI,* 28, no. 1451, 15 March; no. 1452/53, 2 March/1 April).

Various Communist-influenced groups seek to obtain support among the population for DKP activities and objectives. Communist-influenced organizations represent themselves frequently as "non-partisan" or "independent." Some of them were founded by Communists, others came into being without Communist influence but were later infiltrated by Communists, who as a rule occupy decisive organizational positions, such as those in the Secretariat. The spectrum reaches from locally organized "initiatives" and "ad hoc committees" to well-established organizations. Among the most important of the latter, in addition to the DFU, are the following: The League of Persons Persecuted under National Socialism-League of Anti-Fascists (VVN-BdA), which celebrated its thirtieth anniversary on 12 March and held a federal congress during May. It has about 10,000 members.

The German Peace Society-United War Service Resisters (DFG-VK), with 20,000 members, is the largest organization of this type (Arbeitskreis fuer Landesverteidigung, *radical-info,* no. 1, Bonn, January-February, pp. 5-6).

The Committee for Peace, Disarmament, and Cooperation (KFAZ), with only about 420 members, has been very successful in forming unity of actions of Communists with Young Socialists, Young Democrats, SPD members, trade unions, Protestant churches, and public figures for such purposes as "disarmament demonstrations" and the collection of signatures demanding a stop to the arms race. The KFAZ, led by a committee of eight (the majority are members of Communist or Communist-controlled organizations), performs a double function as (1) a coordinating office of the organizations under DKP influence and (2) the main organizer of the "anti-militarist" struggle outside the FRG armed forces (*Linksextremismus und Bundeswehr,* September, pp. xi-xiii).

The Christian Peace Conference (CFK) is closely aligned with the World Peace Council and promotes Moscow's policies among Protestants (*DI,* 28, no. 1450, 28 February). The CKF held a seminar in East Berlin in February on the topic "Churches and World Religions in Cooperation for Peace," in preparation for the "World Conference of Religious Representatives for Lasting Peace, Disarmament and Just Relations between Peoples," scheduled for June in Moscow (ibid., no. 1451, 15 March).

Other organizations of this type, addressed to specific segments of the population, include the Association of Democratic Jurists (VDJ), with about 600 members in nineteen regional groups; the League of Democratic Scientists (BdWi), which in 1977 supported the World Peace Council's disarmament campaigns; the Democratic Culture League (DKBD), with numerous local committees contributing to the "democratic struggle" in the FRG (*DI,* no. 1451, 15 March), and the Democratic Women's Initiative (DF), which held a congress in April in Oberhausen.

Party Internal Affairs. Following a meeting in October 1976, the DKP Directorate's "Organization and Personnel Policies" section published "Directives for Group Work." It explains that the DKP can only accomplish its tasks when the party is united, disciplined, and stable. Every party member must work among the masses, promote the official party newspaper *Unsere Zeit,* and continue to improve his political-ideological competency. The members are reminded that, according to the party statute, they are obliged to participate in the activities of the party group. These party groups, the basic organization of the party, are, according to Lenin, the "life cells" of the party. The "factory group" is the most important basic unit of the DKP because "the factory is the most important place of struggle" (*DI,* no. 1447, 12 January 1977).

At its meeting on 26-27 February 1977 the Directorate appointed a twenty-four-member commission to draft a new DKP program. Heading the commission was DKP chairman Herbert Mies (*JPRS,* 6 April, p. 50).

During the "Week of the DKP" (15-23 January), party members were supposed to propagate DKP aims among the masses (*Unsere Zeit,* 7 January). The party organized the traditional 1 May demonstrations and rallies and the annual "*Unsere Zeit*-Press Festival" at Recklinghausen, 1-3 July, attended by about 300,000 persons (ibid., 8 July).

Most activities were related to the day-to-day struggle for specific short-range objectives and to the ideological schooling of the members. The "Marxist Workers' Education" (MAB) prepared forty-five seminar outlines for the study of "Basic Knowledge of Marxism." The material was used by the Marxist Evening Schools (MASCH) and for individual self study (*DI,* 28, no. 1450, 28 February; no. 1451, 15 March).

Another DKP educational topic was the "class struggle as striving force for social progress." The significance of the economic struggle in the present crisis situation was stressed. The DKP pointed out, however, that the working class must also pursue the political struggle in order to eliminate exploitation. The third important form of the struggle is the ideological fight: the educational work within the DKP must point out that "at present the fight for the minds of the working population is of a higher priority than ever." Another important educational objective is the presentation of the Communist party as the highest form of class organization. (Ibid. no. 1462, 25 August.)

In January a first-year course of instruction for factory workers was organized in Frankfurt am Main by a DKP front, the August Bebel Society (ibid., 28, no 1449, 16 February).

As in previous years, DKP and SDAJ functionaries attended courses of varying length at political educational institutions in the GDR, such as the SED Franz Mehring party school in East Berlin. In 1976, about 240 persons from the FRG took part (ibid., no 1460, 3 July).

Domestic Attitudes and Activities. DKP chairman Mies stated in his New Year's Message that 1977 was to bring about a further deterioration of the political, social, and ideological climate, in which the economic, political, and ideological class struggle would be intensified. Hence the DKP would attempt to create "the unity of action of the working class and the alliance of all democratic, all left-wing forces." Mies referred to the sixtieth anniversary of the October Revolution as additional proof that "we Communists are on the correct side of the historical development" (*DI*, 28, no. 1447, 12 January).

The DKP participated in the local elections in Hesse on 20 March, getting 0.8 percent of the vote in communities (0.7 in 1972) and 1.1 percent in districts (0.8 in 1972). The Communist League of West Germany got 0.1 percent in communities and districts. (Ibid., no. 1452/53, 2 March/1 April.) On 23 October, in eighteen Land districts in parts of Lower Saxony, the DKP won one seat in the district legislature of Bentheim (1,177 votes; 780 in 1976). In nine of the districts the Communist share went from 1,456 votes (in 1976) to 4,218 votes. (Ibid., no. 1466, 29 October.) In spite of the poor results, the DKP decided to take part also in the Land elections in 1978 in Hesse because the party leaders claim that many voters are trying to find an alternative to the parties represented in the legislature, which, according to the Communists, are not operating in the interests of the working people (ibid., no. 1450, 28 February).

Chairman Mies at the October 1976 session of the Party Directorate enumerated the tasks of the DKP for 1977. Most were bread and butter issues, suited to "unity of action" with other "progressive" forces: the fight against unemployment and for the creation of jobs; against increases of prices, rents, and taxes; against the decrease of social services, lower pensions, and higher contributions for social services; for improving the buying power of the masses as result of an active wage policy; for better educational and vocational training, and for the defense of the democratic rights and freedoms and against the so-called *Berufsverbot*, a prohibition to carry on one's profession if one engages in radical activities directed against the state (*DI*, no. 1448, 25 January 1977). Especially the *Berufsverbot* continued in 1977 as a most useful "unity of action" issue, and there was an intensification of the internationalization of the anti-*Berufsverbot* campaign.

On 16 May the DKP published a "Declaration for the Realization of Human Rights in the Federal Republic of Germany" by way of initiating a domestic "human rights" movement. (*Unsere Zeit* published this declaration on 18 March, but without the list of signers which included Communists, sympathizers, intellectuals, and persons affected by the *Berufsverbot*.) The declaration may be seen as an addition to the effort to provide a new basis for unity of action, and as a means to relieve pressure on the Communist-ruled East European countries for their consistent violations of human rights in view of the forthcoming follow-up Conference on Security and Cooperation in Europe (CSCE) in Belgrade (*DI*, no. 1454, 18 April).

The DKP recognized the importance of the so-called citizen initiatives and declared its willingness to give them support in their endeavors. In the FRG there are about 50,000 citizen initiatives, of which 1,000 belong to the Federal Alliance of Citizen Initiatives for the Protection of the Environment (BBU). Sixty percent are of strictly local significance, 30 percent operate on Land level, and only 10 percent are national groups (ibid., no. 1463/64, 16 September). The communiqué of the DKP Directorate meeting on 26-27 February paid special attention to the continuing potential of citizen initiatives, especially those opposed to the establishment of nuclear power plants (*JPRS*, 6 April, pp. 15-16).

Communists and Social Democrats are working together in spite of the SPD directive prohibiting common actions with Communists not only in citizen initiatives but also in a number of committees and organizations, such as the International Niemoeller Foundation or the Society for the Promotion of Relations Between the Federal Republic of Germany and the Soviet Union (*DI*, no. 1449, 16 February). It also has been reported that popular-front alliances (*Volksfrontbuendnisse*) exist among Communists, Social Democrats and occasionally Liberals in twenty-five out of seventy-three institutions of higher learning (*Die Welt*, 29 January).

The "anti-militaristic" activities of the German Communists directed against the federal armed forces (Bundeswehr; Bw) is carried on within the military by about forty groups of the Working Committees of Democratic Soldiers (ADS) with varying success. Military Counter-Intelligence (MAD) reported that in 1976 there were 694 actions by DKP and Communist organizations against the Bw (ibid., 1 September). SDAJ publishes *Informationsdienst fuer Soldaten,* a monthly "information service for soldiers" (*Linksextremismus und Bundeswehr,* September, pp. xvii-xviii).

The DKP makes extensive use of the KFAZ and other Communist-infiltrated organizations for the massive propaganda against Western defense measures. For example, the "Bonn Peace Week, 1977" was a popular-front activity scheduled from 4 to 14 May. Large demonstrations for disarmament and detente took place on 21 May in Munich, Essen, Frankfurt am Main, and Bremen with typical popular-front participation (*Unsere Zeit,* 27 May). The anniversary of the dropping of the atomic bomb on Hiroshima, 6 August, was selected as a day for demonstrations against the neutron bomb. The organizers of this action, the DFG/VK, received endorsement from the DKP and SDAJ. Protest actions and demonstrations were planned in more than forty cities in the FRG (ibid., 29 July, 5 August).

According to the DKP, the new basic program of the German Trade Union Alliance (Deutscher Gewerkschaftsbund; DGB) should include the "perspectives of peace." All the other objectives of the DGB found complete Communist endorsement (*DI,* no. 1452/53, 2 March/1 April). The political activities of the factory groups are a task for the entire party because this work is considered decisive for the orientation of the working class (*JPRS,* 6 April, pp. 36-37). Factory newspapers are considered the most effective means for developing links between the factory personnel and the DKP factory group (ibid., p. 45). The Communist share of the roughly 2,000 shop stewards is about 0.5 percent. The DKP maintains about 300 factory groups, with 400 factory newspapers. The SDAJ has 6 factory groups and 130 factory newspapers (*DI,* no. 1450, 28 February).

The DKP continued its penetration of the Protestant church. In June, seven DKP members were appointed as non-tenured ministers by the Evangelical Church in Hesse-Nassau (*Frankfurter Allgemeine,* 7 June). In October DKP chairman Mies and other party functionaries met with 40 Protestant ministers and members of the Evangelical Church. It was agreed that Christians, Social Democrats, and Communists should pursue their common objectives together (*Die Welt,* 19 October).

International Views and Party Contacts. The strong dependency of the DKP upon the SED and the Communist Party of the Soviet Union (CPSU) requires that the party follow closely the international views held by East Berlin and Moscow. For example, DKP statements regarding the relations between the FRG and the GDR have the same content as those of the SED and the CPSU. Deputy party chairman Hermann Gautier attacked "the attempts of Federal Chancellor Schmidt to include the capital of the GDR, Berlin, in the Four Power Agreement concerning West Berlin." He further declared that Helmut Schmidt's statements contradicted the assertion of the federal government that it would continue to work for detente. On the other hand, Gautier endorsed the declaration of SED chief Erich Honecker, which indicated his policy of continuing the course of peaceful co-existence. Gautier stated that the DKP and the working people of the FRG expect agreements to be strictly followed and relations with the GDR to be based on existing realities and political prudence (*Unsere Zeit,* 20 May).

The DKP, like the SED, repudiates Bonn's views concerning the "unity of the German nation" and the further existence of the "German Question," and demands "normal" relations between the two German states based on international law (*Verfassungsschutz 1976,* pp. 61-63). Contacts between the DKP and SED were maintained by means of mutual visits of party leaders and delegations throughout 1977 (*JPRS,* 6 April, p. 21). The chairman of the DKP's Central Revision Commission, Willi Mohn, received the Karl-Marx-Order from Honecker in East Berlin, an indication of the intimate relationship of the two parties (*DI,* no. 1452/53, 2 March/1 April).

A leading DKP official, paying tribute to the "global impact of the October Revolution," wrote that "the DKP is eager to see its strong and friendly ties with the CPSU—the leading force of Soviet society—furthering a normalization between the FRG and the USSR," and that the German Communists were "helping to strengthen class ties between workers in the FRG and their Soviet class brothers" (*WMR*, September). The DKP celebrated the October Revolution anniversary in Düsseldorf. The SDAJ sponsored a Week of Friendship (19-29 October) between the youth of the FRG and of the Soviet Union, and organized about 400 meetings during this week (*DI*, no. 1466, 29 October).

The DKP strongly endorsed the proposal by the Warsaw Treaty countries that all signatories of the Final Act of Helsinki should commit themselves not to be the first to use nuclear weapons against one another. This proposal, according to the DKP, is of special significance to the FRG because the nuclear weapons depots on its territory are a constant threat to the lives and security of the population (*IB*, no. 23-24, p. 97). The DKP asserts that the Warsaw Treaty states have declared their willingness to reduce their armaments and that the Soviet Union has during recent years decreased its defense expenditures. The party demands that the FRG reduce its military budget by 15 percent (*DI*, no. 1458, 20 June).

The direct elections for the European Parliament planned for 1978 have been of concern to the DKP because of its poor results in past German elections. DKP functionaries addressed themselves to all political parties in the national parliaments of the European Community and declared that these direct elections in the FRG can neither be free nor democratic because of the 5 percent provision of the FRG election law. According to them, an attempt is being made to have this discrimination against the political left, resulting from the 5 percent provision, also superimposed on the European Parliament. (Ibid.) The DKP Directorate decided in June to participate in the direct election of the European Parliament and to have its own list of candidates. It will attempt to strengthen the collaboration of the Communist and workers' parties of the countries of the European Community. (Ibid., no. 1461, 12 August.)

DPK delegations and party representatives visited the Soviet Union, the GDR, Czechoslovakia, Hungary, Bulgaria, Poland, Belgium, France, Luxembourg, and Austria. Party leaders met with representatives from the Revolutionary Socialist Party of Somalia. The DKP in turn was host to visitors from several countries, including the Soviet Union, the GDR, Romania, and Spain.

The SDAJ maintained close relations with a number of Communist youth organizations abroad and organized at least two international meetings. One, at the end of March, drew representatives of twenty national youth organizations to Hamburg to discuss the preparations for the "Eleventh World Festival of Youths and Students, 1978," in Havana and for the Olympic Games in 1980 in Moscow. The other brought thirteen European Communist youth organizations to Dortmund (30-31 July) to decide on "common actions." (Ibid., no 1454, 18 April; no 1461, 12 August.)

DKP dependency on Moscow was decisive for the party's attitude toward "Eurocommunism" and "Charta 77" in Czechoslovakia. The latter was accused of working against Socialism under the disguise of "reform" and "human rights" (*Unsere Zeit*, 18 March). Chairman Mies characterized the concept of Eurocommunism as a creation of the Western news media whereby right-wing Social Democratic leadership and the bourgeoisie hope to divide the Communist movement (ibid., 25 February).

Publications. The official DKP organ, *Unsere Zeit*, appears six times a week and has an estimated circulation of about 50,000. The Friday edition has a weekend supplement and sells between 60,000 and 70,000 copies. *Unsere Zeit* also issues a number of local supplements. About 800 voluntary "worker and people's correspondents" supply the paper with news from factories and local communities.

Since the beginning of 1976 the Directorate has published the *DKP-Report.* During the election campaign several hundred thousands of this eight-page publication were circulated. Other DKP publications are the *Marxistische Blaetter;* the Directorate magazine *Praxis;* a cultural journal, *Kuerbiskern;* the *DKP-Landrevue;* and the information services *DKP Pressedienst* and *DKP-Informationen.* In 1976, there were about 400 factory newspapers and about 490 local papers (*Verfassungschutz 1976,* pp. 70-71).

The Institute for Marxist Studies and Research (IMSF) is responsible for a quarterly, *Marximus-Digest; Informationsberichte;* and *Beitraege des IMSF* (ibid., p. 87). (For publications of related youth organs see *YICA, 1976,* pp. 153-54.)

Seventeen publishing houses and thirty-seven "collective" bookshops belong to the Association of Socialist and Democratic Publishers and Bookstore Managers, which is controlled by the DKP (ibid., p. 88).

Among other leftist periodicals are *Sozialistische Korrespondenz* (Hamburg), *Express* (Offenbach), and *Links,* published by the Sozialistisches Büro (Offenbach). The DFG-VK launched the *Eifel-Echo* in January 1977 (*DI,* no. 1449, 16 February). Orthodox Communists, left-extremists of many shades, and even anarchists are working together in the so-called Alternative Press/People's Newspaper Movement (Alternativpresse/Volksblatt Bewegung) in spite of their great ideological differences. Such left and local "people's newspapers" in the FRG number about seventy and issue a total of about 100,000 copies (ibid., no. 1454, 18 April).

The Federal Security Service (BVS) prepared a calculation of orthodox-Communist and pro-Communist periodicals for 1976. These publications numbered 1,495 (1975: 1,420), with a weekly edition of 850,600 (1975: 801,500). The "New Left" was credited with an additional 458 periodicals (1975: 417), with a weekly editon of 404,000 (1975: 389,000). The total of Communist and left-extremist periodicals was 1,953 (1975: 1,837), with a total of 1,254,600 copies (1975: 1,190,500) distributed weekly (*Verfassungsschutz 1976,* p. 58).

Other Leftist Groups—Rival Communists. Aside from the orthodox, Moscow-loyal Communist organizations, the Federal Security Service identified 159 left-extremist groups in 1976. Some consider themselves to be political parties. At least one, the Communist League of West Germany (Kommunistischer Bund Westdeutschlands; KBW) participated in local elections during 1977. It received 0.1 percent of the vote in Hesse. The more significant of these organizations are Maoist-oriented and claim to follow a dogmatic Marxist-Leninist line. There are also a number of Trotskyist and anarchist groups. The "Spontis" (the term is probably derived from "spontaneity") or anti-dogmatist groups increased rapidly during 1977 at the expense of some of the Maoist organizations. The Maoists are losing their dominant role in the "New Left," while the Socialist Bureau (Sozialistisches Büro; SB) in Offenbach, founded in 1969, is gaining influence. The SB is the communication and coordination center of the unorthodox supporters of a new society. Ideologically it has taken a position between Social Democracy and Trotskyism. It characterizes the Communist-ruled countries as "transitory societies" which are neither capitalist nor Socialist. At present twenty-three groups and eighteen university associations are affiliated with the SB, in addition to about 700 individual members. In May 1977 the SB organized a congress in Frankfurt am Main "against political suppression and economic exploitation" with 12,000 to 15,000 followers attending. Rudi Dutschke is a member of the Working Committee of the SB (*Frankfurter Allgemeine,* 7 May; *DI,* no. 1456/57, 5 June).

It is most difficult to keep track of the organizations of the "New Left" because they are in a continuous state of flux organizationally as well as along ideological lines. They emerge, sometimes combine with other groups, often form splinter groups, and frequently disappear as rapidly as they were formed. For example, it was reported that the number of left-extremist organizations in Bavaria increased by 32 to a total of 197, while the total membership showed only a small increase of 100 to a total of 10,200 (*Die Welt,* 21 April).

The doctrinaire Maoist and Trotskyist Communist groups, as well as the anti-dogmatic organizations, subscribe to armed struggle, although they believe that conditions must be ripe for revolution. This does not preclude their use of violence under certain conditions, as the so-called K-groups, another term used for the violent Maoist organizations, have frequently demonstrated. On the other hand, the terrorist camp, which also has its origin in revolutionary Marxism, insists that the armed struggle must begin in the present and that individual actions give impetus to the revolutionary situation. The FRG experienced during 1977 a number of terrorist activities, including assassinations, murders, kidnapings, bombings, and bank robberies, committed by remnants or successor groups of the Red Army Fraction (*Rote Armee Fraktion;* RAF).

The violent actions of the K-groups, such as the mass violence in March at Grohnde against the construction of a nuclear power plant, where a few hundred members of the KBW transformed a peaceful demonstration of about 15,000 persons into a fierce struggle against the police, are supposed to serve two purposes: (1) to show the masses that the state is vulnerable and (2) to train their own cadres in the organized and disciplined use of violence. The Communist Party of Germany/Marxist-Leninist (KPD/ML) also has decided to create its own "armed forces" (*Die Welt,* 27 May). Leaders of the KBW and the KPD/ML publicly declared that their revolutionary struggle, aimed at the overthrow of the "capitalist state," is of a violent nature and includes political murder (ibid., 12 October).

In spite of pressure from Peking for the Maoist parties and organizations to combine, they continue to insist on their own identity, their own "correct" interpretation of Marxism-Leninism and maintain a rather hostile relationship toward each other.

The strongest Maoist "party" is the KBW, founded in 1973. It has about 2,500 members and twice as many sympathizers. The new organizational structure divides the party into three regions and forty district units. Hans Gerhard Schmierer is secretary of the Central Commitee. In 1977 the KBW bought a large building in Frankfurt for more than $1 million to serve as its new headquarters and training center. It also bought an expensive computer communication system to keep in close touch with its field organization. The costs allegedly were covered by membership fees (about $40 per month) and voluntary contributions (*Christian Science Monitor,* 16 June). Its affiliated organizations are the Communist University Group (KHG) and the Communist Youth League (KJB), with together about 1,500 members (*Die Welt,* 28 September). The KBW has an official weekly, *Kommunistische Volkszeitung* (35,000 copies), and a monthly theoretical organ, *Kommunismus und Klassenkampf.* The KBW is considered to be the most violent of the Maoist organizations. In Heidelberg the KBW succeeded in clearing the 5 percent hurdle in the last local elections and obtained one seat in the city council (*Frankfurter Allgemeine,* 13 March).

The KPD has the same name as the Moscow-loyal underground KPD but is not to be taken as a successor organization (for background see *YICA, 1975,* pp. 183-84; *1976,* p. 154). The membership went down from 900 to 700 during 1976. The KPD was able to mobilize only up to 2,500 sympathizers for its various actions, or half of the number of the previous year (*Die Welt,* 28 September). Its Second Congress, held in strict secrecy on 28-31 July, adopted a resolution in favor of an alliance policy and work within the trade unions. The KPD chairman is Christian Semler. The "party" follows the policies of the Chinese Communists. It has a youth organization, the Communist Youth League of Germany (KJVD).

The KPD issues a weekly, *Rote Fahne* (14,500 copies), and a theoretical organ, the irregularly appearing *Theorie und Praxis.* The KJCD monthly is *Kaempfende Jugend.* The League of Socialist Teachers and Educators, affiliated with the KPD, published in 1977 the first issue of its organ, *Neue Erziehung* (*DI,* no. 1450, 28 February).

The KPD/ML, founded 31 December 1968, is the oldest Maoist party in the FRG. The party follows the teachings of Mao Tse-tung and Albanian leader Enver Hoxha. It has about 800 members. On 5 February 1977, the KPD/ML held its Third Congress in Ludwigshafen. The congress unanimously approved the program and the new constitution of the party and reelected Ernst Aust as chairman. The KPD/ML fights for a united, independent Socialist Germany (*FBIS,* 17 February). During 1977 the KPD/ML became more conspiratorial in character. The official paper is the weekly *Roter Morgen* (10,000 copies), and the theoretical organ the irregularly published *Der Weg der Partei*. The youth organization, Rote Garde, issues *Die Rote Garde* as a monthly supplement to *Roten Morgen* (*Linksextremismus und Bundeswehr,* September, pp. xiv-xv).

Another Maoist organization, the Communist League (KB), has 1,500 members and is comprised of several more or less independent groups. The Hamburg unit, with 800 members, is the most influential group. Its organ is the *Arbeiterkampf,* published every second week in about 24,500 copies. (Ibid., p. xvi.) Yet another Maoist organizatin is the Communist Workers' League of Germany (KABD). It issues its *Rote Fahne* every two weeks. The KABD youth organization, the Revolutionary League of Germany (RJVD), publishes *Rebell.* (Ibid., p. xv.)

The largest among the several Trotskyist groups is the Group of International Marxist-German Section of the IVth International (Gruppe Internationaler Marxisten-Deutsche Sektion der IV. Internationale; GIM), with about 600 members. Its weekly paper is *Was tun?* (Ibid., p. xvi.) (For the smaller Trotskyist groups see *YICA, 1977,* p. 167.)

$$*\qquad*\qquad*\qquad*$$

West Berlin. West Berlin is still an "occupied" city. The three Western powers maintain troops in their respective sectors and have set aside that part of the Basic Law of the FRG which included West Berlin as one of the *Laender.* The Quadripartite Agreement concerning Berlin of 3 September 1971 restated the fact that West Berlin is not part of the FRG and still has its "special status," the outcome of Allied agreements of 1944 and 1945. These arrangements were to apply to the area of Greater Berlin, the former German capital. However, the German Democratic Republic has for all practical purposes incorporated the Soviet Sector, the eastern part of the city, and declared "Berlin" as its capital. Various steps taken by the Communist regime of the GDR during 1977, such as the introduction of visa requirements for foreigners visiting East Berlin, the elimination of control points from the city borders of East Berlin adjacent to the territory of the GDR, and the discontinuation of the official Gazette for Greater Berlin, are implementations of this policy. Both Moscow and East Berlin insist that West Berlin is an "independent political entity" and have pursued a consistent policy to isolate it from the FRG as the first phase of an eventual absorption of the three Western sectors into the GDR (see Eric Waldman, *Die Sozialistische Einheitspartei Westberlins und die sowjetische Berlinpolitik,* Boppard am Rhein, 1972). The FRG, encouraged by the Western Allies, maintains close ties with West Berlin, a situation reaffirmed by the Quadripartite Agreement of 1971.

The SEW. The special status of Berlin, though only implemented in the Western sectors, enabled the Socialist Unity Party of Germany (SED) to establish a West Berlin subsidiary. Thus the present Socialist Unity Party of West Berlin (Sozialistische Einheitspartei Westberlins; SEW) is the creation of the East German SED and was not founded by the Communists in West Berlin. In the beginning, it was de facto the SED organization in the three Western sectors of Berlin. Therefore, up to the time of the artificial "separation" from the "mother party," it has the same history as the SED.

The first change came as a result of Khrushchev's demand in the spring of 1959 that West Berlin be made a "free city." This required the appointment of a separate leadership for the SED in the

Western sectors in order to give the impression of the existence of an independent and indigenous Communist party. The next step came in November 1962, when a "conference of delegates" changed the name of the party to Socialist Unity Party of Germany-West Berlin. This change became necessary as a result of the erection of the Wall (13 August 1961), which physically separates East and West Berlin. A special congress changed the name in February 1969 to the present SEW designation. The removal of "Germany" was done to support the notion of West Berlin as an "independent political entity." Only the ruling Communist party in the GDR carries "Germany" in its name, implying that the other German Communist parties (DKP and SEW) are merely subsidiaries of the SED.

Leadership, Organization, and Domestic Activities. The SEW's fifth congress, held in West Berlin on 15-17 April 1977, was attended by about 700 delegates and the representatives of 16 fraternal parties. The CPSU and the SED were represented by high party officials. The Report of the Party Directorate emphasized ideological work, aimed primarily at improving the Marxist-Leninist education of the cadres (*IB*, no. 8, pp. 36-38). No reference was made to the number of party members probably because, according to the Federal Security Services, the party membership had decreased from 8,000 to about 7,500. (West Berlin's population is close to 2.1 million.) The majority of the party members are only rarely willing to participate in active party work (*Verfassungsschutz 1976*, p. 73). Apparently there was dissent within the SEW as a result of the annulment of the GDR citizenship of polit-singer Wolf Biermann. No fewer than 44 SEW members and 197 party sympathizers signed a declaration protesting this act of the GDR (*DI*, no. 1456/57, 5 June).

Gerhard Danelius, SEW chairman since 1969, was reelected in a secret ballot with 438 of 455 votes (*Die Welt*, 18 April). Horst Schmidt and Dietmar Ahrens were elected as his deputies (*Pravda*, 18 April). (For a discussion of the organization, structure, and additonal leadership personnel and the affiliated organizations, such as the Free German Youth-West Berlin and other "mass organizations," see *YICA, 1976*, p. 157.)

The impact of the activities of the SEW is minimal. At the last elections in West Berlin in 1975, the party obtained 25,585 votes (1.9 percent), a decrease of 8,262 as compared with the previous elections in 1971. The losses in the twelve districts of West Berlin varied between 11.3 and 38.9 percent (*Die Welt*, 16 April). Attempts of the SEW to obtain a foothold in factories and trade unions were as a rule unsuccessful, although the party was able to take over a number of important functions (*Verfassungsschutz 1976*, p. 73). The SEW also succeeded in increasing its influence among a number of student groups in institutions of higher learning, primarily with the Working Group of Democratic Students (ADS) at the Free University (ibid., 13 April). The ADS suffered a decline in membership for the first time since its founding in 1971, down from 1,500 (1975) to 1,400. The membership of the SEW University Groups remained unchanged with 900 members. (Ibid., p. 85.)

SEW propaganda statements reflect the party's concern about the worsening economic situation of West Berlin, the high unemployment rate, and the alleged violation of human rights by the city government. The party proposes to fight together with all "progressive" forces for the interests of the working class. Its call for unity of action, however, had only limited appeal.

The SEW remains a valuable asset to the GDR and the Soviet Union, in spite of its actual insignificance in the political life of West Berlin. SEW declarations can be and are being used by Moscow as the indigenous West Berlin voice supporting Soviet policies concerning the city's future.

International Views and Party Contacts. The SEW's international views, including its views on West Berlin's relations with East and West Germany, are without exception the same as those expressed by Moscow and East Berlin. Emphasis is placed on strict adherence to the Four Power

Agreement of 1971, as interpreted by the Communists. The SEW considers itself a part of the international Communist movement and gives full support to proletarian internationalism (*Pravda,* 15 April 1977). The resolution adopted at the party congress stated the SEW's solidarity with all peoples fighting for freedom and national independence in Africa, Asia, and Latin America, and with the Palestinian people in the Middle East (*IB,* no. 8, pp. 41-42).

The SEW maintains close relations with fraternal Communist parties, especially with the SED, from which the party receives most of its financial support as well as its political direction. Mutual visits of party leaders and delegations and participation of the SEW at international Communist conferences, such as the consultation of representatives from seventy-five Communist and workers' parties in Prague (27-29 April) continued in 1977.

Publications. *Die Wahrheit,* the militant organ of the SEW, appears six times weekly in about 16,000 copies. (For publications of the "mass organizations" affiliated with the SEW see *YICA, 1975,* p. 191.)

Other Leftist Groups—Rival Communists. Several of the left-extremist groups operating in the FRG are also represented in West Berlin. The institutions of higher learning provide them with most of their members. Their influence among the population is insignificant, although the KPD and KBW obtained in the 1975 elections 10,277 and 802 votes respectively. (For further details see *YICA, 1977,* p. 169.)

University of Calgary   Eric Waldman

Great Britain

The Communist Party of Great Britain (CPGB) was founded in 1920. It continued in 1977 to be Great Britain's most significant Marxist party despite pressure from ultra-leftist groups. A recognized political party, the CPGB contests local and national elections except that it does not operate in Northern Ireland. It has had no members of the House of Commons, Britains's principal legislative assembly, since 1950 when it had two. At present it has one member of the House of Lords and eight council members at various levels of local government.

Currently membership of the CPGB is officially given as 25,293 but is probably more like 24,500. The population of Great Britain is almost 56 million.

Leadership and Organization. The CPGB is divided into four layers: the National Congress, the Executive Committee and its attendant departments, the districts, and the various local and factory branches.

Constitutionally, the National Congress is the supreme authority in the party. It meets once every two years and is responsible for electing the forty-two member executive, considering documents on future policy and activity, and listening to reports on the party's activities since the previous meetings. Delegates consist of representatives from districts and branches. The Congress serves as a rubber stamp for the party leadership and opposition is unusual.

The Executive Committee, which meets once every two months, has overall responsibility for party activity on individual issues. It also chooses the members of specialist committees and full-time heads of departments, and selects the sixteen-member Political Committee, which is the party's effective controlling body. The Political Committee meets every week or when the occasion merits.

During 1977 the leading officers and heads of department were Gordon McLennan (general secretary), Reuben Falber (assistant secretary), Mick McGahey (chairman), Dave Cook (national organizer), Bert Ramelson (industrial organizer), Geroge Matthews (press and publicity), Jack Woddis (international department), Betty Matthews (education department), Dennis Ellward (national treasurer), Malcolm Cowle (national election agent), and Jean Styles (national women's organizer).

The Young Communist League (YCL), affiliated to the CPGB since its foundation, continued to decline in 1977. Membership is down to 1,600. Students play a prominent role in the YCL and there are fifty-five Communist organizations in the universities. The YCL general secretary is Tom Bell.

The real strength of the CPGB is in the trade union movement. Here its influence is considerable, with a party member on nearly every union executive in Great Britain—a phenomenon largely attributable to the low polls in most trade union elections and the fact that the Communists are the only effective organization within the trade union movement seeking to control the outcome of elections. This source of strength is potentially of profound importance. Labour Party funds are based 80 percent on trade union contributions and, moreover, 88 percent of votes at the annual Labour Party conference are controlled by the trade unions.

In 1977 the Communists significantly strengthened their position in the trade union movement with the appointment of George Guy, general secretary of the 79,000-member National Union of Sheet Metal Workers, to the TUC general Council. He became the second Communist on the 38-member General Council alongside Ken Gill, general secretary of the Technical and Supervisory section of the AUEW, who was elected in 1974. Another noteworthy trade union succcess for the CPGB was the election of Joseph Whelan as general secretary of the traditionally moderate Nottinghamshire miners.

The Communists continued to sponsor the Liaison Committee for the Defence of Trade Unions (LCDTU), founded in 1966, as the party's principal instrument for the promotion of industrial campaigns and propaganda. In recent years the LCDTU has gone into relative decline. It has not mounted any major action since December 1970 when it was the principal organizer of a strike of 600,000 against the Industrial Relations Bill. However, in February 1977, it called its largest conference since June 1972. Attending were 1,293 delegates (representing 132 shop stewards' committees, 61 trades councils, 34 union district committees, 4 executive committees, and 272 trade union branches) who demanded a return to free collective bargaining. The LCDTU secretary is Kevin Halpin. The CPGB claims to have about 200 workplace branches.

Party Internal Affairs. On 1 February the CPGB published its draft of *The British Road to Socialism.* This first revision of the party program since 1968 differed little from the 1951 original version, allegedly produced with Stalin's personal endorsement. The goal remained the election of a left-wing Labour government, with Communist support, pledged to the destruction of "monopoly capitalism." Though not a new direction in policy, it was the clearest statement yet of the need for Labour and Communist parties to work together. "Socialism," the document said, "can only be won and built on the basis of Labour-Communist unity."

Tactically, the Labour Party and the Labour movement as a whole were to be pushed further to the left by a broad democratic alliance of forces including women's liberation, environmental, immigrant, and anti-racialist groups. The definition of "working class" was broadened considerably to include alliance with white-collar workers, professional people, middle management, small farmers and businessmen, and some self-employed. The document further held that "Britain's road to socialism will be different from the Soviet road." In Britain there would be no need for a civil war because Parliament had a relative autonomy from the capitalist class and "can be transformed into the democratic instrument of the will of the vast majority of people." While "mass struggle outside Parliament" would be necessary, the only real danger of an armed coup lay with the right. This could be obviated by democratizing the armed forces. Most importantly, the party emphasized its commitment to political pluralism and claimed that "a left government will stand down if defeated in an election" and asserted that relations with the world Communist movement would be based on the equality of each party.

As its initial program a left government would abolish the monarchy and the House of Lords, introduce proportional representation, break up monopoly newspaper groups and ensure democratic control of the two television companies. Elected parliaments for Scotland and Wales would be guaranteed. In defense, Britain would withdraw from NATO and join an all-inclusive European security system which would include East European states.

The draft program was due to be endorsed at the party's Thirty-fifth Congress in November. It was the subject of protracted ideological debate, attracting no fewer than 2,591 branch amendments in four volumes on a document on 1,922 lines in length. Considerable discussion took place in the party press. Indeed, Reuben Falber (assistant secretary) went so far as to describe the discussion as "one of the most democratic ever organized by a political party" (*Morning Star,* 12 August).

The more explicit statement of the revised *British Road to Socialism* was taken by many hard-liners as an indication of a further drift from the Soviet line and a shift towards Eurocommunism. Sid French, the head of the Survey branch, was particularly contemptuous of the new program: "The draft looks like an essay for which prizes are awarded for the number of times you can mention the word 'democracy' ." He subsequently led a group of hard-line opponents of Eurocommunism to break away from the party and found the New Communist Party (see below) on 16 July.

This trend towards Eurocommunism in the mainstream party was underlined in a full-page interview given to the *Morning Star* on 4 July by Gordon McLennan. In it he rebuked the Soviet and Spanish Communist parties for discussing their differences through accusation and counter-accusation. Though he did not say so explicitly, it was clear that McLennan blamed the Soviet magazine *New Times* for the breach of etiquette in its vituperative attack on Santiago Carrillo's *Euro-Communism and the State.* McLennan apparently placed the CPGB in the Eurocommunist mold by claiming that there is "no single leading communist party." He further stated: "It must be clearly understood that each party will not only decide its own analysis and policy, but will work out its policy in its own country, and no one else can do so."

At the November Congress hard-line opposition to the draft centered on the East Midlands district committee and fourteen branches, including the intensely pro-Soviet Pollocksfield branch in Scotland. The opposition motion to refer the draft back to the Executive Committee on the grounds that it departed from "the scientific principles of Marxism-Leninism" was overwhelmingly defeated, 330 votes to 48. When the draft document was finally presented for approval, 29 actually voted against it with 4 abstaining. Earlier an amendment to ban or restrict parties "hostile to socialism" attracted 66 votes. The only amendment which was carried was a composite resolution supported by the executive which strengthened the wording concerning the importance of the future role of the Communist Party in the bringing of Socialism to Britain.

Aside from the draft, resolutions were passed demanding a campaign against racism and facism, state action to end unemployment, and an end to the alleged use of torture in Northern Ireland. A resolution expressed solidarity with "the popular struggle in South Africa." Party Chairman McGahey moved a motion warmly congratulating the CPSU on the 60th anniversary of the Russian Revolution. In it he minimized "certain little differences" between the parties. Only ten delegates voted against the motion, with fifteen abstaining.

A further interesting reminder of the limits of de-Stalinization occurred with an abrupt change to the "recommended list" of 42 names out of the 150-odd standing for election to the Executive Committee. When McGahey announced that one candidate was off the recommended list and another was on it, no explanation was given, implying that the party had already made its decision.

The YCL's national congress in April emphasized the need to build a broader-based youth movement. There was clear evidence that the deep ideological division between pro-Soviet and Eurocommunist attitudes had been particularly damaging to membership.

Communist Party income in 1977, largely from donations and dues, is estimated at about £250,000. A national fund campaign, 5-12 March, sought to raise £75,000. The same figure was the target for a national campaign to be held in 1978, 12 February-19 March. A National Finance Conference, in Birmingham on 24 September, consisted of twenty-eight delegates from fourteen districts and was largely concerned with raising money for the branches and districts, which, compared with the executive, were felt to be underfinanced.

The Communist daily newspaper the *Morning Star,* is financially independent of the party organization. It is expected to have a £187,000 deficit in 1978. Furthermore, circulation had dropped to a mere 38,533 in June 1977. The government's decision to take advertising space in the paper is not expected to be of great help.

The CPGB has a wide range of business interests, many of which are nominally independent organizations. These include Central Books Limited; Lawrence and Wishart, publishers; Farleigh Press and London Caledonian, printers; Rodell Properties Ltd; the Labour Research Department; and the Marx Memorial Library.

Two prominent British Communists died in 1977, both in September: John Gollan, general secretary from 1956 to 1975, and James Klugmann, editor for twenty years of the theoretical journal *Marxism Today.*

Domestic Attitudes and Activities. The most striking feature of the CPGB is the vast discrepancy between its ambitious goals and its actual strength. Voting strength has declined markedly from the days of 1945 when twenty-one candidates secured 102,000 votes and two MPs. The accompanying chart shows a picture of steady decline.

	1945	1950	1951	1955	1959	1964	1966
Candidates	21	100	10	17	18	36	57
Votes	102,780	91,736	21,640	23,144	30,897	44,567	62,112
Average vote per candidate	4,894	917	2,164	1,950	1,716	1,236	1,089

	1970	February 1974	October 1974
Candidates	58	44	29
Votes	37,966	32,773	17,008
Average vote per candidate	654	744	586

In other words, the number of Communist voters has actually fallen to being less than the number of card-carrying members. This decline coincides with a steady drop in membership now even officially only just above 25,000. Sid French, head of the breakaway New Communist Party, claimed that the picture is even bleaker for the CPGB with only 12,000 dues-paying members and a mere 430 active members of the YCL.

The same downward trend was confirmed in local elections. In 1977 the Communists fielded 273 candidates polling 52,000 votes, in contrast to 75,000 votes for 306 candidates the previous time these elections were held. Only one result stood out from this record of failure. Jimmy Sneddon regained his seat in Motherwell with a considerably increased majority over his Labour opponent.

The Communist Party does play a parliamentary role through its influence on left-wing members of the Labour Party. Many members of the Labour Party's Tribune Group hold opinions which coincide with Communist policy. Labour MPs have openly supported Communist causes or joined leading Communists on political platforms. Several Labour MPs have written articles in the *Morning Star,* including the chairman of the Tribune Group, Ron Thomas. In a remarkable article which appeared in a June issue of the *Morning Star,* a leading left-wing MP, Sidney Bidwell, described his differences with the Communists as "negligible." The development of such views in the Labour Party may well damage the specific identity of the CPGB, with extreme-left power seekers tending to join the Labour Party and revolutionaries the Trotskyist groups.

This was suggested by the decision of Jimmy Reid, a former executive member, to join the Labour Party in November. There are signs, however, of growing resistance to Communist influence in the Labour Party. Dr. Owen, Labour foreign secretary, in a speech on 18 November attacked the democratic credentials of the Communists and asserted that the new "respectable" form of the British Communist party did not change its underlying reality. On the contrary, he said, there had been a "dangerous conscious blurring of the edges between communism and socialism." It was a trend which had to be resisted. The development of this dispute in the Labour Party probably will be the decisive factor in determining the Communist party's future.

The Communists continued to campaign against the Labour government's economic strategy throughout 1977. Using its trade union influence, the party played a prominent role in combating the government's incomes policy and continued to agitate for the implementation of its own economic policies, which were unchanged from previous years. (See *YICA, 1977,* p. 172.)

Notable successes were scored for the Communists in elections to the executive of the National Union of Students (NUS). Here the Communists are part of a "Broad Left" alliance of Communists, Labour Marxists, and unattached Marxists. Susan Slipman became the first woman and fourth Communist president of the NUS, and Penny Cooper, also a Communist, became treasurer. Attempts to deepen Communist influence in higher education continued with the ninth Communist University of London (CUL). The nine-day event was generally successful, with some 1,000 signing on for the entire event and some 1,500 for part. Courses included the Student Movement; Socialism and Feminism; Modern Marxist Theories of the State; the Strategic Perspectives of the PCI; Literature and Politics; Science and Society; Popular Front Strategies; Socialist Democracy; Racialism; Schools and Society; and .the Politics of Popular Music. Many of the students taking part were foreign, largely from West Germany, Scandinavia, Italy, and Greece, but also the United States and the Middle East.

Approximately half the lecturers were Communist party members. Lecturers included R. Hilton, professor of history at Birmingham University; Martin Milligan, lecturer in philosophy at Leeds; Maurice Levitas, senior lecturer at the Neville Cross College of Education, Durham; David Craig, senior lecturer at Lancaster University; Arnold Kebble, professor of literature at the Open University; J. de Groot, lecturer in history at York University; Ron Bellamy, senior lecturer in economics at Leeds; and Brian Simon, professor of education at Leicester University.

From the Communist viewpoint the success of the event was only marred by the fact that an invitation sent to Zhores Medvedev had to be hastily withdrawn. The organizer said she knew of no pressure from Moscow to withdraw the invitation.

A Communist University Feminist Weekend was held 19-20 March at Bristol University. Sessions included women and literature, art, history, anthropology and discussions on such items as sexism in education.

In general, CPGB policy statements differed only in emphasis from previous years. The party continued to campaign on themes of opposition to public-spending cuts, unemployment, rising prices, and pay restraint. A notable innovation was the collection of signatures for a "protest prices" petition. Supporters were also asked to work against the Abortion (Amendment) Bill.

A perceptible strengthening of the Communist campaign on Northern Ireland entailed giving more support to the Irish trade unions' "Better Life for All" campaign. This largely took the form of resolutions of support from British trade union branches and the twinning of trades councils in Britain and Northern Irleand. Protests were mounted against alleged use of torture in Northern Ireland and the continuance of the Prevention of Terrorism Act. The CPGB also presented evidence to the Royal Commission on the health service. The plan was for a National Health Service based on salaried primary-care teams of doctors, nurses, health visitors, and social workers. All medical treatment should be free and financed through taxation and the nationalization of the pharmaceutical industry. In evidence before the Armitage committee the Communists called for the removal of all restrictions on the rights of civil servants to take part publicly in political activities according to their convictions.

The most successful 1977 campaign in which Communists were prominent was the one directed against the government's social contract and in favor of a return to free collective bargaining. Though the general lines of the government's economic strategy were maintained, it necessitated considerable modification to pay-restraint proposals. The Communists maintained an unremitting propaganda barrage against the social contract in public and inside the trade unions. A Day of Action against the social contract on 20 April had the complete support of the CPGB. In Scotland the LCDTU organized a march of over 1,000 workers; in Dundee some 8,000 engineering, shipbuilding, and construction workers stopped work for the day; in Sheffield about 5,000 engineering workers went on strike; and sizable demonstrations occurred in Sunderland, Huddersfield, Manchester, and Liverpool. In the capital itself 8,000 demonstrators went to Parliament to lobby their MPs.

Two other notable Communist campaigns were those conducted against the National Front (NF) and the Grunwick photo-finishing company. The CPGB sought a ban on the extreme-right-wing NF and supported counter-marches held on the same day as NF demonstrations. The Grunwick dispute is presented by the party as a straightforward bid for trade union recognition although none of the strike committee is a Grunwick employee and there is no question of unfair dismissal. Mass picketing, often punctuated by violence, has been a staple characteristic of the Grunwick dispute, and the Communist-sponsored LCDTU has been prominent in mobilizing demonstrators. Violence on the picket lines has consistently been presented by the *Morning Star* as being a result of police action to "intimidate trade unionists carrying out their lawful right to picket" (14 June).

Attempts were made to change the image of the party by celebrating an alternative to the Queen's Silver Jubilee. The "People's Jubilee" at Alexandra Palace was clearly successful, attracting some 11,000 persons to various events including chess, drinking, dancing, trampolining, and listening to bands like Soft Machine and Shakin' Stevens. It will now be held every year. "Festival of Marxism" was held in Glasgow in January for four days and again on 2-3 July at Sheffield Polytechnic.

The CPGB expressed its full support for the two-day National Assembly for Disarmament and Peace due to be held in London on 28-29 January 1978.

A controversy concerning the early days of the CPGB arose in 1977 about the controversial "Zinoviev letter" which helped to bring down the first Labour government in 1924. In it Zinoviev, president of the Comintern, was alleged to have urged British Communists to put pressure on Labour Party members to prepare for a revolution. The letter has for many years been regarded as a forgery, but the research of Christopher Andrew, a Cambridge University lecturer, changed this picture. Though vital M16 and KGB files remain closed, he felt confident enough to say: "The balance of evidence at present available makes the authenticity of the letter more probable than its forgery."

International Views and Party Contacts. Internationally, the most outspoken statement of CPGB views in 1977 was with regard to Czechoslovakia. On 21 January the party's Political Committee condemned the Czechoslovak authorities' attempts to destroy the human rights campaign focused around "Charta 77." The statement recalled official allegations that "Charta 77" was an "anti-state, anti-socialist, anti-people and demagogic pamphlet which grossly and falsely slanders the Czechoslovak republic." The CPGB expressed its alarm at the use of such methods and language, which it considered a discredit to the Communist movement. It then continued: "Nowhere in the course of a 3,000 word article are these allegations backed by a single quotation from the document." In November the Communist president of the NUS wrote to Brezhnev demanding action in the case of detained British student Andrei Klymchuk. However, CPGB foreign policy statements tended to be simply endorsements of Soviet objectives.

Solidarity with Chile remained a major subject for Communist protest. The CPGB is affiliated to the Chile Solidarity Campaign. An emerging campaign is the movement against the West German *Berufsverbot.* Here a provisional action committee has been established.

McLennan and executive member Jack Askins were guests at the congress of the Vietnamese Workers Party at Hanoi in December 1976, while Ramelson attended the 18th Congress of the Rakah Israeli Communist party. Falber had talks in August in East Berlin with Politburo member Herman Axen of the Socialist Unity Party. McLennan and Woddis visited Japan in January and had discussions with Sanzo Nosaka, and other leaders of the Japan Communist Party. In May a delegation from the Communist Party of Turkey visited London for discussions with the CPGB. McLennan made a notable speech in honor of the Russian Revolution, in Moscow on 3 November. He reiterated the CPGB's aim to build a society in which even parties opposed to Socialism could exist and take part in the political process.

Publications. The principal CPGB organ is the daily *Morning Star.* Its other leading papers are *Comment* (fortnightly) and *Marxism Today* (a monthly theoretical journal). The YCL publishes *Challenge* and *Cogito.*

In addition the Communists publish several magazines of specialist interest. The quarterlies include *Link,* a woman's paper; *Science Bulletin; Red Letters,* a literary paper; *Country Standard; Medicine and Society;* and *Euroed,* on Western Communist parties. Irregular publications are *Socialist Europe,* on Eastern Europe; *Economic Bulletin; Music and Life;* and *Portugal Information Bulletin.*

Other Marxist Groups. A new Marxist party emerged on Britain's far left in 1977 when a hardline pro-Moscow group within the CPGB broke away to form the New Communist Party (NCP) at a meeting in Islington, North London, on 16 July. The decision was precipitated by the CPGB's new draft program (see above) which was felt to be social-democratic and not Communist. The group particularly objected to the dropping of the "dictatorship of the proletariat" and to the surrender of power if the party lost an election. An NCP statement declared: "Working class power, once gained, can only be held on to and consolidated by a proletarian dictatorship."

CPGB failures—feeble electoral performance, a scarcely visible YCL, falling *Morning Star* circulation, no more than about 7,000 members still active—were attributed to the party's change of direction in recent years. The CPSU itself did not issue a statement on the split.

NCP policies were outlined in a pamphlet, *The Case for the New Communist Party*. Its outline of the "crises of capitalism" is conventional and the solution is revolution. The central dynamic of the NCP clearly lies with its intense pro-Soviet feelings: "There will never be room in our party for the slightest trace of anti-Sovietism or any other form of international Communism." Its version of the Soviet invasion of Czechoslovakia in 1968 also makes interesting reading: "The workers of the socialist countries showed their determination to defend hard-won gains when their armies moved into Czechoslovakia to prevent an imperialist-backed counter revolution."

Sid French, former district secretary of the CPGB's Surrey branch, heads the NCP, and Jean Geldart, daughter of the former Communist MP for Mile End, is the national vice-chairman. The NCP claims to have sixty-four branches; its main strength is in the South Yorkshire coalfields. On 16 September the NCP launched a new weekly paper, *The New Worker*. Membership is estimated at 800 and though small it represents some of the most deeply motivated and hard working ex-CPGB members.

Britain's largest and fastest growing Trotskyist organization is the Socialist Workers' Party (SWP), formerly International Socialists (IS). The change of name in December 1976 was intended to indicate a change from pressure-group to party politics. Following a period of decline in the first years of the present Labour government, the SWP showed a sharp upsurge of support in the latter half of 1976 and in 1977. It now claims 4,500 members at an average subscription of £3 per month. Its principal front organization, the Rank and File movement, attracts a lot of people broadly sympathetic to the SWP. *Socialist Worker*, the SWP's chief newspaper, is a weekly with a circulation of between 20,000 and 30,000. A publishing company, Pluto Press, is also associated.

The SWP now has small groups in the car industry, the docks, the railways, the National Union of Mineworkers, the National Union of Teachers, and the National Association of Local Government Officers. In 1977 it played a role in the engineers' dispute at Heathrow Airport, the docks wage claim, and the various stoppages at the Chrysler car factory. SWP members took part in large numbers at the mass picketing of the Grunwick film processing factory.

Two campaigns have formed the basis of SWP recruitment successes. One is the Right to Work campaign, which has made headway among the young unemployed. Its main event of the year was a Right to Work march to Blackpool on 5 September which won considerable publicity. The other is its anti-racialist activity. It is making strenuous efforts to attract unemployed West Indians and has a section for black people called Flame, and a paper of that name. A group of Irish SWP members runs a paper called *Irish Worker*. Recruitment of Asians is going well and there is an SWP section called Chingari (The Spark) which produces papers in Bengali, Punjabi, and Gujerati. Violent opposition to the racialist National Front occasioned two riots, one in Lewisham on 13 August, 1977 which led to the first use of riot shields by the police in Britain, and one shortly afterward at the Ladysmith bye-election.

The Central Committee has ten members, including James Nicholl and Stephen Jefferys. All are full-time and are paid out of party funds, as are an unknown number of staff people, printing workers, and organizers. The party is centrally organized and has about seventy districts and branches. Its main support is claimed to be in Glasgow and the north of England. The party chairman is Duncan Hallas.

While the SWP is just beginning to establish a degree of industrial support, being for many years very middle-class in composition, the Workers' Revolutionary Party (WRP) retains a strong factory base. It has groups in the docks and in engineering, mining, the theater, and the car industry. It controls the All Trade Union Alliance (ATUA), an organization similar to the LCDTU. Founded 4

November 1973, the WRP is a Trotskyist organization, a successor to the Socialist Labour League (SLL), and an affiliate of the Fourth International (International Secretariat). It publishes a daily newspaper, *Newsline,* and an irregular journal, *Fourth International.* Its youth movement, the Young Socialists, is the largest Marxist youth body in Britain. The WRP operates in an atmosphere of intense secrecy and information about it is scarce, but its membership is estimated at about 1,000.

In public campaigns it was notable for its hostility to other Trotskyist groups. Most striking have been its allegations that Joseph Hansen and George Novack, two leading figures in the U.S. Socialist Workers' Party, had links with the Soviet GPU at the time of Trotsky's murder. Prominent members include the actress Vanessa Redgrave.

A fresh departure for the WRP was its involvement in making films. A new company, Vanessa Redgrave Productions Ltd., was set up and one film, *The Palestinian,* has been produced.

The British section of the Trotskyist United Secretariat of the Fourth International is the International Marxist Group (IMG). The national secretary is Bob Pennington. Membership is about 1,200. It publishes a well-produced weekly paper, *Socialist Challenge* (successor to *Red Weekly*) and a journal, *International.* (*Socialist Challenge* circulation is 8,000). It specializes in single-issue campaigns, notably on unemployment, solidarity with Chile, and the coloured peoples of Southern Africa. It gives praise to the Provisional IRA and is closely involved in the *Troops Out Movement.* Its publishing of some private remarks of Sir Richard Dobson, chairman of British Leyland, which had been secretly taped, obliged him to resign. Like the SWP, the IMG now campaigns at elections with other small left groups under the label Socialist Unity. At the Ladywood by-election the Socialist Unity candidate won 54 votes.

The Workers' Socialist League (WSL) was formed on 22 December 1974, following the expulsion of over 200 members from the WRP. It bases its actions entirely on Trotsky's Transitional Program. Its head is Alan Thornett, known as "The Mole," a shop steward at British Leyland's Cowley assembly plant at Oxford. Its fortnightly paper, *Socialist Press,* became a weekly in November 1977. The WSL has inspired the campaign for "Democracy in the Labour Movement," a body similar to the Communist-controlled LCDTU. This held a conference on 27 March. An even more militant body than the LCDTU, it demanded not a return to free collective bargaining but "substantial increases now."

Other small Trotskyist groups include the International Communist League, David Yaafe's Revolutionary Communist Group, and the Workers' League.

There are eight tiny pro-Chinese Marxist groups in Great Britain, the most important of which is the Communist Party of Great Britain-Marxist-Leninist. It has a membership of some 400 and is headed by Reg Birch, a member of the General Council of the TUC.

London   Richard Sim

Greece

The Communist Party of Greece (Kommunistikon Komma Ellados; KKE) evolved from the Socialist Workers' Party of Greece, which was formed in November 1918. In the 1950s and 1960s, the KKE, outlawed since 1947, operated through a front organization, the United Democratic Left (EDA). In April 1967 the EDA was banned along with all other political parties. During the military dictatorship (1967-74), the KKE split between those Communists who had lived in Greece and those who had been in Eastern Europe and the Soviet Union since the collapse of the guerrilla campaign (1946-49). The split led to the emergence of two separate political organizations which became known as "KKE (interior)" and "KKE (exterior)." The latter, which is recognized by the Soviet Union as the legitimate party, does not use the suffix "exterior" and claims to be the only Communist party in Greece. The KKE (interior) is closer to the ideological positions of Eurocommunism and maintains fairly close relations with the European Communist parties.

The Revolutionary Communist Movement of Greece (EKKE), which claims to be the genuine spokesman for proletarian revolution, often attacks Moscow's "revisionism" and "social-imperialism," and appears to uphold a Maoist version of Marxism-Leninism. In the parliamentary election of 20 November 1977 its ticket received 11,657 votes (0.23 percent) in a total of 5,130,420 valid votes.

All political parties returned to legal status following the collapse of the military dictatorship in July 1974. In the 1977 parliamentary election the pro-Soviet KKE received 9.29 percent of the total vote and 11 seats in the 300-seat legislature. The KKE (interior) had formed an electoral coalition, known as the "Alliance," with EDA, two other leftist organizations, Socialistiki Poreia (Socialist Course) and Protovoulia (Initiative for Democracy and Socialism), and the mildly leftist Christian Democracy, an organization which equates Socialism with social justice and humanism. The "Alliance" received 2.72 percent of the total vote and only two seats in the legislature. Babis Drakopoulos, KKE (interior) secretary general, was not elected. One seat was given to EDA chairman Elias Iliou as the leader of the "Alliance."

There are no verifiable figures as to the membership of any of these parties. It may be noted, however, that the ticket of KKE received 470,892 votes in the November election. It may also be noted that its 9.29 percent of the electorate is almost identical with the 9.40 percent abstention in March 1946 attributed to Communist influence by the Allied Mission for Observing the Greek Election (AMFOGE).

Greece has a population of 9,150,000 and 6,794,999 registered voters.

The KKE and the other Marxist-Leninist organizations, whether more moderate, like the KKE (interior) and EDA, or more radical, like the EKKE, remain a marginal force in Greek politics. Especially since the 1977 election, the Greek left is represented by the Panhellenic Socialist Movement (PASOK) under the leadership of Andreas Papandreou. This party, which in many respects holds positions similar to and at times even more radical than those of the KKE, received 1,282,577 votes or 25.33 percent, and emerged as the major opposition party with 92 seats in the 300-seat legislature. Although as a rule Papandreou avoids the use of Marxist-Leninist jargon, his ideological theses are in line with the basic Marxist-Leninist orientations, with variations ranging from the Yugoslav model of workers' councils to Chinese agricultural communes. PASOK is strongly anti-American, anti-NATO, critical of detente, critical of Greece's entry into the European Common Market, and fiercely nationalistic. Prior to the last election, Papandreou toned down his pronouncements considerably and thus increased his appeal among the voters.

Leadership and Organization. The KKE is directed by its Politburo, which includes Kharilaos Florakis as secretary general and Nikos Kaloudhis as first deputy secretary. The party follows the traditional organizational pattern, with "cells" at the grass-roots level, regional committees, Central Committee (which meets usually once a year), and congress (which is supposed to meet every four years but which has not met on schedule in the last forty years). The Ninth Congress, the most recent, met in February 1974. The party has a youth organization, Greek Communist Youth (KNE).

The KKE (interior) is led by Babis Drakopoulos, as noted earlier. Its organization remains small and ineffectual. It has a Communist youth organization under the name of "Rigas Fereos," a hero of the Greek War of Independence. The KKE (interior) tacitly accepted its differentiation from the KKE when it designated its June 1976 congress as its "first." Following the dismal showing of the KKE (interior) and the EDA combined in the November 1977 elections, one may expect these two organizations to play an even less prominent role in Greek politics.

Party Internal Affairs. During 1977 the KKE Central Committee met three times (March, July, and September). The July meeting set the date for the party's Tenth Congress as late February 1978. The "extraordinary plenum" in September decided, "because of the election," to postpone the congress to May.

The KKE (interior) held a conference of professional men on 8 March in an effort to show its appeal to leftist intellectuals. In June the Central Committee discussed the possibilty of closer cooperation with other leftist organizations. Earlier, party secretary Drakopoulos met with PASOK leader Papandreou and discussed the same matter, as did the KKE's Florakis and EDA's Iliou, but the talks were unproductive because Papandreou wanted all leftist forces, in effect, to join PASOK and accept his leadership.

Domestic and International Views. The KKE calls for immediate and complete disengagement from NATO and opposes Greece's entry to the European Economic Community. It calls also for restrictions on the activities of "local and foreign monopolies" in Greece and for the removal of any American bases. With regard to the economic system, it basically favors the Soviet model of command economy. Up to now it has made no concessions to the concept of political pluralism. Nevertheless, due to the repeated failures of the Greek Communists to advance to power by force, the party is tacitly leaving force out of its present avenues toward power.

Although PASOK is not ordinarily included among the Marxist-Leninist parties, its views merit consideration at this point. PASOK calls for the complete and immediate disengagement from NATO, opposes Greece's entry into the EEC, insists on the removal of any remaining NATO or American bases on Greek soil, and calls for an end to the presence of multi-national corporations and "domestic and foreign monoplies." PASOK's views on the economic system call for a radical "change" somewhat along the lines of Yugoslav "self-management" for industrial enterprises and a variation of the Chinese communes for the countryside. Past pronouncements by Papandreou indicate that he is not committed to the preservation of the pluralist political competition if he has the power to impose the drastic changes he visualizes.

The KKE (interior) opposes a return to the military wing of NATO but reluctantly accepts Greece's political ties with the alliance. Its opposition to the presence of American bases is voiced on occasion but without excessive vigor. The party does not oppose Greece's entry into the EEC but favors an extensive revision of the related agreements to assure "better protection of the Greek workers and farmers." In the economic sector, it favors the nationalization of the remaining major enterprises but appears to be flexible on the organization of the farms and the status of small business. Drakopoulos has often said that the party now accepts the basic elements of pluralism.

The EDA also opposes Greece's return to the military wing of NATO but otherwise it does not press for a total withdrawal from the alliance. Its position is also moderate on the question of American or NATO bases. In politico-economic philosophy it is slightly to the left of most social-democratic parties in Europe. The EDA has repeatedly declared its commitment to pluralism.

The EKKE, of course, is totally opposed to NATO, the EEC, foreign military bases, "foreign and domestic monopolies," and "American and Soviet imperialism." It advocates a revolutionary transformation of society, by force if necessary, leading to the dictatorship of the proletariat. An interesting illustration of EKKE's anti-Soviet position was given by an article in the party's weekly *Laikoi Agones* in March, on the alleged "overt invasion of Zaïre by mercenaries of the Soviet Union." The action, the article went on, "shows once again the ugly feature of Soviet social-imperialism."

The moderate, ambivalent Communism of the KKE (interior) and EDA and the strange anti-Soviet Communism of EKKE remain alien to the broad masses of Greek leftists. The KKE and PASOK reflect more accurately the attitudes of the Greek leftists. One may add that PASOK attracted a considerable number of voters in the November 1977 election, drawn mostly by Papandreou's virulent anti-Americanism and advocacy of "change," who were not familiar with or influenced by his socioeconomic ideological positions.

Other Marxist-Leninist Organizations. Several organizations continued to make their presence felt through 1977 by distributing leaflets or bulletins, participating in an occasional demonstration, or trying to foment a strike or a work stoppage. Their memberships and their effectiveness remain dismally limited. We may mention the following only as a matter of record: (a) The Organization of Marxist-Leninists of Greece (OMLE) is anti-Soviet and pro-Chinese. It often attacks "Soviet social-imperialism" and has sided with Hua Kuo-feng and against the "Gang of Four." (b) The Greek Revolutionary Liberation Front (EEAM) often accuses the KKE of opportunism. It is Stalinist in orientation and critical of the present Soviet leadership. Its Union of Struggle of Leftist Students (EPAS) has a limited influence among leftist university students. (c) The Greek Communist Party/Marxist-Leninist (KKE/ML) is Stalinist in orientation. A marginal organization, it tries to make itself visible mostly through "militant" activists within existing student organizations.

Publications. The KKE's official organ is the daily *Rizospastis*. The KKE (interior) and the EDA share the daily *Avgi* (Dawn). The KKE's theoretical review is *Kommunistiki Epitheorisi* (Communist Review). Other organizations publish from time to time tabloids such as OMLE's *Laikos Dromos*, the EKKE's *Laikoi Agones*, and the KKE/ML's *Kokkini Simaia*. These publications do not have very wide circulation. However, a great deal of anti-American, "anti-capitalist" fare is published daily in non-Communist publications with very wide circulation such as *Epikaira, Oikonomikos Takhydromos, Politika Themata,* et al., a legacy of the 1967-74 military dictatorship and the anti-Americanism it generated. PASOK's electoral success in the 1977 election is likely to legitimize and encourage the leftist orientation of such non-Communist publications even more.

Howard University   D. George Kousoulas

Iceland

Iceland's political culture, with its emphasis on egalitarianism and fervent nationalism, has produced various left-Socialist and Communist movements over the years. As is so often the case with Icelandic political institutions, analogies can be made with other Western European countries, but there inevitably emerge unique Icelandic characteristics. For the past decade the main party of the Socialist left has been the People's Alliance (Altydubandalagid; AB), which while advocating fairly radical alternatives to current domestic and foreign policy, nevertheless does so without any reference to Communist pronouncements and clichés from abroad. The AB is thus the latest form of a solidly established native radical tradition. The AB is supported by a heterogeneous collection of trade union members, radical teachers and students, extreme nationalists, and disenchanted Social Democrats. The relative strength of the AB is to be compared to the much weaker, reformist Social Democratic party (Altyduflokkurinn; SDP); Iceland is the only Nordic country in which the Social Democrats are not the largest political party. The People's Alliance has an estimated 2,500 members, out of a total population of about 223,000. Its main strength rests in the Reykjavik area (where half of Iceland's population lives) and in the smaller fishing and processing towns along the eastern and northern coasts.

Communism has had a rather confusing and maverick history in Iceland. Its first organizational form was a secessionist left-wing splinter from the Social Democratic party in 1930. There have never been any legal prohibitions against the Communists. In 1938—now considered its birth year—the Icelandic Communist party (Kommunistaflokkur Islands; ICP) withdrew from the Comintern, reconstituted itself to include more radical Social Democrats, and took the name of United People's Party-Socialist Party (Sameiningarflokkur altydu-Sosialistaflokkurinn; UPP-SP). Even before this realignment the ICP had actively sought a "popular front" with the Social Democrats. The new UPP-SP based their ideology on "scientific socialism-Marxism," and although there were no longer organizational ties to Moscow, the UPP-SP generally echoed Moscow's viewpoint on international affairs. In 1956 an electoral alliance was formed between most of the UPP-SP, the National Preservation Party, and dissident Social Democrats. This "People's Alliance" of 1956 paved the way for the UPP-SP's participation in a broad national coalition government (1956-58). Moreover, the merger with the National Preservation Party (formed in 1953 to protest NATO membership, the NATO airbase at Keflavik, and to promote a return to neutrality in foreign policy) made the AB the principal opponent of NATO membership. The AB became an avowed "Marxist political party" in November 1968 and so replaced the UPP-SP. Several elements in the National Preservation Party objected and under the leadership of Hannibal Valdimarsson formed the Organization of Liberals and Leftists (Samtök frjalslyndra og vinstri manna; OLL). In domestic policy the OLL is more pragmatically Socialist than the AB's leading elements. There is also a pro-Soviet Marxist faction, the Organization of Icelandic Socialists, and a Trotskyist Revolutionary Communist League (Fylking Bytingarsinnadhra Kommunista; FBK), but both groups are without political significance. In April 1976 still another leftist group, the Icelandic Communist Party-Marxist-Leninist (ICP-ML), was established by thirty delegates. Its chairman, Gunnar Andresson, claimed that the new party was the rightful heir to the original ICP. The new group's program was to lead Icelandic workers against modern revisionism and the greatest danger of all, Soviet "social imperialism" (*Nordisk Kontakt,* 1976, No. 10). The ICP-ML has close ties to the Chinese Communist Party and is mentioned frequently in *Peking Review* (see issues of 10 December 1976, 4 February 1977).

The principal left-Socialist/Communist group, currently represented by the AB, has consistently polled between 12 and 20 percent of the popular vote in postwar parliamentary elections. In 1971 the AB received 17.1 percent of the vote and won ten of the sixty Althing (parliament) seats. A coalition government was formed by the Progressive (agrarian centrist) leader, Olafur Johannesson, including the AB and the OLL. The AB thus became with the Communist Party of Finland, one of the two Western European Communist parties to participate in a democratically elected government. Two leading AB politicians held cabinet posts; Ludvik Jósefsson became minister of commerce and fisheries, and Magnus Kjartansson minister of health, social security, and industry, in the seven-man Johannesson government. (For additional details see Trond Gilberg, "Patterns of Nordic Communism," *Problems of Communism* (Washington), May-June 1975.)

The June 1974 parliamentary elections brought the AB electoral gains (18.3 percent of the vote and eleven seats), but the OLL lost both votes and seats (down from 8.9 percent to 4.7 and from five seats to two). The result was a thirty-thirty tie in the Althing and two months of intense political negotiations. The election's biggest winner, the Independents (moderate conservatives), persuaded the Progressives to join a new majority coalition under Independent leader Geir Hallgrimsson. The AB was thus forced back into the opposition.

Leadership and Organization. Ragnar Arnalds, former leader of the anti-NATO campaign, remains AB chairman, and Adda Bara Sigfusdottir is vice-chairman. Parliamentary leader of the AB group is Ludvik Jósefsson, and Steingrimur Hermansson is second vice-president of the parliament. The Management Council is the party's highest authority between meetings of the thirty-two member Central Committee.

Party Internal Affairs. Personalities weigh heavily in Icelandic politics, and over the years Communists have had their full share of factionalism, splits, and realignments. This has been especially true of the AB, whose parliamentary strength has fluctuated more because of intra-party disagreement than from changing public support. The struggle between Hannibal Valdimarsson and the Communists for control of the People's Alliance in 1968 resulted in the formation of the OLL, which captured parliamentary mandates that might otherwise have gone to the AB.

There have also been personality clashes within the remainder of the AB, such as that between the AB's two most influential members, Jósefsson and Kjartansson. During the past two years, however, intra-party strife has been generally absent, and as an opposition party the AB has been able to present a united front.

The OLL appears to be in the process of disintegrating after years of factionalism and eroding electoral support. The party's Reykjavik section intends to continue as a distinct party organization, but the rural groups are anxious to cooperate closely with the Social Democrats. In October 1976 the OLL Executive Committee decided to cancel the party's National Congress and dissolve itself in favor of the small OLL parliamentary group. One of the OLL Althing members has already announced his intention to join the AB (*Nordisk Kontact,* 1976, No. 15). This party's future after the upcoming 1978 parliamentary elections is in doubt.

Domestic Attitudes and Activities. In 1977 the Icelandic economy showed a marked improvement, primarily as a result of improved fishing and the agreement with Great Britain giving Iceland nearly exclusive fishing rights within a 200-mile coastal economic zone. Nevertheless, Icelandic society was challenged by growing labor unrest and strikes. This, coupled with the country's chronic inflation, which again in 1977 will be 31 to 32 percent per year, provides most of the focus for AB's political attacks against the Independent-Progressive government. With the sharp improvement in the national economy and a greatly reduced balance-of-payments deficit, AB statements on economic policy were increasingly specific. Growing foreign investment in large industrial projects was a prime target for AB's criticism during 1977.

There have been energetic efforts during the past few years to develop alternatives to Iceland's economic dependence on fishing, which is still the source of about 75 percent of the country's export earnings and which together with the fish processing industries provides for most private employment. No other Western society is so dependent on a single commodity. An important economic alternative has been the country's underdeveloped energy resources; these include mainly hydroelectricity and, of less industrial importance, geothermal power and heat. Large industrial projects require outside capital assistance, and in recent years this has attracted large multinational concerns in consortium with public and private Icelandic capital. Such joint ventures are strongly opposed by the People's Alliance. In 1977 this opposition was reflected in the debate concerning a large ferro-silicon plant at Hvalsfjördur in which the Icelandic state is to hold 55 percent and a Norwegian firm the remaining 45 percent. In parliament, AB spokesman Jósefsson registered his party's opposition to foreign investment and to the plant's environmental impact (*Nordisk Kontakt,* 1977, No. 4). This was followed by an extensive AB parliamentary motion calling for planning and reallocation of energy resources so as to promote Icelandic enterprises without foreign involvement. A special danger from foreign investors might be the country's accession to the European Economic Community (EC). This despite the fact that the foreign firms concerned have been Swiss and Norwegian, i.e., from non-EC countries (Ibid., No. 6). The declaration followed the proposal in December 1976 of a constitutional amendment providing for the common ownership of natural resources on land and in the sea. (Ibid., 1976, No. 16.)

Labor strife punctuated Icelandic politics throughout 1977. Until the 1968 split in the People's Alliance, Communist influence in the Icelandic Trade Union Federation (Altydusamband Islands; ASI) was significant. Direct control has been less during the past decade, but the AB consistently supports the more radical demands of organized labor. In the private-sector collective agreement of June 1977, average wages were to be increased up to 45 percent, so it was not surprising when public-sector unions demanded similar settlements for their members. Failure to reach an agreement resulted in the first widespread public-sector strike in Icelandic history. Between 11 and 25 October, when an agreement was finally reached, nearly all public activity in Iceland was halted. In parliament AB spokesmen supported the right of public employees to strike and criticized the government's negotiating position. (Ibid., 1977, No. 13.)

The national and municipal elections scheduled for the spring of 1978 began to appear in partisan debates during the fall of 1977. An important issue supported by several parties is a reform of the distribution of parliamentary districts. The current system severely penalizes urban areas such as Reykjavik in favor of rural districts. Parties such as the AB, which draw most of their votes in larger urban centers, would probably benefit significantly from such a reform. (Ibid., No. 14.)

International Views and Positions. No Icelandic party is more consistently suspicious of things foreign than the People's Alliance. This has meant consistent opposition to Icelandic membership in NATO and to retention of the U.S. Icelandic Defense Force (the Keflavik base) in any form. The Communists' long-term objective has been and is an unarmed (except for the coast guard) and neutral Iceland.

The AB brought such sentiments to bear with its hard line in the 1974 Icelandic negotiations with the United States over the Keflavik NATO base. The AB advance in the 1974 elections may have been promoted by anti-NATO feelings, but the even larger gains of the Independence Party and the mass "Defend Our Land" petition campaign indicated that many Icelanders favor a more moderate security policy. The NATO base continues, however, to give the Icelandic government considerable leverage in political and economic dealings with other Western states. This was reflected during the 1975-76 "Cod War" between Iceland and Great Britain, which ended with an agreement greatly favoring the position of Iceland. The use of the British navy to protect British fishing trawlers provided the context of an attack on NATO membership by an AB foreign policy spokesman who characterized the connection as a "political swindle." (Ibid., 1976, No. 15.)

For years Iceland has had substantial trade with the USSR, and the AB has been among the most vociferous in extolling the advantages of trade with non-Western nations. About 10 percent of Iceland's foreign trade is with the USSR (but nearly 30 percent is with the United States). During 1977 Iceland also signed large-scale agreements with China for the purchase of 11,000 tons of Icelandic aluminum. (Ibid., 1977 No. 13.)

International Party Contacts. The Icelandic Communists have been consistently absent from international Communist meetings and have avoided contacts with foreign Communist movements. In fact, no other Western European Communist party has maintained such an isolationist position (see Gilberg, *op. cit.,* pp. 34-35).

The AB does not maintain formal ties with the Communist Party of the Soviet Union, and it condemned the Warsaw Pact invasion of Czechoslovakia in 1968. Accordingly, there have been no AB representatives present at periodic gatherings of pro-Soviet parties such as the CPSU congress in 1976 or the conference of European Communist and Workers' Parties in East Berlin in 1976. In the past the AB has offered moral support for Communist parties, most notably those of Romania and Yugoslavia, which are known for their independent or nationalistic views. The AB has also maintained periodic contact with the Italian Communist Party (PCI), including a visit to Rome by Chairman Arnalds in 1976.

Publications. The AB's central organ is *Thjodviljinn (Will of the Nation),* a daily newspaper in Reykjavik (with national circulation estimated at 10,000). The party also publishes a biweekly theoretical journal, *Ny Utsyn.* Outside the capital, there are at least two pro-Communist weeklies: *Verkamadhurinn* in Akureyri and *Mjolnir in Siglufjördhur.* The Trotskyist FBK publishes a monthly, *Nesti.* The publication of the fledgling Maoist organization is *Stettabarattan* (Class Struggle).

University of Massachusetts   Eric S. Einhorn
Amherst

Ireland

The first Irish Communist Party, founded 14 October 1921 following a schism in the Socialist Party of Ireland, had difficulty making any headway during the Civil War (1922-23) and shortly afterward became extinct. Marxist-Leninist remnants remained organized in Revolutionary Workers' Groups, however, and a conference of these groups refounded it as the Communist Party of Ireland (CPI) in June 1933, the date now adopted by Irish Communists for its origin.

The party was severely disrupted by the Second World War, largely because of the belligerent status of Northern Ireland and the neutrality of the South. In 1941 the southern organization suspended its activities and the present-day general secretary of the party, Michael O'Riordan, was interned. Two separate Irish Communist groups merged in 1948: the Irish Workers' League, later renamed Irish Workers' Party, in the South and the Communist Party of Northern Ireland in the North. At a special "Unity Congress" held in Belfast on 15 March 1970, the two factions reunited to form a unified CPI. Today the CPI has about 500 members, mostly northern Protestants or Dublin based. Marxists in the South usually join the Official Sinn Fein or any of numerous ultra-left groups.

The population of the Republic of Ireland is 3,199,000 and of Northern Ireland about half that.

Leadership and Organization. The CPI is divided into two area branches, northern and southern. Overall direction between congresses is undertaken by the twenty-three member National Executive. The innermost controlling body, the National Political Committee, includes Andrew Barr (chairman), Hugh Moore (secretary, northern area), Sean Nolan, Michael O'Riordan (general secretary), Tom Redmond (vice-chairman), and James Stewart (assistant general secretary).

The CPI holds no seats in any legislative assembly in either North or South. It is an important section of the Left Alternative, itself a small grouping which includes the Liaison Committee of the Labour Left, the Official Sinn Fein-Workers' Party (SFWP), the Socialist Party of Ireland, and the Union of Students of Ireland. The Communists have some influence in the trade unions and the Northern Ireland Civil Rights Association. The CPI controls a small youth organization, the Connolly Youth Movement.

Party Internal Affairs. The CPI's inflexible pro-Moscow stance, which led to the defection of some prominent party personalities in December 1975 and January 1976 (see below, "Other Marxist Groups"), caused further resignations in the spring of 1977. Letters of resignation have accused the party of having gone back on the process of de-Stalinization inititated in the USSR at the CPSU's Twentieth Congress. Most of the dissidents are now organized in a Eurocommunist group called the Irish Marxists Society (see below).

There has been a perceptible strengthening of pro-Soviet sympathies since the party congress of 1971. An arresting example is the Czechoslovak issue. Though originally opposing the Russian invasion of Czechoslovakia, the Political Committee is stifling debate within the party on this issue by bureaucratic handling of political resolutions. The two principal reasons for the CPI's hardening of attitudes on this and other issues are (1) the presence of the Soviet Embassy in Dublin, established in 1975, which has made CPI-CPSU relations more delicate and any deviations from the Moscow "line" more unacceptable, and (2) the small influx from the Official Sinn Fein of members who welcome a strong identification with Moscow.

In October 1977 the CPI moved into new Dublin offices, named Connolly House, near the site of a former party HQ of that name which was burned down by rioters in 1933.

Domestic Attitudes and Activities. The fundamental goal of the CPI is the establishment of a unified Socialist republic in Ireland. To achieve this objective, the party seeks first to build a "broad democratic movement." This idea, first enunciated in 1970, has never actually been defined. Its most tangible result has been the alliance with the renamed Official Sinn Fein-Workers' Party (SFWP) and the Liaison Group of the Left. This tactical formation, under great strain, deteriorated sharply in March 1977 into open rivalry between the CPI and the SFWP. The two parties even ran competing candidates in the 16 June general elections.

The party campaigned on demands for a return to free collective bargaining, an end to cuts in social welfare spending, more taxation for people on high incomes, an end to the Labour Party's coalition with Finn Gael, and state initiative in developing new industrial areas.

All CPI candidates fared badly. Only one, J. Barlow, secured over a thousand (1,238) first preference votes. Overall, the most successful was the candidate in Ballyfermont, who survived until the eighth count on a result which lasted until the ninth count.

This electoral disaster, however, is a misleading indication of the party's influence, which is better gauged by a consideration of its strength in the trade union movement. Here the CPI has a small but not insignificant degree of influence. Most notable is the presence of Andrew Barr, CPI national chairman, a president of the Irish Congress of Trade Unions and member of the Executive Committee of the European Confederation of Trade Unions. The CPI also participated wholeheartedly in the March anti-unemployment demonstration of some 3,000 people organized by the Dublin Council of Trade Unions as part of its Right to Work Campaign. The CPI was active in campaigning against the National Wage Agreement, the restrictions on the right to strike, conditions in Port Laoise prison, and alleged police brutality.

CPI domestic policies for the South remained unchanged in 1977. Its policies include the expansion of state control in productive industry, nationalization of the banks, state development of Ireland's oil, gas, and mineral wealth, withdrawal from the EEC, and increased trade with the countries of Eastern Europe.

In more practical matters, the CPI expressed solidarity with the United Farm Workers' Union of the U.S.A. and mounted a campaign to secure a public boycott of the Californian Red Emperor grape. The party also lent its full support to the actions of the Irish Council for Civil Liberties and the Anti-Apartheid Movement.

Finances remain an acute problem for the CPI and funds are boosted by constant fund-raising campaigns. An "Irish Socialist" bazaar, held in Dublin in January, was particularly successful, raising over £1,200 through sale of East European goods and entertainment provided by Chilean folk singers.

In the North the CPI seeks the withdrawal of British troops. It insists that the way forward for Northern Ireland lies in the implementation of a bill of rights as presented by the Northern Ireland Civil Rights Association and the "Better Life for All" campaign of the trade unions. Thus, it was heartened by the divisions which emerged within the northern Catholic Social Democratic Labor Party (SDLP) when that party's new policy document shifted slightly away from power sharing toward a more anti-British stance. The SDLP's power-sharing strategy, the *Irish Socialist* said in its September issue, was based only on "a blind faith in the good offices of a British Government." Preferring to base its Northern Ireland strategy on a nonsectarian trade union movement embracing both Protestants and Catholics, the CPI is virulent in its condemnation of the Provisional IRA. It also denounced the attempt at a general strike from 3 May to 14 May by the loyalist United Unionist Action Council. In the longer term, the CPI seeks the introduction of secular education in the schools and massive financial aid from the British government to develop industry and create employment. U.S. President Carter's statement on Northern Ireland was dismissed as a "tired series of platitudes."

International Views and Party Contacts. The CPI is totally loyal to Moscow, its Eurocommunist dissenters now having resigned from the party. Its condemnation of Eurocommunism heresies has been forthright. "In times of all-out press campaigns against the ideas of Communism and the unity of the world's anti-imperialist forces . . . there have always been those who for opportunist reasons alone have taken refuge by distancing themselves as far as possible from the Soviet Union. As in the past, we have no intention of doing so, no matter how trendy and fashionable it may be at a given period, and no matter whom it displeases" (*Irish Socialist,* August 1977).

Declarations on foreign policy are straightforward. The CPI continually stresses the need for solidarity with the peoples of Chile, Rhodesia, and South Africa, attacks NATO and the EEC, and criticizes the West German ban on the employment of radicals.

Among recent contacts by the CPI were the sending of a delegation led by O'Riordan to the Eighth Congress of the Portuguese Communist Party and of another to the funeral in Düsseldorf on 22 January of Max Reimann, veteran leader of the German Communist Party. In April Vice-Chairman Redmond and Betty Sinclair visited Czechoslovakia and spoke on Prague radio. Redmond was also received by András Gyénes, secretary of the Hungarian party's Central Committee. O'Riordan toured Britain in April to address several meetings and met Gordon McLennan, general secretary of the Communist Party of Great Britain.

Publications. The CPI publishes a weekly, *Unity,* and the *Young Worker,* in Belfast. In Dublin it publishes the weekly *Irish Worker's Voice* and the monthly *Irish Socialist.* The latter carries Irish-language reports in addition to the English. A theoretical quarterly, *Irish Socialist Review,* appears in Dublin.

Other Marxist Groups. There are several small Marxist organizations in Ireland. The principal one is the Sinn Fein Workers' Party, the political wing of the official IRA, which is closely identified with a pro-Moscow stance. Its mouthpiece is the monthly *United Irishman.* The SFWP ran fifteen candidates in the general elections, securing between 1,000 and 2,000 votes in most constituencies. In total, the SFWP polled 24,469 first preference votes.

Other groups include the Movement for a Socialist Republic, which is the Irish section of the Fourth International. A second Trotskyist group is the League for a Workers' Republic. Another group, the Irish Republican Socialist Party, stems from the official IRA with which it was involved in several armed clashes in early 1975. Its chairman, Seamus Costello, was murdered on 5 October 1977.

The Irish Marxist Society, a Eurocommunist split-off from the CPI, contains four former members of the CPI National Executive: George Jeffares, Sam Nolan, Mick O'Reilly, and Paddy Carmody. Their principal source of disagreement with the CPI leadership was its lack of democracy and free discussion. They further felt that despite the CPI's ostensible intention of seeking to build a broad front the leadership had interpreted this too narrowly. Not enough work had been done in more moderate groups such as tenants' associations, housing action committees, and civil rights groups. This group now has a regular publication, *Newsletter.*

Institute for Study of Conflict   Richard Sim
London

Italy

The Italian Communist Party (Partito Communisto Italiano; PCI) was founded in 1921 by the majority faction of the Italian Socialist Party (PSI). Although municipal returns during 1977 indicated some slippage from the 34.4 percent it received in the 1976 general election, the PCI still retains 228 of the 630 seats in the lower chamber and 116 out of 315 in the Senate. Its claimed membership dropped slightly to just under 1.8 million in a population of 58 million.

During 1977 the PCI increased its influence throughout Italy. In various kinds of coalitions it controlled about 2,800 of the country's 7,900 municipalities, including forty-five of the ninety-four province or regional capitals and Rome itself. In other localities, the network of state-run industries, and national government, it gave the impression that nothing could be done without the PCI. It shared in virtually all normal powers of government: appointment and dismissal in bureaucracy and economy, allocation of resources, and veto over government programs. Significantly, the PCI was able to postpone elections which might have caused problems.

The Communist movement seeks to govern as a potentially hegemonic element in the broadest possible coalition. Its chief objectives are acquisition of ever more important positions of power in the bureaucracy, police, armed forces, economy, mass media, as well as achievement of change within non-Communist parties.

The chief obstacle to PCI advancement is a suppressed but nonetheless widespread fear that, if it has the opportunity, it will deprive Italy of liberty and prosperity which has been the case with every ruling Communist movement in history. Hence, the PCI has spared no effort to portray itself as different from the East European and Soviet parties.

Leadership and Organization. The PCI is organized along Leninist lines. Members belong to one of the 11,000 sections in localities or places of work. Sections elect representatives to plant, town, and area committees, and then to ninety-four province and seventeen other federations. Nearly all officials above the lowest level depend financially on PCI auxiliary organizations. All are expected to contribute part of their salaries to the party. Communist parliamentary deputies sign their paychecks over to the PCI and receive a lesser salary from the party.

The federation committees, and the twenty regional committees into which they are organized, hold biennial conferences and elect delegates to a national congress every four years. The Fourteenth Congress was held in 1975. It elected a Central Committee (177), a Central Control Commission (53), a Central Audit Committee (6), a Directorate (33), and a Secretariat (8 members). General Secretary Enrico Berlinguer remains undisputed leader, but President Luigi Longo is more than a figurehead. Second echelon leaders sometimes debate party policy vigorously, but this has not diminished "democratic centralism." Decisions at a congress or other national meeting are invariably unanimous. Berlinguer ascribed to democratic centralism the reason why the party had come so far (*L'Unità*, 1 February). The PCI expelled a parliamentary former deputy, Rita Macciocchi, for criticism of the PCI (Ibid., 7 September).

During 1977 party membership failed to increase for the first time in this decade. Reaching a peak of 1.8 million in 1976, it declined to just below that figure. Organization and leading personalities remained unchanged during the year. The seventeen working sections are both shadow ministries and party organs.

The published final balance sheet for 1976 showed PCI expenditures of 33.4 billion lire while the projected figure for 1977 was 39.4 billion lire which equals 40 to 46 million U.S. dollars (ibid., 16 January). The only significant difference between these budgets on the income side were 9.7 to 13.8 billion lire from the sale of party cards and 9.4 to 11.3 billion from festivals. The PCI reported increased expenditures for peripheral organizations (20.7 to 24.5 billion) and for propaganda (5.2 to 9.1 billion). This budget is for headquarters only and covers neither local organizations nor auxiliary organizations which make party influence felt throughout Italy.

Auxiliary Organizations. The major auxiliary is the Italian Communist Youth Federation (GIC), headed by Massimo d'Alema, member of the Central Committee. It has grown to 150,000 members and cost the party $450,000 in 1976 (*L'Unità*, 25 January). Local, province, and regional administrations in which the PCI takes part should be counted as auxiliaries. Armando Cossutta is in charge of coordinating party activities in local government. The PCI shares directly in the government of ten regions (ibid., 8 March) and forty-five of the ninety-four province capitals.

Control of local government benefits the party organization by giving it prestige, leverage, and patronage. Under such administrations, PCI business, labor, and mass organizations flourish. In Bologna and other "red cities," cooperatives dominated by the party receive noncompetitive contracts and favorable zoning. Sometimes, land is sold to cooperatives and then its value multiplied by rezoning (*Il Settimanale*, 6 April and 8 June).

City agencies are more efficient in transferring resources to PCI affiliates than in providing services. Bologna, for example, has a per capita debt about twice that of the average municipality (ibid., 13 April). The per-pupil cost at that city's day-care centers is over $220 per month, while the region has the highest ratio of municipal employees to citizens (ibid., 20 April). In Milan, the PCI administration is under attack for allegedly allocating public housing apartments according to political criteria (ibid., 12 October). Policy in such administrations has been to allow Socialists and even Christian Democrats access to prestige, profit, and sometimes influence in exchange for acceptance of the party's leading role.

The National League of Cooperatives is a federation of businesses under control by Socialists and Communists. They provide everything from high-rise buildings to supermarkets and insurance coverage. Annual turnover reaches about a $5 billion equivalent. There is no juridical relationship between the PCI and the League. However, they prosper with the party and take on the role of contractors for local government run by the PCI, e.g., about half of Italy's imported meat. The League has 3 million members (*Il Giornale*, 15 December). Growing PCI influence in Rome has meant increased access for cooperatives to state financing. In 1977 Fincooper, the League's financing agency, received a loan of 100 billion lire to expand operations in the south. the League also took over Duina, a large private steel firm troubled by the rising cost of labor.

The CGIL, with nearly 4 million members and 100,000 proletarian police, is the largest labor organization. Its president is Luciano Lama, member of the PCI Central Committee. The typical union affiliated with CGIL has a party functionary as head and a Socialist functionary as deputy. The Socialists never challenge the Communist hold over CGIL. At most, they lend occasional support to extremists of Workers' Autonomy (AO), Proletarian Democracy (DP), and other "autonomous" groups which rather successfully agitate worker resistance to PCI efforts at moderating wage demands.

In 1977 the CGIL continued to increase its ascendancy over the other two labor confederations (the formerly Christian Democratic CISL and the former Social Democratic UIL) joined in the "Unitary Confederations." Through these "Unitary Confederations," the Communists exercise influence in vital areas of Italian life such as the mass media. Luciano Ceschia, PCI functionary and secretary of the journalists' union, controls the National Press Federation and directs efforts of labor groups within newspapers to set editorial policy and name personnel (*L'Express,* 31 April; *Il Giornale,* 12 May). At the end of the year, the "Unitary Confederations" were close to receiving exclusive right from the government to organize and represent the nation's policemen.

Domestic Views and Activities. In 1976 six Italian political parties—Christian Democrats (DC), Communists (PCI), Socialists (PSI), Social Democrats (PSDI), Republicans (PRI), and Liberals (PLI)—had joined in direct or indirect support of the Andreotti cabinet. The PCI gained assent to the proposition that they constitute a "constitutional arc" beyond which political activities are inimical to the constitution. It built upon this achievement during 1977 by negotiating a common program for the government with the same parties: they committed themselves to passing (1) a law transferring vast administrative powers to regional government, and (2) another to establishing a formula for determining the precise rent on residential property throughout the nation. The PCI believes that the "constitutional arc" which became the "programmatic accord" will lead to an "emergency government" by the six parties in the near future (*La Stampa,* 17 April).

The other foundation of PCI strategy is a promise to individuals, classes, and parties now aligned against it that their economic interests will be protected and that they will have a place in a future ruling alignment under the leadership of the "working class." The Communist party leadership constantly reminds its activists that, given its numerical inferiority, the working class either will "advance to a new and higher level of socioeconomic development" together with "the productive middle state" and Catholics, or it will fail. To make this point, the PCI ascribes the failure in Chile not to any conspiracy but to that regime's excessive sectarianism. The proper relationship between "the working class" and other elements through which it plans to exercise hegemony is the principal basis for the PCI claim that it accepts "pluralism" and a "multiparty system." Thus, Pietro Ingrao wrote that "the debate over hegemony is demystifying: it bluntly recalls the class descriptions of this society. . . . This is why raising the problem of hegemony (which is to say of a helmsman) is not just a clever way to dodge the debate over the institutions of democracy; on the contrary it calls for completely liquidating the dichotomy. . . . I wish only to emphasize to Craxi [leader of the PSI] that we Communists today see the proletariat's standing forth as a general class, as a process aware that it must reckon with the eventuality of conflict between the classes and within the working class itself. . . ." (*Rinascita,* 3 December).

The PCI is trying to accustom as many Christian Democrat leaders as possible to regard their personal safety, interests—their very positions with the DC—as tied to cooperation with the Communists. It points out that, while men such as Moro and Andreotti need DC anti-Communist voters to be elected, they cannot enjoy their offices without PCI support. Communists understand that a Christian Democratic leader who cooperates will weaken himself with his own constituency, and this gives opponents within their own party an opportunity to capture that constituency.

The PCI has long tried to soften Church opposition to Marxism and to elicit acquiescence to its advances. In the decade prior to the 1976 national elections, the Vatican did nothing to discourage its followers from believing that Christianity and Marxism are compatible. At that time, however, the Church seemed to return to the harder line of the 1950s. During 1977 the PCI once again found its efforts to conciliate the Vatican hindered by the need to reduce its role in society. Lucio Lombardo Radice, member of the Central Committee, declared (*La Stampa,* 16 September) that Marxism-Leninism is "inoperative" for the PCI and that, consequently, the party would drop Article 5 in its constitution requiring each member to learn it. Four weeks later, Berlinguer sent a thirteen-page letter to the Bishop of Ivrea which criticized religious intolerance by existing Communist regimes and stated that the PCI is open to people of all religions. He promised that the party would not use its influence to promote atheism (*L'Unità*, 18 October). At the same time, a PCI-sponsored law was going into effect which dissolved all private agencies, principally Catholic organizations, engaged in welfare and transferred "their functions, resources, and personnel to the regions on behalf of the municipalities" (ibid., 22 July).

While PCI strategy aims primarily at precluding opposition from the DC, it could not operate without Socialist Party (PSI) support. Were it not for this, the Communists could govern in only a small number of localities and PCI "mass organizations" would be seen as simple transmission belts. Recently, the PSI Secretariat, after consultation with the Communists, ordered all branches to withdraw from local ruling coalitions with the DC and demand PCI entry (*Il Giornale*, 16 November).

Cooperation of PCI, PSI, and part of the DC could be seen in the September law passed by parliament which postponed for at least six months local elections scheduled for 6 November 1977. The consensus in Italy at that time was that the PCI would have lost the elections. The Communists argued that the six government parties should work together on pressing problems rather than campaigning against one another (Giancarlo Pajetta in *La Stampa*, 20 September). But the DC leadership, despite pressure from the ranks, made the actual postponement motion which shielded the PCI from the charge of suppressing democracy for its own advantage.

The PCI position on elections in general is that they are not the best way to organize popular participation in politics (Luciano Barca in *Rinascita*, 3 June). That is best achieved by direct involvement with political parties, trade unions, work, administrative bodies, and mass organizations. As the head of the Gramsci Institute stated, "We fight for democracy with a new meaning, namely mass democracy, the democracy of the trade unions, the democracy of the parties and relations between the parties; not only this, but also for democracy within the institutions. One must recall the development of a democratic movement inside the organs that administer justice; a democratic movement has developed inside the police force" (cited over Moscow radio, 6 May).

While PCI political stock rose in 1977, its electoral fortunes declined a bit. On 18 April about 400,000 voters elected officials in eighty-five municipalities. In these same places, the PCI had received 37.7 percent of the year before. In 1977, they dropped to 28.8 percent (*Corriere della Sera*, 19 April). In Castellamare di Stabia, the principal city at stake, the PCI dropped from 46 to 33 percent despite an all-out effort by the national leadership. The Communist government, widely accused of corruption, was forced to resign (*NYT*, 10 May).

Whereas the PCI could reasonably hope to limit damage from electoral defeat by increasing its power over other political parties, during 1977 it seemed to lose influence over vast unorganized masses of students and the unemployed. In February, it was profoundly shaken by the first in a series of clashes with these groups. To strengthen Communist organizers at Rome University, beleaguered by ultraleftist and "autonomous" (i.e., politically unattached) students, CGIL head Luciano Lama came to the campus accompanied by a bodyguard of 5,000 proletarian police. However, they were routed by about twice that number of "autonomists" who chased Lama away. For the first time since 1943, the PCI had been physically beaten in the streets by student radicals who had done so much to destroy conservatism in Italian culture.

In an emergency meeting of the Directorate, called for the purpose of self-criticism, the party reversed its heretofore permissive attitude toward student radicals because they had attacked "the workers movement and the Communist Party." Therefore, these "organizations of the so-called autonomy area" had become "fascist" (*L'Unità*, 20 February). It called on the police to take the sternest measures against them. Until then, the PCI had termed "fascist" any attempt by the police to enforce law and order on campuses. The Communists also reversed, in principle, their long-time support of open admission to universities and of near-universal subsistence ("pre-salary") payments to university students. This swung even more students to the "autonomous" revolutionary anti-Communists.

On 13 March several thousand students attacked Communist targets in Bologna. A student was killed by the police. The next day Rome was in a state of seige, with mobs of youth burning and beating. The PCI issued the following statement: "It now emerges clearly that we are confronted by a complex maneuver, a plan with nothing spontaneous about it, centrally inspired and organized by forces keeping in the shadows. The Bologna attack was clearly directed against democracy and the republican institutions and could only have had reactionary, rightist aims." (Ibid., 14 March.) The PCI's shadow interior minister Pecchioli modified the party's previous position when he said that "the police have never been our enemies" (*ANSA,* 14 March).

The PCI sought to present itself to Italians as the only organization capable of controlling the violence which extended throughout the country during 1977. Nevertheless, the latter became the largest PCI asset in its drive for power. With the exception of the "autonomists," the violence centered on prominent anti-Communists. Throughout the year, local DC leaders known for their anti-Communism were hit. During May alone, the three most influential PCI opponents in the media (newspaper editors in Milan and Genoa and a Catholic television newsman) were shot in the legs by members of the Red Brigades. In November newsman Carlo Casalegno of Turin, well known for his independence, was killed by the same group.

The PCI further increased its control over the nation's media. Editors and workers' committees in newspapers and publishing houses could change newspaper stories and determine editorial appointments. Among the major dailies, only Milan's *Giornale,* Bologna's *Resto del Carlino,* Firenze's *Nazione,* and Rome's *Tempo* remained outside of PCI influence. Among serious non-party magazines, only *Il Settimanale* and occasionally *L'Europeo* showed independence. In the field of broadcasting, the party controls one-half of the state radio and television monopoly and continues to make inroads into the other half.

However, a group of journalists opposed to the PCI had begun broadcasting to Italy commercially from Monte Carlo. Telemontecarlo, relayed to most of northern Italy by private stations, became a serious competitor to the state monopoly. A law sponsored by the PCI ordered jamming of Telemontecarlo commercials. Although it disclaimed responsibility for the dynamiting of relay stations, the PCI declared Telemontecarlo illegal (Giancarlo Pajetta in *L'Europeo,* 10 December 1976) and supported injunctions of leftwing magistrates against relay station operations.

By the end of 1977 the PCI was close to its goal of closing the airwaves to opponents. A proposed law, drafted by the parliamentary Post and Telecommunication Committee with a PCI contribution, will allot licenses to a small number of private broadcasters judged by a committee of political appointees to be representative of the political spectrum. Foreign television would be allowed on a rotating basis, whenever another country would agree to reciprocity; but Telemontecarlo would be excluded because Monaco is not competent to make international agreements.

PCI economic policy closely reflects the conflicting requirements of its strategy and of its constituencies. A consensus developed in Italian public opinion that the country's economic troubles (e.g., inflation at over 20 percent during consecutive years) are due to excessive public spending, a huge and inefficient public sector, excessive labor costs, unrealistic indexing of wages and pensions, an almost total lack of confidence by investors.

The PCI has supported union demands that failing companies be taken over by the state. It has done so also because the party now has a large voice in decisions on personnel and policies of government-subsidized industries. Each such industry is now a source of patronage for the PCI as well as for the DC. Thus, with PCI concurrence, Italy's proposed budget for fiscal 1978 shows a deficit of about $23 billion.

By its declarations, the PCI has sought to reassure domestic businessmen as well as Italy's allies that it does not mean to destroy the economy but rather to make it a more viable part of the Western economic system. Giorgio Napolitano, in charge of all PCI economic activities, explained that the Communists would increase expenditures for public housing, public transportation, nuclear energy, and other worthy causes (*Der Spiegel*, 9 May). In every area the party could provide both room and incentives for private investment. Furthermore, according to Napolitano, the PCI believes that the country's resources must now be channeled not to new increases but to creation of new jobs. On the whole, PCI statements on economics satisfied many people. The only exception was Berlinguer's line on austerity. He presented it to the PCI apparatus as a great opportunity. Such a program could be "the way to oppose, down to its very roots . . . a system which is enmeshed in a structural crisis" (*L'Unità,* 16 January).

International Views and Activities. In 1977 the United States became the focus of PCI foreign pronouncements. The party sought to convince American policy makers that they should accept with equanimity Communist assumption of power. At the same time, the PCI sought to convince Italians that Americans already looked benevolently on the party and that Communists would not harm the traditional friendship between Italy and the United States. Even before the U.S. government abolished the policy of refusing entry visas for non-ruling Communist leaders, the PCI took every opportunity to place its members on official Italian delegations bound for the United States.

Ugo Pecchioli and Arrigo Boldrini came to Washington as part of the Senate Defense Committee. Their meetings with American officials as well as "representatives of the U.S. financial and industrial world" were well covered (*L'Unità,* 6 April). The visit by Communist mayor of Florence, Elio Gabuggiani, to Detroit to inaugurate that city's Renaissance center was front-page news. After the visa ban had been lifted, the CPI sent Central Committee member Lucio Libertini to a conference in Washington (ibid., 12 June). Alberto Jacoviello arrived in the United States as *L'Unità's* permanent correspondent in July. Carlo Santoro, a PCI foreign section official, came to New York at the invitation of the Council on Foreign Relations in November.

The PCI description of the United States became more factual (e.g., ibid., 20 January). The party, however, concentrated on difficulties in American society and still portrayed it as a battleground between sane progressives who support detente and mad reactionaries who are the greatest danger to world peace.

As in previous years, the PCI believed that the politics of detente are essential to achievement of its own goals, those of the world Socialist movement, and of its greatest bastion, the USSR. The party believes that detente has contributed to its gains by obscuring the moral distinctions between Marxist and liberal societies and by increasing the Soviet Union's power relative to the United States. Thus it is sensitive to any sign that the United States may no longer be willing to accept these trends (*Washington Post,* 7 May). Whenever this appeared to be the case, the PCI delivered a thorough attack. Thus, when the Soviet Union rejected the American proposal in March that would have provided relatively equal strategic forces, the PCI attributed these events to "pressure from the most extremist U.S. quarters which, on the one hand, fear that, with the development of the detente process, they will lose their traditional capacity for interference in and domination over the politics of other countries and, on the other hand, which see in the arms race the best means of exercising their blackmail" (*L'Unità,* 3 April).

Awareness of Soviet violation of human rights was heightened in Italy by the USSR exchange of Vladimir Bukovsky for Chilean Communist leader Luis Corvalan, East Germany's expulsion and imprisonment, respectively, of Wolff Biermann and Robert Havermann, Czechoslovak regime suppression of signatories to Charter 77, as well as President Carter's statements on human rights. The PCI responded by pointing out that when such things happen, "not only the development of the

Soviet Union suffers, but the international prestige of the Soviet Union and of Socialism all over the world is darkened," that the USSR would have to "face and settle . . . unresolved problems of liberty in the nation's domestic life," and that, for their part, Italian Communists oppose "any form of limitation of individual freedom and collective liberty." (Ibid., 20 December 1976.)

For the most part, the PCI neither said nor hinted that because of their violations of basic human rights Communist regimes should be replaced or even that one should oppose the expansion of their influence. Quite the contrary, Secretariat member Paolo Buffalini spoke of the superior potential for liberty "where, as in the USSR, the bases of a new, egalitarian society have been laid." (Ibid., 19 January.) Berlinguer, speaking to some 2,000 cadres in Milan, said anyone is dreaming who expects the PCI to abandon either the principles or the results of the 1917 October Revolution (ibid., 1 February). Also, although the PCI had steadfastly refused to state which side it would choose in a conflict between the USSR and NATO, Lucio Lombardo Radice admitted that "we would choose the Soviet side, of course" (*NYT*, 17 April).

The PCI maintains good relations with the Soviet Union. It reported the editorial in the December 1976 issue of *Kommunist* which praised the party's political strategy and its "internationalist, comradely, and voluntary cooperation." At the same time, the Chilean Communist leader residing in Moscow, Luis Corvalan, declared publicly that his own party should have followed PCI strategy (*CSM*, 25 February). The PCI also gave wide currency to the Soviet evaluation that "present-day Italy can serve as a graphic example of how the role of the working class and its political parties and organizations is steadily growing in the persistent struggle against reaction . . ." (*Pravda*, 12 May).

The PCI views China as a deeply troubled country in which anything can happen. Its analysis of the purge of the Gang of Four appears to be objective (*L'Unità*, 17 April). The party believes that, given the right circumstances, China could once again cooperate with the world's "progressive forces." But it judges that with a few exceptions, China's present foreign policy is completely reactionary. In 1977 the PCI made no approaches to Peking.

International Party Contacts. During the year, the Italian Communists continued their policy of close cooperation with Moscow-line parties throughout the world. Relations with the CPSU remained cordial, characterized by exchange of congratulations and delegations. Berlinguer received Vadim Zagladin, deputy chief of the CPSU foreign section in Rome, and attended the sixtieth anniversary of the October Revolution in Moscow. He publicly embraced Brezhnev and was granted the podium (*L'Unità*, 8 November). High-level working exchanges between the PCI and CPSU included a visit by Secretariat member Giovanni Cervetti to Boris Ponomarev and of Giancarlo Pajetta to Mikhail Suslov (Moscow radio, 28 January and 2 September). At the end of the year, a "delegation of Italian workers," led by lower ranking PCI personages, took a two-week tour of the Soviet Union to learn "firsthand the life, work and leisure of Soviet people and the work of party organizations for the fulfillment of Twenty-fifth CPSU Congress decisions" (ibid., 22 December).

On two occasions, relations became strained. The USSR denied an entry visa to Vittorio Strada, a Communist professor of Russian literature who was to attend the International Book Fair, on apparent suspicion that Strada would cultivate contacts with dissidents. Subsequently, the Italian exhibit at the fair was harrassed by Soviet authorities. The PCI reported this, explaining that such things are uncharacteristic of the USSR, but it did not endorse these actions (*L'Unità*, 3 September).

As in previous years, the only exception to excelled PCI relations with East European Communist parties was Czechoslovakia. The latter reacted abusively to routinely expressed disapproval of publicized repression. The PCI went further and offered a position at the Gramsci Institute to Milan Hubl, a signer of Charter 77 who has been persecuted by the Czechoslovak regime (*NYT*, 8 May).

Berlinguer visited Janos Kadar, leader of the Hungarian Communist party. In addition to comradely talks "in a spirit of mutual solidarity," they discussed details of the arrangement by which

Budapest supplies meat to Italy via intermediaries controlled by the PCI (*L'Unità*, 3 October). Berlinguer also called on Nicolae Ceausescu in Romania and joined him in a long communiqué endorsing each other's policies. A subsequent visit by Giancarlo Pajetta recognized the "different realities" of Italy and Romania and called for "the autonomy of each party, which does not run counter to internationalism" (Budapest radio, 26 August).

In 1977 the French and Italian Communist parties worked together in what appeared to be harmony. Georges Marchais visited Berlinguer to coordinate strategy in the European communities and other areas. The communiqué (*L'Unità*, 4 May), along with a previous visit to Rome by French party experts on organization, suggests that the French were interested in successful Italian organizational methods.

The traditionally good relations between the PCI and the Spanish Communist Party (PCE) did not appear to suffer from the polemics between the latter and Moscow. Major PCE working delegations visited Rome in December 1976 and January 1977. Berlinguer later saw Santiago Carillo in Madrid. In the summer Spanish and Italian party officials both denied that any coolness had developed between them. (Ibid., 26 July).

On 2-3 March, Berlinguer, Carillo, and Marchais held a widely-publicized conference in Madrid. Contrary to some expectations (*NYT*, 4 March), they established neither principles nor machinery for so-called Eurocommunism. Repression of dissidents by other Communist parties was not mentioned. Instead, they promised to build Socialism "with pluralism of political and social forces . . ." (*L'Unità*, 6 March). In the PCI view, this summit was important above all because it placed the PCE in a good position for the first free elections in Spain since 1936.

The PCI has restored a cooperative relationship with the Portuguese Communist Party (PCP) less than two years after the latter's abortive drive for power. Between 10 and 14 February, a large PCP delegation led by leader Alvaro Cunhal visited Rome. The Portuguese not only conferred with their Italian counterparts but also were introduced to leaders of other political parties. (Ibid., 16 February.)

The PCI also exchanged delegations with the Libyan Socialist People's Congress (ibid., 19 March) and with the Lebanese Communist Party (*IB*, 30 September). While in Beirut, Central Committee member Romano Ledda met with PLO chairman Yasser Arafat (ibid., 6 May).

While the PCI exchanged fraternal greetings with all Moscow-line Communist parties in Latin America, it paid particular attention to the Chilean movement in exile. Luis Corvalan and leaders of other Chilean leftist movements took a tour of the country and were received by the leaders of the other five parties in the Italian "constitutional arc" (*ANSA*, 26 February).

During 1977 the CPI continued the high level of interest in Africa it has shown over the past several years. A PCI delegation attended the MPLA twentieth anniversary celebration in Angola and praised its contribution to tilting the balance of forces in favor of peace and freedom not only in Africa but also throughout the world. A similar delegation attended the third congress of Frelimo in Mozambique (*L'Unità*, 7 February). Another delegation went to Tanzania. In addition, the PCI hosted at Rome large working delegations of guerrilla movements fighting against Rhodesia—Zimbabwe (ibid., 26 July) and South Africa—the African National Congress (ibid., 21 September).

The Asian movement which most resembles the PCI is the Communist Party of Japan (CPJ). A CPJ Central Committee delegation visited Italy early in the year and issued a joint communiqué which stressed the common interest in "the broadest cooperation among all democratic forces" and in "internationalist solidarity" achieved in "full autonomy" (ibid., 20 January). The only other Asian party contacted by the PCI was Vietnam's, whose Fourth Congress was attended by Giancarlo Pajetta and a PCI delegation (*ANSA*, 11 December 1976).

Publications. The PCI's influence in publishing goes beyond its own press. Party newspapers, magazines, and journals, as well as the publishing house Editori Riuniti, are under the working section headed by Renato Zangheri, mayor of Bologna, who also supervises the ideological and cadre schools. The major PCI newspaper is *L'Unità*, appearing daily in both Milan and Rome, edited by Central Committee member Luca Pavolini; Rome's *Paese Sera* is the capital's most popular daily. The weekly *Rinascita*, popular culture journal, is read by intellectuals. The bi-monthly *Critica Marxista* is the theoretical journal. *La Nuova Rivista Internazionale* is a journal of international affairs, while *Politica ed Economia* deals with economics and *Studi Storici* with history. In addition, each PCI auxiliary has a journal, e.g., the women's federation published *Donne e Politica,* a political magazine for women.

Competing Communist Groups. 1977 was a year of turmoil for ultra-leftist competitors of the PCI. Two major groups split and a new one was formed. Moreover, the quarrel between China and Albania weakened the already feeble Maoists. Nevertheless, thousands of frequently violent youths continued to believe themselves the bearers of pure Communism. The ultra-left in Italy consists of about 1,000 guerrillas, some 50,000 activists, about half a million voters, and a few more sympathizers. In descending order of importance, the major groups are the following: Democrazia Proletaria (DP) or "Proletarian Democracy" was formed in 1977 by the followers of Vittorio Foa. They had left the PSI in 1964 as a group called PSIUP, much of which was absorbed by the PCI in 1972. But Foa's supporters, mostly labor organizers who retained influence gained through the CGIL, then formed the PDUP (Democratic Party of Proletarian Unity) by joining with the Manifesto group which had been expelled from the PCI. In 1976 the PDUP formed the backbone in an electoral alliance of the ultra-left, called Democrazia Proletaria (DP) which gained half a million votes and six deputies in the parliament. In 1977 the former Socialists parted company with the former Communists, assuring them of a rapprochement with the PCI and joined with Avanguardia Operaia (AO) to form a party named after the previous year's electoral coalition. Two out of the six deputies joined the new party. AO's 25,000 members (also well connected in the labor movement but with Trotskyite backgrounds) together with Foa's 8,000 should give the new party ability to challenge the PCI leadership over north Italian organized labor, or at least make the PCI task in key industrial centers more difficult by espousing extreme wage demands. DP will be most effective in the Milan-Turin-Genoa industrial triangle. AO's last act before joining DP was to organize a massive demonstration against the PCI in Bologna on 22-25 September. DP continues publication of the former AO daily *Quotidiano dei Lavoratori* and weekly *Politica Comunista.*

Lotta Continua (LC or Continuous Struggle), organized on a national scale since 1972, publishes 20,000 copies of a daily by the same name and exercises great influence in Italy's secondary schools. It suffered disintegration during 1977. Between 1-2,000 of its 12,000 diverse members held a congress on 4 November 1976 (*International Press,* 20 December 1976). In 1977, LC was the label for autonomous groups, some of which retain good relations with PCI-PSI, foreign terrorist groups like the Irish Republican Army, and two violent domestic groups: The Collectives and Workers' Autonomy (AO). LE remains on the edge of legality: one of its members sits in parliament (elected on the DP ticket) and others have served in leftist local government. But its connection with terrorism seems evident.

Workers' Autonomy (AO) split from LC in 1969. This violent, clandestine organization appears quite unstructured. It operates primarily in northern Italy. Like The Collectives, a similar group active primarily in central Italy, AO provides the focus for violent activities of leftists in factories, hospitals and housing projects.

Red Brigades (BR) and Armed Proletarian Nuclei (NAP) are the most spectacular among terrorist organizations in northern and central Italy, respectively. The BR has claimed responsibility for shooting the legs of about fifty prominent Italians during 1976-77, among them the economics dean at Rome University and the liberal editor of Milano's *Giornale*. BR targets have been exclusively well known anti-Communists. In January 1977 most of the Brigatisti imprisoned for the murder of Genoa's prosecutor Cocco in 1976—including Prospero Gallinari—escaped from prison.

In May the trial of BR leader Renato Curcio had to be moved from Turin because after the murder of the prosecutor jurists refused to serve. NAP continued to specialize in violent jailbreaks. The group suffered a setback when its leader, Antonio LoMuscio, was killed in a shootout with police on 1 July.

A number of other groups—Armed Proletarian Units, Communist Unity Fighters, Workers Fighting for Communism, Front-Line Communist Organization—have manifested themselves by claiming credit for widely scattered terrorist acts. The Revolutionary Action Front is the most unusual of these. When it shot Leone Ferrero, movie critic of the PCI's *L'Unita,* it committed the first attack on a Communist carried out by a "competing Communist" organization.

Il Manifesto, expelled from the PCI in 1969, continues to be led by Rossana Rossanda and Luigi Pintor and to publish 20,000 copies of a daily by the same name. In 1977 this group continued its rapprochement with the PCI. It took part in the PCI campaign to brand as "illegitimate" those Soviet and East European dissidents who reject Socialism.

The Communist Party of Italy (Marxist-Leninist) led by Fosco Dinucci since 1966 continued to print the daily *Nuova Unita* and weekly *Voce della Cella.* But in 1966-77, the party shifted its allegiance from Peking to Tirana. A delegation from the Albanian Party of Labor took part in the CPI (ML) national congress—the first time it has sent a delegation to a West European party gathering.

The Organization of the Communists of Italy (Marxist-Leninist) led by Osvaldo Pesce has become the major Peking-line Communist group in Italy. Pesce met with Ghi Ten Kuei, member of the PRC Politburo in February.

Washington, D.C.   Angelo Codevilla

Luxembourg

The Communist Party of Luxembourg (Parti Communiste de Luxembourg; PCL) was founded in January 1921. Before World War II it played an insignificant role in Luxembourg politics. After the war the party increased its influence to some extent, in part because of the enhanced prestige of the Soviet Union. Since 1945 the PCL has been represented in parliament and in the town councils of Luxembourg city and several industrial centers of the South. During 1945-47 the cabinet included one Communist minister. The party's influence decreased thereafter, but increased again following the elections of 1964. It reached a new climax in the elections of 1968 and decreased again in the elections of 1974.

PCL members are estimated to number between 500 and 600. The population of Luxembourg is about 356,400 (estimated 1976).

For many years the PCL recruited its members mainly among industrial workers; gradually it has been able to extend its influence to other segments of the population. In the latest parliamentary elections, 26 May 1974, the PCL received approximately 9 percent of the vote and won five of the fifty-nine seats (six of fifty-six seats in 1968). The next elections are scheduled for May 1979.

On the municipal level, the PCL increased its influence as a result of the decision of the Luxembourg Socialist Workers' Party (Parti Ouvrier Socialiste Luxembourgeois; LSAP) to form a coalition government with the PCL after the municipal elections of October 1969. This occurred in Esch-sur-Alzette, the second-largest town of the country, where PCL Secretariat member Arthur Useldinger, who is also a member of parliament, continued as mayor following the municipal elections of 12 October 1975.

The policy of the LSAP to cooperate more and more with the PCL engendered strong tensions among LSAP members and resulted in a party split in 1970. In 1945 the PCL formed its own trade union, which merged in 1965 with the far stronger LSAP-oriented workers association. This merger permitted the PCL to significantly influence the association in a Marxist direction and paved the way for its opening of relations with East European labor unions.

Leadership and Organization. The PCL, strongly pro-Soviet, presents the image of a united party. Differences of opinion are not made public. Party members vote as a bloc in parliament. The decisions of the party's congress and of its leading bodies are usually passed unanimously. The congress itself meets once every three years, most recently at Luxembourg on 26 and 27 December 1976. At that time, the Central Committee was extended to thirty-one members and four candidates (formerly twenty-eight members and no candidates). The Executive Committee remained at ten members. The three-member Secretariat consists of the new party chairman René Urbany, his father, the honorary chairman Dominique Urbany, and the party treasurer Arthur Useldinger. The PCL leadership is strongly centralized. This point is emphasized by the complete absence of regional party organizations, although local party sections do exist. Members of the Urbany family occupy key party positions. René Urbany succeeded his father, Dominique Urbany, as party chairman at the first meeting of the Central Committee following the Twenty-second Party Congress, held 26-27 December 1976. He remains director of the party press. The post of party secretary is temporarily vacant. The "Réveil de la Résistance" is directed by François Frisch, brother-in-law of René Urbany and member of the Central Committee. René Urbany's sister, Yvonne Frisch-Urbany, leads the Soviet-sponsored "Cultural Center Pushkin." His father-in-law, Jacques Hoffmann, is a member of the Central Committee and Executive Committee, and his brother-in-law François Hoffmann, is a member of the Central Committee and assistant editor of the party press. The PCL moved into new party headquarters at the beginning of 1977.

The party leads the League of Luxembourg Women (Union des Femmes Luxembourgeoises) and has a youth auxiliary (Jeunesse Progressiste). In addition it dominates a group of former resistance members (Le Réveil de la Résistance) and various societies which cultivate good relations with East European organizations.

Domestic Attitudes and Activities. The PCL sharply criticizes the social, economic and political situation in Luxembourg. During 1977 it repeated its offer to work with the Socialist party (Parti Ouvrier Socialiste Luxembourgeois) and confirmed its determination not to deviate from the path of international solidarity with the Communist movement. The PCL asserts that the cordial friendship and solidarity which unite the PCL and the CPSU, as well as the brother-parties of the other countries of the "United Socialist States," agree perfectly with the interests of the working class and of the nation. In the past several years the activities of the PCL have been partly disrupted by Maoist and Trotskyist splinter groups. Initially these leftist groups consisted of high school and university students, but more recently some industrial workers have joined their ranks without, however, increasing their influence.

International Views and Positions. The foreign policy positions of the PCL closely reflect those of the Communist Party of the Soviet Union (CPSU). The Soviet Union's diplomatic representation in Luxembourg far exeeds the number of persons normally assigned to a small country. There also exist strong indications that the PCL is financially dependent on Moscow. Its leading members travel frequently in the Soviet Union and Eastern Europe, and often attend CPSU meetings and congresses or spend their vacations in the Soviet Union.

Publications. The party organ of the PCL is the *Zeitung zum Letzeburger Vollek*, which has a daily distribution of 1,200 copies. The PCL also publishes a weekly, *Wochenzeitung*. Both are printed by the party's publishing company, Coopérative Ouvriere de Presse et d'Editions, which also handles the sale and distribution of foreign Communist publications. The PCL distributes its publications periodically to households and also participates in the political programs of Radio Luxembourg. The value it places on the remarks of PCL members in parliament is underscored by the gratis door-to-door distribution of the parliamentary reports.

Luxemburger Wort,   Leon Zeches
Luxembourg

Netherlands

The Communist Party of the Netherlands (Communistische Partij van Nederland; CPN) was founded as the Communist Party of Holland in 1918, but the official founding date is that of affiliation to the Comintern, 10 April 1919. The present name dates from December 1935. The party has always been legal (with the exception of the World War II period).

CPN policy has been based for more than ten years on the "new orientation" proclaimed at its 1964 congress. It gives primary importance to domestic political goals; relations with international Communism are subordinated to the goal of creating a united front in which Communists and Socialists should play the leading role. Since 1975, however, a tendency toward more involvement in the international Communist movement has been noticeable and has led to the normalization of relations with the Communist Party of the Soviet Union (CPSU), which, in fact, meant the end of the "new orientation policy," although full participation of the CPN in the international movement has not yet come about.

From 1959 (when the party was split) until 1972, the CPN share in elections was steadily increasing (from 2.4 to 4.5 percent of the votes). Elections for the Lower House of the parliament in May 1977 brought a considerable loss. Compared with 1972, CPN votes declined from 329,973 to 143,420 (from 2.41 to 1.73 percent). CPN seats in the Lower House dropped from 7 to 2 (out of 150).

In provincial governing bodies the CPN has 19 seats out of 670, and in the municipal governing bodies 130 out of 12,000. The CPN has aldermen in 16 of some 800 municipalities.

In spite of considerable losses in the elections, CPN membership increased from 10,000 to 14,500 in the last few years. Its followers are scattered over the country, with centers of activity in Amsterdam, The Hague and its environs, and the province of Groningen. The population of the Netherlands is about 13,869,000.

Leadership and Organization. The CPN's Twenty-Fifth Congress, in June 1975, elected a new Central Committee which did not differ much from the previous one. The principal policy-making body is the fourteen-member Executive Committee of the Central Committee, including H. J. Hoekstra (chairman), M. Bakker (chairman of the CPN faction in parliament), G. Hoogenberg (charged with work in industry), and J. IJisberg (administrative secretary). The Secretariat, consisting of three members of the Executive Committee, is the organizational and administrative center of the party. The Central Committee (thirty-six members, three deputies) only meets a few times a year. The influence of former leader Paul de Groot on CPN politics has been on the decline since the 1977 elections.

The most active of the CPN front organizations is the General Netherlands Youth Organization (Algemeen Nederlands Jeugd Verbond; ANJV). The Netherlands Women's Movement (Nederlandse Vrouwen Beweging; NVB), like the ANJV, works to support CPN demands.

Party Internal Affairs. The CPN's national party conference on 15-16 January 1977 drew about 700 delegates from the districts and some 300 other participants, along with the representatives of the domestic and foreign press. The meeting was held to mobilize CPN cadres both for actions in the near future (elections) and with a view to long-range goals of the struggle for Socialism. Chairman Hoekstra analyzed the current political situation and presented his views on the necessary strategy and tactics, while de Groot dealt with the national struggle for Socialism within the framework of the international struggle. The negative election results in May led to internal criticism and weakened the position of de Groot.

Articles in *De Waarheid* (1, 2 August) discussed the election, with de Groot stressing the importance of action in the interest of the unemployed and against the dangers of war. He blamed the party leadership for the election results. The Executive Committee confirmed his views on unemployment and peace, but rejected his criticism of the party leadership.

Domestic Attitudes and Activities. The "national struggle" of the CPN as presented before the 1977 elections did not differ fundamentally from the presentation given afterward. The party called for struggle against the arms race and consequently for peace and security, and recommended a government policy to promote disarmament and arms control. On the domestic front, the main tasks seen by the party were the defense of the standard of living and social achievements and the struggle against unemployment.

In spite of the election results and increasing internal contradictions, some positive developments for the party can be mentioned: first of all, the increasing membership, but also growing influence in some parts of the trade union movement, increasing influence in extra-parliamentary action (particularly in regard to welfare), and finally the normalization of relations with the CPSU.

For the first time in five years the Netherlands had a large-scale strike in February 1977. The main claim was the maintenance of the so-called price compensation. The strike involved more than 200 companies, factories, and building projects. The role of the CPN, although limited to activities supporting the trade unions concerned, was an obvious contribution to the strike as a whole.

On CPN initiative, a group of 130 Dutchmen launched an appeal in *De Waarheid* (20 August) to start a broad movement to petition parliament against the neutron bomb. Some 120,000 signatures have been obtained.

The CPN arranged a national party manifestation in The Hague on 17 September. The purpose was to show that the CPN still is and will be a significant political factor. Some 5,000 participants attended the meeting, which was followed by a demonstration march.

International Views and Positions, and Party Contacts. Normalization of the relation between the CPN and the CPSU, which had been developing since early 1975, really seemed to be settled by the CPN delegation's visit to Moscow in April 1977. The two parties expressed their wish for a further development of relations "on the basis of international cooperation, voluntarily and with equal rights, in the spirit of the great ideas of Marx, Engels, and Lenin."

The CPN was represented by de Groot, Hoekstra, and two members of the Executive Committee. CPSU participants were, among others, the party secretaries Suslov and Ponomarov. The significance of the meeting was also stressed by a simultaneous communiqué in *Pravda* and *De Waarheid*. Mutual satisfaction was expressed in regard to the Helsinki accords and the conference of European Communist parties at East Berlin in 1976.

CPN participation in international Communist events, however, is still limited. There is a certain reluctance to give up the old autonomous policy. Only in a few cases has the CPN sent delegates to West European meetings.

This ambivalent attitude is reflected in the CPN's reaction to Eurocommunism. It neither expresses itself in favor of parties associated with the concept nor criticizes Moscow for its policy toward those parties. In its basic attitude toward principles, such as proletarian internationalism, the party is probably more orthodox than Eurocommunist.

Publications. The CPN daily, *De Waarheid* (The Truth; circulation 20,000), is in constant financial trouble, which the party tries to overcome by collections from time to time. The theoretical bimonthly, *Politiek en Cultuur*, is used for training purposes. The ANJV and NVB have their monthly papers. The CPN's Instituut voor Politiek en Sociaal Onderzoek (IPSO) issues a quarterly, *Info*, which draws attention to articles published by other parties on problems of present-day Communism. The CPN has its own publishing house and bookshop, "Pegasus." In the importation of Russian publications, the pro-Soviet bookshop, "Sterboek," competes with "Pegasus." The CPN has two commercial printing plants, one for *De Waarheid* and one for other printed matter.

Dissident Groups. The autonomous policy of the CPN in the years 1964-75 led to the formation of pro-Soviet groups outside the party. Their influence on CPN politics has always been small, and the improving CPN-CPSU relations endangered their existence. The CPN made it clear that it expects Soviet support of these groups to be stopped. Although the Soviet Union has not cut its relations, it has diminished support. A monthly paper, *Communistische Notities* (Communist Notes) edited by a former CPN Executive Committee member and an official mouthpiece of the CPSU, was discontinued in 1977.

The pro-Soviet Communists in the Netherlands do not have organizational unity. Most are members of the "Nederland-USSR" friendship society, which is not engaged in domestic politics; it promotes cultural relations between the Netherlands and the Soviet Union, hoping to foster appreciation for the Socialist system. Its monthly paper is *NU* ("Netherlands-USSR"). The travel agency "Vernu BV" organizes tourist visits to the Soviet Union. The chairman of the friendship society is also director of the travel agency; he has been awarded the Soviet "Order of the Friendship of the Peoples." Highlights in the life of this society are the annual "Month of the Soviet Union" and the signing of the yearly cultural plan. Similar activities, but on a smaller scale and directed at the Balkan states and the German Democratic Republic (GDR) are fostered by a society for cultural exchange, "Vereniging voor Culturele Uitwisseling" (VCU), which seeks to coordinate its activities with those of the Netherlands-GDR friendship society.

Young members of the Nederland-USSR founded in 1973 a new organization, Jongeren Kontakt voor Internationale Solidariteit en Uitwisseling (Youth Contact for International Solidarity and Exchange; JKU). It issues a paper, *Nieuwsbrief*. Travels to Eastern Europe are organized, with the principal aim to learn more about the system of Socialist society. A travel agency (Kontakt B.V.) created by JKU has developed into a full and independent body. The JKU maintains contacts with similar organizations in other West European countries and with the coordinating Soviet youth organization. JKU is a member of the World Federation of Democratic Youth.

Soviet views are also presented by the "Nederlands Comité voor Europese Veiligheid en Samenwerking" (Dutch Committee for European Security and Cooperation).

The pro-Chinese groups were the result of the autonomous policy of the CPN in the Sino-Soviet dispute. There are eight of these small groups in the Netherlands, all pretending to be governed by Marxist-Leninist principles, but often competing with each other. The three main groups are: the Netherlands Communist Unity Movement, Marxist-Leninist (KEN-ml); the Marxist-Leninist Party of the Netherlands (MLPN); and the Socialist Party (SP).

The KEN-ml participated in the May 1977 elections with very poor results. It has played an important role in the founding of a Netherlands-China friendship organization (Vriendschapsvereniging; VNC). The MLPN is not very much different from KEN-ml, but is smaller. The SP does not maintain relations with China or with foreign pro-Chinese parties. It mainly works through front groups in the fields of public health, environment, and housing.

Oost-West Instituut   C. C. van den Heuvel
The Hague

Norway

The Norwegian Communist Party (Norges Kommunistiske Parti; NKP) remains small and isolated following its decision in 1975 not to merge with several left-Socialist parties and factions. This decision split the party and caused the chairman, Reidar T. Larsen, and several other leaders to leave the NKP for the new Socialist Left Party (Sosialistisk Venstreparti; SV). The NKP is now the weakest of three main parties to the left of the powerful and ruling Norwegian Labor Party (Det Norske Arbeiderparti; DNA), which is a reformist social-democratic movement. In addition to the SV and NKP, current Marxist activity in Norway includes the Maoist (and consistently pro-Chinese) Workers' Communist Party (Arbeidernes Kommunistiske Parti; AKP), which has run in the last two parliamentary elections as the Red Electoral Alliance (Rød Valgallianse; RV).

The NKP was organized on 4 November 1923 by a few radical politicians and trade unionists who split from the DNA. It first demonstrated electoral strength in 1945, when it won 12 of the 150 Storting (Parliament) seats, thanks to Communist participation during World War II in the Norwegian resistance movement and the Soviet liberation of northern Norway. The Cold War quickly eroded NKP strength, and by 1957 the Communists held only a single seat in parliament. In 1961, with the rise of the Socialist People's Party (Sosialistisk Folkeparti; SF) started by dissident Laborites, the NKP lost its last mandate. Not until the formation of the Socialist Electoral Alliance (Sosialistisk Valgforbund—a forerunner of the SV) in 1973 by the SF, NKP, and dissident left Laborites did Communists once again sit in the Storting. Standing alone in the 1977 elections, the NKP polled 8,448 votes (0.4 percent of the total), far short of what was necessary to gain a parliamentary mandate and even down from the party's 1.0 percent in 1969.

NKP membership currently is considerably below the 2,000 to 5,000 estimate before the 1975 schism. The population of Norway is just over four million.

Although the SV was initially an electoral alliance with a common platform, but not a party, the 1975 decision to merge has not created a stronger left-Socialist wing. Its spectacular parliamentary gains in 1973 (11.2 percent of the vote, 16 out of 155 seats) proved to be a singular phenomenon. In the 1975 municipal and county elections, SV electoral strength was down, and in the September 1977 parliamentary elections the party drew only 4.2 percent of the vote and just barely held two seats in the new Storting.

The SV's surprising strength in 1973 resulted from the emotional national campaign against Norwegian membership in the expanded European Economic Community (EC). Supported by many non-Socialist parties and groups, the National Movement Against the EC was victorious in the September 1972 referendum. Parliamentary elections a year later showed severe losses for those parties (especially DNA) which had supported EC membership. By 1975 the EC issue was closed, and surveys showed that many of those who voted SV in 1973 were returning to less extreme parties. Many of those who had supported the SV rejected the party's anti-NATO line. With the results of the 1977 elections and the gains made by the Labor Party (DNA), there is a situation resembling that prior to 1970, when the EC issue arose. Nevertheless, the governing Labor party is dependent upon the two SV parliamentary votes for a majority in any Socialist/non-Socialist confrontation. This situation also resembles the previous parliamentary term and the 1961-65 period (see Ragnar Waldahl, "SV og valgene i 1973 og 1975: fra suksess til nederlag," *Tidsskrift for Samfunnsforskning*, 1974, no. 4). The Marxist left is thus not only divided into three competing factions, but electorally weak—sharing 5.2 percent of the vote among them.

Leadership and Organization. Personalities are important in a small democracy like Norway, and among the three left-Socialist parties there are several prominent names. Current NKP Chairman Martin Gunnar Knudsen emerged as leader of the rump-NKP after the party's divisive Fifteenth Congress (November 1975), which voted 117 to 30 against merger with the SV. Others include Rolf Nettum, organizational vice-chairman; Hans Kleven, political vice-chairman; and Arne Jørgensen, editor of the party's semi-weekly, *Friheten*. The most important affiliate is the Norwegian Communist Youth League (Kommunistisk Ungdom; KU).

The SV can be most easily traced as a modification of the SF group which emerged among anti-NATO Laborites in the early 1960s. Nevertheless, the party has a more outright radical image, which was confirmed by its pre-election congress in Oslo in March 1977. Tromsø University historian Berge Furre was reelected as chairman and Otto Hauglin, Berit Ås, and Bjørgulv Froyn as vice-chairmen. Former SF leader Finn Gustavsen, who remained a prominent SV parliamentarian and played an important role in the party's development, has announced his retirement. All of SV's leaders and prominent MPs lost their seats in the September election (*Aftenposten*, September issues, 1977).

Less is known about the organization of the Norwegian Workers' Communist Party (AKP), which polled 0.6 percent of the vote in 1977 (a gain of .02 percent from 1973). An amalgam of various Maoist groups that arose in the late 1960s, mainly as splinter groups from the SF and NKP youth organizations, the AKP was formally organized in late 1972. Its Second Congress, November 1976, reelected Paal Steigan as chairman. Ideologically, politically, and presumably in organization and finance, the AKP maintains very close ties with the Chinese Communist Party and stresses Maoist thought in a variety of situations (NCNA, 17 November 1976).

Domestic Attitudes and Activities. Increasing North Sea oil production, and revenue from the export of petroleum, again in 1977 spared Norwegians the severe economic difficulties prevalent in most of Western Europe. Nevertheless, oil revenues fell short of official expectations, and costs of production were higher. This plus the "blowout" of an important oil platform in the spring of 1977 forced adjustments in the minority Labor government's economic and oil policies. Increasingly in the forefront of the domestic political debate was the approaching parliamentary election. The relatively calm spring-term of the Storting was followed by an emotional electoral campaign.

Despite the decision of a majority of the NKP not to join the new SV organization, the NKP Central Committee stressed the party's desire to form an electoral alliance (as in 1973), in which each party would remain distinct (*WMR*, October 1976). This proposal was rejected by the SV and AKP, and thus during the campaign there were three distinct Marxist Socialist views competing for votes. Defense issues were to provide the spark for the campaign's more passionate moments, and the SV's views were heard far more prominently than those of either the NKP or the AKP.

Already during the defense appropriations debate in parliament on 26 November 1976, SV spokesman Arne Kielland had demanded an end to NATO membership and a 30 percent reduction in defense expenditures. All other Storting parties supported the current line, which reflected growing public support for NATO during the past few years (*Nordisk Kontakt*, 1976, no. 16). Despite this setback, the SV voted at its congress in March 1977 to oppose all weapons expenditure and to advocate full demilitarization of Norway (ibid., 1977, no. 6). By summer the SV had forced attention on defense issues by claiming that certain NATO installations in Norway were exclusively for use by American nuclear missile submarines. The disclosure of secret defense information by two leading SV parliamentarians (SV Chairman Berge Furre and former SF Chairman Finn Gustavsen) led the government to threaten an impeachment trial. In addition, a journalist attached to the SV weekly *Ny Tid* was arrested for collecting information about Norwegian defense installations and personnel. His activity was condemned, however, by the SV leadership (*Berlingske Tidende*, Copenhagen, 5 September).

These events made it difficult for the NKP to attract voter attention during the campaign. The NKP did issue a twenty-four-point Election Manifesto which summarized its current position. Few of these proposals differed from traditional NKP views: heavier taxes on higher incomes; replacement of the 20 percent value-added tax with luxury taxes; improved working conditions through shorter working hours; greater worker participation in enterprise management; better employment security; and specific promises for special groups—more day-care centers, higher minimum old-age pensions, etc.

The Maoist AKP is less interested in electoral campaigns, even though the party participates through the RV. Committed to "extra-parliamentary" tactics, the AKP has succeeded in gaining influential positions in several issue-oriented and interest organizations. Members have dominated the Oslo University Student Association for several years and have gained some important positions in trade union locals, although the larger unions as well as the Norwegian Trade Union Confederation (Landsorganisasjonen; LO) is firmly controlled by Laborites. With the growing importance of issue organizations in Norwegian politics, the strength and influence of the AKP may be far greater than RV's meager electoral results.

Norwegian Communists have traditionally been stronger in the trade union movement than in electoral politics, but, neither they nor other small left-Socialist groups have been able to challenge the DNA-LO links. Neither the Communists nor the SV have representation in the LO national executive or control any national labor union. At the local level, the NKP is most significant in the construction workers' union, and to a lesser degree in the metal, wood, transport, and electro-chemical fields.

International Views and Positions. The split in the NKP has not significantly changed the party's views on international issues. Both the NKP and the SV are firmly opposed to continued Norwegian membership in NATO and to various cooperative defense measures such as the acquisition of the F-16 fighter aircraft. Both are distrustful of Western economic cooperation and particularly Norwegian participation (subject to special reservations) in the International Energy Agency. NKP and SV statements repeatedly stress the importance of Norwegian "sovereignty" in all foreign policy issues. (See NKP, Election Manifesto, 1977 and SV, Party Program, 1975.) Both parties support increasing economic aid to "progressive" developing countries and national liberation movements.

With the departure of Reidar T. Larsen to the SV, the NKP has lost much of its "nonaligned" orientation and become more strongly supportive of Soviet foreign policy views. The 1975 Helsinki accords and the Soviet interpretation of that agreement form the basis of NKP views on European relations. As the independent Socialist periodical *Kontrast* pointed out, the new NKP Vice-Chairman Hans Kleven, writing in his book *Vår Strategi* (Our Strategy), praised the constructive role of Soviet troops in Eastern Europe and Soviet support of the working class in general.

The SV has continued to make its anti-NATO, anti-military, and anti-functional economic cooperation position a central plank of its party platform. SV founder and foreign policy spokesman Finn Gustavsen, speaking for the last time in the Storting on 6 June 1977, summed up the party's strong anti-American position. Far more attention is devoted to cataloging the evils of American monopoly capital and the CIA than to regretting Soviet civil rights violations (*UD-informasjon*, no. 27, 15 June). A somewhat more balanced view of the Soviet Union appeared in the SV weekly *Ny Tid* (10 November) on the occasion of the sixtieth anniversary of the October Revolution. While calling the revolution "a victory for the working class of every country," the editorial noted the many shortcomings of the Soviet Union today and classified it as a transitional society between capitalism and Socialism.

The AKP, as noted, maintains very close ties with China. It has loyally supported the Chinese leadership through all the changes of recent years. It regularly denounces the Soviet Union and the United States.

International Party Contacts. Under its new leadership, the NKP has moved closer to the Soviet Union and the more conservative Eastern European parties. It refused to criticize the arrest of civil rights advocates in Czechoslovakia (signers of Charta 77) (*Aftenposten*, 29 January 1977). Chairman Knutsen led a delegation for a week of talks with Soviet party officials in Moscow in February (Tass, 19, 26 February). Commenting on the visit, Vice-Chairman Kleven noted his party's agreement with the Soviet view that "Eurocommunism" was an effort by non-Communists to divide the various Communist parties (*Friheten*, 28 February).

NKP delegations visited Hungary (March), the German Democratic Republic (March), Poland (September), and Bulgaria (October). Typical of the new NKP orientation—closer to the Soviet bloc—was the bilateral agreement signed in East Berlin between the NKP and the Socialist Unity Party of the GDR (ADN, 9 March).

A delegation of AKP leaders, led by Chairman Steigan, visited Peking in February. The visit attracted considerable attention because of the prominence given it by the Chinese media. The delegation was given access to the highest Chinese leadership, perhaps as a reward for consistent loyal support (*Far Eastern Economic Review*, Hong Kong, 6 May; *Peking Review*, 18 February). In May an AKP delegation visited Albania (Tirana domestic radio, 3 May).

Publications. The main NKP organ is *Friheten* (Freedom), first published as an underground paper during World War II. Dwindling circulation caused its transition from daily to weekly publication in 1967. Fund raising to keep the paper going is a continuous NKP preoccupation. During the fall of 1977, *Friheten* increased publication to twice a week. The KU publishes a youth bulletin, *Fremad* (Forward). The SV newspaper is *Ny Tid* (New Times), which was intended to absorb much of the readership of the SF publication *Orientering*. The latter was respected by many readers outside the SF party circle. In addition to continuous financial difficulties, the SV weekly was involved in the "espionage" scandal of the election campaign. Nevertheless, given the sharp reduction in the SV parliamentary delegation, *Ny Tid* is likely to be an important party organ. Finally there is the AKP weekly *Klassekampen* (Class Struggle).

University of Massachusetts   Eric S. Einhorn
Amherst

Portugal

The Portuguese Communist Party (Partido Comunista Português; PCP) entered its fifty-seventh year in March 1977 with the largest membership in its history. It claimed 115,000 members, mostly workers and peasants, out of a population of 9,634,000.

Though far less influential than during the first two years following the April 1974 revolution, the PCP continued to be the largest and most powerful left-wing organization in Portugal. Even the governing Socialist Party only claimed 94,000 members. Though appearing to lose strength to the far left in June 1976 presidential elections (see *YICA, 1977*, pp. 217, 221), the party had recovered in December local elections of that year. A radical coalition called the Movement for Popular Unity (Movimento para a Unidade Popular; MUP) received less than 3 percent of the December vote while other radical groups won even less. The revolutionaries were said to be weakened by internal rivalries, poor organization, lack of funds, and the absence of leadership, especially since Major Otelo Saraiva de Carvalho, around whom they had earlier rallied, was barred by the military from further political activity. (*Christian Science Monitor* [*CSM*], 15 December 1976; *NYT*, 16 January 1977.)

Most of the country's far-left parties were formed in 1975 and were outgrowths of a split from the PCP in the early 1960s. The splinter groups had favored an armed popular uprising as a means of overthrowing the fascist dictatorship. After the 1974 revolution, the far-left groups remained bitterly opposed to the PCP, branding its militants as "social fascists" and "Nazi-Cunhalistas" who took their orders from Moscow, the "headquarters of social imperialism." The strongest radical group appeared to be the Maoist People's Democratic Union (União Democrática do Povo; UDP), the only one with a representative in Parliament. It claimed a membership of 10,000 to 15,000 (*NYT*, 16 January). Two other groups active during 1977 were also pro-Chinese: the Communist Party of Portugal-Marxist-Leninist (Partido Comunista do Portugal-Marxista-Leninista; PCP-ML) and the Portuguese Communist Party-Reconstructed (Partido Comunista Português-Reconstruído; PCP-R).

Leadership and Organization. The PCP is organized at the ground level on the basis of thousands of cells, many of them still clandestine-"submarines," as they are known in Lisbon—despite the fact that the party has operated legally since 1974. Vertical cells are formed within individual business firms, rural areas, educational establishments, and the armed forces, though there are also some horizontal "street cells" that include members of different enterprises and institutions. The party claims to have 7,000 "base organizations." (*NYT*, 13 March 1977.)

Since the party was founded in 1921, it has held eight congresses, four of them underground, to determine policy guidelines and to elect a central committee. The latter elects a secretariat and other executive organs and guides party activities between congresses. To inject new blood into the party leadership to help improve its public image, the Central Committee was expanded at the Eighth Congress in 1976 from thirty-six to ninety (fifty-four regular members and thirty-six substitutes). About half of the new members were said to have joined the party after the 1974 overthrow of the Caetano dictatorship. The average age of the members of the Central Committee is now 44.7 years, compared with 48 before, and the number of workers has increased from 63.9 percent to 73.5 percent of the total (*Washington Post*, 15 November 1976).

The secretary-general since 1961 has been Alvaro Cunhal, a staunch supporter of the Soviet Union who reportedly refused to allow suspected Eurocommunists into positions of party power. Smarting from the often expressed charge that the PCP was the last Stalinist party in Europe, Cunhal denied that this was so, if by the word "Stalinist" his critics meant "administration by violence and force, an undemocratic life in the party, decisions controlled by the leaders, the superimposition of the opinion of the chief on the collectivity" (*L'Unità*, Rome, 13 February). According to other sources, the Eighth Congress left the impression of a "well-oiled machine," totally disciplined and lacking in debate (Radio Free Europe Research, 16 November 1976).

Cunhal won a seat in Parliament in 1976 elections but resigned in 1977 to leave more time to direct party activities ("Radio Liberdade," Lisbon, 20 May).

Domestic Attitudes and Activities. The PCP vainly continued its efforts during 1977 to nudge Socialist Prime Minister Mário Soares into embracing the Communists in a majority "government of the left." Grist for the increasingly virulent offensive by Alvaro Cunhal's party was provided by a steady economic deterioration in Portugal combined with official measures of austerity and encouragement to the private sector. Each new initiative by the Soares cabinet was branded by the PCP as a "step to the right" favoring capitalists, big farmers, and imperialists at the expense of the workers. This could only lead the country, it was claimed, toward a new dictatorship. The evident strategy was to encourage an erosion of support for the government among workers in the PCP-dominated unions and farm collectives and to stir up rebellion among the armed forces. (*New Age*, India, 2 January; *CSM*, 8 March; *Expresso*, Lisbon, 3 September.)

By August, popular discontent had emboldened the PCP—as well as parties to the right of the Socialists—to begin demanding new parliamentary elections. The Communists allegedly expected that their disciplined ranks could take advantage of a small voter turnout at the polls to increase their representation in Parliament. However, even while demanding the government's replacement, the party continued to offer the alternative of a Socialist-Communist coalition. Prime Minister Soares responded that he would not resign or waver from his policies, though in October he did make an offer—which was not accepted—to name some members of the non-Communist opposition to his cabinet as "independents." They would replace Socialist ministers who planned to resign, frustrated over their inability to make headway in sorting out Portugal's enormous economic and social distortions. Soares scorned the PCP overtures, warning that its divisive tactics, if pushed hard enough, could lead to the exiling of the party's leaders and to renewed outbursts of anti-Communist violence in the country. (*CSM*, 8 August, 1 November.) Finally, on December 8, Soares was forced to resign when the opposition parties presented a united front against his bid for a vote of confidence. Prodded by President António Ramalho Eanes, he began negotiating with other parties at the end of the month to form a new government (*Washington Post*, 9 December; *NYT*, 30 December).

Soares was severely handicapped in his resolve to keep the Communists at arm's length and at the same time secure support of the Communist-dominated labor sector for his austerity measures and his attempts to upgrade productivity. Especially critical was the fact that the most powerful unions were generally concentrated in the lowest-productivity sectors, such as the hotel industry, which were being kept afloat by massive government subsidies (ibid., 31 March). A four-day congress of trade unions in January underscored the Socialist failure to undermine Communist leadership in the labor movement. The congress, criticized as a "Communist front," was boycotted by 30 Socialist and Social Democratic unions. However, it was attended by 269 unions representing nearly 1.7 million workers—85 percent of organized labor. Of these, 183 belonged to the Communist-controlled Intersindical while most of the others were led by radical leftist groups. The congress set up a central organization to be called the General Confederation of Portuguese Workers-Intersindical Nacional, and it elected a twenty-five-member secretariat composed of Communists and one radical Socialist. (*NYT*, 31 January; *CSM*, 3, 14 February.)

The congress denounced the government for allowing a "capitalist recovery" and demanded an active role for labor in determining and implementing economic and social policy. Throughout the year, there were also numerous strikes and rallies, promoted by the Communists, to protest worker regulation, wage freezes, and price rises as well as such economic measures as cuts in public spending, denationalization of some activities, reopening of the Lisbon stock exchange—"the ultimate symbol of capitalist society"—and the devaluation of the escudo. (*NYT*, 15 January, 27 August; *CSM*, 8 March.) Three Lisbon rallies organized by the PCP in May, June, and September were each attended by up to 150,000 persons (*NYT*, 15 May, 11 July; *Pravda*, 17 September).

In spite of the potential for trouble-making through the unions, the PCP appeared reluctant to provoke as yet a major confrontation with the government through a massive work stoppage. This was in line with an apparent attempt by Cunhal to develop for his party a new image of moderation on the assumption that economic difficulties would soon force the Soares government to turn to other parties for support (*NYT*, 17 April).

Policies suggested by the Communists for reviving the economy included rigorous import quotas for nonessential products and an expanded national production to substitute for imports (*Avante*, 7 July). Cunhal concurred with the government that austerity was necessary but he said it should begin with those "who have a lot of money" rather than being a burden only to the workers (*Diário de Notícias*, Lisbon, 7 March; *NYT*, 17 April). Cunhal also asserted that this year's sharp drop in farm production in the southern Alentejo region could be reversed by abandoning the government's "prolatifundist" agrarian policies. He denounced "setbacks" in the agrarian reform program as a crime against the national economy, against workers, and against social justice (Lisbon domestic radio, 6 April). Agriculture Minister António Barreto was compensating owners for expropriated land and, with the help of national guardsmen, was returning to owners many small and medium-sized farms that had been illegally seized and incorporated into Soviet-style collectives. In March the government revealed "grave irregularities" in the way agricultural subsidies had been used by the Communist-run Agrarian Reform Institute. Credit was then suspended to many collectives accused of fraudulent misuse of funds loaned to them. It was announced in November that the collectives owed the state some $32.5 million in unrepaid loans. It was widely suspected that a considerable part of that money had been diverted to PCP coffers to finance election and poster campaigns. (*CSM*, 15 February, 4, 22 March, 9 November.)

Many agricultural records were destroyed in September when six key land reform offices in Lisbon and Alentejo province were bombed by a group identifying itself as the Red Rose. Though the left apparently benefited from the destruction of documents, the PCP called the bombing a "reactionary provocation." (*NYT*, 9 September; *CSM*, 13 September.)

Critics claimed that workers on most of the Alentejo's 450 collectives worked too little and spent too much time in political meetings. Barreto said that only 30 collectives were efficient. An unusually wet spring combined with the disorder on the farms to reduce wheat production this year to the lowest level in a decade. (*CSM*, 3 August, 9 November.) Many farm workers, dismayed by the inefficiency of the Communist-run collectives, broke away to form independent cooperatives. Though they were supported in these moves by the Soares government and by a new agrarian reform law passed in July, they had to face severe intimidation from the Communist groups, including threats to their lives. In November 1,000 collective workers who reoccupied five farms restored by the government to their original owners had to be evicted again by national guardsmen. Six workers were arrested. The government said it planned to hold elections to offer workers a choice of staying in the collectives, forming private cooperatives or receiving small plots of land. (*NYT*, 27 December 1976, 31 August 1977; *CSM*, 25 July, 9 November.)

Other targets of the PCP campaign against a "resurgence of the forces of reaction" were "fascist" organs of the press whose existence and activities were said to violate the constitution. Especially criticized was the government decision in December 1976 to reorganize the state-owned press, closing some organs and returning others to their original owners. Publication of two of the eight newspapers acquired by the Revolutionary Government in 1975 was suspended, and in September it was announced that subsidies to the others would be ended. (*NYT*, 22 December 1976; Tass, 11 February 1977; *CSM*, 7 September.)

A continuing effort was made by the Communists to recover their leverage in the armed forces, where moderate and right-wing elements had gained the upper hand following the abortive 1975 uprising (see *YICA, 1976*, p. 208). Early in the year, a commander of the central military region accused the PCP and some far leftists of infiltrating the armed forces to incite soldiers to acts of rebellion. Attempted mutinies in Estremoz and Caldas in February led to the jailing of eight soldiers and an officer. The charges were dismissed by the PCP as an attempt to discredit the party's activities and to favor rightist enemies of liberty (*CSM*, 8, 21, 22 March).

Political infighting reportedly continued within the army among Marxist, moderate, and rightist officers, in spite of presidential orders in 1976 that the armed forces were to remain apolitical. To reinforce that decision, the president, General António Ramalho Eanes, named a new chief of staff in April, over the heads of senior officers, with orders to reorganize the armed forces into a nonpartisan force (*NYT*, 7 April).

International Views and Positions. Among the PCP suggestions for improving the Portuguese economy and for countering the "capitalist recovery" was a proposal for a diversification of markets to include Socialist and Third-World countries, especially the former Portuguese colonies. Also proposed were new lines of credit—clearly from Communist countries—to make possible a "patriotic policy of national independence" (*Diario de Notícias*, 7 March). The $750 million loan package that Prime Minister Soares secured from the United States and ten other industrial nations in June was seen by the Communists as a surrender to imperialism (*NYT*, 23 June). Portugal's formal application in March for entry in the European Economic Community was likewise opposed by the party as a political operation seeking the recovery of capitalism in Portugal rather than the recovery of the economy. Membership in the Common Market was seen as a threat to hundreds of small and medium-sized enterprises in Portugal as well as the nationalized sectors, which could not compete with cheaper imports from more developed countries (ibid., 29 March; *WMR*, no. 5, 15 March; CTK, Prague, 23 April).

International Activities and Party Contacts. Speculation that Cunhal was shifting his party's stance toward Eurocommunism was fueled early in the year by visits he made to Italy and France to confer with party leaders of those countries. In contrast with his previous hard-line denunciations of anti-Soviet "calumny," Cunhal now acknowledged, in press conferences and in a joint communiqué following the Italian visit, the need for each party to pursue an autonomous line according to its own national circumstances. Since Portugal was closer to Socialism than other West European nations, he said, its approach had to be different. In this way, he not only struck a more conciliatory note toward the Eurocommunist divergencies, without precisely agreeing with them, but also may have been seeking subtly to justify to Eurocommunist critics the path that the PCP had followed in Portugal since the 1974 revolution. Many had lamented that PCP behavior in Portugal was harmful to Communist prospects elsewhere. Cunhal carefully walked the fence in answering reporters' questions as to whether there was a "leading party" in the international Communist movement. He said there was today "no leadership center" but that some parties played a greater role than others. It was necessary, he said, to stress the value of the October Revolution, without this implying in any way a lessening of each party's autonomy. (ANSA, Rome, 11 February; *L'Unità*, 12 February; Lisbon domestic radio, 14 February; *L'Humanité*, Paris, 14 April.)

Cunhal concluded, following his trip to Italy, that relations had been strengthened between the Portuguese and Italian parties, despite differences of opinion (*Avante*, 17 February). At the same time, he continued to point out that his party's views were closer to those of the Soviet Communist party than to those of any other party and that the PCP would always refuse to take part in any anti-Soviet campaign. However, he insisted that his party was totally independent, only borrowing from the experience of others what was useful to the revolutionary process in Portugal (Tass, 18 February, 18 April; Lisbon domestic radio, 5, 22 March). Even as he was saying this, there was reportedly an accelerated influx of Soviet diplomats in Lisbon. The previous embassy staff of 300 Russians—the largest in Portugal—was expected to rise to 700 (*CSM*, 11 January).

Cunhal made no visit to Spain and, in fact, was not invited to attend a so-called "summit meeting" of Spanish, Italian, and French Communist parties in March. Spanish Communist Santiago Carrillo reportedly commented that it was no secret that "Comrade Cunhal expresses ideas that are not exactly our own" (*NYT*, 13 March). The PCP Central Committee sent a telegram of congratulations in April to Carrillo on the legalization of his party. Cunhal said he "rejoiced" at the dawning of democracy in Spain and denied that he was secretly delighted that Carrillo's party finished a poor third in June elections. He noted, even so, that his own party had taken "amost double" the percentage of votes won by the Spanish party (Lisbon domestic radio, 11 April; *NYT*, 6 July).

In August, Cunhal took advantage of a "vacation" in Moscow to confer with Soviet party officials. He pointed out in a televised broadcast that PCP and Soviet views on all basic ideological questions continued to coincide (Tass, 20 July, 22 August). That visit was followed up by a trip in September by the PCP Central Committee to France, Switzerland, West Germany, Belgium, Hungary, and Romania.

The editors of *Pravda* and *Avante* also exchanged visits during the year, with the latter's chief editor, Dias Lourenço, traveling to the Soviet Union in January and a *Pravda* delegation to Lisbon in September to take part in an "*Avante* festival" (*Pravda*, 5 January, 4 September). A PCP representative visited Bucharest in August to attend the celebration of Romania's "liberation from fascist domination."

In February Cunhal led a PCP delegation to Maputo to attend a congress of the Front for the Liberation of Mozambique (FRELIMO), in which that former liberation movement converted itself formally to the status of a party. In September a delegation of the Popular Movement for the Liberation of Angola (MPLA) visited Lisbon at the invitation of the PCP. Mutual expressions of "solidarity" seemed to belie reports of friction between the two parties resulting from the alleged implication of the Portuguese Communists in an abortive coup in May in the Angolan capital. (*CSM*, 24 August; Tass, 13 September.)

Publications. The PCP's principal publications include the daily *Avante*, which was founded in 1931 and which continued publishing underground during most of the years of the dictatorship; *O Militante*, the theoretical bulletin of the Central Committee; *A Terra*, a peasants' newspaper; *O Textil*, a textile workers' paper; and *Juventude*, press organ of a Communist youth group.

Rival Communist Organizations. Two of the country's numerous Maoist parties, the Communist Party of Portugal-Marxist-Leninist and the Portuguese Communist Party-Reconstructed, held congresses in Lisbon in 1977. At its Seventh Congress, convened in January, the PCP-ML reelected Heduino Gomes (Vilar) as secretary-general (NCNA, Peking, 9 February; *Peking Review*, 18 February). The PCP-R had its Second Congress in April, ending with a rally attended by members of a number of European and Latin American Marxist-Leninist parties. This was said to be the first time that the Albanian Party of Labor had sent a delegation to attend a rally abroad (Lisbon domestic radio, 8 April; Tirana domestic radio, 2 May). In June a delegation of the PCP-R visited Albania at the invitation of the APL Central Committee (Tirana domestic radio, 8 June).

The PCP-ML carried on a bitter anti-Soviet campaign in its publication, *Unidade Popular*. It called for the strengthening of West European unity and the formation of a world front to resist Russian "social imperialism" and the "hegemonies of the two superpowers" (NCNA, Peking, 10 April). In late December 1976, it had denounced a West German journalist, Gunter Wallraff, for a "monstrous mystification" in implicating the PCP-ML in arms purchases by former president General António de Spínola. The latter allegedly sought the arms for the Democratic Movement for the Liberation of Portugal, a clandestine organization of the extreme right. Pointing out that Russian KGB agents were operating in Portugal by the hundreds, the MCP-ML warned that the Soviet Union was a greater threat to Portugal than the right (IPS, Buenos Aires, 29 December 1976; *CMS*, 11 January). A delegation of the PCP-ML Central Committee anounced, on visiting China in May, that this would be the start of regular contacts with the Chinese Communist Party (Lisbon radio in English, 1 May).

The Maoist UDP was the only party to vote in Parliament at the end of 1976 against sustaining Prime Minister Soares with a vote of confidence in his economic plan. The PCP had abstained from the vote, alleging that it would be premature to precipitate the overthrow of the government (*NYT*, 16 January).

The Socialist Party of Portugal charged in January that a group of ten party members, Trotskyist infiltrators known for their radical views, were seeking to destroy the party. The "irresponsible and adventurous acts" of this group, it was said, could weaken the party and thereby facilitate a right-wing takeover of the country (*CSM*, 25 January).

Elbert Covell College   H. Leslie Robinson
University of the Pacific

San Marino

San Marino, whose 23.4 square miles are located in the heart of Italy's Communist-influenced regions, is the world's smallest republic. Of its nearly 20,000 citizens, only 300 are members of the Communist Party of San Marino (PCS). Founded in 1921, as a section of the Italian Communist Party, the PCS is only nominally independent of the latter. In the election of September 1974, it won fifteen of the sixty seats in the General Council which is the country's unicameral legislature.

General Secretary Umberto Barulli presided over the PCS's Ninth Congress in December 1976 and appears to have taken over fully from Ermenegildo Gasperoni. The congress was attended by delegations from Italy, the Soviet Union (Vadim Zagladin), East Germany, Romania, Bulgaria, Czechoslovakia, Hungary, Yugoslavia, and Chile. The Palestine Liberation Organization also sent a delegation. Barulli turned to these foreign representatives to confirm PCS international views. "On its behalf he warmly greeted the Soviet Union, the bulwark of peace and progress, the other Socialist countries, and the people fighting for their freedom." (TASS, 11 December 1976.)

During 1977 the party seems to have felt certain bourgeois radical influences such as feminism. The Ninth Congress expanded its Central Committee from thirteen to twenty-seven members, (*L'Unita*, 13 December 1976) and voted to strengthen relations with the PCI and to push for a "broad based popular government" that would include Socialists, Christian Democrats, and Communists. By the end of 1977, the PCS seemed to be achieving a miniature version of the Historic Compromise the PCI has long sought. The government formed after the December 1977 crisis thus is likely to reject proposals that it allow establishment of commercial broadcasting stations to serve Italian listeners.

A year later, the Communists had an opportunity to form a government in San Marino when the ruling Christian Democrats fell from power. The two captains regent, who comprise the executive, invited the PCS to form a coalition by 29 December. The Communists came within one vote of attaining a majority in the legislature (*NYT*, 25 and 31 December). New parliamentary elections probably will be held in the spring of 1978.

Washington, D.C.   Angelo Codevilla

Spain

The Communist Party of Spain (Partido Comunista de España; PCE) is the largest, most influential, and most moderate of the various leftist organizations in Spain. It was founded in 1920. Forced underground in 1939, it suffered a marked decline in membership, from a pre-Civil War peak of 300,000. By the time the party was again legalized in April 1977, it had rebuilt to a claimed 200,000. The population of Spain is 36,542,000.

The PCE has launched a drive to triple its membership in spite of some alleged misgivings that such expansion could weaken party discipline and lead to embarrassing incidents that might discredit the organization in the long run (*WMR*, January 1977; *Christian Science Monitor* [*CSM*], 11 April). In legislative elections in June the party attracted 9 percent of the vote and won twenty seats in the new Chamber of Deputies; its best showing was in Catalonia and Andalusia.

Financial support for the PCE is said to come from other Communist parties, especially those in Italy and Romania. It is uncertain whether the Soviet Union continues to withhold funds because of the party's independent "Eurocommunist" line. The PCE is the foremost champion of Eurocommunism, the movement of Western Communists who claim to have abandoned revolution in favor of the parliamentary path to power, at the same time rejecting subservience to Moscow. Unhappy with the recalcitrant PCE leadership, the Soviets were said to be interested during 1977 in trying to revive a dormant group called the Spanish Communist Workers' Party (Partido Comunista de Obreros Españoles; PCOE). Members of that Stalinist organization had been expelled from the PCE in 1970. The PCOE is directed by Enrique Líster, a former Civil War general who now lives in southern France (*NYT*, 28 June). Líster announced in late 1976 that a clandestine dissident wing of the PCE had given up hope of correcting the PCE's "reactionary and revisionist" policy and had decided to merge with the PCOE (*ABC*, Madrid, 2 November).

Of the numerous radical parties to the left of the PCE, only two continued systematic terrorist campaigns during 1977. These were the October First Anti-Fascist Resistance Group (Grupo de Resistencia Antifascista Primero de Octubre; GRAPO) and the guerrilla faction of the Basque separatist movement called ETA (Euzkadi ta Askatasuna, "Basque Homeland and Liberty"). GRAPO was said to be the armed wing of the Reconstituted Communist Party (Partido Comunista Reconstituido; PCR), which police identified as an organization that had originally splintered from the PCE. The PCE, insisting that it was not the parent of the PCR, attributed its own low electoral count partly to a confused public impression that the PCE was a terrorist organization (*Mundo Obrero*, 29 June). It claimed that the PCR had actually defected from the Organization of Marxist-Leninist Spaniards (Organización Marxista-Leninista de Españoles; OMLE), which in turn was an offshoot of the Communist Party of Spain-Marxist Leninist (Partido Comunista de España-Marxista-Leninista; PCE-ML). (EFE, Madrid, 13 December 1976; *CSM*, 14 February 1977.) Galician names were prominent among GRAPO militants mentioned by police (*NYT*, 30 January).

The ETA guerrillas have been committing terrorist acts since the organization was formed in 1959 to seek "national liberation" for the Basque country. Militants who renounced violence split into a separate "political" wing of ETA in 1970 and, in early 1977, were said to be moving into the Koordina-dora Abertzle Socialista (KAS). This was a new alliance of Trotskyists, Marxists, and various Basque leftist unions. KAS sources claimed some 5,000 militants and "key sympathizers" among a Spanish Basque population of 2 million; membership in ETA dwindled to an estimated 50 (*CSM*, 21 January). The KAS eschewed terrorism but also demanded Basque independence and scorned participation in the June elections (ibid., 24 May). Total independence from Spain was said to be supported only by an estimated 10 percent of the Basque population (ibid., 21 January).

The remaining radical-left parties in Spain were said to be mainly Maoist, Trotskyist, Marxist-Leninist, and anarchist. They included the Spanish Labor Party (Partido de Trabajo Español; PTE), the Revolutionary Workers' Organization (Organización Revolucionaria de los Trabajadores; ORT), the Organization of the Communist Left of Spain (Organización de la Izquierda Comunista de España; OICE), the Communist Movement of Spain (Movimiento Comunista de España; MCE), the Revolutionary Communist League (Liga Comunista Revolucionaria; LCR), the Revolutionary Anti-Fascist and Patriotic Front (Frente Revolucionaria Antifascista y Patriota; FRAP), the PCE-ML, and others. Unlike GRAPO and ETA, these are open though still illegal parties whose leaders and militants do not hide. (*Washington Post*, 13 February; *Intercontinental Press*, New York, 14 February.) The PCE-ML reported an illegal meeting in July of its Second Congress, at which Eurocommunist "revisionism" was denounced (ATA, Tirana, 30 July).

Leadership and Organization. Basic policy guidelines for the PCE are set at occasional congresses, which also elect the 142-member Central Committee, 36-member Executive Committee, and 7-member Secretariat. As secretary general since 1960, sixty-two-year-old Santiago Carrillo reportedly runs the party "with an iron fist." His Eurocommunist ideas are said to be opposed by party chairman Dolores Ibarruri, who returned to Spain in May after thirty-eight years of exile in the Soviet Union, and by Marcelino Camacho, Central Committee member and chairman of the Workers' Commissions (Comisiones Obreras, or "CC OO"). The latter are PCE-organized trade unions, which were able to operate openly after the Cortes (parliament) voted in March to phase out the old government-sponsored labor syndicates (*CSM*, 4 April). The eighty-two-year-old Ibarruri, known as "La Pasionaria" during the Spanish Civil War, reportedly had long held the party together by forcing the old guard to accept Carrillo's "revisionism." (*CSM*, 11 April; *Washington Post*, 17 April; *Manchester Guardian*, 3 July.)

One of the alleged goals of the PCE's Ninth Congress, scheduled for early 1978, is to "democratize" the leadership so as to make the party more attractive to young people. Communists assert that most party militants are young but that Central Committee members are predominantly middle-aged or older, most having spent many years in Franco's prisons. Saying that the party was still organized "like an underground, with cells and rigid lines of command," one spokesman acknowledged that the present structure had to be scrapped because of criticism from the ranks. He was concerned about the PCE's poor showing at June parliamentary elections. (*Washington Post*, 2 October.)

By occupation, the Central Committee consists of fifty-seven urban workers, six farm workers, twenty-two white-collar employees, and fifty-four engineers and intellectuals. There are only seventeen women in the committee; the party has indicated its intention of expanding this number (*IB*, no. 15-16, 31 July 1976). As an example of its policy favoring women's "emancipation," the PCE claimed in June to be the party with the largest number of female candidates for seats in the legislature. La Pasionaria was among the winners (*Washington Post*, 14 June).

The tight organization of the PCE allows some autonomy for four affiliated Communist parties in the Basque region, Catalonia, Galicia, and Valencia. The latter party was formed in April (Radio Free Europe Research, 15 June).

Domestic Attitudes and Activities. Despite continuing setbacks to public order, Premier Adolfo Suárez moved quickly during 1977 to liberalize political institutions in Spain. In the more open atmosphere, Santiago Carrillo made not insignificant progress in fashioning for himself and the PCE an image of enhanced democratic respectability. He sought constantly to reassure the Spanish government and electorate regarding the party's commitment to democratic processes and freedom from Soviet discipline. He even urged labor union restraint as essential to ease the transition to democracy; however, he dangled a big stick, making it clear early in the year that "we are not going to give gifts to those who ban us" (NYT, 16 January). The party was rewarded for its moderation by being legalized in April, thereby being enabled to take part in June legislative elections. Though disappointed with the meager 9 percent of the vote won by the Communists, Carrillo was not deflected from his image-building strategy. This was in line with his proclaimed conclusion that the path to Socialism in a modern West European industrial state had to be "democratic, parliamentarian and pluralistic." The first need, he said, was to consolidate the democratic system in Spain. (Radio Free Europe Research, 29 April, 20 June; NYT, 22 June.)

Early in February the stage was set for the legalization of the PCE and other political parties when the government decreed new procedures for their registration. Legal status was quickly accorded to most applicants. However, determination of the PCE's eligibility was deferred to the Supreme Court, which was instructed under the new law to decide whether the party was disqualified by being "subject to an international discipline" intent on implanting totalitarianism in Spain (NYT, 9 February). Some thought Suárez expected the sensitive issue would be tied up in the court for months, thereby diminishing the time available to the Communists for campaigning. The court did not indulge the government's evident wish to avoid having to make this hard decision; two months after receiving the case, it tossed the issue back to the Interior Ministry for an "administrative" ruling, arguing that it was a political, not legal, matter (CSM, 4 April). The premier quickly lined up support during the following week for the legalization that was announced on 9 April (NYT, 3 April; Washington Post, 10 April).

An angry backlash from the right-wing power elite was skillfully contained by the premier and King Juan Carlos. The navy minister and five members of the Cortes resigned in protest, allegedly accusing Suárez of having misled the military chiefs and the Cortes on his intentions. A total military revolt was said to have been narrowly averted when the king personally persuaded the army and air force ministers not to resign. Though reprimanding the government for its action, the Army Supreme Council decided grudgingly and "in the higher national interest" to accept the "fait accompli." (NYT, 14, 18, 20 April; CSM, 14 April; Washington Post, 17 May.)

As the armed forces high command continued to be shifted in favor of officers sympathetic to the king, the military's political role became progressively more circumscribed. Also, an April decree further reinforced a February ban on military participation in politics (NYT, 22 April). Even so, the PCE found it prudent to restrain its celebration over its new legal status and to be deferential toward the military. Carrillo warned his party that any unconsidered act could provoke a "catastrophic reaction" (CSM, 19 April).

The Communists reserved their bitterest fire for the Francoist establishment in the Cortes and for former Interior Minister Manuel Fraga Iribarne, who was a candidate for a seat in the new Chamber of Deputies to be elected in June. Representing a center-right party, the Popular Alliance, Fraga sought support from the middle class and financial interests with a bitterly anti-Communist campaign. He denounced the legalization of the PCE as a betrayal of the Cortes and as a "monstrous act equivalent to a coup d'état" (NYT, 15 April; CSM, 19 April). Carrillo countered that Fraga was a "little Caudillo" and that his party offered "the most serious danger of political regression that could befall Spain's incipient freedoms" (Visión, New York, 6 May; NYT, 9 June). He called for a "grand pact" of center and left parties to assure a victory for democracy over the right-wing forces of Francoism (Los Angeles times, 15 April).

The Communists appeared to strike a more moderate pose in the campaign than Felipe González's Spanish Socialist Workers Party (Partido Socialista Obrero Español; PSOE), their chief rival for the leftist vote. The latter had to alternate between placating its more radical and more moderate militants (*CSM*, 19 April). The PCE was not troubled with this problem since Carrillo seemed able to prevail over his dissidents. Party officials declared that the monarchy was "compatible with communism," so long as the king helped complete the task of making Spain a democracy. Even La Pasionaria reportedly stopped giving the leftist clenched-fist salute. The PCE's modest official platform pressed, "for the time being," for nationalization only in manufacturing and distribution of electric power. (*Washington Post*, 17 May; *CSM*, 13 June; *NYT*, 23 July.)

Some observers theorized that Carrillo had been permitted to return to Spain and his party legalized in return for an agreement to support the monarchy and preserve order (*NYT*, 25 June). Others suggested that Carrillo's hope in helping the center was to weaken the Socialists so that in future elections the PCE could wean the working-class vote from the PSOE (ibid., 17 May). It was also evident that the PCE was trying to lure away Socialist votes by insisting that there was no real difference between a true Socialist and a Communist. González pinpointed the main difference when he ridiculed the Communist call for a freer society. He said the party could scarcely offer society something its "anti-democratic and authoritarian" organization did not practice internally (*La Vanguardia*, Barcelona, 30 April; *CSM*, 13 June).

The winner of the June elections was candidate Suárez's coalition of middle-of-the-road parties, the Democratic Center Union (Unión del Centro Democrático; UCD). It drew 34 percent of the vote and 165 seats in the 350-seat Chamber of Deputies, 11 seats short of a majority. The PSOE emerged as the strongest single party, with 28.5 percent of the vote and 118 seats. The Popular Alliance got 3 seats less than the third-place PCE, which won 20. Most of the remaining seats were divided among smaller Socialist and autonomist parties of Catalonia and the Basque provinces (Radio Free Europe Research, 20 June; *Visión*, New York, 1/15 July).

Clearly, the right and left extremes were decisively repudiated by Spanish voters. This was in spite of the PCE's moderate pose, which most voters apparently found unconvincing, and despite the party's formidable organizational strength and the huge campaign crowds it was able to rally. The Communists' final rain-drenched rally in Madrid, for example, drew some 200,000 people. Undaunted, Carrillo continued to urge "national reconciliation" in order to draw up a new constitution and to achieve needed economic reforms. Specifically, he suggested that a government coalition be formed by Suárez and González, since neither leader alone could command the majority necessary to enact a program acceptable to the entire country. While he felt that the Communists and other minor parties should be consulted on the formulation of a common program, he said it was "unthinkable" that the PCE should take part in the new cabinet. He also discarded the notion of a "leftist," i.e., Socialist-Communist, unity. That would polarize the nation, he said, at a time when potential army intervention still threatened the fragile democracy. (Radio Free Europe Research, 20 June; *NYT*, 22 June; *Washington Post*, 2 October.)

Apart from the logic of this position, many felt that it also demonstrated a continuing major objective of the PCE—to weaken the more popular PSOE. If the latter joined the government, it would have to share responsibility for the country's worsening economic plight. At the same time, by moving toward the center, it could lose its hard-core Marxist militants. In the upcoming municipal elections, therefore, the PCE could benefit as the chief leftist alternative. González perceived the danger, and both he and Suárez flatly rejected the possibility of a coalition government. (*Mundo Obrero*, 6 July; *Baltimore Sun*, 25 July; *CSM*, 20 September; *NYT*, 18 October.)

The Suárez minority cabinet sought to govern by forging parliamentary consensus on key issues. The most pressing issue following elections was how to ease a 30 percent rate of inflation, high unemployment, and a substantial deficit in the balance of payments. It was feared that a credit squeeze and heavy wage increases could push thousands of businesses into bankruptcy by the end of the year (*NYT*, 14 October). Clearly, necessary wage restraints would not be possible without the cooperation of the labor unions, which now had the right—granted by the Cortes in March—to organize and even strike free of government control. The unions were primarily linked to the Socialists and Communists, who were jockeying for the right to represent them in forthcoming union elections (ibid., 10 March; *CSM*, 4 April, 31 August).

In order to win PSOE and PCE—and, therefore, worker—support for his economic program, Suárez softened a proposal for holding back wages by also calling for price controls and for tax and social reforms. In this way labor might be appeased by seeing the wealthy share the burden of austerity. The latter were urged by Suárez to go along with this package with the rationale that they would suffer even more at the hands of the Socialists, who would be certain to win the next elections if the economy continued to deteriorate (*CSM*, 31 August).

At a summit crisis meeting of the major political parties early in October, Suárez finally got agreement on an "emergency" austerity program along the lines he had been seeking. Besides a heavier tax bite for the rich, there was to be a 22 percent ceiling on wages and prices during 1978. Suárez also conceded more power to the Cortes to help determine economic policy. During the two-day discussions, the Communists and parties of the UCD were said to be conciliatory while the PSOE and Popular Alliance were characterized as militant (ibid., 12 October; *NYT*, 14 October).

International Views and Positions. With the intent of boosting Communist credibility in Spain, the PCE redoubled its efforts in 1977 to reinforce its Eurocommunist credentials. This was done primarily by engaging the Soviet Union in a belligerent confrontation, a ploy well beyond what the party's less insecure Eurocommunist allies in Italy and France were disposed to go along with (*Wall Street Journal*, 19 April).

In February, the PCE's weekly newspaper bitterly assailed East European governments for trying to silence dissidents through repression or expulsion (*Mundo Obrero*, 24-30 January; Radio Free Europe Research, 4 February). Two months later, Carrillo lashed out—in greater detail than any Western Communist leader had ever done—at the Soviet leadership for failing to dismantle Stalinism and for stifling human rights and economic progress. In a best-selling book, *Eurocommunism and the State*, he lamented that in sixty years of Communist power, the Soviet Union had still not become a "workers' democracy." By contrast, he wrote, advocates of Eurocommunism all agreed on the need to work for Socialism by respecting human rights and freedoms and by accepting a multi-party system and parliamentary elections. They also insisted, he added, upon "full independence from any possible international center." Carrillo accepted U.S. bases in Spain as a counter to the Soviet military threat, but he called for the dissolution of both the North Atlantic Treaty Organization and the Warsaw Pact. He favored Spain's entry into the Common Market. (*Opinión*, Madrid, 2-8 April; Radio Free Europe Research, 29 April; *Washington Post*, 24 June.)

The outraged Soviets waited until after elections in Spain to answer Carrillo's "crude anti-Sovietism." In the official foreign affairs weekly, *Novoye Vremya* (also published in English as *New Times*), Carrillo was accused of trying to split the international Communist movement and of playing into the hands of "reactionary imperialist forces." The editorial also denounced all forms of Eurocommunism as the creation of "bourgeois political theorists" who wanted West European Communists to cease being Communist (*New Times*, 23 June; *Washington Post*, 24 June, 7 July; *NYT*, 24 June; *The Manchester Guardian*, 3 July).

The attack was widely seen as an attempt to stir PCE opposition to Carrillo's leadership at a time when his prestige was diminished by the election results. In the meantime, the Soviet ambassador, who took up his post in Madrid in April after Spanish-USSR diplomatic ties had been restored, reportedly was trying to undermine the secretary-general by courting pro-Soviet elements in the party and in the "CC OO." One PCE theoretician suggested that the Soviets wanted to build a new party around Dolores Ibarruri, who, on her return to Spain, publicly gave an emotional tribute to the "great Soviet nation" and who privately was said to speak of Eurocommunism as "foolishness." (*El País*, Madrid, 26 June, *NYT*, 25, 27 June.)

The Soviet assault backfired by provoking a defiant PCE counter-attack in Carrillo's defense and by reportedly causing the latter's personal prestige to soar in Spain. The PCE Central Committee indignantly rejected the criticism and vowed to continue the Eurocommunist line of independence. Ibarruri called the party line "realistic and skillful" and Marcelino Camacho, hard-line pro-Soviet leader of the "CC OO," denied any anti-Carrillo tendency in the party. Since votes within the committee had reportedly been less than unanimous, outsiders assumed that the apparent solidarity was imposed by party discipline. (Radio Independent Spain, 27 June; *NYT*, 27 June; *CSM*, 28 June; *Manchester Guardian*, 3 July; *Baltimore Sun*, 25 July; *Washington Post*, 2 October.)

Carrillo followed up with a sarcastic article in a popular leftist magazine, *Triunfo*. He assailed the *New Times* for its "string of lies" and for forgetting that "the international Communist movement is not a church, that Moscow is not Rome, that we do not accept the existence of a holy office . . . that can excommunicate or bless us." He sarcastically expressed his gratitude to the Soviets for "confirming . . . that the PCE is an authentically independent party" and regretted that the attack had not come before the elections so that it could have boosted the Communist vote (*CSM*, 5 July).

In the face of the Spanish reaction and of expressions of solidarity that issued from the Italian, French, Belgian, and Yugoslav Communist parties, the Soviets began backtracking. Blaming the Western press for trying to create the "false" impression of a Soviet Union "offensive" against European Communist parties, the *New Times* insisted its only quarrel was with Carrillo (Tass, 6 July; *NYT*, 10 July). Then the Soviets reportedly sent officials to Spain in September and October to mute the public quarrel and to explore differences quietly (*Le Monde*, Paris, 14 September; *Mundo Obrero*, 15-21 September; *Washington Post*, 16 September, 17 October).

International Activities and Contacts. To help support the PCE campaign to win formal government recognition as a legal party, French and Italian Communist leaders George Marchais and Enrico Berlinguer were invited to Madrid in March for a "Eurocommunist" summit meeting. Carrillo was said to feel that the two could best bolster his case in Spain by joining him in condemning political repression in the Soviet Union and Eastern Europe. They balked at this but did agree in a joint communiqué merely to call for full implementation everywhere of the Helsinki agreement on human rights. They also affirmed their commitment to a multi-party society, democratic freedoms, and independence to adapt Communist tenets to the conditions of one's own country (*Washington Post*, 3, 4 March; *NYT*, 3, 4 March).

In the wake of the furor caused by the publication of Carrillo's book and the Soviet response, visits were made by PCE officials to Romania and Yugoslavia in August and September. Following each visit, joint statements made oblique reference to the right of all Communist parties to autonomy and noninterference from abroad (Agerpres, Bucharest, 1, 25 August; Tanyug, Belgrade, 30 September).

In an alleged conciliatory mood, Soviet officials invited Carrillo, he claimed, to speak at the Moscow celebration of the sixtieth anniversary of the October Revolution. He was reportedly told that the Soviets wanted to restore "good relations" with the PCE. However, he was snubbed at the ceremony and not given the floor. Berlinguer, by contrast, was permitted to speak and was invited to meet with President Brezhnev in a session the Soviet press said "underlined the necessity for international . . . voluntary cooperation" (*NYT*, 4 November).

Carrillo accepted an invitation to go to Yale, Harvard, and Johns Hopkins universities in November for a ten-day lecture tour. He sought thereby further to improve his image, but apparently he was not disturbed by the impression he made by crossing AFL-CIO picket lines at Yale to give a speech. The leader of striking maintenance workers accused him of being a "scab" and "choosing to lie in bed with the capitalist host." Carrillo said he was puzzled as to why U.S. labor—"more to the right" than their Spanish counterparts—would want to deny him freedom of speech. He was contemptuous of the American labor movement for having "done nothing to promote democracy in Spain" (*Wall Street Journal*, 17 November).

Other visits abroad by PCE officials were made to Poland in January for official talks, to Belgium in March to attend a world conference promoting Korean reunification, and to North Korea in September to "exchange views" at an international seminar on *chuche*—i.e., independence (PAP, Warsaw, 17 January; KCNA, Pyongyang, 26 February, 8 March, 16 September). In October, Carrillo also attended a British Labour party conference, where he met with several government ministers and made a point of calling for the return of Gibraltar to Spain (*FBIS*, 3, 5 October).

Media. The PCE's principal publication is the weekly *Mundo Obrero*, which was temporarily expanded to a daily during the 1977 parliamentary election campaign. Published since 1931, it claimed to have boosted its circulation from 137,000 in March to 275,000 in June (EFE, Madrid, 16 March; *Mundo Obrero*, 6 July). The party also publishes *Nuestra Bandera*, a bimonthly theoretical and political journal (circulation 25,000), and a number of small regional newspapers.

A June article in William Buckley's *National Review* claimed that *Cambio-16*, Spain's largest-selling newsweekly, was also at the service of the Communists since the director of publications, Ricardo Utrilla, had been an "active PCE member since his student days." This charge was doubted by various other journalists who knew Utrilla (*National Review*, 10 June; *CSM*, 21 June).

After 108,300 shortwave programs beamed by the PCE to Spain from Eastern Europe, "Radio Independent Spain" ended its broadcasts in July. It was announced that this was in recognition that, having accomplished its clandestine mission, it should "abide by the democratic game" in the new Spain (Radio Independent Spain, 14 July; *CSM*, 29 July).

Activities of Basque and Rival Communist Organizations. In spite of the Suárez government's accelerated dismantling of the Francoist police-state, Spain continued to be jostled in 1977 by extremist violence. Both left-wing and right-wing radicals were apparently seeking to derail democracy by provoking government repression and a military coup. In the rightist scheme, the disorder would finally induce the army to restore military rule; in the leftist view, the repression would precipitate a true "revolutionary situation" leading "progressive" officers to revolt and set up a Marxist regime (*U.S. News & World Report*, 14 February; *CSM*, 24 May). The PCE condemned the violence and Carrillo praised the army for not falling into the trap set by extremists who wanted to "put the people and the army at loggerheads" (Radio Independent Spain, 25 January).

Responsibility for most of the terrorist bombings, killings and kidnapings was claimed by the leftist ETA and GRAPO and by the rightist Anti-Communist Apostolic Alliance (AAA) and Warriors of Christ the King. Each side sought to avenge the violence of the other. Leftists demanded amnesty for all political prisoners, suppression of police brutality and right-wing terrorism (which they charged were officially tolerated), and political autonomy for the Basque region. The practical effect of the violence was apparently to delay amnesty and to prevent any possibility that the far leftists might be legalized along with the PCE. Negotiations for the granting of autonomy to the Basques were also stalled. A measure of home rule was granted in September to a less agitated Catalonia, but not until the end of December to the Basque provinces (*NYT*, 7 May; *CSM*, 3 October).

The AAA claimed credit for the January killing in Madrid of a leftist student demonstrator and of five persons in a Communist law office, and for the September bombing of a satiric magazine, *Paus* (*CSM*, 25 January, 30 September; *Washington Post*, 13 February; *NYT*, 29 September). It was widely believed that the rightists were also responsible for violence committed by the mysterious GRAPO.

The liberal newspaper *Diario-16* suggested that GRAPO either consisted entirely of right-wing fanatics masquerading as leftists or was a group of gullible leftists being manipulated by "parallels" (elite super-secret police agents organized during Franco's time to infiltrate leftist groups). *El País* quoted an estimate by a former parallel living in exile in France that there were now 2,000 of these provocateurs in Spain (*Washington Post*, 13 February; *CSM*, 19 August).

GRAPO bombed the offices of *Diario-16* and seven Madrid power stations in June, two weeks before the elections. The organization also claimed responsibility—along with the obscure Revolutionary Anti-Fascist Movement—for having set up explosives in August in a Palma de Mallorca underpass. This was an attempt, foiled by police, to assassinate King Juan Carlos and Premier Suárez as they drove through (*CSM*, 6 June, 19 August; *NYT*, 21 August). Acts less likely to be manipulated by rightists were GRAPO killings of three policemen in Madrid in late January and of two members of the Civil Guard in Barcelona in June (*NYT*, 30 January; *CSM*, 6 June).

In January, GRAPO claimed a second kidnap victim, Antonio María de Oriol y Urquijo, who was an industrialist and president of the Council of State. Lieutenant General Emilio Villaescusa, the president of the Supreme Court of Military Justice, who was abducted in October 1976, was still being held. Their captors warned that if total amnesty were not granted to all "anti-fascist prisoners," they would continue avenging fascist crimes and taking prisoners "among the hierarchs of the state." A few weeks later, both De Oriol and Villaescusa were rescued by police in separate apartments in working-class sections of Madrid. Villaescusa said his captors were Maoist radicals who wanted to destroy the nation's government; both said they had been treated well. (*CSM*, 25 January; *NYT*, 30 January, 12, 14 February.)

A wave of strikes and violence erupted in the Basque country in May to demand release of Basque political prisoners and to protest police brutality against demonstrators. Four persons were killed in clashes between police and protesters, a policeman was murdered by ETA, and a wealthy right-wing Basque industrialist, Javier de Ibarra y Berge, was kidnaped in Bilbao by ETA. A month later, Ibarra was executed by his abductors after a deadline had passed for delivery of a $15 million ransom. (*NYT*, 18, 21 May, 23 June.) ETA also claimed responsibility for the October assassination of the Vizcaya provincial president, Augusto Unceta Barrenechea, and his two police bodyguards. The separatist group vowed to continue attacking "all instruments of domination of the Basque country by the Spanish oligarchy." To the argument that the killings could undermine democracy, they retorted that there was no democracy in the Spanish state. (Ibid., 9, 10 October.)

Police made some headway in apprehending GRAPO as well as right-wing extremist ringleaders but did not succeed in breaking up the organizations or in containing the violence. The extremism continued to be tied primarily to demands for "total" amnesty. The government resisted such intimidation, though it did gradually release most prisoners and exiled many of those convicted of "blood crimes" for the duration of their sentences. Suárez won the support of opposition parties in October for a wide-ranging amnesty law, which freed some ninety prisoners, and for a "defense of democracy" anti-terrorist offensive. There was amnesty for previous political offenses but any new political crimes were to be considered as aimed against the consolidation of the country's new democracy. Nearly twenty-nine extremists were arrested, eleven from rightist groups and eighteen from GRAPO. The entire executive committee of the latter organization was said to be included in the arrests. (*CSM*, 15 March, 28 June, 12, 17 October; *NYT*, 22 May, 14 June.)

Elbert Covell College   H. Leslie Robinson
University of the Pacific

Sweden

A Communist party was founded in Sweden on 13 May 1917 after a split with the Social Democrats. It joined the Communist International in July 1919. Today's party dates from another split, in 1921, when it took the name Swedish Communist Party (Sveriges Kommunistiska Parti; SKP). Next to the Soviet party, Swedish Communists can claim that theirs is the oldest Communist party in the world.

After a period of relative insignificance during the 1950s the SKP profited from the rise of the New Left in Sweden and in 1967 changed its name to Left Party-Communists (Vänsterpartiet Kommunisterna; VPK). A large minority within the party criticized it for being "reformist" and founded the Communist League, Marxist Leninists (Kommunistiska förbundet Marxist-Leninisterna; KFML), under the influence of Maoism. In 1973 the KFML appropriated the name SKP.

During the period 1970-76 the VPK exerted an influence on Swedish politics disproportionate to its number of seats in the parliament. In 1970, Prime Minister Olof Palme and the Social Democrats, with 163 seats in the 350-seat parliament, had to rely on the VPK's seventeen members for the survival of the Palme government. When the Social Democrats in the 1973 elections dropped to 156 seats and the VPK gained 2, the importance of the party increased even more. During 1970-73 the VPK was admitted to such important parliamentary committees as defense and taxes, but after 1973 Palme compromised to the right with the Liberals, thus putting a stop to a real Communist breakthrough in Swedish parliamentary life. With the fall of the Social Democratic government in the elections of 19 September 1976, the VPK seems once more threatened by political insignificance—the more so since the split of the party in February 1977, when the Stalinist faction formed a party of its own.

The VPK membership is reported to number about 17,500. The population of Sweden is about 8,250,000.

Organization and Internal Party Affairs. The party congress is theoretically the all-important organ of the VPK. It elects the thirty-five-member Central Committee, since 1964 known as the Party Board. The board selects the eight-member Executive Committee (Verkställande Utskott), which directs the party work. There are 28 party districts, corresponding to Sweden's electoral regions, and 395 local organizations. The Communist Youth (Kommunistisk Ungdom) is the party's youth organization.

Lars Werner, the current VPK chairman, has been less successful than his predecessor, Carl-Henrick Hermansson, in keeping the party united. The dissension that troubled the VPK during the whole of 1976 continued during the first months of 1977. On 28 February the split took place which had been expected for some time. Three party districts (Malmö, Göteborg, Mälardalen) then formed the "Workers Party (Communists)" (Arbetarepartiet Kommunisterna; K). The immediate reason for the split was the VPK board's decision to exclude party members in the Västernorrland party district and set up a parallel leadership to the elected district board. A few days later the Norrbotton, Västerbotten, Västernorrland, and Halland districts joined the new party.

Leading the revolt was Communist member of parliament Rolf Hagel from Göteborg. In 1975 he ran against Werner for the post of party chairman and received a third of the votes. At a press conference on 1 March 1977 Hagel mentioned several points of disagreement with the VPK as the ideological reason for the split: "The VPK has had a weak position on the question of atomic energy. We have been against nuclear power. We in the Worker's Party (Communists) do not want to reject nuclear power altogether. But we do want real information about the energy supply and how the problem of radioactive waste is to be solved." (*Intercontinental Press,* New York, 21 March.)

On 26-27 March the new party held its first conference, in Stockholm. Hagel was elected chairman. According to him the new party had 4,600 members, of whom 4,000 came from the VPK. There were 200 representatives from 16 party districts present, but according to Bo Hammar of the VPK party board, fewer than 1,000 members of the VPK joined the new party. Hammar also said at the VPK Stockholm party district annual conference that the VPK after the split had received applications from 1,000 new members.

In a speech at the K conference, Hagel attacked former VPK chairman Hermansson for having let the party be "liquidated as a Marxist-Leninist party and become instead a broad leftist party that would attract the middle class. . . . He wanted to create a socialist people's party. . . . the party lacked independent analyses of the economic and political development and willingly allowed itself to be guided by all sorts of petty bourgeois sects." (*Norrskensflamman,* 30 March.)

VPK leader Werner's reaction to the new party was expressed in an interview: "The attempt to divide the party turned out to be a fiasco. If the number of members which the Hagel group says it has attracted were converted, we would be a party of 50,000 rather than the 16,000 to 17,000 which is the accurate figure. The VPK is stronger now than at the time when there was a group within the party which made statements diametrically opposed to those of the party leadership." (*Dagens Nyheter,* Stockholm, 19 March.)

It was not until April that the Soviet press reported on the split, with a very neutral comment: ". . . the party leadership (VPK) took administrative measures, up to expulsion from the party, against those Communists . . . who criticized the policy of the leadership. . . . Many Communists and some of the party organizations announced their decision to withdraw from the party and to establish a new party." (Tass, 7 April.)

In May both the VPK and the K celebrated the sixtieth anniversary of the foundation of the Communist party in Sweden. At the time of its formation the Communist party had 35,000 members and drew 200 representatives from all over Sweden to inaugurate the Left-Wing Social Democratic Party.

Domestic Activities and Attitudes. The result of the 1976 election was a heavy blow to the VPK. The victory of the non-Socialist parties and the formation of the three-party (Conservative, Liberal, and Center) coalition was the end of a long period of Communist influence in Swedish government policies, not directly but through its supporting function for the ruling Social Democratic Party.

Early in 1977 a group of the Executive Committee put forward a proposal for a new cultural program of the VKP. In the outline the group suggested, among other things, that the Swedish Broadcasting Corporation (Sveriges Radio) should remain in its present organizational form, but "capitalist power over the newspapers must be broken and ownership organized in a more democratic way." A law, according to the proposal, should be inaugurated to guarantee the same cultural level in all Swedish counties. Further, it stated: "The Socialist cultural struggle is a struggle to break the existing class system. . . . The goal must be to create already under capitalism an alternative culture, the beginning of a culture which can be developed in a future socialist society." (*Socialistisk debatt,* no. 1-2).

The VPK also criticized the new Swedish Labor Law on Participation (MBL), which opens, it was said, new steering methods in industry: since the framework for participation still is capitalist control of production, there is a danger that participation may mean that the trade unions become responsible for growth and effectiveness of production. Trade unions, the party argued, would then be responsible for matters that should be the responsibility of the capitalists.

The VPK also prepared a Communist alternative to the Social Democratic proposal on Wage Earners Funds. Its criticism concentrated on the view that the proposal did not challenge the capitalist system and its laws. The alternative to capitalism, it said, should be self-determination and not only participation. "This means liberation of the wage-earners, means other power relations within industry and all of society. The self-determination of the wage earners means: democratic rights in the places of work, wage earners' decisions on working conditions, wage forms, investments, production." (C.H. Hermansson, ibid., no. 5.)

In January the VPK proposed in parliament that the monarchy be abolished and that the speaker of the parliament should be made head of state. The party also proposed that the Swedish Lutheran Church be separated from the state, and that grades should be abolished in the school system.

In foreign policy, VPK resolutions were introduced in parliament calling for a ban on Swedish investments in South Africa, and for a boycott action against Chile and a ban on Swedish exports to Chile. It was also proposed that Sweden should leave the World Bank.

Development aid for the Eritrean Liberation Front, the Palestinian Red Half Moon, the Democratic Saharian Arab Republic, and POLISARIO (Western Sahara) was suggested. The VPK also wanted the government to raise the aid to Cuba to 80 million Swedish kronor (U.S. $16 million). Priority for development aid should, according to the VPK, be given to countries such as Vietnam, Mozambique, Guinea-Bissau, Cap Verde, Laos, Somalia, Angola, Tanzania, Cuba, and South Yemen, and liberation movements in South Africa and Eastern Timor.

International Views and Activities. In a speech in January 1977 Lars Werner criticized the measures taken in Czechoslovakia against that country's dissidents. The VPK, he said, was an advocate of full freedom of association and opinion. (Swedish domestic service, 30 January.)

In a newspaper interview, Hermansson said he would welcome it if radical voices were raised in the Social Democratic Party. Referring to the situation in France, he said: "There the Communist and Socialist parties have a common government program. They are prepared to cooperate in a government in the event they win the parliamentary elections next year, which I believe they will . . . this opens interesting prospects for us." (*Dagens Nyheter,* 1 April.)

International Contacts. Bo Hammar of the VPK board was received by Nicolae Ceauşescu in April 1977 on the invitation of the Romanian party's Central Committee. During the discussions it was stressed that each party's right to "draw up its policy independently, without any outside interference, should be respected" (Bucharest domestic service, 16 April). In July, Paul Verner, Politburo member of the East German party, and Lars Werner met for discussions and investigated possibilities of cooperation.

Preparations for the Communist World Youth Festival in Havana in 1978 have started in Sweden. Articles on Cuba have been published in *Socialistisk Debatt* and the Swedish-Cuban Society is in charge of the practical matters.

Other Leftist Groups — Rival Communists. There are a number of extreme leftist groups in Sweden. Among these, the Maoists are split into two "parties," each claiming to have the true interpretation of Marxism-Leninism.

The new SKP, as noted earlier, grew out of the KFML. The size of the membership is secret, but is believed to be around 2,000. In 1973 the party claimed to have 100 local organizations. In January 1977 the SKP sent a message to Chinese party leader Hua Kuo-feng on the first anniversary of the death of Chou En-lai (Peking NCNA, in English, 21 January). The same day the party organ *Spark* expressed fear of Soviet aggression in an editorial: "The North European countries are situated for attack in the Soviet strategy," said the paper. In April, SKP chairman Roland Pettersson and a delegation visited China. Hua Kuo-feng was host at a banquet in honor of the delegation and lauded the party for its progress in recent years and for its opposition to monopoly capital and to the two hegemonic powers, the Soviet Union and the United States, especially Soviet social-imperialism" (NCNA, 4 April).

As in earlier years SKP has been ridden by dissension. In 1976 former chairman Gunnar Bylin, and Ulf Mårtensson were suspended. In May 1977 Bo Gustafsson and Sköld Peter Matthis were excluded. Both Mårtensson and Matthis were prominently active in the pro-Communist Vietnam activities at the end of the 1960s and beginning of the 1970s.

The Communist Association of Marxist-Leninist Revolutionaries (Kommunistiska Förbundet Marxist-Leninisterna; KFML(r) broke away in October 1970 from the KFML. It has been riddled by internal conflicts. The association declared its aim to form a political party at its congress on 28-31 December 1977. The Trotskyists are weak in Sweden. The Communist Workers League (Kommunistiska Arbetarförbundet; KAF) is the Swedish section of the Fourth International.

Publications. *Ny Dag* (New Day) is the VPK's twice-weekly central organ. It appears under the name *Arbetare-Tidningen* (Worker News) in Göteborg. The only daily of the party, *Norrskensflamman* (Blaze of the Northern Lights), published in Luleå, is now the main organ of the new party, K. The VPK theoretical organ is *Socialistisk debatt.* The central organ of SKP is the weekly *Gnistan* (Spark). KFML(r)'s main voice is *Proletären* (The Proletarian). The Trotskyist KAF publishes *Internationalen* (The International).

Ängelholm, Sweden   Bertil Häggman

Switzerland

The Swiss Labor Party—Partei der Arbeit (PdA), Parti du Travail (PdT), Partito del Lavoro (PdL), here referred to as PdA—is pro-Soviet in orientation and is the oldest Communist party in Switzerland. Founded as the Swiss Communist Party on 5 March 1921, it was banned in 1940 and reformed under its present name on 14 October 1944.

Three other Communist organizations also warrant mention, although their influence on Swiss political life is marginal. The Marxist Revolutionary League—Ligue Marxiste Revolutionnaire (LMR), Marxistische Revolutionare Liga (MRL), here referred to as LMR—was established in 1969 by dissident members of the PdA in Geneva and Lausanne. The LMR is a member of the Trotskyist Fourth International and advocates violent overthrow of the system. The Progressive Organizations,

Switzerland (Progressive Organisationen, Schweiz; POCH), founded in 1972, is comprised primarily of young persons. Its general secretary is Eduard Hafner, and POCH concentrates primarily on domestic issues. A pro-Chinese group, the Communist Party of Switzerland (Marxist-Leninist)—CPS/ML—was organized in 1972. (See *YICA, 1977,* pp. 234-38; *1976,* pp. 222-27; *1973,* pp. 227-29.)

PdA membership numbers about 5,000. In the most recent elections, in 1975, the PdA captured 2.5 percent of the vote and put 5 members in the 200-member Swiss parliament. Its greatest strength is in the cantons of Basel, Vaud, Neuchatel, and Geneva. The PdA has more than forty deputies in cantonal parliaments, as well as a number of elected municipal officials.

The population of Switzerland is 6,421,000.

During the year a number of smaller leftist groups were also active in Switzerland. Their political, social, and economic views cover a broad spectrum of leftist ideologies. These groups are probably between fifty and sixty in number and are comprised of primarily younger members.

Leadership and Organization. The PdA is governed by a fifty-member Central Committee with representatives from the German-, French-, and Italian-speaking parts of Switzerland. The fourteen-member Political Bureau has a five-member Secretariat headed by Jean Vincent (Geneva). The other members are Andrew Muret (Lausanne), Jakob Lechleitner (Zurich), Hansjorg Hofer (Basel), and Armand Magnin (Geneva).

The party has youth organizations in most of Switzerland's twenty-two cantons. They are administered by a national organization created at the last party congress, in December 1974. The largest party organizations are located in Geneva, Vaud, Neuchatel, Zurich, Basel, and Ticiono. The next party congress is scheduled for 1978.

Domestic Affairs. In 1977, as in the year before, domestic issues in Switzerland, the sixth financial power in the world, were dominated by economic considerations and the political climate remained relatively quiet. In an article in *World Marxist Review* (June), party chairman Jean Vincent took pride in observing that the PdA was the first to warn (in 1974) of impending economic problems, such as decreased production and investment, and rising unemployment. These developments, he concluded, revealed "Switzerland's original link with the entire capitalist economic mechanism."

While Switzerland is undeniably capitalistic, the economic problems suggested by Vincent were practically nonexistent. The Swiss economy is an especially stable one; and, as Vincent noted, the inflation rate in 1976 was about 1.2 percent and the exchange rate of the Swiss franc had increased about 60 percent since 1971. Moreover, according to Vincent, Swiss bank deposits had risen by 47,000 million francs in 1975, reaching a figure almost twice as large as the gross national product; exports in 1976 had increased by 5.4 percent; and the balance of payments showed a surplus of 6,700 million francs.

Because of all this "evidence of Swiss capitalism's 'durability,' " Vincent stressed that the PdA "intends to rely on the country's democratic institutions. We shall give them real substance, we shall protect and develop them to the maximum." To accomplish this aim, he advocated (1) "unity of action among the working class," (2) "an alliance of leftist forces," and (3) the unification of "the broad masses." He acknowledged, however, that this would be difficult for several reasons. First, each of Switzerland's cantons has its own constitution and its own laws; this requires the PdA to be "constantly alive to local conditions and careful in drafting policy at canton as well as [the] national level." Second, all work of the PdA must be conducted in three languages, which puts "tremendous strain" on party resources. Third, "the proportion of actual proletarians, industrial workers that directly create surplus value, is very small, far less than in other developed capitalist countries. It will be appreciated how this influences the social profile of the masses, what difficulties it creates for us in getting through to the population."

Vincent did claim certain successes, however, in the French- and German-speaking parts of Switzerland, although noting that party work in the Italian-speaking part had not been particularly successful. Of special importance was his conclusion that in the French cantons the PdA had been able "to build up a relationship with the Socialists" (Sozialdemokratische Partei, SP), and that electoral agreements had been made in Vaud, Geneva, and Neuchatel, thus indicating, in his view, the emergence of "a permanent alliance of left-wing forces."

With reference to the future, Vincent said that the PdA would "make use of various spheres and forms of political activity—parliamentary, at confederation and canton level, the mechanism of popular initiatives and referendums, mass movements for achieving specific social aims . . . ." The PdA would support popular initiatives providing for (1) "control of prices and profits," (2) introduction of control over trusts and cartels, including their possible nationalization," and (3) "democratic tax increases on high incomes and large estates" (see also *France Nouvelle,* Paris, 18 April).

Although Vincent was optimistic that the unity of the left would produce election victories on the issues set forth in the popular initiatives, the PdA suffered defeat on a tax referendum in June. The proposal would have adopted the largest tax increase in Switzerland's history and would have raised the Swiss cost-of-living index by 2.5 to 3 percent. On another issue in the same month, however, the PdA considered its position vindicated in the decision of Swiss voters to require local officials to oppose construction of nuclear power plants (*NYT,* 13 June).

International Views and Positions, and International Party Contacts. The international views of the PdA closely coincided with those of the Soviet Union. This was especially evident in an editorial published in the autumn of 1977 in *Vorwaerts* (reprinted in *WMR,* September), eulogizing "the historic significance of the Great October which showed the world the way to a new future." The editorial made clear that the party strongly supported the Communist Party of the Soviet Union while maintaining its belief in following its own road toward achieving Socialism in Switzerland:

It has long been known that there can be no universal model of socialist society. True Marxism has always been creative in character and never indulged in imitation. But one should not ignore the experience of the Soviet Union. Socialism is our common goal, but the ways of attaining it are inevitably different. The huge size of the socialist world, now as well as in the future, the great differences between its nations, their traditions, history, and economic and political conditions—all this presupposes a difference in the ways we follow. (*WMR,* September.)

On general issues, the PdA stressed "the violations of democratic rights and freedoms" not only in Switzerland, but also in the United States, Chile, Argentina, Brazil, Uruguay, Paraguay, South Africa, Rhodesia, Namibia, South Korea, and Indonesia. In this connection, the PdA noted the leading role of the Soviet Union in "the fight for human rights" (*WMR,* September).

A significant development during the year was Jean Vincent's visit to Paris in May where he met with the chairman of the French Communist Party, Georges Marchais. In the communiqué issued following the meeting, both parties agreed (1) "that Socialism constitutes a higher form of democracy," (2) that peaceful coexistence, collective security, arms reduction and disarmament, and international cooperation should be endorsed, and (3) that they would "continue to develop stable and friendly relations and profitable exchanges of experiences . . . in the interest of the French and Swiss workers and democrats" (*L'Humanité,* Paris, 11 May).

This cooperation assumed added significance in June when the party chairman stated in an interview with *France Nouvelle* (7 June) that "the success of the left and the Communist Party in France's municipal elections [in March] has had its repercussions in our country," indicating how closely developments in France were being watched with a view toward the elections to the French National Assembly, scheduled for March 1978.

Publications. The PdA publishes newspapers in three languages: *Voix Ouvriere,* Geneva, daily (8,000 circulation), in French; *Vorwaerts,* Basel, weekly (6,000 circulation), in German *Il Lavoratore,* Lugano, weekly (3,000 circulation), in Italian.

La Breche is the twice-monthly French-language publication of the LMR, published in Lausanne. The monthly organ of the CPS/ML is *Octobre,* published in French. The POCH publishes in German the weekly *POCH-Zeitung* (circulation about 6,000) and *Emanzipation,* for "progressive" women's groups. It also publishes the weekly *Tribune ouvrière,* the French counterpart of the *POCH-Zeitung,* and *Positionen,* a periodical for university groups.

Hoover Institution   Dennis L. Bark

Turkey

Political deadlock, continuing violence, especially among university students, and increased polarization between the extreme right and extreme left remained the rule in Turkey during 1977, despite a parliamentary election.

The elections occurred on 5 June, four months earlier than required by law. Although the democratic socialist Republican People's Party (RPP), led by Bulent Ecevit, scored impressive gains, confirming trends observed in the 1973 elections (see Ozbudun and Tachau, *International Journal of Middle East Studies,* VI, no. 4, October 1975), the party fell short of obtaining an absolute majority of the seats at stake. Polling over 41 percent of the popular vote, the RPP increased its parliamentary delegation from roughly 185 in 1973 to 213, or 13 short of a majority. The conservative Justice Party of Suleyman Demirel also made gains, increasing its share of the popular vote from 30 percent to 37 percent and its share of seats from approximately 150 to 189. Three minor parties suffered severe losses, apparently in favor of the Justice Party. One of these, the religiously-oriented National Salvation Party (NSP), nevertheless retained enough strength (24 seats) to occupy a crucial swing position from which it could provide the necessary parliamentary majority for either a conservative or RPP-led coalition government. Finally, the neo-fascist party of Alparslan Turkes, the National Action Party (NAP), doubled its proportion of the popular vote (to 6 percent) and increased its parliamentary delegation from 3 to 16.

After an abortive attempt by Ecevit to form a minority government, Demirel succeeded in reestablishing a coalition government supported by the NSP and NAP. Thus, the basic lineup of political forces in the country hardly changed at all. No major political issues were resolved, and the terms of political debate also remained unchanged. Demirel and his supporters continued to claim the label of "nationalism," and sought to stigmatize Ecevit and the RPP as supporters or stooges of Communism. In particular, Demirel labeled the RPP decision in late November of 1976 to join the Socialist International as an anti-nationalist move. In turn, Ecevit accused the government, and especially Turkes and his faction, of protecting the so-called commandos (or self-styled "idealists"), the organized groups of young toughs implicated in violent attacks on leftists, particularly among university students.

The level and pace of political violence rose during 1977. A major incident occurred in Taksim, the main square of Istanbul, on 1 May. A May Day mass rally staged by the leftist labor confederation, or DISK, was disrupted when gunfire broke out. Close to 40 people were killed, and hundreds were wounded and arrested. Although the government blamed extreme Maoists for this incident, unconfirmed reports indicated that the identity of those who fired the first shots was unclear, and that many of those who died were trampled in the ensuing panic rather than having been shot. Another indication of the increased scale of violence was the fact that Ecevit himself, perhaps for the first time, became the object of assassination threats, and that a machine gun attack was reportedly staged against his motor convoy during an election campaign tour. By the end of the year, nearly 250 persons had reportedly been killed as a result of such political violence, a total exceeding that of the two preceding years.

One other factor emerged with greater clarity during the year. While the extreme right remained largely united and enjoyed the mantle of protection afforded by its mentor's participation in the government, the left remained fragmented. Ecevit could claim, as he did in an interview with the Italian Communist publication *L'Unità,* that his party had the support of nearly 45 percent of the electorate, while more extreme leftists accounted for less than 2 percent of the vote. Nonetheless, this extremist fringe counted for more than its meager share of the vote might indicate, for two reasons: first, because it is this extremist fringe which is largely involved in violent conflict with the extreme right, as well as in such other violent incidents as bank robberies and kidnapings; and second, because this extremist fringe appeals particularly to the young people who are caught in the middle of the violent conflict in the educational institutions. In any event, in spite of its meager electoral turnout, the extreme left is reportedly made up of at least seven different organizations (*NYT,* 18 December); what is more, most of these are illegal.

Because of its continued illegal status, the Communist Party of Turkey remained relegated to the use of clandestine radio broadcasts from Eastern Europe as a means of communicating with potential supporters in the country. Its main message this year was to grudgingly advocate support of the "bourgeois" Ecevit and the RPP as the most effective means of unseating the Demirel coalition, which it viewed as a stooge for capitalist interests domestically and American imperialism internationally.

Thus, deadlock and a rising tide of violence remained the predominant features of Turkish politics in 1977. None of the outstanding issues of domestic or foreign policy were resolved. At the same time, the economic situation was rapidly deteriorating toward the end of the year. With the extreme left, including Marxists and Communists, badly fragmented, with the moderate leftist RPP unable to transpose electoral strength into governmental power, anti-leftist forces seemed to have a slim margin of advantage. In the face of all this, however, the future of parliamentary democracy appeared to be more clouded than ever.

University of Illinois at Chicago Circle   Frank Tachau

ASIA AND THE PACIFIC

Australia

The Communist Party of Australia (CPA), founded in October 1920, peaked in influence in 1944 when its membership reached 23,000. By 1977 this figure had dropped to about 1,500 and the party had split twice. The pro-Peking Communist Party of Australia (Marxist-Leninist) — CPA(M-L) — was established in 1964 in response to the CPA's rejection of China in the Sino-Soviet dispute. The pro-Moscow Socialist Party of Australia (SPA) was formed in 1971 after the CPA adopted a critical attitude to the Soviet Union. The CPA(M-L) and SPA have current memberships of, respectively, about 200 and 650. The population of Australia is 13,861,000.

The CPA is headed by Laurie Carmichael as president, Bernie Taft as vice-president, and Mavis Robertson, Eric Aarons, and Joe Palmada as national secretaries. These and five others comprise the National Executive (see *YICA, 1977,* pp. 244-45). E.F. Hill is chairman of the CPA(M-L); A.E. Bull and Clarrie O'Shea are the vice-chairmen. Pat Clancy is president of the SPA, and Peter Symon is general secretary.

In March 1975 the CPA(M-L)'s Third Congress stressed that Australia was not yet an independent country and asserted that the main political task was to organize "the broadest united front to abolish the remnants of colonialism" — i.e., governors-general — "and to achieve national independence." Party Chairman E.F. Hill insists that the united front should even include national capitalists.

The CPA condemned this strategy as Maoist, but it acknowledged that the CPA(M-L) had hit upon an immensely appealing theme — nationalism. Eric Aarons declared in February 1977 that this Maoist faction of the Australian Communist movement had made the CPA more sensitive to national concerns as expressed by the public (*Australia and the Economic Crisis: Report by Eric Aarons to CPA National Committee Meeting,* 4-7 February 1977).

Students for Australian Independence (SAI), working-class in composition and aggressive in orientation, is a front organization for the CPA(M-L) and strives to realize Hill's national united-front strategy. It has endeavored to portray Australia's history in terms of a militant, Third World-type struggle for independence from British colonialism, American imperialism, and most recently, Soviet social-imperialism. It has elevated the Eureka gold miners and the bushranger Ned Kelly into heroic freedom fighters.

The Australian left has actively opposed uranium mining. The attitudes of the three Communist parties on this issue reflect their general political orientations and international alignments. The Central Committee of the SPA, for example, called for suspension of the mining and export of uranium because the "sale of Australian uranium to West Germany and the U.S.A. can assist those countries to continue stockpiling nuclear weapons for projected use against the socialist countries" (*The Socialist,* 6 July 1977). The CPA advocates leaving the uranium in the ground, a positon similar to the radical left's policy on the issue. The CPA hopes to harness this radicalism for its own purposes (see Eric Aarons, *Our Party, Its Prospects, and the Way Forward: Report to the National*

Committee, Communist Party of Australia, 2-4 September 1977). The CPA(M-L) has been particularly critical of positions adopted by the Australian Council of Trade Unions (ACTU).

Industrial Relations. Since Malcom Fraser became prime minister in December 1975, he has tried to reduce the influence of the trade union movement in general and its left-wing and Communist officials in particular. Fraser believes that Communists gain support and maintain office in trade unions through the militant few who will turn out and vote for them. To make it more difficult for the Communists, his government amended the Conciliation and Arbitration Act in 1976 to have secret postal ballots held for elective positions in trade unions (see *YICA, 1977,* p. 249).

In February 1977 the minister of employment and industrial relations introduced into Federal Parliament further amendments to the act, endorsed by the prime minister himself, which were designed to put down industrial lawlessness by strengthening the protection of employees against unfair actions by trade unions, providing for the establishment of a statutory body—the Industrial Relations Bureau—to secure observance of industrial law, and extending the highly unpopular penal provisions of the Arbitration Act.

On 4 May the ACTU Executive passed a resolution rejecting the bill and threatening "massive dislocation" of the economy unless it was withdrawn. It also called on the Federal Unions Conference to "recommend to the Executive how our united industrial strength can most quickly and effecitvely defeat the legislation" (*The Socialist,* 11 May). The left was enthusiastic. Pat Clancy, president of the SPA and the federal secretary of the Building Workers Industrial Union (BWIU), said that "a Government faced with . . . the kind of action [envisaged by the Executive] will find it very difficult to survive" (*Tribune,* 11 May). Laurie Carmichael, assistant national secretary of the Amalgamated Metal Workers and Shipwrights' Union (AMSWU) and president of the CPA, said that the ACTU Executive decision should be supported by the whole of the united left (ibid.).

Building Industry Unions. Norm Gallagher, federal secretary of the Australian Building Construction Employees and Laborers' Federation (BLF) and a member of the CPA(M-L), took over the CPA-led New South Wales branch of the union in 1975. This left only one other prominent Communist protagonist in the industry—Pat Clancy. However, Gallagher experienced such severe setbacks in 1977 that Clancy may soon have the whole field to himself.

In June 1977 the BLF joined the BWIU and the other tradesmen's unions in the building industry—Plumbers and Gas Fitters, Operative Painters and Decorators, and Carpenters and Joiners—to wage a joint campaign in support of a $30 weekly wage claim and improved conditions in the National Building Trades Construction Award (*The Socialist,* 22 June). this campaign, coordinated in each state by joint union committees, adopted "guerrilla" tactics aimed at disrupting selected building projects. The BLF, by participating in such methods, broke an agreement it had made with employer organizations the previous year. At that time, Gallagher agreed to lift all work bans in return for an undertaking by the employers that they would not oppose the BLF's application for registration (*YICA, 1977,* p. 251). Judging the moment ripe, Clancy and his colleagues agreed to bring their claims before the Arbitration Commission, where they negotiated a satisfactory settlement with the Master Builders Association (MBA) which demonstrated the worth of SPA and Clancy's broadly based, arbitration-geared industrial relations strategy.

Gallagher, with the full support of the CPA(M-L), refused to submit to arbitration and maintained his work bans into September (*Vanguard,* 29 September), and the BLF's three-month-long campaign actually deprived them—until the end of the year—of wage increases gained by all other unionists.

The comparative success of Clancy's industrial policy was not lost on building industry delegates to the ACTU congress (12-16 September), obliged ot elect either him, Gallagher, or J. McLoughlin of the Carpenters and Joiners to the position of building group representative on the ACTU Executive. Seven right-wing adherents refused to honor an agreement between Gallagher and the right. Instead they gave their second preference to Clancy, enabling him to beat Gallagher by forty-one votes to thirty-six (see R.M. Martin, *The ACTU Congress of 1977*).

After the ACTU congress Clancy made his move, seeking the amalgamation of the N.S.W. branches of the BWIU and the Australian Workers' Union (AWU). A considerable number of AWU members, like their BWIU counterparts, work in the building and construction industry. Accordingly, the industry and the eligibility rules of the new, amalgamated union, should it materialize, would cover workers in both unions. If the BLF were de-registered, Clancy would be able to pick up its N.S.W. membership in one scoop (*Tribune,* 3, 10 August and 21 September; *Australian Finance Review,* 16 August; *The Socialist,* 31 August).

The CPA(M-L) was worried by this development. According to *Vanguard* (8 September) "the amalgamation of the Building Workers' Industrial Union, the Australian Workers' Union and the Shop Assistants' Union (SDA) in New South Wales is a most sinister business. It shows the tremendous lengths to which the Soviet social-imperialists are prepared to go."

In October the Federal Court announced that it would investigate Gallagher's recent electoral victory in the BLF.

International Relations and the International Communist Movement. In 1976-77 the CPA(M-L) wanted to adjust its general line to the new policies of Chinese Party Chairman Hua Kuo-feng. At first the CPA(M-L) leadership was seriously embarrassed by the disgrace of the Gang of Four and the return to power of Teng Hsiao-p'ing; in 1976 Hill had praised some of the former and criticized Teng (see *Australian Communist,* September). On 27 October 1976, two days after the appearance of the *People's Daily* criticism of Chiang Ching, Hill saw his error and wrote an article supporting the actions of the Chinese party against the Gang of Four (*Vanguard,* 4 November). For good measure, he wrote a forty-five-page personal explanation of his change of heart (see E.F. Hill, *Class Struggle within the Communist Parties,* December).

The CPA has shown an interest in the Eurocommunist parties. In the words of the CPA's National Executive: "Because of our experiences, including the interference in our internal affairs which occurred when we sought to take an independent position we thought suitable to Australian conditions, and in principle, we strongly affirm the right and necessity for each party to make its own analysis of its own situation, of the way forward, and of the experiences of the movement for socialism throughout the world" (*Tribune,* 3 August 1977).

This declaration was followed by a most important rider: "Such rights, essential as they are, of course do not of themselves guarantee the correctness of the conclusion reached" (ibid.). In other words, the CPA's National Executive stopped short of endorsing any particular strategies of the European Communist parties. Not all party members share the leadership's approval of the policies adopted by the Italian Communist party. Some, especially in Sydney and Adelaide, believe that the strategies of the Italian and French parties are ill-conceived. They argue that the goal should be to smash the bourgeois state instead of gaining control through elections.

The SPA has likewise been concerned with Eurocommunism, but from the Soviet party's point of view (*The Socialist,* 20 July and 17 August).

Publications. The CPA publishes a weekly newspaper, *Tribune,* a monthly theoretical journal, *The Australian Left Review,* and an occasional internal publication, *Praxis.* The SPA publishes a fortnightly newspaper, *The Socialist,* and a monthly digest, *Survey.* The CPA(M-L) publishes a weekly newspaper, *Vanguard,* and a monthly theoretical journal, *The Australian Communist.*

La Trobe University   Angus McIntyre
Bundoora, Victoria
Australia

Bangladesh

Various Communist movements as well as the Communist parties in Bangladesh are outgrowths of Communism in Pakistan when the country was East Pakistan. The largest Communist party, the Communist Party of Pakistan, was banned by the Pakistan government in 1954. Shortly after this, it joined forces—in a sense merged with or infiltrated—the National Awami Party (NAP), a left-wing secessionist party formerly part of the Awami League (AL). In 1957 the NAP split over Sino-Soviet differences into pro-Soviet and pro-Chinese factions. The pro-Soviet faction in East Pakistan came under the leadership of Muzaffar Almad and became known as the NAP(M). The pro-Chinese faction, led by Maulana Bhashini, was known as the NAP(B); it subsequently split into several generally extremist Maoist groups.

During the struggle for independence from Pakistan, the NAP(M) supported the Awami League's government in exile, and when independence was attained in 1971 it emerged as the Communist Party of Bangladesh (CPB) and claimed to be the country's only legal Communist party. It supported the leadership of Shiekh Mujibur Rahman and had fought alongside the AL against the Pakistan army. The Communists' efforts, although consisting primarily of guerrilla warfare and the disruption of supply and other facilities, earned their leaders a role in the new government. Another factor was the Soviet Union's support and that of India, allied by treaty with Moscow, for the independence of Bangladesh. China, with some qualifications, supported Pakistan, and for this reason the pro-China Communist groups suffered, although the Naxalites, a Maoist faction in India and active in the Indian state of West Bengal, maintained some following in Bangladesh. Four of the Maoist parties—the Banglar Communist Party, the Proletarian Party of East Bengal, the East Bengal Communist Party, and the Bangladesh Communist Party-Leninist—joined in the fight for secession, but whether they were allied with the AL or fighting a "people's war" against both Pakistan and the AL is unclear. The fifth Maoist party, the Communist Party of Bangladesh-Marxist-Leninist (CPB-ML), was criticized for opposing independence and cooperating with the Pakistan army.

With the formation of a parliamentary government in Bangladesh in 1972, political parties were legalized and encouraged. The CPB's electoral platform was not clearly distinguishable from that of the NAP(M), and both were considered as part of or adjunct to the dominant AL, with the result that none of the four CPB-supported candidates won seats in 1973. The following year Maulana Bhashini, head of the pro-Chinese NAP(B), was ordered to remain in his home village. He had persuaded five other leftist parties, chiefly Maoist groups, to join a united front. He then issued a manifesto demanding that the government release political prisoners, repeal the special powers of the tribunals, disband Mujibur's "private army," and introduce grain rationing. He also criticized "unequal treaties" with foreign governments and made charges of corruption. Because he was regarded as a folk hero by many, his political activities were merely restricted; otherwise he would probably have been imprisoned.

In 1975 all political parties, except the AL, were banned. The pro-Chinese leftist parties were for the most part operating underground anyway, and they continued to organize protest demonstrations against the government and the AL (which they regarded as synonymous with the government). The

CPB joined the AL to comprise a faction of left-wing moderates in the ruling party, and supplied some semblance of choice within the single governing group. Although neither the CPB nor the pro-Chinese leftist groups had a large following, and none of them constituted a mass party, their special techniques—working with the AL in the case of the CPB and organizing demonstrations in the case of the others—gave them political influence beyond what their numbers suggested. Their combined strength probably did not exceed 4,000.

Meanwhile the Jatyo Samajtantrik Dal (JSD), or National Socialist Party, became the second-largest party in the nation, though small compared with the AL. As a pro-China and anti-India party, it manifested a policy of protesting Soviet and Indian influence in Bangladesh. In early 1974 it organized a "resistance day," which the government blocked, and in March led demonstrations resulting in eight deaths and scores of injuries. Abdur Ram, the JSD secretary general, was subsequently imprisoned and the party was disestablished.

In November 1975, following a series of coups and countercoups, Shiekh Mujibur Rahman was killed and General Ziaur Rahman assumed de facto political control of the nation as deputy head of the Martial Law Administration. Ziaur promised that national elections would be held in 1977, and in preparation the various parties and political organizations applied for legal status. In July 1976, however, a plot against the government led to trials of those involved—including Major J. A. Jalil, president of the JSD. Jalil was sentenced to life in prison, and a lesser JSD official was executed. By December, seventeen parties had been approved, of fifty-five that had applied. No religious extremist parties were allowed, and several Maoist parties failed to receive government sanction. In August of that year, the chairman of the pro-Soviet CPB, Moni Singh, had returned to Dacca, claiming to have been in the Soviet Union since the death of Sheikh Mujibur, though the pro-Chinese magazine *Holiday* alleged that he had been in India organizing an anti-Bangladesh movement. Thus there was some question whether the CPB would be allowed to participate in elections scheduled for February 1977, but approval was finally given.

In November 1976, the elections were postponed as General Ziaur further solidified his power (see "Domestic Developments"). He ordered the arrest of eleven prominent politicians for "prejudicial activities against the state." Most of those arrested belonged to the AL; one belonged to the NAP(M). A number of parties criticized the postponement since it came just as they were beginning to prepare for the elections. The Maoist Communist parties, including the CPB-ML, supported the decision.

Current Communist and Leftist Parties. The two most important Communist parties to be legalized at the end of 1976 were the CPB, led by Moni Singh, and the CPB-ML, led by Mohammad Toaha. Non-Communist leftist parties included the NAP-Bhashini, led by Mashiur Rahman; the NAP-Muzaffar, led by Muzaffar Ahmed; the Bangladesh People's League, led by Aleem al-Razee; the Jatiya Samajtantrik Dal, or National Socialist Party, led by M. A. Awal; and the United People's Party, led by Kazi Zafar. The CPB and the NAP-Muzaffar are pro-Soviet. The CPB-ML and the NAP-Bhashini are pro-Chinese.

While the CPB sought to work with the AL and to ameliorate the growing antagonism in Bangladesh toward the Soviet Union and India, it was not very active in 1977, due to the government's pressure on political parties in general and differences with the Soviet Union. In late September the CPB Central Committee met and approved a resolution calling on all the country's "patriotic forces" to mark the sixtieth anniversary of the October Revolution in the Soviet Union. It also decided to hold the party's Third Congress in May 1978. Soon after this, the party was banned (see "Domestic Developments").

The CPB-ML supported the military government's stance on almost all issues during the year, including Ziaur's decision to postpone the elections. The main reason for this was the fact that the government had tilted toward Peking, and this improved the appeal of the party and its position in the political arena vis-à-vis the other parties. Its membership grew in 1977, though it is uncertain how large the party is because it publishes no figures on its size or budget. It is still small and there seems little chance that it will become a mass party in the near future.

The other Maoist parties also seemed to benefit from the government's tilting toward China and away from the Soviet Union. However, they remain small and dependent upon small segments of the population, and in some cases tiny areas, for support. There has been talk of the Maoist parties forming a united front, but there was little progress apparent toward that goal.

Domestic Developments: The end of 1976 saw General Ziaur Rahman, who rules the country as chief administrator of martial law and chief of staff of the Bangladesh army, widen his political powers in the context of political unrest and serious economic problems. He canceled the elections scheduled for February 1977 and had many of his opponents arrested, from both right and left of the political spectrum. The opposition to his moves was meager, and the public generally favored his decisiveness and efforts to promote political stability and a favorable climate for economic development. The large number of political parties that had applied for legal status, anticipating the elections in February, and the fact that few of them had announced realistic goals, undermined public confidence in the parties in general. This was further accentuated by the fact that fighting among the parties was widespread.

Local elections were held in late January and February and representatives were chosen to over 400 parish councils, the basic unit of local government. The elections saw a victory for the AL, which won 75 percent of the local seats. The other parties generally performed poorly, especially the rightist parties—as was to be expected in view of the preparations that the AL had made and the fact that the rightist parties were out of favor. The pro-Soviet Communists were also experiencing problems, stemming from Moscow's association with India and the growing unpopularity of both. The pro-Chinese parties were not enthusiastic about the elections and sought political power instead through contacts with the government. The fact that national elections were not held did not cause unrest or serious protest.

In April General Ziaur was nominated president by Justice Abu Sadat Mohammad Seyem, who held that position but resigned because of "failing health." General Ziaur thereupon announced that there would be elections to municipal committees and district councils in August and December, respectively. At the same time he pushed through a constitutional amendment that dropped secularism in favor of the state principle of Islam. He also ordered the release of eleven political detainees, including the former speaker of the parliament, an AL member of parliament, and three pro-Peking militants who had instigated a coup attempt shortly after independence. At the same time he gave freedom to 737 political prisoners. All of this represented a balanced approach toward the right and left.

On 30 May voters went to the polls in a referendum called by General Ziaur to win support for his regime and for his 19-point government program. The turnout was unprecedented—more than 88 percent of the 38 million eligible voters, and the support for Ziaur was an unquestionable 98.97 percent. Some foreign observers reported the election was rigged and called it "overkill," but most agreed that a large majority of Bangladesh's population of nearly 78,000,000 supported General Ziaur and his programs. The vote to some extent repudiated the claim that Ziaur canceled the February elections because the AL would have won.

In August two incidents that might have stimulated opposition to the government, or created political problems for General Ziaur, passed with little notice. On 15 August the "Baksalites" (remnants of the Bangladesh Krishak Sramik Awami League) held a mourning day marking the second anniversary of the death of Mujibur. At almost the same time, rightist parties protested the erection of statues in Dacca commemorating those killed in the struggle against Pakistan. The rightists considered them anti-Islam and wanted to erase the memory of their complicity in the massive killing of intellectuals by the Pakistan army just before Bangladesh attained independence. Neither of these "movements" created any problem for the government.

On 30 September in Bogra and 2 October in Dacca "mutinies" or coup attempts were launched by members of the armed forces. The attempts failed and a number of "rebels" were arrested. President Ziaur subsequently told a group of sixty political leaders that there was "no room for underground politics or terrorism in this country." He went on to condemn "those who conduct their policies with assistance and inspiration from abroad," and made illegal those parties that followed such methods. This included specifically the CPB, NSP, and AL. Moni Singh and Mohammad Ferhad of the CPB were subsequently detained under the government's emergency powers. Nothing was said about the Maoist parties, which apparently remained loyal to the government. Ziaur stated that politics in the future "would be based on Bangladesh nationalism."

Relations with Foreign Countries. In January 1977, General Ziaur went to Peking to confer with Chinese leaders, including Hua Kuo-feng, in the first contact between leaders of the two countries. An economic and technical cooperation agreement was signed, and Peking praised Bangladesh, describing its government as following a non-aligned policy opposed to hegemonism and expansionism. Chinese leaders were invited to Bangladesh. In April it was reported that China was sending four to five squadrons of MIG-21's to Bangladesh to help modernize its air force. Trade increased throughout the rest of the year and relations remained warm.

At the year's onset *Izvestia* criticized Bangladesh as "departing from progressive stands," and commented that "right and left extremists were supported from outside and were playing an active part in the politics of Bangladesh." Relations with the Soviet Union deteriorated during the year, though aid to Bangladesh continued.

Relations with both Moscow and Peking were managed by the government and did not involve pro-Moscow and pro-Peking Communist parties. Leaders of both countries preferred to deal with General Ziaur. The one exception was Mohammad Toha's visit to Peking on 1 October where he met Chinese Communist Party Chairman Hua Kuo-feng and four other top Chinese leaders.

Publications. The CPB publishes a weekly paper in English, *Ekota,* and a daily in Bengali, *Sangbad. Holiday,* a weekly magazine in English, represents Maoist views.

Southwestern at Memphis   John F. Copper

Burma

The Burma Communist Party (BCP) was established on 15 August 1939 with probably thirteen members and Thakin Soe as secretary general. After participating in the struggle for the liberation of Burma under the leadership of the Anti-Fascist People's Freedom League (AFPFL), the Communists more and more disagreed with the Socialists in the AFPFL. In March 1946 Thakin Soe and some followers split from the BCP, where Thakin Than Tun had taken over the leadership, and founded the Communist Party of Burma, also known as the "Red Flag." The Red Flag soon went underground, and in January 1947 it was declared an unlawful association. The BCP or "White Flag" Communists under Thakin Than Tun also went underground at the end of March 1948, and in October 1953 they too were declared illegal.

Except for the years 1948 to 1950 when the government of Prime Minister U Nu nearly collapsed, Communist activities were confined to certain areas (especially the Irrawaddy delta, the Pegu Yoma highlands, and the Shan State) and therefore were a local, though constant, harrassment to the Union government. Large-scale counterinsurgency operations of the Burmese army, undertaken in cooperation with local "People's Militia," together with internal party struggles and purges of "revisionists" critically weakened the BCP after 1967-68. After the death of Thakin Than Tun in September 1968, leadership was taken over at most levels by men subservient to Peking. With Communist Chinese aid given openly after June 1967 and continued secretly after the resumption of full diplomatic relations between Burma and China in 1971, the BCP stepped up its guerrilla activities in the Shan State, first north of Lashio and about 1971 in the Kunlong area east of the Salween River, which it has controlled since the end of 1973.

The Red Flags, whose main base was in the Arakan region and for some time also in the Irrawaddy delta, did not attain any major importance. The capture of their leader Thakin Soe and the loss of other leaders at the end of 1970 critically weakened the group. Thus, the Red Flag and its splinter group, the Arakan Communist Party, numbering perhaps some 100 followers each, declined from even the small local importance they were able to claim during the mid-1960s. They are not noted further in the following survey.

Reliable figures on the membership of the BCP are not available. The estimates range from 5,000 to 12,000 or even 20,000 men under arms with 10,000 to 72,000 being probably the closest to reality. This could include as well some leftist insurgents who are cooperating with the BCP in certain areas. The strength of the government troops is estimated at 130,000 to 150,000. Burma's population is around 31.7 million.

Leadership and Organization. Since the reshuffle following the deaths of Chairman Thakin Zin and Secretary Thakin Chit in March 1975, no changes in the top ranks of the BCP have become known (see *YICA, 1977,* p. 254 for Politburo and Central Committee members). It can be assumed that Thakin Ba Thein Tin (probably mostly residing in Peking) continues as chairman and Thakin Pe Tint as vice-chairman. The only high-ranking member the government claimed to have killed in 1977 was Arakan district military commander and district political commissar Tha Doe Aung (*Botataung,* 25 January; *FBIS,* 27 January).

The organizational structure extends down through divisional and district committees to township and, in some areas, even village committees. Divisional committees exist for all parts of Burma, though sometimes only in name, and other committees only in regions where the BCP is active. Since the Central Committee meeting in May 1975 there is also a "border area people's administrative body" of whose activities nothing is known as yet. The BCP's "People's Army, led by a "Central Military Commission," is structured along traditional Communist lines with party political cadres superior to military commanders at all levels.

Party Internal Affairs and Alliances. The BCP's apparent internal peace since the reestablishment of the top committees in May 1975 was continued during 1977. The lack of information does not exclude internal difficulties but makes them improbable, especially as the message on the occasion of the BCP's thirty-eighth anniversary did not include any exhortations for inter-party unity. Thus it can be concluded that party organization has been fully consolidated in the northeastern frontier regions which form the BCP's military base and strongholds. Furthermore, the BCP at present is not likely to expand its territory by expanding its organizational structure. It evidently aims instead at strengthening its army, as armed struggle again became the main feature of the BAP's activities. Numbers four and six of the nine anniversary pledges read: "We shall emphasize armed struggle as the key link and correctly blend it with other forms of struggle . . . . We shall strengthen and develop the people's army under the unreserved leadership of the party" (Radio "Voice of the People of Burma" [VPB], 14 August; *FBIS*, 18 August).

The obvious contentment with the existing party organization corresponds to another important feature of the present policy of the Burmese Communists: the endeavor for alliances with minority insurgent groups. Such alliances have been made often in the BCP's history (e.g., in 1948-50 with the People's Volunteer Organization and the Karens, or between 1959 and 1963 with the Karen National Union and others as the "National Democratic United Front"). However, these were never very effective. It could be different with the treaties concluded in 1975-76, and officially announced in early 1977, with the Shan State People's Liberation Army and the Shan State Progressive Party (both, VPB, 30 January; *FBIS*, 1 February) and with the Kachin Independence Organization (KIO) (VPB, 21 January; *FBIS*, 26 January). Of those three, the KIO can be regarded as the strongest group and was the only one treated on equal terms, which also led to an agreement "written in both the Kachin and Burmese languages." The others had to recognize the leadership of the BCP, which the BCP internally assumes also in its relations with the Kachins. The Burmese government claimed that the following directives were issued by the BCP to its forces in dealing with the KIA (Kachin Independence Army):

(1) The alliance with the KIA is temporary; therefore, sufficient arms and ammunition must not be given to start a revolt.

(2) Divide the leadership and smaller ranks within the KIA and maintain control over it.

(3) The KIA previously trusted and relied on the agrarian forces and, therefore, it cannot be totally trusted.

(4) Indoctrinate the KIA, which is brainwashed with religion (*Loktha Pyeithu Nezin*, 31 May; *FBIS*, 9 June).

The future will show if the BCP this time will be more successful in its strategy of establishing leadership over minority insurgent groups.

Domestic Activities. The main form of the BCP's underground activity against the Rangoon government continues to be armed struggle (see below). In this regard the Burmese Communists not only present themselves as true followers of Mao Tse-tung—"the seizure of power by armed forces, the settlement of the issue by war, is the central task and the highest form of revolution" (VPB, 28 March; *FBIS*, 1 April)—but also as the true and only heirs of the anti-Japanese and anti-British resistance movement which liberated Burma from colonialism in 1948. According to the Communists, the present government has betrayed "the spirit and goals of this revolution:

> The Ne Win-San Yu military government as well as its main "pillar"—the mercenary army—are destroying the prestige and tradition of the anti-Japanese revolution. They are stumbling blocks to the goals and ardent desires of the people evisaged during the anti-Japanese revolution. They represent obstacles on the path of the people's militant march. Undeniable facts and their own actions clearly prove that they are counterrevolutionaries. (VPB, 27 March; *FBIS*, 31 March.)

From this feigned connection with Burma's founding ideology and from their claim to be the only representatives of the peasants and workers, the BCP derives its right to criticize present conditions in Burma. Mostly its criticism is aimed at the bad economic situation, from which it often passes on to other points:

> The decline in industrial and agricultural production, the setbacks in and destruction of transportation, the scarcity of consumer goods, soaring prices of commodities and degeneration of the education, health and social sectors are proof for the whole world to see. Due to economic hardships throughout the country; difficulties in finding food, clothing and shelter; setbacks in and deterioration of health, education and social sectors; lack of democratic rights; oppression and exploitation; people have found the military government increasingly repugnant and have risen and struggled against the Ne Win-San Yu military government. It brutally crushed the uprisings and struggles of workers, students and other laboring masses in 1974, 1975 and 1976. However, the basic conditions causing the uprisings and struggles have not yet been alleviated; they have become worse. (VPB, 7 April; *FBIS*, 11 April)

The BCP stresses that the government's "plans in the agricultural, industrial, and trade sectors have been failure," and that "every time it fails, the military government changes its tactics," so that "the country has become poorer day by day and is listed among the world's poorest nations" (VPB, 12 May; *FBIS*, 17 May).

The BCP elaborated on special economic problems such as: housing for workers (VPB, 16 January; *FBIS*, 4 February); soaring prices of consumer goods, and the government's constant wavering between controlling and decontrolling foodstuffs and other items (VPB, 12 May; *FBIS*, 18 May); allegedly growing unemployment and "how the military government's labor exchange offices are exploiting the unemployed" (VPB, 15 May; *FBIS*, 14 June). The BCP also attacked the education system—up to now generally regarded as one of the few real successes of the Ne Win government—as being ineffective and favoring the "children of the members of the military clique" (VPB, 27 March; *FBIS*, 22 April), and notes rising crime rates (VPB, 10 February; *FBIS*, 17 February). The BCP's radio propaganda paints a very gloomy picture of today's Burma.

The main aim of this propaganda is to present the Ne Win government as a "self-seeking, exploitive, and privileged class which is suppressing and destroying the democratic cause and impoverishing the people" (VPB, 27 March; *FBIS*, 31 March). The "Pyithu Hluttaw," the parliament created by the new constitution of 1974, is termed "puppet assembly" or "showcase assembly," and the election of delegates to the recent congress of the ruling Burma Socialist Programme Party is described as prearranged:

> In order to insure that only those handpicked by the leaders of the military clique were elected, conciliation, blackmail threats, [and] repeated elections to get the desired results . . . were used in various regions. These tactics were so widespread that they cannot be recounted in detail.
>
> Some sham democratic procedures had been practiced before . . . . But this time the leaders of the military clique did not trust their own mercenary troops, which they had nurtured, and they did not even bother with such pretences.

> At the third congress of the military party only the top brass of the mercenary army were asked to be delegates. In some regiments, every time elections were held only NCOs and junior NCOs were elected, but fresh elections were held every time for various excuses. (VPB, 3 April; *FBIS*, 5 April)

The BCP's statements about the Rangoon government present a mixture of facts, exaggerations, and falsifications in which the Burmese listener more often than not may be unable to distinguish one from another. With this policy the BCP can renege on presenting a program of its own. Being "the sole proletarian party in Burma" and "a genuine Marxist-Leninist party that is exercising Marxism-Leninism and Mao Tse-tung Thought as its basic and guiding ideology" (VPB, 30 January; *FBIS*, 1 February) is regarded as sufficient. Thus, even one of the rare definitions of the BCP's understanding of "people's democracy" centers on the negation of present conditions:

> What is people's democracy? It is opposition to imperialism, feudalism-landlordism and bureaucratic capitalism under the leadership of the working class, based on the worker-peasant alliance and participated in by workers, peasants, petty bourgeoisie, patriotic capitalists, democratic people and the oppressed people of all nationalities. This democratic power of the people will totally eradicate the reactionaries who are protecting imperialism, feudalism-landlordism and bureaucratic capitalism. (VPB, 3 April; *FBIS*, 5 April)

Since 1948 the BCP has been in the position of an opposition party without any chance to become the ruling party. Moreover, the only necessity for it has been to fight. The absence of an even slightly evolved program is a consequence of this continued fight.

Armed Struggle. The armed struggle was continued in 1977 as before. It was centered in the northern and eastern Shan State and the Kachin State northeast of Myitkyina. The BCP's broadcasts throughout the year reported successes of guerrilla activities, especially in the Kengtung District (areas of Kengtung, Mong Yawng and Mong Yang) and Lashio District (areas of Hsipaw, Namhsan, Namtu, Kutkai, and Namhkam). From 1 January to 31 December 1976 the BCP claimed "479 small and large-scale engagements," in which "2,016 enemies were incapacitated," of whom 888 died, 1,008 were wounded, 104 were taken prisoner, and an uncertain (16?) defected to the People's Army side (VPB, 2 January; *FBIS*, 4 January). For 1977 no total figures have been published yet; however, the figures given for the first half indicate that the BCP has stepped up its activities considerably.

> During the first half of 1977, according to incomplete reports, more than 447 small-and large-scale battles were fought in some areas of the Shan and Kachin States, in which more than 2,200 enemy were crushed. More than 250 assorted weapons and more than 50,000 rounds of assorted ammunition were captured from the enemy including artillery, mortar, bazooka and assorted shells. (VPB, 14 August; *FBIS*, 18 August.)

The other side of the coin is given by the government, as follows:

> From February to June this year the Tatmadaw [Burmese army] fought and destroyed the CPB insurgents in 93 skirmishes including 42 major battles. The enemy lost over 500 men including 275 bodies which were captured by the troops. The Tatmadaw also captured two insurgents alive and a large amount of arms and ammunition. Altogether 130 Tatmadaw men gave their lives for the country and 142 received injuries. (*The Guardian*, Rangoon, 12 July)

More than in previous years the Burmese Communists tried to infiltrate into the central Shan State. The regions south of Lashio and around Mongtung were mentioned several times in BCP reports, e.g.:

> The people's armed forces in central Shan State fought 24 battles against the enemy from 1 January to 31 December 1976. The enemy suffered 38 dead and 20 wounded, and 5 were captured. A total of 63 enemy were thus annihilated. (VPB, 12 May; *FBIS*, 13 May)

The effectiveness of the guerrilla attacks in the central Shan State seems to have increased in 1977, as the BCP claimed to have put out of action 132 men in only seven attacks between February and April (VPB, 5 June; *FBIS*, 8 June). This includes the battle around Momeik, where, according to government sources, on "April 11 CPB rebels with a force of about 300 surrounded and attacked the forward camp of 12th Battalion, Burma Regiment," entered Momeik, and "destroyed the Trade godown, Co-operative godown and the treasury." On the government side four officers and fifteen soldiers were killed as against fifty-two Communists. (*The Guardian*, 15 April).

The government confirmed the close alliance to the Communists and the Shan rebels by reporting a clash "with about 200 CPB-led Shan rebels" in Mong Hsu township and describing the "Shan insurgents" as "members of the group which had gone for training with the CPB at Pang Hsang," a spot near the Namhka River at the border with China (ibid., 6 January).

Successes of Kachin insurgents or of combined actions were never reported in the combat news broadcasts of the Communists, in spite of the alliance mentioned above and a high degree of Communist guerrilla activity in the Kachin State. Probably because of this fact the Communists could boast of comparatively fewer battles there.

> During the first half of 1977, from 1 January to 30 June, the people and people's army in (Songlin) and Lauhkaung—east and northeast of Myitkyina—attacked and crushed the enemy. There were 16 small and large-scale battles in which 55 enemy soldiers, including a mercenary officer, died; 33 others, including a military column commander, were wounded; and 17 were taken prisoners—a total of 105 enemy soldiers put out of action. (VPB, 29 July; *FBIS*, 11 August)

Even without exact information on the activities of the Kachin Independence Army it seems, however, the rumors that "Burma's Kachin State has been taken over by the rebels" (*Far Eastern Economic Review*, Hong Kong, 9 September) are incorrect. The KIA, partly rightist, partly allied to the Communists, probably dominates or even controls vast parts of the mountainous forests and jungles, but not any economically important territory. This situation has prevailed for many years without major changes.

The BCP repeated, as in previous years, its effort to get larger parts of Kengtung District under its direct control as this would not only improve their provisions base but also the connection to Laos and Thailand. Entering Mong Pu region southeast of Kentung in February, they were repulsed. This evidently resulted in a change of strategy, as in March, May, and June columns of 500 to 800 BCP troops crossed the Salween and proceeded up to 25 miles west of Ke-hsi (*The Guardian*, 12 July). Whether the BCP troops were driven back over the Salween is not known, but it does not seem very likely that they were.

The situation in the northeastern part of the Shan State obviously deteriorated for the government troops during 1977. The BCP made all-out efforts to expand its territory and to tighten its grip on areas already dominated. "A force of more than 1,500 men made up of two BCP brigades and six regiments, backed up by supporting weapons, infiltrated into Ho-pang" and other government outposts in the Northern Wa State. According to the government, "the BCP's plan to occupy Ho-pang failed," and in "25 major battles—including 10 hand-to-hand fights" from 3 to 27 October a total of more than 500 dead . . . . Thirteen officers and 113 soldiers from the armed forces gave their lives for the country, while 237 of them were wounded. Thirty-nine are missing. A Vampire plane from the air force crashed and was lost" (Burma Broadcasting Service, 1 November; *FBIS*, 2 November).

With a "total of 552 enemy mercenaries . . . put out of action" (among them 24 taken prisoner and more than 130 killed), the BCP reported slightly higher figures on the government losses (VPB, 4 November; *FBIS,* 8 November).

The deteriorating situation in the frontier areas, the high losses (for the BCP is, although by far the strongest, only one among several insurgent groups in Burma), and the dwindling readiness of youths to risk their lives for some army privileges evidently have prompted the government to announce the early introduction of compulsory military service (*The Guardian,* 29 May).

International Views and Contacts. Firmly aligned with the People's Republic of China, the BCP praised the Chinese leaders in greetings on several anniversaries during 1977. Also the "successful conclusion of the third plenary session of the Tenth Central Committee" of the Chinese Communist Party (CCP) was greeted "with boundless joy." The appointment of Hua Kuo-feng ("good student and successor of Chairman Mao and good leader and supreme commander") as chairman, the reinstallation of Teng Hsiao-p'ing, and the resolution against the Gang of Four were celebrated as "a very heavy blow to imperialism, revisionism and all reaction and a great encouragement to the revolutionary forces in the world and the further development of the world revolution" (NCNA, Peking, in English, 27 July; *FBIS,* 28 July). In all these cases the BCP showed an absolute submission to the Chinese position, such as could not be remarked (or not to this extent) before Thakin Ba Thein Tin became its chairman.

The main problem of Sino-Burmese relations continued to be the existence side-by-side of full diplomatic relations between the governments and full recognition of the BCP by the CCP. At about the same time as President Ne Win had "a cordial and friendly talk" with the Chinese ambassador, Ba Thein Tin "paid respects to the remains of Chairman Mao Tse-tung" (NCNA, 10 September; *FBIS,* 12 September). And in the report on China's National Day reception on 30 September, Ba Thein Tin was mentioned second, preceded only by Pol Pot from Kampuchea, among the "distinguished guests at the main table" (NCNA, 30 September; *FBIS,* 3 October). This event took place just ten days after Ne Win, on his way to North Korea, had concluded a friendly visit—the second in 1977!—to the PRC.

The extent of the support the BCP receives from China is not known. A Thai correspondent's report that "700 soldiers of a cavalry unit of the People's Republic of China" attacked army bases far inside Burma (Siang Puangchon, Bangkok, 7 March; *FBIS,* 8 March) can be regarded as a distortion, if not a falsification, of news. Nevertheless, the BCP reacted in an unusually sensitive way to Ne Win's first China visit, in April, by calling perhaps with the aim to warn the Chinese leaders against him—New Win "the man who shows his colors to the imperialists as the staunchest anti-communist in Asia," and saying that the visit was "designed only to hoodwink the Burmese people and the world, to gain political profit, seek temporary relief from the crises, accelerate the brutal oppression of the people and increase their reliance on imperialists . . . while pretending to be friendly with China (VPB, 8 May; *FBIS,* 12 May). As a close understanding between China and Burma could deprive the BCP of its most important base and resource, the suspicion that it is now heavily dealing in opium "to gain some independence of Peking" (*FEER,* 15 April, p. 28) makes sense, because arms and ammunition surely cannot only be procured from the enemy as the BCP pretends (VPB, 12 June; *FBIS,* 16 June).

Aside from the CCP, the BCP apparently has no real relations with other Communist parties. Following the general Chinese line, the BCP attacked the "Soviet social-imperialists" for their fleet's "infiltration into Southeast Asian waters . . . not for economic profit but for carrying out [their] evil design of world hegemony" (VPB, 12 July; *FBIS,* 15 July).

Publications. The only first-hand information on the BCP comes from the broadcasts of its clandestine radio station, the "Voice of the People of Burma," inaugurated on 28 March 1971 and supposedly located in southwest Yunnan Province in China.

Köln-Weiss   Klaus Fleischmann
Federal Republic of Germany

Cambodia

Communist organizations have existed in Cambodia since before World War II. They have always been secretive, conspiratorial, and highly sensitive about their links with foreign organizations, notably the Indochinese Communist Party. The most obvious reason for concealing such foreign links is that most Cambodians are taught from birth to fear and detest the Vietnamese as national enemies. Mutual racial hostility has not been altered by any of the events of the 1970s.

On 27 September 1977, Premier Pol Pot acknowledged the KCP's existence for the first time. Pol Pot's September 1977 speech contains what amounts to an official history or legend of the KCP. Since all of the purported facts are self-serving, none can be taken at face value, except by the party faithful. Yet the speech repays careful analysis. Compared with earlier statements, such as his long interview with Vietnam News Agency in July 1976 (see *YICA, 1977*), Pol Pot's speech reveals much about how the KCP leadership views itself, Cambodia, and the world beyond.

Pol Pot's September 1977 speech lasted five hours and was divided into three parts: (1) a summary of Cambodian history "from slavery" until 1960; (2) events from the KCP's alleged founding date, 30 September 1960, to the Communist victory in 1975; and (3) the "new era of the Cambodian revolution." Pol Pot described a number of activities which he and other Khmer Communists carried out in Cambodia during the 1950s. He noted the poor showing of Communist candidates in Cambodian elections of 1955 and 1958, and he alleged massive persecution of Communists by the Khmer regime of that period, which he said was dominated by U.S. imperialism. During Pol Pot's subsequent visit to Pyongyang, in October 1977, Khmer ambassador to North Korea, Sim Son, gave the date of the founding of the Communist movement in Cambodia as 1951. These statements seem to indicate that the present Cambodian leaders distinguish, at least implicitly, between their Vietnamese-dominated organization of the 1950s and a more nationally-based Communist organization that they formed sometime in the 1960s. In his speech, Pol Pot also dismissed all other Khmer political parties formed since World War II as tools of western imperialism.

"Democratic Kampuchea" remained nearly isolated from foreign contacts during 1977 while its leaders pursued their quest for national self-sufficiency through brutal regimentation of the people. The year began with reports that all surviving members of Lon Nol's army had been ordered executed. For the rest of the people, however, available data suggest that living conditions became slightly less intolerable during the year. The hand-built hydraulic system which will eventually cover the entire country, was said to be partly complete. Food production began to approach prewar levels. While some rice was exported, the very meager domestic food ration was also increased, and the government spent some of its Chinese aid funds to buy pharmaceuticals. Traditional medicines were produced in Cambodia, and the sixteen-hour work day was shortened. These changes seemed to reflect no basic change of policy but only a more orderly approach to the KCP's basic goal of social reconstruction—a revolutionary realization that healthy people can work harder than people racked by dysentery, malaria, and malnutrition.

Leadership and Organization. The KCP is run by a Central Committee which acts as the collective leadership of Cambodia. Although its membership is secret, press speculation has focused on a few individuals long active in Cambodian left-wing political circles. Saloth Sar has been variously described as chairman, secretary general, and secretary of the KCP. Pol Pot, who was named premier in April 1976, is probably a pseudonym for Saloth Sar. Pol Pot reappeared in September 1977, after a year's "sick leave," to deliver the speech discussed above. Khieu Samphan, Ieng Sary, and Son Sen—who were named deputy premiers in August 1975—are believed to be members of the KCP Central Committee and dominant political personalities in Phnom Penh. All are in their forties. Since 17 April 1975, Khieu Samphan has played a prominent but not preeminent role in the very limited public activity of the new regime. In the April 1976 reshuffle, he was named head of the Presidium, replacing Prince Sihanouk as chief-of-state. An internal purge of KCP officials evidently took place in the Northern region (Siem Reap and Oudar Mean Chey) and perhaps in other parts of the country. But apart from the disappearance of the information minister, Hu Nim, there were no known major changes in the inner ruling circle.

National Political Leadership.

State Presidium

Chairman	Khieu Samphan
First deputy chairman	So Phim
Second deputy chairman	Nhim Ros

Cambodian People's Representative Assembly, Standing Committee

Chairman	Nuon Chea
First deputy chairman	Nguon Kang
Second deputy chairman	Peou Sou

Members, Ros Nim, Sor Sean, Mey Chham, Kheng Sok, Mat Ly, Thang Si, and Ros Preap

Government of Democratic Cambodia

Premier	Pol Pot
Deputy premier, foreign affairs	Ieng Sary
Deputy premier, national defense	Son Sen
Deputy premier, economy	Vorn Vet
Minister, information and propaganda	Hu Nim
Minister, public health	Thiounn Thioeunn
Minister, social affairs	Khieu Thirith (Mrs. Ieng Sary)
Minister, public works	Toch Phoeun
Minister, culture, education and learning	Yun Yat (Mrs. Son Sen)

Auxiliary and Mass Organizations. During the 1970-75 war, refugee reports indicated that the usual range of mass organizations (e.g., for peasants, women, students, and Buddhist monks) was created by the KCP to aid in the reconstruction of Cambodian society. This was the central nonmilitary goal of the KCP during the war and has been its main concern since military victory. It is not known how important a role mass organizations have actually played in the process of reconstruction. Many refugees have reported that virtually their only contact with the new regime was with gun-wielding guerrillas and anonymous cadres, who lectured them on political subjects or on practical matters such as farming.

International Views and Policies. Avoiding economic dependence on foreign powers—and particularly any form of domination by Vietnam—seems to be the main foreign policy goal of the new Khmer regime. In 1975 they established close relations with China—Pol Pot visited the PRC for the 1 October celebrations in 1977—and correct relations with Thailand, the latter improving during the year after bilateral talks in Vientiane. Still, the Khmers continued to provoke frequent border clashes with all three of their neighbors, apparently reflecting incompetence on the part of KCP leaders rather than coherent foreign policy objectives. In an unusual bow toward Moscow, Khieu Samphan sent greetings to the Soviet Union on the sixtieth anniversary of the CPSU and the Soviet press was quick to publish a message of congratulations to the KCP leaders on "the occasion of the official announcement of their party's existence." Ieng Sary attended the 1977 session of the United Nations General Assembly and visited several Southeast Asian capitals. In mid-1976 Cambodia began to improve or expand relations with a number of non-Communist countries, having meanwhile allowed several pro-Peking Communist countries to set up embassies in Phnom Penh, though under extremely tight restrictions. With the non-Communist countries, including Japan, Great Britain, and most ASEAN states, they issued joint communiqués expressing their intention to establish relations at the ambassadorial level on the basis of the five principles of peaceful coexistence. Some non-Communist ambassadors accredited in Peking have flown to Phnom Penh for this ceremony. France condemned human rights violations in Cambodia at the 1977 UN General Assembly and Great Britain has cited human rights violations as its reason for refusing to accredit an ambassador to Cambodia. There were virtually no contacts with the United States.

Publications. Radio broadcasts, by the two relatively weak transmitters of Radio Phnom Penh, are almost the only means the KCP has of communicating news and commentary on internal developments to the outside world—and indeed to the Khmer people, though batteries for transistor radios are probably in very short supply in Cambodia. No printed publications are known to circulate in the country.

Old Dominion University   Peter A. Poole
Norfolk, Virginia

China

The First Congress of the Chinese Communist Party (Chung-kuo kung-ch'an tang; CCP) was held in Shanghai in July 1921. The eleventh and latest congress met in Peking on 12-18 August 1977. As the only legal party, the CCP provides "absolute leadership" for all other organizations in China (Eleventh Party Constitution, II, 14).

The CCP is the largest Communist party in the world. During the Eleventh Party Congress, in August 1977, the CCP claimed "more than thirty-five million" members (*Peking Review,* 26 August, p. 6), a considerable increase from the twenty-eight million reported in August 1973 and the thirty million in October 1976.

The population of the People's Republic of China (PRC) is still a matter of speculation and debate. Chinese sources refer to "more than 800 million," but reportedly in 1977 Chinese officials confided to visiting Western delegations that the figure used for planning purposes is 950 million (official informants at the U.S. Consulate-General, Hong Kong, 17 October).

The Eleventh Party Congress was attended by 1,510 delegates elected by party organizations throughout the country. (See below, "Domestic Party Affairs.") Delegates from among the workers, peasants, soldiers, "and other working people" constituted 72.4 percent, revolutionary intellectuals 6.7 percent, and revolutionary cadres 20.9 percent of the total; women constituted 19.0 percent, minority nationalities 9.3 percent, and middle-aged and young members 73.8 percent (*Peking Review,* 26 August, p. 7).

Organization and Leadership. According to the party constitution, the "highest leading body" of the CCP is the Party National Congress, convened every five years. Under "special circumstances" the party congress may be convened early or postponed, and each congress to date has been called under such circumstances. The congress elects the Central Committee, which leads when the congress is not in session and which elects the committee's Political Bureau (Politburo), the Standing Committee of the Politburo, and the chairman and the vice-chairman of the Central Committee. The Politburo and its Standing Committee exercise the functions and powers of the Central Committee when the latter is not in plenary session.

The Eleventh Congress elected the Eleventh Central Committee, with 201 full members and 132 alternates. (The 1973 committee originally had 195 full members and 124 alternates, and the 1969 committee, 170 and 109.)

On 19 August the Eleventh Central Committee elected its chairman, vice-chairmen, and the members and alternate members of the Politburo as follows.

Chairman:	Hua Kuo-feng
Vice-chairmen:	Yeh Chien-ying, Teng Hsiao-ping
	Li Hsien-nien, Wang Tun-hsing
	(These five comprise the Standing Committee of the Politburo.)

Members of the Politburo (22), in the order of the number
of strokes in their surnames:

Wei Kuo-ching	Wu Teh
Ulanfu	Yu Chiu-li
Fang Yi	Wang Tung-hsing
Teng Hsiao-ping	Chang Ting-fa
Yeh Chien-ying	Chen Yung-kuei
Liu Po-cheng	Chen Hsi-lien
Hsu Shih-yu	Keng Piao
Chi Teng-kuei	Nieh Jung-chen
Su Chen-hua	Ni Chih-fu
Li Hsien-nien	Hsu Hsiang-chien
Li Teh-sheng	Peng Chung

Alternate Members of the Politburo (3), similarly listed:
    Chen Mu-hua
    Chao Tzu-yang
    Saifudin

(Source: *Peking Review,* 26 August)

The Eleventh Central Committee, compared with the Tenth Central Committee, which it displaced, has a much different character. It is dominated by much older, experienced cadres, many of whom (76) had been purged in the Cultural Revolution, and many others of whom had been at least criticized at that time. Seventy-one new people (35 percent of the total) were added to the Central Committee's list of full members, while 110 were carried over from the previous committee and 20 were promoted from alternate status. Of the Tenth Central Committee, 59 full members were dropped, though not all are completely disgraced, while 16 full members and one alternate had died. Of the alternates, only 52 were carried over, while 80 were new appointees (5 of these had been demoted from previous full membership). According to Jurgen Domes (using information available on 163 of the 201 full members), the average age is sixty-three years. Apparently only 10 percent of the full members are under sixty, as against more than 20 percent in the Tenth Committee, and only 8 are under the age of fifty (lecture talk at the Universities Service Centre, Hong Kong, 6 October).

Greater prominence is now given to the provincial leaders, who for the past decade had been under attack by the ousted radicals. The first secretaries of all twenty-nine of China's provinces, autonomous regions, and municipalities are full members. Seven provinces and autonomous regions not previously represented, now are. There has been a great changeover in the military representation, especially among political commissars, but the overall military presence remains strong, and it has been reinforced in the Politburo.

Among those who have received full membership are also the ministers of metallurgy, oil, and finance; the president of the Academy of Military Science, the heads of the air force and navy, the chief commissar of the railway bureau of the People's Liberation Army (PLA); and the president of the Supreme Court. The radical leadership has allegedly been removed from the Central Committee. Activists from the trade unions, youth league, and women's federations, and from the fields of education and culture were ejected. The former ministers of sport, culture, health, and public security have disappeared, presumably because of association with the Gang of Four.

Both the Eleventh Central Committee and the new Politburo have only a few people with experience in foreign affairs. Those with experience include Hua Kuo-feng, Teng Hsiao-ping, Li Hsien-nien, Fang Yi, and Keng Piao in the Politburo, and Huang Hua, Huang Chen, Li Chiang and

Yao Yi-lin in the Central Committee (see David Bonavia, *Far Eastern Economic Review* [*FEER*], Hong Kong, 9 September, p. 16).

Below the Central Committee extends a network of party committees at the provincial, special district, county and municipal levels. A similar network exists within the PLA, from the level of the military region down to that of the regiment. According to the party constitution, primary party organizations or party branches are located in factories, mines, and other enterprises, and people's communes, offices, schools, shops, neighborhoods, PLA companies, and elsewhere as required.

Throughout 1977 many expected the Fifth National People's Congress (NPC) to be held before the end of the year, and it appeared to be forthcoming sometime soon after the party congress in August. In late October, however, at the plenum of the Fourth NPC's Standing Committee, Hua Kuo-feng announced that the Fifth NPC would not be convened until the spring of 1978, and indicated that it would be preceded by further purges. Protracted delays in the holding of NPCs have been the rule in China. The Fourth NPC had been held ten years after the previous one, in January 1975. A new one would not be due for two more years; nevertheless, the purge of the Gang of Four and their supporters had created many vacancies in government posts. The Fourth NPC had cleared the air in a number of respects, and conferred, if only briefly, a new aura of legitimacy in the Chinese government after years of uncertainty and post vacancies in the wake of the Cultural Revolution; but by 1977 another NPC was clearly needed.

According to the 1975 PRC constitution, the powers of the NPC (see *YICA, 1977,* p. 266) are exercised contingent upon recommendation by the party's Central Committee (for names of NPC Standing Committees, see ibid., p. 267).

The State Council, according to the 1975 PRC constitution, formulates administrative measures and issues decrees and orders, exercises leadership over ministries and commissions and local state organs, drafts and implements the national economic plan and the state budget, and directs state administrative affairs. It is also to exercise such other functions and powers as are vested in it by the NPC or its Standing Committee. As premier, party chairman Hua Kuo-feng heads the State Council. There are eleven vice-premiers (see ibid., p. 268, for names; Teng Hsiao-ping, purged as vice-premier in 1976, was reinstated in July 1977), and twenty-nine ministries or commissions, and five offices—the General Office, the Staff Office, the Political Work group, and those in charge of Environment Protection and Work Concerning Educated Young People. Finally, there are twenty special agencies of the State Council, ranging from the Bank of China to the Written Chinese Language Reform Committee.

The president of the Supreme People's Court is Chiang Hua.

The 1975 PRC constitution is much shorter than the one adopted in 1954, having only 30 articles (previously 106). It redefines the PRC as a "socialist state of the dictatorship of the proletariat" rather than as "a people's democratic state." The Fifth NPC is expected to adopt a new constitution, particularly since the Gang of Four had a large role in drafting the present one.

The 1975 constitution states (I, 15) that the PLA and the people's militia are "the workers' and peasants' own armed forces led by the Communist Party of China." It gives command of the armed forces to the chairman of the CCP Central Committee (then Mao, now Hua), in contrast to the 1954 constitution, which invested command in the chairman of the PRC, a post eliminated in 1975.

The PLA for many months after the Great Proletarian Cultural Revolution was prominent on the newly established revolutionary committees. Following the Lin Piao incident of 1971, the party reasserted its dominance; and by the fall of 1976 more than 200 transfers of military leaders had taken place, perhaps as part of an effort to weaken old alliances and to make the PLA more responsive to civilian party control. Party dominance, particularly under the influence of Maoist or radical priorities, resulted in greatly reduced investment in conventional arms and equipment. Defense spending in 1972-74 dropped about 25 percent lower than the peak period of 1970-71. This reduced attention to military needs continued with few exceptions into 1976. Most of China's military equipment is ten to twenty years out of date, although the nuclear and missile program continues to develop. On 12 September 1977 China disclosed that it had tested guided missiles with nuclear warheads. On 16 September its twenty-second nuclear explosion (since the first test in 1964) was successfully detonated (Reuter, Peking, 12, 16 September).

Toward the end of 1976 and as 1977 wore along, the military became much more influential. The PLA participated in the campaign against supporters of the Gang of Four and took over civilian-type responsibilities at Chengchow in order to keep the trains running. Since 1976 the military has increased by a half-million to a total of 3.95 million, according to the Institute of Strategic Studies, *Military Balance 1977.* Of this number, 400,000 are air force and 300,000 are navy personnel. The watchword is modernization, and perhaps an overall reduction in size (Drew Middleton, *NYT,* 6 April). Modernization will be a lengthy process, because the needs are many and the means for supplying them are limited. The country's large industry base must first be expanded before tanks and other heavy equipment can be supplied in large quantities. Meanwhile, there is a greater stress on sharpening military skill and a deemphasizing of political study. A campaign was launched in February to learn from the "hard-bone Sixth Company," a model army unit which "adheres to rigid requirements in training and is always in combat readiness" and which did not listen to "the stuff peddled by" the Gang of Four (AP, Tokyo, 26 February). The Chinese also shopped abroad for arms in 1977. A large military delegation visited France in September, and visiting retired Japanese defense planners were told in Peking on 7 October that China would purchase new weapons and introduce new technology from other countries (*Hong Kong Standard,* 8 October). Drew Middleton said in June that modernizing China's military forces and training them to use new weapons would take at least ten years (*NYT,* 24 June).

The PRC armed militia numbers about five million men and women; the "backbone militia" has about twenty million loyal party members and "positive elements," including PLA veterans; the "ordinary militia," a national force of about seventy-five million, comprises mostly younger able-bodied peasants and urban workers. Although the urban militia was supposedly becoming a base for the radicals, it failed to act to forestall the downfall of the Gang of Four in October 1976.

Mass organizations experienced an overhaul of leadership in 1976-77, and they now have less say in the top levels of decision making. Regarded as a principal support for the radical faction of the Politburo, they too failed to provide support to the radicals when the need arrived. These organizations particularly were weakened by the changes in the Central Committee in August (see below).

Domestic Party Affairs. For new party chairman Hua Kuo-feng, 1977 was a year of political consolidation. It was also characterized by continuing change in policies as a result of a succession of conferences, which probably will continue into 1978. The expectation of a more pragmatic stance of the new leadership—by and large a revivified gerontocracy—was largely borne out by events. Many observers noted a more relaxed climate, although the freer expression of ideas is tempered by an appeal to order, discipline, and production. The Gang of Four, who had appeared to be puristically Communist and closely identified with Mao's radical notions, were condemned as counterrevolutionaries. The new leadership claims the mantle of Mao, though it appears that many of the policies and practices long advocated by Mao are being rejected or greatly modified.

The year's events actually began in late 1976, with the Second National Tachai Conference on 10-27 December, attended by some 5,000 delegates. Of special interest was the circulation among the delegates of Mao's talk of 25 April 1956, "On the Ten Major Relationships." This essay, not previously made public officially, was published with great fanfare on Mao's birthday, 26 December. Politburo member Chen Yung-kuei and Hua Kuo-feng gave major speeches in which Chen sharply criticized the Gang of Four and advocated the extension of Tachai-like counties throughout the country, and Hua reviewed the crucial events of 1976 and put forward the "fighting tasks" for 1977. Hua said that the current internal and international situation was excellent and added, "It is our belief that 1977 will be a year in which we shall smash the Gang of Four completely and move towards great order . . . (*People's Daily,* 26 December).

The New Year's Day joint editorial of the *People's Daily, Red Flag,* and *Liberation Army Daily* continued the hopeful theme:

> We are certainly able to create a completely new situation in which there are political liveliness and economic prosperity, and in which a hundred schools of thought contend and a hundred flowers blossom in science and culture, and the people's livelihood steadily improves on the basis of the development of production. We will certainly be able to achieve the magnificent goal of accomplishing the comprehensive modernization of agriculture, industry, national defense, and science and technology and build China into a powerful socialist country before the end of the century. (*Peking Review,* 1 January 1977, p. 47)

There had been considerable strife in China during 1976, and many news reports in January 1977 spoke of serious fighting, which, in addition to the natural disasters of the year (it was reported in January that 655,237 people died and 739,000 were injured in the July 1976 quake, making it the second-worst quake toll in history—AP, Hong Kong, 5 January), further disrupted industrial production and rail transportation. Violence reportedly peaked in the city of Paoting, 100 miles south of Peking, in April 1976, when soldiers were sent in to quell factory sabotage, looting, bank robberies, murders, and rape (*NYT,* 4 January), and then flared again in late December and early January. Unrest in Fukien, Hupeh, Yunnan, Szechuan, and elsewhere continued into 1977. There were reports of wall posters opposing Hua Kuo-feng in Sian, Shensi, and Tsinan, Shantung (*FBIS,* 11 January, from a Taipei source, 6 January). A number of executions—some for political crimes relating to the Gang of Four—were reported in Yunnan, Wuhan, Shanghai, Hangchow, Anyang, and elsewhere (e.g., *FBIS,* 21 January, from Taipei's CNA, 20 January, 25 March, citing *Agence France Presse* and Reuters; ibid., 2 March, from AFP, Peking, 1 March; ibid., 14 March, from AFP, Peking, 12 March; Peter Weintraub, *FEER,* 19 August, p. 8). On 30 October the London *Sunday Telegraph* reported a wave of executions during the purge of followers of the Gang of Four, which "must be well into the thousands." In later November it was learned that Ross Munro, correspondent for the *Toronto Globe and Mail,* would be denied an extension of his visa, presumably because of his articles on human rights in China.

The first anniversary of the death of Chou En-lai, 8 January, was commemorated by thousands of tearful Chinese who marched into Tien An Men in Peking. The event became also a demonstration in support of Teng Hsiao-ping; many posters demanded that he be reinstated in his posts, from which he had been removed in April 1976. Although the twice-purged Teng may have been secretly given office or assignments early in 1977, it was not until late summer that the public was informed that he had been restored to his previous offices (see below).

There were some indications of a thaw on the cultural scene. The *People's Daily* criticized official newspapers for being "stereotyped, noxious, long-winded and monotonous" but blamed this on the Gang of Four. The paper pledged that great efforts would be made to "improve the style of writing and editing and produce short, good stories" (see Fox Butterfield, *NYT,* 31 January). A number of films and plays that had been banned by Chiang Ching were revived, and some well-known singers and musicians whom she disliked reappeared (ibid., 22 January). Reports circulated in Hong Kong about a new underground literature in China, taking the form mostly of manuscripts of novels and other writings, implicitly or even explicitly critical of various aspects of life or the system, which were passed from hand to hand (see, e.g., *Time,* 19 September). In November Mao Tun called for new literary works to be produced. Meanwhile, works from the time of the May Fourth Movement (just before the 1920s) were scheduled to reappear; Pa Chin's early novel *Home* was to be among the first of these. Lao She (Shu Ching-chun), the famous novelist (*Rickshaw Boy*) who committed suicide during the GPCR, was posthumously rehabilitated.

In December 1976 some 1,800 delegates attended a preparatory meeting in Peking for national conferences on "learning from Taching" in industry, in crude oil enterprises, and in the chemical industry and oil refining enterprises. A light-industry learn-from-Taching conference convened in Peking on 11 January 1977. The major national conference convened at Taching on 20 April with 7,000 delegates in attendance; on 27 April it moved to Peking, where it was completed on 13 May. Key speeches were given by Hua Kuo-feng, Yeh Chien-ying, and Yu Chiu-li. The latter's speech of 4 May stated that the six major regional administrations, twice-earlier utilized and abandoned, would play a role once again, this time in conjunction with the "grand plan of the two-stage development" (*Peking Review*, 27 May, p. 17). Earlier, 3,000 delegates attended a national conference of the coal industry on learning from Taching, and also "catching up with Kailuan" (NCNA, 23 January). In July a national geological conference on learning from Taching was held in Peking, and also a national foreign trade conference to exchange experiences in learning from both Taching and Tachai.

Given the great difficulties that were being experienced on the country's rail system, it was no surprise that a national conference on railroad work took place in Peking (*FBIS*, 22 February). It was acknowledged that "railway transportation has now become a strikingly weak link in the national economy." To resolve the problem, railway workers were to be turned into "a semi-militarized production army" (ibid., 22 February). The important Chengchow Railway Bureau was placed under military control in January, and a veteran official, Tuan Chun-yi, was appointed as minister of railways (Jacques Leslie, Los Angeles Times Service, Hong Kong, 2 March). A conference on railway public security work was held 1-13 March in Peking. It conceded that embezzlers, persons guilty of graft, speculators and profiteers were active and seriously affected rail transport safety (*FBIS*, 17 March).

In September, 200 delegates attended a preparatory meeting in Peking for a national conference on science to be held in the spring of 1978 (*Peking Review*, 30 September).

On 15 April the long-delayed fifth volume of Mao Tse-tung's *Selected Works* was published in Peking. The 500-page volume covers the period from the establishment of the People's Republic of China in 1949 to 1957 (the period prior to the Great Leap Forward program when China made rapid progress in economic development). Plans were announced for issuing 200 million copies. On 30 April the NCNA released an article by Hua Kuo-feng, "Continue the Revolution under the Dictatorship of the Proletariat to the End," which was an interpretive review of the new Mao volume.

The Central Committee plenum of 16-21 July confirmed Hua Kuo-feng as chairman of the CCP; restored Teng Hsiao-ping to his posts as a member of the Central Committee, the Politburo and its Standing Committee, vice-premier of the State Council, and chief of the General Staff of the PLA; and expelled the Gang of Four from the party. It was said that the struggle against the "Wang-Chang-Chiang-Yao antiparty clique" was the eleventh major two-line struggle in the history of the CCP, and that a "vast amount of evidence collected and verified through investigation" showed "Chang Chun-chiao [to be] a Kuomintang special agent, Chiang Ching a renegade, Yao Wen-yuan an alien class element, and Wang Hung-wen a new bourgeois element" (*NYT*, 23 July).

News of Teng's restoration to high office was greeted by Peking's millions going "on a joyful rampage . . . in one of the most deafening and chaotic street parties ever seen," according to the *Washington Post* (23 July). Teng made an official public appearance at the ceremony marking the fiftieth anniversary of the PLA on 1 August—the first since his delivery of Chou En-lai's funeral eulogy almost a year and a half earlier.

The Eleventh Party Congress was held in Peking on 12-18 August. As noted earlier, 1,510 delegates attended.

Hua Kuo-feng delivered the four-hour political report on 12 August. He praised the late Chairman Mao, saying that all the victories won in the Chinese revolution over more than half a century had been due to Mao's leadership and the guidance of his revolutionary line. Hua summed up the "eleventh struggle between the two lines," pointing out that Mao became aware of the anti-party activities of the Gang of Four long ago and had sternly admonished them on many occasions and led the party in repeated struggles against them. Mao's greatest contribution to the theory of the proletarian revolution and the dictatorship of the proletariat, Hua said, was that he established the theory of continuing the revolution under the dictatorship of the proletariat. As for the eleventh struggle, the Gang of Four had completely perverted this great theory, as well as the party's basic line for the entire historical period of Socialism and Mao's comprehensive thesis on the question of capitalist-roaders inside the party. The Gang of Four had equated veteran cadres with "democrats," and "democrats" with "capitalist-roaders," had slanderously alleged that there was a "bourgeois class" inside the party and the army, and altogether had reversed the relationship of the people to the enemy in the historical period of Socialism, hoping to destroy the party and the army, overthrow the dictatorship of the proletariat and restore capitalism.

Hua argued that as long as supreme party and state power rests with a leading core that adheres to the Marxist-Leninist line, the capitalist-roaders cannot grow into a bourgeois class inside the party because they are only a handful and are constantly being exposed and weeded out. Very significantly, he declared that the smashing of the Gang of Four was another signal victory of the Great Proletarian Cultural Revolution. Hua stressed the tremendous achievements and historic significance of the GPCR, pointing out that it would go down in the history of the dictatorship of the proletariat as a momentous innovation. However, he said, now that the "Gang" had been overthrown, "we are able to achieve stability and unity and attain great order across the land in compliance with Chairman Mao's instructions." "Thus," Hua announced, "the smashing of the Gang of Four marks the triumphant conclusion of our first Great Proletarian Cultural Revolution, which lasted eleven years."

Analyzing the international situation, Hua said that the United States and the Soviet Union are the source of a new world war, and that Soviet social-imperialism presents the greater danger. Mao's thesis differentiating the three worlds, Hua said, establishes the correct orientation for the current struggle in the international arena, as it clearly defines the main revolutionary forces, the chief enemies, and the middle forces that can be won over and united, thus enabling the international proletariat to unite with all the forces that can be united to form the broadest united front in class struggles against its chief enemies. (This reaffirmation was a stinging rejection of recent criticism of the thesis by Albania.)

At the plenary session on 13 August, Vice-Chairman Yeh Chien-ying, giving the report on the revision of the party constitution, emphasized that Hua had been chosen by Mao himself as his successor, and that Hua would lead the party triumphantly into the twenty-first century.

On 18 August the delegates adopted a resolution on the political report and on the new constitution and the report on the revision of the constitution, and elected 201 full and 132 alternate members to the Eleventh Central Committee. Vice-Chairman Teng Hsiao-ping then gave the closing address. His short speech said that the traditions and style of work which Mao fostered must be revived and carried forward—that is, "following the mass line, seeking truth from facts, conducting criticism and self-criticism, being modest and prudent and free from arrogance and impetuosity, keeping to the plain living and hard struggle and practicing democratic centralism," while the smashing of the Gang of Four had "changed the face of the whole party and the whole nation," and scored tremendous victories, Teng cautioned that there were "many problems to be tackled and many difficulties to be surmounted."

In the weeks and months following the party congress, it appeared that a working compromise had been established among the "top five" leadership. However, although much publicity was focused on Hua, on the triumvirate of Hua, Yeh, and Teng, and on the "top five" as a whole, it seemed obvious that in reality China was being governed by a Teng Hsiao-ping administration. The Politburo has several strong Teng supporters, and there was a general consensus that what the country needed was Teng's administrative experience and no-nonsense directness. It would appear that fifty-six-year-old Hua has little choice but to bide his time, meanwhile making the best use of seventy-four-year-old Teng's formidable talents. Teng himself may be reconciled to this arrangement, figuring that any attempt to take the party chairmanship for himself would have consequences that would threaten economic development; in September he told a Japanese delegation that he had no wish to become premier (AFP, Peking, 14 September). Li Hsien-nien, the fourth in the "top five," is a solid contributor and full supporter of the new pragmatic line to move the economy effectively toward the ambitious goal of the "four modernizations"—in industry, agriculture, the military, and in science and technology.

The fifth in the "top five" is Wang Tung-hsing, the late Mao's bodyguard, who organized the arrests of the Gang of Four and whose rise to a top leadership role was the most dramatic and unexpected. Wang is a somewhat enigmatic figure. On 8 September he published a lengthy article in the *People's Daily*, extolling the role played during the past twenty years by the Central Committee's security units which he headed: the 8341 guards detachment and the General Office, which is responsible for archives and documents. Wang revealed that Mao had been using these units ever since 1955 for reconnaissance, propaganda, and security purposes, bypassing regular CCP and state channels.

Despite the compromise arrangement among the "top five" there appeared to be signs of strain late in the year, and this may partially account for the delay in convening the Fifth NPC. One possible example may be the case of Wang Huai-hsiang, former first secretary of Kirin Province and political commissar of the provincial military district, who was dropped from the Central Committee in August. However, Wang (who had been called the "right hand" of Mao Tse-tung's fallen nephew, Mao Yuan-hsin, and who is believed to be the person denounced as the "overlord" of the northeast) was reappointed as a deputy political commissar in the Wuhan Military Region. There is speculation that this implies protection of him by Li Teh-sheng, the Shen-yang region commander, and is one possible indication that the military may be shielding some of its own people (David Bonavia, *FEER*, 4 November).

The Mao Memorial Hall in Peking was dedicated on 9 September. Missing from the ceremony were three close relatives, Mao's wife Chiang Ching (who remained under house arrest), his daughter Li Na, and his nephew Mao Yuan-hsin. His son Mao An-ching (by first wife Yang Kai-hui) and daughter Li-min (by second wife Ho Tzu-chen) were present. On 12 September Peking newspapers published ten photographs showing Mao's living quarters in Chungnanhai, near the former Forbidden City. However, for all the continued attention being lavished on the late chairman, it was becoming increasingly clear that China was now leaving behind many of Mao's cherished notions. This was given succinct expression in the caption accompanying a photo of the Mao memorial, in an article by John Roderick in Tokyo: "Here lie Chairman Mao's boldest socialist ideas, together with his body" (AP, 11 September).

At the National Day celebrations on 1 October, Chou Yang, former deputy director of the party's propaganda department, reappeared for the first time since the GPCR. Also reappearing on this occasion were former vice-minister of culture Hsia Yen and playwright Tsao Yu.

On 6 October, the first anniversary of the arrest of the Gang of Four, the "anti-gang of four" campaign moved into its "third stage" (*People's Daily*, 6 October). The Fifth NPC, which was supposed to have been held by this time, apparently had been postponed because of internal disagreement among the "top five" and the leadership's dissatisfaction with the purge thus far, especially in the provinces (*South China Morning Post,* Hong Kong, 7 October). Also it was indicated that the Gang of Four were still drawing salaries while under house arrest. On 24 October Hua Kuó-feng informed a session of the Standing Committee of the Fourth NPC that there would be a widespread purge in every administrative organ of the state, leading up to the convening of the new NPC in the spring of 1978. Only a few days earlier it was reported that both the "mayor" of Peking, Wu Teh, and Chen Hsi-lien, commander of the Peking Military Region, had been asked to make self-criticisms. Both men had been criticized in wall posters during the Chou En-lai memorial demonstrations in January (AFP, Peking, 20 October).

Hu Yao-pang, who had been branded a supporter of Liu Shao-chi during the GPCR, was named deputy principal of the Central Communist Party School in Peking. The school, which had been closed for some time, presumably because of the Gang of Four, was reopened on 9 October. Its principal and first deputy principal, respectively, are Hua Kuo-feng and Wang Tung-hsing (AP, 11 October). Party schools at lower levels are to be opened too. There is speculation that the party schools may displace the famous May Seventh Cadre schools.

The philosopher Feng Yu-lan came under fire yet one more time, although because of his advanced age of eighty-two, he is now being attacked only indirectly as "a certain scholar." He is considered to have been too soft on the radicals in his latest self-criticism following the fall of the Gang of Four (AFP, Peking, 17 October).

In mid-November it was revealed that Tao Chu, one of the more prominent victims of the GPCR, had been rehabilitated in 1973, but had died in that same year before he could be reappointed to office. There were unconfirmed rumors in late November that former Peking Mayor Peng Chen, also purged in the Cultural Revolution, had reappeared in Canton (*South China Morning Post,* 20 November).

The Chinese economy did poorly in 1976. The value of industrial output probably rose, at the maximum, 5 percent over 1975, in contrast with the estimated 10 percent increase in 1975. Although the economy began to recover in the fourth quarter, clearly the Fifth Five-Year Plan was off to a poor start. Grain production in 1976 was to set a new record, but the estimated increase was very small, perhaps no more than 1-2 percent, just keeping even with the population growth.

It was expected that in 1977 industrial growth would begin to recover toward its post-1970 average annual increase of approximately 8 percent, and by October the total value of industrial output was reported to have increased by 12 percent over the same period in 1976 (NCNA, 25 October). In China's increasingly complex economy, long-term development in particular is likely to remain difficult. There are hard decisions to be made on the allocation of resources. Policies pursued since the early 1960s have stressed agriculture and light industry as the keys to rapid development, and the revival of and attention given to Mao's 1956 speech "On the Ten Major Relationships" suggest that this priority will continue. Coal, steel, and transport have been targeted for emphasis, all three sectors having had problems and having been badly hurt by the July 1976 earthquake. If the new leadership keeps to its intention to improve living standards, additional pressures may build in 1977 and 1978 on the usual Chinese exports such as foodstuffs, light industrial goods, and textiles (*Current Scene,* April-May 1977).

Yet internal pressures to improve both the economy generally and living standards have been mounting. A particularly outspoken and lengthy wall poster in Canton charged that for the past ten years China's economy has been greatly outperformed by Japan's and that, because of China's low standard of living, social order has broken down and crime has increased. The poster advocated devoting a larger share of industrial production to consumer goods, raising wages, giving workers more control over the economy, and introducing advanced technology. The poster asked: "Are the Chinese people inferior to the Japanese people in intelligence and talent?" "Does it [the lesser performance] mean that Chinese natural resources are inferior to those of Japan or that our social system is somehow lacking?" The correct answer, it concluded, was: "Our relative backwardness is attributable to the interference of the Gang of Four" (Fox Butterfield, *NYT,* 2 February; Peter Weintraub, *FEER,* 11 February).

In October 50 to 60 percent of China's urban workers received wage increases for the first time in at least ten years. These raises were to improve the wages of factory workers at the bottom levels of the eight-grade wage system. Schoolteachers and some lower-level party and government cadres also benefited; but higher-paid workers, factory managers, and technicians were excluded. According to Li Hsien-nien, the raises averaged somewhat less than 15 to 20 percent, with workers in the lowest two grades getting the biggest hike in pay. Some believe that the raises were designed to give the economy a shot in the arm. While serving to narrow the differential between the highest- and lowest-paid of the urban workers, there is a danger that they may widen the gap between city and countryside (Fox Butterfield, NYT Service, 11 October).

According to a U. S. Central Intelligence Agency study of China's oil production, released in July, China will not soon become a world oil power. Offshore reserves apparently are smaller than had been estimated, the quality is questionable, and the financial and manpower restraints are considerable, aside from the technological problems in extracting the oil. A large and growing domestic demand for oil must be taken into consideration, and there are also "geopolitical considerations" which argue against increases in exports. Hence, China is not likely to export oil in the foreseeable future (Daniel Southerland, *Christian Science Monitor* [CSM], 7 July).

China plans to earn more foreign exchange by admitting tourists in larger numbers. The government-run China Travel Service and two Hong Kong agencies have developed a cooperative scheme to offer tours which feature China as an extended transit stop between Hong Kong and a third country. These arrangements depart from the past policy of using tourism as an educational and propaganda vehicle, rather than as a means to earn cold cash. In late February the Greek-registered vessel *Danae* with 214 passengers spent several days at Whampoa near Canton, the first foreign cruise liner to call at a Chinese port in three decades. It was followed by a Norwegian ship, and later passengers from the *Queen Elizabeth II,* the world's largest ocean liner, visited Canton and Peking during its Hong Kong stopover (Peter Weintraub, *FEER,* 10 June).

The Forty-second Canton Trade Fair (15 October-15 November) had a record volume of trade and attendance. More than 17,000 businessmen visited the fair (Reuter, Canton, 16 November).

Despite the relative popularity of the new Peking regime, the relative cultural thaw, and the up-turning economy, the number of illegal immigrants entering Hong Kong from China more than doubled in the first nine months of 1977, as compared with the same period (reportedly a much more restless one) in 1976. The figures are 1,400 against 650) (*Hong Kong Standard,* 24 October).

International Views and Positions. "Chairman Mao's revolutionary line in diplomacy" remained unaltered in 1977. Relations with the Soviet Union remained strained, the Sino-American detente remained intact despite the Taiwan problem, and China received many foreign visitors, most notably U.S. Secretary of State Cyrus Vance in August and Yugoslav President Tito in September. Diplomatic relations were established with two more countries (Liberia, 17 February; Barbados, 30 May) so that by the end of the year there were diplomatic ties with 112 countries. Only 22 countries have formal relations with Taiwan. (For complete listings, exclusive, of course, of the changes made in 1977 and noted here, see *YICA, 1977,* pp. 277-78.)

Relations with the Soviet Union. By the fall of 1976—with the death of Mao and the subsequent purge of the radical leadership in China—conditions were such that a dramatic change in Sino-Soviet relations could have taken place. The Soviets, on their part, made overtures and refrained from highly publicized or sharp criticism of China for several months as a clear indication of their interest in improving relations. The Chinese, however, did not change their posture one iota. While many aspects of this relationship may be hidden from sight so that it is difficult to assign blame confidently to one side or the other, it may be that the Chinese are basically offended by the military pressure the Soviet Union continues to bring to bear on the border.

On 14 May the Soviet Union expressed a loss of patience by publishing in Pravda another article by V. Alexandrov (a pseudonym) entitled "The Peking Road to the Breakdown of International Detente under the Cloak of Anti-Sovietism." This was specifically in response to Hua Kuo-feng's 1 May review of the fifth volume of Mao's *Selected Works*. Hua called on the Chinese people to "follow the legacy of Chairman Mao Tse-tung and carry to its conclusion the struggle against Soviet social-imperialism," and "to speed up the process of revolutionizing and modernizing the People's Liberation Army and to enforce war preparations." (The Russian translation of Hua's statements into English is used here.) The Soviet article claimed that the Chinese talk about Soviet hegemonism merely served to justify Chinese military expenditure, "which is out of all proportion," and to "direct world public opinion away from Peking's expansionist plans, especially with regard to the countries around the Pacific Ocean and of Southeast Asia." The article referred to a statement in the report of the U.N. Commission on Disarmament that "military expenditure in the PRC is increasing; whereas it used to account for 16 to 20 percent of the national budget, it now comes to more than 40 percent." It further claimed that at a CCP Central Committee meeting in September 1959 Mao said: "We must rule the world. Our objective is the whole world, and we will create a great power . . . . We must, without fail, take possession of Southeast Asia, including South Vietnam, Thailand, Burma, Malaysia, and Singapore." At a session of the "Conference of the Military Council," in June 1958, the article added, Mao reportedly said: "The present situation in the Pacific Ocean is not really so peaceful. In the future, when it is under our control, we will be able to say it is peaceful."

The Chinese responded with a lengthy article in *Red Flag* (4 July) entitled "Soviet Social-Imperialism is the Most Dangerous Source of World War," which declared that "arrogant and ambitious craving for world hegemony is driving Soviet social-imperialism to rush all over the world like a wild beast running amok . . . ." The Soviets had "massed a million troops along the Chinese border with the spearhead first and foremost directed at the United States and Japan and posing a serious threat to China's security as well." The article linked domestic Soviet policies with such behavior externally: "In its acquisition of maximum profit, Soviet state monopoly capital is both sucking the life-blood of its own people and madly pursuing a policy of aggression and committing most ruthless colonialist plunder abroad."

On 25 September Teng Hsiao-ping told Manfred Woerner, chairman of the Defense Committee of the West German Bundestag, that resumption of friendly Sino-Soviet relations would not come about in his (Teng's) lifetime, nor in that of Hua Kuo-feng's or even the next generation. He reportedly said that the Sino-Soviet conflict could go on for thousands of years! In the week just before these remarks were made, diplomats from the Soviet bloc, Mongolia, and Cuba walked out of two banquets in Peking because of verbal attacks on the Soviet Union by Li Hsien-nien (AFP, Peking, 25 September).

In July the deputy director of the Sinkiang Revolutionary Committee's Foreign Affairs Department told Western journalists, who were making an unprecedented visit to Urumchi, that "nearly every day we have border problems with the Soviet Union at some point or another in our territory" (Radio Liberty Research, 14 July). According to John Dillin, China has more than one million troops deployed well back from the border in order to better absorb a Russian thrust if it should come. The Chinese forces along the border may consist of seventy-five regular divisions, thirty-two militia divisions, and thirty-six independent regiments. The Soviets have approximately 800,000 men very close to the border, because the Trans-Siberian railway runs there (CSM Service, 29 May). The

Chinese continue to encourage publicity in the West about their nuclear shelter system which is still being dug in various places (e.g., see Harrison Salisbury, NYT Service, 28 October).

On 30 October the *Yomiuri Shimbun* (Tokyo) reported that Marshal Hsu Hsiang-chien told a delegation of retired Japanese military officers in Peking that Soviet troops illegally occupy 386,000 square miles (one million square kilometers) of Chinese territory, and that Soviet troops make night raids along the disputed border between the two countries in order to move boundary markers back into Chinese territory. He said that in some cases the signs have been moved back by as much as 43.75 miles (100 kilometers). Hsu told the Japanese that it is a good thing for an independent country to have the power of self-defense and asked if Japan's policy, which is based on the U.S.-Japanese Security Treaty (i.e., dependent on the United States) might not gradually become unfeasible (UPI, Tokyo, 30 October).

On 1 November the *People's Daily* published a 35,000-word editorial department article entitled "Chairman Mao's Theory of the Differentiation of the Three Worlds is a Major Contribution to Marxism-Leninism." A Hsinhua "introduction" to this major pronouncement summarized one of its most important discussions on why the Soviet Union is the most dangerous source of world war:

> This is because: first, as a late-comer among the imperialist countries, Soviet social-imperialism has to employ an offensive strategy to encroach on the sovereignty of all other countries and has to try and grab areas under the control of the other imperialist superpower—the United States, and is, therefore, more aggressive and adventurous; second, as comparatively speaking Soviet social-imperialism is inferior in economic strength, it must rely chiefly on its military power and recourse to threats of war in order to expand; third, it has a highly centralized state-monopoly capitalist economy without its equal in any other imperialist country and it is a state under fascist dictatorship; it is therefore easier for Soviet social-imperialism to put the entire economy on a military footing and militarize the whole state apparatus; fourth, it still flaunts the banner of "socialism" to bluff and deceive people everywhere. Although the paint on its signboard of "socialism" is peeling day by day, it must not be supposed that Soviet social-imperialism has completely lost its capacity to deceive.
>
> In these circumstances . . . if we should still undiscriminatingly put the two superpowers on a par and fail to single out the Soviet Union as the more dangerous instigator of world war, we would only be blunting the revolutionary vigilance of the people of the world and blurring the primary target in the struggle against hegemonism. Therefore, in no circumstances must we play into the hands of the Soviet Union in its deception and conspiracy and give the green light to its war preparations and acts of aggression. (*Hsinhua News Bulletin*, 1 November)

Despite this continued antagonistic confrontation, there were indications that some effort was being made to maintain contact and to improve relations where this would be mutually advantageous. Veteran diplomat Wang Yu-pin was sent to Moscow in August as the new Chinese ambassador, after this important post had been left vacant for sixteen months (AP, Tokyo, 26 August). On 7 October the Chinese and the Russians reached an agreement for the first time in eight years on the navigation of the Amur (Heilung) and Ussuri rivers (AFP, Peking, 7 October). Foreign Minister Huang Hua attended the Soviet reception in Peking celebrating the sixtieth anniversary of the October Revolution, the first ranking Chinese official to do so since Chou-En-lai attended such a reception in 1967.

Relations with the United States. U.S.-Chinese relations proceeded cautiously in 1977. Early in the year there were indications that the Chinese considered the Taiwan problem a secondary issue that would wait. This was a point made by Keng Piao, a former diplomat who heads the Central Committee's International Liaison Department (and in August 1977 became a member of the new Politburo), in a speech on 24 August 1976 at a graduation ceremony of the Institute of Diplomacy in Peking. (The text was obtained and made available in 1977 by Chinese Nationalist intelligence sources.) He said that both Moscow and Washington are enemies, but the danger of Soviet aggression is so great that for the sake of survival China has to "give up one and win over the other

. . . . From the strategic point of view, if we shelve the China-United States controversy, we will be able to cope with one side with all-out effort and even gain time to solve our domestic problems first." He conceded that even if Sino-American relations were to be normalized, it would still be impossible to liberate Taiwan immediately. Keng Piao's candid (because they were intended for internal use only) remarks included these observations:

> Just let the United States defend us against the influence of Soviet revisionism and guard the coast of the East China Sea so that we can have more strength to deal with the power in the north and engage in state construction. When we regard the time as right, we will be candid and say: Please, Uncle Sam, pack up your things and go. [Incidentally, this comment was included in the *Pravda* article of 14 May by V. Alexandrov.] From now on, we will invite more American guests who are influential in the United States political and military circles and in United States society . . . . The purpose is to explain to them our views on the situation and point out that it will not do, and is capitulatory and retrogressive and not a positive way of solving the world problem, to promote detente with the USSR. (Fox Butterfield, *NYT,* 27 January)

The Chinese reportedly informed David Rockefeller, chairman of the Chase Manhattan Bank, during his visit to Peking in January, that a solution of the frozen assets issue "was no longer a problem" (Peter Weintraub, *FEER,* 25 February). The United States has $76.5 million of Chinese assets, while the Chinese have $196.9 million of American corporate and private property in China. In May it was revealed that talks on the subject had been under way for several weeks in Washington, D.C. (Bernard Gwertzman, *NYT,* 2 May). In April Christopher H. Phillips, the president of the National Council for United States-China Trade, noted the unexpected interest the Chinese had shown in receiving specialized American trade missions since President Jimmy Carter's inauguration; by this time China had invited four groups for the year, and possibly two more, which seemed significant inasmuch as only one such group had been invited in the previous four years (ibid., 12 April). On 11 April Secretary of State Cyrus Vance invited Huang Chen, head of the Chinese Liaison Office in Washington, to his office to discuss the recent Vance mission to Moscow and to inform the Chinese diplomat that the Carter administration desired normal relations with Peking and an increase in Chinese-American aid (ibid.). When Thomas S. Gates, who served for a year as head of the American Liaison Mission in Peking, returned to the United States in June, he counseled early recognition of the PRC: "I'm afraid that if another year passes and this administration doesn't make some important moves [toward a normalization of relations], the pride of the Chinese may be hurt and they may get very sticky on details." He also said that the administration had failed to educate the American public on the necessity of moving in the direction of devising a formula under which it would break diplomatic relations with Taiwan while maintaining other relations with the island (Daniel Southerland, *CSM,* 17 June). Gates was replaced in Peking by Leonard Woodcock, former head of the United Auto Workers union.

Publicity was given in June to a major Carter administration policy review regarding the sale of military technology to China. The paper, Policy Review Memorandum No. 24, was the subject of much debate in Washington. The document takes a position against the sale of military technology, on the grounds that it would lead to a "fundamental reassessment" of Soviet policies toward the United States and an increase of Sino-Soviet tensions. The opponents of this majority position contend that the paper did not take into account the potential diplomatic advantages to the United States with regard to the Soviet Union if arms sales were made to China (Bernard Weintraub, *NYT,* 24 June). By July, it was noted that Peking was taking a harder line regarding Taiwan. Li Hsien-nien told visiting Admiral Elmo R. Zumwalt, Jr.: "As to when and in what way the Chinese people are to liberate their sacred territory of Taiwan, that is entirely China's internal affair, which brooks no interference" (Ross H. Munro, *CSM,* 6 July).

Secretary of State Vance visited Peking on 25 August and met with Huang Hua, Teng Hsiao-ping, and Hua Kuo-feng. This was the first high-level meeting between representatives of the new leaderships in both countries. Since there had been no expectations of breakthroughs during the Vance visit, the meetings were generally regarded as useful. Vance hinted that Peking became more aware of the political pressures on President Carter not to break with Taiwan; the American position was currently complicated by the administration's need to retain conservative support for the impending new Panama Canal Treaty (Barry Schweid, AP, Peking, 27 August). Vance was praised by former CIA Deputy Director Ray S. Cline for "not doing something unwise" about Taiwan (AP, Washington, 30 August). An incongruous note was sounded a few days later by Teng Hsiao-ping, who told the Associated Press in an off-the-record interview that reports of the Vance visit were wrong. Teng said that former President Gerald Ford had indicated in December 1975 that if he were reelected he would break diplomatic relations with Taiwan and establish normal ties with the PRC. (Ford later acknowledged such speculation but said he made no promises.) By contrast, Vance reportedly suggested switching the U.S. embassy from Taipei to Peking, and the liaison office from Peking to Taipei (Reuter and AFP, Washington, 8 September). Some have suggested that Teng was appealing directly to the American public with such remarks; another view is that Teng was speaking directly to the administration and to Congress. There was consternation in Washington that Teng had revealed alleged secret American positions with regard to Taiwan, even though Teng's tone had not been strident. Teng also said that if the United States did not interfere, China would not rule out the possibility of a peaceful solution of the Taiwan problem, thus softening Li Hsien-nien's earlier comment to Admiral Zumwalt. Several days later, Teng told a visiting Japanese parliamentary group that it was regrettable that Washington was "playing with two cards," and that the stance adopted by Vance was a step backward from that of his predecessor, Henry Kissinger (Kyodo, Tokyo, 12 September). Vice-Foreign Minister Yu Chan later told editors of the *Wall Street Journal* that any supply of arms to Taiwan after the normalization of Sino-American relations would be intolerable, and also that any declaration of intent by Washington that it has vital interests in the peace and stability in the Taiwan region would be unacceptable (V. F. Kulkarni, *Hong Kong Standard*, 8 October).

On 12 September U. S. Secretary of Defense Harold Brown announced a key decision that was expected to spur the sale of American technology to China, i.e., to quietly move to ease the export of some defense-related equipment while restricting the transfer of design and manufacturing skills (NYT Service, Washington, 12 September). A high-level Chinese trade delegation headed by Wang Yao-ting was currently in the United States surveying American technology.

Relations Elsewhere. Although China's trade with Japan continued to stagnate in 1977, there was expectation of an upsurge. This optimism was based on discussion begun in April during an enthusiastically welcomed visit by Japanese business leaders (the president and most of the vice-presidents of the important Keidanren, the federation of business organizations). This was followed by the lengthy visit to Japan of China's vice-minister of foreign trade and by a large number of Chinese technical "exchange" missions. In October the Japanese accepted a Chinese-proposed eight-year private trade pact, to begin in 1978 (UPI, Tokyo, 15 October). The peace treaty, still unsigned, remained an unresolved issue because of the anti-hegemony clause, which is insisted upon by the Chinese, but which the Japanese remain reluctant to include in deference to the Soviets. However, the Chinese appear to have applied pressure during the year, and the Japanese have been annoyed at the Russians because of the tough fisheries agreement to which it finally agreed. China, for its part, was upset over the Tokyo-Seoul agreement on the joint development of the continental shelf (Susumu Awanohare, *FEER*, 7 October).

China's changing complexion was dramatically signaled in late summer by the simultaneous cooling of relations with Albania and the highly successful visit of Yuoslav President Tito to Peking. Albania, for years China's most loyal ally, had become increasingly critical since the fall of the Gang of Four and because of China's closer ties with the West. It has been suggested that a reduction of Chinese aid to Albania may be a factor, although it is not clear whether this began before or after Albania's criticisms. It is ironic that Albania would choose to attack Mao's own concept of the three worlds in international relationships. The Albanians could hardly have been pleased to see Tito, who only a decade earlier had been reviled as the arch-revisionist, get a hero's welcome in Peking.

On 10 May Chen Chu took over as China's chief delegate to the United Nations, a position which had been vacant for more than six months since Huang Hua had been promoted to foreign minister. Chen Chu, sixty years of age, is a Soviet specialist, and was Huang Hua's deputy at the U.N. for about a year.

On 1 November the *People's Daily* published (as noted earlier) the 35,000-word editorial-article entitled "Chairman Mao's Theory of the Differentiation of the Three Worlds Is a Major Contribution to Marxism-Leninism." This was undoubtedly the major foreign policy statement of the year.

Publications. The official and most authoritative publication of the CCP is the newspaper *Jenmin jih-pao* (People's Daily), published in Peking. The theoretical journal of the Central Committee, *Hung Chi* (Red Flag) is published approximately once a month. The daily paper of the PLA is *Chiehfang-chun-pao* (Liberation Army Daily). The weekly *Peking Review*, published in English and several other languages, carries translations of important articles, editorials, and documents from the three aforementioned publications. The official news agency of the party and government is the New China News Agency (Hsinhua; NCNA).

University of Hawaii   Stephen Uhalley, Jr.

India

The Communist Party of India was formed in 1928 and from the start was divided in social character, base of support, and ideological stance. These factional cleavages were difficult to contain, and the party split in 1964. As a consequence, two antagonistic organizations emerged: the Communist Party of India (CPI) and the more militant Communist Party of India— Marxist (CPM).

In part, the dispute was about domestic strategy, separating those who thought the best way forward was in alliance with the leftist elements within the dominant Congress Party, and those who wanted a more radical alternative. But what made it impossible to hold the party together was the Sino-Soviet split, and more directly the border clash between India and China in 1962.

The CPI remained loyal to the international goals of the Soviet Union, while the CPM took a more independent line. The CPI, the smaller fragment of the split, retained the bulk of the party bureaucracy, the larger number of members of central and state assemblies, and the trade unions;

the larger group, the CPM, carried off the main geographic areas of the party's strength: West Bengal, Kerala, and Andhra Pradesh. The radical left of the CPM itself later fragmented into a number of groups which protested against the CPM's participation in united front ministries in West Bengal and Kerala during 1967-71. Most of these radicals—popularly known as "Naxalites," after rural revolutionary activity in West Bengal—were opposed to parliamentary democracy and were committed to the Maoist conception of guerrilla warfare and armed revolution. Some met in March 1969 in Calcutta to proclaim the formation of the Communist Party of India, Marxist-Leninist (CPML), though most remained loyal to the dozen or more factions of this radical movement. The various "Naxalite" groups were banned during the 1975-77 State of Emergency. The ban was not lifted until after the Congress Party's defeat in the March 1977 general elections.

The two major Communist parties, the CPI and the CPM, took opposing stands to the State of Emergency declared by former Prime Minister Indira Gandhi's Congress government on 26 June 1975. The CPI initially supported the restrictions on political activity and on civil rights as a legitimate effort to curb a "rightist" challenge, but became increasingly estranged from the ruling Congress Party when the latter began to use the special Emergency powers against the CPI. The CPM, which claimed from the beginning that the Emergency was a tactical move to shore up the position of the "big bourgeoisie," cooperated with other opposition parties to get the Emergency lifted.

When the government announced in early 1977 that general elections would be held, the CPM continued to work closely with the opposition Janata Front, an alliance of the four largest non-Communist opposition parties. The CPI, despite its strained relations with the Congress leadership, refused to abandon completely its "unity and struggle" relationship with the Congress, and along with the ruling party it met with major electoral reverses. The Congress Party, which held about two-thirds of the parliamentary seats after the 1971 elections, emerged this time with only about a third of the 542 seats, most of them in the four southern states where the Emergency had been less vigorously enforced. The CPI's parliamentary representation dropped from 23 to 7 seats, all from the south, and its share of the vote from 4.73 percent to 2.82 percent. In contrast, the CPM retained its strength. With some 4.30 percent of the vote, it won 22 parliamentary seats, including 17 in West Bengal. It probably could have won several additional seats in West Bengal had it contested the seats allocated to the Janata Front.

Elections for legislative assemblies were held three months later in ten of India's twenty-two states and in two union territories, where the Congress had already fared poorly in the general elections. These states and union territories, containing some 60 percent of India's 620 million people, witnessed a repetition of the March elections. The Janata Party won large legislative majorities in seven states and one union territory. In three states, regional parties won: the Akali Dal (a Janata Party ally) in Punjab, the All-India ADMK (which supported the Janata government in parliament) in Tamilnadu, and the CPM in West Bengal. The CPM captured 205 of the 2,458 legislative assembly seats, 178 of them in West Bengal's 294-seat assembly. The CPI and the Congress were virtually wiped out in these states. In late 1977 the CPM gained a solid legislative majority in the eastern state of Tripura. The 1977 electoral results enhanced the CPM's claim to leadership of India's Communist movement, although its support is restricted to a few regions of the country. The CPI and the Congress formed a united front government in Kerala after the March elections.

The CPI. *Organization and Strategy.* The CPI is an all-India organization based on the principle of "democratic centralism." Its structure, however, has been essentially regional in orientation. Tactics and election strategy frequently have been determined more by local circumstances than by directives from the top.

The party's major decision-making unit is the 9-member Central Executive Committee, led by the party chairman, S. A. Dange (who resigned in late 1977), and the general secretary, C. Rajeswara Rao. Other national CPI bodies are the 31-member National Executive Committee and 138-member National Council. The party in October 1977 claimed 546,000 members, an increase of some 60,000 over the previous year. Approximately 80 percent of its members are in six states: Bihar (132,000), Andhra Pradesh (97,000), Kerala (77,000), Tamilnadu (44,000), Uttar Pradesh (41,000), and West Bengal (40,000). (*New Age,* 16 October 1977; this English-language weekly is published in New Delhi by the CPI central organization.)

The CPI's major auxiliary organizations are the All-India Students' Federation (105,000 members), the All-India Trade Union Conference (2,600,000), and a peasant group, the All-India Kisan Samiti (175,000). The Jan Seva Dal, the party's "educational" auxiliary, conducts indoctrination camps. The party publishes more than twenty weeklies.

The CPI's strategy of using the Emergency to enhance its influence proved a failure. By the end of 1976 it was clear that the government did not need the CPI to consolidate its power. There had been little overt opposition to the Emergency or to the series of constitutional amendments which institutionalized the Emergency. Indeed, the CPI had become something of a nuisance to the Congress government, and relations between the two reached the breaking point in late 1976 and early 1977. Both Indira Gandhi and her politically ambitious son, Sanjay, charged that the CPI was interfering in Congress Party affairs; even more damaging was their contention that it had collaborated with the British during India's freedom struggle. Sanjay claimed that the CPI leaders were "more corrupt than anybody else" (*Far Eastern Economic Review,* Hong Kong, 21 January 1977). A Congress chief minister, like many of his colleagues, joined the campaign and stated that the CPI was "the most reactionary party of the country" (ibid.).

Meanwhile the CPI continued to antagonize the government by charging that the bureaucracy, while vigorously enforcing Sanjay's Five-Point Program (sterilization, slum removal, etc.), was lax in carrying out what it considered the more important Twenty-Point Economic Program of Prime Minister Gandhi (*New Age,* 9 January). C. Rajeswara Rao, the general secretary, wrote in the party's official journal that the CPI was "not one of those who claim that the burning problems of the country like poverty can be solved through the five point programme" (*New Age,* 2 January). To protest a resurgence in the prices of basic commodities, the CPI organized a national protest on 1-10 January in direct defiance of government orders against such events. Despite these developments, the CPI national leadership refused to abandon the "unity and struggle" line.

When Prime Minister Gandhi on 18 January made the surprise announcement on All-India Radio that national elections would be held in March, the CPI was forced to reconsider its strategy. It had four options: mend its relations with the Congress (i.e., strengthen the "unity and struggle" line); build up its links with other leftists, particularly the CPM; move toward the four-party opposition Janata Front; or fight the elections alone. Although the last offered the least chance for success, the political isolation of the party virtually forced it into this position. A move toward the Janata Front was impossible since the constituent units of the front were deeply suspicious of the CPI and tended to be critical of India's close ties with the Soviet Union. A leftist coalition was improbable, as the CPM, to defeat the Congress, had allied itself with the Janata. The preferred option was a linkage to the Congress, then considered a sure victor at the polls. The CPI's Central Executive Committee met on 25-26 January and declared: "Our policy towards the government continues to be one of supporting its progressive policies . . . and opposing everything which is anti-democratic." (Ibid., 30 January.) The ruling party's response, however, was cool, though the public attack on the CPI virtually ceased after 18 January.

The resignation of Jagjivan Ram, the most senior cabinet member and a leader of India's large

Harijan (i.e., untouchable) community, along with the resignation of several prominent leftists from the Congress Party on 2 February, made the political outcome less certain. The CPI reacted ambiguously to the new situation. It publicly welcomed Ram's resignation and agreed with his attacks on the "violation of accepted norms of democratic standards" and on the prime minister's efforts to "build up a personality who had no official status (i.e., Sanjay)" (*Christian Science Monitor,* 7 February). There were reports that it attempted to negotiate electoral understandings with the Congress for Democracy, the party founded by Ram, although Ram's party was allied to the Janata Front (*Current,* 19 February; *India Weekly,* 24 February 1977). Ram's dramatic act, however, made the CPI a more valuable electoral partner for the Congress, and in a few states electoral arrangements were worked out between the two parties. Even so, the CPI's efforts for a Congress victory were tempered by the knowledge that the CPI could regain an influential role only if the Congress' parliamentary majority were small.

The electorate, as already noted, gave a huge parliamentary majority to the Janata Front and administered a severe drubbing to both the Congress and the CPI. The Central Executive Committee of the CPI met immediately after the elections to evaluate the results. It declared that the public had turned against the rightward drift that had taken place under Indira Gandhi, but that it still supported "economic self-reliance," "strengthening the public sector," "radical socio-economic reforms," and "anti-imperialist nonalignment" (*New Age,* 2 April). The CPI halfheartedly admitted that its defense of the Emergency was a factor in its defeat (ibid., 10 April).

The problem now was to devise a strategy to recoup its strength. A reconciliation with the Janata remained impossible. Rather, the CPI leaders increasingly spoke of a leftist alternative to the two major political parties, and the National Council worried that the talk of a two-party system was in fact an attempt to "consolidate the capitalist system" and "squeeze out [the] left and democratic parties and forces." (Ibid., 10 April.) The CPI, however, did not sever its links with the defeated Congress. In Kerala, as noted, the CPI and the Congress formed a united front government. The proposed cooperation between the CPI and the CPM was a non-starter since the CPM insisted that the CPI first sever its links with the Congress and withdraw from the Kerala coalition (ibid., 15 May). The CPI was unwilling to do either. When the government called for state elections in June, the CPI negotiated electoral adjustments with the Congress in five states and two union territories. The two again fared poorly.

The argument for a leftist coalition appeared even more compelling. The CPI called the CPM's victory in West Bengal a "positive development which can pave the way for a broader mobilization of all left and democratic forces in the people's interests" (*NYT,* 22 June). The CPM, however, refused to include the CPI in its government or to cooperate politically with it elsewhere. A major obstacle, according to Rajeswara Rao, was, the "line of the CPM leadership which takes the Janata Party as its ally" (*New Age,* 16 October).

As the CPI considers its strategic options, the likely debate will be between those who support the formation of an independent leftist party and those who seek to retain the ties with the Congress Party and various regional parties. The 30 December resignation of S. A. Dange, a proponent of the "unity and struggle" relationship with the Congress, as chairman of the Central Executive Committee, could tip the scales toward the former option. The formal split in the Congress Party in the first week of 1978 could so weaken the Congress as to make it an unreliable political ally. While there are occasional references to "progressives" in the ruling Janata Party in CIP literature, the distrust between the leadership of the two parties is so great that cooperation of any kind in the near future is improbable. In the present shifting of political forces, the CPI remains discredited and politically isolated. The very fluid nature of the political situation could change its fortunes, but the immediate task for the CPI is to build its organizational base and its public image.

Domestic and International Attitudes. Image-building began even before the 18 January 1977 announcement of new elections. The early January protest was a public move that served both to demonstrate the party's independence and to place distance between itself and the increasingly unpopular policies of the government, particularly the sterilization and slum removal campaigns. The indirect criticism of Sanjay Gandhi served the same purposes.

After the 18 January announcement of general elections, which was accompanied by a relaxation in the Emergency restrictions on the press and political activity, the CPI began to demand the unconditional lifting of the Emergency (*New Age,* 30 January). To justify its shift, the party issued a declaration on 3 February which stated that the Emergency had been necessary in 1975 to combat the challenge from the right, but that the "emergency powers came to be more and more misused against the working class, peasantry and common people . . . Even our parliamentary democratic systems were sought to be weakened on one pretext or another" (ibid., 6 February). Immediately after the general elections, the party's official journal noted in an editorial that "the Congress Party as a whole had to pay the heavy penalty for the crimes of the unspeakable reactionary caucus around Indira Gandhi" (ibid., 27 March).

The lifting of the State of Emergency after the Congress' defeat provided the CPI with the freedom to criticize openly the policies of the "bourgeois" Janata government. The West Bengal State Council, for example, claimed that national power had passed to a coalition (the Janata Front did not become a united party until 1 May 1977) "predominating in which were those who had been opposed to nationally accepted progressive policies, radical socio-economic reforms, secularism, anti-imperialism, non-alignment and peace." (Ibid., 24 April.)

The CPI did welcome the government's dismantling of the various restrictions on civil liberties. Indeed, it demanded the full repeal of all preventive detention acts still in force and the release of all political detainees. At the same time, it charged the new government with throwing India open to multinationals, restricting the role of the public sector, and moving away from centralized planning. The new government's plan to shift investment priority from large-scale industry to labor-intensive, small-scale consumer industries was considered a retrograde step that would make India dependent on the "capitalist West." (Ibid., 17 July).

On the international front, the party suggested that under its announced policy of "genuine nonalignment" the new government might attempt "to play down imperialism and to tilt the foreign economic policies in a pro-imperialist direction" (ibid., 17 July). Many of the Janata Party's leaders, including the leftists within it, had in the past expressed reservations over the close ties to Moscow and the 1971 Indo-Soviet Treaty of Peace and Friendship. It was well known, moreover, that the Soviet Union had strongly backed Indira Gandhi during the campaign. *Pravda* (12 March), for example, stated in a signed editorial one week before the elections: ". . . reactionaries from Bharatiya Lok Dal, Jana Sangh, the Organization Congress, and the Socialist Party are now united under the demagogic sign of the Janata Party." They had "nothing in common" with the people of India, and, according to the editorial, the Janata Front was "the defender of the interests of landowners and local and foreign monopolies." Shortly after the elections, the same journalist wrote that the Congress' defeat was due to the influence of its conservative wing, particularly Sanjay Gandhi, who had blocked the implementation of economic reforms and misused the emergency powers (*Za rubezhom,* March 24).

Relations with Moscow, however, did not deteriorate. Foreign policy had not been an issue in the campaign, and all the major parties apparently agreed that the general shape of India's foreign policy served its interests. Soviet Foreign Minister Gromyko, nevertheless, flew to New Delhi in late April to confer with the leaders of the new government. Both sides stressed the continuity in Indo-Soviet relations. Gromyko offered a $200 million loan, gave a commitment to supply 5.5 million tons of crude oil in the next few years (at favorable terms of repayment), and made proposals for increased trade

(*NYT,* 28 April). Subsequent high-level visits of Indian cabinet ministers and military figures reaffirmed the continuity of close relations, culminating in the October visit of Prime Minister Desai to the Soviet Union. The communiqués released at the conclusion of these visits, however, suggested a new basis for the relationship. There was almost no reference in them to common political goals, as had been the case earlier in such documents. Rather, relations were rather self-consciously based on self-interest. Janata leaders repeated frequently that Indo-Soviet relations would not be allowed to stand in the way of New Delhi's relations with other countries. Moscow, for its part, did not allow India's internal political developments to affect state-to-state relations. The Soviet Union's stand seems to be one of protecting its present position rather than aiming for substantial gains.

The CPM. *Organization and Strategy.* The CPM, with an organizational structure roughly parallel to that of the CPI, reported some 120,000 members in 1974. Its membership, concentrated in Andhra Pradesh, Kerala, and West Bengal, remained stable during the 1975-77 Emergency. Its record of consistent opposition to the Emergency, its subsequent electoral successes, and its friendly relations with the ruling party are likely to create opportunities for an expanded base of support. The same is probably the case with its auxiliaries. Its trade union, the Centre of Indian Trade Unions, has about 900,000 members. The Students' Federation of India (160,000 members) has won a number of college unions since the Emergency was lifted. Its peasant front, the All-India Kisan Sabha, with some 1,100,000 members, is far larger than the CPI's peasant affiliate.

Its Ninth Congress (1972) set the CPM firmly in opposition to the Congress Party. During the next three years, it increasingly cooperated with the opposition parties grouped around Jaya Prakash Narayan to protest corruption, economic scarcities, and the concentration of political power. That cooperation deepened during the Emergency, and when elections were declared, the CPM worked closely with the Janata Front. It emerged from the elections with a sizable parliamentary representation, though its support was still concentrated in a few regions, particularly West Bengal.

When state elections were called for June, the CPM worked out an electoral arrangement in those states where it was the junior partner; but in West Bengal, where it was the major political force, the Janata and the CPM had drifted apart. The underlying cause was probably the fear of the middle class and business that the CPM would resort to the radical policies and the agitational style it had adopted between 1969-71 if it came to power again.

The CPM management of the state government this time has proved quite different. It campaigned on a very moderate political platform and won an overwhelming victory. The Janata won only 20 of the 294 legislative seats, while the CPM won 178. The CPM chief minister in West Bengal, Jyoti Basu, instructed magistrates to show no favoritism in enforcing the law. Business houses were encouraged to invest and were informed that pacts with Communist unions would be honored *(Far Eastern Economic Review,* 29 July). Indeed, the CPM government supported the expansion plans of the Electric Supply Corporation, a foreign-owned company, and a fiber unit in which one of India's largest private business houses is a partner (ibid., 18 November). Basu told four Calcutta-based chambers of commerce on 19 August that "we must get together to see that conflicts are minimized through bipartite talks and government mediation." He warned the revolutionary Marxists that "if they go back to their ways, "the government will have to deal with them firmly" (noted in the international press, 17 October).

The party's moderate policies in West Bengal and its cooperation with the Janata Party in New Delhi were not universally accepted within the party. Disagreements over this line may have been the proximate cause for the shifting of General Secretary P. Sundarayya, associated with a more confrontational approach, to Andhra Pradesh and his replacement with E. M. S. Namboodiripad, formerly chief minister of Kerala.

While the CPM has cultivated its ties with the ruling party and kept the CPI at arm's length, it has not completely shut the door to increased cooperation with the CPI. Indeed, there has been cooperation between the front organizations at the local level. However, the CPM will work closely with the CPI only if it snaps its links with the Congress, still considered the major threat to a progressive evolution to the left (*New Age,* 16 May). Over the long run, the CPM, according to its powerful West Bengal secretary, intends to replace the Congress as the major political alternative to the Janata Party at the national level. CPM leaders expect that ideological differences within the ruling party will eventually weaken its cohesion. The Janata Party is, according to General Secretary Namboodiripad, "a collection of different political parties" that "cannot remain as a single united political party." According to him, its positive contribution to Indian political history is the dismantling of the authoritarian regime forged by the Congress Party. The CPM's relationship with the ruling party, he further maintained, is necessary to ensure that the process is completed. But he has emphasized that the Janata has the same class base as the Congress and consequently cannot be expected to handle the next economic crisis that strikes the country (*Link,* New Delhi, 15 August).

Attitudes on Internal and External Issues. The two major Communist parties differ widely over the appropriate model for economic development. The CPM view, similar to the economic policy of the Janata Party in several key respects, is that rural-oriented, small-scale, labor-intensive industry requires priority consideration. This contrasts sharply with the CPI's emphasis on urban-based, large-scale, capital-intensive industry. The two Communist parties also differ on the issue of state/center relations. The CPI advocates a strong center, while the CPM favors a greater devolution of power—a stand close to that of the Janata Party. This difference could reflect the more regional orientation of the CPM and its recent history of strained relations with the ruling party at the center.

There are a number of issues where the two Communist parties agree. Both favor the social ownership of the means of production, distribution, and exchange (*Patriot,* New Delhi, 7 November 1977). The CPM government in West Bengal, however, is at present willing to live with a wide expansion of private enterprise, including increased foreign investment, and to encourage labor peace to stimulate the state's sluggish economy.

The CPM was as vehemently opposed to the Emergency's restrictions on civil liberties as the Janata Front. Indeed, the CPM has demanded that the new government expunge all provisions in the constitution that sanction preventive detention. It has also demanded the scrapping of the forty-second constitutional amendment, passed during the Emergency to strengthen the power of the executive. The CPM Politburo has demanded additional constitutional changes that would introduce the right of recall and enhance the autonomy of the states. (Ibid.)

On foreign policy, the CPM has tended to take an even-handed policy on the Sino-Soviet dispute. During the 1970s, it criticized the government's close relations with the USSR and Moscow's support for Indira Gandhi. Since the March elections, it has toned down considerably such criticism. The CPM has spoken out more forcefully for a reconciliation between India and China than either the Janata or the CPI.

The CPM's campaign manifesto called for a "speedy development of friendly relations with People's China." In that same document, the party expressed support for friendship with Socialist countries and increased economic ties with them. It complained that "the trend of the Indian economy is towards greater dependence on the capitalist market, on aid and loans from imperialist countries." The party has generally agreed with the Janata Party's policy of "genuine nonalignment." The one major foreign policy difference has been the October Indo-Bangladesh agreement to share the waters of the Ganges, though its criticism was expressed in a low-key manner. Its charge was that India had been overly generous to Bangladesh, a stand that finds wide support in West Bengal.

The CPML. The various factions of the revolutionary Marxist movement were banned during the Emergency; the ban was promptly lifted after the March elections. The revolutionary Marxists had operated secretly in the past and had made almost no provisions for building mass organizations. This policy was based on the premise that mass organizations would lead to the domination of them by the rich peasantry and the "bourgeois," thus resulting in the "revisionism" that had occurred in the CPM. During the late 1960s and early 1970s, the "Naxalites" engaged in violent attacks on the "class enemy," a tactic that brought down upon them severe government reprisals and the arrest of its leaders. The restoration of law and order, however, also involved the long-term incarceration of many Naxalites.

The Janata Front in its electoral campaign had demanded the release of all political prisoners, including the Naxalites. On coming to power, the new home minister advised the states, which have original police power, to expedite the release of political detainees. He also revealed that he had met with Naxalite representatives who assured him that the Naxalites desired to "eschew the path of violence," and that consequently he had ordered the states to release those who promised to adhere to the democratic process (Ministry of Home Affairs, *First Hundred Days in Office,* New Delhi, 1977). The government reported in July that only 784 political detainees out of 6,851 held in March under the Maintenance of Internal Security Act (MISA)—one of the legal tools used to arrest political opponents—were still in prison (ibid.). The home minister also advised the states to release all Naxalites held under MISA, and reported in July that all but 5 had been released (ibid.). Similarly, the government ordered that members of banned organizations charged with offenses under the Defense of India Rules have their cases dropped except for "economic offenders" and those charged with specific criminal offenses. The home ministry reported in July that some 20,000 cases had been withdrawn and another 5,500 cases dropped (ibid.). A nonofficial body was formed in April by the Citizens for Democracy, a group with close ties to influential Janata figures, to investigate police brutality against Naxalites. Yet, a revolutionary Marxist wrote to a leading Indian journal in April that most Naxalites were not classified as political prisoners and therefore would not benefit from the releases (*Economic and Political Weekly,* Bombay, 12 April).

It would be difficult to say how many Naxalites will abandon revolutionary Marxism for parliamentary democracy. One of the groups, led by Satyanarain Singh, has done so publicly (Delhi Domestic Service, 11 December). While most of the Naxalites have probably not given up their revolutionary ideology, they seem at present to have adopted a wait-and-see attitude. If economic conditions should deteriorate, they would be tempted to resort to their traditional practices, perhaps with some support from the radical fringe within the CPM in West Bengal, the state where most Naxalites are located. West Bengal's CPM chief minister has warned that he would deal harshly with the Naxalites if they should again use violent methods.

Arlington, Virginia   Walter Andersen

Indonesia

Although Communism as a political issue plays an important role in Indonesian domestic affairs today, the Indonesian Communist party, split between Moscow- and Peking-oriented factions, itself remains proscribed, and its handful of adherents in the country are engaged either in deep-cover infiltration or in supporting guerrilla movement along the frontier with East Malaysia (see *Malaysia*). Meanwhile, Indonesia's relations with the USSR are improving, but diplomatic ties with People's China remain suspended.

The Communist Party of Indonesia (Partai Komunis Indonesia; PKI), the oldest Communist party in Asia, was founded on 23 May 1920 by Dutch Marxists, but Indonesians shortly assumed leadership. Uncertain in its relationship with the Executive Committee of the Comintern and over the position to be adopted toward Islamic and other manifestations of Indonesian nationalism, the PKI soon ran afoul of the Dutch colonial authority. It plunged into disaster in 1926-27 when a poorly planned coup attempt in West Java and West Sumatra was quickly quelled, and several hundred party cadres and others were arrested and imprisoned. Not until independence was proclaimed in August 1945 was the PKI again permitted to function legally.

Active in the Indonesian revolution (1945-49), the party was represented in the Republic's parliament and in several cabinets. It also developed paramilitary armed "volunteer" groups, whose strength eventually aroused alarm. In September 1948 the party attempted for a second time to seize power, this time in Madiun, East Java. Failure plunged the party once more into disarray, with the added stigma of having tried to "stab the revolution in the back." After the Dutch recognized Indonesia's independence in December 1949, the PKI began an ideological and organizational rebuilding under younger leaders, and in the first parliamentary elections in 1955, won 16 percent of the popular vote.

In subsequent years the PKI developed a broad-based organization of more than three million members, with additional tens of thousands of supporters in trade unions, farmers', youth, women's, and other front groups, and allied itself with President Sukarno's militant nationalist ideology, from which it drew protective coloration in its struggle with the anti-Communist Indonesian Army. In the Sino-Soviet dispute the PKI followed a nominally independent course, but leaned toward Peking.

Because of concern over Sukarno's failing heath, encouragement by Chinese Communists (see Masashi Nishihara, *The Japanese and Sukarno's Indonesia*, Honolulu, 1976, pp,. 169-70), or fear that the Army might stage a preemptive coup, top PKI leaders, along with a handful of dissident Army and Air Force officers, attempted to seize power in Djakarta on the night of 30 September 1965. Six Army generals were murdered by Communist youth and women's front members in this third coup venture. Sukarno probably tacitly approved it, but loyal Army units, led by General Suharto, quelled the rebels in Djakarta within two days. Party cadres and rebellious army units, however, continued to fight for several weeks in Central Java.

As Suharto and defense minister General A. H. Nasution established their authority, anti-Communist Muslim youth groups massacred several tens and probably hundreds of thousands of suspected Communists and sympathizers, including masses of innocents. On 12 March 1966 the PKI was banned, despite Sukarno's efforts to preserve its legality. In July the propagation or public discussion of Marxism-Leninism was prohibited, except for the purpose of academic study. In 1967 Suharto assumed the remaining vestiges of authority left to the discredited Sukarno. Meanwhile, ceaseless issuance of public reminders of the nation's narrow escape in the abortive *Gestapu* affair (from *Gerakan Tiga Puluh*, "September Movement" or "Thirty September Movement") became standard policy in Suharto's New Order.

In the period since then the detention of hundreds of thousands of political prisoners suspected of Gestapu involvement has drawn international criticism. Severe prison conditions, slow adjudication, uncertainty as to how many prisoners there actually are, and confusion in prisoner classification procedures have aggravated the problem, although the government has denied that the detainees are "political" prisoners at all. It also has stated that, in any case, all or most are to be set free in the near future (Justus M. van der Kroef, "Indonesia's Political Prisoners," *Pacific Affairs*, Winter, 1976-77, pp. 625-47). In mid-1977 probably about 60,000 prisoners remained.

The government continues to emphasize that Communism remains a "latent" threat, but overt Communist resistance has been only minimally evident since 1965. In 1968 an underground PKI movement in Central and East Java briefly crystallized in an "Indonesian People's Republic" center at Blitar, East Java, whose adherents were soon killed or arrested in military sweeps. Since that time scattered Communist deep-cover resistance—the *PKI malam* or "night PKI"—has reportedly focused on infiltration of anti-Suharto groups in West Java, including orthodox Muslim and university student militants, and on assistance to guerrillas along the Sarawak border.

Organization and Tactics. As early as March 1976 the Indonesian Information Ministry connected the "latent danger" of PKI activity with the general elections to be held in May 1977 (*FBIS*, 17 March). The threat of subversion, however limited it may be, is clearly being utilized as a spur to national modernization and official development efforts, which are considered the best means for countering Communist influences. As the press is sensitive to government wishes, it is difficult to obtain data not influenced by the regime's stake in preserving an overdrawn picture of "latent" PKI dangers.

The emphasis on domestic political stability as a *sine qua non* for sustained development became particularly apparent as the general elections approached. In August 1976 the nation's chief domestic security agency warned against unspecified "irresponsible rumors," the spreading of which was "clearly an act of subversion" (ibid., 5 August). In January 1977 the military commander of East Kalimantan, at a gathering of Muslim scholars and clerics in Balikpapan, described "Communist remnants and subversion" as two major threats to national development; the warning was reportedly given because the country was "entering the campaign period" for the May elections (*Indonesia Times*, Djakarta, 24 January). How "rumor mongering" could be laid at the door of the Communists (or indeed what rumors exactly might have been spread), or how specifically Communist "remnant" activity was threatening national development and the elections, was not explained. After the May elections, attention was focused on the March 1978 election for the presidency, and military commanders saw potential Communist influence in a campaign of opposition to incumbent President Suharto. "Clandestine" posters allegedly had appeared, calling for the formation of an "opposition front" as soon as "a competent leader has been found." General Widodo, the military commander in Central Java, characterized the posters as a "provocative movement penetrated by Communist remnants." (Ibid., 27 July.) The extent to which either of the two factions of the PKI is involved in underground activity is not known with certainty.

The Maoist-oriented faction, usually calling itself the "Delegation of the PKI Central Committee," has as its chairman Jusuf Adjitorop, a former Politburo member who escaped the post-Gestapu holocaust because he was in China at the time. The "Delegation" apparently consists of about forty persons based in Peking and twenty in Tirana, Albania, whence most of its publications issue. The number of "Delegation" followers in Indonesia is unknown, but several scores of Indonesian Chinese who live in West Borneo are believed to be sympathizers with the Sarawak Communist guerrillas and can be considered informal supporters.

Other than Adjitorop, "Delegation" literature makes no mention of its leadership. Moreover, as a small group of exiles who appear to be financed entirely by the Chinese and Albanian Communists, the "Delegation" has little need for extensive organization. On the other hand, its publicity campaign is quite extensive, and its materials have appeared with regularity. A statement, purportedly issued by its Politburo in August 1966, and an *otokritik* (self-criticism) in the following September have provided much of the theoretical foundation of this Maoist group, and a new party program in November 1967 has specified courses of action (both documents reprinted in *Build the PKI Along the Marxist-Leninist Line to Lead the People's Democratic Revolution in Indonesia*, Tirana, 1971).

In September 1976 a statement over the signature of Adjitorop commemorated the tenth anniversary of the aforementioned "self-criticism." The new PKI leadership, it said, through criticism and self-criticism, had overcome its "opportunistic and revisionist mistakes" and was now on the "correct path," defined as an "armed agrarian peasant revolution under proletarian leadership." The PKI, it added, has appealed to workers, peasants, and to "all Indonesian revolutionary, anti-imperialist and antifeudalist forces" to unite in the face of the Suharto government's "anti-national, anti-people and anti-Communist policy," with which "Soviet social imperialism" was said to be in league. (*Voice of the Malayan Revolution*, clandestine radio, 4 November 1976; *FBIS*, 8 November.)

Organization and Tactics. In March 1977 "Delegation" chairman Adjitorop reviewed the achievements of his faction in countering the "Indonesian revisionist renegade clique" (the Moscow PKI faction) and their mentors, "The Soviet modern revisionists." The Moscow faction, he said, had sought to impose their revisionist line on the party, and been trying "frenziedly" to split the PKI, while "Soviet revisionists" were giving aid to the Suharto regime and, in essence, denying the necessity of "making revolution by force." (Ibid., 16 April, in *FBIS*, 21 April; *Peking Review*, 6 May, pp. 46-48; NCNA, 23 April.)

A "Delegation" broadcast on 28 May excoriated the 2 May general elections in Indonesia, charging the "fascist regime" with chicanery, violence, and political assassination to insure its victory. Also the disparity between the privileged few and the masses of poor was alleged to be steadily widening, while foreign monopoly capital was strangling the national economy and Soviet "social imperialism" was intensifying its "collusion" with the regime.

However, apart from their policy value to their supporters in People's China, the Indonesian Maoists, like the Moscow faction, appear mainly interested in capitalizing on the long-term effect in Indonesia of the political and economic difficulties of the regime, and on the pressures for a less authoritarian government. If the latter were to come about, accommodation of now repressed leftist intersts would probably re-legitimize in Indonesia the dissemination or propagation of some Maoist tenets (Justus M. van der Kroef, *The Indonesian Maoists: Doctrines and Perspectives*, University of Maryland School of Law, Baltimore, 1977).

The Moscow faction of the PKI refers to itself as the "Communist Party of Indonesia," usually without indicating that it is a smaller entity than the whole PKI. Its statements, not often signed by a single, regular chief spokesman but rather by various or previously unknown authors, sometimes identified as members of the Central Committee, or of the "leadership of the CP, Indonesia," appear in Moscow-oriented media such as the *World Marxist Review*.

The principal policy document of the Moscow faction, issued in February 1969, is called "Urgent Tasks of the Communist Movement in Indonesia." (*IB*, Prague, no. 7, pp. 27, 33-37). It stresses the importance of reestablishing public credibility for the PKI and tends to minimize the use of armed resistance and revolutionary violence, unless careful preparation has been made. Its statements have become fewer in the past five years or so as Soviet-Indonesian relations have begun to recover from the effects of the Gestapu incident. Its statements customarily parallel the Maoist faction's pronouncements in alleging foreign economic exploitation and political repression in Indonesia under the Suharto regime (e.g., "Ten Years of Repression in Indonesia," *IB*, 1975, no. 20-21, p. 75).

In December 1976 the Moscow faction termed the forthcoming general elections a "sham" whose only purpose was to strengthen the existing regime. It also alleged that "tens of thousands of innocent partiots" were still being incarcerated in Indonesia, and that the regime, having opened the doors wide to the exploitation of foreign capital, today "obediently follows in the wake of imperialism, chiefly U.S. imperialism." According to the statement, Indonesian Communists today demand: (1) restoration of all political freedoms and release of all political prisoners; (2) freedom of religion and the lifting of the ban on "scientific socialism" and on Sukarno's doctrines; (3) restoration of constitutional rights of parliament and the abolition of special domestic security and intelligence agencies; (4) fiscal reforms and elimination of corruption; (5) control over foreign capital; (6) implementation of the 1960 agrarian laws; (7) protection of students' rights, of the interests of professional persons, and of national culture; and (8) return to an "active anti-imperialist foreign policy," including opposition to turning the Association of Southeast Asia (ASEAN), to which Indonesia belongs, into a military bloc, and instead support of the principle of making Southeast Asia a "zone of peace, security, and mutually beneficial cooperation among all countries of the region" (*IB*, 1977, no. 2, pp. 22-25).

Domestic Developments. Indonesian government and media statements in 1977 continued to give prominence to the arrest and trial of Gestapu defendants. In May a prison sentence of nineteen years was meted out by a military court to a former Bandung mayor and army colonel who had been arrested in 1968 and was found guilty of "abusing his authority" as local military commander in connection with the preparation of the Gestapu affair (*FBIS*, 4 May). in Mid-July a court-martial sentenced a former Air Force sergeant to death for alleged "full responsibility" for the killing of the six Army generals at the Halim Air Force base near Djakarta, an incident that marked the beginning of the 1965 coup attempt (ibid., 16 July). On 18 July the official news agency Antara announced the capture of an important, hitherto fugitive Gestapu conspirator, former Brigadier General Suharjo, onetime military commander in East Kalimantan (ibid., 19 July). On 27 October military sources claimed the arrest of "several hundreds" of PKI members during the year, notably in and around Surabaya and in Central Java. Their identities were not further specified, nor was it revealed how, in view of repeated government assurances in the past that the PKI had been destroyed, such a large number had been able to remain at large. On 31 October the military commander of Java and Bali, Lieutenant General Widodo, announced the arrest of nineteen "underground Communists" who had been trying to organize via telepathy. (Ibid., 1 November.)

The threat of subversion was perceived as coming from quarters other than the PKI, however. In December 1976 the government announced that 499 illegal immigrants from mainland China would shortly be tried (ibid., 29 December). These Chinese are believed to be part of a stream of thousands who had left Indonesia, some because of a ban on Chinese carrying on rural retail trade, others in the aftermath of widespread pogroms in Java and Sumatra resulting from popular suspicion of Chinese involvement in the Gestapu affair. Suspicion of People's China's policies and of the loyalty of 4.5 million ethnic Chinese domiciled in Indonesia provide additional dynamics for the Suharto regime's domestic anti-Communist campaign, though the Chinese have made some effort to assimilate more fully since 1965.

There were also reports of the emergence of a clandestine movement for the liberation of Aceh, a province at the northern tip of Sumatra. The "Aceh free state movement" was denounced by

Indonesian foreign minister Adam Malik, and Security Command chief Admiral Sudomo called it a "subversive and separatist plot" (ibid., 7, 8 June). The Aceh movement is one more in a range of secessionist groups, most comprising a few hundred followers or less, that include the guerrillas of the Papua independence movement in West New Guinea, the "South Moluccan Republic" on Seran in eastern Indonesia, and the freedom movement in former Portuguese East Timor which, after an invasion by Indonesian militarized volunteers, became Indonesia's twenty-seventh province on 17 July (Justus M. van der Kroef, *Patterns of Conflict in Eastern Indonesia*, London, Institute for the Study of Conflict, January 1977). Additionally, Indonesia regularly has engaged in military discussions with the Malaysian government to safeguard the Sarawak-Indonesian frontier, where several scores of ethnic Chinese Communist guerrillas seeking an independent Sarawak are still active.

On 2 May about sixty-three million voters, more than 90 percent of the electorate, cast ballots in the general elections. The government's party organization, Golkar (from *Golongan Karya*, "functional group"), one of only three parties participating, won about 61.7 percent of the votes. This was a drop of about 1 percent from its share in 1971, and considerably less than the 70 percent that Golkar spokesmen had predicted. At stake were 360 elected seats in parliament; there are an additional 100 government-appointed seats for the military and special interest groups (who usually vote with Golkar). Because of its electoral drop, Golkar lost 5 of its 236 elected seats. The Indonesian Democratic Party, primarily a fusion of Christian confessional and secular nationalist parties, won about 8.7 percent of the vote (also about 1 percent less than in 1971) and gave up one seat. The evident gainer was the Unity Development Party (PPP), a merger of four theologically disparate Muslim parties, which won 29.6 percent of the vote (almost 2.5 percent more than in 1971) and added six seats to its ninety-four-member parliamentary delegation.

The election results, and particularly the PPP's victory in restive metropolitan Djakarta (44 percent of the votes, compared with 39 percent for Golkar), were a blow to the Suharto regime, giving encouragement to critics. Student, intellectual, and some business circles began mooting the possibility of supporting a candidate in opposition to President Suharto, whose term of office expires in March 1978. While it seemed unlikely that Suharto would not continue as president, the opposition campaign led to sharp warnings by Malik and General Widodo not to create confusion through dissent (*National Review*, Bangkok, 2 July 1977; *Straits Times*, Singapore, 29 June). Widodo subsequently appeared to link the opposition campaign to the PKI's "united national front" building efforts (Antara dispatch, Djakarta, 4 August). In mid-June, military authorities in Central Java warned, in connection with electoral violence there, that a number of Indonesian youths, known to have been trained in terrorism abroad by "certain elements hostile to Indonesia," were responsible for the violence, which was called a "warming-up activity" (*Straits Times*, 13 June).

The problem of the *tapol* (from *tahanan politik*, "political prisoners") continued to give the Suharto regime difficulties, particularly in the light of the new emphasis on "human rights" in the policies of the Carter administration in Washington. In the Gestapu aftermath some 580,000 Indonesians were arrested for alleged complicity in the coup plot or for Communist activity. A trickle of arrests has continued, and though Gestapu detainees have been released, re-arrests have been common. Estimates differ as to how many *tapol* still remain incarcerated—from around 30,000 (the usual figure in official accounts) to 100,000 and even higher (Justus M. van der Kroef, "Indonesia's Political Prisoners," pp. 625-47), with a probable figure being about 60,000 as of September 1977. While the *Tapol* issue becomes increasingly controversial, the government insists that those detained are not "political prisoners" at all, but were arrested because of various statutory offenses. Repeated promises that the bulk of them will be released have sometimes been qualified by references to budgetary and other planning considerations (*Tapol Bulletin*, British edition, June 1977). Skepticism persists among some observers that release or trials of the prisoners in fact will be accelerated, especially of the nearly 10,000 confined on the island of Buru. There is not sufficient evidence to bring them to trial (by the government's own admission), but the regime views their confinement as desirable for domestic security reasons.

International Aspects. Indonesia's relations with People's China, suspended in 1967 in the Gestapu aftermath, remain so though not formally broken. During 1977 official statements repeated the familiar theme that efforts at normalization of relations were continuing, but that the time for completion of that process was not yet ripe. Foreign Minister Malik said that Indonesia would first have to "re-educate and register the approximately 5 million Indonesians of Chinese descent" (*FBIS*, 1 August). On other occasions Malik had seemed more sanguine, saying that normalization would take place after the May elections, that the Chinese People's government had promised not to assist subversion in Indonesia, and, hence, that "the time has come for Indonesia not to ignore a country of 800 million people any longer" (*Straits Times*, 1 January). Malik also reportedly said that the two countries had "promised each other" to normalize relations after the elections, although "in any event" the problem would have to be considered from the standpoint of Indonesia's national interest (*FBIS*, 3 January). On 30 September, after returning from the UN General Assembly meeting in New York, Malik said that "activities toward normalization" were "being initiated." He added that Indonesia would send a delegation to the October trade fair in Canton.

Suspicion of Chinese loyalty, fed by undercurrents of resentment of Chinese commercial and financial prowess in Indonesia bolstered by Japanese interests, is pervasive, and other prominent public figures, such as State Intelligence Board vice-chief and Suharto confidant Lieutenant General Ali Murtopo, have asserted that China must stop her "hostilities" and "discontinue support to Indonesians" involved in the Gestapu affair (*Antara Daily News Bulletin*, 12 February). Apprehension was augmented when, on 18 May, Hua Kuo-feng and other members of the Chinese Politburo and Central Committee had a well-publicized meeting with and tendered a banquet to Adjitorop, described as "Secretary of the PKI Central Committee" (*Peking Review*, 27 May, p. 3). It was the first time in many years that such an official gesture of approbation had been given the Maoist PKI faction. Indonesia's interim foreign minister declared that this, "as well as other like acts of the People's Republic of China," had "slowed down the rehabilitation and normalization" of relations (*Sinar Harapan*, 21 May; *FBIS*, 31 May).

Two other factors influence normalization. One is the problem of citizenship. The legal status of an estimated one million Chinese now in Indonesia "remains unclear and is still under investigation," according to General Murtopo (*FBIS*, 7 February). Just how many of these lived in Indonesia, left during the anti-Chinese pogram in 1966-67, and have since then illegally returned is not known. In Hong Kong, reportedly, several thousand former Chinese residents desirous of returning are stranded as "stateless persons because the Djakarta government does not permit them to enter" (*Asian Student*, San Francisco, 1 January). In a statement to a Singapore daily in May (which did not appear in the Indonesian press), Malik stated that, as per a recent agreement with Peking, all stateless persons of Chinese descent age fifteen or older in Indonesia would be registered and would have to choose between becoming Indonesian or Chinese citizens (*FBIS*, 18 May). There has been no significant implementation of this agreement.

The other factor concerns the hostility of some Indonesian business circles, and their bureaucratic and military ancillaries in the power structure, toward Chinese-owned and -run enterprises, often financed by Japanese or multinational interests. As so often in the past, the government seems concerned to curtail the scope of Chinese business operations in favor of the so-called *pribumi* (i.e., autochthonously Indonesian) enterprises. On 21 February Indonesian trade minister Radius Prawiro declared that foreign trading corporations in the country would have to be transferred to Indonesian management by the end of the year; about 15,000 companies, mostly Chinese, would be affected by the decision, according to Prawiro (*StraitsTimes*, 22 February). While the measure is designed to enhance "pribumization," one consequence, as in the past, will be the growth or covert continuance of Chinese enterprises with paper Indonesian owners or front men. These arrangements are open to corruption and malversation that can sharpen the legal uncertainties already facing some of the more productive elements of the Chinese community.

Relations with the Soviet bloc, following (1) a new trade agreement between the two countries signed in March 1974, and (2) Moscow's readiness, announced in November 1975, to provide technical and financial assistance in connection with the construction of two hydropower plants in West and Central Java (*Indonesia Times*, Djakarta, 19 November 1975), have officially continued to improve, and have particularly been marked by a steady Soviet-Indonesian trade expansion. Though strained, post-Gestapu Soviet-Indonesian diplomatic relations were never suspended. Between 1975 and 1976, according to the Soviet news agency "Novosti," trade grew by 48.2 percent (from 28.6 million rubles to 42.4 million), with the Russians buying rubber, copra, and palm oil, and Indonesia importing machinery, cars, and chemicals (Antara despatch, 20 April 1977).

Soviet media these days only briefly and without editorializing mention the ongoing trials and convictions of PKI leaders, and even find occasion now to praise the historically anti-Communist Indonesian armed forces. On 4 October 1976, the founding anniversary of Indonesia's armed forces, for example, Radio Moscow, in an Indonesian-language broadcast, praised the "valor of Indonesian officers and soldiers" and asserted that the "armed forces' endorsement" of Indonesia's "active anti-imperialist policy" had made Indonesia a "recognized leader among developing countries" (*FBIS*, 20 October). Such fulsome praise is perhaps the more remarkable because other Soviet commentators at this time noted critically that "some Indonesian leaders" were stressing the desirability of U.S.-Indonesian military cooperation, in the context of alleged "pro-imperialist" U.S. interest in converting ASEAN into an anti-Communist alliance as a replacement for the now defunct SEATO (A. Yuryev, "Indonesia and Her Problems," *International Affairs*, Moscow, November 1976, pp. 90-91). The official Soviet outlook on Indonesia is today generally quite positive, despite the strong anti-Communist dynamic of most major Indonesian policies of the Suharto regime. Moscow appears to be committed to a long-haul, gradual liberalization of the domestic political climate, and hopes to assist it by demonstrating less need for reliance by Indonesia on Western and Japanese capital. Advantage is thus seen to lie in small achievements; the first post-Gestapu exhibition of books published in the USSR, Bulgaria, Czechoslovakia, Hungary, and Poland occurred on 6 June at the residence of the ambassador of the German Democratic Republic in Djakarta.

In the meantime, however, the PKI "Delegation" in Moscow is of sufficient importance to the Soviets to have been permitted to hold its own "scientific conference" there in August. Participants (not further identified) hailed the "bonds of friendship and solidarity" which had "traditionally" linked the Indonesian and Soviet Communist parties (*Pravda*, 28 August; *FBIS*, 2 September).

Publications. The Maoist PKI faction relies on the "Voice of the Malayan Revolution," the clandestine radio transmitter of the Peking-oriented Communist Party of Malaya, for relatively quick dissemination of its major policy and party anniversary statements. The faction's bimonthly *Indonesian Tribune* and tabloid *API* (*Api Pemuda Indonesia*, "Flame of Indonesian Youth"), both edited primarily from Tirana, Albania, have been slow and irregular in appearing. People's China media noted the faction's statements with greatly declined frequency in the past decade.

The Moscow PKI faction primarily uses the Prague-based *World Marxist Review* and *Information Bulletin*. Its Indonesian-language *Tekad Rakjat* ("Will of the People") appears somewhat irregularly.

University of Bridgeport   Justus M. van der Kroef

Japan

The Japan Communist Party (Nihon Kyosanto; JCP), founded 15 July 1922, was illegal until the end of World War II. During that period it had little influence and the party membership did not exceed 1,000. Japan's surrender brought the postwar Allied Occupation, and on 4 October 1945 General Douglas MacArthur, as Supreme Commander for the Allied Powers, ordered the Japanese government to release all political prisoners and legalized several political parties, including the JCP. Among those freed were Tokuda Kyuichi and Shiga Yoshio, two of the JCP's three founding members, who had been in prison for twenty years. the third, Nosaka Sanzo, returned in 1946 from China, where he had been working with the Chinese Communists on the indoctrination of Japanese war prisoners.

During the next five years the attitude of the JCP toward the emperor and the constitution was ambiguous. The party won a base of support, although not a broad one. JCP members also gained some influence in labor unions and led several strikes in 1945-47. In February 1947 the Occupation authorities moved against a general strike, forcing several JCP-backed unions into submission—thus causing the party to lose considerable prestige. Because of its anti-American stance, however, the JCP became known as the only real "opposition" party, and in the 1949 elections it won 10 percent of the popular vote and thirty-five seats in the lower, more important house of the Diet, the House of Representatives, in which it was the fourth-largest party.

In 1950 the JCP's policy of "peaceful revolution" to achieve Socialism, advocated particularly by Nosaka, came under criticism by the Cominform. The successes of Communist revolutions in China and Southeast Asia strengthened the aggressive factions of the JCP and brought Tokuda to the top of the leadership heirarchy of the Communist movement in Japan. Following these internal changes, in May 1950 the JCP led violent demonstrations against the Occupation authorities. Arrests of participants then prompted the JCP to make propaganda attacks against the U.S. and the Japanese government, with the result that MacArthur ordered the prime minister to purge the Central Committee of the JCP from political life.

In June, when the party newspaper *Akahata* openly favored the cause of North Korea, it and other Japanese Communist publications were banned. Many Communist leaders went underground and some engaged in subversive activities. Having become a symbol of terrorism and extremism, the JCP lost in the 1952 elections, retaining no seats in the Diet. Compared with 1949, the popular vote given to the JCP dropped from around 3 million to 897,000. Party membership fell from 150,000 in 1949 to somewhere in the vicinity of 20,000.

Following the death of Tokuda in 1953, Nosaka became undisputed leader of the JCP. Alterations were made in the party's aggressive policies and in 1953 one JCP member was elected to the House of Representatives and in 1955 two won seats. In 1961 the Sino-Soviet dispute came into the open and th JCP took the stand that each party in the international Communist movement had the right to choose its own policies, tantamount to denying Moscow's predominant role in Communist affairs in other countries. This marked the beginning of a nationalist, parliamentary policy on the party of the JCP.

The "parliamentary road" became even more definite after 1964 when the JCP broke with

Moscow over the issue of the test-ban treaty, and with China after 1966 when the Cultural Revolution came into direct conflict with the policies of the mainstream of the party. Shiga, who opposed the official party line, was expelled from the JCP. He subsequently organized another party, "Voice of Japan," which followed the Soviet line. The Shiga group, although active, was not success-ful in winning much support in elections or on major political or social issues. Meanwhile, Fuwa Tetsuzo, who articulated "people's parliamentarianism," became the most important JCP theoretician and Miyamoto Kenji became the formal and recognized head of the party. Under their leadership, in 1969 the JCP began to achieve election victories. In December of that year the JCP polled 3.1 million votes and won 14 seats in the House of Representatives. It also won 1,600 seats in various local assemblies and was reported to have a membership of more than 250,000.

In 1970, at its Eleventh Congress, the JCP reaffirmed its policy of the parliamentary path to power, adopted a policy of working toward a "democratic coalition government," and expressed considerable flexibility on economic matters. Perhaps more important for attracting the electorate were resolutions which stated that the party would not institute a one-party dictatorship if it won political power, and that it would willingly return power to the ruling Liberal Democratic Party (LDP) if it should win an election in coalition with other opposition parties and later lose to the LDP.

As a result of these changes in party doctrine, as well as shifts in the style of Japanese politics and the aspirations of the electorate, the JCP gained a major election victory in the 1972 House of Representatives election, polling more than 5,479,000 votes (10.5 percent) and winning 38 seats. These gains made it the second opposition party in Japan and were followed by successes in local elections in 1973. For example, the JCP increased its seats in the Tokyo Metropolitan Assembly from 18 to 24 and became the third-largest party in Tokyo. In 1974 it matched its 1972 lower house victory with similar gains in the upper house, the House of Councillors, winning some 6.4 million votes (about 12 percent) and 20 seats (out of 252). The 1975 local elections gave the party 3,165 (out of 76,216) seats in prefectural, municipal, town, and village assemblies; included in its victories was the reelection of the governor of Osaka—supported solely by the JCP.

By 1975, however, many observers of Japanese politics speculated that the JCP had possibly reached its zenith. This view reflected the reversal of some election gains in urban areas, a drop in subscriptions to *Akahata,* and faltering membership drives—about the same number dropped out as joined the party during 1975-76. Efforts to win labor union and individual worker support also noticeably bogged down. The two largest Japanese unions, Sohyo and Domei, consistently voted against the JCP proposal that union members should have freedom of party choice. Meanwhile the JCP lost ground with Nikkyoso (the Japan Teachers' Union).

The JCP also failed in its efforts to form a coalition with other opposition parties. In 1974 the Democratic Socialist Party (DSP) announced that it would not cooperate with the Communists. The Clean Government Party (Komeito) opposed working with the JCP less adamantly; but when it was learned that JCP officials had made a secret agreement with the Value Creation Society (Soka Gakkai), the Buddhist organization upon which Komeito depends for its support, Komeito persuaded Soka Gakkai leaders to rescind the agreement. The Japan Socialist Party (JSP) was more willing to ally with the JCP, but a feud over the routing of financial support to *Burakumin* (social outcast) groups, the revision of election laws, and the JCP's role vis-à-vis the major labor unions made meaningful cooperation impossible.

A major reversal in the December 1976 House of Representatives election cost the JCP more than half of its seats and was repeated in the July 1977 House of Councillors election (see below), suggesting that the party may at present be in a state of crisis and may be destined to decline as a force in Japanese politics. On the other hand, the poor showing in recent elections could be due simply to shifts in support to which election strategy has not yet been accommodated, and to the anti-Communist campaigns undertaken by several other parties and several major magazines and newspapers.

The JCP claimed 370,000 members in 1976, and a government source reported the same number in September 1977. The party's goal of 400,000 was not attained. An official Communist publication puts the occupational status of JCP as follows: manual and office workers, 59 percent; the remainder being farmers, merchants, professionals, students, and others. In age and sex, 54 percent are between eighteen and thirty years of age, 40 percent are between thirty-one and fifty, and women make up 31.7 percent. The population of Japan is about 112 to 113 million.

Organization and Leadership. Officially the supreme decision-making organ of the JCP is the party congress, convened every two or three years and elected from local party organizations. It elects the Central Committee, which acts for the congress when it is not in session. The committee has varied in size, generally growing larger over recent years. In 1977 it had a total of 165 members (122 full and 43 alternate) until the party congress in October, which chose a new committee of 195 (141 full and 54 alternate). The Central Committee elects a chairman and also the Presidium (some 40 members), which in turn elects the Standing Committee or Secretariat. The Secretariat chairman—the secretary general—is the actual head of the party. The Central Committee meets at least every three months; while it is not in session, the Presidium and the Secretariat carry on the party's business.

The committee also elects (in reality, appoints) the Central Control Commission (responsible for discipline, it can expell members who do not follow the party line) and the Central Auditing Commission (party finances). Some twenty other committees are responsible in such areas of interest as mass movements and international affairs. Prefectural and district organizations interpret and relay Central Committee decisions to local organizations in schools, towns, and villages—in essence, wherever there are three or more party members. Presidium Chairman Miyamoto Kenji is de facto leader of the JCP. Fuwa Tetsuzo, chairman of the Secretariat, is generally regarded as his "second," and others of the Secretariat as "Miyamoto's men." Fuwa was acting chairman of the Secretariat until Miyamoto, preparing to run for a seat in the House of Councillors, turned over the chairmanship to him.

The JCP members of the Diet are directed by an executive council, consisting of its chairman and their group and floor leaders in the House of Representatives and House of Councillors.

In spite of slower growth in recent years, the JCP is still the second-largest party in Japan, outnumbered only by the ruling LDP. This is compensated for by the fact that other parties have a base of support: the JSP and DSP depend upon the two major labor unions for votes, while the Komeito relies upon its parent organization, the Buddhist group called Soka Gakkai. While the JCP depends for its support almost entirely on individual members, it has affiliation with some activist groups (see below).

The JCP has a full-time headquarters staff of more than 900, and there are more than 5,000 employees at lower levels. About 300 of the full-time central organization worker are attached to *Akahata,* which has in addition 13,000 unpaid correspondents and 50,000 delivery personnel.

Since 1972 the JCP has been the richest political party in Japan. In 1975 its revenue was over $40 million, and its budget has increased since then, though not markedly. The party is also solvent, with a surplus of nearly $1 million. In 1977 the JCP's budget included revenues of slightly over 17 billion yen and expenditures of 15.5 billion yen. More than 90 percent of the party's revenue comes from the sale of its publications, and most of the rest from dues; since nearly all party members subscribe to JCP publications, more money comes from them than the percentage of dues indicates.

Although the party is financially sound, its status as the richest party is deceptive. The reason for its high ranking is that it manages its own funds. The LDP spends much more on campaigning even though its budget is smaller, because much money is spent by factions within the LDP. Also, contributions often don't enter the budget because they are held by campaign organizations; the same is true to a lesser extent of the other parties.

Mass and Auxiliary Organizations. The JCP supports and depends upon support from a large number of affiliate, sympathetic, and common-interest groups and organizations. About forty to fifty could be classified as important nationally, and some are international; many more are small or local in scale.

The most important affiliate organizations are the Democratic Youth League (Minseido) and the Japan Council against Atomic and Hydrogen Bombs (Gensuikyo). Other important organizations with which the JCP has close ties include the All-Japan Students' Federation (Zengakuren), New Japan Women's Association (Shin Fujin), All Japan Merchants' Federation (Zenshoren), Democratic Federation of Doctors (Min-i-ren), Japan Peace Committee (Nihon Heiwa Iin Kai), and the Japan Council of Scientists. Membership in this group of organizations varies, with the largest listed first, from over 500,000 to around 10,000.

In past years, the JCP has also supported the National Movement for the Return of Okinawa and the National People's Council for the Settlement of the Okinawa Problem. In February 1977 *Akahata* expressed JCP opposition to the "Temporary Use Law" as applied to land in Okinawa, which it claimed would extend the "illegal" use of both private and public land by U.S. military bases and the Japan Self-Defense Forces (JSDF). The JCP vice-chairman and four Dietmen subsequently visited Okinawa on a land record survey mission, apparently aimed at winning public acclaim in Okinawa for the JCP and accentuating the issue of U.S. nuclear weapons on the island. In May *Zenei* carried an article critical of the government's position on Okinawa relating to citizens' standard of living and the bases.

Democratic Youth League. Minseido, organized by the JCP in 1923, is the training organ for future party leaders. It also serves to promote youth support and long-range propagation of JCP goals. It is limited to those from fifteen to twenty-five years of age. Membership in recent years has been fairly constant at about 200,000.

Party Vice-Chairman Kaneko addressed Minseido's Central Committee meeting on 13 May and spoke of common goals, particularly in the upcoming House of Councillors election. He also pointed out to the group that the main purpose of the JCP is to reform Japanese politics. In this context, he stressed fighting anti-Communism in Japan.

Japan Council against Atomic and Hydrogen Bombs. Gensuikyo was formed in 1954 and within a year was taken over by the JCP, Zengakuren, the JSP, and Sohyo, the largest labor union in Japan. Gradually the JCP increased its influence and broadened Gensuikyo's objectives to include opposition to U.S. "imperialist" policies and support for national liberation movements. The 1960 Gensuikyo conference adopted an "appeal" stating that the banning of atomic and hydrogen bombs could be accomplished only by struggle against the U.S. Subsequently, moderate elements withdrew from Gensuikyo and the DSP established its own organization, called the Congress for the Prohibition of Nuclear Weapons (Kakkin Kaigi). In 1961-62, when the JCP defended Soviet nuclear testing, the JSP similarly formed a rival organization, the Japan Congress against Atomic and Hydrogen Bombs (Gensuikin).

Early in 1977 Gensuikyo and Gensuikin began discussions of a merger, long advocated by JCP. The two agreed to (1) convene a unified world conference in the summer, (2) merge within the year, and (3) adopt a policy of absolute opposition to nuclear weapons. Subsequently, the JCP put its position on unification in more specific terms to include support for the Pugwash Conference, the International Peace Bureau, and the U.N. Non-Governmental Organization. From this it was clear that the JCP wants to coordinate the Japanese anti-nuclear movement with such movements elsewhere.

In August the "World Conference against Atomic and Hydrogen Bombs" was held in Hiroshima, sponsored by the united forces of Gensuikyo and Gensuikin. Sit-in demonstrations by local residents against nuclear tests conducted by the Soviet Union at the time gave the meeting added publicity and seemed to have no ill effects on the unity of the sponsors, as both refused to take a stand for or against the demonstrations. Several commentators in the Japanese press noted that there was real unity between the JCP and the JSP, and one suggested that it might pave the way for a more general coalition between the two parties (*Chou Koron*, October).

Party Congress. On 17 October 1977 the JCP's Fourteenth Congress convened in Atami City. Six thousand delegates attended the six-day meeting and a number of items were discussed and crucial decisions made. Policy decisions reached at the six-day meeting included: (1) to improve the political lines of opposition parties, with special reference to the JSP, which is in a state of confusion, and the JCP, which is isolated; (2) to internationalize the opposition parties' line; (3) to influence the Komeito to revolutionize and repudiate the influence of the DSP's centrist, anti-Communist line; (4) to help the JSP rid itself of factional strife. Important themes were the restoration of the JCP's strength and the strategy for its activities and work in the future. Non-activists in the party were criticized, and it was agreed that the education of new members must be given additional stress. The congress resolved to raise the party membership to 500,000 and *Akahata's* readership to 400,000 by mid-1978. Representatives of foreign Communist parties came from Italy, Australia, Cuba, Spain, France, Vietnam, Mexico, Yugoslavia, and Romania—two more countries than were represented at the previous congress. Vietnamese and Romanian delegates spoke at the meeting; Korean and Yugoslav representatives were also active at the session.

The new Central Committee chosen at the meeting consists of 141 full and 54 alternate members. The average age of the full members is fifty-five years (compared with sixty before) and forty-seven for the alternates (fifty-three before). The youngest full member is forty-two, and there are two alternates aged thirty. Thirteen alternates are women (7 before). Four alternates are part-owners or managers of large companies.

The leadership remained essentially the same. Nosaka retained his chairmanship of the Central Committee despite his advanced age. Miyamoto kept his position of real authority even though the party had suffered two serious election defeats in just over six months. Other top leaders stayed in their pre-congress jobs. This reflects both the view that the recent election losses were caused by external factors and that there is no feasible alternative to Miyamoto's leadership and the currently espoused national, Eurocommunism style and line taken by the JCP.

A party congress resolution was adopted on 22 October, the closing day of the session. It contained three parts dealing with the world situation and Japan's role in world affairs, national administration reform tasks and struggles, and the JCP's international activities. The first and third were more detailed.

Regarding the former, the JCP hailed the "total victory" of the Vietnamese, Lao, and Cambodian people in their anti-imperialist struggles. According to the resolution, the defeat changed the international balance of power in favor of anti-imperialist and revolutionary forces. But it also noted that the United States is now pursuing new aggressive policies, mentioning specifically Washington's policy of pre-emptive nuclear attack, the neutron bomb, and the tripartite alliance of the U.S., Western Europe, and Japan. However, the resolution went on to mention "deep-rooted arguments" within the international Communist movement and those "who misdirect international struggles." Mention was made of those who "give top priority to U.S.-Soviet cooperation" and others who take the attitude that "U.S. imperialism is beautiful so as to deal with the major enemy the Soviet Union." This was an unveiled criticism of both the Soviet Union and China. The resolution went on to say that the JCP supports solidarity among the three revolutionary forces: the Socialist countries, the revolutionary movements in the capitalist countries, and the national liberation movements. In this context the role of Eurocommunism was given a specific significance because it "represents developments and variations in the theory and practice of scientific socialism."

Concerning the JCP's international activities, the resolution specifically mentioned continued support for the countries of Indochina, struggles against the governments of Chile and South Korea, close relations with Eurocommunist parties, better ties with parties in the Socialist countries, and improved bonds with the Palestine Liberation Organization and the Algerian National Liberation Front. A special call was made to close the ten-year-old split in the world Communist movement by "getting rid of national chauvinism and accepting scientific socialism while helping promote unity in the international socialist movement."

Domestic Attitudes and Activities. The central domestic issue for the JCP during 1977 was its relations with the other political parties, especially the opposition parties. It has long advocated an alliance of opposition parites and a coalition in order to win an election victory over the ruling LDP. (The New Liberal Club, a new party on the political scene, is not classified as "progressive" by the JCP and therefore does not qualify.) The DSP and the Komeito oppose the JCP's participation in a coalition allegedly because of its inclination toward violence, its opposition to the emperor system and its stance on the U.S.-Japan Security Treaty. The secret agreement worked out in 1974 with Soka Gakkai, the parent organization supporting Komeito, was to the effect that the JCP would shelve its anti-religious stance if Komeito would not espouse anti-Communism. When the agreement was publicized in 1975, Komeito repudiated it and relations between the two parties deteriorated. This situation remains. The DSP has been antagonistic toward the JCP for some time, and this became even more pronounced during 1977. Two months before the July House of Councillors election, DSP Secretary General Tsukamoto Saburo rebuffed a JCP proposal for a coalition of all opposition parties, stating that his party would not align with the JCP. While not changing its stance on a broad coalition, the JCP criticized the DSP and Komeito for their anti-Communist stance, which it said worked to the advantage of the LDP. After the election, in which "moderate" tendencies seemed to help the DSP and Komeito, JCP spokesmen repudiated the idea of a "centrist trend." They also stated that more seats in local government could have been won by progressives had it not been for the two parties' unwillingness to cooperate.

An anti-Communist campaign, carried out not only by these two parties but also by the LDP and the press, prompted JCP officials to assail the press for its bias. This attack was particularly directed against two prominent Japanese magazines, *Bungei Shunju* and *Shukan Bunshun,* which carried a series of articles very critical of the JCP.

Relations with the JSP remained cordial and may be said to have improved somewhat. On the other hand, Sohyo, Japan's largest labor union, which supports the JSP, continued to reject the JCP's suggestion that members be allowed to choose their political party freely. Also, the JCP opposes the right of teachers to strike (it calls teaching the "sacred profession"), while the JSP supports this right.

The JCP continued to publicize the Lockheed scandal (see *YICA, 1977,* p. 314), but this was gradually shifted to a lower priority and supplanted by interest in the "Korean" scandal. In January the JCP demanded that the government provide a written explanation of alleged bribery of Japanese officials by the Korean Central Intelligence Agency (KCIA) and a release of information on the agency's 1973 abduction of South Korean opposition leader Kim Dae-chung from Japan. Later the party sent one of its Diet members to the U.S. to seek further details. Upon his return he stated that members of the LDP had received KCIA bribes to hush up the abduction case. Subsequent articles in *Zenei* alleged that former Prime Minister Tanaka had received a 300 million yen bribe from the KCIA to suppress the case and that pro-South Korea members of the Diet were also on the take, including members of parties besides the LDP. In August, after a second visit to the U.S., the JCP member stated that he had received documented evidence from a number of high U.S. officials that proved that the KCIA had committed crimes in Japan and that it was originally going to murder Kim Dae-chung. He said also that Prime Minister Fukuda had in July sent a secret emissary to the U.S. to obtain a statement from Kim Jae Kwon, who was responsible for the abduction, to the effect that the testimony before the U.S. Congress by the former head of the KCIA was not true. In subsequent months the JCP continued to demand that the government obtain testimony regarding the case and the associated bribery, but was unable to expand the importance of the issue.

The most important foreign policy issue for the JCP during the year was Japan's territorial claim to the Kurile Islands. This issue is an old one, but it became more controversial in mid-1977 as a result of the Soviet Union's extending its 200-mile sea jurisdiction. At the end of World War II, Japan's unconditional surrender meant giving up claim to territory occupied by Allied forces. Since the Red Army was in the Kuriles, this gave Moscow title to them, which Tokyo yielded in 1951 under the San Francisco Treaty. However, five years later, the Japanese government made the claim that Kunashiri and Etorofu (the two southernmost islands) were not included. Since the two islands were the home of nearly 17,000 Japanese fishermen and their families when the Soviet army occupied them for only one week at the close of World War II, many in Japan feel they should be returned. Also, the waters around these islands constitute one of the world's richest fishing grounds, and the area is rich in lumber, seaweed, gold, silver, copper, and various minerals. It has been estimated that the islands would produce $30 million a year in products for Japan. At present more than a half million Japanese tourists visit the area annually, and the "Northern Territory Association" and the "Council to Return the Northern Territories" are pushing the issue, which, needless to say, is an important one in Japanese politics. It also gives the JCP an opportunity to capitalize on Japanese nationalist sentiment and to prove itself a nationalist party. The JCP's consistent attitude on the issue in the past and its efforts to persuade Moscow to return the islands are in its favor.

The issue became heated when Moscow, in retaliation for the government's refusal to return the MIG-25 flown to Japan by a defecting Soviet pilot, made Japanese who wanted to visit the islands (where 4,000 ancestral tombs are located) obtain visas. It was amplified by the Soviet's 200-mile ocean territorial claim and controversy with Japan over a fishing treaty. In April, Presidium Chairman Miyamoto told a JCP conference, which newsmen were invited to attend, that the government had erred in abandoning Japan's claim to them by signing the San Francisco Treaty. Later, Miyamoto told reporters that in 1971 when he visited the Soviet Union, Kremlin leaders had agreed to return the adjacent lesser islands, Habomai and Shikotan, once a peace treaty was signed between the two countries. He went on to say that the Soviet attitude was now "obscure" and that the issue should not be tied to the fishing rights agreement being discussed between the two countries.

In May, the JCP Central Committee wrote an open letter to the Communist Party of the Soviet Union (CPSU) on the Kuriles issue. The letter pointed out that the islands were not territories that Japan had originally "plundered by violence and greed" and thus are not covered under provisions of the Cairo Declaration, which provided for the return of such territories to their original owners; rather, they were acquired from Russia in 1855 by peaceful agreements and were from that time on inhabited by the Japanese. The letter also noted that in 1959 Miyamoto Kenji, then secretary general of the JCP attended the Twenty-first Congress of the CPSU and at that time the Kremlin specifically promised the return of the southern Kuriles chain, and that this agreement was reaffirmed in 1971. The Soviet attitude, the letter said, "openly violates the principles of scientific socialism, which oppose the merging of territories of one nation into those of another."

This letter provoked a rebuttal in *Pravda* ("International Views and Party Contacts"). The JCP, however, kept the issue alive by answering the rebuttal and further clarifying its stand. The JCP apparently sought to improve its image in Japan by countering the claim that it is foreign-controlled. The case also gave it opportunity to criticize the government for slavishly following U.S. orders to the detriment of Japan's national interest.

While supporting the right of the Soviet Union to adopt a 200-mile exclusive fishing zone as a part of a general world trend, JCP leaders maintained that Moscow should respect existing fishing agreements, and that the Soviet zone should not include the Kuriles. A JCP spokesman criticized the Soviet Union for its stance on both issues as well as its request for the right to fish in Japan's 12-mile territorial water area. The main thrust of the party's policies was toward separation of the Kuriles issue from the 200-mile sea jurisdiction zone and Japan's 12-mile territorial sea claim. This included a demand that the Soviet Union negotiate a fishing treaty on the basis of previous agreements and that it rescind its demand to fish in Japan's waters. At the same time, the party demanded that the government move promptly on compensation and relief measures to help fishermen who were forced to stop fishing as a result of the breakdown in negotiations with the Soviet Union.

Later, in September, the JCP took up the issue of the Democratic People's Republic of Korea's 200-mile fishing zone, established on 1 August, and the right of Japanese fishermen to fish in the zone. The JCP expressed praise for the fact that North Korea would allow Japanese fishermen into the zone. It assailed the government for not negotiating directly with North Korea and pointed out that because an agreement had to be worked out instead by the Dietmen's "Association for Japan-Democratic People's Republic of Korea," Japanese fishermen would sacrifice 20,000 tons of fish annually and 600 fishing boats would be put out of business.

The JCP retained its policy of a neutral Japan and criticized increased activities of the Japan Self-Defense Forces. In 1976 a JCP Diet member broached the issue of clandestine activities by units of the JSDF, which he said had begun in 1957. In early 1977 the party raised this issue again, charging JSDF involvement in the MIG-25 "incident." *Akahata* suggested that the delayed order to Japanese planes to scramble was intentional, to make it appear that Japan's defenses were grossly inadequate, and that the U.S. CIA and the JSDF may have colluded in the "maneuver." Also, the JCP charged that a communications base in northern Japan operated by a JSDF unit (since the U.S. Army "spy base" there closed down) was in violation of Article 38 of the International Communications Treaty (which bans organizations other than military units from intercepting radio transmissions and decoding messages) as well as domestic law in Japan.

In April the JCP announced an investigation of the Kodaira "spy school" in Tokyo, which it said had been in operation for over two years. A JCP Diet member presented the results of the investigation in a Diet budget session and charged that the school used intelligence agents from the Nakano Gakko, which trained spies and agents for the Japanese Army before the end of World War II, and was teaching techniques of espionage, sabotage, and political provocation to be used against Socialist countries. He also asserted that graduates of the school operated through law schools all over Japan.

As part of its neutral policy for Japan, the JCP criticized the creation of a "triple military" bloc (U.S., Japan, South Korea) to defend the Republic of Korea after the withdrawal of U.S. forces. JCP leaders assailed the Federation of Economic Organizations, especially its defense committee, which the JCP claimed was trying to involve Japan actively in the modernization of South Korea's armed forces. Hence, taking what might be considered an unusual stand, it opposed the U.S. withdrawal. On the U.S.-Japan Security Treaty, the JCP continued to express strong opposition. Although this stand hurts the party at the polls, it makes the JCP unique in Japan and appeals to Japanese nationalism.

Reacting to criticism that the JCP would not respect human rights if it came to power, *Akahata,* in a May issue, pointed out that the International Covenant on Human Rights unanimously adopted in 1966 by the U.N. General Assembly had been ratified by the Soviet Union and most East European countries but not by the U.S., Japan, France, Italy, Spain, and a number of other "capitalist" countries. Particular reference was made to "Charta 77." *Akahata* made it clear that the JCP did not condone the infringements on human rights in Czechoslovakia and summed up its position by citing

Miyamato's statement in January that it was the duty of all people to help protect human rights that are internationally recognized, even to the extent of interference in the internal affairs of another country.

JCP spokesmen also appealed to Japanese nationalism, and particularly residents of Okinawa, by writing about and discussing crimes committed by U.S. soldiers and violations of property rights by U.S. bases. They assailed the government's weak stand in these matters.

Elections. The JCP entered 1977 reeling from a major defeat in the December 1976 House of Representatives election, from with it emerged with less than half of its previous seats. The fact that its share of the popular vote dropped only 0.1 percent (from 10.5 to 10.4 percent) suggests that the defeat was in large part the result of a shifting electorate. Because of its defeat, the party immediately decided that Presidium Chairman Miyamoto would run in the upcoming House of Councillors election in July. To ensure victory by a sizable margin lest the party suffer a loss of prestige, the JCP started to campaign in January for Miyamoto and its six other candidates running in the national constituency, although overt electioneering is prohibited in Japan before the official announcement of elections. Since political parties can campaign indirectly by scheduling "speech meetings," the JCP blanketed much of Tokyo with posters about such meetings.

A comprehensive poll taken in June by *Yomiuri Shimbun* revealed that the major issues were commodity prices, business conditions, welfare, education, and tax reduction. Welfare and to some extent tax reduction were the only major issues that voters would associate in a positive way with the JCP. Clean politics, the fisheries issues, diplomacy, and defense were of far lesser importance and were issues that the JCP had pushed as part of its campaign program for several months. When the question of supporting a political party was asked, only 3.8 percent of those polled said that they supported the JCP, which thus took fifth place, behind the LDP (with 35.6 percent), the JSP (15.9 percent), Komeito (5.1 percent), and the New Liberal Club (4.2 percent), and little ahead of the DSP (3.6 percent). It also ranked number one among parties that Japanese dislike (31.4 percent).

The July election confirmed the JCP's difficulties. The party won only five seats in the upper house, which, together with its eleven seats not up for reelection, put its strength at sixteen seats—compared with twenty before the election. In the national constituency, the JCP won 4,027,007 votes, or 8.33 percent of the total cast, and in local constituencies, 5,159,141 votes, or 9.96 percent. In both cases its popular vote declined (from the 9.4 percent in the national constituency and 12.0 percent in local constituencies attained in the House of Councillors election in 1974).

Miyamoto Kenji won a seat for the first time, but received only 440,000 votes, which put him number forty-one out of fifty victorious candidates in the national constituency. His ranking among JCP winners was below Shimoda Kyoko, a female candidate who placed twenty-seventh. Sasaki Toshio, who campaigned with Miyamoto and who ran in the Tokyo local constituency, won 120,000 more votes there than Mayamoto. The JCP returned its candidate to office in Osaka and won a new seat in Kyoto. However, this was more than offset by defeats in the Tokyo and Aichi elections. In the Tokyo Metropolitan Assembly election, JCP strength declined by half.

Assessing the results, Miyamoto told the Central Committee on 16 July that (1) there is no error in basic JCP policy, but (2) the theory calling for unification of the opposition parties in a "renovationist front" was unable to penetrate the mood of the electorate, which favored stability of political power and thus leaned toward the LDP and the moderate parties; and (3) the party's capabilities for carrying on day-to-day work had declined, as had the circulation of *Akahata*. On the first point, other officials said that had the party acted violently the election results would have been much worse, and that the "flexible" policy, meaning the parliamentary road to power, must be retained. Elaborating on his second point, Miyamoto noted that cooperation with the JSP had not materialized because of elements in the JSP that favored cooperation with the Komeito and the DSP. He assailed the Komeito and the DSP for not joining in a broad united front and thus not grasping the opportunity of defeating the LDP. On the third problem, he called for "emergency" measures for reconstructing the party, including stepping up mass activities and propaganda, improving theoretical training, "quickly" increasing the circulation of *Akahata,* and making earlier preparations for future elections.

It seems clear that the party's past successes—doubling its strength in the Diet in every major election of the past decade—has had an inauspicious effect in recent months. A vote for the JCP, which was in the past seen as a harmless form of protest, is no longer that. Due to its gains, many voters now see the JCP as a real opposition party and consequently a threat. All of the other parties except the JSP have made efforts to further this view, as have several major magazines and newspapers. JCP opponents pictured the party as a radical organization that espouses extreme policies, does not accept individual freedoms, and is a member of the Soviet camp. The party's efforts to counter the contention that it is violence-prone were generally ineffectual and probably only attracted attention to its past record. Likewise, the effort to prove itself a nationalist party and not an appendage of the Soviet Communist party, by taking an almost militant stand on the return of the northern islands, may have been counterproductive. It called for an association between the JCP and the Soviet Union in the minds of voters and probably was seen as "overkill" by some and perhaps as hypocrisy or a trick by others.

The JCP's relations with the LDP have never been good and the latter was quick to take advantage of the JCP's vulnerabilities. The DSP and Komeito also adopted policies that in many ways were openly anti-Communist. The JSP continued to cooperate, but efforts by the DSP and Komeito to form a coalition excluding the Communists had some impact, which was underscored when the right-wing faction of the JSP bolted and formed a new party, the Socialist Citizens' League. The formation of the United Progressive Liberals, a party of celebrities, and the Japanese Women's Party, together with more independent candidacies, no doubt also hurt the JCP. The JCP was critical of the celebrities and some of them reacted in kind. The Women's Party undermined to some extent the JCP's image as a party that supports women's rights. Although neither was able to elect its candidates, their efforts probably cost the JCP a sizable number of votes.

Another factor in the centrist or moderate parties' attraction was the rapid growth of a middle class in Japan, or at least a middle-class mentality on the part of voters. According to a poll conducted just a few months before the election, 90 percent of the Japanese regarded themselves as middle class. Other polls indicated that the Vietnam War, which had helped the JCP, was no longer an issue. Also, young people showed less interest in Socialism and leftist political views because of the business recession. Several scholars analyzing recent trends have argued that the voters now have little interest in fast economic growth, but do want to maintain their standard of living. In addition, the Japanese are now seen as more individualist and interested in participating in smaller groups. None of these trends seem to favor the JCP.

International Views and Party Contacts. In 1977, as in the recent past, the JCP's relations with the Communist Party of the Soviet Union (CPSU) and the Chinese Communist Party (CCP) were not good. Because of its poor relations with the CPSU, the JCP's contacts with the Communist parties of Eastern Europe have been limited. Its ties with the Communist parties of African, Middle Eastern, North and South American countries have not been considered important. The JCP maintains formal ties with the Communist parties, or their equivalents, of North Korea and Vietnam and is trying to increase its contacts with them. Relations with several Western European Communist parties are good and are given a special position of importance by the JCP.

A proposed visit by the JCP to Moscow was postponed in December 1976 at the behest of the Kremlin. Following this, Miyamato in an interview in *Akahata* outlined in a critical manner the reasons for the strained relations. Twelve years ago, the CPSU sought to interfere in internal JCP affairs by supporting the Shiga faction of the party (see "Splinter Parties and Factions") in the issue of the nuclear test ban treaty, on which the JCP decided to take an independent stand. Miyamoto went on to say that "as long as this state of affairs is unchanged, a beachhead of interference exists." At the same time *Akahata* published an unattributed article criticizing the Shiga faction's *Voice of Japan* for "anti-Japan" views on the northern territories and fishermen's rights, and the faction for its anti-party activities.

Late in January a JCP delegation led by Presidium Vice-President Nishizawa Tomio visited Moscow and held talks with CPSU officials. The substance of the talks was not announced and the short visit probably was little more than exploratory. Shortly afterward, the CPSU invited representatives of the JSP to Moscow. Relations between Moscow and the JSP were strained, owing to the JSP's willingness to recognize the anti-hegemony clause in the proposed Sino-Japanese treaty, and this may have prompted the invitation. CPSU party leader Brezhnev's subsequent comments suggested that relations between the CPSU and the JSP may improve— news not received happily by the JCP.

In April— when the JCP proposed talks with the CPSU over the fishery agreement, the Soviet Union's 200-mile sea jurisdiction announcement, the northern territories problem, and other issues— Miyamoto at the same time promised that he would try to patch up ideological differences with the CPSU, but that the JCP would take an adamant stance on the issues of importance between the Soviet Union and Japan. Moscow's reaction was to refuse the proposed visit. The JCP then took an even tougher stance on territorial and other issues and strongly criticized Soviet policies on these matters. The CPSU retaliated by accusing the JCP of chauvinist, nationalist attitudes and of "trying to revise the outcome of World War II."

In September *Akahata* found an opportunity to criticize the CPSU when the Soviet weekly *New Times* assailed Spanish party chief Santiago Carrillo's book *Eurocommunism and the State.* According to *Akahata,* the CPSU had attacked the book as anti-Soviet and as an attempt to perpetuate the division of Europe and help strengthen NATO. The JCP instead interpreted it as representative of differences in Communism in the advanced countries and the right of Communist parties to pursue independent policies.

Late in the year the CPSU and Moscow chose to invite other Japanese groups to the Soviet Union. In September *Pravda* cited improved relations with Japan after the resolution of the fishing problem, but didn't mention the JCP.

As for the CCP, Miyamoto pointed out in January an official JCP representative was attacked by terrorists and expelled from China during the Cultural Revolution, and that the *Akahata* correspondent was seriously injured at the same time. He charged that the CCP was to blame for these incidents and that it encouraged and supported the Yamaguchi faction of the Japanese Communist Party-Left. Miyamoto concluded that since the removal of the Gang of Four there may be some hope of an improvement in JCP-CCP relations. During the year, while other political parties in Japan sent representatives to China and various other groups were invited and feted by the Chinese, apparently there were no contacts or talks between the JCP and the CCP or Chinese government officials. In August Watanabe Takeshi, a JCP member of the Diet, was granted a visa by China and became the first JCP representative to visit China in ten years. The significance of this, however, must be seen against the fact that Watanabe was a member of a Japanese parliamentarians' delegation and that the leader of the group, a member of the LDP, requested the visa for him. Also, the visa was only a transit visa which allowed Watanabe a short stay in China en route to North Korea. Furthermore, at nearly this same time the JCP took China to task for interference in its internal affairs. An October issue of *Akahata* specifically cited the CCP for attempting to impose the thought of Mao on other Asian parties and for actively supporting the U.S.-Japan security pact. The former criticism was made in the context of CCP contacts with other Communist parties in Japan and the latter's praise of the newly published revised edition of Mao's works.

The JCP maintained friendly contacts with the (North) Korean Workers' Party (KWP). In February the JCP sent representatives to a meeting of pro-North Korean citizens of Korean descent living in Japan and to a meeting in Brussels on the unification of the two Koreas. In July the KWP sent a congratulatory message to the JCP on the fifty-fifth anniversary of its founding. However, relations were limited by the influence of the CPSU and the CCP on the KWP.

The JCP maintained somewhat better relations with the Vietnamese Communist party. In February the JCP contributed 3.7 million yen for the reconstruction of Vietnam to the "Japan Committee for Support of the Vietnamese People." In October a representative of the JCP Central Committee visited Vietnamese party chief Le Duan in Hanoi. In January *Akahata* published joint communiqués with the Communist parties of Italy and Great Britain. The communiqué with the Italian party followed a visit by Fuwa Tetsuzo, chief of the JCP Secretariat, to Rome and underscored the two parties' commitment to Eurocommunism. The other followed a visit by the British party's Secretariat chief to Japan. It endorsed the new type of Socialism through parliamentary democracy and majority revolution, and common policy goals for Communists in advanced capitalist countries.

Publications. Most JCP publications are advertised or delivered by party members, especially activists, and this word is often seen as a measure of party loyalty. In addition, members are asked to read party publications and other works on recommended lists. Related to this ideological training are the Neohe Central Party School, founded in 1962, and the Social Science Institute, founded in 1970. Part-time party schools give qualification tests for ideological workers. Most of the reading materials used by these schools are written and published by the party.

Akahata (Red Banner), the JCP newspaper, appears each weekday and also in a special Sunday edition. Officially, the daily circulation is 700,000 and the Sunday circulation is 2,500,000. These figures are known to be inflated, and 400,000 has been cited by JCP leaders as the present daily circulation. *Akahata* also is printed in Braille.

Zenei (Vanguard), a monthly, is the JCP's most important theoretical and political review. Its circulation is reported at more than 100,000.

Gejjab Gakushu (Educational Monthly) deals with educational and propaganda issues. It is written especially for new members. Other publications include *Gikai to Jichitai* (Parliament and Self-Government) and *Bunka Hyoron* (Cultural Review), both monthly; *Sekai Seiji Shiryo* (International Politics), a fortnightly; and *Gakusei Shimbun* (Students Gazette), a weekly newspaper.

The JCP *Bulletin,* an information pamphlet, contains major resolutions, decisions and articles reprinted from *Akahata.* It is published in English, French, and Spanish, for dissemination abroad, and appears from ten to twenty times per year. *Problems of Peace and Socialism* is a quarterly dealing with theoretical issues, particularly those related to world peace.

The Proletarian, Rono Senbo (Workers' Report), and *Jinmin Shimbo* (People's Newspaper) are organs of the National Committee of the JCP-Marxist-Leninist, the Central Committee of the Workers' Party of Japan, and the Provisional central guidance group of the JCP-Left, respectively.

Splinter Groups and Factions. The most well-known splinter group of the JCP is Nihon no Koe (Voice of Japan), founded by Shiga Yoshio when he broke from the party over the issue of the nuclear test ban treaty in 1963 and JCP relations with the Soviet Union. Shiga had a considerable following in Osaka and among Japanese intellectuals, and the break weakened the JCP. Now seventy-six, he still actively heads the Voice of Japan group, which maintains a pro-Moscow position. His faction, though quite small, is regarded as a Communist party with some influence.

Other splinter groups or factions include the Yamaguchi (Prefecture); the Kanto (Tokyo area) factions of the JCP-Left; the Japan Labor Party; the Japan Worker's Party; the Japan Revolutionary Communist League (JRCL); and the Japan Communist League. These can be categorized as either "new left" or pro-Chinese groups.

The Japan Communist League, known as the League or (by its German name) the Bund, has been active in student radicalism. In mid-1977 it attracted attention in Tokyo by protesting the building of an additional airport at Narita, northeast of the city. In June the League organized demonstrations which resulted in battles with police and 400 injuries and one death among the protestors. Harada Hideaki, the leader of the organization, said its objective is to stop the building of the airport because it would be used by U.S. military forces (citing as evidence the fact that Haneda, Tokyo's major airport, was used by U. S. transport planes to supply troops in Vietnam during the Vietnam War), would be destructive to the environment, and represented business as opposed to agricultural interests.

Publications of non-JCP Communist groups include Nihon no Koe's newspaper of the same name (Voice of Japan) and the JRCL's *Sekai Kakumei* (World Revolution).

The Japanese Red Army, often associated with the JCP and other Communist organizations, but not known to have any connection now or in the past with the JCP, is the most notorious leftist group in Japan. The Red Army was formed by a Kyoto University assistant professor, Takaya Shiomi, in 1969 during the height of the anti-Vietnam protest. He argued that demonstrations were useless against well-trained riot police and instead advocated armed urban guerilla warfare directed against specific targets. Since then the Red Army has amassed quite a record for terrorism: in 1969 members of the group threw Molotov cocktails into the U.S. and Soviet embassies; in 1970, highjacked a Japan Air Lines plane to North Korea; in 1972, killed twenty-four people in the lobby of Lod Airport at Tel Aviv; in 1973, highjacked a jumbo jet to Libya and subsequently destroyed the plane; in 1974, seized the French Embassy in The Hague; in 1975, seized the U.S. and Swedish Embassies in Malaysia. In September 1977 five members of the group highjacked a DC-8 en route to Dacca, Bangladesh, from India. Subsequently, they obtained $6 million in ransom from the Japanese government— the biggest on record in Japan— plus the release of prisoners from Japanese jails, including some that were not in any way political prisoners.

The highjacking was led by Maruoka Osamu, twenty-six, though some sources reported that it was masterminded by Shigenobu Fusako, the wife of Okudaira Takeshi, one of the gunmen killed in the Lod Airport massacre. The highjack team ended up in Algeria and most of the members of the group are now thought to reside in the Middle East. They are believed to have ties there with the Marxist Popular Front for the Liberation of Palestine and other radical groups.

Meanwhile, the Japanese minister of justice resigned over the incident and the Japanese government promised to organize a special police unit to track down members of the organization in Japan. Subsequent investigative work showed possible links between the Red Army and a small group known as the 1980 Action Committee that is active in the Kyoto area and the employees of the *Jinmin Shimbun* in Osaka. In late October Mitsui Osamu, chief of the National Police Agency's Guard Bureau reported that the Japanese Red Army had more than 100 active supporters in Japan and "efficient" overseas support. He cited specifically the Proletarian Revolution group of the Red Army Faction of the Communist League and the Keihin Ampo Kyoto (Tokyo-Yokohama Anti-U.S.-Japan Security Treaty Joint Struggle Committee).

Southwestern at Memphis   John F. Copper

Korea: Democratic People's Republic of Korea

The Korean Communist Party (Choson Kongsan-dang; KCP) was formed at Seoul in 1925 during the time of the Japanese rule; in 1928, due chiefly to suppression, it ceased to function. Shortly after World War II, a revived KCP appeared briefly in Seoul. Control of the Communist movement in Korea soon shifted to the northern part of the country, then occupied by Soviet forces, where the "North Korean Central Bureau of the KCP" was formed in October 1945 under Soviet auspices. The three major factions of the movement—comprising Korean Communists who during the Japanese period had gone to China, or to the Soviet Union, or had remained in Korea—subsequently merged, and on 23 June 1949 the Korean Workers' Party (Choson Nodong-dang; KWP) was established. The KWP is today the ruling party of the Democratic People's Republic of Korea (DPRK).

Kim Il-song, Korean-born but Soviet-trained, who had been an anti-Japanese Communist guerrilla leader in southern Manchuria in the 1930s, consolidated his dictatorial power by eliminating rival factions, and today his Manchurian partisan group (the Kapsan faction) holds unassailable supremacy in the North Korean leadership.

KWP membership was estimated in 1972 at 2,000,000 by the party newspaper, *Nodong Shinmun* (editorial, 29 August). A recent outside estimate is 1.8 million. The population of the DPRK is 17.5 million.

Leadership and Organization. North Korea has a typical Communist administrative structure. The center of the decision making is in the KWP, and the government merely executes party policy. All important leaders hold concurrent positions in the party and government.

The present top leaders of the DPRK, eight of whom were elected at the KWP's Fifth Congress on 13 November 1970, include the following (note: since the 1970 congress, the DPRK has not announced the membership of the KWP Political Committee, and this list is based on an analysis of fragmentary information):

KWP Political Committee	Other Positions Held Concurrently
Regular (Voting) Members	
Kim Il-song	KWP secretary general; DPRK president; supreme commander of armed forces; chairman of KWP Military Committee; marshal
Kim Il (semi-retired)	KWP CC (Central Committee) secretary; 1st DPRK vice-president; member of Central People's Committee
Choe Hyon (semi-retired)	Colonel general; vice-chairman of DPRK National Defense Commission; member of Central People's Committee
O Chin-u	Colonel general; KWP CC secretary; minister of People's Armed Forces; Armed Forces chief of staff; vice-chairman of DPRK National Defense Commission; member of Central People's Committee

Pak Song-chol	DPRK vice-president; member of Central People's Committee
So Chol	Colonel general; member of Standing Committee of Supreme People's Assembly; KWP CC secretary
Kim Tong-kyu	KWP CC secretary (retired or purged?)
Im Chun-chu	Secretary and member of Central People's Committee
Kim Yong-chu	Kim Il-song's younger brother; KWP CC secretary
Yi Kun-mo	Member of Central People's Committee
Yon Hyung-muk	KWP CC secretary; member of Central People's Committee
Yi Yong-mu	Colonel general; chief of Political Bureau of (North) Korean People's Army
Yang Hyong-sop	KWP CC secretary; director of KWP Inspection (Control) Committee
Yi Chong-ok	Premier of State Administration Council; member of Central People's Committee
Kim Chong-il	Kim Il-song's son; KWP CC secretary; director of KWP CC Departments on Organization and Guidance, and on Culture and Arts

Candidate (Non-Voting) Members

Kim Yong-nam	KWP CC secretary; director of KWP CC International Department; member of Standing Committee of Supreme People's Assembly
Hyon Mu-kwang	KWP CC secretary; member of Central People's Committee
Han Ik-su	Colonel general; KWP CC secretary; member of Standing Committee of Supreme People's Assembly
Chong Chung-ki	Deputy premier of State Administration Council; member of Standing Committee of Supreme People's Assembly; chairman of Pyongyang Municipal People's Committee
Kang Song-san	Deputy premier of State Administration Council; Secretary of KWP Pyongyang Municipal Committee; member of Standing Committee of Supreme People's Assembly; chairman of Transport and Communications Committee of State Administration Council
Chon Mun-sop	Colonel general; director of Escort Bureau (for Kim Il-song)
O Paek-yong	Colonel general; commander of People's Militia
Kim Chol-man	Colonel general; first deputy chief of staff of (North) Korean People's Army
Kim Chun-hu	Director of KWP Liaison Bureau (General Bureau of South Korea)
Chong Kyong-hui	(Chong is a shadowy figure, so his other positions held concurrently are unknown. He is believed to be active in secret intelligence service.)

The 25-member KWP Political Committee and the 15-member Secretariat constitute the core of important decision makers in the DPRK and act as a controlling nucleus for the Central Committee (123 regular and 60 alternate members at the Fifth Congress, November 1970; about 20 of these seats were vacant in 1977 due to either death or retirement).

The present central government structure consists of three pillars of power: the 32-member

Central People's Committee (basically a policy-making and supervisory body under KWP guidance), the 27-member State Administration Council (an organ to execute policies already made by the Central People's Committee), and the 19-member Standing Committee of the 579-member Supreme People's Assembly (a symbolic and honorific body which functions as a legislative branch).

The KWP controls the following mass organizations: the 2 million-member General Federation of Trade Unions of Korea (GFTUK), the 2.7 million-member League of Socialist Working Youth of Korea (LSWY), the Union of Agricultural Working People, the Korean Democratic Women's Union, and the General Federation of Korean Residents in Japan (Chongnyon, or Chosen Soren).

At least two subordinate political movements exist under tight KWP control: the Korean Democratic Party (Choson Minju-dang) and Young Friend's Party of the Chondogyo Sect (the sect being the Society of the Heavenly Way—Chondogyo Chong-u-dang). No membership figures are available on these movements. Their function is to enhance acceptance of the United Democratic Fatherland Front (Choguk Tongil Minjujuui Chonson), created by seventy-one political and social organizations in June 1949, which is assigned the task of uniting "all the revolutionary forces of North and South Korea" under the leadership of the KWP, in order to implement the "peaceful unification and complete independence of the country." The KWP also controls the "Committee for Peaceful Unification of the Fatherland," established in May 1961 and consisting of representatives from the KWP, the subordinate "democratic" parties, and the mass organizations.

The first session of the new sixth 579-member Supreme People's Assembly, which was elected on 11 November 1977, was held in Pyongyang from 15-18 December. The session unanimously reelected Kim Il-song as president of the DPRK for a four-year term and accelerated efforts to bolster the country's troubled economy, announcing major changes in the cabinet. Yi Chong-ok, 72, a veteran industrial administrator, was chosen to head the cabinet, and a group of young technocrats were given a number of key cabinet posts. The appointment of Yi as the DPRK's new premier indicated that the Pyongyang regime has put first priority on straightening out the country's economic crisis.

Yi Chong-ok replaced Pak Song-chol, 67, a veteran North Korean diplomat, who had held the job since April 1976. Pak was elevated to a largely ceremonial post as vice-president.

The DPRK constitution provides for four vice-presidents, but only three of the slots were filled before Pak's promotion. Radio Pyongyang said that Vice-Presidents Kang Ryang-uk, 73, and Kim Il, who is about 65, retained their posts. It did not mention Vice-President Kim Tong-kyu, 62, who had been inactive or gradually out of favor with Kim Il-song this year.

Kim Yong-chu, Kim Tong-kyu, Yang Hyong-sop, and Kim Yong-nam were not reappointed to the new fifteen-member Central People's Committee. (The members of the Central People's Committee were reduced to fifteen in December 1977.)

Kim Yong-chu, Yi Kun-mo and Choe Chae-u were not retained as the DPRK's deputy premiers. (The number of deputy premiers was reduced from eight to six in December 1977.)

On 1 March 1977 North Korea announced the death of its vice-minister of defense, Colonel General Chi Byong-hak, 60, a long-time associate of Kim Il-song.

Ko Jung-taek, 81, former vice-president of North Korea (late 1950s, early 1960s), died 6 March.

Kim Yong-chu, Kim Il-song's younger brother, once believed slated eventually to succeed to his brother's position, has not been seen in public since April 1975. He is believed to have taken ill with an incurable disease in late 1973.

The cult of the North Korean dictator and his family members continued unabated in 1977. DPRK media constantly stressed that the loyalty to Kim Il-song and his ideology of *chuch'e* (self-identity or national identity) should continue from generation to generation, and the program of perpetuating his ideology and policies was given further institutional muscle.

Foreign press speculation that Kim Il-song was quietly laying the groundwork for a Communist dynasty with his son, Kim Chong-il, as heir apparent, had persisted. For example, the Japanese Kyodo

News Agency, quoting "well-informed" but unnamed pro-North Korean sources in Japan, reported 23 February that the DPRK had officially designated Kim Chong-il, 36, Kim Il-song's eldest son and only surviving son by his long-deceased wife, Kim Jung-sook, as the "sole" successor to his father. The same sources claimed that this decision was made by the Political Committee of the KWP. The sources forecasted that North Korea would probably make the designation public either on the occasion of Kim Il-song's 65th birthday (15 April) or during the long-overdue sixth KWP National Congress scheduled for the end of the year. It was further said that Chongnyon leaderes in Japan had been informed of the decision, and that they had in turn briefed key cadres at a meeting in Tokyo on 12 February.

In an editorial commemorating the birthday of Kim Il-song, *Nodong Shinmun* hailed the president as one who has "provided solid groundwork on which we can fulfill our revolutionary tasks from generation to generation." It added that all North Koreans "must implement the Great Leader's teachings and party policy without a moment of delay or hesitation under all conditions." Some observers interpreted this as hinting that Kim Chong-il's succession was being effected institutionally while presenting it to the North Korean people as a foregone conclusion.

In recent months Choe Chae-u (candidate member of the KWP Political Committee, deputy premier), Yu Chang-sik (candidate member of the Political Committee, secretary of the Central Committee and director of its External Affairs Department), O Tae-bong (Central Committee secretary, chairman of the Supreme People's Assembly's Budget Committee), Hong Song-nam (chairman of the State Planning Commission, deputy premier), and Pak Su-tong (director of the Department of Organization and Guidance of the Central Committee until September 1975) have been demoted or fallen into oblivion. Most were Kim Yong-chu's close followers.

Im Chun-chu, O Paek-yong, Chong Chung-ki, Kang Song-san, Yi Chong-ok, Ho Tam, and Yun Ki-bok have been promoted in party ranks and all of them, except perhaps Yi, are believed to be work-horses in the campaign to groom Kim Chong-il to succeed his father.

Kim Chun-nin, a once powerful political figure, believed in eclipse since late 1975, returned to the DPRK political scene in early November. He led a delegation at Pyongyang Airport on 1 November to welcome Mrs. Pak Jong-hyon, leader of the Democratic Union of Korean Women in Japan, but was not listed among the VIPs attending sessions of the Supreme People's Assembly.

Domestic Attitudes and Activities. DPRK media constantly stressed during 1977 that the "three revolutions"—ideological, technical, and cultural—must be carried on after the establishment of the Socialist system and "until Communism has been built."

The KWP Central Committee session in Pyongyang on 6-7 September adopted the "Thesis on Socialist Education," authored by Kim Il-song, as a programmatic document.

In an effort to draw world-wide attention to the Kim Il-song ideology, an international seminar on the *chuch'e* idea was held in Pyongyang on 14-17 September, attended by delegates from 73 countries and four regional organizations. Significantly enough, no Communist bloc countries, except for Yugoslavia, sent representatives. The delegates adopted a declaration strongly criticizing the United States.

The Supreme People's Assembly session on 26-29 April heard reports on the state budget and a new land law. The 1976 state budgetary revenues amounted to 12,625,830,000 *won* (the official exchange rate is about 43 U.S. cents = one *won*) and the expenditures to 12,325,500,000 *won*, according to Finance Minister Kim Kyong-yon's report, while 1977 revenues and expenditures amounted to 13,762,150,000 *won* (about U.S. $6,881,075,000), an increment of 9 percent in revenue and 11.6 percent in expenditures. Kim also said that defense expenditure would amount to 15.4 percent of the government's total budget (roughly U.S. $1,059 million), an increase of about U.S. $30 million from 1976. (The actual defense budget would be higher because the Pyongyang regime makes it a rule to hide defense expenditures in other sectors.) Total armed forces in 1977 were believed to number around 470,000 actives and 1,600,000 civilian militia.

On 29 April the new land law was adopted by the Supreme People's Assembly. The new law emphasized (a) the complete abolition of feudal landownership and all manner of exploitation, and (b) full establishment of Socialist landownership and the dynamic progress of land construction and conservation.

North Korea has been suffering from foreign debts for quite some time. Figures on external debts vary, but according to reliable sources the DPRK owed a total of U.S. $2 billion to the Communist bloc, Western Europe, and Japan at the end of 1976. Of this U.S. $400 million was already overdue for repayment to non-Communist creditors alone. Imports from non-Communist countries have dropped sharply because of payment difficulties, and to a lesser extent so have exports to those countries. Trade with the Communist nations was also reported to have shrunk severely. Renegotiations during 1977 apparently resulted in a five-year moratorium on repayment of Pyongyang's long overdue debts to West European creditors, in return for an increase in interest rates.

These balance-of-payments difficulties indicated a serious bottleneck in North Korea's economy and appeared to contradict claims made in April 1976 by the Pyongyang regime that the Six-Year (1971-76) Economic Plan had been completed a year and four months ahead of schedule except in cement and steel production. Other serious factors included an unbalanced industrial structure, continued heavy military expenditures, low industrial productivity, and lack of social overhead capital. Fragmentary Western intelligence reports indicated that economic problems were increased by a drastic drop in aid from the Soviet Union and China.

For the first time in its 31-year history, North Korea in 1977 appeared to be operating without a long-term economic plan. As the six-year plan launched in January 1971 officially came to an end, there was no announcement of a new plan. The first session of the sixth Supreme People's Assembly, held in mid-December, approved a new seven-year economic development plan (1978-84) to be launched on 1 January 1978. Recent KCNA reports said that the production targets had been reduced considerably, although full details of the new plan have not yet been made public. On 6 April the DPRK ordered its 17 million people to begin a massive well-drilling campaign to counter a severe drought threatening agriculture and industry. The current economic hardships, however, appeared not to have deprived the population of the essentials of life or to have cause internal political crisis.

South Korea. During 1977, more than five years after a limited dialogue between North and South Korea started, relations between them continued to deteriorate. Talks on rapprochement have been suspended for more than four years. Meanwhile the DPRK resumed violent propaganda attacks on the Republic of Korea in the South, and the tension between the two Koreas was at its highest level since the end of the Korean War in 1953. DPRK propaganda campaigns claimed that the danger of war was steadily increasing because of the Southern regime's "war preparations."

Since the collapse of the talks, North Korea has taken the line that the road to unification lies through a revolution in the South, and has reiterated its opposition both to any "cross-recognition" of Seoul and Pyongyang by outside (especially, great) powers, and to a simultaneous admission of the two Koreas to the United Nations. If Korea is to become a UN member before the country is completely reunified, Pyongyang said, it must be as a single state in the name of a confederate or federal republic.

Indeed, the military situation in Korea in 1977 was potentially as explosive as ever. More than a million men were under arms in the divided peninsula, each side possessing the most sophisticated modern weapons short of the nuclear variety. While none of the great powers was encouraging either Pyongyang or Seoul to attempt to reunify the peninsula by force, Korea presented at least as great a threat to world peace as did the Middle East.

International Views and Positions. On 1 August 1977 the DPRK established a 200-mile economic zone off its coast (the Sea of Japan and the Yellow Sea), and a Pyongyang broadcast said that, without prior approval of the North Korean authorities, foreigners, foreign fishing boats, and foreign aircraft would be banned from engaging in fishing, establishment of facilities, or exploration and development within the zone. The broadcast added that North Korea would also ban all activities contaminating the sea or atmosphere and causing harm to the people and resources.

On the same day the DPRK established a 50-mile "military sea boundary" off its shore, and all foreign ships and planes—both civilian and military—were banned from entering the area without prior permission. (All nations have territorial waters off their coasts and many have been adopting economic zones, but North Korea is the first to declare a coastal defense zone in peacetime.) North Korea said that the military zone was "demanded by the situation prevailing in our country" and was designed to "safeguard the economic sea zone and to defend militarily the national interests."

South Korea promptly declared that it would not recognize the DPRK's military and economic zones, calling them "provocative acts intended to create new tension on the Korean peninsula." (On 1 August a South Korean ferry carrying 465 passengers reached a South Korean-held island off the North Korean coast without interference in the first test of Pyongyang's new military sea border.)

The United States rejected the claim to a 50-mile military sea boundary as a unilateral breach of international law. The American-led UN Command (UNC) officially told North Korea that the military sea border could not curtail the UNC's military operations under the 1953 armistice agreement. Japan also reacted negatively. A chief cabinet secretary termed the military sea border "counter to international law and practice," and the Foreign Ministry said that it would study what countermeasures should be taken.

During 1977 the DPRK established diplomatic relations with Spain. But this gain was more than offset by several diplomatic setbacks. In late December 1976, Peru expelled a North Korean citizen for involvement in "contraband" activities. In late February 1977 three North Koreans were expelled from Ecuador after they were found to have printed seditious publications propagating Communist ideologies. The Argentine military government broke diplomatic relations with the DPRK on 14 June, stating that the entire diplomatic staff of the North Korean embassy had left the country without advising the government. In late September, Upper Volta asked the North Korean ambassador to leave, apparently in connection with his allegedly having helped an African newspaperman depart illegally to participate in an international gathering at Pyongyang.

During 1977 Pyongyang supplemented its efforts on the unification of Korea "without foreign interference" by becoming active on the foreign policy front, partly to undermine the international position of its rival regime in South Korea and partly to develop world support for North Korean policies. Parliamentary, trade, and other good-will missions were dispatched abroad and invited to North Korea, and friendly diplomatic gestures were made to every corner of the earth, especially the Third World countries whose bloc has increasingly dominated actions at the UN. In particular, the DPRK sought (a) to prevent recognition of "the two Koreas" concept by the world community, (b) to isolate South Korea from both the Third World and the Communist bloc, and (c) to drum up diplomatic support for the annual UN debate on the withdrawal of UN (actually U.S.) forces from South Korea.

Yugoslav President Tito (August), President Ne Win of Burma (September), and Cambodian Premier Pol Pot (October) visited the DPRK at the invitation of Kim Il-song.

In April the DPRK participated in a six-day meeting of foreign ministers of nonaligned countries at New Delhi. The resulting joint communiqué adopted phrases much more moderate than before on the Korean issue, in comparison with the politically-oriented statement issued in August 1976 following the nonaligned summit conference in Sri Lanka, which mentioned a northward invasion threat on the Korean Peninsula. The New Delhi communiqué dropped such allegation.

Unlike the Vietnamese, who turned down the invitation, North Korea attended the opening and closing ceremonies of the second ASEAN (Association of Southeast Asia Nations) summit conference held in Malaya in August.

Indications were that North Korea's courtship of the Third World had not been going well because of its diplomatic rigidity and rudeness. According to some UN diplomatic sources, a substantial number of the nonaligned countries in 1977 were voicing disinterest in North Korea's aggressive and provocative diplomatic maneuverings, and such formerly strong-supporting countries as Algeria and Yugoslavia appeared to be removing themselves from direct involvement in the DPRK's diplomatic maneuverings. Noting that these nonaligned countries had apparently come to realize that their militant support had brought about nothing but face-losing damage to their national prestige in the international political arena, the sources said that their attitudes toward Pyongyang now seemed to be "let it alone." The sources attributed the North Koreans' present moderation and calmness on the UN diplomatic scene to such atmospheric changes among the nonaligned nations.

Relations with the Soviet Union and China. During 1977 the DPRK continued to pursue a nationalistic, independent, and self-reliant foreign policy in Communist bloc affairs by playing off the Soviet Union against China. But its relations with the two major Communist powers remained equally correct and cordial. According to U.S. Defense Department figures declassified in August, North Korea had received US $180 million in various forms of military aid from the Chinese and US $145 million from the Soviet Union during 1974-77 (*Washington Post*, 9 August). Toward Moscow and Peking, Pyongyang endeavored to strengthen its diplomatic contacts by sending many good-will missions. By June North Korea had concluded three economy-related agreements with the Soviet Union and China.

In mid-year Kim Il-song expressed sympathy for the independent course pursued by several West European Communist parties (Eurocommunism). In an interview with *Le Monde*'s editor in chief on 20 June the DPRK president said: "We [North Koreans] know that for some time the Communist parties of a number of [West] European countries have been stressing independence in the communist movement. We consider it a very correct attitude, for every communist should adapt his activities to the concrete realities of his country." (*The Guardian*, New York, 3 July.)

The United States had obtained assurances from both the Soviet Union and China that they had no intention of increasing tension in Korea after the American pullout, the Japan Broadcast Corporation quoted Japanese government sources as saying on 5 June. It added that this came from two U.S. presidential envoys (Gen. George Brown, chairman of the Joint Chiefs of Staff, and Under Secretary of State Philip C. Habib) who stopped over in Tokyo in May en route from consultations with South Korean leaders.

The Soviet Union urged withdrawal of American troops from South Korea several times during 1977. An official Soviet newspaper alleged in mid-June that U.S. President Carter's plan to withdraw ground forces was "too limited and nominal" and also that in return for the Seoul government's consent to the troop withdrawal, all weapons of the departing U.S. military units would be left behind. In short, Moscow said that "the United States was trying to reenter Korea through a window after leaving it through the door."

DPRK Premier Pak Song-chol visited the Soviet Union in late January, technically on what the Soviets called a "friendly visit" rather than an official one. Pak held talks with Soviet party leader Brezhnev, Premier Kosygin, State Planning Chairman Nikolai K. Baibakov, and foreign trade and economic aid experts. The presence of aid officials at the talks led Western observers to conclude that Pak had come mainly in search of support for Pyongyang's shaky economy. It is possible that Carter's proposed pullout of troops was discussed.

No communiqué was issued following Pak's departure from Moscow on 26 January, and a statement in *Pravda*, headlined "Negotiation Ends," was only seven paragraphs long. "They discussed measures to expand and deepen economic and trade relations between the USSR and the DPRK," the statement said, but failed to mention a single area of agreement which had been reached. According to Western intelligence, Pak had sought a new aid agreement and obtained only a postponement until 1983 of the repayment of Pyongyang's debts to the Soviet Union. In late May the *Christian Science Monitor* reported that the second-largest Soviet bank in Western Europe, the Banque Commerciale pour les Pays du Nord in Paris, had decided to extend an unspecified loan to the DPRK.

Publicly, China reiterated its long-held position in requesting withdrawal of U.S. forces from South Korea and dissolution of the UNC. In one of its strongest attacks on the American policy in months, Peking's *People's Daily*, marking the 29th anniversary of the DPRK in September, said: "The root cause for the failure to realize reunification of Korea up to now lies in the fact that U.S. troops are still hanging on in South Korea."

China continued to send the United States signals that it wanted Washington to maintain a strong military presence in the Pacific to counter Soviet attempts to gain influence in the area. This position had been expressed or suggested by Chinese officials in private talks with foreign visitors, but it had never been reflected so clearly in the official press.

Peking reacted negatively to Washington's proposal of a joint step for a peace settlement on the Korean Peninsula, reiterating its previous stand supporting Pyongyang's negative stand. According to Kyodo News Service in Japan, Chinese vice-premier Teng Hsiao-p'ing told visiting retired Japanese defense planners in early October that China did not expect North Korea to start a war on the Korean Peninsula in the future. "The best way to achieve the peaceful unification of Korea," Teng was quoted as saying, "is for both North and South Koreas to hold direct negotiations."

U.S. congressman Lester Wolff, chairman of the House International Relations Subcommittee on East Asia, said on 4 August that in the event of a North Korean attack on the South, China would not appear ready to provide the North with a "resupply" of arms which, he said, would be crucial for a North Korean victory. In a news conference on triangular relations between the United States, Russia and China, the New York Democratic congressman said that his view was based on the conversations with Chinese leaders last year during his China visit.

Relations with Japan. Relations between North Korea and Japan have never been warm. In mid-October 1977 Prime Minister Takeo Fukuda rejected a Japan Socialist Party proposal which urged the establishment of diplomatic relations with the DPRK. Pyongyang viewed Japan as being excessively partial to Seoul, pursuing a policy of "two Koreas" and hostility toward North Korea, as exemplified by the Japanese government's strong opposition to a drastic reduction of U.S. ground forces in South Korea. North Korean media continued to denounce the growing Japanese "imperialistic" stakes in South Korea and the alleged collusion of Tokyo and Washington to preserve their mutual "colonial interests" in the Korean Peninsula.

At the end of 1976 Japan was stuck with about U.S. $220 million worth of outstanding trade loans to North Korea. Of this amount, U.S. $70 million already was overdue for repayment. On 29 December Japan agreed to the North Korean proposal for a two-year moratorium on its overdue debts to Japanese trade firms, at annual interest of 7.5 to 8 percent. According to Japanese Foreign Ministry sources, the DPRK failed to pay the interest charges after June. Some Japanese trading firms were moving to apply for export insurance through the Japan-North Korea Trade Association.

On 6 September Japan and North Korea signed a private interim fishery agreement which would allow Japanese fishermen to operate within the DPRK's newly-declared 200-mile economic zone up to its 50-mile military sea boundary, to be effective from October to the end of June 1978. Japanese Foreign Ministry officials said that the Tokyo government was prepared to endorse the fishery accord, but that endorsement would not constitute a step toward recognition of the Pyongyang regime.

Relations with the United States. The advent of the Carter Administration coincided with a softening of North Korean pronouncements on the United States. In January 1977 Kim Il-song reportedly sent a message of congratulations to President Carter through Pakistani President Zulfikar Ali Bhutto, hoping for improved relations. Kim's overture intensified the friendship offensive mounted since Carter took office. Pyongyang largely dropped the use of such hostile phrases as "U.S. imperialists" and appeared eager to exploit the present cool relations between the United States and South Korea, caused by the troop-withdrawal plan and the South Korean lobby scandal in the U.S. capital.

In April Pyongyang reacted favorably to Washington's end to a tourist ban against North Korea. (In early March the Carter Administration lifted travel restrictions on North Korea, Cuba, Vietnam, and Cambodia.)

In a television interview with a news commentator from the Japan Broadcasting Corporation on 4 June, aired in prime time in Japan in July, President Kim called Carter's troop-withdrawal plan "a very good thing" that removed a major obstacle to the reunification of Korea. Although he criticized Carter's intention to leave Air Force units in South Korea and the continuing American support for the Seoul government, his comments were moderate in tone. The DPRK had proposed a dialogue with the United States "quite a long time ago," Kim said. He added that although there had been no response, he stood ready to meet with U.S. diplomats at any time.

North Korea's desire not to strengthen the hand of American opponents of troop withdrawal and also to open a dialogue with Washington was evident in mid-July, when after shooting down a U.S. helicopter that had strayed into North Korea across the DMZ on 14 July, it speedily returned the bodies of three dead crewmen and released a wounded fourth two days later. Absent was the usual propaganda about "imperialist warmongers."

The Soviet Union and China had refused to provide any new aid to North Korea to help underwrite its new seven-year economic plan, and thus the DPRK was anxious to improve relations with the United States and Japan for various reasons, the *Boston Globe* reported on 31 August, quoting a leading Japanese television commentator, who had returned from two weeks of reporting in North Korea. The same dispatch said that the commentator quoted Kim Il-song and other ranking DPRK officials as saying that they wanted trade and technology from the United States to bolster their shaky economy and modernize their industry.

The Carter Administration assured the Seoul government that the U.S. security commitment to South Korea remained "firm and undiminished," despite the planned withdrawal of American combat troops. It also reaffirmed a long-standing U.S. policy: (1) that the United States would not hold direct talks with the DPRK on the future of the Korean Peninsula unless South Korea was a full participant, (2) that it was prepared to improve relations with North Korea if the DPRK's allies would take steps to improve relations with South Korea, and (3) that it would support the entry of North and South Korea into the UN without prejudice to ultimate reunification.

In mid-1977 North Korean attacks on the United States began to escalate by expressing Pyongyang's disappointment over the slow pace of the American military withdrawal. In early July *Nodong Shinmun* criticized the plan for phased withdrawal, asserting that President Carter had "stepped back" from a campaign promise for speedy withdrawal: "The talk about the withdrawal of U.S. troops over a period of four to five years cannot be interpreted as a sincere stand for the solution of the Korean question. . . . There is no reason or condition for the United States to need so long a period . . . ." In late July the DPRK denounced the phased withdrawal plan as "war preparations" with the intention to make the division of Korea permanent.

In late September the U.S. government granted an entry visa to North Korea's foreign minister, who had applied for it to attend a foreign ministers' meeting of the nonaligned countries in connection with the 1977 session of the UN General Assembly in New York. Washington assured Seoul that the visa was merely in line with its customary practice to delegates attending the UN General Assembly and thus did not mean any change in policy toward the DPRK.

United Nations. The DPRK was admitted in 1977 to the International Civil Aviation Organization—a world aviation regulatory body sponsored by the UN.

The Korean question—a Cold War issue that has plagued the UN for more than two decades—was not included in the agenda of the 1977 fall session of the UN General Assembly. China and Yugoslavia, along with other moderate East European and nonaligned countries, played key roles in persuading the DPRK to give up the Korean debate this year, according to reliable UN diplomatic sources. Those countries probably concluded that the pro-North Korean resolution would win less support than it did previously, and thus did not see any necessity of repeating it. Because of President Carter's pullout plan, the DPRK virtually has lost appealing momentum for its call for foreign troop withdrawal.

Publications. The KWP publishes a daily organ, *Nodong Shinmun*, and a journal, *Kulloja*. The DPRK government publishes *Minju Choson*, organ of the Supreme People's Assembly and the cabinet. The *Pyongyang Times, People's Korea,* and *Korea Today* are weekly English-language publications. The official news agency is the Korean Central News Agency.

Washington College   Tai Sung An

Laos

The Lao People's Revolutionary Party (Phak Pasason Pativat Lao; PPPL) emerged in February 1972 from the Second Congress of the Lao People's Party (Phak Pasason Lao; PPL), which had been secretly established with 300 members on 22 March 1955. Party membership was estimated in 1975 at 15,000 (*NYT*, 5 October). The population of Laos is approximately 3.4 million.

Leadership and Organization. The members of the PPPL Political Bureau are reported to be: Kaysone Phomvihan, general secretary; Nouhak Phoumsavan; Phoumi Vongvichit; Phoun Sipaseut; Khamtai Siphandon; Sisomphon Lovansai; and (formerlyPrince) Souphanouvong.

Full members of the Central Committee are reported to be the seven Politburo members and Chanmi Douangboutdi, Khamsouk Saignaseng, Ma Khaikhamphithoun, Maichantan Sengmani, Maisouk Saisompheng, Meun Somvichit, Nhiavu Lobaliayao, Sali Vongkhamsao, Sanan Soutthichak, Sisayat Keobounphan, Somseun Khamphithoun, and Souk Vongsak. Alternate members are Khambou Soumisai, Mrs. Khampheng Boupha, Saman Vilaket, and Sisana Sisan.

Beyond these names, little is known to the outside world concerning PPPL leadership and organization. Although the PPPL has moved into the open, its procedures and deliberations are still secret.

Auxiliary and Mass Organizations. The Lao Patriotic Front (Neo Lao Hak Xat; NLHX or NLHS) was founded on 6 January 1956. It served as the PPPL's principal mass-mobilizing instrument during the long years of warfare and for the successful seizure of power through a combination of armed force and negotiation. Perhaps its last significant action was its participation in the National Congress of People's Representatives which met in Vientiane on 1-2 December 1975 and established the new organs of state power in the Lao People's Democratic Republic (LPDR).

The NLHX has not been disbanded, however. As Phoumi Vongvichit told Front members in a speech marking the twenty-first anniversary of its founding, the Front, "which led our people in the revolution, has not ceased to function and has not relinquished its position; however, it has accomplished its task." The PPPL, which in the past "hid in the background to provide leadership" to the Front, was now taking direct charge of leadership. But the Front "is a mass organization and is cooperating with the Party in leading our people to march toward socialism in the new period." (Radio Vientiane, 8 January 1977, in *FBIS*, 18 January.) And in the same vein an editorial in the official organ *Siang Pasason* called for the strengthening of the Front's work in the new stage of the Lao revolution (Pathet Lao News Agency, 13 August 1977, in *FBIS*, 17 August).

From the point of view of the exercise of power in Laos, the change in the relative positions accorded the PPPL and the NLHX has meant the thrusting into the background of the prominent leaders of Laos' ethnic minorities who held high positions in the NLHX and whose names had almost come to symbolize the national resistance struggle. One of these NLHX leaders, Sithon Kommadam, whose father and grandfather before him had won fame among the Lao Theung people of southern Laos for their resistance against the French, died in Vientiane on 1 May 1977. He was given a state funeral, with all the leading figures of the regime present, but he was really a relic of a past era. Others, like NLHX Vice Chairman Faidang Lobaliayao, a leader of the Meo, have been given sinecures like the vice presidency of the Standing Committee of the Supreme People's Council. Even Souphanouvong, the NLHX chairman, has lost his royal title and has become just another member of the PPPL Political Bureau, although he is also LPDR president.

Party Internal Affairs. Few details of the PPPL's internal affairs are known, although it is providing the leadership of the LPDR and controls all the important positions in the government of the LPDR.

Domestic Attitudes and Activities. PPPL organs describe the party as "the organizer and leader of all victories of the Lao revolution." In the words of *Siang Pasason*:

> The Lao People's Revolutionary Party is the party of the Lao working class and its vanguard, its highly-organized militant staff and highest organization at present. Realities of our revolution have proved that the Lao People's Revolutionary Party is the only party representing the interest of the working class and the entire nation of Laos. (Pathet Lao News Agency, 23 March 1977, in *FBIS*, 24 March.)

On the same anniversary occasion, the PPPL Central Committee drew attention to a number of deficiencies among the party's followers, saying:

> . . . our ideology and viewpoints have not caught up with the development of the situation and tasks in the new stage of the revolution. Our organizational work to carry out the party's line and policies is also still weak. All this has greatly affected and limited our successes. . . . our party and people must overcome many difficulties and obstacles caused by the enemy who, although having sustained defeats, has not yet given up his dark designs against our revolution. On the other hand, our material and technical foundations are still weak and the consequences of the war and vestiges of the old regime are still heavy. We have not gained much experience in socialist transformation and construction. (Pathet Lao News Agency, 22 March 1977, in *FBIS*, 23 March.)

The difficulties referred to above stem in part from the poor economic situation faced by Laos in 1977. The recent record in agriculture, the mainstay of the economy, is perhaps the poorest. While the party has been compelled to maintain private agricultural production temporarily, because of its inability to collectivize agriculture except by brute force, it imposed a graduated agricultural tax in November 1976 which it was widely believed was responsible for failure of food production to meet needs, a failure officially attributed to drought.

Another major source of difficulties has been the flight from Laos of many trained persons (including in 1977 seven employees of Radio Vientiane) and the active resistance to the regime by armed bands in the countryside, some but by no means all of whom were survivors of the former royal government and army.

Thousands of refugees from Laos were housed in temporary camps in Thailand, where they became a source of tension between the two countries. For foreign consumption, the regime paid scant attention to the flight of these people, or even pretended to welcome their departure as the riddance accorded "reactionaries." But the Lao domestic press and radio carried descriptions of the miserable living conditions in the camps, obviously intended to discourage others who might be tempted to flee (e.g., Pathet Lao News Agency, 17 February 1977, *FBIS*, 17 February). A large number of shooting incidents by the Lao police occurred along the Mekong River boundary triggered by attempted escapes.

The number of former officials and soldiers of the royal government sent to Vietnam-style "re-education" centers in Laos is variously estimated at 30,000 (*NYT*, 3 May 1977), 37,600 (*Agence France Presse* dispatch from Bangkok, 23 June, in *FBIS*, 24 June), or 50,000 (*Washington Post*, 10 July). Whatever the number, the inmates of these centers, who have been providing manpower for dangerous or unhealthy tasks and reconstruction work, have become an important facet of the present situation in Laos.

PPPL organs continued in 1977 to report sporadic armed resistance to the regime in many parts of the country. While this resistance is generally regarded as being hopeless, it has tied down a large number of security forces and prevented the regime from entirely overcoming the effects of the long civil war. Units of the Vietnam People's Army, totaling an estimated 30,000 men, are still stationed in Laos, and these are believed to have been engaged against the "counter-revolutionaries." The regime took the threat of widespread resistance in the countryside seriously enough in March to remove the former King of Laos, Savang Vatthana, from his residence near Luang Prabang to safe keeping at Vieng Sai (the old Pathet Lao headquarters near the Vietnam border), thereby preventing his person from becoming a rallying point for rebels.

International Views and Policies. A top-level delegation of the Communist Party of Vietnam and the government of the Socialist Republic of Vietnam visited Laos between 15 and 18 July, principally to sign a number of historic documents cementing further the "special relationship" declared to exist in 1976.

The speeches marking the occasion were replete on both sides with references to the bond formed during the war to overthrow the pro-Western governments of Laos and South Vietnam. Alluding to the thousands of Vietnamese soldiers who lived permanently on the Laos side of the Annam Cordillera, Kaysone Phomvihan declared:

> The special internationalist combatants of Vietnam working in Laos, implementing orders from the Central Committee of the Communist Party of Vietnam and President Ho Chi Minh, have shown a high degree of proletarian internationalism. They loved the Lao people as their own parents or brothers and sisters. They shared weal and woe with us, shared with us each grain of salt and each blade of vegetable and assumed difficult jobs while giving us advantages. They fought shoulder to shoulder, lived and died together with our soldiers and people in each trench and on battlefields throughout the country with exceptional heroism.

. . . The conclusions drawn from half a century of struggle side by side have fully proved that the Vietnam-Laos relationship is a life-and-death relationship, a law of development of the revolutionary process of our two countries. (Vietnam News Agency, 16 July 1977, in *FBIS*, 18 July.)

Le Duan repeated these sentiments and likewise praised the side-by-side struggles of the two peoples over the past 30 years (see ibid.).

Prior to the departure of the Vietnamese delegation from Vientiane on 18 July, three documents were signed dealing with friendship and cooperation, border delimitation, and assistance and loans from the SRV to the LPDR during the 1978-80 period. Article 2 of the friendship treaty provided for mutual assistance and cooperation in security and defense matters, and although this article did not specifically mention the stationing of Vietnamese troops in Laos, it could be interpreted as giving legal sanction to this. (For additional details see *FBIS*, 19 July.) The border delimitation agreement represented the fulfillment of the long-standing aim of Vietnam's Communist leaders to effect certain modifications of the tracing of the long boundary between Laos and Vietnam left by French cartographers of the colonial period, most notably in Savannakhet and Xieng Khoung provinces. In fact, the Laos-Vietnam border has had only a relative meaning for many years past since the Hanoi government freely used the territory of Laos for passage of its agents and soldiers into South Vietnam. Under the assistance and loan agreement Vietnam will presumably continue the aid it has been giving to Laos since the founding of the LPDR, in some sense a partial repayment for services rendered by Laos in the war to "liberate" South Vietnam.

In accordance with practice to date, the PPPL and LPDR continued in 1977 to follow the lead of Hanoi in expressing views and determining policies vis-à-vis international issues, including relationships with third parties. This included expressions of support for the reunification of Korea and for Third World liberation movements. While maintaining correct relations with both the CCP and the CPSU, the PPPL leans more to the latter than to the former in its present stage. The state-owned book shop in Vientiane displays a mass of publications from the Soviet Union, but none from China. Of 176 Lao students sent abroad for study in 1976, 148 went to the Soviet Union; none went to China although scholarships were reported to be available.

International Activities and Contacts. The·PPPL takes pride in its record to date of contacts with other Communist parties and with representatives of Third World liberation movements. Among important international contacts over the past year, Kaysone Phomvihan led a delegation to the Fourth Congress of the Vietnam Workers Party in Hanoi in December 1976; Souphanouvong paid visits to India and Burma in January 1977; Kaysone headed a PPPL delegation which visited East Germany from 11-16 May and stopped in Moscow for talks with Leonid Brezhnev on the way home; Kaysone headed a PPPL delegation which visited the DPRK from 13-18 June and stopped over in China on the return.

Publications. The central organ of the PPPL is the newspaper *Siang Pasason* (Voice of the People), published in Vientiane. Official news is released by the Pathet Lao News Agency, Khaosan Pathet Lao (KPL). Sisanan Sengnanouvong is at the same time editor-in-chief of *Siang Pasason* and director-general of KPL.

Bethesda, Maryland   Arthur J. Dommen

Malaysia

Malaysian Communism is organized geographically. In West Malaysia (the Malay Peninsula) activity emanates from the Communist Party of Malaya (CPM) and two small splinter groups, the Communist Party of Malaya (Marxist-Leninist) or CPM-ML, Peking-oriented like the parent CPM, and the Communist Party of Malaya (Revolutionary Faction), or CPM(RF), whose ideological character is unclear. Each has its "mass" front organizations, with bewilderingly similar names, all concerned with infiltration and terrorism. The three are also engaged in an ongoing guerrilla war along the border with Thailand, where the guerrilla bases are concentrated on Thai territory. Terrorist activity has also occurred in the towns. In East Malaysia, Communist activity consists of severely limited operations in Sarawak by the North Kalimantan Communist Party (NKCP) and its guerrilla units, usually collectively referred to as the North Kalimantan People's Guerrilla Force (NKPGF). There is no significant Communist activity in the other East Malaysian state, Sabah.

The division in the operations reflects deliberate policy of the parties and satellite organizations. Malaysian Communists claim that the formation of the Federation of Malaysia in 1963 occurred illegally and undemocratically. The ultimate objective of the CPM is, therefore, a "democratic" Republic of Malaya comprising only the Peninsular Malayan states and Singapore. The aim of the NKCP is an independent Republic of North Borneo in Sarawak but with the opportunity for both Sabah and the oil-rich Sultanate of Brunei (a British protectorate) to join. The NKCP rarely refers to this long-term objective, being more concerned with severing Sarawak from Malaysia by means of a plebiscite or referendum.

In both East and West Malaysia the ranks of the Communist movement consist overwhelmingly of Malaysian-born Chinese, with a sprinkling of *bumiputras* (the Malaysian term for indigenous non-Chinese population groups, like the Malays and the Sarawak Ibans). In West Malaysia the CPM, reportedly, interacts with Thai Communist guerrilla elements and secessionist-minded Thai Muslims in the southern Thai provinces of Yala, Pattani, and Songkhla. Malaysian authorities commonly use the designation CTS (Communist Terrorists) for all rural or urban guerrillas in Malaysia. The older SCO (Sarawak Communist Organization) is still used on occasion for the activity in East Malaysia.

Founded in April 1930 in Singapore, the CPM was the crystallization of more than a decade's proselytizing among Chinese trade unions, private schools, and other interest groups in Peninsular Malaya, including Singapore. This proselytizing reflected the intense concern of Malayan Chinese with events in Mainland China during this period. A shadowy Nanyang (South Seas) Communist party, dominated by Chinese Communists, had already been founded in 1928 under Comintern auspices to coordinate Communist activity in most of Southeast Asia. But Malaysian and some expatriate Indonesian Communists wanted an organization of their own in the Peninsula, so the CPM was born.

Before World War II, CPM recruitment remained heavily Chinese, and its following and influence among Malays and local Indonesian and Indian residents was minimal. The total membership numbered probably not more than 5,000. Not until the Japanese invasion in December 1941—which led to a broad, multiracial resistance movement and encouraged nationalist postwar expectations among all population groups—did the CPM begin winning a measure of legitimacy and significant popular following (Gene Z. Hanrahan, *The Communist Struggle in Malaya,* Kuala Lumpur, 1971).

British policy after 1945 undercut CPM efforts for control of Malayan nationalism, and the more moderate Chinese business interests joined Malay leaders in a phased movement toward independence. In August 1957 Malaya became independent, though it remained within the Commonwealth. Since 1948 the CPM, having failed to retain broad-based popular support, had resorted to guerrilla war and terrorism, thus creating what became known as "The Emergency." Buoyed by moderate Chinese and Malay support, British counterinsurgency tactics by the early sixties reduced the one time 6,000-man Malayan People's Liberation Army (MPLA) to a few score remnants in the jungle, an often inaccessible region along the border with Thailand (Anthony Short, *The Communist Insurrection in Malaya, 1948-1960,* New York, 1975; Noel Barber, *The War of the Running Dogs,* London, 1975). Here, tolerant Thai officials allowed the insurgents to mix with the local population, contributing to a complex interaction, pervaded by the common racketeering and brigandage not unknown in other frontier zones of the world, between the CPM guerrillas, Chinese farmers, rubber estate owners and workers, small shopkeepers, youths, Muslim dissidents on both sides of the border, corrupt bureaucrats and security officials, and Thai mining entrepreneurs—to name but some of the principal constituencies. By the middle sixties the CPM had developed a new guerrilla force, now usually called the Malayan National Liberation Army (MNLA), with a network of border jungle camps, arms caches, and spies and sympathizers in "new villages" of resettled Chinese who had been moved on government orders from their former interior communities during The Emergency (Justus M. van der Kroef, *Communism in Malaysia and Singapore,* The Hague, 1967).

Despite the CPM's ability to reconstitute itself during the sixties and seventies, the seemingly endless guerrilla struggle, the relative effectiveness of the government's countermeasures, and persistent leadership quarrels led to deep fissures in the party organization (see *YICA, 1977,* pp. 338-39). In 1967 fear of being infiltrated by Malaysian security forces caused party leaders to assassinate twenty recent recruits. In January 1970 a CPM Central Committee directive reportedly ordered the killing of all MNLA members thirteen years or older who had joined since 1962. At that time the MNLA's Eighth Regiment "seceded" from the CPM, its commanders claiming that the Central Committee had been betraying its plans to the security forces. These dissidents established a rival organization, the CPM(RF). Similar dissension in the MNLA's Twelfth Regiment led to the formation of the CPM-ML in August 1974. Both splinter groups initially adopted the MPLA name for their guerrilla forces. Later the CPM-ML also formed the Malayan People's Liberation League (MPLL) as a back-up organization for infiltration purposes, and the CPM(RF) formed a support group known as Malayan People's Liberation Front (MPLF). (On the origins of the CPM split, see *YICA, 1976,* pp. 334-36.)

Since then other tactical differences in West Malaysian Communism have surfaced (e.g., over the desirability of waging "urban guerrilla warfare" and over the use to be made of the radical "New Left," and often undisciplined student community in West Malaysia), and there have been reports of periodic clashes between rival party factions. The parent CPM still remains the most important of the three groups, however, and has effective control over the movement's chief media conduit, the clandestine radio transmitter "Voice of the Malayan Revolution." The active insurgents in all three CPM factions today are estimated by Malaysian authorities at 2,500 to 3,000. There are perhaps 3,000 to 4,000 sympathizers. There has been no credible new estimate of the overall strength of the CPM(RF) and the CPM-ML since the Malaysian government's figures of 100 and 200, respectively, made public in early 1976 (*YICA, 1977*, p. 343), but some estimates go as high as 1,000 for the CPM-ML (*Far Eastern Economic Review* [FEER], 2 September 1977). Despite reports of successful security operations, the government apparently has been able to eliminate comparatively few of the guerrillas.

In Sarawak, too, local Communism had its roots well before World War II in the private Chinese schools and school associations. Even before the Japanese occupation, the Sarawak Advanced Youth's Association (SAYA), served as a recruiting vehicle for proselytizing Chinese schoolteachers, and during the war this group provided much of the core of the Sarawak Liberation League, a major resistance organization. During the 1950s there emerged a complex of Communist-infiltrated organizations (Government of Sarawak, Information Service, *The Danger Within: A History of the Clandestine Communist Organization in Sarawak,* Kuching, 1963). The Communist complex, usually designated as the SCO, along with the Sarawak United People's Party (SUPP) opposed Sarawak's entry into the Malaysian Federation when it was formed in 1963 and made common cause with Indonesia, which at the time also opposed the creation of Malaysia (Harold James and Denis Shiel-Small, *The Undeclared War: The Story of the Indonesian Confrontation 1962-1966,* Totowa, N.J., 1971). While the SUPP gradually abandoned its more radical course and in the seventies began joining in various government coalitions, the SCO in 1967 crystallized into the North Kalimantan Communist Party (NKCP), with its own guerrilla force, the North Kalimantan People's Guerrilla Force (NKPGF). In October 1973 the Malaysian government's Sri Aman (Lasting Peace) program of amnesty to the Sarawak insurgents eventually led some 600 NKPGF followers to come out of the jungle, put down their arms, and submit to rehabilitation. About two score redefected, however, and the NKPFG, estimated today at about 150 cadres and active sympathizers, has continued its proselytizing and occasional hit-and-run attacks in the interior. A few underground cadres of the Communist Party of Indonesia along the Sarawak-Indonesian border, sheltered by local Chinese, reportedly continue to coordinate their activities with those of the NKPFG.

Organization, Tactics, and Program. The CPM-MNLA is led by a Central Committee of about 45, headed by Chin Peng as party secretary general. Among committee members are the leaders of such party fronts as the Islamic Solidarity Party (Parti Persuadaraan Islam; usually called by its acronym "Paperi") and the Malayan Peasants' Front (Barisan Tani Melaya). Paperi, founded in 1965 by the MNLA's Tenth Regiment in order to recruit followers among the Muslim ethnic Malay village populations along the Thai-Malaysian border, has its own executive committee, but its membership overlaps with that of the Peasants' Front (which also includes Chinese). Other CPM fronts, like the Malayan Communist Youth League, are relatively ephemeral organizations which, on occasion, issue statements depending on the CPM's tactical needs. More significant is the Malayan National Liberation Front (MNLF), an action group of urban terrorists and proselytizers, which the government views as a principal Communist vanguard in areas other than the frontier zone where the MNLA principally operates. According to some police sources, the MNLF was formed in 1970 to accommodate dissidents in the CPM who otherwise might have left the organization. The extent to which the CPM continues control over MNLF operations is uncertain. A smaller CPM-affiliated terrorist front, the Malayan National Liberation League (MNLL), which has had supporters in Singapore also, was all but smashed in June 1977 (see below). The degree of its coordination with the CPM main group also is not certain. The MNLF cadre core is estimated at about 150 (despite a wave of arrests during 1977).

The MNLA is the CPM's principal combat organization, however, and party recruits have customarily been funnelled into MNLA units. These have included (1) the Twelfth Regiment, with underground headquarters in the border district of Betong, a strip of Thailand's Yala Province that juts into Malaysia's Perak State, but reported today to be mainly based in Thailand's Pattani

Province; (2) the Tenth Regiment, largely composed of Muslims (both Thais and Malays), usually stationed in the border zone of Thailand's Narithiwat Province, across from Malaysia's Kelantan State; and (3) the Eighth Regiment (now usually called Eighth Assault Unit), located along the southwestern border of the Thai province of Songkhla, whence it has forayed into Malaysia's Perlis and Kedah States. CPM announcements claim that the main bodies of all these regiments have remained loyal and are active in the field (but see other analyses in *FEER*, 2 September 1977). There has also been informal contact between the MNLA and such Thai Muslim secessionist movements as the Pattani Liberation Movement (see Astrid Suhrke, "Irredentism Contained: The Thai Muslim Case," *Comparative Politics*, January 1975, pp. 192-203). During the joint Thai-Malaysian anti-insurgency campaign of 1977, however, Malaysian spokesmen stressed that there were "no links at all" between the Muslim secessionists and the Communists *(Sarawak Tribune,* Kuching, 7 August), though these disclaimers may have been politically inspired. According to both Thai and Malaysian military sources in May, the CPM has begun active cooperation with the Communist Party of Thailand in implementing "joint" insurgent actions (*FBIS,* 16 May).

A CPM review of achievements during 1976 said that "under the correct leadership of the party Central Committee led by Chin Peng," the MNLA had "fought about 100 battles," killed or wounded "more than 350 enemies," including an assistant police superintendent and "many middle and lower class military officers." The statement reaffirmed MNLA tactics, claiming gains "in our advance southwards" and the forging of "extensive ties" between the "people of all nationalities" and "our army's shock troops and mobile teams." (Ibid., 7 January 1977.) Additional claims of victory were made in a statement on 1 February which declared "420 enemy" to have been annihilated in 1976. The statement stressed that in expanding the "people's war," the party and the MNLA "must mobilize the masses and rely on them," while solving the problems of the "people's livelihood" and of their "work methods" by, among other means, implementing the party's land reform program. (Ibid., 10 February.)

The CPM's annual theoretical statement of 30 April, the party's official founding date, explicitly acknowledged the value of Mao Tse-tung's thought, in particular the "three basic principles": "practice Marxism not revisionism," unite and "don't split," and be open and aboveboard and "don't intrigue and conspire." It urged further consolidation of the party under "democratic centralism" and "discipline," whereby the "entire membership is subordinate to the central committee," and declared that the "imperialists and their running dogs" (the followers of Malaysian Premier Hussein Onn and Singapore Premier Lee Kuan Yew) were "frenziedly expanding their police as they attempt to cling to power." The CPM viewed the "international situaiton" as developing "favorably," as "Socialist China" had become more "consolidated and powerful," and as the "people's revolutionary armed struggle" throughout Southeast Asia was winning "new victories." (Ibid., 3 May.)

The government's counterinsurgency efforts, including increased border surveillance and the joint Thai-Malaysian so-called "Sacred Ray" campaign (see below), were viewed as having no effect. In the opinion of the CPM, all this stepped-up Malaysian "collusion" with Thai "reactionaries" provided "eloquent proof" that the party's proselytizing labors in the frontier zones, and in particular in such states as Perak, Kelantan, and Pahang, were producing "remarkable results." (Ibid., 7 September.)

Notwithstanding the CPM's favorable analysis of its policies and achievements, its statements appeared to devote more space than ever to the rival CPM-ML faction and its alleged doctrinal and tactical errors. The CPM-ML was accused of being the agent of the Malaysian government, of opposing the principle of using the countryside to encircle the cities, and of attempting to separate the "national liberation" struggle from the "national democratic revolution." (Ibid., 2 December 1976.) However, the mutual recriminations between the CPM factions sometimes appear to be more reflective of personality conflicts than of genuine theoretical differences.

Principal CPM fronts also issued policy statements during the year. Paperi, the CPM's conduit to the more orthodox Malay Muslim community, claimed in September that the Hussein Onn regime, like the governments before it, had always been "hostile toward Moslems in our country," bloodily oppressing them even as the Moslems sank "into poverty and destitution." At least 16,000 peasant families have been rendered destitute annually according to Paperi, while "foreign" and "imperialist capitalist" interests (a reference usually to British investment and estate capital in West Malaysia) are reaping huge profits. Government programs such as those of the Federal Land Development Authority are charged with keeping tens of thousands of farmers in bondage under the promise of giving land to them. Paperi, as also in the past, charged the Malaysian government with malfeasance in the state-run Pilgrim Management and Fund Board, which assists Malay Muslims in making the pilgrimage to Mecca. Money at the disposal of the board was said to have found its way into the pockets of "various foreign monopoly capitalists" and to have helped board members to "buy big houses" and finance their own palm oil, rubber, and other estate interests. The Hussein Onn government, further, was accused of flouting Muslim mores by assisting in the spread of a "sex-dominated culture" which originates in countries dominated by "imperialist monopolist capital." This evil, in turn, had encouraged the spread of "drug abuse." A final "diabolical crime" was the "reactionary" government's accommodation of "Zionist Jewish" capital in Malaysia's development and encouragement of a secret "Jewish Zionist movement" in the country, called "Premesa." (Ibid., 29 September.) The Malayan Peasants' Front issued a statement in July stressing the need to carry out the CPM's program in order to realize fully the interests of the Malayan peasantry (ibid., 20 July). (On CPM land reform and agrarian policies, see Justus M. van der Kroef, "New Trends in Malaysian Communism," *Issues and Studies,* June 1977, pp. 56-61.)

Little is known of the organizational structure and leadership of Paperi (estimated membership about 300) and of the Malayan Peasants' Front (about 100 followers), although a central committee structure is claimed for both.

Similarly, the year brought little news of the operations of the CPM(RF) and CPM-ML, although security forces reported periodic small-scale clashes with units of the MPLA—the name of the guerrilla forces of both CPM(RF) and CPM-ML—and with the MPLL and MPLF. The CPM-ML's guerrillas are said to have their base area west of the Jungei River in Thailand's Patani Province, while the CPM(RF) operates from the Sadao area of southern Thailand (*FEER,* 2 September).

According to Malaysian security officials in conversation with this author in early July 1977, the CPM-ML's units disseminate literature calling for intensified armed struggle and continue their clashes along the border of Thailand and eastern Kedah, while the faction's pamphlets and covert proselytizers also have made their appearance in Kuala Lumpur and on university campuses. The explicit commitment of both the parent CPM and the CPM-ML to Maoist ideology and "people's war" tactics, makes the split meaningful only in the context of intra-organizational quarrels. The CPM(RF)'s media resources and tactical operations appear much more limited than the CPM-ML's and are confined primarily to Sadao and to parts of the border area between Perlis and Kedah States.

In Sarawak, where continuing defections and joint Indonesian-Malaysian counterinsurgency operations limit the scope of NKCP and NKPGF activity, a party Central Committee headed by Wen Ming-chuan as chairman, is concerned with rebuilding the guerrilla infrastructure so severely damaged in the aftermath of the Sri Aman amnesty and rehabilitation campaign. The NKCP's organizational front complex appears to be largely dormant. No new NKCP tactical statement was published during the year, but on 24 July Wen Ming-chuan sent a letter to the Central Committee of the Chinese Communist party, subsequently released by the New China News Agency. (Ibid., 10 August.) Wen's letter eulogized Chinese party leader Hua Kuo-feng. The NKCP's ideological and tactical commitments are identical with those of the CPM-MNLA. But the NKCP has been careful to avoid giving an impression of having any organizational or doctrinal unity or any sort of tactical collaboration with the West Malaysian Communist movement. The reason lies in the earlier noted position of Malaysian Communists that West and East Malaysia 'were undemocratically and unlawfully joined in 1963, and that their future properly lies in the independence of both regions.

Domestic Developments. Besides its ongoing anti-guerrilla operations, the Malaysian government continued an extensive political anti-subversion and surveillance campaign in 1977. In mid-January twenty-three "Communist underground" members and terrorist "supporters," some later identified as members of the MNLF, were arrested in raids in different districts in Perak. In February a vaguely worded announcement reported police discovery of a "Communist plot" to infiltrate "certain areas" of Perak, Pahang, Kedah, Perlis, and Kelantan. The MNLF was charged with preparing for a protracted "armed struggle" by establishing food dumps in districts where MNLF activity was to be deployed and by sending cadres to "secret camps in the jungle" for training. Exact locations of the "infiltrated' districts or other details of MNLF methods of operations were not disclosed, but a senior police spokesman called attention to the activities in connection with the reported infiltration attempt by the CPM-ML's Malayan People's Liberation League, which he said was "active in both urban and rural areas," and whose cadres were trained in the use of firearms. An "Underground Mobile Squad" of the MPLL, he said, was moving from state to state with the "primary aim of assassinating police personnel," and "many" such personnel had already fallen victim to the squad (*Sarawak Tribune,* 17 February; *FBIS,* 13 January).

At the close of June, just as the faction-ridden United Malays National Organization (UMNO), a mainstay of the Alliance party government, was to hold its annual meeting, eighty-six cadres and members of the CPM-front Malayan National Liberation League (MNLL) were reported to have been arrested in West Malaysia as part of an ongoing operation code named "Planet." The Home Affairs minister, Tan Sri Ghazali Shafie, declared that the arrests had "virtually crippled" the CPM's organization, so that its "remnant elements" were now doomed to lead a "fugitive existence" (*Straits Times,* Singapore, 30 June). The arrests were said to have included senior CPM cadres "in the forty-fifty age group," as well as younger members and supporters, but not among them was the chief MNLL leader, fifty-two-year-old Communist veteran Fong Chong Pik, who under the code name "The Plen" (for Plenipotentiary) had already been identified as a major Communist figure by Singapore Premier Lee Kuan Yew some sixteen years ago (Lee Kuan Yew, *The Battle for Merger,* Singapore, pp. 45-47). The arrests were said to have begun as early as September 1975 in Kuala Lumpur and have extended subsequently as far south as Johore, including such areas as Trengganu, not previously in the spotlight of Communist activity.

These and other arrests (*Straits Times,* 4 July, 13 August) tended to accentuate the atmosphere of national danger. Rising public concern over this danger had already reached a new high with the arrests on 22 June 1976 of two leading Malay intellectual figures, Abdul Samad Ismail, former editor of the Kuala Lumpur daily, *The New Straits Times,* and Samani bin Mohammed Amin, news editor of the leading Malay daily, *Berita Harian.* They were charged with propagating Communist ideology. These arrests were followed by the detention on 3 November 1976 of a number of prominent political figures on grounds of allegedly subversive activities. Among those arrested were the former Science, Technology and Environmental Affairs deputy minister, Datuk Abdullah Ahmad, and former Labor Minister deputy, Tengku Abdullah Majid. The subsequent confessions of most of those arrested in June and November also tended to implicate the embassy of the Soviet Union as a source of subversion in the country, and gave the impression that the process of Communist infiltration had reached the most influential figures in public life (*Asia Research Bulletin,* Six-Monthly Political Supplement, 30 April 1977, pp. 315-16).

Some observers, however, saw the arrests and confessions as part of the ongoing intra-UMNO political infighting and jockeying for power. In legal circles, meanwhile, there was increasing apprehension over the erosion of fundamental civil rights because of the application of the Internal Security Act and its correlate, the 1975 Essential (Security Cases) Amendment Regulations. Application of the death penalty in August 1977 by the Penang High Court to a thirteen-year-old boy, under the security regulations, for possession of a gun aroused further widespread criticism (*FEER*, 8 April, 9 September, 7 October). Approval by the UMNO conference on 2 July of a resolution calling for a detailed investigation of the activities of Freemasons in Malaysia suggested to some that concern over subversion was geting out of bounds, and brought a statement by Ghazali Shafie that the requested investigation should be conducted cautiously and with due regard for human rights. Ghazali also urged UMNO delegates to stop making "wild allegations" (*Morning Express*, Bangkok, 3 July).

In the meantime, joint Malaysian-Thai anti-insurgency operations were being stepped up, under a new border agreement between the two governments, signed on 4 March, which eases operations on both sides of the frontier, including "hot pursuit" into the national territories of both (*Straits Times*, 5 March). Already, in January, some 5,000 Thai and Malaysian troops had begun Operation Big Star (Daoyai-Musnah) in the Sadoa area of Thailand, and on 4 July they continued their flushing out of the Communist guerrillas of all three party factions, and of the Communist Party of Thailand besides, in the first phase of Operation Sacred Ray (Cahaya Bena), which was initially centered on the Betong salient.

Overrunning and destroying guerrilla camps, seizing food and arms dumps, breaking up the underground network of guerrilla intelligence, and killing, capturing, as well as scattering insurgents in all directions, these joint counterinsurgency operations were said to have had significant success. (Ibid., 12 April; *Asiaweek*, 4 February, 15 April; *FBIS*, 3 August.) Yet, not even Malaysia's home minister has claimed that the much-vaunted operations have, in fact, destroyed the guerrillas. Ghazali, rather, has said that it had been the two governments' intentions all along to "disperse" the insurgents and to "make them run," and to "reduce the status" of the insurgency in the critical Betong salient (*Straits Times*, 13 August). Earlier, in an address to foreign journalists, Ghazali had said that the fight against the Communist insurgents was "an unending one," adding paradoxically that the problem would be "resolved," although "not that soon" (*FBIS*, 5 August).

Other observers noted that some 800 Communist insurgents, though flushed from their jungle hideouts, were concealing themselves in Betong town, apparently with impunity, while elsewhere the Betong rebels were carefully avoiding all clashes with security forces (*Straits Times*, 22, 28 July). Moreover, as they were being driven out of their southern Thai sanctuaries, the Malaysian Communist rebels were proceeding to set up new training centers further south, in Peninsular Malaysia itself, including some in Selangor, and Pahang, according to Major General Mahmud Suleiman, commander of Armed Forces Region I (*FBIS*, 18 April).

With increasing frequency, too, there have been reports of coalescing of Thai and Malaysian Communists. Indeed. General Suleiman noted as early as January that dissident leftist Thai students, who had gone underground in the wake of the October 1976 coup in Bangkok, had joined the CPM(RF), and that the latter party even was seeking a rapprochement with the Communist Party of Thailand (CPT) (*Sarawak Tribune*, 31 January). In May it was reported in the Bangkok press that the joint counterinsurgency operations in recent weeks had provided evidence that the CPM and CPT were joining forces (*Nation Review*, Bangkok, 16 May *FBIS*, 16 May). Meanwhile, CPM media proclaimed that the "revolutionary situation has been getting better every day" (*FBIS*, 17 March).

The Malaysian government's counterinsurgency campaign includes a program of rapid economic development of the rebel-infested frontier area. In early July Home Minister Ghazali announced government intentions to clear and open up large tracts of land for agricultural settlement in the northwestern part of the country, as the government continued construction of a 200-mile east-west highway along the frontier. Because it is hacked through the dense jungle area, the road, which will eventually connect Kota Bahru on the east coast with the port of Penang in the west, is costing a million dollars a mile to asphalt. Ex-servicemen will be encouraged to settle along the road, thus forming a spine of loyal communities in the surrounding wooded body of frontier insurgency (*Wall Street Journal,* 22 February; *China News,* Taipei, 5 July).

In Sarawak, counterinsurgency operations involve armed confrontation as well as the rehabilitation of guerrillas who have surrendered. At the end of March, an executive of the government's counterinsurgency program (RASCOM) declared that there were still "107 CTS lurking in the jungle," and further that during the past year a total of 7 insurgents were killed by security forces, 3 were captured, and 1 had surrendered, while "numerous food and arms dumps" were seized. Sarawak's chief minister, Abdul Rahman Yakub, said at the same time that half of the "Communist terrorist remnants" in Sarawak's First Division area had now been "wiped out" following a series of security operations, and he warned the insurgents that unless they gave up their "meaningless anti-national activities," the government would hunt them down "to the last man" (*Sarawak Tribune,* 28 March). It was, nevertheless, apparent that the NKPGF hard core not only had managed to survive, but also could continue to count on the covert support of elements of the Sarawak Chinese community. In May Chief Minister Rahman threatened "stern action" against those who persisted in helping the insurgents, adding that he regretted that there were still people "who were taking the government's warnings lightly." A new strategy, though not revealed in detail, would, according to Rahman, aim at denying to the insurgents occupation of any area and support from the population. The announced objectives suggested that complete success in dislodging the NKPGF was still eluding the government. (Ibid., 5, 18 May.)

Sarawak's difficulties point up persistent sources of economic disparity and social unrest throughout the country that help feed the insurgent movement. While Malaysia's estimated per capita income of $720 in 1975 is surpassed in Asia only by Japan and the Republic of China (Taiwan), and by the city states of Singapore and Hong Kong (*Malaysian Digest,* Kuala Lumpur, 28 February), the Third Malaysia Plan (1976-80) is at present "running at less than half the goals set two years ago," with investors, both domestic and foreign, showing little confidence in the country's future (*NYT,* 5 September). Racial animosities between Chinese and Malays persist in the context of programs favoring the advancement of the latter as so-called *bumiputras,* while there is little indication that the poorer strata of society, predominantly Malay, are benefiting from national development efforts. For example, according to data from the government's Statistics Department, between 1957 and 1970 income distribution in Malaysia worsened, so that the top 10 percent of households increased their share of total income from 35 percent to 41 percent, while the poorest 20 percent of families experienced a drop in their share of income from 6 percent of total income to 4 percent. According to another calculation, the top 5 percent of the population alone earned more than the bottom 60 percent combined ("Poverty in Malaysia—A Review," *Sarawak Tribune,* 9 July).

Many of Malaysia's higher education graduates have not found employment, especially those holding degrees in the humanities—for whom a government bureaucratic position remains highly prized (*Asiaweek,* October, p. 100). At the same time, the government appears particularly concerned to control student political activity (e.g., through the new University and University Colleges Amendment Act of June 1975), as a result of student agitation on behalf of the rural poor three years ago. Leaders of such student organizations as are now permitted are held criminally responsible for any violation by their group, "even if no individual involved were found guilty," but in the meantime "the problem of Malay rural poverty and land hunger has not gone away" (Stuart Drummond, "Malaysia's Two Years of Stress," *The World Today,* London, March p. 114). To be sure, the Third Malaysia Plan seems particularly to address itself to the conditions of poverty of all major Malaysian population groups, not just Malays (Colin MacAndrews, "The Politics of Planning: Malaysia and the New Third Malaysia Plan, 1976-1980," *Asian Survey,* March, pp. 305-6). But neither the sense of ethnic grievance, nor the effects of income disparities, nor again the problems of specific social groups like the young educated unemployed Chinese, or the Malay rubber cultivators and urban poor, seem likely to be ameliorated at any time soon. Malaysian Communism, whatever the efficacy of ongoing government counterinsurgency programs, will not want for new recruits in the foreseeable future.

Relations with Communist Countries. Though Malaysia, in the aftermath of the Communist conquest of Saigon, had led its fellow members of ASEAN (Association of Southeast Asian Nations, the regional cooperative organization founded in 1967 and comprising Malaysia, Singapore, Thailand, Indonesia, and the Philippines) in urging friendly relations with the new Socialist Republic of Vietnam (SRV), its efforts in this regard have met with but limited success, in large part because of the Hanoi government's suspicions of ASEAN and the residual military relations of some ASEAN members with the U.S., U.K., Australia, and New Zealand (Justus M. van der Kroef, "ASEAN, Vietnam, and Southeast Asia's Search for Security," *Asian Thought and Society,* December 1977). Malaysia and the Hanoi government had already agreed to establish diplomatic relations in 1973, but no agreement on an exchange of ambassadors was reached until 1975, and not until 28 May 1976 did SRV officials arrive in Kuala Lumpur to open their embassy.

On 22 August 1977 Malaysian Premier Hussein Onn declared that he did not have "negative thoughts" about the new Communist regime in Indochina. Indeed, according to Onn, Malaysia preferred to view the recent struggle of these Indochina countries as a "legitimate" part of the elimination of "colonial" influences. He further expressed the hope that the Indochinese states, in view of Malaysia's feelings of friendship toward them, would adopt the same attitude and "respect our rights to practice the system of government elected by the people and not to misunderstand it as a form of domination by Western colonial influence" (*FBIS,* 23 August). In October the premier called on the Soviet Union (whose embassy in Kuala Lumpur has reportedly been linked to alleged recruitment of prominent Malays to the Communist cause) to use its influence to foster better relations between the Southeast Asian states and the SRV. Onn said that he would not make a formal approach to Moscow in this regard, however, because "Moscow can always take note of such public statements" as he had made (ibid., 12 October). Onn said that he felt justified in making the appeal because the USSR "is very friendly with the Indochina states" and therefore should be able to play a part in bringing about a better understanding, thus contributing to peace in the Southeast Asian region.

Relations with People's China have remained formally correct, but continue to be adversely affected by Peking's verbal encouragement of the CPM and by the latter organization's ideological connection with Maoism and Chinese policies. CPM statements, relayed over the "Voice of the Malayan Revolution," whose transmitter is located in southern China, are often prominently noted in the Peking media (see e.g. *Peking Review,* 1 July, p.26). In turn, the CPM, in the course of any year, is wont to eulogize such events as congresses or plenary meetings of the Chinese Communist party or its committees, or to commemorate the anniversary of the Chinese "People's Liberation Army," or note other important dates in the public life of the People's Republic of China. On such occasions CPM acknowledgement of the alleged invincibility of "Marxism-Leninism-Mao Tse-tung Thought," and of the "revolutionary friendship and militant unity" between the Chinese and Malaysian Communist parties, or of the applicability of Mao's tactical thought to Malaysian conditions ("Surround the cities from the countryside," and "Seize political power by armed force") is *de rigueur* (*FBIS*, 8, 26 August).

Malaysian officials, mindful of their country's leadership in the development of ASEAN, have gone out of their way to note Peking's approving attitude toward the association. On 18 August, Malaysia's deputy minister of finance returned from Shanghai where he had taken formal delivery of a 3,700-ton coastal vessel built in People's China, the first such vessel exported by the Peking government. He declared that People's China "fully supported" the concept of ASEAN economic cooperation and "wishes it all success" (Bernama despatch, Kuala Lumpur, 18 August).

Malaysian-Indonesian joint military surveillances of the Sarawak frontier, in conjunction with anti-guerrilla activities, have continued. On 27 July, Malaysia's Home Affairs Minister Ghazali said that the government had asked the Indonesian government for assistance in arresting twenty-five Malaysian Communists who, more than a decade ago, during the Sukarno regime's "confrontation" campaign against Malaysia, had "infiltrated" into Indonesia. Ghazali also said that Indonesia's President Suharto "appreciated" the current joint Thai-Malaysian operations against Communist insurgents, added that, insofar as similar Indonesian-Malaysian anti-guerrilla operations were concerned, these would be continued "until the Communist remnants have been totally wiped out" (*FBIS,* 28 July).

Publications. The "Voice of the Malayan Revolution" (Radio Suara Revolusi Malaya), whose transmitter is believed to be located in Hengyang in southern China about 200 miles south of the city of Changsha (*FEER,* 2 September, 1977), is the CPM's principal medium of communication, with broadcasts mainly in Mandarin, and occasionally in Malay and Indonesian. The "Voice" usually also transmits major party statements of the NKCP, which now has no regularly appearing publication of its own. Such Sarawak Communist publications as *Masses News* (in Mandarin and English) have ceased appearing. Another transmitter, which made an initial broadcast on 4 May 1976 and which identified itself then as "Voice of the People of Malaya" (Suara Rakyat Malaya) (*YICA, 1977,* p. 348), is heard only irregularly and with a very weak signal. This transmitter appears to be affiliated with the CPM-ML, although this is not certain.

The CPM(RF) and the CPM-ML appear to rely on poorly printed or stenciled leaflets for local and very limited proselytizing or propagandistic purposes; it is obvious that recruitment and indoctrination occur primarily by word of mouth. Until the early 1970s, CPM supporters in the U.K. regularly published a monthly, the *Malayan Monitor & General News,* but its appearance has become much rarer, possibly reflecting the division within the Malayan Communist movement itself. People's China's media, both foreign-language and domestic, also devote much less attention to the CPM than they used to in the dcades of the fifties and sixties.

University of Bridgeport   Justus M. van der Kroef

Mongolia

A fusion of two revolutionary groups produced the Mongolian People's Party in 1921. The party held its First Congress in March of that year at Kyakhta, on Soviet territory. It became known as the Mongolian People's Revolutionary Party (MPRP) in 1924. Fiftieth anniversary celebrations in November 1974 commemorated this shift to "socialism" in 1924, but Russian dominance had already been established in 1921. The designation of the country as the Mongolian People's Republic (MPR) was adopted in 1924, as was the name of the capital, Ulan Bator (formerly Urga). At that time a non-capitalist and anti-bourgeois line was announced by the party's Third Congress and the first Great Khural (the structural equivalent of the USSR Supreme Soviet).

In 1976 the MPRP claimed 67,000 members (compared with 58,000 in 1971). The population of the MPR in 1977 was estimated at just over 1,500,000.

Organization and Leadership. Confirmation of Tsedenbal as first secretary of the MPRP at the Seventeenth Congress in mid-1976 and as president—chairman of the Presidium of the Great Khural—in mid-1977, along with similar confirmation of Batmunkh as prime minister and Politburo member, indicated establishment of a hierarchy of rank, with Tsedenbal clearly recognized as senior. Since his removal from the Politburo in mid-1976, S. Luvsan has also lost his former positions as first deputy chairman of the Great Khural, and chairman of the Mongolian-Soviet Friendship Association, probably due to age rather than political disfavor. T. Ragcha, sixty years old, serving as a first deputy prime minister, advanced to full membership in the Politburo and was reelected as a deputy prime minister. D. Gombojav, a new candidate-member of the Politburo, replaced S. Luvsan as chairman of the Mongolian-Soviet Friendship Association. In the government, M. Pelje was confirmed as deputy prime minister and replaced Gombojav as principal representative to CEMA. The promotion of Pelje, with his ten-year experience as minister of geology, indicates the increasing importance attached to the development of Mongolia's mineral resources. Batmunkh, a comparative newcomer to a top position in the Mongolian power elite, had duplicated a major step in Tsedenbal's career by heading the Institute of Economics in Ulan Bator. The men—and they are all men—rising fastest are all trained in economics and experienced in jobs dealing with economic planning, foreign trade, or resource development. The veteran Politburo members of more than fifteen years' service—Molomjamts, Jagvaral, Luvsanravdan, and Maidar—continue their by now traditional roles in the system, while Jalan-Ajav's appointment in 1977 as one of two vice-presidents (deputy chairman of the Presidium of the Great Khural) represents a small promotion. Altangerel continues unchanged as first secretary of the Ulan Bator City party organization and candidate member of the Politburo. Thirty-five of the ninety-one full Central Committee members were on the Central Committee by 1963, and twenty other occupied leading party and/or government positions in that year. Eight of the nine Politburo members and candidate-members from 1963 were confirmed as Central Committee members in 1976. Stability and continuity in the system has been dramatized by Tsedenbal's unbroken hegemony since the death of Choibalsan in 1952. Still, Batmunkh (b. 1926) is ten years younger than Tsedenbal, and a substantial number of the new Central Committee members and top-job appointees are younger men. Identifiable categories of Central Committee membership include heads of sections of the Central Committee of the party, Aimak (province) first secretaries, government ministers, ambassadors, and military. Of named heads of Central Committee sections, eleven are full members of the Central Committee, nine are candidate-members, and only one is not listed as either member or candidate-member. Of Aimak first secretaries, six are full members, ten are candidate-members, and three are neither. Among the many government ministers, twenty-five hold full membership, twenty-one candidate-membership, and nine are not listed on the Central Committee at all. Three ambassadors are full Central Committee members, six are candidate-members, and ten are not on the Central Committee. The Mongolian ambassador to the USSR, serving since 1973, is a full member of the Central Committee, and the new ambassador to China is a candidate-member. Of top military leaders, five are full members, ten are candidate-members, and nine hold no Central Committee position. While almost all of the full members of the Central Committee were readily identifiable by party or government positions, twenty-one of the sixty-one candidate members seemed to be "new people" unmentioned in any connection other than the published Central Committee list.

The intelligentsia—bureaucrats and professionals—continued to constitute about 50 percent of the party, while livestock-herding arats (nomads) declined slightly to 19 percent and factory workers increased slightly to 31 percent. The steady but slow increase in the number of women party members continued, but still falls short of 25 percent. Ethnic Khalkhas continue to dominate all the top positions, with little sign of political significance or prominence for any Kazakh or Oirat (western Mongol). The role of Buryat Mongols, who certainly are important and influential among the elite, is deliberately and systematically masked statistically and downplayed publicly.

The Presidium of the Great Khural, elected in mid-1977, includes no new political figures. Institutional recognition is provided the military, trade-unions, women, youth, and the party, but omitted are the nomads and agriculture, whether livestock or grain farming. The cities—Ulan Bator, Darkhan, and now Erdenet—are the favored places in politics as in all other matters. Of the 354 deputies elected to the Great Khural, 341 were members of the party or its subordinate youth organization.

The public image of Tsedenbal's Russian wife, which had been markedly prominent in press accounts and photographs in 1975, had already receded in 1976. Neither press notices nor pictures of her appeared in 1977. Most other standard phenomena and rituals of the party and regime continued: meetings of the full Central Committee twice a year, in June and December; Tsedenbal's two-month summer vacation in the USSR and August meeting with Brezhnev in the Crimea; regional conferences of secretaries of primary party organizations chaired by the various Politburo members.

Domestic Attitudes and Activities. Domestic affairs, and especially economic development questions, are inseparable from relations with the USSR. The most important domestic project, the Erdenet copper-molybdenum mining complex, is a Russian conception under Russian supervision, and the whole of its product is destined for the Soviet Union. Old coal mines at Nalaikha (near Ulan Bator), newer ones at Sharyn-gol (near Darkhan), and new open mines not yet producing at Baganur, receive extensive modern mining machinery from the USSR. The existence of open coal and copper mines suggests the likelihood of extensive pollution and erosion previously unknown in Mongolia. There is at least nominal attention to such problems within the State Committee on Science and Technology. Inclusion of north central Mongolia in the large East Siberian long distance electric power grid has not reduced attention to production of coal. Mongolian imports of Soviet oil and petroleum products increase every year. The trade imbalance—the surplus of Mongolian imports from Russia over its exports to Russia—increased from 166 million rubles in 1974 to 335 million in 1976. Copper and molybdenum production of Erdenet should go a long way toward eliminating that imbalance. The political sensitivity of Soviet imports of fluorspar was underlined when the 1976 trade statistics for the first time omitted quantities and masked value-figures. Nonetheless it appears that the value of Mongolian fluorspar to Russia remained approximately the same in 1976 as in 1975, while the value of Chinese fluorspar to Russia doubled.

Serious problems of weather and of organization have led to decreasing livestock herds. Less than 23 million total head of livestock probably decreased even further in 1977. January-February 1977 was marked by exceptionally low temperatures and heavy snows, and an ad hoc Extraordinary Commission was established to cope with the problem of livestock survival. The export of livestock-on-the-hoof to the USSR decreased from 1.3 million head in 1973 to 974,000 in 1976. But, at the same time, the shipment of meat and meat products, tinned and frozen, has more than doubled, to 41,000 tons in 1976. While new lands opened to agriculture increased by 40,000 hectares in 1976, and were to increase by an additional 90,000 hectares in 1977, the 1976 grain harvest of 340,000 tons was below target. Soviet export of flour to Mongolia increased from 23,000 tons in 1975 to 42,000 tons in 1976. The USSR encourages Mongolian grain farming so as to eliminate requirement for imports, but bad weather and many other factors do not permit that goal to be attained.

International Views and Contacts. "A new qualitative stage is opening in the development of Mongolian-Soviet relations," Tsedenbal stated in August. The strands of infrastructural web, which bind Mongolia to the Soviet Union, continue to multiply, thicken, strengthen, and tighten. Convergence and even absorption proceed. A new development with striking historical resonance, following a pattern established by the Russian Tsarist government in 1914, was the announcement in September that a representative of the Soviet Ministry of Finance will be stationed directly in the offices of the Mongolian Ministry of Finance. Russian control over Mongolian use of Russian funds has always been close.

In June Batmunkh led an MPR delegation to Warsaw for the thirty-first session of CEMA and in August the fifteenth meeting of the Joint Mongolian-Soviet Intergovernmental Commission was held. Mongolian-Soviet Friendship Month took place this year, as it does every year, and the sixtieth anniversary of the Bolshevik Revolution was extensively celebrated. The Sixth Congress of the Mongolian-Soviet Friendship Association met in June. Mongols and Russians on joint scientific expeditions searched for dinosaurs (the Joint Paleontological Expedition) and for mineral resources (Joint Geological Expedition). A special festival of Mongolian and Soviet Youth was held in Ulan Bator in July. Some 4,000 Mongols pursued studies in the USSR. The Institute of Oriental Studies in Moscow and the Far Eastern Institute at Vladivostok maintain Mongolian sections and close ties with Mongolian scholars. The selection of the new head of the Institute of Oriental Studies concerns Mongols, for that Institute has functioned as one instrument of Soviet ideological control in the MPR.

Special regional connections also continue. The first secretaries of the Irkutsk Oblast Committee and of the Chita Oblast Committee of the CPSU visited the MPR, as did the Kalmyk Mongol first secretary. A Mongolian delegation went to Uzbekistan in April, and Kazakh experts directed the Selenga River Erdenet water-pipeline construction. A Soviet Ministry of Defense delegation paid a formal visit in March and General Altunin, Chief of USSR Civil Defense, visited Mongolia in June.

A brief verbal truce with China followed MaoTse-tung's death in September 1976 and the arrest of the Gang of Four in October but the Mongols were again attacking China in November, and the Chinese retaliated in December. Mutual accusations and verbal hostilities continued throughout 1977. Mongolian attacks came especially often and in a particularly slashing style in June and July. These included the specific charge that Chinese policy aimed at annexation of the MPR. In mid-September the Mongols hurled a wide ranging barrage of accusations, although most of them constituted Mongolian defense of the USSR. In October a long article based on Western sources charged that Peking participates actively in the narcotics trade, supplying opium and heroin through the Burma-Thailand Golden Triangle, Macao, and Hong Kong. In April, the Mongols warned of their intention to incorporate the Chinese in Mongolia into the regular school system, posing a clear threat to Chinese schools which had operated for the small number of Chinese residents in Mongolia.

The Chinese charged that Soviet domination of the MPR was increasing, that the USSR continued "tsarist Russia's reactionary policy," and forecast assimilation of the Mongolian people. They specifically attacked direct governmental ministry-to-ministry cooperation, and Russian language training and use. When the Mongols requested permission to enter China to honor their war dead interred in Manchuria and Inner Mongolia, the Chinese refused, although in March they ostentatiously laid a wreath for the "fallen heroes" of the Mongolian Army at a monument to them. The Mongols called the Chinese charges about intensification of Soviet control "slander." In January a Chinese deputy premier received the new Mongolian Ambassador to China, L. Chulunbator. A Chinese trade delegation arrived in Ulan Bator and signed a trade protocol in June. In August a meeting of the Mongolian-Chinese Friendship Association was held in Ulan Bator though no letup in violent language ensued. Harrison Salisbury reported from Inner Mongolia that the local population had been moved back from the border some years ago, and a kind of no-man's-land maintained.

East European bloc countries generally follow the pattern of the USSR in their relationship with Mongolia, though trade and other activities are only one-quarter of the Soviet volume. Joint Intergovernmental Commissions supervise bilateral relations between Mongolia and individual East European countries. Trade relations and mutual official visits continue with North Korea, Vietnam, and Laos, but not Cambodia. Establishment of the Laos-Mongolian Friendship Association in Vientiane in July and the considerable volume of Mongolian publicity about anything concerning Laos suggests continuation of a deliberate special relationship. The head of a department of the Central Committee of the Mongolian Party attended the Third Congress of the Mozambique Liberation Front (FRELIMO) in January, and the MPR recognized Djibouti on 29 June.

In addition to regular diplomatic relations with more than eighty countries (still not including the United States), trade relations with all the Communist bloc countries and a few non-Communist countries, and U.N.-related activities, Mongolia sends its "Parliamentary Group," led by Deputy Prime Minister D. Tsevegmid, to international conferences and countries of a wide variety of political persuasions.

Publications. The MPRP issues *Unen* (Truth), *Namyn Amdral* (Party Life), the Russian language *Novosti Mongolii* (News of Mongolia), and a Chinese-language weekly *Meng-ku Hsiao-hsi Pao* (News of Mongolia). *Ediyn Dzasag* (Economics) is issued by the party Central Committee, and *Shine Hodoo* (New Countryside) by the Ministry of Agriculture. The MPR assigns a representative to the editorial board of *Problems of Peace and Socialism.* There are radio broadcasts in Mongolian, Russian, English, Chinese, and Kazakh. Television broadcasting was begun in 1970.

University of North Carolina   Robert A. Rupen
Chapel Hill

Nepal

The Communist Party of Nepal (CPN) was formed in 1949, and its membership is estimated at 6,500. All political parties have been banned in Nepal since 1960 when the late King Mahendra dissolved the Nepali Congress party (NC) government. A "partyless" panchayat (assembly) system of government was later established. The CPN's major competitor among active political groups is the democratic-socialist NC. Nepal's population is approximately 13,199,000.

Leadership and Organization. The CPN has been openly split since 1960 when the King's actions exacerbated internal ideological and personal disagreements. The moderate faction, led by Keshar Jung Raimajhi, the general secretary, has retained party control. Through its pro-monarchy stance and support of "progressive" government measures such as land reform, the Raimajhi CPN and its sympathizers have gained positions in government and officially sponsored political organizations.

Dissidents Pushpa Lal Shrestha, Tulsi Lal Amatya, and their supporters, militantly opposed to the monarchy, fled to India where they formed a parallel CPN organization at the "Third Party Congress" in May 1962. Further factionalism has developed in the revolutionary CPN. Pushpa Lal remains in India, but the less militant Man Mohan Adhikari, a CPN founder who was imprisoned for several years, now leads an extremist faction in Nepal.

Both CPN organizations operate within Nepal, concentrating their activities in the Kathmandu Valley and in the Tarai, the southern plains adjoining India, but in general their influence appears limited. Communist sympathizers appear most numerous among students, educators, and urban elements.

Among student groups, the pro-revolutionary CPN All Nepal National Independent Students' Union competes with the National Student Union, sponsored by the moderate CPN. Their major non-Communist rival is the NC student organization, the Nepal Students' Union.

Domestic Attitudes and Activities. Although the moderate CPN has supported the monarchy, its policies and views as outlined at Raimajhi's own "Third Party Congress" in 1968 were critical of the present political system. The congress criticized the ban on parties, demanded the release of all political prisoners, and proclaimed the need for restoring democratic rights. Working with the system, the moderate faction's ultimate aim was establishment of a national democracy. Immediate targets in this task were "workers, peasants, students, youth, traders, and professionals." (*New Age*, New Delhi, 12 January 1969.)

The extremist CPN has called for reinstatement of political parties, restoration of parliamentary democracy, and distribution of surplus land among the peasants. Pushpa Lal and Adhikari differ over strategy: while Pushpa Lal has advocated overthrow of the King, Adhikari has been working for domestic political reforms.

Terrorist activity in Nepal, allegedly involving CPN extremists and NC dissidents, has declined since 1974. A number of the extremist "Naxalites," who waged the 1972-73 terrorist campaign in the southeastern Jhapa area, remain in prison, although a small group escaped in late April (*Far Eastern Economic Review*, Hong Kong, 20 May).

The detention of Nepali Congress leader, B. P. Koirala, for subversion became the focus of political activity during 1977 and intensified the debate between conservative and liberal elements over political reforms. Koirala, an advocate of parliamentary democracy, was arrested in December 1976 on his return home from self-exile in India; he later received expressions of international support from human rights organizations and prominent Indian politicians, among others.

Both CPN extremist Man Mohan Adhikari and moderate K. J. Raimajhi were reportedly among Nepalese politicians involved in an unsuccessful effort to make the panchayat system more "dynamic" (*Pratignya*, Kathmandu, 14 May; *Rastra Dhwani*, Kathmandu, 19 May). Widespread criticism of the policy of consensus in panchayat elections did appear, however, especially among panchayat workers and in the press. Both CPN leaders also continued to press for reforms such as an amnesty for political prisoners and press freedom (*Matribhumi*, Kathmandu, 16 August; *Samaj*, Kathmandu, 22 September).

These various pressures undoubtedly contributed to the appointment of a new prime minister, K. N. Bista, in September and to limited government steps toward liberalization. Following formation of the new cabinet, which included CPN co-founder D. P. Adhikari as a minister of state, most of the officially acknowledged political prisoners were released, some dissidents were given amnesty, and the ban on several newspapers, including the pro-Soviet *Samiksha*, was lifted. King Birendra also directed that the panchayat system should become "even more people-oriented within the constitution," emphasizing public participation (*Rising Nepal*, Kathmandu, 23 September).

CPN leaders are among those who nevertheless remain skeptical of the government's commitment to reform. Man Mohan Adhikari declared that the government's amnesty and releases discriminated against leftists, such as the Jhapa "Naxalites" and Pushpa Lal Shrestha and Tulsi Lal Amatya in India (*Asiali Awaj*, Kathmandu, 28 October). Pushpa Lal, in fact, claims that there are still over 1,000 political prisoners in Nepal (*Times of India*, 30 September).

International Views and Policies. The moderate CPN is recognized by, and receives financial assistance from, the Soviet Union, and favors closer Nepal-Soviet relations. It is critical of China's views. Competing factions of the revolutionary CPN have appealed to China for closer working relationships, but Chinese involvement appears limited to some financial support.

Publications. The weekly *Samiksha* has reflected the views of the moderate CPN. The Pushpa Lal Shrestha revolutionary faction reportedly publishes *Nepal Patra*.

Alexandria, Virginia   Barbara Reid

New Zealand

The Communist Party of New Zealand (CPNZ) was founded in April 1921. For more than forty years it was the only Marxist party in New Zealand, but from the late sixties onward a process of fragmentation began which led to the establishment of several Communist organizations, including for the first time a number of Trotskyist groups. The three major bodies at present are the CPNZ, the New Zealand Socialist Unity Party (SUP), and the Socialist Action League (SAL). The SUP was founded in 1966 when Soviet supporters broke away from the CPNZ, which had turned toward Peking. The SAL, founded in 1969 by a group of university students, is a Trotskyist organization affiliated to the Fourth International.

Other minor bodies are the Socialist Labour League, a Trotskyist group linked with the International Committee of the Fourth International and the Workers Revolutionary Party in Great Britain, and various local groups formed by defectors from the CPNZ: the Wellington Marxist-Leninist Organisation, the "Struggle" group (in Porirua near Wellington), the Communist Party of Aotearoa (in Wellington) and the New Zealand Marxist-Leninist Workers Party (in Auckland).

These parties and organizations all operate legally. None of them publishes membership figures, but their combined membership is probably in the vicinity of 500. The SUP is the strongest party, with an estimated memberhsip of up to 200; the CPNZ has perhaps 150 members, and the SAL up to 100. Although these figures are small, there has been a definite increase in membership in recent years which parallels the declining state of the economy. The SUP claimed an increase of 23 percent during 1976 and has grown further in 1977. The SAL in May claimed a growth of nearly 30 percent since the beginning of the year (*Socialist Action*, 27 May).

The population of New Zealand is 3,100,000.

Leadership and Organization. According to its constitution, the CPNZ holds a conference at intervals not exceeding three years. Conference delegates elect the National Committee, which in turn elects the national president and secretary and the Political Committee. The latter then elects a small National Secretariat which is responsible for the day-to-day running of the party. This is the theory, but in practice no conference has been held since 1966 and national offices have been filled by co-optation rather than election. No names of officers have been divulged for many years now, with the major exception of V. G. Wilcox who has been national secretary since 1951. Next in importance in the national leadership is R. C. Wolf. The party's headquarters is in Auckland, New Zealand's largest city, where most of its mainly working-class members are concentrated.

The SUP constitution is very similar. It too prescribes a triennial conference which elects a National Committee including the national president and secretary. This committee in turn elects a small National Executive. The fourth national conferene of the SUP met in Auckland in October 1976 and reelected G. H. Andersen as national president and G. E. Jackson as national secretary (an office he has held since the party's foundation). From the triennial membership census presented to the conference it appears that the average age of party members is forty-five (down from forty-seven in 1973), 18 percent of members are women (down from 26 percent), and 21 percent are under 30 years of age (up from 16 percent). The party's main strength is in the trade unions, where members hold some key positions. According to the census, two-thirds of SUP members are union members (52 percent in 1973), and fully a third hold office. (*Socialist Politics*, December-March.) The SUP too has its head office in Auckland, where five of its ten branches are located. In 1976 it set up a district organization in Auckland, and the second Auckland regional conference met in August 1977.

SAL conferences meet every two years under the League's constitution. The latest, fourth conference was held at Otaki near Wellington in the last week of 1976, attended by a hundred delegates and observers. It elected a new leadership, including K. Locke, G. A. Fyson, and R. Johnson. The SAL has its headquarters in Wellington, New Zealand's capital city. Its only other branch was in Auckland, but in 1977 the Christchurch branch was revived and new branches and study groups were formed in working-class districts near Wellington (Petone and Porirua) and Auckland. While the SUP is pleased that its average age is falling and that it is attracting more young people, the SAL is probably equally pleased to find its average age rising. In its early years the League was essentially an organization of university students; it is now attracting older age-groups as well as a growing number of workers, including Maoris and other Polynesians.

Auxiliary Organizations. The three major parties are each closely linked with a youth organization. The CPNZ has sponsored the Progressive Youth Movement, founded in Auckland in 1965. It has failed to establish itself in any other center and its activities rarely come to the notice of the public, apart from the occasional appearance of its news sheet, *Rebel*, once published fortnightly but now every three months approximately.

The SUP's Democratic Youth Front was until recently an even more shadowy organization, also confined to Auckland. In 1977, however, the Front experienced an upsurge in membership and activity. It has expanded by forming branches in Hamilton, New Plymouth, and Wellington and establishing contacts in other centers. It has redrafted its constitution to stress its Marxist-Leninist character, and has begun irregular publication of the *D.Y.F. Bulletin*. It has also sent delegates overseas, to the congress of the Australian Young Socialist League in April, and to the Soviet Union (for an international children's festival at Artek in July and a conference of Pacific Basin young researchers at Nakhodka). The first national conference of the Democratic Youth Front is planned for 1978.

The Young Socialists, linked with the SAL, were until this year the only nation-wide Marxist youth organization in the country. They held their third national conference in Wellington in April, attended by about 75 people, including the national secretary of the Australian Socialist Youth Alliance. They publish a journal, *Young Socialist*, which appears three times a year.

Another Trotskyist youth organization, also called Young Socialists, first made its appearance in New Zealand in 1975. It is linked with the Socialist Labour League and was at first confined to Auckland, but has now formed groups in Wellington as well. The first national conference of these Young Socialists met in Auckland in April, attended by delegates from Australia and Great Britain (the actor Corin Redgrave).

A small women's organization in Auckland, the Union of New Zealand Women, has links with the SUP. In March it was host to a delegation from the Women's International Democratic Federation, led by their president, Freda Brown.

There are also moves to revive a peace organization (the New Zealand Peace Council dissolved in the early seventies) in connection with the campaign for signatures for the new Stockholm Peace Appeal. An International Convention for Peace Action met in Wellington in February, attended by delegates from the World Peace Council, the Soviet Peace Committee, and other eastern (but not Chinese) delegates. In May a New Zealand delegation which included Ella Ayo, vice-president of the SUP, attended the World Assembly of Builders of Peace in Warsaw.

Friendship societies are active to promote closer relations with the Soviet Union, China, and the Democratic People's Republic of Korea, and Chile solidarity committees have been formed in several centers. Luis Meneses, general secretary of the Chilean Central Union of Workers, visited New Zealand in May and addressed the annual conference of the New Zealand Federation of Labour.

Domestic Attitudes and Activities. According to SUP president G. H. Andersen, the main difference between his party and the CPNZ is that the SUP "believes that the basic prerequisite for the change to a socialist society in New Zealand is a wide and powerful political movement of the people educated and organised to win the socialist objective." While not underestimating the strength of the anti-socialist forces, the SUP stresses "the desirability and possibility of peaceful change to socialism." The CPNZ on the other hand, adheres "to the 'all power from the barrel of the gun' philosophy which is advanced as the alternative to building the mass political movement." (*New Zealand Truth*, 19 July.)

The CPNZ in turn charges that "the Jackson-Andersen clique discarded the red banner of revolutionary Marxism-Leninism and put in its place the yellow flag of opportunism, class collaboration and capitulation to imperialism," trading "revolutionary politics for trade union politics," and the "democratic centralist organisation of a disciplined vanguard party of the working class for a loose, amorphous set of rules suited to a party of social democrcy" (*N.Z. Communist Review*, June).

Both parties concentrate their efforts among industrial workers but the SUP has been more successful in this field and has been able in recent years to overtake the CPNZ in both membership and influence. As far as the government is concerned, the CPNZ is hardly ever mentioned, while the SUP has been the target of frequent attacks by the prime minister, R. D. Muldoon, and his cabinet colleagues. Thus in March Muldoon claimed that the Soviet embassy in New Zealand was financing the activities of the SUP, which was denied by both the embassy and the SUP. The only staff employed by the party, it was stated, was one full-time organizer, while its journal had a staff of two full-time employees and one part-time.

In July, Muldoon launched a personal attack on G. H. Andersen, whom he described as "a sinister figure," and in October he told the Auckland Provincial Employers' Association that "the time may come when the Socialist Unity Party will be banned because of its undue influence in industrial unrest." Militant unionists who damaged New Zealand's economy, he said, were traitors and saboteurs and deserved to be treated accordingly. (*Auckland Star*, 18 October.)

Trade union leaders retorted that the government was merely seeking a convenient scapegoat for its own failure to halt inflation and lift the economy out of the doldrums. The SUP has certainly benefited from the persistent attacks which ascribe to it an importance out of proportion to its real strength. It is seen, among trade unionists in particular, as a major opponent of the government's economic policies, which have reduced the standard of living of all wage and salary earners. The party's increased support was shown at the annual conference of the New Zealand Federation of Labour in May, when an SUP member, K. G. Douglas, gained a seat on the National Executive—the first Communist ever to be elected to national office in the Federation. SUP members also hold key positions in the country's three major trades councils in Auckland, Wellington and Christchurch, as well as the secretaryships of some important trade unions.

In parliamentary and municipal elections, on the other hand, support for the extreme left has remained small, and the Labour Party, which forms the opposition in the New Zealand Parliament, has retained its hold over the working-class vote. In a parliamentary by-election in March in the working class electorate of Mangere, the SAL put up a candidate while the SUP urged support for the Labour Party candidate (the CPNZ as usual ignored the election). The SAL candidate obtained a mere seven votes in a total poll of about 14,000. In municipal elections in October the Communists did somewhat better. The SAL put up three candidates, all women, for the Hospital Board elections in Auckland, Wellington and Christchurch, while the SUP contested the Council elections in Auckland and

Dunedin. G. H. Andersen polled 3,513 votes for the Auckland City Council (compared with 2,539 votes at the previous election in 1974), while the SAL candidate for the Auckland Hospital Board gained 3,544 votes. In Dunedin, however, the SUP vote was below the 1974 figures.

International Activities and Contacts. In 1977, although again no CPNZ visits to China have been announced (Wilcox's last visit to Peking was in 1974), the party has maintained its loyal support for Chinese policies, sending the customary message of fraternal greetings on China's national day in October. Only a year earlier, as *Socialist Action* pointed out (23 September), the CPNZ had denounced the now restored Teng Hsiao-ping as a "capitalist roader" and as "the general representative of the bourgeoisie inside and outside the party." The CPNZ used to maintain close links with the Albanian Party of Labour, but now, perhaps because of the growing coolness between China and Albania, Albanian materials are less frequently reprinted in the New Zealand Communist press. The Communist Party of Australia (Marxist-Leninist), another former close friend, is never mentioned since there are profound ideological differences between the two parties.

The New Zealand government, which frequently stresses its anti-Communist stand in international affairs, has made an exception for China. When a high-powered Chinese delegation visited New Zealand in September, the acting prime minister explained that New Zealand friendship with China was "a natural and rightful state of affairs" (*New Zealand Herald*, 22 September). In October New Zealand's minister of foreign affairs visited Peking, where he was received by Hua Kuo-feng.

The SUP has maintained its close contacts with the Soviet Communist Party, and SUP leaders have visited the Soviet Union and other Communist countries as members of party or trade union delegations. Thus G. E. Jackson was in Moscow in January, and K. G. Douglas in March. G. H. Andersen, who has never yet visited the Soviet Union, was invited to attend the sixtieth anniversary celebrations, but he deferred his visit in view of "the present industrial and political climate, including the present irrational behaviour of the Prime Minister." (Ibid., 21 October.) His place was taken by Jackson and B. Skilton, a member of the party's National Executive. The SUP also has close links with the Australian Socialist Party, whose chairman Pat Clancy visited Auckland in August.

The SAL arranged New Zealand speaking tours for a Malaysian Trotskyist in April, and for a South African student leader from Soweto in August.

Publications. The three main parties each publish journals of similar tabloid format. The CPNZ's *People's Voice* is the oldest, launched in Auckland in 1939 (banned 1940-43), and it is the only one published weekly, with eight pages. The SUP's *New Zealand Tribune*, first published in Auckland in 1966, has eight pages and is published fortnightly. The SAL's *Socialist Action*, published in Wellington since 1969, appears fortnightly and has raised its size from eight to twelve pages from the beginning of 1977. A fourth journal, *Bulletin*, has been published fortnightly (with gaps) by the Socialist Labour League in Auckland since January.

The CPNZ also publishes a monthly theoretical journal, *N.Z. Communist Review*, in which all local contributions are anonymous. The SUP theoretical journal, *Socialist Politics*, appears about three times a year. More regular has been the quarterly *Struggle*, subtitled "For the Study and Application of Marxism-Leninism-Maotsetung Thought in New Zealand," which is published by former CPNZ members in Porirua near Wellington.

The circulation of each of the three major journals is in the vicinity of 2,500 within New Zealand. *Socialist Action* is probably the most widely read. Far more political pamphlets from a variety of Communist sources became available in 1977 than before.

University of Auckland   H. Roth

Philippines

The Communist movement in the Philippines consists of two proscribed, underground party organizations. The larger, the Communist Party of the Philippines-Marxist-Leninist (CPP-ML), is oriented toward Peking. It has an active guerrilla force, the New People's Army (NPA). The other is the parent group, the Philippine Communist Party (Partido Komunista ng Pilipinas; PKP), which has abandoned armed resistance and is striving to relegitimize itself.

The PKP was formally established on 7 November 1930, although Filipino Marxists and also Indonesian and Chinese Comintern agents had been active in trade union organizations in the islands for more than a decade. This relative lateness, compared with other Communist parties in Asian countries, seems in part to have stemmed from a jurisdictional dispute: the Communist Party, USA (CPUSA), according to the Comintern, was to have initial responsibility for Philippine affairs. Filipino Marxists were not pleased with this arrangement and, acccording to some PKP sources, had already organized the party in August 1930, or perhaps earlier. For some time the PKP remained dependent on CPUSA directives and assistance.

Early PKP cadres were lower-middle-class white-collar workers, with some extensive trade union experience. At first, the party had but little outreach to the peasantry, which was becoming restive because of changing tenant-landlord relationships. Cristano Evangelista, an activist in a Marxist labor union (Association of the Sons of Sweat of the Philippines; KAP), became the PKP first secretary general. Both PKP and KAP were banned in September 1931, after a series of ill-planned strikes and anti-government demonstrations. The leaders were subsequently jailed on charges of sedition, and on Comintern instructions what was left of the party embarked on a policy of front building, allying itself with nationalist demands for complete independence from the United States

In 1935 a visiting CPUSA functionary, Sol Auerbach, persuaded Philippines Commonwealth President Manuel Quezon to grant (and Evangelista and other jailed PKP leaders to agree to) a limited executive pardon which would permit them to be discharged from prison and begin building an anti-fascist national front. In October 1938 the CPP entered a short-lived merger with the small Socialist Party of the Philippines. (See Alfredo B. Saulo, *Communism in the Philippines: An Introduction,* Manila, 1969, pp. 33-35.)

The Japanese occupation of the Philippines during World War II opened new opportunities to the PKP and others in a popular resistance movement which crystallized in the founding of the Anti-Japanese People's Army (Hukbo ng Bayan Laban sa Hapon; Hukbalahap, or "Huks" for short) on 29 March 1942. The roots of the Huk movement, however, lay in the discontent of the land-poor peasantry in Central Luzon which the PKP sought to exploit both during and after the Japanese occupation (Benedict J. Kerkvliet, *The Huk Rebellion: A Study of Peasant Revolt in the Philippines,* Berkeley, Los Angeles, London, 1977).

After the war, the PKP and its front-group associates faced a newly independent government little inclined to accommodate them or even to seat their duly elected congressional representatives. When the call of Philippine President Manual A. Roxas that the Huks surrender their arms was not heeded, an executive order outlawed them on 6 March 1948 (*The Communist Movement in the Philippines,* Southeast Asia Treaty Organization Short Paper, no.46, Bangkok, March 1970, pp. 20-21). The PKP attempted with some success to direct the rising of the new Huk "People's Liberation Army" led by PKP Politburo member Luis Taruc. Nevertheless the uneasy alliance of doctrinaire, Maoist revolutionary principles and more conservative peasant demands for land reform, together with intra-PKP quarrels and the reform policies of President Ramon Magsaysay, doomed the new Huk rising (Renze L. Hoeksema, "Communism in the Philippines: Historical and Analytical Study of Communism and the Communist Party in the Philippines and Its Relation to Communist Movements Abroad, unpublished Ph.D. dissertation, Harvard University, 1956). In October 1952 PKP Secretary General José Lava and most of the Politburo fell into government hands. As the party's fortunes further declined, most of the Huk organization degenerated into mere brigandage and racketeering, although some leaders retained vague ideological commitments to needed social reforms and dispensed a rough, Robin Hood style of justice on rapacious landlords in the Luzon countryside. On 17 June 1957 both the PKP and the People's Liberation Army were outlawed.

In the 1960s important, if often unfocused, impulses from various groups of students, intellectuals, laborers, and peasants provided the radical left with new life (Justus M. Van der Kroef, "Communist Fronts in the Philippines," *Problems of Communism,* March-April 1967, pp. 65-75). Nationalism (frequently perceived in terms of the need for the Philippines to rid itself of U.S. economic dominance and U.S. military bases on Philippine soil), various demands for social reform (particularly for a more consistent and vigorous campaign against the pervasive corruption in Philippine political life and business), and a generalized call for improvement in the standard of living were all part of these impulses.

On Mao Tse-tung's 75th birthday, 26 December 1968, young radical leftists—long dissatisfied with the ineffectual and shattered PKP, whose principal leaders continued in confinement—took the lead in "reestablishing" the Philippine Communist party at a secret congress near the town of Capas in Southern Tarlac Province, Luzon. Thus was born the Communist Party of the Philippines, Marxist-Leninist (or Communist Party of the Philippines-Mao Tse-tung Thought). The CPP-ML dedicated itself to the revolutionary liberation of the country, and on 29 March 1969, at another meeting near Capas, CPP-ML leaders and a handful of old Huk and People's Liberation Army cadres founded the New People's Army. The NPA, which has since remained the principal Communist guerrilla movement in the Philippines, eventually expanded its organization and its hit-and-run attacks through much of the northern and central Philippines and, according to government spokesmen, also formed a working alliance with the Muslim rebel movement of the Moro National Liberation Front (MNLF) in Mindanao. Spokesmen for the parent PKP denounced the "adventurist" course of violence of the CPP-ML, and after finally repudiating party connections with some of the more unsavory remaining Huk leaders, proceeded to organize a small fighting force, the "Army ng Bayan" (National Army), of their own. But the latter appeared to be little more than a paper organization, and as CPP-ML raids on government posts and other clashes and terrorist bomb attacks even in the city of Manila underscored a deepening constitutional crisis in the country, Philippine president Ferdinand Marcos, himself already a target of bitter partisan political attacks, proclaimed martial law (22 September 1972). Marcos blamed the NPA for making the measure necessary and claimed that the NPA had seized power in "thirty-three" municipalities" and had established communal farms and production bases (Eduardo Lachica, *Huk! Philippine Agrarian Society in Revolt,* Manila, 1971; Justus M. van der Kroef, "The Philippine Maoists," *Orbis,* Winter 1973, pp. 892-926).

It is generally conceded, however, that Marcos used and magnified the NPA threat to justify his seizure of power and to avoid losing the presidency. Even so, the attempted reform and stabilization measures of Marcos' "New Society" program found considerable popular support. Military and business circles welcomed the stability promised by martial law. And while the Philippine Congress and other deliberative bodies were suspended, and the press, at least initially, was severely curtailed, Marcos' policies were repeatedly upheld by the Philippine Supreme Court and by nationwide popular referenda (*YICA, 1974,* p. 525). Some 50,000 Filipinos, including prominent opposition politicians, were arrested in the aftermath of the martial law proclamation, but all but some 5,000 have, according to the government, been released. Well-documented instances of torture of political prisoners have aroused international criticism of the Marcos government. Meanwhile, NPA guerrilla attacks, despite the periodic capture of key commanders, have continued, in keeping with the CPP-ML's principle that liberation is possible only through violence. The PKP, whose older leadership was gradually released in the early 1970s, appears to be committed to a policy of peaceful support for the Marcos government's "progressive policies," such as its land distribution program. This policy of qualified support is in keeping with current Soviet attitudes toward the Philippines.

The PKP is estimated to have perhaps 100 members, the CPP-ML and NPA together may have 2,000. The population of the Philippines is about 40 million.

Organization and Tactics. CPP-ML Chairman José Sison, a former instructor at the University of the Philippines in Quezon City, has described his party's objective as a "people's democratic state" under the "joint dictatorship" of all revolutionary classes, and led by the proletariat. Writing under the pseudonym Amado Guerrero ("Beloved Warrior"), Sison calls for the elimination of U.S. "imperialist" control over the Philippine economy and foreign relations, and the removal of "feudal" and "bureaucratic capitalist" domination of domestic Philippine life (*Philippine Society and Revolution,* Manila, 1971).

On 11 September 1976 Sison (Guerrero) issued a statement reviewing the growth of the party, and claiming success despite arrests and other adversities. Party cadres, he said, were "coming forward continuously from among the revolutionary masses." Calling on lower units to be flexible and tactically pragmatic, he said further that centralized leadership was being maintained notwithstanding "dispersed operations." (Voice of the Malayan Revolution, clandestine in Mandarin, to Malaysia and Singapore, 11 November; *FBIS,* 17 November).

On 26 December the CPP-ML Central Committee's anniversary statement reaffirmed its "resolute" opposition to (1) "modern revisionism pushed by Soviet social imperialism" and its PKP promoters, and (2) "dogmatic and empirical tendencies within the party." The latter opposition was in line with the party's realization that "no complete ready-made plan" for solving the nation's problems is available "in books or foreign countries." The statement acknowledged that the NPA and mass organizations could not, as yet, break through "the enemy's large-scale encirclement and suppression," but added that the party's forces were "learning how to sabotage" the operations of its opponents, that weapons were being seized "through guerrilla warfare" and "surprise attack," and that, without neglecting the cities, the party was "putting above all else" its work in the countryside. The statement noted further the party's four "emergency tasks," as announced in June 1976: (1) intensification of the struggle against "fascism, feudalism, and imperialism," (2) strengthening of the party organization, (3) launching "revolutionary mass movements" in the rural areas, and (4) further development of the NPA and revolutionary armed struggle (Voice of the Malayan Revolution, 22 March 1977; *FBIS,* 5 April).

Sources friendly to the NPA emphasize its rural work:

> In hundreds of villages all over the Philippines today, NPA cadres are talking to poor peasants about their plight, about landlessness, the indebtedness, the chronic poverty which plagues their daily lives . . . . They have instilled confidence among the people that by acting together they can slowly work to regain their lands and their democratic rights. In most cases, peasants start by asking that land rents be lowered. If landlords refuse, they may simply report lower harvests, keeping the remainder for themselves. If recalcitrant landlords use armed goons to enforce high rents as they often do, they are warned by the local

NPA unit. It is only if the landlord persists, despite repeated warnings, that his land is confiscated altogether. (*Philippine Liberation Courier,* Oakland, Ca., 29 March, p. 2a)

The government's capture of various NPA and CPP-ML figures, disclosed in August 1976, left only Party Chairman Sison at large among the principal leaders. On 19 November 1977 President Marcos announced that José M. Sison, chairman of the CPP-ML, had been captured "without a battle." The arrest occurred on 10 November in San Fernando. According to Marcos, documents linking Sison's party with the Moslem rebellion in the southern Philippines, and possibly with leftist elements in the Roman Catholic Church, had also been seized. The president added that he believed the party would revive, "as such movements usually do" (*NYT,* 20 November). Philippine Defense Secretary Juan Ponce Enrile and senior Philippine military commanders claim that new young cadres have emerged and that the party is very much alive, as demonstrated by continuing clashes with and ambushes of government forces in Central Luzon and the Visayas. CPP-ML "propaganda units" are also said to be active in various poverty-stricken rural areas where covert sympathy for the NPA reportedly remains considerable (Rodney Tasker, "Philippine Communists Pose a Latent Threat," *Far Eastern Economic Review [FEER],* 17 June 1977, pp. 36-37).

CPP-ML pronouncements refer to a party Central Committee and Politburo, but these probably are largely paper organizations, since the NPA guerrilla operations are so dispersed as to make centralized control virtually imposible. In the above cited anniversary statement, the CPP-ML was said to comprise a number of regional organizations, only four of which received financial support from the Central Committee. The statement said that "the time has arrived" when "all regional party organizations can deliver the remainder of their cash incomes to the Central Committee"—which says something of the relative autonomy of local party units.

Little was heard of the parent PKP during 1977. Principal leaders, such as the brothers Jesús and José Lava, both at different times secretary general, have been reported as traveling or staying in Central and East European countries, and even as serving as informal contacts for the Marcos regime with the Soviet bloc. There has been no major PKP policy statement since the party's 1973 congress and its November 1974 "new policy orientation" toward the Marcos government (see *YICA, 1976,* pp. 362-63).

As part of its drive to legitimize itself and to underscore the "foreign" (i.e., China-oriented) character of the rival CPP-ML, and to become more identified with nationalist aspirations, the PKP Central Committee late in 1976 issued a statement stressing that the party, from its inception, was the "indigenous product of domestic conditions." The PKP, according to the statement, although admittedly at one time considered a branch of the CPUSA, was never dominated by any foreign party or government, and also today does not take direction from the Communist Party of the Soviet Union (CPSU), although relations between the two have "always been warm and fraternal." In keeping with its concept of "progressive, democratic, and revolutionary nationalism," it is possible for the PKP to give qualified support to the Marcos government:

In this period of martial law the PKP again proved its readiness to cooperate with the government on areas which redound to the welfare of the masses, primarily land reform. Although it differs with the Marcos administration on several points, especially on the suspension of democratic rights and the encouragement of foreign investments and new-colonial industrialization, the PKP nevertheless recognizes the merits of the government's more independent stance in foreign affairs, its bid to renegotiate the U.S. bases, its close relations with Socialist and Arab countries, its progressive positions in the United Nations, and the increased participation of the state sector in the oil, sugar, and transportation industries." ("The Communist Party of the Philippines Is a Truly Filipine Party," *IB,* 1976, no. 15-16, pp. 39-45)

In a letter to a leading Asian newsperiodical at the close of October, PKP Secretary General Felicismo C. Macapagal noted that while his party had entered into a "national unity agreement" with the government in order to "push certain reforms," which the Marcos regime had initiated, this did not mean that the PKP no longer was critical of other aspects of government policy—precisely because it gave "honest criticism," the PKP was able to give "meaning and substance" to its pledge of cooperation (*Asiaweek,* Hong Kong, 28 October, pp. 3-4).

In different ways, both the CPP-ML and the PKP seek to exert pressure on behalf of the process of liberalization of Marcos' martial law policies, and to capitalize on the significant, but repressed, domestic opposition to the government. The NPA's guerrilla struggle, which calls into question the viability of the regime, and the PKP's more parliamentary emphasis in moving the Marcos government toward greater "independence" in foreign affairs and state control over major, including multinational, enterprises, thus supplement each other, and also interact with non-Communist Filipino demands evident in the Catholic Church and in university and trade union circles for a return to representative government and individual liberties.

Domestic Developments. During 1977 NPA, now led by Commander Rodolfo Salas, was said to have been able to stage widespread new attacks. Already in November 1976, an NPA band of more than a hundred successfully attacked some hamlets close to Clark Field, the principal U. S. airbase in the country, and captured a quantity of weapons. During 1977 Communist insurgent activity ranged from Cagayan Province in the north to Davao City in the south. In Davao an NPA terrorist named "The Jackal" was reportedly responsible for killing twenty-one persons in four months, including eighteen military ("The NPA Returns," *Asiaweek,* 26 August, pp.9-11). In mid-June NPA units were able to seize the towns of Arteche and San Policarpion in Samar Province, in the Central Philippines (*Straits Times,* Singapore, 15 June). According to an alleged estimate by the Philippine army, and published by sources friendly to the NPA, in Mindanao alone there are up to 2,000 NPA guerrillas, with a "mass base" support among the population of from 750,000 to 1,000,000 ("NPA in Mindanao Gaining Strength," *Philippine Liberation Courier,* May-June 1977, p.4).

Throughout the year, however, government sources claimed serious NPA losses. Sometimes mass surrenders were said to have occurred—at the end of March, fifty-four insurgents reportedly surrendered in Cagayan Province, taking an oath of allegiance to the government and in mid-May fifty-nine surrendered or had been captured in Mindanao (*FBIS,* 1 April, 18 May). Also in March thirty-nine "ranking Communist guerrillas" were said to have been killed in twenty-one clashes during the previous ten months in Southern Luzon (ibid., 9 March). Those claimed to have been killed included top NPA commanders like Renualdo Cruz, a regional CPP-ML committee member, slain along with members of the "Black Orchids," an NPA "liquidation squad" specializing in killing government informers and agents, in a clash at the town of Mauban, Quezon Province, in the middle of August (ibid., 19 August). In mid-September Philippine military sources claimed that the "backbone" of the NPA in Mindanao had now been smashed, that only a few NPA members were still in hiding, and that it was only "a matter of time" before these remnants would be rounded up (ibid., 13 September).

Even so, the government's reports also give the impression of persistent and even widening NPA operations. For example, senior military men reported in July that Samar Province had become "heavily infested" with the NPA guerrillas who were harassing and committing atrocities among the civilian population (ibid., 29 July). Elsewhere one reads that mayors of a number of towns in Pampanga Province, confronted by a "resurgent Communist guerrilla threat," had begun to form an anti-guerrilla "commando strike force"; the overall NPA strength in the province was estimated at about 2,000 or "double last year's figure" (ibid., 17 August).

Trials of Communists or alleged Communists continued to focus public attention on the threat to the nation. During the trial of former Senator Benigno S. Aquino, a prominent figure in the opposition to Marcos, a specialist on Philippine Communism and prosecution witness asserted that Aquino was a "top leader" of the CPP-ML (*Straits Times,* 30 March). And in May the government announced that ninety-two leaders and cadres of the "Philippine Communist movement," including former NPA Commander Victor Corpuz and former party Secretary General José Luneta, would be tried shortly by a military court in what was described as one of the "biggest rebellion trials" in recent years (*FBIS,* 24 May).

On 7 February, before a military court near Manila, the trial began of two prominent politicians, Eugenio López, Jr., nephew of Marcos' vice-president, and Sergio Osmeña III, whose father opposed Marcos in the last presidential election. The accused are charged with having fomented rebellion, along with three lesser Philippine political figures and an American, August M. Lehman, of Nashville. All denied the charges, and the trial has been seen as part of Marcos' continuing power struggle (*NYT,* 8 February). López and Osmeña were reported on 2 October to have escaped and, supplied with U.S. travel documents, to have fled to the United States. There was immediate speculation that their flight had occurred with the tacit connivance of the Marcos government seeking to avoid further embarrassment and adverse publicity concerning its political prisoners problem.

Government sources claim that the NPA continues to involve itself in the rebellion of Muslim dissidents in the Mindanao and Sulu Islands area (*YICA,* 1977, pp.367-68). A cease-fire and agreement to establish a "Muslim Autonomous Region" in Mindanao, reached on 24 December 1976 between Mme. Imelda Marcos, the president's wife, and Libyan President Muammar al-Qaddafi (widely suspected of having supplied weapons to the Moro National Liberation Front), was initially implemented by Marcos' proclamation on 26 March 1977 of an autonomous zone for Muslims with a provisional regional government, comprising thirteen provinces in Western Mindanao and the Sulu Archipelago areas (*Asia Research Bulletin,* 28 February, p.296; *NYT,* 27 March).

Marcos had indicated that the proposed autonomy would not mean the creation of a separate state. The MNLF concept, however, included a separate chief minister, chief justice, a flag for the autonomous region, and the right to conclude separate external aid and loan treaties (*Asia Research Bulletin,* 31 March, p.305; *FBIS,* 30 March). The MNLF boycotted the referendum in the thirteen provinces, and on 23 April final returns on the referendum were announced, indicating that 98 percent of eligible voters had voted against a government run by the MNLF in the proposed autonomous region (*NYT,* 24 April).

In Tripoli, MNLF leader Nur Misuari vowed to continue the struggle to achieve total independence for the southern region. The government claimed in July that 1,289 Muslim and Communist rebels had surrendered since the December 1976 cease-fire (*FBIS,* 6 June, 27 July). It is apparent that the long-standing Muslim-Christian conflict in Mindanao will not easily be resolved by periodic dialogues between MNLF commanders and government officials (*Bulletin Today,* Manila, 28 June; "The Mindanao Struggle: A Second Phase," *Asiaweek,* 10 June, pp. 14-26). Meanwhile, the continuing inroads of NPA units in Mindanao have facilitated extension of the uneasy alliance between the Communist guerrillas and the MNLF, notwithstanding the fact the CPP-ML is opposed to the secessionism and demand for full independence of the MNLF. Although at the beginning of October representatives of the Philippines' military "Southern Command" and of the MNLF agreed to lower the level of their conflict and attempt to strengthen their cease-fire with a view to improving negotiations, on 11 October the government announced that an army general and thirty-two other officers and men had been ambushed and killed in Jolo, in the Sulu Archipelago, as they came to discuss possible surrender by local MNLF insurgents (*NYT,* 3 October; *FBIS,* 11 October).

The government showed increasing sensitivity to the rising international criticism of its arrests and inhumane treatment of persons since the martial law declaration of September 1972. On 3 June 1977 President Marcos said that 4,774 persons were being held, that 3,913 of these had been seized as "common criminals," and that 598 were detained on rebellion or subversion charges. He added that the military tribunals for martial-law-related cases would be phased out, and that civilian courts would be instituted (*NYT,* 4 June). In its report sent to the Marcos government in May 1976, Amnesty International noted that according to President Marcos' own estimate some 50,000 persons had been arrested since the proclamation of martial law and that 70 percent of the prisoners interviewed by a visiting Amnesty International mission said that they had been tortured. The same report claimed that a pattern of wide-scale arrests had continued (*Report of Amnesty International Mission to the Republic of the Philippines, 22 November-5 December 1975*, London, 1976, pp. 4-7). Communist and other opposition sources claim that an undetermined number of political prisoners, some allegedly kidnaped by the military, are missing (*Ang Bayan*, 15 May 1977, also cited in *Ang Katipunan*, Oakland, Ca., 27 July-10 August, p. 12).

On 30 July the International Commission of Jurists, in a study published in Geneva, accused the Marcos regime of extensive violations of human rights, including detention without charge or trial and the use of torture, and with attempts to perpetuate itself by undemocratic means (*NYT*, 31 July). According to a U.S. State Department report, however, "instances of torture and maltreatment represent aberrations and are not the result of explicit Government policy at the political level" (*Human Rights Practices in Countries Receiving U.S. Security Assistance. Report Submitted to the Committee on International Relations, House of Representatives, by the Department of State, in accordance with section 502B(b) of the Foreign Assistance Act, as amended*, Washington, D.C., 1977, p.17).

President Marcos, though earlier having branded a State Department report of human rights violations as a "provocation" (*NYT*, 8 January), subsequently ordered immediate trials for two military officers charged with inhuman treatment of a woman prisoner, and in an address to the Foreign Correspondents Association of the Philippines on 3 June 1977, Marcos indicated that "no one shall go unpunished" who had violated the "sacred principle" of "humane regard" for every person (*Philippines Daily Express*, Manila, 25 June). At the close of June Marcos ordered the release of two groups of 500 detainees each, including several hundred held for security offenses. In an address to the Eighth World Law Conference, in Manila on 22 August, he said that he had issued a new decree granting amnesty to those "guilty of subversion" and providing for the release of detainees not thus far brought to trial. He also announced the end of the curfew at night, and of foreign travel restrictions for Filipinos. (*FBIS*, 22 August).

Uncertainty over the number and status of political prisoners caused Marcos' new amnesty decree to be greeted with some skepticism. And while another presidential announcement, also made to the World Law Conference, that elections for local officials would be held "not later than next year," has been praised widely, so long as there is no across-the-board rescission of martial law authority, opposition to the Marcos regime, often sparked by former senators like Jovito Salonga and clergy like Bishop Francisco Claver, is likely to continue (*NYT*, 3 October 1976, 15 August 1977). Heightened concern for the preservation of domestic security has, according to government spokesmen, gone hand-in-hand with a "nationwide crackdown on erring policemen and other law enforcement personnel following reports of a resurgence of abusive conduct" (Juan Ponce Enrile, "The Main Thrusts of the National Security Program," *Fookien Times Philippines Yearbook, 1976*, pp. 72-77). Observers have questioned, however, whether the regime can continue much longer to appease the deep frustrations and criticisms of such interest groups as the military, the nation's intellectuals, youth, the Church, and others; and a deepening mood of public cynicism about Marcos' "New Society," spurred by the old and persistent corruption and the stark contrasts in life-styles between rich and poor, suggests continuing sources of left radical recruitment in the future (David Wurfel, "Martial Law in the Philippines: The Methods of Regime Survival," *Pacific Affairs*, Spring 1977, pp. 5-30; Harvey Stockwin, "Inside the Marcos Volcano," *FEER*, 5 November, 1976, pp. 30-36).

There remains the question also as to whether, with the influx of foreign development capital and much-vaunted plans for economic growth, the mass of Filipinos are necessarily better off now than five years ago when martial law government began. If 1972 is taken as a base year of 100 index points, the real wages of skilled laborers, for example, dropped to 71.2 in 1976, according to central bank statistics, while unskilled laborers saw their wages decline to 72.2 in 1976. In 1977 skilled laborers' wages rose by about 1.4 percent, but those for unskilled laborers fell further by 1.8 percent. On the other hand, inflation has dropped from 34 percent in 1974 to 6 percent in 1976, but though the growth in real gross national product has averaged around 5-6 percent per annum, it is unlikely to be adequate to meet the needs of a burgeoning population (*FEER*, 30 September).

International Aspects. During the year the Philippine relations with both People's China and the USSR cautiously expanded, following exchanges of diplomatic recognition between Peking and Manila in June 1975 (*YICA, 1976*, p. 369) and between Moscow and Manila a year later (ibid., 1977, pp. 368-69). The pattern of commercial contacts between the Philippines and the USSR, which preceded the mutual diplomatic recognition on 2 June 1976 (Manuel Collantes, "The Establishment of Relations Between the Philippines and the Soviet Union," *Fookien Times Philippines Yearbook 1976*, Manila, 1976, pp. 34-37), has been interspersed with continuing, guarded Soviet media approval of Marcos' agrarian reform and foreign policies (see, e. g. *Selskaya zhizn*, Moscow, 16 June, 1976; *FBIS*, 18 June). In June 1977 Mme. Imelda Marcos had been scheduled to visit the USSR on an undisclosed "special mission" for the president, but an announced illness prevented the journey (*Bulletin Today*, Manila, 23 June). Soviet media and spokesmen have generally continued to focus on the remaining U.S. bases in the Philippines and the ongoing U.S.-Philippine negotiations in the past two years to change the terms of the bases' operations.

On 21 June 1977 Miss Imee Marcos, daughter of the president, arrived in Peking at the head of a visiting delegation of Filipino youth leaders. Her visit was given prominent attention in the Chinese media and her reception by high-ranking Chinese officials was believed to demonstrate the Peking leadership's interest in maintaining proper and even cordial relations at a level other than formal, state-to-state, interaction (ibid., 23 June).

Chinese media still, on one or two occasions during the year, briefly relay excerpts of statements of the CPP-ML. But no CPP-ML leader has been officially received in Peking in recent years. Meanwhile, in the wake of the mutual diplomatic recognition, the Philippine government has begun to relax naturalization procedures for Chinese and other alien residents. Some 20,000 heads of families of such Chinese residents had registered under the new easier regulations granting Philippine citizenship by the end of 1975. At the same time, to further facilitate the assimilation of Chinese residents, the 120 language schools in the Philippines gradually are being phased out (Juan T. Gatbonton, "Manila Tries the Hua Ch'iao Blend," *Insight*, Hong Kong, March 1977, p. 58). On 6 June a trade agreement was signed, providing for the Peking government's purchase of copper concentrates, coconut oil, sugar, lumber, and machinery, including small hydraulic turbine generator units (*FBIS*, 8 June). Sino-Filipino trade has been growing significantly: the value of Filipino exports to China rose from $13.3 million in 1974 to $38.2 million in 1976, while imports from China climbed in the same period from $23.9 million to $53.7 million (*FEER*, 7 October).

Publications. Neither the PKP nor the CPP-ML has regularly appearing publications. *Ang Komunista* (The Communist), and stenciled brochures are the PKP's principal media. Such Moscow-oriented publications as *World Marxist Review* and *Information Bulletin* occasionally carry statements by the PKP or its leaders. *Ang Bayan* (The Nation), with both English and Tagalog editions, is the principal and more regularly appearing journal of the CPP-ML. Both the clandestine radio transmitter of the Communist Party of Malaya, "The Voice of the Malayan Revolution (see *Malaysia*) and the journal of the Maoist branch of the Indonesian Communist Party, *Indonesian Tribune* (see *Indonesia*) regularly relay CPP-ML statements. Chinese media today play a decreasing role of importance for the CPP-ML.

University of Bridgeport   Justus M. van der Kroef

Singapore

Communists in the island republic of Singapore, according to statements by the government over the years, are usually considered to be associated with the Communist Party of Malaya (CPM) or its satellite organizations (see *Malaysia*). One reason for the absence of a distinctive local party is that, in the view of the CPM and its adherents, the 1963 merger of Singapore with the Malay states, Sabah, and Sarawak into the Malaysian Federation and the subsequent departure of Singapore from the federation in 1965 to become an independent republic within the Commonwealth all occurred illegally and undemocratically. The CPM and the Singapore Communists remain committed to the breakup of Malaysia and to a new merger of Malaysia and Singapore, letting Sabah and Sarawak go their own way.

The government charged for a long time, though not in recent years, that the Barisan Sosialis Malaya (Malayan Socialist Front) was an organizational vehicle for Communists in Singapore—a charge which the Barisan chairman, Dr. Lee Siew Choh, repeatedly denied. The ineffectiveness of the Barisan at the polls has caused a drift of leftists elements, who oppose the People's Action Party (PAP) government of Premier Lee Kuan Yew, to other small opposition parties, such as the Workers' Party (WP), but with no electoral successes thus far. At the same time, the Communists' dependence on the CPM has found increasing disfavor among younger Singapore radicals, who see the need for an independent organization. Intensive political surveillance and control by the government, under the Internal Security Act and related statutes, leave the prospects of any left-oriented, let alone Communist, opposition party in Singapore very dim for the foreseeable future.

In 1928, Communists in Singapore founded the Nanyang (South Seas) Communist party as a rallying point, under the leadership of the Comintern's Far Eastern Bureau, for Communist and radical nationalist movements throughout Southeast Asia. Already proselytizing efforts had been made by members of the Communist Party of Indonesia and the Chinese Communist party, and considerable impetus was also given by the Malayan Revolutionary Committee of the Kuomintang, which at the time was more or less allied with the Chinese Communists. (See Gene Z. Hanrahan, *The Communist Struggle in Malaya,* Kuala Lumpur, 1971, and *The Communist Movement in West Malaysia and Singapore,* Short Paper, no. 54, Southeast Asia Treaty Organization, Bangkok, 1972.)

In the 1930s the Nanyang party became the Communist Party of Malaya (CPM) and succeeded in creating a network of militantly nationalist and Communist-sympathizing students, white-collar workers, trade union activists, and young professionals. In the post-World War II period, the English-educated and politically more moderate segment of the Chinese community broke away from the radical Chinese-educated and CPM-influenced component. A struggle within the PAP, founded in 1954, ended with expulsion of the radicals and the founding of the Barisan Sosialis in 1961 after PAP moderates, controlling the government, had repeatedly quelled Communist-inspired riots, strikes, and school demonstrations (*The Communist Threat in Singapore,* Legislative Assembly Sessional Paper, Singapore, 1957). By October 1961, as PAP leader and Singapore Premier Lee Kuan Yew put it, the Barisan Sosialis had become "the main open front Communist organization," with a "subsidiary" in the smaller Party Rakyat and a few cadres in the WP (*The Battle for Merger,*

Singapore, 1961, p 93; Justus M. van der Kroef, "Singapore's Communist Fronts," *Problems of Communism,* 1964, no. 5, pp. 53-62).

Since then, effective security controls have forced CPM activity deeply underground. Most of Singapore's electorate, despite the authoritarian policies of PAP-controlled governments led by Lee Kuan Yew, has for nearly two decades not shown itself inclined to support the development-oriented program of Premier Lee, which puts a premium on preserving the kind of political stability that attracts foreign investors.

Barisan membership appears to have dropped steadily during the past decade and, despite claims of a following of "several thousand," probably today stands at less than 400. Since party activity is only permitted around elections and then only for a brief period, the Barisan and other opposition groups give the impression of being somnolent, although the combined opposition has been estimated as comprising from one-fourth to one-third of the electorate. The population of Singapore is about 2.4 million.

Organization, Aims and Tactics. Barisan Sosialis spokesmen have told this author over the years that the tight government control over press and political opinion—including intimidation of and occasional court suits against opposition candidates, limited time for electioneering, and difficulty even in finding printers willing to produce the party's materials—has made it very hard for the party to function or to articulate its program. Government spokesmen attribute the Barisan's problems to declining support and to leadership squabbles surrounding its aging chairman, Dr. Lee Siew Choh. The party's Central Committee, headed by Lee Siew Choh, has about a dozen members; cadres are scattered through the electoral districts.

The Barisan Sosialis usually contests the government in elections for the legislature. The main lines of its program, remaining much the same over the years, envision a merger of Malaya and Singapore in a "democratic, Socialist, and independent Republic," the reorientation of the economy and foreign policies away from alleged dependence on British and American "imperialism," and the fostering of interracial harmony (about 76 percent of the population is Chinese, about 15 percent Malay, and the remainder Indian or other South Asian extraction).

Immediate Barisan demands call for greater freedom to strike, improvements in general working and living conditions, and freedom for "political prisoners." According to an authoritative estimate, about sixty men and women currently are being detained on grounds of being members or supporters of the CPM or its affiliated groups, and some of these have been held without trial since 1963. Although some twenty prisoners were freed in 1975, arrests have continued (*Amnesty International Report 1975-1976,* London, 1976, pp. 146-47).

Lee Siew Choh's report to the Barisan Congress in August 1969 continues to be distributed to visitors to party headquarters. It states that the party's aims are being thwarted by the alleged collusion of American and British "imperialism," by Soviet "revisionism," and by the alleged police state tactics of the Lee Kuan Yew regime. The general line has a Maoist flavor, and closer relations with the "Socialist" countries, in particular with People's China (with which Singapore has no diplomatic ties at the present) are advocated. The economy of Singapore would undergo a transformation into a far more state-controlled system if the Barisan were to achieve power. This tends to make the party less attractive to other critics of the government, even if they agree with Barisan on other points.

Post-World War II infiltration efforts of the CPM (Lee Ting Hui, *The Communist Orgnaization in Singapore: Its Techniques of Manpower Mobilization and Management, 1948-1966,* Institute of Southeast Asian Studies, Singapore, Field Report Series, no. 12, August 1976) as of today must be considered a failure. Some observers question whether the CPM, apart from its residual influence in the Barisan has anything like a front organization left.

Domestic Developments. In the December 1976 general elections, the PAP returned to power for the sixth time since 1959, winning 72.4 percent of the votes (69 percent in 1972) and making a clean sweep of all sixty-three contested seats for the third time since 1968. Four opposition parties—the Barisan Sosialis, the Singapore Malays National Organization, the United Front Party (UFP), and the Singapore Justice Party—formed the Joint Opposition Council (JOC) for the 1976 election, and made an agreement with the leftist, but non-Communist, opposition (WP) not to run candidates in the same districts. The combined opposition won 27.5 percent of the votes.

Lee Kuan Yew dismissed the opposition as having no "rational alternative" to PAP policies. This characterization overlooked the fact that the JOC-WP program had more to offer than just the abolition of the Internal Security Act—for instance,improved social welfare policies. During the campaign other PAP spokesmen took up the Communist theme, declaring without further elaboration, for example, that the real oppositon in Singapore was "the CPM" (*FBIS*, 18 November, 14 December 1976; *Far Eastern Economic Review* [*FEER*], 12 August 1977, pp. 38-39). The Barisan chairman commented that "the people are afraid to help us, afraid to support us, even afraid to vote for us" (*NYT*, 6 February).

While there is no evidence of fraud in the election, within days of its victory at the polls the Lee Kuan Yew government moved against some of its opponents, repeating a pattern begun in previous elections. A spokesman, convicted of having made false accusations against the law firm of Premier Lee's wife during the campaign, was sentenced to four months in jail. The premier himself sued WP leader J.B. Jeyeratnam for slander. The People's Front secretary general was sentence to eighteen months for having slandered the premier.

Journalists also ran afoul of the government. The former editor of the daily *Nan Yang Siang Pau*, Shamsuddin Tung Tao Chang, who had been arrested in 1971 for allegedly stirring up "Communist sentiments," was arrested for having "played on" the issue of Chinese language and education, an action which, according to the Singapore Home Ministry, could result in "racial violence." Ho Kwong Ping, the Singapore correspondent for the *Far Eastern Economic Review,* was charged with having published classified military information, but his "real offense" appears to have been that he had written critically of the Lee government's educational and language policy (*Manchester Guardian,* 6 February).

One of the arrests took a more disquieting turn when the correspondent reportedly confessed that he had been used by Malaysian intelligence in a "black operation" to discredit and "topple" the Lee Kuan Yew government, a charge subsequently denied by the Malaysian inspector general of police. The incident did not expand beyond the stage of revelations, accusations, and Malaysian denials, but did, perhaps, suggest as much about the continuing strain in Singapore-Malaysian relations as about the political sensitivities of the Lee Kuan Yew government.

On 10 February a Singapore lawyer, G. Raman, counselor to the Singapore University Students Union in 1971-76 and to the Singapore Polytechnic Students Union in 1975-76, was arrested for allegedly having worked with a group of Eurocommunists to exert pressure on the government to release "hard-core Communist detainees." He was also accused of agitating to foster the development of a Communist united front in Singapore that would have included students and workers (*FBIS,* 11 February). Raman was said to have run an "indoctrination team" to further his aims, and nine persons, among them another lawyer, a public accountant, and several business executives, were arrested subsequently (*Straits Times,* Singapore, 17 February).

Another journalist, Arun Senkuttuvan, formerly correspondent for the *Far Eastern Economic Review* in Singapore and more recently, among others, for the London *Economist,* was also arrested, though not as part of Raman's group. In a purported confession Arun declared that he had sought to portray the Singapore government as "undemocratic, totalitarian and oppressive." (Ibid., 12 March.) Controversy also erupted around the question of the accuracyof a tape and the propriety of its release, in which the editor of the *Far Eastern Economic Review,* Derek Davies, recorded impressions of an interview he had with Premier Lee Kuan Yew. Copies of the tape had been made by Arun a year earlier without Davies' permission, according to Davies, and in his confession to the Singapore government Arun reportedly also referred to the tape (Derek Davies, "Putting the Record Straight," *FEER,* 25 March, pp. 14-18; *FBIS,* 14 March). According to Arun's confession, relayed by the Singapore govenrment, Davies intended the tape to be circulated "thereby causing a rift between Singapore and Malaysia." Davies denied that the tape contained anything that could prejudice "Singapore's relations with its neighbors," and said that its contents had been misrepresented (see also *Straits Times,* 11 March).

On 16 April the Singapore Home Ministry reported that the earlier named and still detained Ho Kwong Ping had made a full confession as to his "pro-Communist activities," both in Singapore and in the United States, and of having used the *Far Eastern Economic Review* to "promote his pro-Communist ideas" (*FBIS,* 18 April). In a comment on Ho's confession, Derek Davies denied that Ho's articles had been slanted, saying further that the *Review* stood by "the accuracy and objectivity of Ho's reports" and that Ho's dispatches "gave no cause for any suspicion" of an "anti-Singaporean direction" (*FEER,* 29 April).

In the aftermath of all these arrests, Singapore deputy premier and defense minister, Dr. Goh Keng Swee, announced that "selected senior commanders and staff officers" of the armed forces would be given a course in Marxism-Leninism. He said that he had yet to meet one among these officers who had "even a smattering of knowledge of the subject," and this notwithstanding the fact that "communist insurgencies are the greatest threat to Singapore's security" (*FBIS,* 27 February). Goh particularly criticized "fellow travellers" who are providing "safe" support to the Communists, and who should realize that they would not escape "the killing game" when "the revolution hots up" (*Asia Research Bulletin,* 31 March, p. 303).

On 26 March the Home Affairs Ministry announced that G. Raman had given details about a "pro-Communist group" in Singapore which had been interested in setting up a "human rights committee." According to Raman, an engineer now in hiding had approached him to form a "human rights committee" to oppose the practice of detention without trial and also to discredit the PAP government and pressure it to release detainees, thus allegedly aiding the CPM cause (*FBIS,* 28 March). WP Secetary General J.B. Jeyeratnam, a leading political opposition figure in Singapore, said that it was "a lot of nonsense" that he had lent himself to the Communist cause by also having been interested in creating such a committee, and added: "Why should we assume that if anyone shows interest or concern in human rights that he is a pro-Communist, or that he is being used by the Communists?" (Ibid., 30 March.)

On 14 May three of those who had been arrested in February as part of the Raman group were released, but remained restricted in their movements. The government said that the three—an investment manager, a lawyer, and a former bookstore manager—had "renounced Communism," the implication being that they had been Communists in the first place, an allegation for which it thus far has supplied no proof. At the close of July, a letter by the earlier named Shamsuddin Tung Tao Chang to Premier Lee was made public, in which Chang said: "I am not and never have been a Communist, a pro-Communist or even a Communist sympathizer," and went on to express his "abhorrence" of the use of force to oppose the Singapore government (*FEER,* 5 August).

On 15 October the Internal Security Department announced that since July of 1976 thirty-nine persons, including "leading cadres" of the Malayan National Liberation Forces had been arrested. The thirty-nine were members of four underground units which reportedly had been covertly supplying the Communist guerrilla forces in West Malaysia with books pharmaceuticals, radios, and other articles (*FBIS,* 17 October). The arrests and the particular concerns and sensitivities of the Singapore government which they reflected, led to repeated sharp criticisms broadcast over the

CPM's clandestine radio transmitter "Voice of the Malayan Revolution." In one such broadcast the government was charged with "concocting so-called confessions" by detainees and with starting a "succession of sinister anti-Communist drives," which revealed the "ferocious fascist nature" of "Lee Kuan Yew and his men" (ibid., 11 April). An earlier broadcast termed the 1976 elections a "farce" and said that "parliamentary democracy has long been bankrupt" in the island republic (ibid., 27 December).

Whatever the Singapore electorate may have thought about the arrests and the charges of opposition politicians, the PAP continued to retain its following at the polls. In a by-election for the parliament on 14 May in the Radin Mas constituency, the PAP candidate won handily over WP leader Jeyeratnam. About 30 percent of the voters in Radin Mas voted against the PAP. After the election the WP announced that it would boycott further elections unless the PAP agreed to changes in existing voting procedures, including discontinuance of the numbering of ballot papers, and establishment of a commission to oversee elections. In the background of these demands was a much-discussed fear that the PAP government knows the choices made by voters through the numbered ballots (*FEER,* 27 May; *Asiaweek,* 3 June). Another PAP candidate had no difficulty in defeating his Barisan Sosialis opponent, Dr. Lee Siew Choh, in the parliamentary by-election in the Bukit Merah constituency at the close of July (*Asiaweek,* 5 August). The Barisan chairman drew significant crowds during this campaign, however, and his attacks on the "fascist and oppressive" character of the Lee government did not go unappreciated in a segment of the electorate.

PAP government strategy is to emphasize orderly economic development and to use education, national military service, and public welfare facilities such as housing construction as "nation-building" efforts to rivet the electorate's loyalties to the regime (John S. T. Quah, "Singapore: Towards a National Identity," in Kernial S. Sandhu, ed., *Southeast Asian Affairs 1977,* Singapore, 1977, pp. 207-19). Steady improvements in the standard of living (in 1965 40 percent of Singapore's households earned less than $50 a month; in 1975 only 24 percent earned less than $100 a month) have been spurred by development-oriented policies and by stressing a no-nonsense work ethic based on traditional Confucianist values (Brewster Grace, "The Politics of Income Distribution in Singapore," *American Universities Field Staff Reports, Southeast Asia Series,* vol. 25, no. 1, 1977, pp. 3, 6).

Foreign Relations. During 1977 Singapore retained its foreign policy posture of wariness toward the USSR (with which it has diplomatic relations) and toward the People's Republic of China (with which it has not), and at the same time sought to improve its recently established relations with the new Communist regimes in Indochina. In an interview given to the German radio service *Deutsche Welle* on 15 April, Premier Lee declared that a "Sino-Soviet competition" for influence in Southeast Asia was "inevitable" in the long run. He said that both Moscow and Peking would be competing for "more parties to be installed as the governments of neighboring countries" in Asia. When asked whether the danger of war in Southeast Asia had diminished or increased since the U.S. withdrawal from Vietnam, he said:

I think the danger of more Communist guerrilla insurgency spreading from Laos— and occasionally we hear reports even of clashes between Cambodia and Thailand, not just of Lao and Thai, but Cambodians and Thai— has increased. . . . Of course, we must expect the Communist governments to help Communists in Thailand to create revolution, but as long as that is done without sending in foreign troops into Thailand, I believe the situation is containable by the Thai themselves." (*FBIS,* 27 April).

In line with an increased trade outreach by other ASEAN countries individually toward the Comecon countries, the Singapore association of manufacturers, with the encouragement of the Lee government, announced in February that it would be attempting to expand commercial ties with the

Soviet Union and Eastern Europe. The government is promoting direct contact between Singapore firms and foreign trade organizations in the Eastern and Central European zone. This development, according to the government media, is desirable in view of the "instability" of the capitalist market and its "discriminatory" measures against Singapore. (Ibid., 11 February.)

A new trade outreach also was being made toward People's China and Vietnam. A fact-finding mission of the Singapore Chinese Chamber of Commerce visited both countries in April, including the Canton Trade Fair (ibid., 5 April). The Lee government appears, however, to retain informal contacts with the Republic of China on Taiwan. According to the CPM's "Voice of the Malayan Revolution" (7 April), Lee Kuan Yew had quietly visited Taiwan for discussions with Chinese leaders on 12 March, the fourth of such visits in recent years. According to the same broadcast, since 1973 the Republic of China government has trained troops, including marine and naval units, and "counter-intelligence organizations" for the Singapore government (*FBIS*, 13 April).

On 24 March Ieng Sary, Cambodian deputy premier and foreign minister, concluded a four-day visit to Singapore. A communiqué stated the two countries reaffirmed their adherence to principles of mutal respect for each other's independence, sovereignty, territorial integrity, nonaggression and noninterference in each other's affairs, equality, and mutual benefits. It was noted with "satisfaction" that "relations between democratic Cambodia and Singapore had continued to develop." (Ibid., 24 March.) In mid-June 1977 the Lee Kuan Yew government encouraged Singapore's national shipping line, Neptune Orient Lines, to study the feasibility of a regular shipping service with Vietnam "in anticipation of increased trade between the two countries." At about the same time two oil companies, Shell and BP Singapore, began preliminary discussions with the national Singapore trading corporation, Intraco, to promote the oil trade between Vietnam and Singapore. Singapore refinery products reportedly are finding their way to Vietnam again, after a virtual standstill following the fall of the Thieu regime in Saigon three years ago. (Ibid., 22 June.)

Singapore's interest in greater trade has not prevented frequent sharp retorts to Hanoi in the past two years whenever the SRV government has expressed itself critically on the role of ASEAN (Association of Southeast Asian Nations, founded in 1967 and comprising Singapore, Indonesia, Thailand, Malaysia, and the Philippines), or on the bilateral security arrangements existing between individual ASEAN members. Singapore's leading daily, the *Straits Times*, whose editorials on foreign affairs frequently reflect government policy, took Hanoi to task on 19 January for its criticism of recent joint Thai-Malaysian border security campaigns against Communist insurgents. "Vietnam's vituperation," the paper said, "shows again the clear interest of the SRV in fomenting guerrilla wars in neighboring states," not just to extend Vietnam's ideological influence, "but also for promoting Vietnam's own dominance in the area." The Lee Kuan Yew government has been among the most articulate ASEAN regimes today in calling attention to the regional security problems presented by Hanoi's assistance to the Thai guerrillas and its persistent political hostility to the ASEAN regimes (Justus M. van der Kroef, "ASEAN, Vietnam and Southeast Asia's Search for Security," *Asian Thought and Society*, December 1977).

Publications. Barisan Sosialis spokesmen claim that it remains difficult if not impossible to obtain necessary government permits to print its partisan political publications, and also that printers feel intimidated by the Lee Kuan Yew regime. Major Singapore printing firms have indicated, however, that they would print Barisan materials if these were not "defamatory" and if the "price is right." Smaller printers admit that they are frightened off by the Barisan's "fiery" language (*Straits Times*, 16 July 1977).

The Barisan's biweekly *Plebeian* has not appeared with any regularity for more than five years. Stenciled leaflets are circulated at election time. The CPM's clandestine radio transmitter, "Voice of the Malaysian Revolution," during the past year had a few broadcasts attacking the Lee Kuan Yew government, but it does not customarily devote much attention any more to Singapore develoments. The government claims, from time to time, to have discovered leaflets or other propaganda materials which it attributes to West Malaysia-based Communist action groups. People's Chinese media rarely deal with the Barisan Sosialis or other opposition groups in Singapore.

University of Bridgeport   Justus M. van der Kroef

Sri Lanka

Sri Lanka's oldest Marxist party, the Ceylon Equal Society Party (Lanka Sama Samaja Party; LSSP), was formed in 1935. From the original LSSP, a number of parties and groups have emerged. The present LSSP, generally referred to as Trotskyist, although it was expelled from the Fourth International, is the country's major Marxist party.

The Ceylon Communist Party was formed in 1943 by an LSSP founder, S. A. Wickremasinghe. In 1963 it split into pro-Soviet and pro-Chinese factions led by Wickremasinghe and N. Sanmugathasan, respectively. Membership in the pro-Soviet Sri Lanka Communist Party (SLCP) is estimated at 5,000. The now-divided pro-Chinese groups probably have fewer than 1,000 members and are much less influential than the SLCP or LSSP.

In 1968 the LSSP and the SLCP set aside their antagonism for each other and joined in the United Front (UF) with the social-democratic Sri Lanka Freedom Party (SLFP). Following the May 1970 general elections, the three parties formed a coalition government headed by SLFP leader, Mrs. Sirimavo Bandaranaike. In September 1975 the LSSP was ousted from the coalition, and, when the SLCP withdrew in February 1977, the alliance ended altogether.

The SLFP government was defeated in the July 1977 elections. Neither the LSSP (with 3.9 percent of the popular vote) nor the SLCP (1.9 percent) won any seats. Sri Lanka's population is 14,349,000 (estimated 1977).

Leadership and Organization: *The LSSP.* The Trotskyist party's most prominent leaders are N. M. Perera, Colvin de Silva, and Leslie Goonewardena, all of whom were cabinet ministers until September 1975. Bernard Soysa is general secretary. The labor movement has long been identified politically with the Marxists, and the LSSP is a major influence in trade unionism. The party controls the Ceylon Federation of Labor and receives support from the Government Workers' Trade Union Federation and the Government Clerical Service Union. The Ceylon Students Federation also supports the party.

The Pro-Soviet SLCP. In the 1975 elections to the Politburo and Secretariat, Pieter Keuneman was chosen general secretary, S.A. Wickremasinghe president, and K.P. Silva secretary for organizational matters (*Pravda*, 16 September 1975). Keuneman was also minister of housing until February 1977. Party affiliates include its Youth League, Women's Organization, and the Ceylon Federation of Trade Unions. Keuneman claimed in 1975 that the party had leadership in unions with memberships totaling 250,000 and that youth leagues supporting the party had nearly 30,000 members.

The Pro-Chinese Communist Parties. In 1972 Central Committee member Watson Fernando broke away from N. Sanmugathasan's pro-Chinese SLCP to establish the Communist Party of Sri Lanka (Marxist-Leninist). Sanmugathasan's faction is now called the Ceylon Communist Party and has retained the support of the Ceylon Trade Union Federation.

The Revolutionary JVP. In April 1971 the traditional Marxist parties found themselves challenged by a young radical movement—the People's Liberation Front (Janatha Vimukthi Peramuna; JVP). Rohana Wijeweera and other JVP leaders had been members of the orthodox Communist parties. Although their armed attempt to overthrow the government in 1971 failed, sporadic violence has continued. The ban on the JVP was lifted when the six-year-old state of emergency ended in early 1977. The JVP candidates and other young radicals who contested the elections fared poorly, but with little hope of winning seats, they probably campaigned primarily to publicize their long-term objective of a revolutionary government. Wijeweera and the other insurgent leaders still imprisoned were later released by the new United National Party Government.

Domestic Attitudes and Activities: *The LSSP.* The LSSP seeks extensive political and economic reforms through parliamentary activity; some of these objectives were achieved through such government actions as land reform, an income ceiling, greater press regulation, and the 1972 constitution. The younger and more militant party members considered the UF's progress toward Socialism too slow, and their pressure probably contributed to the LSSP's ouster from the United Front in 1975. In late 1976 the LSSP stepped up its opposition to Mrs. Bandaranaike's government and was actively involved in widespread strikes which the government finally cracked down on in January 1977.

In early 1977 with elections coming up, the LSSP intensified its efforts to organize a new leftist united front and by June had formed the United Left Front (ULF) with the SLCP and a small group of defectors from Mrs. Bandaranaike's SLFP. The ULF partners bitterly criticized the prime minister for abandoning Socialist goals, and their manifesto called for "a radical social-oriented turn in policies" (*FEER*, Hong Kong, 10 June). In the July elections fought over economic issues, the left in general, and the LSSP in particular, suffered unprecedented losses. The ULF lost all 134 seats contested; LSSP leader Perera, for example, lost his first election in thirty-five years and all the leftist parties together obtained only about 7 percent of the popular vote. In a post-mortem, the former coalition partners of the SLFP, which itself was badly defeated, admitted that they had been tempted into "opportunism and corruption" while in the government (*Ceylon Daily News*, 11 August).

The SLCP. The pro-Soviet SLCP has also followed the parliamentary strategy. The Wickremasinghe faction, however, became increasingly disenchanted with the party's participation in the government and had long criticized the government's failure to take over all foreign banks, industries, and plantations. The bulk of the party supported the strike action, and some SLCP unions participated (*FEER*, 14 January). The strikes brought SLCP-SLFP tensions to a head, and in February 1977 the SLCP resigned from the UF government, stating that "a more decisive shift toward Socialism" was necessary. The party noted, nevertheless, that it still considered the tactic of the united front to be valid (*WMR*, May). Like the LSSP, the SLCP is going through a period of reassessment following the elections. Its intentions are still unclear, though the general secretary has raised the possibility of such extra-parliamentary activities as demonstrations, industrial action, and non-violent civil disobedience against the new conservative government (*FEER,* 26 August).

International Views and Policies: *The LSSP.* Although the LSSP rejects Soviet domination, it has supported the "socialist" USSR against "imperialism" and "capitalism." It has accused the United States of subversive activities in Sri Lanka and called the U.S. military presence in the Indian Ocean a threat to littoral states.

The SLCP. During Pieter Keuneman's April visit to Moscow, where he met with CPSU officials, *Pravda* "noted with satisfaction . . . the unity of views" on problems of the international Communist movement (*FBIS,* 22 April). Keuneman was awarded the Soviet Order of People's Friendship on his sixtieth birthday (*FBIS,* 7 October).

Party Publications. The SLCP's publications are *Aththa, Mawbima, Deshabimani,* and *Forward.* The current orientation of pro-Chinese publications, such as *Kamkaruwa, Tolilali,* and *Red Flag,* is not clear, but at least *Kamkaruwa* and *Tolilali* may favor the Ceylon Communist party. LSSP newspapers include *Samasamajaya* and *Janadina.*

Alexandria, Virginia   Barbara Reid

Thailand

Since October 1973, when Thailand's military regime was overthrown and a civilian government established, Thai politics have been in a state of constant flux; the country has witnessed seven different administrations under five constitutions in four years. The "democratic period," from October 1973 to October 1976, was characterized by vigorous and open debates, press freedom, labor participation in strikes and demonstrations, and a move away from total reliance on the United States regarding security policies toward a more balanced policy which included the establishment of diplomatic relations with the People's Republic of China. A violent military coup in October 1976 led to the establishment of Thanin Kraivichean, a civilian Supreme Court judge and confidant of the King, in the position of prime minister. Thanin's rule was characterized by rigid restrictions on press and speech freedoms, the banning of all demonstrations, including labor strikes, and a doctrinaire ideology of anti-Communism in both domestic and foreign policies. However, the military coup group, acting as an Advisory Council to Thanin, became disillusioned by his leadership, and without opposition or bloodshed, deposed him on 29 October 1977. Three weeks later the supreme commander of the armed forces, Kriangsak Chamanond, was designated prime minister. Whereas in the past military coups have taken place against regimes considered leftist or weak, the Thanin government appears to have been overthrown at least in part because the military leadership felt it was too conservative.

Communist Insurgency. The Communist Party of Thailand (CPT) remains one of the most secretive groups in Southeast Asia. The CIA's National Basic Intelligence *Factbook* (July 1977) estimates CPT insurgents to number 9,400. Prime Minister Thanin announced that "there are about 9,000 armed communist guerillas carrying out subversive activities against the government from the jungles." (*Bangkok World,* 30 August, 1977). In February 1977 Major General Prayun Bunnak of the Internal Security Operation Command (ISOC) put the strength of the combat forces of the CPT at around 6,750. Some 2,300 of them, he said, were concentrated in the northern provinces, around 2,650 in the northeastern provinces, 500 in the central areas, and 1,200 in the southern provinces (ibid., 3 February 1977).

When Vietnam, Laos, and Cambodia changed governments in 1975, it was widely believed that the Communist victories would enhance the strength of the Communist insurgency in Thailand. Yet official estimates of CPT strength have shown no dramatic numerical increases. It is difficult to judge the degree to which the Communist victories in Indochina boosted insurgents' morale. The advantage to the CPT from the changes in Indochina has been offset by the large number of refugees from the three Communist nations with their stories of repression and hardship. By focusing on the plight of the refugees, the mass media have given credence to the Thai government's anti-Communist program.

The violent and polarizing 6 October coup was also thought to strengthen insurgent forces by encouraging large numbers of students and left-leaning politicians to join the anti-government forces. Clearly, the coup provided the CPT with a focus for their propaganda and information efforts. During the "democratic period." the Voice of the People of Thailand (VOPT) had been cautious in its denunciations of the Thai government. Beginning in October 1976, however, the VOPT concentrated on the "fascistic, renegade, piratic, country-selling, criminal Thanin government under the control of the vicious, imperialistic United States and its lackeys."

In addition, the CPT was thought to be strengthened by an estimated 500 university students who fled to the jungle to join the insurgents following the 6 October coup. One group of students has been used to make broadcasts over the VOPT to add legitimacy and credibility to the CPT. Government officials believe that the increased role of the students is responsible for the unprecedented attacks made by the VOPT broadcasts on the Thai monarchy. During 1977, the monarch was vilified as the chief feudal landlord and overseer of the corrupt reactionary Thanin regime. On 1 April 1977, the VOPT broadcast a statement by Thirayut Bunmi wherein the former student leader declared that "the monarchy is obsolete and deteriorating. I think that if our people were to destroy it, there would be no bad effects." (*FBIS,* 4 April 1977.)

Since many of the students are ethnically Thai—in contrast to the Chinese or tribal ethnicity of most CPT members—some have been used to recruit new members among the Thai peasantry. Because there have been very few student defectors from the CPT there is no reliable information on the capacity of the formerly urban intellectual students to cope with the conditions of camps in rural Thailand, Laos, and Vietnam. It is not yet clear what contributions the influx of students will make toward the success of insurgency efforts.

CPT Organization and Strategy. Very little is known about the organization and leadership of the CPT but it is thought that the organization follows classical Communist party lines. The membership of the central committee is not known. Even the name of the CPT secretary general has never been announced by the party, although Thai intelligence agencies have identified Mit Smanant or Chat Wanngam as possible leaders.

The CPT has been regionally based with the following persons thought to be acting as regional commanders: Udom Sisuwan in the Northeast, Song Napakun in the North, and Prasit Thiansiri in the South. For the most part, the regional leaders have a large degree of autonomy and there does not appear to be effective coordination among the regions.

On 28 September 1977 the VOPT announced the formation of a "Committee for the Coordination of Patriotic and Peace-Loving Forces." The representatives of the CPT, the Socialist Party of Thailand, the Socialist United Front Party, and other political groups met from 26 to 28 September "to discuss cooperation in the struggle for national independence and democracy." (*FBIS,* 4 October 1977.) The meeting appointed a coordinating committee consisting of Udom Sisuwan, chairman; Bunyen Wotong, vice chairman; Mongkhon na Nakhon; Samak Chalikun; Thoetphum Chaidi; Sithon Yotkantha; Chamni Sakdiset; Si Inthapanti; and Thirayut Bunmi, a prominent student leader during the 1973 revolt, as secretary.

The purpose of the united front is to mobilize students, labor leaders, intellectuals, farmer group leaders, and Socialist party members. Greater support for the CPT was also expected following the announcement on 1 December 1976 of a ten-point policy program designed to be acceptable to many sectors of the society. The program includes the following points: guaranteed freedom of speech and political activity; racial and social equality; agrarian reform; full employment; guaranteed education and health care; and an independent foreign policy (*Far Eastern Economic Review (FEER)* 7 January 1977.)

The united front reorientation signals a significant transformation of CPT strategy. However, the change, emanating from the 6 October 1976 coup does not seem to have had major impact on the predominant Chinese orientation of the party. The pro-Peking attitude has traditionally been strong in CPT leadership, at least partially because of the Chinese ethnicity of most of the leadership. Throughout 1977, the VOPT continued its strong attacks on "Soviet imperialism."

On 20 September 1977 the VOPT criticized the Soviet Union's effort to gain influence in Southeast Asia. The broadcast accused the Soviets of attempting to fill the void left by the United States imperialists to exploit the rich resources of Southeast Asia, to control the Southeast Asian waterways, and to overthrow legitimate governments through KGB agents and military means. "The Soviet social imperialists are no less dangerous an enemy of the peoples of this region than the U. S. imperialists." (*FBIS,* 26 September 1977.)

Communist insurgency in Thailand during 1977 continued to be concentrated in the border areas, specifically in rural jungle sites. The northern, northeastern and southern provinces remained the principal focus of insurgency activity. The central provinces and urban areas remained relatively free from terrorist activity.

Northeast Thailand. Communist insurgency strategy in Thailand's Northeast has been reported to visualize an "L-plan, cutting off the Northeast from Bangkok by domination of the Phetcha range of mountains running north-south from the Laotian border to connect with the Dangrek Range shooting off eastward to the Cambodian border north of Aranyaprathet." (*FEER,* 16 September 1977). The "L-plan" strategy led to increased terrorist activity and the proclamation of "liberated areas" in the mountains of the northeast.

It is now claimed that the CPT radio, the VOPT, has been transferred from Yunnan province in southern China to the "red triangle" of Loei-Phetcha-bun-Pitsanaloke in the northern part of the country (ibid., 23 September 1977). The move means that insurgents in the Northeast can receive political and tactical information far more quickly than formerly.

The insurgency in the Northeast is complicated by the fact that the Khmer Rouge in Cambodia have initiated attacks against certain northeastern villages. Refugees at Aranyaprathet insist that the Cambodians train and supply the CPT in every possible way. (Ibid. 16 September 1977.) The purported collusion of the CPT with the Khmer Rouge brings a new dimension to insurgency in Thailand's Northeast.

During 1977 an estimated 100 Thai citizens were killed by Cambodian troops who crossed the border in more than 400 incursions. The purpose of the Cambodian raids appears to be the creation of a strip of no-man's land which would stop refugees from leaving Cambodia and anti-Communist Cambodian guerrillas based in Thailand from entering the country. Reportedly, the Cambodians have depopulated a twenty-five-mile-wide strip in the jungle area near Aranyaprathet.

The pattern of incidents along the 500 mile-wide Thai-Cambodian border indicates the desire to seal the border where it is most open, namely the 50-mile stretch of open forest both north and south of Aranyaprathet. This 50-mile strip is called the Watthana Pass and is the main strategic corridor between Thailand and Cambodia as well as Vietnam. The military on both sides of the border have viewed this pass as an avenue of aggression.

The Thai-Cambodian border has never been clearly demarcated and hence both sides accuse the other of illegal forays. According to the Thai account, in early August Khmer soldiers ambushed a routine army border patrol resulting in a twenty-eight hour fight between 300 Khmer regulars and heavy Thai reinforcements backed by aircraft and artillery. Seventeen Thais were killed and an unknown number of casualties were suffered by the Khmers. (Ibid., 5 August 1977.) The Thanin government used the Cambodian strikes to help justify its anti-Communist policies. The official Cambodian version of the incident, broadcast over Radio Phnom Penh on 8 August, stated that "enemies of all stripes, near and far, big and small have always nurtured criminal ambitions of swallowing our territory and subjugating our people." (Ibid., 19 August.)

A further complication for northeast insurgency is the belief that the Communist government in Laos is supporting guerrilla insurgents. The Laotian government claims that Thai border commanders have been aiding anti-government forces in Laos, particularly during the short anti-Communist government siege and occupation of Ching Chu, a Mekong River island about ten miles from Vientiane. (*Christian Science Monitor,* 12 April, 1977). Thai officials, however, claim that Laos is being used by the Vietnamese Communist government to aid insurgency in the northeast. The evidence to support both claims is sparse and unsubstantiated.

Northeast Thailand is the home of approximately 63,000 Vietnamese who fled to Thailand during the French-Indochina war or at the closing phases of the Vietnam war in 1975. Thai officials tend to view the Vietnamese with suspicion. Periodic mass confinement, restrictions on movements, and onerous registration procedures, have caused discontent among these Vietnamese. The problem is exacerbated by the influx of thousands of Laotian and Cambodian refugees since 1975. Most recent refugees live in camps administered by the Thai government but financed by the United Nations High Commission for Refugees.

Southern Thailand. Communist insurgency in Southern Thailand received increasing attention from Thai government officials and the mass media in 1977. Insurgency in the south has included the activities of remnants of the Malaysian Communist Party (MCP)—led by Chen Peng and involving two to three thousand persons who are using Thai territory as a sanctuary—the Communist Party of Thailand, non-Communist Muslim separatists, and non-Communist bandits. Neither the Thai Muslim separatists nor the MCP should be confused with the Thai Communist guerrillas who also operate in southern Thailand considerably north of the Thai-Malaysian border. Malaysian and Thai military authorities have established that there are no clear links between the Communist terrorists and the Muslim separatists in southern Thailand. There had been reports earlier that the MCP was giving training to Thai Muslim irredentists in the Communist sanctuaries in Betong and Weng on the Thai-Malaysian border. However, Major General Datuk Mahmood Sulaiman, co-chairman of the Malaysian-Thai border committee, reported that the Muslim separatists were in fact taking great pains to keep themselves away from the Communists and vice versa. He said the mass of documents captured in counter insurgency operations conclusively proved no relationship existed between the two movements. (*FBIS,* 6 August 1977.)

The focus of the insurgency was in Betong, a town of some 37,000 persons, mostly ethnic Chinese, who at the beginning of the year were under the loose control of the MCP. The Thai government had allowed the Malaysians to keep a small police force detachment of almost 500 persons in the Betong area for intelligence gathering purposes. However, in early 1976 a series of anti-Malay "demonstrations" in Betong persuaded the Thai government under Seni Pramoj to abrogate the existing border agreement with Malaysia and oust the Malaysian troops who were said to be violating "Thai sovereignty." With the forced withdrawal of the Malaysian detachment, full control of Betong passed on to the MCP. Beginning in late 1976 the Thanin government attempted to reverse Seni's policies and to move toward cooperation with Malaysia in countering insurgency along the common border. Communiques were drafted by the two nations pledging joint campaigns against the insurgents. In January 1977 some 2,000 Malaysian troops penetrated more than five miles into Thailand to counter what Thai military analysts saw as increased insurgency strength. At the same time over 1,000 Thai soldiers and police attacked the south in a pincer movement to choke off the insurgent base camps. The joint effort, which lasted from 14 January to 4 February and was referred to as Operation Big Star, was seen to be significant not because of any military victories, but because it symbolized cooperation with Malaysia, demonstrated a willingness to take on the MCP directly, and reversed the previous government's "passive" policy of acquiescence to the MCP use of sanctuaries in Thailand.

On 4 March 1977 Thailand and Malaysia signed a border agreement providing for joint military operations in the border area and for "hot pursuit" across the border of either country by troops trailing guerrilla bands. The agreement does not specify how long troops will be allowed to stay in the other's territory nor is it clear what limit exists, if any, to the depth of territorial penetration allowed. The articles of the agreement set up an elaborate array of task forces to assure the most effective communication between the two nations. The preamble specifies that the agreement is to deal with Communist terrorists and members of their related agencies. No mention is made of Muslim separatists. (The full text of the Thai-Malaysian Border Agreement is printed in *FBIS,* 8 March 1977, and in the *Bangkok Post,* 4 March, 1977.)

The signing of the border agreement initiated the second phase of Operation Big Star which began on 14 March and lasted about five weeks. A total of about 1,400 Thai troops and 3,200 Malaysian counterparts were involved in the operation in Sadao district of Songkhla province against an estimated 300 members of the MCP Revolutionary Faction—a splinter group out of favor with Chen Peng. As with Operation Big Star I, the second phase achieved no major military victories. However, military commanders seemed satisfied with breaking up the MCP's infrastructure and disrupting the ease of operation they have enjoyed for a decade.

Operation Big Star I and II were modest operations compared to the combined Thai-Malaysian assault named Operation Sacred Ray which began on 4 July in the Betong area with 16,000 troops. For the most part, the operation involved few direct ground engagements against the insurgents who were thought to be remnants of the MCP that sought sanctuary in Thailand. Instead, the operation's function was to disrupt MCP supplies and communications, utilizing combined Thai and Malaysian forces. The major thrust of Sacred Ray was in Weng district to the east of Betong where the 10th Regiment of the MCP had been stationed. The 10th Regiment is composed mostly of Malays rather than Chinese and is under the leadership of Rashid Mydin, a senior aide to MCP leader Chen Peng. Elements of the MCP under attack by the joint operations were forced to run and were absorbed in the local population. According to the Thai intelligence chief, some fifteen insurgent camps were seized, thirty-seven suspected insurgents arrested, and at least twenty-three killed at the end of the operation. Sacred Ray was more effective than Operation Big Star I and II because Thailand and Malaysia had created a workable command structure, established a joint air operations center, and worked out liaison on the ground. A small residual unit of Thai-Malaysian combined forces was stationed in Betong "for the protection of the life and property of the people and to prevent communist terrorists from reestablishing control in the area."

Northern Illinois University   Chark D. Neher

Socialist Republic of Vietnam

Communism in Vietnam dates from the 1920s (for history, see *YICA, 1977*, p. 387). The Vietnamese Workers' Party was renamed the Vietnamese Communist Party (VCP) at the party congress in December 1976. The 1976 congress set the post-Vietnam war course for the VCP, confirmed the party's top leadership, amalgamated the two Communist parties of North and South Vietnam, ordered the party and country to begin an all-out economic development effort, and set out a policy of "independence" in industrial affairs.

The Setting in 1977. A number of important developments occurred in the Socialist Republic of Vietnam during 1977. (1) The nation moved rapidly into the international community, opened new diplomatic relations, sent abroad dozens of high and intermediate level delegations, and welcomed to Hanoi a seemingly endless parade of visitors. (2) Little economic progress was achieved during the year. Agriculture experienced a particularly bad year because of poor weather and because many agricultural cadres were confused about the plan to collectivize southern agriculture. (3) An important doctrinal issue emerged for the VCP, namely, how far can the party and the society go in subordinating domestic politics and ideology to the laws of economics and even more importantly, how far can it go in international relations? (4) The society experienced more extensive social control, especially in the South, and discipline over the populace was tightened. (5) No significant military demobilization occurred during the year. A few of the armed force's professional and technical personnel were released for work on farms and factories, but this number was small compared to the total under arms.

The official assessment of the year 1977 can be summed up as a recognition of monumental problems confronted with unabashed optimism. Such a description characterizes the official view of Vietnam's future as well. On the one hand, Vietnam has scored "astounding revolutionary gains, defeated poverty and backwardness, scored achievements in the fields of economics and national defense . . . faces an extremely bright future," as the National Day anniversary editorial in *Nhan Dan* (1 September) expressed it. But there was a long list of problems, shortcomings, failures, and shortages due to the past. In short, the official overview for 1977 was that the new system was performing well overall, and where it did not, the party was not to blame.

Leadership. No change in the top level party leadership occurred during the year. The average age of the Politburo at year's end stood at sixty-six; the average age of the Central Committee was fifty-eight. Membership of the Politburo (enlarged by the Fourth Party Congress in December 1976 to fourteen seats, with three alternates) was.

1. Le Duan, party Central Committee secretary general
2. Truong Chinh
3. Pham Van Dong
4. Pham Hung
5. Le Duc Tho
6. Vo Nguyen Giap
7. Nguyen Duy Trinh
8. Le Thanh
9. Tran Quoc Hoan
10. Van Tien Dung
11. Le Van Luong
12. Nguyen Van Cuc (alias Nguyen Van Linh)
13. Vo Toan (alias Vo Chi Cong)
14. Chu Huy Man

Politburo alternate members:

1. To Huu
2. Vo Van Kiet (alias Sau Dan)
3. Do Muoi

This small, tight leadership seemed to rule harmoniously, as has generally been the case during the past forty years. The single, credible report of doctrinal differences to emerge was to what extent Vietnam should become accessible, especially for trade, to outsiders. Apparently a compromise settlement of limited entry was reached.

Scattered reports provide this picture of Vietnamese leadership during the year: Pham Van Dong became increasingly intransigent on the question of pragmatism as opposed to ideology, throwing his weight to the former. General Vo Nguyen Giap seemed more concerned with research and development and less with military affairs, possibly a step toward easing him out of national defense matters in favor of General Van Tien Dung. A Japanese visitor to Hanoi described Le Duan as "a fading movie star." Truong Chinh lost some status and prestige, which must be inferred to mean power as well. Nguyen Duy Trinh, the foreign minister, has returned to the economic scene. An economist by training, he played a key role in economic construction in the North during the late 1950s. Pham Hung moved up in importance during the year and may well prove to be Le Duan's successor. Two other figures appear on the ascendent: Le Thanh Nghi, czar of planning, and Le Duc Tho, the CPV's all-position man. Vo Van Kiet, the party's chief official in the South, made more public appearances. But unsubstantiated mid-year reports contend he is in serious political difficulty because of failures in southern agriculture. However, Nguyen Van Cuc (alias Nguyen Van Linh) still probably remains the most important figure in the South (if Pham Hung is considered a national rather than a regional figure). Vo Toan (alias Vo Chi Cong) proved as durable as ever, moving into the Ministry of Agriculture to replace the sacked Vo Thuc Dong. Chu Huy Man is the fastest-rising high level military figure and is likely to become number two in PAVN if General Giap leaves and is replaced by General Van Tien Dung.

Roughly 50 percent of all party cadres in the North are now on duty in the South, where they live with and monitor the activities of the southerners. Reportedly one *to chung* or northerner is responsible for a *phuong* or bloc of ten-fifteen families. This southward shift of from 350,000 to 500,000 cadres seems overly ambitious. Districts are required to add 60 cadres (6 with college degrees) to each of the country's 500 districts. Some 20,000 PAVN cadres also are being trained as economic cadres and 40 will be added to each district's administrative staff.

Party Internal Developments. All party members spent the year absorbing the results of the Fourth Party Congress. Congress documents, guideline (policy) papers, memoirs, and other forms of rhetoric flooded the land. One speech by Le Duan lasted eight hours. More than 100 speeches were delivered by members of the Politburo, the Central Committee and visitors. The Congress issued a political report, five major party resolutions and many minor ones, new party by-laws, detailed discussions of the current Five Year Plan, and biographical data on new Central Committee members. Finally it ordered that every party member read and study these documents.

The spring brought the "second round" of provincial/municipal party congresses—the "first round" having been held in November 1976, prior to the Fourth Congress. There were explanations of Fourth Congress decisions, discussions of the local application of the Five Year Plan, and reports on agricultural production in their areas. Each congress hosted 300 to 500 party representatives, each delegate representing some thirty party members. Each elected a provincial/municipal central committee of twenty-five to forty members. The selected members had to attend a special forty-five-day course to study the Fourth Party Congress documents at Nguyen Ai Quoc Party School in Hanoi, run by To Huu, the party's agitprop chief.

The overriding theme was that the party must remain central to all. The party must plan the society's future, lead the economic development work, motivate and, when necessary, discipline the masses. Such a monumental task for the party means that its 1.5 million membership must be made more qualified. The party would have to become stronger, better organized, more disciplined, and thoroughly permeated with a spirit of unity. Its members and cadres also should become better qualified and trained, more politically conscious, more selflessly dedicated, more ethical in their behavior. Vietnam cannot evolve into a new society unless the party upgrades its activities, and this could only be achieved if each member improved his qualifications.

Five organizational and structural objectives emerged during the year: to increase both party responsiveness to society's needs and internal ideological purity; to proletarianize the party by altering membership requirements; to raise the quality of party leadership by training and better recruitment; to strengthen loyalty to Marxism-Leninism as set down by the leadership and resist any left and right deviations. (The main slogan for the year was: "All for the Unity of the Party.")

The thrust in achieving these changes is organizational—tinkering with the party machinery to make it more effective and efficient. Among the changes effected by the new party by-laws are these: (1) strengthening the role and increasing the responsibility of the district party central committees, especially in the South. (2) increasing upper-lower coordination to strengthen the center's supervisory function over lower levels, and allow more effective upward communication. (3) creation of more specialized party units within the State, and especially in the agricultural sector, party activity is to be more tailor-made within specific institutions. (4) more "verticalization," that is, party units within major institutions, such as the armed forces, the heavy industry sector, and so forth, with a more independent chain of command. In the past the party structure tended to be laterally organized; now the VCP has introduced the idea of the "party within," and it is expected to make the party more flexible in its leadership role. (5) development of a new party control mechanism, not for control of internal party affairs but for control of state and production activities. The government set up a new State Inspection Commission in January and it was soon revealed that party elements will be the inner core of the commission. (6) tightening up on party admission. A candidate must now be eighteen years of age and have five years service associated with the party. usually in a Ho Chi Minh Youth Group; he must be vouched for by two party members and voted in by two-thirds of his local chapter. He is then placed on probation for eighteen months.

Some party members were expelled during the year. *Nhan Dan* (7 February) reported that expelled party members were those whose behavior had degenerated, who were caught engaging in economic speculation, or who simply were no longer fit to be members. The paper added cryptically, "orders were issued which unmasked or eliminated enemy elements still hiding in the party." No figures were given. Throughout the year there were hints of a full scale purge, but at year's end this had not taken place; the leadership apparently decided not to shake up the party at this critical moment.

The previous "Seven Responsibilities" of each party member were trimmed to the "Five Duties," and these became the major guides for rank and file members. The five are: (1) devotion to the cause of Communism and what it stands for; (2) individual self-improvement through study and training with a view to increasing political awareness, improving ethical behavior, and perfecting occupational skills; (3) allegiance to the masses and their interests; (4) maintaining party discipline as a contribution to raising the quality of the party; (5) fulfilling the party's international obligations in a spirit of international proletarianism.

It was not an easy year for party cadres who were, once again, blamed for all sorts of failures. Le Duan at the Fourth Congress complained that some cadres had degenerated, that individual cadres often violated the law, intimidated the population, and generally abused their powers. At the same gathering Le Duc Tho described the cadre corps as arbitrary, corrupt, autocratic, and illegal in behavior. Said one editorial: the cadre boasts like a roaring lion, eats like a hungry dragon and works like a sick kitten. The party also tried to control the cadre corps through specialized training courses, more careful personnel assignments, rewarding good performance, and paying more attention to cadre salary structure and fringe benefits.

The party continued to experiment with techniques to overcome the tendency of members to lose their sense of *elan* and become bureaucratized, defined as failing to act as a proper link between the party's plan for the society and the masses. These included cultural revolution innovations, various proletarianizing experiences—such as consignment to the New Economic Zones—and other status reversal techniques.

While the leadership attempted to restore elitism to the party it appeared to be going in the opposite direction with the party's youth arm, the Ho Chi Minh Youth Union. A massive drive has been underway for more than a year to recruit youth. One Ho Chi Minh City newspaper said the plan was to recruit eight out of every ten youths into the organization. Apparently officials want to convert the Union into a mass movement, though they will carefully select youths from the Union for membership in the party. In August the party named Dang Quoc Bao the new head of the Union.

Domestic Developments. The most important internal development of the year was the generally bad situation in agriculture. Poor weather and inept management by party, state cadres, and officials in the communes and state farms were the reasons cited for the state of affairs. The country's rice harvest for 1977 was significantly lower than 1976, possibly by 5 percent although final figures had not been released at year's end. Bad weather affected the rice crop, first cold, then drought, heavy rains and flooding. Rice shipments from China were reportedly halted. The total grain shortage for the country at year's end was estimated at from one to two million metric tons, a 5 to 10 percent shortfall. Shipments of wheat and other grains from the USSR, reportedly 500,000 metric tons, helped ease the shortage. Even so, rice rations were cut by 20 percent on 9 June. The rice ration for individuals varies according to occupation, but the nationwide average in late 1977 was half a pound a day, as low as that of the North in wartime and far lower than it ever was in the South. The poor harvest was made worse by bungling and errors frankly admitted by the leaders. In a Politburo resolution in late June and again in Prime Minister Pham Van Dong's National Day address (1 September) agricultural officials and workers were castigated for the organizational problems on the communes and state farms and for ignoring detailed agricultural production plans sent down from Hanoi in the spring. These mistakes, the premier stated, were the most important cause of the agricultural failure. The party fired Vo Thuc Dong, the minister of agriculture, and replaced him with Vo Chi Cong, a capable southerner who has little experience in managing food production.

Another problem has been how to collectivize southern agriculture. The party has recognized this problem since mid-1975 but has not solved it so far. In June a Party Plenum apparently ordered full scale collectivization in the South to begin. Unofficial reports said cadres had to spend 1977 planning the collectivization program, to begin it officially in January 1978, and complete it by December 1979. Vo Van Kiet, the party's chief official for agricultural affairs in the South, indicated such a schedule in his July speeches. His remarks did not clarify whether the decision was taken because of worsening food production in the South. At year's end the question of how rapidly to collectivize agriculture in the South was still uncertain.

Elsewhere on the economic scene there were continued efforts to keep "economics in command," that is bring it to the forefront in policy-making and increase public consciousness of the imperative nature of the drive for socialist transformation. A new Vietnam investment code has been promulgated. Foreign investments are welcome, although the scope of the code was not clear at year's end. Vietnam joined the International Monetary Fund, the World Bank, and the Asian Development Bank during the year. It also sought bilateral relations with Japan, France and other capitalist nations. Reports on an imminent oil development agreement continued to surface, but at year's end still no agreement has been finalized.

The Third Five Year Plan (1976 through 1980) is supposed to carry a U.S. $15 billion price tag, half of which is to come from abroad. Vietnam's central problem at the moment is where to get that kind of money. Two economic systems continued to operate, one in the North and the other in the South, with the Hai Van pass dividing the two. The North-South exchange rate is fixed to benefit the North. A steady supply of food, raw materials, and consumer goods flows to the North. This "pauperization plan," as it is guardedly termed in the South, greatly enriches the North, though economic life in the North still remains threadbare with essential commodities very difficult to obtain. In short, two years after the war officially ended, the Vietnamese economy has still developed very little. An estimated 40 to 50 percent of the factory capacity stands idle. Agriculture production has dropped, as noted above. Development of the infrastructure has barely begun. The economy is hardly able to absorb the economic aid already received at the Haiphong docks and Vietnam can offer little in return for trade.

Socialist transformation of Vietnam continues, especially in the South. The party has restructured the social order, and moved many to the countryside. The middle class loses its property when it relocates in the New Economic Zones. Agitprop campaigns socially ostracize the middle class by encouraging many to criticize it.

The regime's massive population relocation program, blandly called the state redistribution of labor program, continued during the year with unflagging vigor. This highly ambitious undertaking eventually will affect one out of every two Vietnamese living in the South and will fundamentally alter the social structure of the region. It may produce a more lasting effect than any other Communist effort in the South. While not as bloody as the program in Cambodia, it involves relocating a majority of all Vietnamese villagers into some 15,000 to 20,000 "agricultural production units" or giant agro-farms. The nation's 1.5 million Montagnards will be resettled. By the year 2000, when Vietnam's population is expected to reach 100 million, there will be no villages, merely agro-farms of 50,000 or more grouped around the nation's 500 district towns.

Widespread resistance to the regime in the South continues although it is scattered, poorly organized and generally ineffectual. Armed resistance—by an estimated 12,000 active resistance fighters—diminished during the year, but passive hostility and low grade sabotage was not uncommon. Japanese correspondents returning from South Vietnam report that virtually all of the educated, the middle class and the Catholics, as well as most Buddhists, are anti-regime. One Japanese journalist with long experience in Vietnam estimated that 40 percent of the adult population is actively hostile. Regionalism still survives in some areas.

The armed resistance has no national character; rather it is a series of regional groups linked by the generic term *Phuc Quoc* (national restoration) and is strongest in five areas: the Hao Hao villages along the Cambodian border in the Mekong Delta; the Montagnard communities in Lam Dong province and west of Kontum, an area the official press terms "the nameless front"; the Catholic villages of the Ho Nai complex (north of Ho Chi Minh City) and in the Phan Thiet region; Tay Ninh province among the Cao Dai; and the Hue and Quang Nam region, home of the two old nationalist organizations, the Viet Nam Quoc Dan Dang and the Dai Viets. Fourteen divisions of troops and 250,000 internal security police are trying to pacify these areas but as a French reporter in Vietnam recently wrote, the South still must be conquered.

Armed resistance is poorly led because the able people are still in re-education camps. The regime admits having 50,000 such prisoners—the SRV ambassador to France said in a July interview—although estimates by others range as high as 300,000. About 2.5 million South Vietnamese have gone through the re-education process in the past two years. The "five year sentence" prisoners are persons deemed by security officials to be potential leaders of the resistance and thus too dangerous to release. They must number around 30,000 and are true political prisoners as defined by Amnesty International. Late year reports indicated that these prisoners are being sent to prisons in the North.

Teams of special security police have attempted to seal off escape routes from Vietnam, but Vietnamese continued to flee at a rate of about 500 a week, often becoming pitiful "boat cases," that is refugees at sea with no place to land. At least 90,000 have fled Vietnam since the Communist takeover of the South, including 20,000 during 1977, most being working-class or professionals rather than the rich or upper class. Of the 275,000 who have left Vietnam since May 1975, about 150,000 are in the U.S., 100,000 in Asia (including 80,000 in Thailand), and the rest in Europe and elsewhere.

Foreign Relations. Vietnamese diplomats and party officials received foreign visitors, granted interviews and made pronouncements. Relations with the outside world still remain tenuous without firm commitments being made. SRV leaders view their country as a major force in Asia. Vietnam's population of nearly 52 million makes it the sixteenth of the world's 145 nations, and the third largest Communist nation. It has the fourth largest standing army in the world and is battle-hardened and well equipped. The country has considerable natural wealth and economic potential. Finally, it is strategically located. Much external activity during the year involved economic assistance, trade, and the transfer of technology.

Probably the most significant SRV external development during the year was its successful effort to achieve closer relations with Laos. An extraordinarily high level Vietnamese delegation (three of the top four Politburo figures) flew to Vientiane in July and signed a mutual cooperation treaty, an economic aid agreement, and a treaty redefining the Laos-Vietnam border, the latter implying that Laos will make no major foreign policy decision without first clearing it with Hanoi. A series of other Vietnam-Laos ties were established during the year, leading some foreign observers to believe that Laos has become little more than another province of Vietnam. In Cambodia the opposite situation prevailed. Relations steadily worsened. In late summer came reports of military clashes along the common border. In one instance PAVN forces reportedly used tanks.

Relations with China apparently improved over the previous year which probably marked an all time low in Sino-Vietnamese relations. The offshore island controversy remained unsolved but quiescent. Ties with the USSR remained close and if anything became even warmer. The USSR is now supplying Vietnam an estimated US$1.5 billion annually in economic aid, or half of all foreign aid Vietnam receives. Still officially dedicated to healing the Sino-Soviet rift, Hanoi officials act on the assumption that the dispute will continue into the forseeable future and that Vietnam's economic needs depend on Moscow. Diplomacy in Southeast Asia had ups and downs. Relations with ASEAN remained distinctly cool, as they have been since the 1976 Colombo conference imbroglio. The SRV joined the United Nations.

Relations with the U.S., which seemed to promise much forward movement early in the year, by mid-year had slowed. By year's end it was apparent that American-Vietnamese relations were at a standstill.

Publications. The party's theoretical journal, *Tap Chi Hoc Tap* (Studies), returned to its original 1943 title, *Tap Chi Cong San* (Communist Review). The party's military journal is still called *Tap Chi Quan Do Nhan Dan* (People's Army Studies). Major newspapers are the party's *Nhan Dan* (People) published in Hanoi and Ho Chi Minh City editions, and the PAVN daily, *Quan Doi Nhan Dan* (People's Army). Other publications include *Tien Phong* (Youth), the party youth group organ; *Lao Dong* (Workers), a weekly publication of the Vietnam General Confederation of Trade Unions; *Cuu Quoc* (National Salvation), the official organ of the Vietnam Fatherland Front; and a series of technical journals dealing with military science, economic development and agriculture.

The Voice of Vietnam operates radio (including wired broadcasting in the villages) and television stations. As Radio Hanoi it broadcasts in twelve languages on both medium wave and short wave frequencies. The Foreign Language Publishing House issues books, pamphlets and periodicals in foreign languages for distribution abroad.

Washington, D.C.   Douglas Pike

THE AMERICAS

Argentina

The Communist Party of Argentina (Partido Comunista de Argentina; PCA), founded in 1918, is said to be the oldest Communist party in Latin America. Its estimated membership in 1977 was between 50,000 and 85,000, a considerable decline from 1976. The Revolutionary Communist Party (Partido Comunista Revolucionario; PCR) is still considered pro-Chinese; its active membership is thought to have dipped to less than 10,000 due to government repression against the Marxist sector generally. The same is true of the Socialist Workers Party (Partido Socialista de los Trabajadores; PST), which has links with the Fourth (Trotskyist) International and is estimated to have had no more than 15,000 members in 1977. Other parties of the Marxist spectrum include the Social Democratic Party (Partido Socialista Democrático; PSD), which showed a slight membership increase to about 20,000 members and is probably the party on the left with the greatest chance of becoming a real force in Argentine politics. Parties associated with the guerrilla movements within the country, such as the Revolutionary Workers Party (Partido Revolucionario de los Trabajadores; PRT) have, by and large, been eliminated by the military regime's counterinsurgency offensive. The same is true of the People's Revolutionary Army (Ejército Revolucionario del Pueblo; ERP) and the Peronist Montoneros, though a Peronist Montonero Party (Movimiento Peronista Montonero; MPM) was formed in exile.

Understanding the Marxist spectrum of parties and influence groups in Argentina during 1977 requires a brief preface. First, the various groups of Marxists, Socialists, and Communists proliferated, often using spurious names. They formed a continuum from cautious collaboration with the military regime (which came to power via a coup on 24 march 1976) to outright advocacy of anarchy and violence. Second, the Argentine violence continued despite government claims to have liquidated the principal guerrilla groups and evidence mounted that many of the paramilitary terrorist squads were either officially sponsored or at least tolerated. Third, although the policies of Economics Minister Martinez de Hoz were successful in reducing inflation, the cost of living continued to rise nonetheless and by the end of 1977 had reduced the average Argentine's purchasing power since the coup by some 40 percent. In contrast to this was the fact that incomes for wealthy landowners increased. Fourth, the government became increasingly aware that it could not expect to govern indefinitely without the acquiescence of organized labor (the General Confederation of Labor, a Peronist creation sprinkled with both Marxist and fascist elements). Fifth, there was the international Graiver scandal. This series of revelations forces a reexamination of the status of the Montonero guerrilla organization.

The population of Argentina is 26,224,000 (estimated 1977), about half of which is concentrated in the capital city, the focus of this report, and the province of Buenos Aires.

The Setting. Government restrictions on the press and arrests of journalists made reporting on Marxist groups difficult during 1977. A *New York Times* story (4 January) cited the continuation of terrorism both by leftist guerrillas and by government and/or other paramilitary squads, but argued that "the balance of terror has tilted heavily in favor of the government." In particular it should be noted that when the military ended the chaotic Peronist regime in March 1976, some 10,000 bodyguards in the city and province of Buenos Aires were put out of work. The military had to either absorb them, or risk having them pass over to the Marxist guerrillas, a not uncommon practice in Latin America. That the military was unable to control all such groups is a partial explanation of the ambiguity surrounding the thousands of lives reported lost since the military took over in 1976. It is clear that many deaths go unreported, and that many of the attributions of such deaths are spurious.

The military government is sensitive to the impact of the terrorism, reports of political prisoners— Amnesty International estimated there were 5,000 of these at various times during 1977— and Argentina's economic malaise. The potential influence of the Argentine labor movement is well known. The position of labor was confused by the emergence of a break-away labor group from the large General Confederation of Labor (CGT), known as the CGT in Resistance, some of whose workers declared a Marxist motive. The labor activity of the year involved slowdown strikes by railway and transport workers and acts of sabotage by some telephone workers.

The PCA: Leadership, Organization, and Activities. The Argentina Communist Party is considered the nation's principal Marxist organization. It is not prohibited, but its legal status is indefinitely suspended. The titular head of the party is Rodolfo Ghioldi, though the bulk of the party's operations are handled by Gerónimo Arnedo Alvarez, secretary general, and Ghioldi's brother, Orestes Ghioldi, a member of the central executive committee. Other party leaders include Rubens Iscaro, Fernando Nadra, Jorge Pereyra, and Irene Rodríguez.

In February the PCA reiterated its support for the military government of General Videla, saying that the general's ideas and policies, except for the human rights violations, reflected the sentiments of most Argentines (*IB,* no. 4). In an interview published at mid-year, Orestes Ghioldi warned of creeping "CIAism" in Latin America and defended his party's support of the Argentine junta, arguing that it was not manipulated by the CIA, as he alleged to be the case in Chile and Brazil (*Latinskaya Amerika,* Moscow, May-June). The PCA urges generals Jorge Videla and Roberto Viola to maintain a soft line (*dictablanda*) against the hard line (*dictadura*) of such figures as Admiral Emilio Massera. The PCA wants to see Peronism destroyed so that Marxism (as contrasted with Peronist fascism) can take the leading proletarian role in Argentina's political life. (Alberto Kohen, in the September issue of the *World Marxist Review,* admitted that the bulk of the working class now adheres to Peronism but argued that a process is underway in which "the advocates of Peronism are coming nearer to the class positions of the communists.")

The PCA was put in an awkward position, and Soviet-Argentine relations were tested, when in October the Argentine navy, under Admiral Massera, fired on several Russian trawlers that had violated the 200-mile limit and then forced them into detention at a port some 800 miles south of Buenos Aires. Nonetheless, this did not weaken the dialogue of the PCA with the generals, nor did the government's decision to break diplomatic relations with the regime of North Korea in June, and reports of the harassment of North Koreans in Argentina, evoke formal protests from the Communists. It seems a fair judgment that the PCA was being used by the junta as a proletariat control mechanism, and by both junta and the Soviet Union as a way of protecting mutually-beneficial trade relations. Thus, although some rank-and-file Communists have lost their lives under military repression, the PCA as a whole has probably suffered less than most groups on the Marxist left. The PCA's willingness to assume this role accounts for the decline in party membership since 1976. Still, sensitive to the charge that it was a Soviet puppet, the PCA held several clandestine meetings during 1977 in which the "Europeanization" of Argentine Communism was discussed, stressing that allegiance to the Soviet Union comes after Argentine nationalism.

The pro-Soviet Communists of the PCA continued their propaganda campaign against the "eastern brand" of Marxism (Maoism) and denounced all anti-Soviet activities going on in Argentina. Orestes Ghioldi lauded the military regimes of Peru and Panama, without mentioning their human rights and press censorship records, and thanked the Soviet Union for its contributions to easing international tensions. He warned that the United States was looking enviously at the Patagonian oil reserves of Argentina and said that Brazil, at the behest of the United States, has geopolitical goals which make democratic regimes on its borders intolerable (*Latinskaya Amerika,* May-June).

Publications. The PCA began publication of the journal *Elementos,* on a semi-clandestine basis, as a replacement for the magazine *Movimiento Obrero,* which was shut down by the military. The journal *Fundamentos,* unofficially associated with the PCA, continued to circulate on a restricted basis.

The Revolutionary Communist Party. The PCR remained on the junta's 1977 list of prohibited parties. Due to the severe repression against the PCR by the military government, it is impossible to identify the group's leadership or to describe its organization. One Argentine political observer informed me that during 1977 the PCR tried to retain its limited influence among some student and professional groups but that, lacking proletarian support, its "revolutionary" activities usually amounted to little more than writing slogans on subway walls. The PCR has been severely denounced by the PCA for its previous support of the Isabel Perón-López Rega regime and for its advocacy of violence. It is likely that conflict with the predominant Argentine Communist Party has undermined the PCR almost to the point of nonexistence, and that military repression has finished off the rest. I am told that a significant number of PCR members became alienated during 1977 and joined the proscribed Peronist left (discussed below). At the moment of this writing it seems that the PCR may be headed for extinction.

The Socialist Vanguard Party. The proscribed PSV is still Elias Semán and his tiny group of sympathizers. Semán was described by one who knew him personally as a hard line Leninist-Maoist who would sympathize with guerrilla tactics against the regime. Informants in Buenos Aires state that this party operated in near total clandestinity during 1977. Semán himself left the country under mysterious circumstances late in 1976 and returned early in 1977, but details of this trip are not available. There is no reason to believe that the PSV increased its membership during the year.

The Socialist Workers Party. Sources in Buenos Aires report that the prohibited PST is one of the fastest growing Marxist parties in the country, but not necessarily the best organized or the one most likely to acquire real power. It renounces violence as a political tool, yet it has been strongly suppressed. This writer was told that military sources admitted their crackdown on the PST was excessive and probably unjustified, this repression alone bringing some popular sympathy to the party. (It is believed that some of the military regime's antagonism toward the PST stems from the alleged past association of one of its leaders, Nahuel Moreno (a pseudonym), with Argentine Trotskyism, though Moreno has disavowed this allegiance.) The PST benefited from the divisions within Peronism toward the end of the Isabel Perón regime; some alienated Peronistas of the moderate left began to identify more and more with the PST and its primary leader, Juan Carlos Coral. Unlike the PCA, the PST does not have to defend its ties to a foreign power since it has none, or pretend, transparently, that such do not exist. Knowledgeable sources suggest that the PST could probably win more popular votes in an honest election in Buenos Aires than could the PCA. Coral, who remained cautiously silent during 1977, has a broad personal following and certain charismatic attributes. He is known to many as a former deputy who served in the Radical administration of

Arturo Illia (1963-1966). The party has contacts with the Socialist Workers Party in the United States. Its official publication, *Los de Abajo,* was not permitted to circulate during 1977.

The Social Democratic Party. The suspended PSD is one of the most potentially promising of the groups in the Marxist spectrum. It has long been a powerful, middle-class, Socialist-oriented party in the important city of Mar del Plata in southern Buenos Aires province. Although the PSD lacks the proletarian base of the PST, it derives support from a party-created lending and investment institution called "El Hogar Obrero," a kind of credit union, which some say is successful precisely because it is independent of the government. This institution functioned during 1977. The most important leaders of the PSD are Américo Ghioldi, titular head, whom the military government retained as ambassador to Portugal, Juan Antonio Solari, Luis Pan, and Raúl Dellepaine. The party suffered no major internal divisions during the year, avoided involvement with Argentine exile groups, and apparently sustained a slight membership increase.

During 1977 the PSD began to establish "study centers" (in place of party offices) in an effort to evade the government's ban on political activity. As of late November, these "study centers" were moderately successful and had not been closed down by the military regime. Cooperative action as opposed to free enterprise was a theme stressed by the PSD both in these centers and in the party organ, *La Vanguardia*, edited by Dellepaine, though this is done with great care so as not to threaten the PSD rapprochement with the Videla junta. On other subjects *La Vanguardia* was sometimes more critical (albeit usually subtly) of the government than in 1976, and the paper was hard to find at many newsstands. For example, an editorial on 11 August said the Social Democrats will not participate in any action that is not intended to bring domestic peace to Argentina, this being prefaced by a resume of remarks by President Videla, all done in such a way as to suggest, without being too obvious, that the PSD has confidence in Videla's good intentions. However, the article then urged the government to "adopt an intelligent policy of peace" concerning those prisoners being held without proof that they were involved in subversion. The 1 September edition devoted its principal editorial to an analysis of the serious tax evasion problem in Argentina, a direct and clearly written attack on the upper classes which has to include some of the military. In this criticism the PSD was clearly taking a risk which could affect its immediate future.

Marxism and the Guerrilla Sector. Most of the guerrilla sector of 1976 had been eliminated and/or fractionalized by the Argentine security forces by January 1977. Still, a *New York Times* report on 4 January estimated the total strength of the left-wing extremists at around 5,000. Their main leaders were not in Argentina, however, but rather exiled in Italy. On 20 April a group of Montoneros (formally attached to the Marxist wing of the Peronist movement despite their having been forced underground by Perón himself in 1974) held a secret exile press conference in Rome, the substance of which was subsequently made public. The conference signaled one of the most significant events for the entire Marxist spectrum of Argentina during 1977. Mario Firmenich, Rodolfo Galimberti, Oscar Bidegain (ex-governor of Buenos Aires province), Rodolfo Puiggros (ex-rector of the University of Buenos Aires), and others proclaimed the formation of a new party, the Peronist Montonero Party (MPM), which will be directed temporarily from European exile. Its leaders plan to return to Argentina when democratic political conditions are reestablished following a predicted collapse of the Videla government.

The Argentine government classified the Montoneros as Marxist subversives and Firmenich, the titular leader, never disavowed Marxism which had been the group's official ideology (*La Prensa,* Buenos Aires, 22 April). The general public belief in Argentina is also that the Montoneros are a Marxist organization. However, while this may be true for many within the rank-and-file, there is now reason to doubt that Firmenich and some of his leadership colleagues are or ever were in fact genuine Marxists.

Briefly, the doubt about Firmenich and some other Montoneros comes from two sets of phenomena: (1) a history of right wing involvement by Firmenich and others, including participation in the Tacuara anti-semitic and fascist-type organization in the 1960s, and (2) the David Graiver case in 1977. The second point must be touched upon here. In about the same week that the Montoneros's Rome press conference was held, Argentina learned that the financier Graiver had managed the Montoneros's financial affairs for a number of years, including the investment of millions of dollars from kidnaping ransoms in European stock markets. Graiver also created banks in Belgium, New York, and elsewhere, and deliberately allowed them to go bankrupt, with himself as principal beneficiary in these transactions. Subsequently Graiver was reportedly killed in an airplane accident in Mexico, an event shrouded in mystery and thought by some to have been staged to provide Graiver with a new identity. What seems clear is that Graiver was a kind of financial advisor to the Montoneros for a number of years. It is not clear, however, whether the Montoneros's kidnapings, ransoms and bank robberies were carried out primarily to finance Marxist activities, as claimed, or whether they were part of a deliberately concealed "commercial communism" with strictly financial motives for the benefit of Firmenich and other Montoneros leaders.

Finally, reports of Firmenich's movements and statements during the year are contradictory. According to an interview published in the *Manchester Guardian* (13 March), allegedly taken in Buenos Aires, Firmenich expressed optimism about the future of guerrilla warfare and the Montoneros in Argentina. And yet some believe the guerrilla leader was in exile permanently from late 1976. Confidential sources in Buenos Aires even assert that Firmenich visited the Soviet Union early in 1977.

The March 1977 edition of the Montoneros's underground publication *Evita Montonera* contains articles by Firmenich and Horacio Mendizábal, painting the movement essentially as a political party but one which would engage in armed struggle when necessary. The publication announced that special tapes containing talks by Firmenich would be circulated about Argentina so that people would know the true program of the Montonero Party, and urged former Peronists to join the Montoneros with "aerosol, chalk, and faith in victory" in writing their slogans and symbols in public places about the country. This same pamphlet called for a restoration of democracy, respect for human rights, removal of military intervention in worker syndicates, and other demands. What is significant about this pamphlet is that it does not contain any of the Marxist rhetoric used by the Montoneros in previous years. Aside from its proletarian appeal, the document does not mention class struggle and could just as easily be termed fascist (with Firmenich occupying the critical leader position). Also, the organic metaphor of the state, another fascist characteristic, is clearly implicit in this document.

On 22 November 1977 the "high command" of the MPM (*Movimiento Peronista Montoneros*) in exile issued a communiqué in Rome stating that its motive was to reestablish democracy in Argentina via strikes, sabotage, and demonstrations (*La Prensa*, 23 November 1977). Montonero leader Mario Firmenich declared that the forthcoming world championship soccer matches during 1978 in Argentina would give the world an opportunity to know the truth about the Argentine political situation. The communiqué concluded with a call for free elections and a safe conduct guarantee for former President Cámpora who was completing more than a year of exile in the Mexican Embassy in Buenos Aires. No mention of Marxist ideology or Communist goals was reported from this late 1977 press conference by the Montoneros in exile.

Thus is now seems possible that the Montoneros leadership never was Marxist as the government of Argentina insists and as many scholars, including myself, were led to believe. Clearly, however, the Montoneros did and do contain Marxist cadres even if the status of certain leadership elements is currently in doubt.

Not all Peronists remaining in Argentina have agreed to accept orders sent from Italy by Firmenich and others. In 1977 handbills began to appear signed by a rival Peronist group calling itself the Carlos Caride Peronist-Montonero Column (Columna Montonera y Peronista "Carlos Caride"). One of these documents (communique no. 2) denounced Firmenich and the others for their financial involvements with Graiver and for misuse of "popular funds" for their personal benefit. The "Carlos Caride" group says it will carry on the revolution at home, now that the traitor Firmenich has fled. But the handbill cited contains no language that is even mildly Marxist.

University of Missouri
St. Louis

Kenneth F. Johnson

Bolivia

The Communist Party of Bolivia (Partido Comunista de Bolivia; PCB) was founded in 1950 and is pro-Soviet in orientation. A pro-Chinese splinter group became the Communist Party of Bolivia Marxist-Leninist (Partido Comunista de Bolivia, Marxista-Leninista; PCB-ML) in 1965. the Trotskyist Revolutionary Workers' Party (Partido Revolucionario de los Trabajadores; POR) is split into several factions. The National Liberation Army (Ejército de Liberación Nacional; ELN), founded in 1966, formed the Bolivian Revolutionary Workers' Party (Partido Revolucionario de los Trabajadores de Bolivia; PRT-B) in 1975. The Movement of the Revolutionary Left (Movimiento de Izquierda Revolucionaria; MIR) was formed in mid-1971 and reorganized after the 21 August 1971 coup in which rightist Colonel Hugo Banzer overthrew the government of leftist General Juan José Torres and seized the presidency for himself, a position he retained throughout 1977. Although Banzer lifted the ban on moderate political parties in anticipation of the announced July 1978 presidential and congressional elections, the Marxist-Leninist parties remained illegal during 1977. Although arrests of revolutionaries were reported periodically during the year, the only major incident occurred in February when the interior minister announced the breaking up of an alleged "subversive plot" by more than twenty members of the PCB, MIR, and POR. The PCB and PCB-ML are estimated to have approximately 300 and 150 members, respectively. The population of Bolivia is 5,500,500 (estimated 1977).

The PCB: Leadership and Organization. The first secretary of the PCB is Jorge Kolle Cueto. Others prominent in the party include Mario Monje Molina, a former first secretary, and Central Committee members Simón Reyes, Arturo Lanza, Carlos Alba, and Luis Padilla, the latter a frequent international spokesman for the party.

The basic organization of the PCB is the cell, which consists of no fewer than three party members. District committees, elected at national congresses (the most recent of which was in June 1971), reportedly exist in each department and in most mining centers. The national congress of the party elects the Central Committee, the latter guiding the party between congresses. The Central Committee elects the Political and Control-Auditing Commissions and the first secretary, and convenes national conferences to discuss current organizational and political affairs not requiring the convocation of the national congress. The PCB emphasizes its determination to provide an effective working class vanguard, the absence of which, the party claims, led to revolutionary failures over the past quarter-century (*WMR*, September).

The PCB's youth organization, the Communist Youth of Bolivia (Juventud Comunista de Bolivia; JCB), is illegal. Among its leaders in recent years have been Jorge Escalera, reported arrested in the February plot incident, and Carlos Soría Galvarro. Simón Reyes, the head of the PCB's mining activities, in exile during 1977, was reelected in absentia to a top leadership position in the miners' federation (FSTMB) congress in May 1976.

The PCB: Domestic and International Attitudes and Activities. The PCB classifies Bolivia as a backward dependent capitalist country whose backwardness is due to its dependency. Government measures are directed toward disorganizing the masses, eliminating bourgeois freedoms, and obtaining total ideological supremacy. The country is in the midst of a serious economic crisis, the entire burden of which falls upon the working people. Analyzing the failure of the Torres government, Kolle Cueto has written that the PCB learned several important lessons: (1) it is necessary to be prepared for any variety of armed struggle; (2) whenever possible, it is necessary to rally progressive members of the military to the side of the masses; (3) it is essential to "unmask the provocative and counterrevolutionary" positions of the "ultra-left adventurists," with whom "it is wrong to enter into alliance even for the sake of the highest ideals"; (4) it is necessary and possible to create a broad, progressive, political front with the working class playing the key role. The PCB claims to have learned that a leftist alliance is inadequate since ultra-leftists tend to bring matters to a split. Now the party favors a united front of all "genuinely anti-fascist forces" in the country, a National Democratic Front which will include a portion of the left wing of the National Revolutionary Movement (MNR), the Socialist Party, certain circles of the Christian Democratic Party, and other parties and groups. (*Latinskaya Amerika,* Moscow, January 1977.)

The current government in Bolivia, according to Padilla, is not different from the "fascist and fascist-minded regimes" established recently in other southern Latin American countries. The "new order" in Bolivia is more of a "terroristic dictatorship of Bolivia's pro-imperialist bourgeoisie than a state mechanism for the domination of the right wing of the armed forces." The "new order" is simply "the face of fascism in Bolivia." Padilla told an international meeting in Prague that strikes, manifestations, protests, and other disruptions are increasing in the country since public discontent is on the rise. One of the key results of this struggle is "the formation of a broad democratic movement in defense of civil rights and freedoms on which numerous public figures and leaders of the opposition parties, including former ministers of the Banzer government, are represented." The movement is "working hard to establish a democratic, independent and progressive regime in Bolivia." (*WMR*, October.)

PCB and JCB members were alleged to form the majority of the participants in the February plot. According to the Bolivian interior minister, the objectives of the internationally-funded extremist movement were: (1) promotion of class struggle to increase social conflict; (2) division of civic and other organizations to prevent them from participating in national development; (3) infiltration of student and labor organizations in an effort to provoke political and social disruptions; and (4) unleashing of violence to disrupt the current administration. Toward the end of the year, the PCB was reportedly trying to work out an electoral front through discussions with the leftist MNRI, the MIR, the underground leaders of the FSTMB, and other parties and groupings (*Latin America Political Report,* London, 18 November).

The PCB remains firmly in the pro-Soviet camp and responds to international issues in accordance with Soviet positions.

Publications. The PCB publishes the irregular, clandestine newspaper *Unidad* and occasional pamphlets and bulletins distributed among workers, peasants, and intellectuals.

*   *   *

The PCB-ML. The pro-Chinese Communist party has long been torn by dissension. The faction headed by Oscar Zamora Medinacelli has given its blessing to Hua Kuo-feng and continues to be recognized by the People's Republic of China. A delegation from the PCB-ML met with representatives of six other Latin American pro-Chinese parties in Albania at the end of 1976 and early in 1977 published a "joint declaration of Marxist-Leninist parties of Latin America" in the Argentine paper *No Transar* (see *Chile*).

*   *   *

Other Revolutionary Organizations and Activities. The Revolutionary Workers' Party (POR) and the MIR were reportedly involved in the February plot and a dozen of their members were taken into custody. Members of the MIR, the ELN, and other groups were arrested periodically during the year in La Paz and outlying cities and communities. While the MIR expressed some interest in participating in the 1978 election, at least one faction of the POR called upon the Bolivian people to fight against the "electoral farce" in a Revolutionary Antifascist Front of workers, peasants, and students (AFP, 15 November). Some revolutionary objectives were achieved with the assistance of foreign parties and organizations, among the latter the British National Union of Mineworkers (NUM). The NUM was instrumental in persuading the British government to kill a proposed $32.7 million grant to the Bolivian state mining company (Comibol), a move urged by the Bolivian FSTMB. (See *Financial Times,* London, 13 May; *Latin America Political Report,* 12 August.)

Hoover Institution   William E. Ratliff
Stanford University

Brazil

The original Communist Party of Brazil (Partido Comunista do Brasil), founded in March 1922, remains the most important Marxist-Leninist organization in the nation. Several small groups that broke away or were expelled from the party in the first decade formed a Trotskyist movement which subsequently split into several factions. Two of these factions still maintain a precarious existence. In 1960, in a bid for legal recognition, the original pro-Soviet party dropped all international slogans from its statutes and changed its name to Brazilian Communist Party (Partido Comunista Brasileiro; PCB). A pro-Chinese element broke away the following year and in February 1962 adopted the original party name, Communist Party of Brazil (PCdoB). Another source of far-leftist groups was Popular Action (Ačao Popular; AP), which originated in the Catholic student movement in the late 1950s. In the following decade a segment of AP identified itself as the Marxist-Leninist Popular Action (Ačao Popular Marxista Leninista; APML).

Dissidence within these parties after the military coup of 1964 led to the formation of numerous splinter groups, predominantly of Maoist and Castroite tendencies, which strongly advocated the use of armed violence to overthrow the regime. There may have been as many as sixteen such organizations at one point. Some of them, using urban guerrilla or terrorist tactics, gained considerable notoriety for a time, but between 1969 and 1972 the deaths of their most prominent leaders, the wholesale arrests of militants, and continued public apathy or hositility, drastically reduced their number and effectiveness. An attempt to launch a rural guerrilla movement in the early 1970s, undertaken by the PCdoB and three other groups, was suppressed by the military.

The Communist movement has been illegal in Brazil throughout most of its existence, though it has at times operated with varying degrees of freedom. The military regime which came to power in March 1964 drove the PCB and other far-left groups underground and banned the existing Communist-influenced organizations. Since 1969 certain acts of subversion have been punishable by banishment or death. In practice, the death penalty has not been applied by the courts, but several dozen Brazilian terrorists have been exiled and others have died in prison or have been killed in clashes with the police and the military.

PCB membership in 1977 was certainly well below the 1974 estimate of about 6,000. The PCdoB was said to have some 1,000 members in 1974; no later estimates are available. Little is known of the strength of other Marxist-Leninist groups. The population of Brazil is 110,000,000 (estimated 1977).

The PCB: Organization and Leadership. The PCB apparatus is supposed to include a twenty-one member Executive Commission (some of whose members are resident abroad), a Central Committee (which functions chiefly in Brazil, although some of its members also reside abroad), state committees, municipal committees, and local cells in residential districts and places of employment. Government persecution has made it impossible for the party to maintain a full panoply of organization.

The last congress of the PCB (the sixth) took place in December 1967. Since then occasional plenary sessions of the Central Committee have been held. A meeting of the Executive Committee was held in February 1977. Party secretary general Luiz Carlos Prestes has resided in the USSR since

1971 and his second-in-command, Giocondo Alves Dias, reportedly now lives in exile as well. Government repression continued in 1977.

The party draws its leadership and members from the ranks of students, intellectuals, and organized labor. Consistently, there has been a substantial turnover in membership, especially among white collar elements, as individuals become inactive because of boredom, fear of arrest, or—in the past dozen years—impatience with the non-violent policies of the PCB.

Domestic Activities and Attitudes. The PCB is an orthodox pro-Soviet party which seeks to mobilize and manipulate the masses to achieve power. It long ago recognized the impossibility of achieving power in Brazil by violence, and thus advocates popular front tactics. Within its limited possibilities, the PCB seeks to identify with—and to claim responsibility for articulating—the legitimate grievances and aspirations of broad sectors of Brazilian society. The total failure of the "reckless adventures" of extremist left-wing guerrilla organizations has reinforced the belief of the PCB leaders in the correctness of the party's domestic policies.

On various recent occasions representatives of the PCB have published analyses of the current Brazilian situation and the party's reaction to it. These statements have insisted that the existing regime in Brazil is "fascist." An article in the *World Marxist Review* (August), signed by representatives of four Latin American Communist parties, including José Soares, alternate member of the Executive Committee of the PCB, defended this definition with reference to the 1935 definition of fascism by the Seventh Congress of the Comintern, and concluded: "Fascism, as seen in some Latin American countries, is essentially an outright terroristic dictatorship of the most reactionary and aggressive foreign monopoly circles, the local oligarchy, and the big bourgeoisie which is connected with imperialism and . . . shows signs of becoming a monopolistic bourgeoisie, although in a distorted and immature form." In an earlier article, Sofia de Castro noted with regard to Brazil: "The escalation of fascism proceeded in a favorable economic situation, and this helped to extend its social base somewhat. In the days of the 'economic miracle,' civil servants, civilian and military technocrats, who were now enjoying a higher standard of living and more political influence, joined the reactionary section of the middle strata. The fascists were able to win the support of even part of the laboring population with their slogan of a 'great-power Brazil.' The regime also exploited the rise in consumption." De Castro argued that the military regime engaged in "the inculcation of fascist ideology, based entirely on rabid anti-communism and social, nationalist and chauvinist demagogy," and added: "The underlying tenet of fascist ideology is 'economic development and national security.' This is meant to justify not only the methods used to bring the country out of its social and economic crisis, but, more important, assure stability for the development of dependent capitalism." De Castro insisted, however, that the regime's policies are "bound to narrow its social base." To take advantage of that eventuality, the Communist party is working for the unity of the "democratic forces." Its platform calls for respect for "human rights and democratic freedoms." She concludes that the PCB "closely links the fight for democracy with the defense of national interests, with the struggle against the anti-national, capitulationist, expansionist and aggressive policies of the regime, which is closely tied to the most reactionary monopoly groups opposed to detente and world peace." (*WMR*, November 1976.)

In February the Executive Committee of the PCB issued a statement concerning the opposition's good showing in municipal elections of the previous November. It was a positive assessment of elections which "clearly point to the Brazilian people's refusal to remain on the margin of political life and their desire to participate in selecting the country's leaders." The statement added that as part of the government's reaction to its defeat, "we are witnessing attempts to split the opposition, either by raising the banner of anti-communism, or by selective repression against communists and the most active anti-fascists." After commenting that the forthcoming parliamentary elections of

1978 present new opportunities to show up the government, the statement set forth the "directions" of PCB activity, namely: (1) united action by all social forces and political trends, relying on the platform of the "anti-fascist patriotic front" proposed by the PCB; (2) more broadly-based actions designed to establish the front on a countrywide scale; (3) struggle for the "timely holding of elections and for the direct election of state governors"; and (4) campaign against the anti-Communism and anti-Sovietism "used by the dictatorship to justify its 'national security' doctrine and its oppressive actions." (*IB*, No. 4.) On the fifty-fifth anniversary of the founding of the PCB, Prestes issued an appeal for a joint struggle for "amnesty, national reconciliation of the great majority of the people on the basis of freedom, the right to strike, the free organization and independence of trade unions, and the right to free organization of political parties, including the Communist Party, which represents a substantial part of the population" (*IB*, 15 April). The PCB was apparently willing to go quite far in its overtures to other elements in Brazilian politics. It was reported in September that the party was backing the presidential aspirations of José de Magalhaes Pinto (one of the principal civilian architects of the 1964 coup), the only declared civilian candidate in the 1978 election.

Although two congressmen (one national and one state) proposed legalization of the PCB, most non-Communist political groups opposed such a move. The government and its supporters continued to stress the threat of the Communists as a major justification for maintaining the military-dominated regime. One opposition member of the Federal Chamber of Deputies was attacked by a pro-government colleague for making a speech in the Chamber which had been taken largely from the underground Communist Party newspaper *Voz Operaria*. Three weeks later, he was removed from Congress and deprived of his civil rights by President Geisel. (*Latin American Political Report*, 17 June.) On another occasion a pro-government newspaper in Brasilia attacked the National Conference of Brazilian Bishops for its criticism of the human rights violations of the regime, arguing that the bishops were working for the Communists since *Voz Operaria* had praised the position assumed by the clergymen (*Correio Braziliense*, 13 March).

International Views and Contacts. The fifty-fifth anniversary of the foundation of the PCB, a party which has remained firmly pro-Moscow in its international positions, brought in many greetings from pro-Soviet Communist parties around the world; the Cuban Communist Party held a special meeting to celebrate the anniversary, presided over by Central Committee member Manuel Piñeiro. Brazilian Communists took part in international meetings of pro-Moscow Communists, including an international symposium on natural resources and national independence held in Havana (*WMR*, April). Luiz Carlos Prestes went to Mozambique in July; he was interviewed by the country's principal newspaper, and issued a joint communiqué with the governing party, Frelimo, which expressed support for armed struggle of blacks in Zimbabwe (Rhodesia) (*FBIS*, 11 July). He also visited the Soviet republic of Azerbaijan.

Publications. In January 1975 the Brazilian government seized the PCB's two principal printing facilities and the PCB daily, *Voz Operaria*, did not circulate for some months thereafter. However, the periodical was back in circulation throughout 1977. It was quoted by a number of sources both inside Brazil and abroad.

The PCdoB. The organizational structure of the PCdoB, which was founded by men who had long held leadership positions in the PCB, is believed to be patterned after that of the parent party. Little is known about the number or distribution of currently functioning units. Just before Christmas in 1976, the army raided a house in São Paulo, in the course of which three members of the Central Committee of the PCdoB were killed. One of these was Pedro Pomar, a deputy between 1945 and 1947, who before his break with the PCB had been one of that party's principal leaders. (*Latin*

America Political Report, 7 January.) Another was Angel Arroyo, another important leader of the pro-Chinese party (ibid., 4 February). Mauricio Grabois, perhaps the PCdoB's most important leader, was reportedly killed in guerrilla activities in the Amazonian state of Para (ibid., 8 July). Members of the PCdoB were also prosecuted by the government during the year. For example, thirty-nine members of the party were tried in the northeastern city of Fortaleza on charges of trying to reorganize the party (*Folha de São Paulo,* 27 April). In spite of these difficulties, the PCdoB continued to be active. In September it was reported that the party supported a campaign for a new constitutional assembly which would replace the military-imposed constitution written in 1967 and the oppressive amendments of 1969 (*Latin America Political Report,* 23 September).

The PCdoB maintained its contacts with other pro-Chinese Communist parties. In January the Central Committee of the Communist Party of China sent a message of condolence to the PCdoB after the deaths of Pomar and other party leaders (*FBIS,* 26 January). The PCdoB was present at a meeting of pro-Peking Communist parties in Albania (see *Chile*).

Other Organizations. Of the numerous extremist and terrorist organizations operating in Brazil in the late 1960s and early 1970s, only a few appear to have survived into 1977. Some of the leaders of the MR-8, a terrorist group of Castroite persuasion, were tried in the middle of the year by a secret session of the Superior Military Court. Although the defendants were convicted, some of the members of the court questioned the legality of the proceedings. (*O Globo,* Rio de Janeiro, 9 August.) There were other trials of groups seeking to organize the pro-Maoists, the Revolutionary Communist Party (PCR), and the Popular Revolutionary Vanguard (*O Estado de São Paulo,* 1 July, 24 March).

The Movement for the Emancipation of the Proletariat (Movimento pela Emancipacao do Proletariado; MEP), apparently a dissident faction of the PCdoB, seemed to receive special attention from the police during the year. Eighteen members of the group were indicted in June although only seven were then under arrest. (*Jornal do Brasil,* 15 June; *O Globo,* 22 July.)

Trotskyists of various persuasions were also apparently active in 1977. The São Paulo police arrested a number of leaders of the Trotskyist Liga Operaria in May (*O Globo,* 5 May). During the year another Trotskyist group, aligned with the United Secretariat of the Fourth International, also appeared to be active. Its periodical, *Independencia Operaria,* campaigned against the workers cooperating with the legal opposition party, the MDB (*Intercontinental Press,* New York, 7 March).

Rutgers University   Robert J. Alexander

Canada

The Communist Party of Canada was founded in 1921. The legal party claims a membership of under 5,000; some sources estimate its membership at about 2,000. The population of Canada is 23,437,000 (estimated 1977). There are several other small Communist parties or groups. The Communist Party of Canada/Marxist-Leninist (CPC/M-L) is Maoist and now takes its orientation from Albania. It is especially active in the province of Quebec and has its headquarters in Montreal. The Canadian Communist League (M-L) apparently enjoys a better relationship with the present government in Peking. The League for Socialist Action/Ligue Socialist Ouvriere (LSA/LSO) is the most important Trotskyist organization in Canada. It has a youth wing, the Young Socialists. The Revolutionary Marxist Group (RMG) was founded in 1973 by LSA/LSO breakaways. The Red Circle group is composed of some left wing members of the New Democratic Party and the Old Mole, a student group at the University of Toronto. The Groupe Marxist Revolutionnaire (GMR) is the RMG's "sister organization" in Quebec, its founders being Trotskyists in Quebec who broke away from the LSA/LSO in the summer of 1972. The Workers League of Canada, which is the Canadian section of the International Committee of the Fourth International in Paris, confines its activities to Montreal. The Canadian Party of Labour (CPL) was founded by breakaways from the Progressive Workers Movement, the first pro-Maoist organization in Canada. Like the Progressive Labor Party in the USA, the CPL followed a pro-Chinese line until the improvement in Sino-U.S. relations.

It used to be said that most CPC members were elderly persons of East European origin, but that is no longer true. There has been energetic recruitment of younger members and these are active in the party. In the provincial election in Ontario on 9 June 1977 there were thirty three CPC candidates, more than half of whom were under forty years old. None were elected though altogether these candidates won some 8,300 votes. In federal by-elections in Quebec in May 1977, the CPC ran four candidates. Again none were elected. In Manitoba's provincial election there were five candidates, all unsuccessful. Thus the CPC has no federal or provincial representation. There are, however, CPC members or sympathizers who serve on municipal councils and local school boards.

The United Fishermen and the Allied Workers Union, on the West Coast, and the United Electrical, Radio, and Allied Workers Union, are unions in which Communists hold some leadership positions; also, a number of CPC members are officers in union locals and regional labor councils. Communists are influential on several district and town labor councils and in the British Columbia Federation of Labour. The CPC's influence is also to be seen in a half-dozen ethnic organizations of Canadians of East European origin.

CPC Leadership and Organization. William Kashtan continues as the CPC's general secretary. Alfred Dewhurst, the editor of *Communist Viewpoint,* is a member of the party's Central Executive Committee and director of its ideological work, writing a regular column on Marxist-Leninist theory, as it relates to contemporary problems, in the *Canadian Tribune.* Bruce Magnusson serves as labor secretary and contributes a labor column to the *Tribune.* Mel Doig and Gareth Blythe continue as members of the Central Committee along with Elizabeth Hill, who until recently was general secretary of the Young Communist League. William Stewart is the leader of the party in Ontario, William Ross in Manitoba, and John Bizzell is the chairman of the metropolitan Toronto organization. Mike Gidora is now the general secretary of the Young Communist League.

Sam Walsh is the president of the Parti Communiste du Québec (PCQ), which enjoys a certain autonomy within the CPC. Norman Freed, long a CPC organizer who had been editor of *Communist Viewpoint* and served on the council of the *World Marxist Review,* died in January. Jean Paré, former vice-president of the United Electrical Workers and leader in the CPQ, died in September.

Domestic Attitudes and Activities. The electoral success of Rene Levesque's Parti Quebecois, in late 1976, with its commitment to an independent Quebec outside the Canadian federation, created a crisis in Canadian politics. Originally Pierre Trudeau had been elected in 1968 on a one country-one nation principle which rejected the notion of French Canadians as a separate nation within Canada. The CPC has actively supported a united Canada but called for a constitution which would affirm Canada as one country composed of two founding nations—France and England. The CPC considers the Parti Quebecois a bourgeois middle class group and it fears the breakup of Canada would leave it more vulnerable to takeover by an imperialistic USA. The CPC called for the removal of wage and price controls imposed in October 1975. Unemployment has remained at a relatively high percentage of the work force and the demand that the Trudeau government create more jobs has been a theme of the weekly editorials in the *Tribune.* Since the signing of the arctic gas pipeline agreements with the U.S., the CPC has mounted a campaign to protect the native northern peoples from exploitation by multinational corporations. Revelations in Canada's parliament in Ottawa regarding the illegal acts carried out by the R.C.M.P. in the name of national security have provided further grist for the CPC mills of protest. The generally poor economic year Canada experienced in 1977, with its devalued dollar, inflationary pressures, and high unemployment, provided occasions for the CPC to emphasize what it regarded as the shortcomings of capitalism and the virtues of Communism. Economic difficulties provided the impetus for the recruitment drives of the Young Communist League (YCL).

International Views and Policies. The CPC generally supports positions taken by the Communist Party of the Soviet Union (CPSU) on international issues. The sixtieth anniversary of the October Revolution was celebrated in the CPC press and favorable attention was given to discussions in the USSR of the fourth Soviet constitution—discussions held up as an example of how a "real democracy" functions.

By contrast, the inauguration of U.S. President Carter and his campaign for human rights throughout the world were subject to unfavorable treatment. Whereas the Soviet Union was said to provide housing, health care, education, and employment for its citizens, such rights were deemphasized in Western countries and repudiated outright in Western support for repressive regimes in Chile. Thailand, South Africa, Israel, Brazil, Haiti, Uruguay, and other countries. Soviet dissidents such as Bukovsky, Solzhenitsyn, and Sakharov were dismissed as "darlings of the Western press" and it was charged that this press delighted in stories concerning Commmunist dissenters while ignorning the demonstrations of workers in their own countries. There was the usual negative treatment of NATO and NORAD agreements and a plea for Canada to withdraw from these organizations.

While there was praise for Cuba, Angola, and Ethiopia, the racial policies of South Africa and Rhodesia came in for criticism. The Pinochet government in Chile was regularly castigated and the released Chilean Communist leader Luis Corvalán was praised extensively. Israel received negative treatment as did those Canadians who criticized the Arab boycott of firms dealing with Israel. There was almost no mention of China nor of Mao Tse-tung's successor, Hua Kuo-feng. The notion of

"Eurocommunism," as expressed by Santiago Carrillo, general secretary of the Communist Party of Spain, was condemned.

While there was approval for everything President Carter did which increased detente, the neutron bomb project was the subject of unfavorable editorials and cartoons. The party was particularly critical of U.S. exploitation of Canadian natural resources.

International Activities and Contacts. In January 1977 William Kashtan attended the Fourth Congress of the Vietnam Workers' Party in Hanoi and Alfred Dewhurst was a delegate at the World Forum of Peace conference in Moscow. Kashtan was on the reviewing stand in Red Square for the Soviet Union's May Day parade. Dewhurst visited Warsaw, for the May meeting of the World Assembly of Builders of Peace, and the German Democratic Republic. Mel Doig and Gareth Blythe of the Central Committee represented the CPC in Baghdad for the thirtieth anniversary of the founding of Iraq's Arab Baath Socialist Party. Maggie Bizzell and Peter Boychuck represented the CPC at a meeting of the editorial council of the *World Marxist Review* in early May.

Communist Publications. The CPC publishes a theoretical journal, *Communist Viewpoint,* six times a year, and two weeklies, *Canadian Tribune* (Toronto) and *Pacific Tribune* (Vancouver). The PCQ issued the fortnightly *Combat* (Montreal). The organ of the YCL, *Young Worker* (Toronto) appears irregularly. Party members edit and publish various pro-Communist ethnic papers in languages other than English and French; the first issue of *Lotta Unitaria,* an Italian language paper edited by Orlando Buonostella, appeared in April.

The North American edition of the Prague-based *World Marxist Review* and its companion publication, the fortnightly *Information Bulletin,* are published in Toronto.

The CPC (M-L) organ, the *People's Canada Daily News,* appears regularly and follows a Maoist line—as set forth on Radio Tirana, Albania—primarily by its main Quebec spokesman, Hardial Bains. The Canadian Communist League (M-L) supported two fortnightlies, *In Struggle* and *The Forge.* The LSA/LSO publishes the bi-weekly *Labor Challenge* (Toronto). The French-language monthly, *Liberation,* continued to follow the labor strife and the separatist movement in Quebec. The *Young Socialist* (Toronto) is the organ of the LSA/LSO's youth wing. The Workers League of Canada has a monthly, *Labor Press,* in English and French, printed in the USA. The CPL monthly, *Worker* (Toronto), publishes articles in English, French, and Italian.

University of San Francisco   Desmond J. FitzGerald

Chile

The Communist Party of Chile (Partido Comunista de Chile; PCCh) was first established as the Socialist Workers' Party in 1912 by Luis Emilio Recabarren. The name PCCh was adopted in January 1922 following the party's decision in 1921 to join the Communist International. The party was illegal between 1948 and 1958. A pro-Chinese party, the Revolutionary Communist Party of Chile (Partido Comunista Revolucionario de Chile; PCRCh), was established in May 1966, primarily by a group of Communists expelled from the PCCh in 1963. The Movement of the Revolutionary Left (Movimiento de Izquierda Revolucionaria; MIR) brought together several leftist groups in 1965 and soon developed an affinity for the form of revolutionary struggle advocated during the middle and late 1960s by Che Guevara and Fidel Castro. All of these groups have been illegal since the military coup of September 1973.

The PCCh, which reported a membership of 60,000 at the time of its last congress in 1969, claimed 200,000 members in early 1973. Many party leaders have been killed, imprisoned, or forced into exile since September 1973, though most PCCh members remain free in Chile. At its height before the military coup the PCRCh probably had several hundred active members but, after internal dissension, there are fewer today. The MIR, which may have had 5,000 active members in mid-1973, has been hardest hit by Chilean security forces; its membership has been greatly reduced and its top leaders are dead, in jail, or abroad.

Movement for Leftist Unity. Between 1956 and 1969 the PCCh allied itself for electoral purposes with the Socialist Party of Chile (Partido Socialista de Chile; PSCh) in the Popular Action Front (Frente de Acción Popular; FRAP). Realizing that a still broader front had to be established to secure victory at the polls, the PCCh led in forming the Popular Unity (Unidad Popular; UP) in 1969, an alliance of leftist parties which enabled Salvador Allende to win a narrow plurality in the elections of September 1970. At the beginning of 1977 members of the UP—all of which were outlawed in Chile—were: the PCCh, the PSCh, the Radical Party (PR), the Christian Left (IC), the Movement of United Popular Action (MAPU), a MAPU splinter group calling itself the Worker-Peasant MAPU (MAPU-OC), and the Independent Popular Action (API), essentially the composition of the original 1969 alliance.

The Popular Unity alliance, under the leadership of Socialist Salvador Allende, controlled the Chilean executive branch of government during the 1970-73 period despite ongoing dissension within its ranks with respect to the proper strategy and tactics of revolution. During the Allende period the unity of the Popular Unity alliance was further weakened by disputes with non-UP revolutionary groups that adopted a more militant revolutionary line, particularly the MIR. Since the coup the PCCh has led the drive to build a broader and more secure leftist front, ranging from the Christian Democrats (PDC) on the right to the MIR and other groups on what it has long considered the "ultra-left." Other Marxist parties have supported this drive in varying degrees, some PSCh members in particular playing an active role.

A UP document signed in Santiago in December 1976, and circulated widely abroad in early

1977, asserted that the majority of Chileans had come to oppose the military government and noted that "sectarianism, the source of so much harm, is noticeably on the wane under the impact of harsh and bloody lessons" (*IB*, No. 4, 1977). The Popular Unity Political Committee met in Stockholm at the end of March and published a declaration (in *Neues Deutschland,* East Berlin, 29 March) presenting the analyses and objectives of the UP Marxist left. The declaration commented on what the Popular Unity leaders saw as the "positive attitudes of the Catholic Church" on some issues, such as human rights, and took particular note of the outlawing of the middle-of-the-road parties (most importantly the Christian Democrats), concluding that this latter action proved the military government could not maintain control in the country while even a semblance of democratic practice remained. Another document, released on 1 November after a meeting in Berlin, claimed UP leadership of increasing opposition to the Pinochet government by labor unions, slum dwellers, workers, and the unemployed. It found the Christian Democratic statement "A Homeland for All" an important contribution to leftist unity. It called for "democratic renovation rather than restoration" since the political system overthrown in 1973, with its "vices of politicking," had not been a true democracy. The UP asserted the legitimacy of resorting to violence to eliminate the military government, but added that this general affirmation did not imply the indiscriminate acceptance of violence nor anticipation, lacking in real content, of the concrete forms which the defeat of the government would take. (*Granma,* Havana, English edition, 13 November.)

Representatives of the Popular Unity and the MIR met in Mexico City in January 1977 to set up the Secretariat of Solidarity with Chile, with headquarters in the Mexican capital, to coordinate solidarity activities of the Chilean Left throughout the continent. Luis Maira, a former congressman from the Christian Left, was chosen executive secretary. The official publication of the Secretariat is the bulletin *Chile Informativo,* edited in Havana and published in Mexico. But this meeting did not resolve the differences between the UP leaders and the MIR. UP executive secretary, Socialist Clodomiro Almeyda, met with representatives of other UP parties and the MIR at UP headquarters in East Berlin in mid-August and pledged to "overthrow the Chilean military dictatorship." A communique, released at the end of the month in Paris, called for united activities on a number of fronts and established a calendar of meetings between the UP and the MIR "which should serve as the basis for solving theoretical, political, and practical problems on which they still differ." (AFP, Paris, 28 August.) According to the Cuban press, the declaration stated that, following a study of the main issues on which the two organizations differ, it was thought that these differences could be ironed out through "frank and respectful ideological struggle on the basis of mutual respect, with stress on unity in the struggle against the common enemy" (*Granma,* Havana, English ed., 28 August). Although several of the most left-wing Christian Democrats have been close to the UP since the coup, a declaration released by exiled PDC leaders in Caracas in October rejected the formation of a "resistance front" with the UP. This has not prevented a degree of cooperation on labor and other issues in Chile (see below).

PCCh: Leadership and Organization. Luis Corvalán, PCCh general secretary, was released from prison in December 1976 in exchange for the freedom of a Soviet political prisoner. Political commission members and alternate members who are active in exile include Orlando Millas, Rodrigo Rojas, Volodia Teitelboim, José Cademártori, Jorge Insunza, Manuel Cantero, and Gladys Marín, the latter also general secretary of the Communist Youth (Juventud Comunista de Chile; JCCh). Carvalán said in mid-March that although the party "has been the target of many savage blows" its "organization and vitality have been preserved" (*IB,* No. 6). Most party members remain in Chile, but maintain a fairly low profile. The once-powerful, Communist-dominated Single Center of Chilean Workers (CUT) has been outlawed and the Communist Youth, for years a powerful force in university politics, has been driven underground. Both the CUT and the Communist Youth remain active abroad, the labor central in particular getting powerful backing from such international labor organizations as the World Federation of Trade Unions.

During the year, General Secretary Corvalán received a number of awards for his "outstanding achievements in the international communist movement and his active participation in the struggle for peace, social progress and against imperialism and fascism" (words of Soviet Presidium President Podgorni), among them the Order of Lenin from the Soviet Union and the Georgi Dimitrov Order from the People's Republic of Bulgaria.

The party held its first Central Committee plenary session since the coup during the month of August in Mexico City. Corvalán read a 166-page report to the meeting which examined the domestic and international issues surveyed below.

PCCh: Domestic Attitudes and Activities. Although isolated Communist statements were circulated within Chile during the year, most published analyses were made by party leaders in exile. Commentaries focused primarily on two interrelated topics—the "lessons" to be learned from the Allende period and the organization of a broad leftist front to overthrow the military government. A third, but less seriously examined topic, was what kind of political system should be established if (or, as they put it, when) the military government is vanquished.

A "Manifesto" issued in May stated that the PCCh proposals, "in a nutshell," were: "First, let us engage in a joint action to overthrow the tyranny; second, let us seek the community of ideas that will permit the construction of a new democracy; and third, let us establish a government in which all the antifascist forces are represented" (*Granma*, Havana, English ed., 3 July).

The revolution the PCCh seeks has been set forth by the party: "We view the Chilean revolution as a movement of the working class and organized population which, by means of the mass struggle, removes the ruling classes from power, liquidates the old state apparatus and production relations obstructing development of the productive forces, and carries out profound transformations in the country's economic, social and political structure, opening the way to socialism" (*WMR*, June).

Lessons of the Allende Period. The reasons for the failure of the UP government between 1970 and 1973 have been discussed at great length for several years, but never so fully as in 1977. A crucial problem was the failure of the UP government to maintain a solid and homogeneous revolutionary leadership which could mobilize the masses and act decisively. According to Gladys Marín: "Many of the decisive debates on whether or not the revolutionary process was being led correctly were only held 'at the summit' or in very narrow circles. As a result, difficulties arising from the lack of a single leadership increased, which repeatedly found expression in divisive and anarchist moves and at times tended to paralyze the government." (*WMR*, July.) Ultra-leftists, who, according to PCCh officials prevented leftist unity in UP leadership, took advantage of UP mistakes to attack the government and its potential allies and gave the traditionalists ammunition in their important psychological war against President Allende and those who sought to assist him (*WMR*, February, March, July). According to Manuel Cantero, "imperialism drew up the strategy, stages and forms of counter-revolutionary struggle against the UP government." Still the many difficulties created by the imperialists then and now are "not insurmountable when the consciousness and efforts of the people are merged with solidarity and assistance from all parts of the world." (*WMR*, August.)

United Front Tactics During 1977. As Jorge Insunza said in the *World Marxist Review* in May, the PCCh blames much of the failure of the early 1970s on its inability to unite all democratic forces against the country's fascists. Resistance from both the UP and PDC had prevented essential compromises, according to Gladys Marín (*WMR*, July). Thus throughout 1977 the party sought to increase pressure on the military government by pulling together the UP and the Christian Democrats in a broad, loose, anti-fascist alliance. The need for such a front was elaborated in a party

"Manifesto" drawn up in May, which said: "If we look the facts straight in the eye, we can conclude that Popular Unity cannot today reinstate democracy by itself, and neither can the Christian Democratic Party, by itself. Reality decrees that an alliance of all those opposed to the tyranny is required." The "Manifesto" recognized that differences which could not be ignored remained between the two groups but maintained that the UP could reach an understanding with the PDC without compromising its principles. (*Granma*, 3 July.) In line with this position, early in the year the PCCh put three proposals to the PDC with respect to an alliance: (1) that the Christian Democrats agree to work with the UP; (2) that both groups look for common ground with respect to a future political system for Chile; and (3) that an understanding be reached on the formation of a new government of all democratic forces following the downfall of the military regime (*WMR*, February). Moderate and conservative Christian Democrats did not respond warmly to these proposals, however, and although the party continued to call for a working agreement, as it did at the August plenary session of the Central Committee, statements by individual PCCh leaders sometimes became more barbed. Addressing a Cuban labor audience in Havana in June, Corvalán commented that the PDC "does not want the sudden overthrow of the dictatorship; it wants gradual change . . . . It is against the dictatorship and fascism, but only wants half-baked change." (*Granma*, 19 June.)

The post-military government sought by the PCCh has been described briefly on many occasions. The May "Manifesto" spoke of "a joint government of all antifascists, chiefly of Popular Unity and the Christian Democratic Party, because such a government would really represent the majority of the people." This government would "totally eradicate fascism and give way to a new democratic regime and the resumption of social transformations." (*Granma*, 3 July.) Drawing lessons from past experiences, Insunza gave a slightly more specific picture of what state structure the Communists think would best carry out major transformations in the future: "The decisive factor is the deep-going democratization of the state apparatus, the creation of mechanisms instituting genuine popular control over the functioning of the state, and transfer of as many as possible of its powers to the masses." He pointed in particular to the positive and encouraging experiences in this field in the control, distribution, and pricing of staple goods. Control "from below," he argued, allows the masses "to realize their power in practice and to promote essential changes in the state apparatus from outside, changes that are effected with the assistance of the revolutionary leadership from within." (*WMR*, May.)

Some cooperative actions which might be called "converging plans of action" (*Le Monde*, Paris, 22 February) have taken place. Communist leaders have claimed cooperation with other "progressives and democratic forces" in the universities, unions, and local communities, such as a petition to the government by 122 union leaders seeking permission to celebrate May Day, and assorted "human rights" protests, including exile campaigns against the docking in foreign ports of the Chilean training vessel "Esmerelda" (Corvalán interview in *Tribuna Popular*, Caracas, 17-23 June).

PCCh: International Attitudes and Activities. Prior to the 1973 coup, the PCCh was extraordinarily interested in international affairs, but since then its concerns have shifted. Although pro forma denunciations of the Chinese Communists continued, in 1977 proletarian internationalism meant chiefly international support for efforts to overthrow the Chilean military government. Exiled PCCh leaders travelled ceaselessly, particularly in Eastern and Western Europe and the Soviet Union, promoting international opposition to the Chilean government and support for its "anti-fascist" front. Support groups operate in and out of many countries, the most important in the Western Hemisphere being Cuba, the United States, Canada, Venezuela, and Mexico. With the support of assorted pro-Soviet international front organizations, such as the World Federation of

Trade Unions, and other groups, it played an important role in a variety of international meetings, campaigns, and declarations.

*   *   *

The Revolutionary Communist Party. The PCRCh has been weakened in recent years by Chilean government suppression and by internal dissension, the latter resulting from disputes over domestic strategy and tactics, on the one hand, and confusion over the direction of Chinese international policies. As party leaders have disputed among themselves, membership has fallen. Policy statements are rare. The most recent comprehensive elaboration of PCRCh positions emerged following the Seventh Congress of the Albanian Workers Party in November 1976, a meeting attended by so-called "Marxist-Leninist" Communist parties from seven Latin American countries (Chile, Argentina, Bolivia, Brazil, Colombia, Ecuador, and Uruguay). According to a joint statement published in January 1977 in *No Transar,* the organ of the Communist Party of Argentina (ML), the PCRCh and its fraternal parties concluded the following:

1. The present situation in Latin America favors the peoples and their revolutionary struggles;
2. Both imperialist superpowers, the United States and the Soviet Union, are "actively preparing a new world war" and are "the major enemies of the peoples" of the world;
3. Progressive forces around the world, assisted by Socialist China and Albania, are building a broad international front in opposition to both superpowers;
4. Latin American peoples cannot liberate themselves unless they smash the predatory and aggressive Yankee imperialism which now dominates the continent in cooperation with dictatorial, military and fascist regimes in power in most countries;
5. The Russian social-imperialists, like U.S. imperialists, have no interest in helping liberate the Latin American people, but rather seek only to exploit and dominate the continent;
6. Only the proletariat and its Marxist-Leninist party can lead the national democratic and popular revolutionary movements in each country by uniting the peoples and showing them the way to victory through armed struggle of the masses;
7. The "revisionist (i.e. pro-Soviet) Communist parties merely seek to check the struggle of the masses, deceive the workers, and "open the way for Soviet domination" of the continent; they are the "agents of Russian social imperialism, its fifth column in the patriotic and popular movements."

The parties concluded by expressing their sorrow over the death of Mao Tse-tung and their support for the "brilliant successes" of the Albanian congress.

The Movement of the Revolutionary Left. The MIR has been particularly hard-hit by government security forces since September 1973. The organization has lost important leaders through death and defection; Edgardo Enriquez, Bautista Van Schowen, and Jorge Fuentes are among those in prison or missing. Ex-president Allende's nephew, Andres Pascal Allende, is in exile. The most outspoken MIR leader abroad in 1977 was Central Committee member Victor Toro, formerly head of the MIR's Revolutionary Workers' Front (FTR), who was released from prison and expelled from the country in December 1976. In an interview given in Cuba in early 1977 (see *Chile Newsletter,* Berkeley, February-March), Toro recognized the need for leftist unity in order to overthrow the military government, but pointedly excluded any cooperative efforts with former Chilean President Eduardo Frei and his followers in the PDC. According to Toro, a Popular Resistance Movement within the country must employ "diverse and unusual means to undermine the dictatorship." These are said to include legal, semi-legal, and clandestine forms of struggle, including the sabotage of such facilities as railroad tracks and docks. Resistance Committees, he said, are being organized in factories, poblaciones, schools, and army barracks. Under the impact of domestic and foreign criticism, the MIR leader argued that the Chilean government was trying to "introduce policy readjustments" without changing its actual objectives, which are to perpetuate itself in power and repress the activity of the working class. He argued that "the dictatorship's strength or weakness depends fundamentally on the degree of imperialist aid it receives," adding that International solidarity with the Resistance Movement plays an important role in weakening the military government.

Publications. The illegal Marxist and Marxist-Leninist parties and organizations of Chile circulate irregular clandestine papers and leaflets domestically and publish limited-circulation but legal newspapers abroad. These include *Unidad Antifascista* and *Principios* (PCCh), *Liberación* (JCCh), *El Rebelde* (MIR), *La Chispa* (PSCh), *Frente Antifascista* (UP), and three publications of the ultra-leftist factions of the PDC, *Resistencia Democrática, Venceremos,* and *Pueblo Cristiano.* Communist Party statements circulate most widely in the regular journals of individual pro-Soviet Communist parties around the world, as well as in the *World Marxist Review* and its *Information Bulletin.* MIR (as well as PCCh) statements appear periodically in Cuban and sympathetic U.S. and European papers and journals.

Hoover Institution   William E. Ratliff
Stanford University

Colombia

The Communist movement in Colombia began within the ranks of the Socialist Revolutionary Party (Partido Socialista Revolucionario; PSR) shortly after the party's formation in December 1926. Contacts between the PSR and the Communist International during 1929 and 1930 inspired a group of PSR members to proclaim publicly the creation of the Communist Party of Colombia (Partido Comunista de Colombia; PCC) on 17 July 1930. The party has retained this designation ever since except for a short period (1944-47) during which it was called the Social Democratic Party (Partido Social Democrático). In July 1965 a schism within the PCC between pro-Soviet and pro-Chinese factions resulted in the latter's becoming the Communist Party of Colombia, Marxist-Leninist (Partido Comunista de Colombia, Marxista-Leninista; PCC-ML). Only the PCC has legal status. It has been allowed to participate in elections under its own banners since 1972.

The PCC participated in the 1974 general elections as a member of the leftist coalition National Opposition Union (Unión de Oposición Nacional; UNO), founded in September 1972. The coalition won two seats in the 112-member Senate and five seats in the 199-member Lower Chamber. Of these, PCC members occupy one of the Lower chamber seats from Cundinamarca and the seat from Cauca. In the 1976 midterm elections for state assemblies and municipal corporations, the UNO coalition was severely weakened by the defection of the pro-Chinese Independent Revolutionary Workers Movement (MOIR), which offered a separate slate of candidates. The PCC-dominated UNO won slightly more than a third of the nationwide vote of 9 percent for leftist parties. The MOIR secured approximately 1.5 percent, while the other major opposition party, the National Popular Alliance (ANAPO), obtained the balance. The concentration of UNO support in Bogotá was sufficient to elect two deputies to the Cundinamarca Assembly, both of whom are members of the PCC's Central Committee. Congressional, assembly and municipal elections are scheduled for 25 February 1978. Colombia's next presidential election will be held on 4 June 1978.

According to U.S. intelligence estimates, the PCC has 10,000 to 12,000 members. Although confident that the party's rank and file has increased in recent years, the PCC concluded at its Sixth Organizational Conference in January that the party's growth has been "less than hoped for" in general, and "especially disappointing in the large cities" (*Voz Proletaria*, 20 January). The PCC exercises only marginal influence in national affairs. The population of Colombia is estimated at 24,880,000 (1977).

Guerrilla warfare, although not a serious threat to the government, has been a feature of Colombian life since the late 1940s, the current wave beginning in 1964. The three main guerrilla organizations are the Revolutionary Armed Forces of Colombia (FARC), long controlled by the PCC; the pro-Chinese People's Liberation Army (EPL), which is the guerrilla arm of the PCC-ML; and the Castroite National Liberation Army (ELN). The FARC and the ELN probably have between 250 to 300 guerrillas each, along with an undetermined number of urban supporters. The EPL is believed to have fewer than 100 members.

According to Colombian intelligence services, the success of the army in combatting guerrilla militants has increased their willingness to overcome ideological differences in seeking some degree of unified action. It was reported in February that efforts were being made to hold a guerrilla summit meeting to study the situation (*El Tiempo*, 20 February). Although EPL spokesmen continue to resist attempts at guerrilla unification, Colombian sources indicated in May that the ELN and the FARC had agreed to modify their strategy and operate separately in rural and urban sectors. According to the agreement, the FARC would continue to operate in rural sectors, while the ELN, because of its broader connections in the cities, would concentrate its activities in the urban sector, especially within university circles (*El Siglo*, 4 May). On 13 May Colombia's defense minister stated that military operations in the northeast and middle and lower Magdalena areas had reduced FARC and ELN units "to a state of impotence" (*El Tiempo*, 14 May). However, by October the ELN was rumored to be in the process of reorganization under its former leader, Fabio Vásquez Castaño, while the FARC appeared to be gaining strength in the southeast of the country. On the basis of bulletins issued during the course of the year, leaders of both groups, along with the urban movement M-19, continued to advocate guerrilla unity as the only means to avoid their dissolution.

The urban guerrilla movement M-19 marked its third anniversary on 25 February by pledging to continue its revolutionary struggle. On 29 March the M-19 issued a twelve-page bulletin to newspapers proposing the formation of a popular army by means of "revolutionary violence." In analyzing the country's situation, the document called for "a revolution to expel Yankee imperialism, to end monopolies and the oligarchy, to nationalize and distribute land, and to turn the government and power over to the people." (Ibid., 30 March.) In a communiqué released on 28 July, the M-19 proposed the nomination of a single opposition candidate for the 1978 presidential elections and called for unity among Colombia's guerrilla forces in order to carry forward "a popular revolution of national liberation aimed toward socialism" (AFP, Paris, 29 July). In an independent operation, the M-19 claimed credit for the 20 August kidnaping of a former agriculture minister, now the manager of the Indupalma Company, who was released unharmed on 16 September after the company signed a labor contract favorable to striking workers. The M-19, which achieved notoriety in 1976 with the kidnaping and "execution" of José Rafael Mercado, president of the powerful Confederation of Workers of Colombia (CTC), warned that it would "continue struggling for the welfare of the working class" (*El Tiempo,* 17 September).

In response to the periodic intensification of rural and urban guerrilla activities in 1977, which included a rash of ten kidnapings during the first three months of the year, various attacks on military outposts, and the occasional ransacking of small towns, the minister of justice declared on 1 November that the "promoters of terrorism" would soon be overcome. He dismissed the possibility that guerrilla forces had gained strength during the year, stating that "recent attacks are isolated incidents which do not disrupt the nation's order" (*El Tiempo,* 2 November).

The PCC: Leadership and Organization. The PCC is headed by its twelve-member Executive Committee and fifty-four-member Central Committee. The highest party authority is the congress, convened by the Central Committee at four-year intervals. The PCC held its Twelfth Congress on 5-9 December 1975 in Bogotá. The party congress elects the Central Committee, which is responsible for all party activity between congresses. The Central Committee meets at six-month intervals and in turn is responsible for the election of a national Secretariat and the all-important Central Executive Committee. Gilberto Vieira is general secretary of the PCC. Members of the Executive Committee include, besides Vieira: Alvaro Vásquez, Jesús Villegas, Joaquín Moreno, Roso Osorio, Hernando Hurtado, Julio Posada, Gustavo Castro, Teodosio Varela, Gustavo Osorio, Juan Viana, Manlio Lafont, and Manuel Cepeda Vargas. The first four named are also members of the National Secretariat.

A major source of the PCC's influence lies in its control over the Trade Union Confederation of Workers of Colombia (CSTC), which claims a membership of 300,000. The CSTC was granted legal status by the Colombian government in August 1974 and is a member of the World Federation of Trade Unions (WFTU). The president of the CSTC is Pástor Pérez. Other prominent members are General Secretary Roso Osorio, Luis Hernán Sabogal, Luis Carlos Pérez, Julio Poveda, and Alcibiades Aguiree.

In what was perhaps its most active and successful year of operation, the CSTC helped to achieve an unprecedented degree of cooperation among Colombia's four major labor centrals in 1977. The CSTC issued a plea to other labor centrals for a unified plan of action at its Fifth Plenum held on 8-9 December 1976. On 17 February the CSTC and the PCC organized a public demonstration to protest the high cost of living and the state of siege decreed in effect since June 1976 (*Voz Proletaria,* 20 February). In March the CSTC participated in a demonstration march of solidarity against the government's handling of a strike by state petroleum workers. According to Roso Osorio, the CSTC provided the occasion with "the physical presence of the working class" and gave incentive to prepare for a demonstration of unity on 1 May (ibid., 10 March). In April the CSTC and the General Confederation of Workers (CGT) issued a joint communiqué calling for solidarity in the defense of workers' rights. In a separate manifesto, the CSTC protested against the rising cost of living, growing unemployment, and the scarcity of food staples (ibid., 21 April). Significantly, impartial reports on the various acts held throughout Colombia on 1 May noted that for the first time in many years, all four major labor centrals participated in joint protests in many cities.

Buoyed by the relative success of the May Day demonstrations, the CSTC took the initiative in calling for a unified national strike to manifest popular discontent. On 2 August the CSTC headed a list of leftist labor organizations, student associations, and political parties that communicated their protest to President López Michelsen. Specific demands called for a general wage increase of at least 50 percent; a freeze on the price of staples; the lifting of the state of siege; the reopening and demilitarization of universities; land reform; and the abolition of administrative regulations that violate the rights of association, bargaining and striking for state workers (*El Espectador,* 7 August). On 12 August the Confederation of Workers of Colombia (CTC) voted to participate along with the Union of Workers of Colombia (UTC) in the national strike called for by the CSTC (*El Tiempo,* 13 August). In ratifying the strike order, the executive committees of the country's major labor centrals formalized their unity of action and broke off talks with the government. The government responded on 30 August when a government minister categorically warned that the administration would not allow itself "to be overthrown by political strikes" and reaffirmed its authority "to apply the law" against the total cessation of labor activities (*El Siglo,* 31 August). Government spokesmen subsequently denounced the "subversive motives" of the strike and censured the labor leaders for their "senseless and unpatriotic attitude" (*El Tiempo,* 3 September). During the course of the strike on 14 September, 23 persons were killed, hundreds were injured, and an estimated 4,000 persons were arrested. On 11 October the presidents of the four labor centrals met in Bogotá to lay the basis for a demonstration to protest the "deaths, detentions, and disappearance of workers resulting from the 14 September strike" (ibid., 11 October). Tulio Cuevas, president of the UTC and one of the most authoritative trade union leaders in Colombia, emphasized the fact that the unity achieved by the trade unions in the September strike would be maintained. He also spoke of the possibility of forming "a permanent council of a consultative nature in which the organizations that came together to launch the recent strike will be represented" (*Alternativa,* 17 October). In contrast to the violent disorders that broke out during the September strike, the demonstrations organized on 18 November in at least twenty cities were conducted without major incident. According to Gustavo Osorio, an estimated three million workers participated in activities throughout the country to protest "the government's total indifference to the workers' just demands which had led to the civic strike on 14 September" (*Voz Proletaria,* 24 November).

At the Twelfth Party Congress, the PCC stated that it was necessary to work through the organizations of the one-million-member National Peasant Association of Land Users (ANUC) for the purpose of involving them in unitary action with the working class. Although founded by the government in 1968 to encourage peasant participation in the development and implementation of agrarian reform, the "Sincelejo" faction of ANUC soon established a militantly independent policy. Its leadership also adopted and maintained a strongly anti-Communist policy to the point of refusing to seat PCC delegations at regional and national meetings. On 3-6 December 1976 the CSTC organized its first National Peasant Congress in Bogotá, signaling an end to the PCC's efforts to overcome the anti-Communist sentiments within ANUC and marking the beginning of an attempt to establish direct links with the rural proletariat and landless peasants. In a series of editorials leading up to the congress, the PCC attributed ANUC's "ruination" to the "corrosive presence" of Maoists and their "systematic divisiveness" (ibid., 11 November 1976). The congress created the National Federation of Agrarian Syndicates (Federación Nacional Sindical Agraria; FENSA), which functions as part of the CSTC. FENSA has a national directorate composed of thirty-five members and an executive committee which includes, among others, Saúl Zambrano, president; Isidro López, vice president, Luis Hernán Sabogal, head of agrarian relations in the CSTC and one of the principal organizers of the congress, general secretary; and Raúl Herrera, treasurer. The creation of a separate, Communist peasant federation attests to the PCC's failure to prevent ANUC's independent leadership from focusing exclusively on agrarian problems, to the exclusion of the working class.

The PCC's youth organization, the Communist Youth of Colombia (Juventud Comunista de Colombia; JUCO), was organized on 1 May 1952 and has an estimated membership of 2,000. JUCO has its own national directorate, executive committee, and central committee. The general secretary is Jaime Caicedo. JUCO held its Fourth National Congress in Bogotá from 10-14 November 1976. According to party sources, the social composition of delegates was: 28 percent university students, 17 percent high school graduates, 17 percent white-collar workers, 17 percent peasants, 8 percent student-workers, 6 percent salaried workers, and 5 percent university professionals. Approximately one-third of the delegates working within specific mass organizations were involved with student-related activities. The average age of delegates was twenty-three, with the largest percentage having been active in JUCO for a period ranging from one to five years (*Voz Proletaria,* 18 November 1976). The central document approved by the congress called for opposition to "imperialist influence" among educational circles and renewed efforts to unify the student movement. JUCO reaffirmed its support for the National Union of University Students (UNEU), organized in 1973, and the corresponding Union of High School Students (UNES), indicating its intention to establish a broader and more flexible affiliation with both organizations in 1977. The document also noted the role assigned to JUCO in raising the class consciousness among the working youth associated with the CSTC in both the industrial and agrarian sectors. (Ibid.) In April JUCO's leadership called for poltical unity among all "democratic and progressive youth" in protesting against "military repression in rural areas and the dangerous advance of reactionary forces seeking to militarize the country" (*Voz Proletaria,* 14 April). The MOIR and other anti-Soviet groups continued to hamper JUCO's efforts to establish unity within the university student movement. MOIR's opposition to the PCC-dominated UNEU and its role leading up to the suspension of classes at the National University for much of the year produced numerous editorials in the Communist press denouncing the Maoist groups' "anarchist tendencies" (ibid., 9 June). As a militant adjunct of the PCC, the JUCO supported the national strikes of 14 September and 18 November. JUCO is among the youth organizations comprising the National Committee preparing for the Eleventh World Youth Festival to be held in Cuba in 1978.

The PCC has controlled a peasant guerrilla group since 1966, the Revolutionary Armed Forces of Colombia (FARC). Party leaders have maintained an ambivalent attitude in recent years toward the use of armed struggle in furthering the revolutionary process. Although the political resolution adopted at the Twelfth Congress affirmed that "the guerrilla movement in the rural areas [has] always been a notable factor in the general popular struggle [and] is a component of the tactics of correctly combining all forms of action," the general position of the party is that armed struggle cannot yet be the chief means of resistance (*IB*, 31 January 1976). At this point in time, the PCC does not wish to jeopardize its quest to achieve power through an electoral coalition of opposition groups. The party's lack of total commitment to armed struggle is a continuous source of irritation to FARC leaders. Early in the year, the FARC circulated a bulletin blaming the PCC for the recent setbacks suffered by guerrilla groups and for the failure of attempts to seize power by force (EFE, Madrid, 16 February). In February, Mario Marulanda Vélez, the supreme commander of FARC and a member of the PCC's Central Committee, broke his silence of several years to propose the creation of "a single front of popular struggle to seize power." With regard to the lack of unity among the various guerrilla movements, Marulanda stated: "Our purposes are the same, but we disagree on methods, on ideological conceptions, on military and political strategy, and to some extent on tactics" (*El Espectador,* 23 February). Marulanda completely rejected any possibility of reaching an understanding with the EPL, which he criticized as an anti-Communist and anti-FARC movement. He suggested the possibility that an agreement could be reached with the ELN for the formation of a single liberation front, although the same self-centered policies that have prevented any unification of political positions among Colombia's guerrilla groups in the past are unlikely to be overcome in the immediate future.

The FARC maintained five active guerrilla fronts in 1977: the first and second in Caquetá; the third in the central Cordillera; the fourth in middle Magdalena; and the fifth in Antioquia. According to FARC leader Jacobo Arenas, the political nucleus of each unit is in essence a Communist cell. The minimal guerrilla unit consists of twelve men. The leadership mechanisms and general policy of the FARC are determined by the PCC's bylaws and political resolutions emitted at various congresses and plenums, and presumably transmitted to the various fronts through Marulanda's directives. Arenas admitted that as of May, no agreement had yet been reached with the ELN to synchronize guerrilla action (*Alternativa,* 7 May).

The FARC was most active of Colombia's rural guerrilla movements in 1977. In April FARC units attacked and looted small towns in Cundinamarca and Huila departments. Similar attacks were reported in Antioquia, Caldas, and Córdoba in May, where guerrillas confiscated supplies of food and medicine (*El Expectador,* 11 May). In July the FARC claimed credit for the execution of ten persons accused of "using the name of the guerrillas to commit crimes." In separate bulletins sent to local news media, the FARC and the ELN announced that they would continue to execute criminals who, posing as guerrillas, engaged in extortion and murder. Both guerrilla groups vowed to continue their revolutionary struggle, while simultaneously fighting against bandits and drug traffickers (AFP, 4 July). Meanwhile, the FARC continued to carry out its own kidnapings for ransom and the assassination of peasants and former guerrilla members accused of cooperating with military authorities. In September FARC guerrillas claimed responsibility for separate bombing incidents that destroyed sections of the oil pipeline running from Barrancabermeja to Antioquia (*El Tiempo,* 23 September). On 23 September FARC spokesmen confirmed that they were holding Richard Starr, a Peace Corps botanist who was kidnaped in a small village in La Macarena mountains on 28 February. According to a clandestine communiqué, Starr admitted to being a member of the CIA and requested that the U.S. Embassy intervene to obtain his release (AFP, 23 September). A subsequent report published in *Resistencia* claimed that Starr had been kidnaped in reprisal for the foreign exploitation of Colombia's natural resources (RCN, 1 December). A rash of kidnapings and clashes with military patrols in the Cimitarra region of Santander was reported in October, including the execution of two ranchers who were apparently killed when ransom demands went unmet (*El Espectador,* 27 October). Although military authorities periodically announced "heavy" guerrilla casualties and the seizure of arms caches from FARC units, there appeared to be no reduction in the FARC's varied and widespread operations at year's end, especially in Tolima, Huila, and Caquetá departments.

Domestic Attitudes and Activities. The PCC's Central Committee held a plenary session in Bogotá on 17-18 January to discuss the general political situation and to consider the resolutions adopted at the Sixth Organizational Conference held earlier in the month. The plenum adopted the basis of a common program "to take a new step forward on the way to creating a patriotic front of national liberation." Specifically, the PCC proposed to struggle (1) against the economic, political, military, and cultural infiltration of imperialism; (2) for democratic and trade union rights; (3) for an agrarian reform that would ensure transfer of land to the peasants; (4) for the nationalization of oil and other natural resources; (5) for popular unity; and (6) to overcome anti-Communist and anarchistic tendencies which induce splits (*Voz Proletaria,* 20 January).

In support of its position that greater unity is necessary to further the struggle for "democratic changes," the Executive Committee issued a statement in April calling upon popular forces to agree on a single candidate for the 1978 presidential election (ibid., 7 April). By May it was evident that the acceptance of a common political program and the selection of a candidate capable of unifying opposition groups were becoming increasingly unrealistic goals. PCC spokesmen expressed growing concern over factionalism and the threat represented by the Socialist wing of ANAPO. In the face of increasing dissension, the PCC adopted the position of moving ahead with an electoral campaign organized around UNO (ibid., 19 May).

During an interview in Prague, Gilberto Vieira declared that the PCC and its allies within UNO were preparing an election platform which would "state the demand for profound changes in the country's economic and social structure and show the people of Colombia a real solution to their current difficult problems." He added the platform would define the ultimate prospects for building a Socialist society in Colombia, demanding, among other things, "the abolition of the state of emergency, the implementation of a genuine land reform, and the safeguarding of national independence." In discussing the PCC's domestic policies, Vieira defined the main task of the party as "the struggle for the unity of the Colombian working class." He attributed existing divisions within the workers' movement to the influence of the ruling classes, North American imperialism, and the reactionary forces within the heirarchy of the Catholic Church. Vieira also emphasized the PCC's activity aimed at strengthening the alliance between the working class and the working peasants on the basis of their common struggle for fundamental demands (*Voz Proletaria,* 20 June.)

The PCC's concern over factionalism proved to be well-founded. By mid-year UNO's efforts at unification were being seriously challenged by the creation of a new coalition of opposition groups consisting of the largest faction of ANAPO, headed by José Jaramillo Giraldo; members of the broad-based Movement of Colombia (MAC); the Popular Revolutionary Democratic Committees (CDPR); and the MOIR. During a large rally in Bogotá on 15 July, ex-ANAPO Senator Jaime Piedrahita Cardona was nominated presidential candidate for this coalition of the "Revolutionary Left" (*El Tiempo,* 16 July). The new movement's platform differs from that of the UNO mainly in the desire to establish a Socialist state free from any foreign domination, including that of the Soviet Union. This obviously reduces the probability of collaboration with the PCC-dominated UNO.

On 7 August the UNO and the PCC announced their decision to launch the presidential candidacy of ex-ANAPO Congressman Julio César Pernía. The coalition outlined a presidential platform based on policy positions consistent with PCC views on domestic and international issues. (Ibid., 8 August.) On 24 November spokesmen from the PCC, UNO and a faction of ANAPO held a news conference at which they confirmed the establishment of a broad, democratic front in which they and the Independent Liberal Movement (MIL) had joined forces to promote the candidacy of Pernia and the joint platform agreed upon by the respective movements and parties (Radio Santa Fe, 24 November).

In January, and again in July, the Political Commission of the PCC denounced the "repression and the terror to which the peasants, workers, and militants of the UNO are being subjected in the militarized districts of Uraba, Cimitarra, and Yacopi" (*Voz Proletaria,* 13 January; 28 July). In a report sent to President López, the commission claimed that thirty-seven peasants has been killed by anti-guerrilla troops in Antioquia, while the military asserted that the dead were all FARC guerrillas killed in armed clashes.

Ideological friction continued among the various factions of the Communist party in 1977. The PCC condemned the anarchist tendencies of Maoist and Trotskyist groups and charged the EPL with committing "the most heinous and merciless crimes." Notwithstanding its own association with the FARC, the PCC stated that EPL attacks "discredit the revolution because they are carried out by the petit bourgeoisie who have no political experience" (*Voz Proletaria,* 14 July). Given the resurgence of FARC guerrilla activity in 1977, the PCC's position appears to be somewhat inconsistent with that expressed in December 1976 when the party's congressional delegates affirmed that "the Communist party's philosophical principles and political orientation are incompatible with anarchism, the use of terrorism or personal attacks as a method of struggle" (ibid., 2 December 1976).

International Views and Positions. The PCC faithfully follows the Soviet line in its international positions. In the Executive Committee report at the January plenum. Vieira called for continued support for the policies of the Soviet Union, which he identified as the "firm, unbreakable and most reliable bulwark in the struggle for peace throughout the world." He called on Communists to organize the collection of signatures under the Stockholm Appeal to solidify detente and "to stop the dangerous arms drive not only between the big powers, but also among the Latin American countries" (*Voz Proletaria,* 20 January). Writing in the *World Marxist Review,* Alvaro Mosquera criticized anti-Sovietism of every type, whether from the rightists, the Maoists, or the Trotskyists. He singled out the interpretation of freedom and democracy in the context of "the present imperialist campaign about so-called human rights" as an example of anti-Sovietism that "undermines international solidarity at its most important link" (*WMR,* September). Within the hemisphere, the PCC maintained its support for the position of Venezuela and Ecuador in their effort to abolish the trade discrimination law adopted by the U.S. Congress. Party statements also proclaimed support for "the liquidation of imperialist domination in the Panama Canal Zone" and consistent solidarity with the revolutionary government of Cuba.

Party Contacts. Julio Posada attended a symposium in Havana in April. A PCC delegation headed by Gilberto Vieira visited Hungary and Czecholsolvakia in May and returned home by way of Cuba where it met with Castro on 28 May. In Cuba, views were exchanged on the general situation in Latin America and the state of bilateral relations between the two countries and their respective parties (*Voz Proletaria,* 2 June). A delegation led by José Cardona Hoyos and Alvaro Mosquera visited Romania in June. In September Carlos Romero, former general secretary of JUCO and now a member of the PCC's Central Committee, visited Hungary and Poland and exchanged views with local party leaders on issues of the international Communist movement and problems concerning cooperation between their countries. A delegation of the Hungarian Socialist Workers Party visited Colombia in November at the invitation of the PCC. The PCC sent a congratulatory message to the Central Committee of the CPSU on the occasion of the sixtieth anniversary of the October Revolution (*Pravda,* 11 November). On 9 November Gilberto Vieira was decorated in Moscow with the Order of the October Revolution for his "active contribution to the struggle for peace and the development of friendly relations with the Soviet Union" (Moscow, 9 November).

Publications. The PCC publishes a weekly newspaper, *Voz Proletaria* (reported circulation 40,000), a theoretical journal, *Documentos Políticos* (5,000), and a Colombian edition of *World Marxist Review* (7,500). The FARC publishes a clandestine bulletin, *Resistencia.*

*　　　*　　　*

The PCC-ML. The Communist Party of Colombia, Marxist-Leninist, is firmly pro-Chinese. Its present leadership hierarchy is not clearly known, although Arturo Acero has been cited by the Chinese press as the political secretary of a group referred to as the Marxist-Leninist League of Colombia (Peking, 27 September). The PCC-ML has not recovered from the serious setback it received in July 1975 when its general secretary, Pedro León Arboleda, was killed by police in Cali. The PCC-ML has an estimated membership of 1,000. Unlike the PCC, it has not attempted to obtain legal status. Its impact in terms of national political life is insignificant. Within the labor movement, the party has exercised some influence in the past over the Bloque Independiente, a small trade union organization with an estimated membership of 20,000.

A delegation of the PCC-ML attended the Seventh Congress of the Albanian Workers Party in late 1976 and exchanged ideas on issues of common interest with Maoist groups from other Latin American countries, including Argentina, Bolivia, Brazil, Chile, Ecuador, and Uruguay. The delegations from Latin America stated that the liberation struggle is directed against both imperialist super-powers. U.S. imperialism was charged with being the "inciter and supporter of tyrannical anti-national and anti-popular regimes," while the Soviet Union was accused of carrying out an intensive activity "whose aim is to capture economic, political and strategic positions in this area of the world." The Marxist-Leninist delegations participating at the meeting also pointed out the "counter-revolutionary activity of the Communist revisionist parties of Latin America . . . who are striving everywhere to check the struggle of the masses, to deceive the workers, and to serve their social imperialist masters." (See *Chile.*)

On 21 August the National Direction of the Marxist-Leninist League of Colombia sent a letter to the Central Committee of the Communist Party of China acclaiming the holding of the Eleventh CCP National Congress and congratulating Hua Kuo-feng upon his election as chairman of the

CCP's Central Committee. The People's Republic of China also reported the receipt of a letter dated 9 September commemorating the first anniversary of the death of Mao Tse-tung.

The official organ of the PCC-ML is *Revolución*. The Marxist-Leninist League of Colombia has a monthly publication called *Nueva Democracia*. PCC-ML statements are sometimes found in Chinese Communist publications and those of pro-Chinese parties in Europe and Latin America.

The basic form of struggle adopted and approved by the PCC-ML is rural guerrilla warfare, peasant indoctrination, and the creation of a Popular Liberation Army that will eventually achieve revolutionary victory. The PCC-ML's guerrilla arm, the EPL, was the first attempt to stage a revolutionary "people's war" in Latin America. The EPL has limited its operations largely to urban areas since 1975, although several rural attacks and kidnapings were attributed to the group in 1977. In mid-April, the "Pedro León Arboleda" urban cell operating in Bogotá issued death threats to several business executives and claimed responsibility for the shooting of the major shareholder of one of Colombia's largest textile enterprises (*El Espectador,* 19 April). An unrban cell of the EPL claimed credit for the 1 July assassination attempt on Colombia's air force chief-of-staff who was accused of "issuing orders to kill" from his office (AFP, 8 July). On 28 October special police forces in Bogotá captured four alleged terrorists and charged them with belonging to an EPL unit that had carried out of a number of killings and attacks against members of the national police and special security forces (*El Tiempo,* 29 October). On 22 November police announced the arrest of three persons who claimed to belong to an EPL urban cell responsible for the slaying of a Colombian industrialist in Bogotá on 3 November (*El Espectador,* 23 November).

The Independent Revolutionary Workers' Movement (MOIR), established in 1971, also follows a pro-Chinese orientation, although its leadership and organization are independent from those of the PCC-ML. The general secretary is Francisco Mosquera. A former director and leading spokesman for MOIR, Ricardo Samper, was expelled from the movement on 31 May, approximately six months after his marriage to the daughter of ex-liberal President Alberto Lleras Camargo. An announcement by the executive committee in MOIR's official organ, *Tribuna Roja,* branded Samper an "opportunist" and explained that his marriage had "unavoidable political implications" that necessitated his expulsion from the movement (*El Tiempo,* 31 July). Although the MOIR has been active in supporting the formation of an independent labor movement free from PCC domination, the movement's leadership declared on 25 August that it would support the national strike organized by the leading labor centrals on 14 September (EFE, 26 August). Politically, the MOIR has committed its electoral support to the new coalition of the revolutionary left.

The ELN. The National Liberation Army was formed in Santander in 1964 under the inspiration of the Cuban Revolution. It undertook its first military action in January 1965. Once recognized as the largest and most militant of the guerrilla forces operating in the country, the ELN has never recovered from the toll exacted on its leadership and urban network in recent years, including the defection in 1976 of its principal founder and greatest leader, Fabio Vásquez Castaño, rumored to have returned to the group at the end of 1977. Nevertheless, individual units continued to carry out operations in rural areas in a number of departments, and evidence points to considerable reorganization of the movement's urban networks in 1977.

According to Colombian military intelligence services, one of the ELN's top urban leaders, Daniel Navarro Ospina, was captured on 17 February (*El Tiempo,* 19 February). The "Domingo Laín" guerrilla cell claimed credit for the 11 March kidnaping of Italian banker Guiseppe Mondini. According to police sources, ransom and the release of political prisoners, including Navarro Ospina, was demanded. A clandestine bulletin released by the ELN called upon the Latin American proletariat to "fight to the death against imperialist capitalism and those who represent it, the multinational concerns, the CIA, and the national bourgeoisies" (ibid., 29 March; 2 April). On 5

April the military high command announced the creation of special security measures in Bogotá to handle the increasing wave of kidnapings. A military spokesman warned that "we are going to fight the bands of organized kidnapers and we will not give up until we have exterminated them" (*El Siglo*, 6 April). The army officially reported in May that the ELN had succeeded in reorganizing an armed group of some thirty men in the border area of north Santander after having suffered "serious setbacks" in that region (Emisoras Caracol, 17 May). In the May issue of its clandestine bulletin *Insurrección*, the ELN confirmed that it had reactivated its forces in April and that the 23 April attack on a military post near Taratá, Antioquia, was "a war cry to awaken those who believe guerrilla warfare is about to die" (RCN, 26 May).

In a communiqué issued on 8 June, the ELN announced an escalation in its struggle on both rural and urban fronts and a number of incidents occurred during the months following. A copy of *Insurrección* stated that "in view of the success in the urban struggle achieved by other organizations, its members had asked that the ELN's attitude on this type of struggle be defined. The ELN has always considered the urban struggle to be secondary to the rural areas because the development of the latter guarantees the struggle's continuity" (AFP, 8 June).

At mid-year the ELN's rural activities were divided into three major fronts. One, headed by Nicolás Rodríguez Bautista, was operating principally in the San Lucas mountains on the borders of Santander, Antioquia, and Bolívar. A second front, led by Elías Awad, operated in Antioquia and in certain areas of César. The third front is led by José Vera and by the former Spanish priest, Manuel Pérez. Other fronts were reportedly undergoing a period of reorganization (*El Tiempo*, 7 July). A new bulletin entitled *Nupalom* began circulating in Bucaramanga in late July and confirmed the existence of severe internal strife within the movement. A document criticized the leadership of Vásquez Castaño, *Insurrección*, and in general those associated with the ELN's central organization of the late 1960s. Members of the group noted that Vásquez had tried to impose a centralization of authority within the ELN in order to rule it according to his personal need (*El Espectador*, 24 July). On 24 July the secret police reported the capture of Javier Naranjo Ochoa, an ELN urban guerrilla leader they say was second in command of the group headed by Hernando Tamayo, who was killed by authorities on 9 July (*El Tiempo*, 25 July). In a pamphlet entitled "The Militant," the ELN admitted in August that the movement was facing a series of crises brought about by "demoralization and individual breakdowns due to a lack of revolutionary awareness." The document grimly predicted that if "personality cults" continued, guerrilla action would disappear (*Alternativa*, 19 August). On 20 October an urban group seized control of two radio stations in Bucaramanga and broadcast its commitment to "liberation or death," a slogan associated with the *Nupalom* faction of the ELN, which authorities believe to be headed either by Alonso Ojeda Awad or Rodríguez Bautista (*El Tiempo*, 21 October).

The ELN faction headed by Ojeda Awad supports a policy calling for a coup d'état by strengthening the urban networks. In an October bulletin, Ojeda's faction affirmed its opposition to the formation of a single guerrilla front on the grounds that the merger "would facilitate its destruction by reactionary forces" (*El Espectador*, 24 October). For their part, Colombian civil and military authorities feel that the ELN will not survive its current internal divisions. On 23 October the governor of Santander announced that the ELN "is virtually liquidated." Military spokesmen were more cautious. They recognize the continued existence of the ELN, but no longer consider the group "a menace" (ibid.). A new wave of kidnapings carried out by ELN units in El Valle and Antioquia in November suggests that it would be unwise to predict an early and permanent end to the movement's existence.

Washington College   Daniel L. Premo

Costa Rica

The Communist Party of Costa Rica (Partido Comunista de Costa Rica) was founded in 1931 and accepted as a full member of the Communist International in 1935. In 1943, following the wartime policy of many Latin American Communist parties, it was reorganized under a new name, the Popular Vanguard Party (Partido Vanguardia Popular; PVP). The PVP and its youth and labor affiliates basically follow Soviet-line policies. No splinter Communist groups exist in Costa Rica.

Primarily because it backed the losing side in the civil strife of 1948, the PVP was proscribed between that year and 1974. Despite the proscription, the PVP operated with some freedom in the early 1970s, and in the 1974 elections it ran party members as candidates of the legal Party of Socialist Action (PASO), a leftist coalition of splinter groups. Two PASO candidates were elected to the fifty-seven-seat National Assembly: Eduardo Mora Valverde, brother of PVP founder and Secretary General Manuel Mora Valverde, and Antonio Ferreto Segura, a full-time worker in PVP affairs for many years with Under Secretary General Humberto Vargas Carbonell. However, upon assuming office in 1974, the National Liberation Party (PLN), victor in the 1948 conflict, found itself in a minority position and unable to govern without a coalition with the PVP. Part of the price extracted by the PVP for its cooperation was the rescinding of Article 98 of the constitution which proscribed it. The PASO deputies in the Assembly now call themselves the PVP faction. In anticipation of the February 1978 national elections, the PVP has again formed a coalition with PASO, now renamed the Unified People's Party (PPU), and is fielding the dean of the University of Costa Rica medical school, who is not a PVP member, for the office of president. The party is likely to retain the two seats it holds in the National Assembly because of the Costa Rican system of proportional representation. In addition, it hopes to pick up additional seats in San José province, where candidates include Vargas Carbonell, Mario Devandas, and Fabio Araya.

The PVP probably has between 500 and 1500 members out of a Costa Rican population of 2,100,000 (estimated 1977).

Leadership and Organization. Manuel Mora Valverde has been secretary general of the PVP since its founding. His brother Eduardo is assistant secretary general and Ferreto Segura is organizational secretary.

The PVP-controlled General Confederation of Costa Rican Workers (CGTC), one of four national labor federations, is believed to enroll in its affiliates about 3,600 of the estimated 30,000 unionized workers in the country. The CGTC is strongest in the banana growing coastal regions although major efforts are being made to shift into the urban central plateau area. Alvaro Montero Vega continues as secretary general.

The PVP affiliate for work among young persons is the Vanguard Youth of Costa Rica (Juventud Vanguardia de Costa Rica; JVCR). The JVCR regained control of student government at the University of Costa Rica in late 1977, but was roundly defeated in the election of the student government at the National University of Costa Rica in Heredia which had been considered a Communist stronghold.

Domestic and International Attitudes. The PVP maintains a three-pronged domestic program which focuses on enlisting worker support for its programs through the CGTC, influencing and enrolling young persons at the universities, and strengthening its position in the political arena. But problems of aging leadership coupled with inflexible ideology and party discipline make it difficult for the PPU to markedly improve its situation even though the PPU electoral campaign is largely non-ideological and focuses on such issues as taxation, better socialized medicine, control of foreign investment, and the similarities between the two major candidates.

The PVP continues to support Soviet international policies and opposes United States AID programs.

Publications. The weekly *Libertad* is the official PVP newspaper. The CGTC publishes *El Orientador.*

National Univesity of   Charles F. Denton
    Costa Rica
Heredia, Costa Rica

Cuba

The Communist Party of Cuba (Partido Comunista de Cuba; PCC) is the country's ruling party and the only one permitted under the 1976 constitution. The PCC was formed on 26 August 1925 by a few Moscow-trained Cubans and non-Cuban Communists who were members of and responsible to the Comintern. For the next three decades the leaders followed faithfully the policies of Stalin and his successors. They collaborated closely with the regime of Fulgencio Batista and later, for a while, with President Ramón Grau San Martín, opportunistically adapting their line to the mercurial political situation in Cuba. In 1940 the PCC supported Batista's candidacy for president; in return, during his 1940-44 presidential term, Batista rewarded the Communists with high positions in his government and with control of the organized labor movement. Lázaro Peña, a top party leader, became secretary-general of the Cuban Confederation of Labor (Confederación de Trabajadores de Cuba; CTC). In 1944, Carlos Rafael Rodríguez, one of the most prominent pro-Soviet Communist leaders (today a member of the PCC's Political Bureau, vice-president of the Council of State, and vice-president of the Council of Ministers), became one of Batista's ministers without portfolio. In that year the party changed its name to People's Socialist Party (PSP), under which it functioned through a period of legal existence, 1944-52, and of clandestine activities, 1952-59. In July 1961 the PSP merged with Fidel Castro's victorious 26th of July Movement and the Revolutionary Directorate (a student anti-Batista group) to form the Integrated Revolutionary Organization, which in 1961, after a purge of members, became the United Party of the Socialist Revolution. On 5 October 1965 that party was dissolved and in its place the PCC came into being, organized along orthodox and Soviet Communist lines. After ten years of slow, problem-ridden organizational work and the building of cadres and middle-level leadership, the PCC held its First Congress in December 1975.

There were no official figures for the PCC membership in 1977, but the total of some 204,000 members and alternate members given by Fidel Castro in 1976 is not believed to have changed since. In June 1977 one announced result of a plenary session of the Central Committee was the intention to renew all party cards and to tighten "disciplinary measures within the party," which could lead to another cleansing of the PCC rank and file (*Granma*, Havana, 11 June).

The population of Cuba at the end of 1977 was close to 9,700,000.

Leadership and Organization. In 1977, called in Cuba "The Year of Institutionalization," the PCC leadership continued its dominant role in the country under the 1976 constitution, whose Article 5 says: "The Communist Party of Cuba, the organized Marxist-Leninist vanguard of the working class, is the supreme leading force of the society and of the State, which organizes and guides the common effort toward the goals of the construction of Socialism and the progress toward a Communist society."

The 13-member Political Bureau consists of Fidel Castro Ruz (first secretary), Raúl Castro Ruz (second party secretary), Juan Almeida Bosque, Osvaldo Dorticós Torrado, Guillermo García Frías, Armando Hart Dávalos, Ramiro Valdés Menéndez, Sergio del Valle Jiménez, Blas Roca Calderío, José Ramón Machado Ventura, Carlos Rafael Rodríguez, Pedro Miret Prieto, and Arnaldo Milián Castro. Comprising the 10-member Secretariat are Fidel Castro Ruz, Raúl Castro Ruz, Blas Roca Calderío, Carlos Rafael Rodríguez, Pedro Miret Prieto, Isidoro Malmierca Peoli, Jorge Risquet Valdés, Antonio Pérez Herrero, Raúl García Peláez, and Arnaldo Milián Castro. Milián was appointed to the Secretariat in June 1977 when the Central Committee, at a Havana meeting, decided to increase the Secretariat membership from nine to ten. The Central Committee lost one of its 112 members (it also has 12 alternates), when Juan Marinello, at one time president of the party during the Batista period, died at the age of seventy-eight.

Lower on the pyramid-like structure of the PCC are 14 provincial and 169 municipal committees, and the Isle of Pines party committee under direct supervision of the Central Committee. There are basic party cells in virtually all centers of work and military units above company level. The PCC has thirty-seven schools, with an enrollment of over 6,000 students. These institutions, including the five-year Ñico López National School attended by almost 600 students, are intended to improve the ideological and political standards of party cadres. There are also national and provincial schools operated by the Union of Young Communists (USC).

Under the 1976 constitution, Cuba, divided administratively into 14 provinces and 169 municipalities, has a three-tier governmental structure: municipal, provincial, and national. The Municipal Assemblies, elected by all Cubans sixteen years of age or older, have powers over education, health, culture, local industries, and, in general, matters that affect the daily life of a community. The assemblies have a five-year term and meet every four months to "render account to electors." Between sessions, their Executive Committees handle all matters. Executive Committee members, elected by the Assembly, are the only ones to receive pay.

The Provincial Assemblies are responsible for matters that affect the life of a province. The elections are indirect; the members are chosen from among the delegates to the Municipal Assemblies in the given province and the PCC makes the list of candidates. The Provincial Assemblies also meet every three months and have executive Committees. The assemblies tend to rubber-stamp their Executive Committees' decisions. According to a Havana newspaper, a session of the Havana Provincial Assembly held in July 1977 looked like an "information meeting." The delegates did not prepare themselves adequately for the session, with the result that "there was no debate, and the sessions suffered from the lack of any analysis." (*Juventud Rebelde*, 1 August.)

Of the approximately 30,000 registered candidates in the October 1976 Municipal Assemblies elections (in which 10,725 delegates were chosen), 70 percent were PCC and UJC members (Blas Roca, *WMR*, February 1977). An even higher percentage of PCC and UJC members were deputies of the National Assembly. Its 481 deputies serve for five years and meet once a year, mainly to approve the state budget. (In 1977, no budget was submitted for approval at the July session.)

The executive arm of the National Assembly is the thirty-member Council of State, which has legislative powers while the Assembly is not in session, executive powers to name and remove ministers and heads of state agencies, and judicial powers, because it gives instructions of "general character" to the courts and the attorney general. The Council of State also appoints ambassadors and other high-level diplomatic representatives abroad. It watches over the performance of forty-three central organizations, thirty-four of which are state committees of ministries, whose heads hold ministerial rank and, along with the president of the Council of State and the vice-presidents, comprise the Council of Ministers. The supreme authority within the State Council is its president, who is also prime minister, and "it is on his recommendation that the Assembly appoints ministers and elects to the Supreme Court" (Blas Roca, op cit.).

The Council of State's Executive Committee consists of Fidel Castro, president; Raúl Castro, first vice-president; and vice-presidents Juan Almeida Bosque (who also has an honorary title of "Commander of the Revolution"), Ramiro Valdés, Guillermo García, Blas Roca, and Carlos Rafael Rodríguez. The secretary of the Council is Celia Sánchez Manduley.

The Council of Ministers' Executive Committee consists of Fidel Castro, president; Raúl Castro, first vice-president; and vice-presidents Osvaldo Dorticós Torrado, Carlos Rafael Rodríguez, Ramiro Valdés, Guillermo García, Diocles Torralba Gonzáles, and Belarmino Castilla Mas. The secretary is Osmany Cienfuegos Gorriarán. (For other Council members, unchanged from 1976, see YICA, 1977, p. 435.)

President Castro's dominant role was accentuated in 1977 by his extensive trips abroad, foreign press and television interviews, and policy-making speeches. At home, he was often on the move, visiting the provinces. In April, at the Third Congress of the YCL, a resolution extolled the "leadership of the invincible party and the teachings of Fidel—guide of all the people and founder of the first workers' and peasants' state in Latin America" (*Granma*, 8 April).

Throughout 1977 the government continued to make efforts to introduce at every level less erratic economic, political, and judicial structures than those that existed in the preceding 17 years. The process, which is to end by 1980, appeared to be making only slow progress. Implementation of the new Economic Management System, which would regulate relations between different state production and nonproducing enterprises, was apparently behind schedule. In 1977, as an important step in the new economic look, the government was supposed to announce its first national budget in a decade. Without explanation the first session of the National Assembly failed to mention the budget.

The Economic Management System, described by some foreign observers as "State capitalism with a tropical flavor," introduces a certain autonomy in the state production units, which now would be allowed to sell and lease (from other state organizations) idle basic resources, and engage in sideline production utilizing leftover materials on their own decision, without affecting their main production plans. Thus, in effect, the system rejects the Guevara concept of moral incentives and institutionalizes the position that state investments would be based on the premise of profitability. State enterprises must cover their expenditures with their income and also be able to create a fund with the profits that will enable them to finance at least part of the investments necessary for expansion and development. The Cuban structures, both political and economic, are not sui generis. In shaping them, wrote Blas Roca, "we carefully studied the experiences of the Soviet Union and of other Socialist countries. We studied their constitituions, sent comrades to other countries to learn more about the way a popular government works. We also took into account our own traditions." (Op. cit.)

Mass Organizations. Cuba's mass organizations are the Confederation of Cuban Workers (Central de Trabajadores de Cuba; CTC), the National Association of Small Farmers (Asociación de Agricultores Pequeños; ANAP), the Committees for the Defense of the Revolution (Comités de Defensa de la Revolución; CDR), and the Federation of Cuban Women (Federación de Mujeres Cubanas; FMC). Four other groups, the Union of Young Communists (Unión de Jovenes Comunistas; UJC), the Union of Cuban Pioneers (Unión de Pioneros de Cuba; UPC), the University Student Federation (Federación Estudiantil Universitaria), and the Federation of High School Students (Federación de Estudiantes de Enseñanza Media), are not regarded as mass organizations. Rather, they are institutional steppingstones in the selection process of the ruling elite—the PCC and the government officialdom.

The mass organizations have two basic functions set by the party: they constitute a source of cadres and militants, and they enable the party leadership to keep in touch with and exercise control of every sector of the population whose specific interests these groups represent.

The CTC. The Confederation of Cuban Workers is headed by PCC Central Committee member Roberto Veiga Menéndez, who is secretary-general of the CTC national committee.

The CTC's principal task is to improve, quantitatively and qualitatively, the country's production and productivity by fostering a "new collective attitude toward work and social property." The CTC consists of twenty-three national unions and has about 2,200,000 members. The CTC is supposed also to collaborate in the direction of centers of work as a harmonious counterpart to management because it often tends toward sectorial, managerial mentality to the detriment of the work. But because of the relatively low education level of most workers and many labor officials, there has been little evidence of the CTC assuming any managerial prerogatives.

There are various methods for stimulating production: the "millionaire movement," a drive to cut a million or more *arrobas* (one *arroba* equals twenty-five pounds) of sugar cane per harvest per brigade of twenty-one workers; the "Vangard Movement," concerned with volunteer labor; national "emulation"; working competition and the like. There are "National Hero of Labor" awards, medals so far given to some sixty persons.

The ANAP. The National Association of Small Farmers has been headed since its inception in 1961 by José Ramírez Cruz, a Central Committee member. There were about 220,000 ANAP members, including 150,000 farm owners, operating some 5,500 private farms, but these numbers were slowly but steadily decreasing. About 20 percent of Cuban land (3.7 million acres) is in private hands, although individual farmers have to sell practically all their produce—mostly vegetables, coffee, tobacco and some sugar cane—to the state. There are no free markets like those in most European Communist countries, where farmers can freely sell their products. In 1977, in a new and apparently determined effort to reduce the private agricultural sector to a minimum, President Castro urged small farmers to voluntarily merge their plots into state agricultural cooperatives: "Only by integrating the land and by developing rural committees on this land can there be a radical change in living conditions in rural areas. . . . But the farmers' free will will be respected." (*Granma*, 7 May.) In June, *Granma* announced the creation of a new cooperative in Pinar del Río Province, where 132 families gave up their land to the state. The newspaper indicated that this was one of many such conversions to production farms that resemble the Soviet *kolhozes*, which had not existed in Cuba before. In July, Castro visited Guantánamo Province as part of the campaign to persuade the peasants to join the cooperatives. He announced that 33 percent of the farmers interviewed expressed willingness to "join the higher form of production and cease production on individual plots." (Ibid., 4 July.)

The CDR. There are more than 5,000,000 members of the Committees for the Defense of the Revolution, comprising more than 80 percent of the country's population over the age of fourteen years, the minimum age required to join. Organized initially to combat all manifestations of "counterrevolutionary activities" as an open branch of the Ministry of Interior, in recent years the CDRs have been performing primarily social and economic—frequently productive—functions. There are CDR committees for every city block, factory, farm, and office in the country. But of late, according to Castro, the CDRs have been dedicating more and more of their time to combating common criminals and have requested that more regular policemen be recruited in view of the "attack against property," apparently a growing problem.

The FMC. The Federation of Cuban Women, constituted in 1960 and headed since then by Vilma Espín, PCC Central Committee member and wife of Raúl Castro, had some 2,230,000 members as of June 1977 (*Juventud Rebelde*, 19 July). The FMC also had 169 municipal directorates and 40,472 rank-and-file groupings. The organization's principal objective is to incorporate as many women as possible into productive work, and to mobilize them for educational and social tasks set by the PCC. Second to Mrs. Castro, FMC president, is Central Committee alternate member Dora Carcaño Araujo. Cuban women seem to have a long way to go to reach the level of equality desired by FMC leaders, because of the inherent "machismo" in Cuba. "You have to fight against the vestiges of discrimination," members were told in August. "The FMC's future goal," said Mrs. Castro, is "to struggle for the eradication of a number of remnants from the past so that women . . . will be able to assume under equal conditions to men greater responsibilities in the country's economic, social, cultural, ideological and political spheres." (*Granma*, 4 September.)

The UJC. The Union of Young Communists, the Cuban counterpart of the Soviet Komsomol, had approximately 390,000 members in 1977 (*O Estado de São Paulo,* São Paulo, 26 April), of whom 30 percent were girls. A young Cuban who has political ambitions can join the UJC at the age of fourteen and is either promoted to the PCC, after he becomes twenty-one years of age, or is dropped from the youth organization at twenty-seven because he is not considered of party caliber. The UJC was created in 1962 and is designated as the "organization of vanguard youth and a militant source and reserve" of the PCC. By definition, the UJC is the most radical and the least politically sophisticated of these groups. Yet certain problems appear to be affecting the group, and the rest of the Cuban youth. Speaking at the Third Congress of the UJC, Antonio Pérez Herrero, a party leader, said that "young people should be warned about being gullible with regard to the developed capitalist societies, unthinking admiration of luxury items and foreign made products, and about swallowing the poisonous bait of the bourgeois propaganda." He also said that a "certain amount of antisocial behavior still persists," and that UJC members should not "get alarmed by and despair in the face of shortages of consumer goods." (*Granma*, 2 April). The UJC supervises the activities of the Union of Cuban Pioneers, the Federation of High School Students, with some 500,000 members, and the University Students Federation (FEU), to which some 40,000 out of 100,000 university students belong.

The UPC. Equivalent to the Soviet Pioneers, the Union of Cuban Pioneers was created in 1961 in an effort to introduce the young generation to regimentation—an essential characteristic of Cuban life today—at the earliest possible stage, and to instill respect for and acceptance of PCC ideas. The UPC, to which almost all students between the ages of five and fourteen belong, also organizes the children's leisure time, which includes periods of productive work in communal vegetable or fruit gardens. The Pioneers wear blue uniforms, white socks, a blue or white kerchief tied around the neck and sometimes a blue or white beret.

The Revolutionary Armed Forces. The FAR (Fuerzas Armadas Revolucionarias) is considered by Western intelligence specialists to be the strongest and best trained and equipped military force in

Latin America. With about 120,000 men on active service, and 180,000 in reserve, the FAR can mobilize some 300,000 troops in forty-eight hours and up to one million men in a week, according to the Strategic Service Institute of London. It is essentially a defensive force and it is in a constant state of readiness. Its officer corps and NCOs are disciplined and well trained by a large number of Soviet military instructors. The FAR is closely tied to the party and government power structure. Between 85 and 90 percent of the officers belong either to the PCC or the UJC. They have their considerable share of governmental perquisites such as private cars, best housing, and private clubs. In late 1975 and early 1976, Cuban regular troops were sent to Angola. They helped the pro-Marxist Popular Movement for the Liberation of Angola to defeat its two rivals and to seize control of the country. Late in 1976, Cuba began withdrawing its units from Angola, where its force, according to Western observers, had grown to some 20,000. In early 1977, however, troop withdrawals were halted. This was confirmed by President Castro in his televised interview with Barbara Walters. He said that the troops had to stay in Angola because France and Morocco had intervened in the fighting in neighboring Zaire. Although the fighting in Zaire's Shaba Province proved to be brief and practically bloodless, the withdrawal of Cuban troops was not resumed. According to American estimates, Cuba had at the close of 1977 between 12,000 and 15,000 troops in Angola. In May, in an interview with the magazine *Afrique-Asie*, Castro said that Cuba "will consider an attack against Angola to be an attack against Cuba. We will defend [Angola] with all the means we have at our disposal." But it appears likely that the presence of Cuban military units in Angola is due to the continuation of internal struggle there rather than to external threats. During the year the Angolan guerrilla movement UNITA made several claims of having captured and killed Cuban soldiers in the course of its fighting against government forces of President Agostinho Neto.

In addition to its forces in Angola, according to U.S. State Department officials, Cuba had about 1,000 military advisers in Congo, and military personnel numbering more than a few hundred in six countries: Ethiopia, Equatorial Guinea, Sierra Leone, Guinea-Bissau, Somalia, and Mozambique. (*NYT*, 26 May.) Later in 1977 there were reports that the number of Cuban military advisers in Ethiopia had increased from the initial 50 to 400 or 500.

Domestic Affairs. More slowly than was planned, the Cuban government is introducing the Economic Management System, which is expected, among other changes, to decentralize the economic direction of the country and to make all state enterprises profitable. Implementation has revealed that the majority of Cuban production centers have a large surplus of workers, which poses a new and complex economic and social problem. According to foreign estimates, the 1977 sugar harvest, the mainstay of the economy, totaled 5.6 million tons, virtually the same as in the last several years. Cuba continued to withhold most of the meaningful economic data, making it difficult to assess the country's economic situation, which, on the face of it, appeared unchanged from 1976. While Cuban officials, in talks with American businessmen visiting Cuba, or in the United States, expressed willingness to renew commercial relations, they recognized that the volume of exchanges would have to be small because of Cuba's trading limitations. Trade Minister Marcelo Fernández, who visited Washington in October, said later that even if commercial relations with the United States were normalized, the Soviet Union would continue to be his country's major trading partner (*NYT*, 25 October). In his talk with a Minnesota businessman in Havana, President Castro frankly admitted Cuba's economic problems: "We have difficulties, lots of difficulties" (ibid., 25 April). According to a Cuban publication, the difficulties mentioned by Castro were principally financial, "caused by the decrease in sugar prices and the increase in the foreign market of raw materials and other articles that we need for national development" (*Bohemia*, Havana, 24 June). "We must produce more with the same resources; economize on raw and other materials, fuel and energy; eliminate any superfluous expenses," said Raúl Castro (*Granma*, 5 April). Thus there appeared to be no early prospects that

Cubans would discard their two ration books, which they have been carrying for nearly fifteen years, or that they would stop queueing for products of every kind every day—the rite which has become the hallmark of daily Cuban life.

Another domestic issue troubling the Cuban leaders was that of political prisoners. Because of more frequent contacts with foreign journalists, Cuban officials were asked more often about their alleged violations of human rights, especially since the Castro government has refused repeated requests by the International Committee of the Red Cross and Amnesty International to study the situation on the spot and visit Cuban prisons. In its 1975-76 report, Amnesty International placed the number of political prisoners in Cuba at 4,000 to 5,000 (*Washington Post*, 30 July). President Castro, in his interview with Barbara Walters, said that there are "maybe two to three thousand" political prisoners in Cuba, down from a peak of more than 15,000 in the early days of the revolution (*NYT*, 9 June). In 1967 he had put the peak figure at 20,000. He also told Miss Walters that Russian writer Alexander Solzhenitsyn was "politically mediocre."

International Positions. Cuba moved on two principal fronts in its international activities during 1977: enlarging its African involvement and improving its relations with the United States. The Cubans were in Africa to stay, principally for political reasons. President Castro and Soviet leaders conferred in the Kremlin in April on what appeared to be their joint African strategy, which reportedly is aimed at eliminating Western as well as Chinese influence. "Africa," Castro noted, "today is the weakest link in the imperialist chain. [It offers] splendid prospects for a practical transition from tribal relations to Socialist, bypassing certain stages that other parts of the world had to go through. If we are revolutionaries, we should support the struggle against imperialism, racism and neo-colonialism." (*WMR*, September.) In March, during his trip to Africa, Castro tried to mediate the armed conflict between Ethiopia and Somalia. The effort, which involved shuttling between Addis Ababa and Mogadiscio, was unsuccessful. But it resulted in a marked tilt of the Cuban government toward Ethiopia in preference over Somalia, essentially following the lead of the Soviet Union. Also following Moscow, Havana repeatedly criticized the government of China and the Chinese Communist Party.

Castro had kind words to say about the United States, especially President Jimmy Carter. He said that Carter was the first American President in more than sixteen years "not committed to a policy of hostility toward Cuba." Castro took cognizance of the fact that Carter ordered cessation of American surveillance flights over Cuba and allowed American tourists to spend dollars in Cuba. In April, as a result of direct talks between Cuban and U.S. officials, Havana and Washington signed a fishing agreement. Castro indicated that even though the 1973 bilateral anti-hijacking agreement had lapsed, Cuba would continue to abide by its provisions. On 1 September the United States in Havana and Cuba in Washington opened diplomatic missions, called "interest sections," that began to carry out some diplomatic, consular, and cultural functions. But Castro rejected the idea suggested by Washington that its lifting of the sixteen-year-old economic embargo against Cuba was conditional on the Cuban withdrawal of troops from Angola.

In a continuing effort to strengthen ties with and influence in the Caribbean, Castro traveled to Jamaica, where he impressed the population with his apparent moderate stance; Havana signed an educational agreement with Guyana, which already has an economic and scientific-technical collaboration accord with Cuba; and the PCC was host to a meeting of the Communist parties of the area. At the May meeting—with parties of Cuba, Guadeloupe, Guyana, Haiti, Martinique, Puerto Rico, the Dominican Republic, and Venezuela participating—it was agreed that "under new conditions determined by the recent governmental change in the United States of America, there is an evident intent to use new forms of moving the imperialist policy ahead [by] resorting to more subtle methods. . . . This new situation demands an adequate response in order to prevent imperialism from attaining its objectives." (*Granma*, 17 May.)

International Contacts. Although 1977 was supposed to be a year dedicated principally to Cuba's institutionalization, it was one of the busiest in a long time in foreign contacts and issues. *January:* Georges Marchais, general secretary of the French Communist Party, visited Havana; Politburo member Sergio del Valle represented the PCC at the Fourth Congress of the Vietnamese Communist Party in Hanoi. President Castro met in Havana with a delegation of the Democratic Front for the Liberation of Palestine, led by Nayef Hawatmeh, its secretary-general; with Kamel Almaghur, special envoy of Mu'ammar Qaddafi, president of Libya's Revolutionary Command Council; with the foreign minister of Jamaica and a Jamaican delegation; and with the foreign minister of Guyana. General of the Army Raúl Castro traveled to the Soviet Union and Bulgaria. Havana was site of the seventy-ninth meeting of the Executive Committee of the Council for Mutual Economic Assistance, at which it was announced that COMECON countries would help Cuba (a member since 1972) to build a new nickel-processing plant increasing the country's present annual production of 30,000 tons to 100,000 tons. *February:* Visiting Cuba were General of the Army Heinz Hoffman, defense minister of the German Democratic Republic; the defense minister of Bulgaria; and Cheddi Jagan, general secretary of the People's Progressive Party of Guyana. General Arnaldo Ochoa, commander in chief of the Cuban military force in Angola, visited Ethiopia. *March:* President Castro began his six-week-long foreign trip which took him to seven African countries—Libya, Somalia, Ethiopia, Tanzania, Mozambique, Angola, and Algeria—and to the Soviet Union, East Germany, and South Yemen. A meeting of several Latin American and Caribbean countries took place in Havana, with the participants urging that the minimum price of sugar should not be under fifteen cents a pound. Juan Almeida, Major of the Revolution, traveled to Brazzaville for the funeral of the president of the People's Republic of the Congo. *April:* General Raúl Castro met with U.S. Senators George McGovern and James Abourezk and Congressman Les Aspin, who traveled to Havana with a group of businessmen. *May:* Leaders of Communist parties of the Caribbean area traveled to Havana, as noted before. President Castro received in Havana delegations of the Communist Party of Lebanon, led by its secretary-general Nigula al-Shawi, and a delegation of the Communist Party of Colombia, led by its secretary-general, Gilberto Vieira. *June:* Travelers to Havana were René Urbany, chairman of the Communist Party of Luxemburg; Luis Corvalán, secretary-general of the Communist Party of Chile; Juan Mari Bras, secretary-general of the Socialist Party of Puerto Rico; Arnold Becchetti, member of the Politburo of the Communist Party, USA; the prime minister of Jamaica; a delegation of the Polisario Front's Sahara-based, Algeria-supported guerrillas; and a delegation of the League of Communists of Yugoslavia. Cuba's foreign minister visited Guinea and Benin. *July:* The prime minister of Guyana met with President Castro in Havana, also visited by the chief of the General Staff of the Hungarian Army. The visit to Cuba of Barbara Walters of ABC TV was regarded as an important event by Havana. Not only was she able to tape a long interview with President Castro, but also the text was printed in *Granma*, occupying over a dozen pages of the newspaper. *August:* Gen. Raúl Castro visited East Germany and Algeria. President Neto of Angola traveled to Cuba. *September:* The chairman of the Presidential Council of Yemen visited Cuba. *October:* The president of Mozambique spent five days in Cuba. Also visiting were Oliver Tambo, general secretary of the African National Congress of South Africa, and Colonel Feleke Gedle-Giorgir, foreign minister of Ethiopia. As noted, President Castro went for a week-long state visit to Jamaica. Later that month he received in Havana the foreign ministers of Denmark, Ghana, and Zambia.

Publications. *Granma*, the official organ of the PCC Central Committee, is published six times a week in Havana, with a daily average circulation of 600,000. Its editor is Jorge Enrique Mendoza, a Central Committee member. *Granma* also appears in weekly editions in Spanish, English, and French, which circulate widely abroad. The Central Committee's Secretariat publishes a journal, *Militante Comunista*, which gives news about the PCC and its contacts with other "fraternal" parties. Its circulation is 150,000. The UJC publishes the daily *Juventud Rebelde*, the country's second national newspaper, with a circulation of 200,000. National weeklies are *Verde Olivo*, the organ of the FAR, and

Bohemia, a general news magazine whose circulation is 300,000. Among the provincial party dailies are: *Guerrillero*, Pinar del Río (circulation 15,000), *Girón*, Matanzas (15,000), *Vanguardia*, Santa Clara (25,000), *Adelante*, Camagüey (25,000), *Sierra Maestra*, Santiago de Cuba (45,000), *Ahora,* Holguín (10,000), *Venceremos*, Guantánamo (4,500).

University of Miami   George Volsky

Dominican Republic

Intense disagreement over leadership and policy issues, especially since the civil war of 1965, has led to fragmentation of the Communist movement in the Dominican Republic. The three principal organizations from which the presently existing far left groups emerged are the Dominican Communist Party (Partido Comunista Dominicano; PCD), founded in 1942 as the Popular Socialist Party, now officially recognized by the USSR; the Dominican People's Movement (Movimiento Popular Dominicano; MPD), which for some years was pro-Chinese; and the Revolutionary Movement of 14 June (Movimiento Revolucionario 14 de Junio; MR-1J4), which is pro-Chinese, but for some years also the group most sympathetic toward Cuba. Splits within these groups have created several other factions and parties, including the Popular Socialist Party (Partido Socialista Popular; PSP), the Communist Party of the Dominican Republic (Partido Comunista de la República Dominicana; PCRD or PACOREDO), and the Red Flag (Bandera Roja), Red Line (Línea Roja), Red Fatherland (Pátria Roja), and Proletarian Voice (Voz Proletaria) factions of MR-1J4. There has recently been some indication of activity by elements with Trotskyist sympathies. There are also several small guerrilla groups.

Until 1977 all Communist factions were officially proscribed. However, President Joaquin Balaguer has allowed the various groups to operate with relative freedom. For their part, most of the Marxist-Leninist groups have tended to seek respectability in recent years; the more important of them have denounced terrorism, though threats against political leaders—if not many actual assassinations—continue. In 1977 the PCD was finally legalized by an act of congress.

Estimates of membership vary widely. The PCD has approximately 1,000 members, and the MPD, reputed to be the largest of the Communist groups, perhaps twice that number. The MR-1J4 may have 300 members, the PCRD 150, the PSP 40. The population of the Dominican Republic is 5,051,000 (estimated 1977).

Sources of support for the Communists include the universities, secondary schools, and labor unions, and reflect the fragmentation of the movement. At the university level, "Fragua" is led by the Red Line of the MR-1J4; the League of Democratic Youth (LJD), or Communist Youth (JC), by PCRD members; the University Committee "Julio Antonio Mella" by PCD members; and the Flavio Suero Committee by MPD members. The powerful Federation of Dominican Students (FED), which is said to enroll about 200,000 university and secondary school students, has since 1969 oscillated between control by the MPD and by non-Communist but left-wing students of the Dominican Revolutionary Party (PRD) and a PRD splinter, the Dominican Liberation Party (PLD). In March student unrest led to a temporary closing of the Autonomous University of Santo Domingo, the country's largest, and the occupation of its grounds by military troops (*FBIS*, 14 March).

Communist support is more limited within the labor movement, which in general has been very weak since the 1965 civil war. The small "Foupsa-Cesitrado" labor confederation, reportedly in MPD hands, is only one of several central labor bodies. There is also some Communist influence in the General Confederation of Workers (CGT). The Autonomous Confederation of Christian Workers (CASC) is more or less assoicated with the Revolutionary Social Christian Party (PRSC). The powerful "Unachosin" chauffers' union inlcudes Communist members, mostly of the MPD, although the influence of the PRD in that union is greater than that of any Communist group.

The PCD: Domestic Attitudes and Activities. Most political activity in the Dominican Republic in 1977 centered around the presidential and congressional elections scheduled for mid-1978. In this maneuvering, the PCD seemed to adopt a position favorable to the re-election of President Joaquin Balaguer.

The PCD held its Third National Conference in December 1976. Discussion at this meeting centered on economic, social, and political developments since 1973. An article by Pedro Juan Persia, a member of the PCD Central Committee, discussing the party's position after the Conference, noted that in spite of considerable economic development, the country's grave economic and social problems persisted. Persia claimed: "It has become perfectly clear that an economic policy founded entirely, or mainly, on the uncontrolled inflow of foreign investment, has proved utterly ineffectual and is contrary to the widespread demand for independent development."

Reflecting the increasingly friendly attitude adopted toward Balaguer, a PCD spokesman wrote that in recent years there have been significant changes in the alignment of political forces. "Since 1972, the Balaguer government has been following a reformist policy. Signs of a tendency opposed to the traditional policy of the oligarchy can be seen, in particular, in a series of draft laws generally known as 'The Agrarian Code of the Balaguer Government.' Some have been rejected by Congress, but the very fact that they were put before Congress is, in the opinion of the Communist Party, indicative of the sharp contradiction between government policy and the interests of the right-wing forces who have supported the president since 1966." After discussing the opposition parties, Persia wrote that "the outlook for further political action and deep-going structural change depends not on this 'opposition,' but rather on the formation of a new socio-political movement capable of giving voice to the aspirations of the people." He added that "though the perspective is for continued aggravation of the crisis of the existing system, the government is still in a position to change to a new course in its economic and social policy." Persia then put forward the elements of such a new course, which included nationalization of foreign companies, accelerated agrarian reform, strengthening of the state sector, nationalization of foreign banks, and gradual transfer of foreign trade to the state (*WMR*, May).

President Balaguer reciprocated the friendly approaches of the PCD. Although as early as 1973 he had sent congress a bill to legalize the party, it languished for four years. However, after the PCD had unsuccessfully sought in the middle of the year to get the Supreme Electoral Tribunal to recognize the party without a change in the law, President Balaguer pushed for enactment of the law to legalize the PCD. This law was finally passed by both houses of congress early in November (*Latin America Political Report,* London, 11 November).

International Views and Positions. The PCD is the officially recognized pro-Moscow party in the Dominican Republic. Thus, Political Committee member Carlos Dore attended a meeting of

Caribbean Communist parties in Havana in May. Subsequently he met at some length with Manuel Piñeiro Losada, head of the American Department of the Central Committee of the Cuban Communist Party (*Granma,* 23 May).

Publications. Until 1976 the PCD published a clandestine weekly, *El Popular.* Now it is issuing a legal magazine, *Impacto Socialista.*

*　　　*　　　*

The MPD. The MPD was formed by Dominican exiles in Havana in 1956. It became a formal party in August 1965 when it was pro-Chinese and one of the most active and violent leftist groups in the country, with considerable support among students and slum dwellers and some following in organized labor. More recently, like the PCD, the MPD has sought a more respectable image, a development which has led to the desertion of its more violence-prone members. In 1977 the party was reported to be seeking legal recognition, so as to be able to participate in its own right in the 1978 elections. However, there was no indication that the legalization of the PCD would lead to similar action with regard to the MPD. The MPD publishes an irregular clandestine paper, *Libertad.*

The MR-1J4. The Revolutionary Movement of 14 June derives its name from an unsuccessful attempt to overthrow the late dictator Trujillo on that day in 1959. The MR-1J4 currently exists in several factions, most of which were Maoist by the middle 1970s. These include the so-called Red Flag, headed by Juan B. Mejia; the Red Line, headed by Juan Rodríguez; the Red Fatherland; and the Proletarian Voice. By 1977 all MR-1J4 factions were fringe groups in the country with little or no general political impact; they had only marginal influence in the labor movement and only the Red Line group had a significant following in the universities. At least two of the MR-1J4 factions have received a degree of recognition from Peking. In December 1976 the *Peking Review* published a long message from the Red Line group to the new Chinese leadership; the following April Juan Mejia of the Red Flag group visited China and attended a banquet where Li Hsien-nien was the major speaker.

Other Groups. The PSP, the PCRD, and the Twelfth of January Liberation Movement, formed as an MPD splinter in 1973, were inactive in 1977. In September, Claudio Tavares was arrested in Santo Domingo for circulating *Perspectiva Mundial,* a Spanish-language journal of the United Secretariat of the Fourth International. The only groups to attempt any form of guerrilla warfare during the year were the ineffectual Los Trinitarios, the Army of National Liberation, and other such organizations.

Rutgers University　　　　　　　　　　　　　　　　　　　　　　　　Robert J. Alexander

Ecuador

In 1926, representatives of Marxist discussion groups founded the Ecuadorian Socialist Party, from which the "Friends of Lenin" group split two years later, adopting the name Communist Party of Ecuador (Partido Comunista del Ecuador; PCE) in October 1931. A Maoist splinter group, the Marxist-Leninist Communist Party of Ecuador (Partido Comunista Marxista-Leninista del Ecuador; PCMLE) dates from 1963. Factional disputes have repeatedly fragmented the Socialist Party. The most important offshoot is a frankly Fidelista group, the Ecuadorean Revolutionary Socialist Party (Partido Socialista Revolucionario Ecuatoriano; PSRE). The PSRE has generally stood to the left of the PCE, embracing the most radical elements of Ecuadorean Marxism. Membership for all of the parties is small, led by the PCE with an estimated 800 members; the PCMLE and PSRE have perhaps 200 each. The population of Ecuador is about 7,680,000.

The PCE, although the oldest and most prominent Marxist party, has only marginal importance in national affairs. Vigorously persecuted in the early 1960s, the PCE reemerged later in the decade. Its Eighth Congress, in 1968, adopted the basic program in effect today. In broad ideological terms, it commits the party to national liberation from imperialism and feudalism, seeking the ultimate achievement of Socialist revolution.

In 1968 the PCE organized the Popular Democratic Union (Unión Democrática Popular; UDP), a coalition movement whose candidates for president and vice-president both finished last in a five-man race that year, receiving about 2 percent of the vote. The UDP was being reorganized when General Guillermo Rodríguez Lara assumed power on 15 February 1972 and cancelled elections. The PCE was swift to praise the military regime as "revolutionary and nationalist." Legalized in 1973, the party held its Ninth Congress that year and repeated its approval of the government—the only party to do so. The PCE continued this support until Rodríguez was deposed by fellow officers on 11 January 1976. Policies of the new junta, called the Supreme Council of Government, were greeted by the PCE as a continuation of those of Rodríguez. Hence it would "resolutely support all steps of the government to translate into reality the aspirations of the people," while opposing "any intentions of the oligarchic and imperialist forces to maintain their positions in the national economy," (*IB*, 31 January 1976). The PCE similarly applauded the official announcement that power would be returned to elected civilian authorities in January 1978.

The Supreme Council of Government appointed three special commissions: one to draft a new constitution, another to revise the 1945 charter, and a third to produce a new Law of Parties. A nation-wide plebiscite was to choose between two drafts for a new constitution; only then would elections take place. Progress was slow, and in April 1977 the return to civilian government was postponed to September 1978. The delay was attributed to bureaucratic obstacles in preparing a new national voter registration, but there was widespread disbelief. Although the public commitment of the Supreme Council of Government remained intact at the close of the year, the PCE and other parties were warily pessimistic.

The PCE, which had agreed to participate in the drafting by the commissions of the alternate constitutions, nonetheless became more critical. It announced an official break with the government in November 1976 and periodically attacked the regime in 1977. In June the PCE charged it with unleashing "reactionary violence," and alleged that it sought to impose a fascist regime while trying to paralyze the constitutional reorganization (*El Tiempo*, 8 June). The Central Committee announced in August its decision to participate in the referendum, but warned the government not to intervene in the process (EFE, 7 August). When the PCMLE condemned PCE participation in government commissions, PCE Secretary General Pedro Saad attacked the Maoists as reactionaries affiliated with the CIA and the Ecuadorean right. PCE involvement was necessary, he said, "inasmuch as war must be waged against the ruling classes on all fronts" (*El Comercio*, 23 June).

The party also undertook extensive discussions with others in hopes of creating a broad-based leftist alliance. In June Saad advocated formation of a Broad Front of the Left (Frente Amplio de la Izquierda; FADI) in conjunction with the PSRE, the left wing of the Christian Democrats, and various Marxist splinter groups. The proposed platform was to call for total nationalization of oil, electricity, and foreign trans-national corporations. Foreign banks would also be taken over, and strict controls placed upon private banking. In sum, the PCE promised through FADI "a popular government, the fruit of the alliance and struggle of all workers and Ecuadoreans who are determined to forge the basis of an Ecuador that is socialist, democratic and free of all dependence" (*El Comercio*, 14 July).

Organization and Leadership. The PCE is noteworthy for its stability, continuing for over three decades under the domination of Pedro Antonio Saad. Only minor revisions have been made recently on the Central Committee (twenty-seven full members, fifteen alternates), chosen at the November 1973 congress. Saad himself, founder of the Communist-dominated Confederation of Ecuadorean Workers (Confederación de Trabajadores Ecuatorianos; CTE) in 1944, remains influential within this, the oldest of Ecuador's three national labor organizations. The CTE, a member of the Communist-front World Federation of Trade Unions (WFTU), is the largest of the three, with an estimated 60,000 workers on its rolls.

Labor unrest increased markedly during 1976 and grew even more pronounced in 1977. The CTE worked with the two non-Communist labor federations—the Ecuadorean Central of Class Workers (CEDOC) and the Ecuadorean Confederation of Free Union Organizations (CEOSL)—in applying pressure on the government. In opposing the regime's anti-inflationary wage policies and its generally unsympathetic attitude toward labor, the CTE played a major role in sharpening hostility. On 16 January came the arrest of forty-five union leaders, including PCE and PSRE members, in response to a strike by hospital personnel in Guayaquil (*FBIS*, 17 January). A more serious confrontation occurred in May, when the three federations called a general strike in support of demands for salary increases, oil nationalization, agrarian reform, and the resolution of existing labor disputes.

Although the CTE claimed that 60 percent of the work force had participated, the planned stoppage was relatively ineffective. In the aftermath some fifty leaders were arrested, including the CTE president and the pro-PCE president of the Pichincha Workers' Federation. The latter two received two-year prison sentences. In the wake of the May strike and a concurrent month-long stoppage by the National Teachers' Union (UNE), much of the top labor leadership went underground. Labor-government clashes climaxed in October when some 700 striking sugar workers at the Zatra plantation near Guayaquil were forcibly expelled from the sugar mill by an estimated 1,500 police. The government announced that twenty-four sugar workers had been killed, while unofficial figures ran higher. By the close of 1977 the Supreme Council of Government had adopted an unyielding stance toward labor, and the CTE and the radical wing of CEDOC had assumed a dominant role on behalf of the workers.

PCE influence over labor is exercised through the CTE and also through two peasant organizations, the Coastal Farm Workers Federation (FTAL) and the Ecuadorean Federation of Indians (FEI). These are less important, however, than the party's youth wing, the Communist Youth of Ecuador (Juventud Comunista Ecuatoriana; JCE). In 1976 and 1977, the JCE lost ground in its struggle with

Maoists for control of the Federation of Ecuadorean University Students (FEUE). Its position was eroded during the UNE-sponsored teachers' strike in May and June, for the UNE was largely under pro-Chinese Communist leadership. While government firmness led to the eventual collapse of the strike, it left Marxist elements strengthened within the ranks of both teachers and students, notwithstanding the enduring strains between pro-Moscow and Maoist activists.

Party Internal Affairs. At the 23 May 1976 celebration of its fiftieth anniversary, the PCE had reiterated its unquestioning allegiance to Soviet Communism, and in November at Guayaquil, its spokesman further praised the domestic and international successes of the Soviet Union (Tass, 12 November). A year later the Central Committee named a special delegation, led by Saad, to attend the Moscow festivities in celebration of the sixtieth anniversary of the October Revolution.

Domestic Views. Despite its November 1976 break with the military government following years of qualified approval, the PCE indicated a month later its willingness to withhold final judgment on plans for reestablishment of constitutional government. Secretary General Saad announced that the party was less concerned with legal reorganization of the state than with specific policy problems. He demanded the promised structural transformations announced earlier while General Rodríguez had held power, arguing that otherwise oligarchical power would remain unchallenged. More specifically, the PCE insisted upon total nationalization of the petroleum industry, state ownership of social security and welfare assistance services, swift implementation of agrarian reform, and a staunch defense of national sovereignty over the 200-mile oceanic limit (*EFE*, 8 December 1976).

This attitude was largely maintained through 1977, with much of the criticism directed at official handling of oil. In a press release on 6 February, the PCE charged the regime with establishing an unacceptably low price for oil being sold to and exported by Texaco. An estimated $0.54 per barrel was supposedly being lost (*EFE*, 7 February). At the same time, the PCE publicly proclaimed its doubts about government intentions toward the process of restoring elected government. In March Saad rejected the bases for the proposed Law of Parties in a letter to the commission chairman, characterizing them as representing "a new attack on democracy" (*El Universo*, 29 March). Following release of the law in final form, the PCE asked that it be voided, on the grounds that it was unduly restrictive in the regulation of parties and therefore encouraged an antidemocratic system serving the interests of the oligarchy (*FBIS*, 27 June). Despite its later agreement to take part in the referendum, the PCE continued to attack the government throughout 1977.

International Views. In addition to attending Moscow celebrations of the October Revolution anniversary, the PCE in 1977 sent representatives to an international symposium in Havana sponsored by the *World Marxist Review* and the Communist Party of Cuba. Efraín Alvarez of the PCE's Executive Committee spoke of foreign exploitation of Ecuadorean agricultural exports, especially cacao, coffee, bananas, and rice. Industrial enterprises were described as being largely controlled by international monopoly, and government contracts with the oil industry during the preceding decade were also attacked as reflecting oligarchical anti-nationalism. The Texaco-Gulf Consortium, from which Gulf had recently withdrawn, was criticized for an array of interventionist measures designed to preserve its privileged position in Ecuador (*WMR*, April).

The PCE also continued to echo its support for Soviet leadership of world Communism. Typical was a resolution of the CTE which praised Russian domestic and international policies, lauded Cuba, and expressed working-class solidarity with the peoples of Chile, Paraguay, Uruguay, and others engaged in a struggle for the restoration of democracy and creation of genuine national liberation (*FBIS*, 10 February).

Publications. The PCE publishes the weekly *El Pueblo* in Guayaquil. Since the 1972 military coup d'état, it has appeared with intermittent interruptions, owing both to financial difficulties and to occasional temporary closings by the government.

The PCMLE. In November 1976 the Marxist-Leninist Communist Party of Ecuador sent a delegation to the Seventh Congress of the Albanian Party of Labor. Joined by Maoists from six other Latin American countries, they issued a declaration charging the United States and the Soviet Union with being "imperialist superpowers" engaged in conspiracies against the peoples of the world. Alleging that "Russian social imperialists" were opposed to the liberation of Latin America, the participants were similarly critical of the "revisionism" demonstrated by pro-Moscow Communist parties. China was hailed as a modern Socialist country which through the wisdom of Mao, had made "a decisive contribution to the reconstitution of the international Marxist-Leninist communist movement" (*FBIS*, 8 February; see also *Chile*).

The PCMLE presented similar views through its central organ, *En Marcha*, which is published roughly on a monthly basis. Its February issue applauded the victory of the Chinese Central Committee over the Gang of Four while elaborating upon Mao's contributions.

The PSRE. The Revolutionary Socialist Party of Ecuador became more active during 1977 in preparation for the forthcoming referendum and national elections. Secretary General Fernando Maldonado Donoso committed the PSRE to participation with the PCE and other organizations in the FADI coalition, although questioning the intentions of the Supreme Council of Government. Pessimistic about the prospects for meaningful change in the near future, Maldonado nonetheless contended that conditions for political struggle were improving. Plans were initiated for a special congress to detail tactics for the 1978 elections.

The University of North Carolina   John D. Martz

El Salvador

The Communist Party of El Salvador (Partido Comunista de El Salvador; PCES) was officially founded in March 1930, but has been illegal since the Communist-led uprising of 1932. Although illegal, the PCES is tolerated by the present government, and its leadership is openly known. It is active in politics through the front group known as the National Democratic Union (Unión Democrática Nacionalista; UDN), which has joined the Christian Democrats and the left-wing but non-Communist National Revolutionary Movement to form the National Opposition Union (Unión Nacional Opositara; UNO). The PCES has repudiated violence and does not currently back any of the guerrilla movements active in the country.

The current PCES membership is estimated to number about 150.

El Salvador, the most densely populated nation on the mainland of America, with about 4,310,000 persons, is also one of the most unreformed and economically backward. Since 1960 power has been in the hands of a military oligarchy linked to a landholding aristocracy jealous of its position and prestige. The ruling Party of National Conciliation (Partido de Conciliación Nacional; PCN) holds regular elections, but arranges them so that its candidates are victorious.

Leadership and Organization. The secretary general of the PCES continues to be Jorge Shafick Handal. The PCES controls the country's major industrial union, the Federation of Salvadorean Unions (Federación Unida de Sindicatos Salvadoreños; FUSS). It does not appear to have any great strength in the growing peasant movement.

Domestic Activities. The central event of 1977 in El Salvador was the election of a new president, which took place on 20 February. The most dramatic problem, however, continued to be land reform. In August 1976 President Arturo Armando Molina put forth a timid land-reform proposal which would have involved some 57,000 hectares, to be divided in four-hectare plots benefiting some 20,000 people. This was welcomed by the PCES, but denounced by the country's main guerrilla groups, the FPL and ERP (see below). The Catholic Church, and especially the Jesuit order, which the government absurdly claims to be an arm of the PCES, demanded greater reform through the Farm Workers' Union and the Christian Federation of Peasants. On the other hand, the conservative National Association of Private Enterprise denounced Molina and his reforms as communistic, and the more extreme UGB (see below) was formed to oppose any land reform. This confrontation was responsible for much of the violence in the country during the year.

The election came off as scheduled, and the PCN candidate, General Carlos Romero, was declared to have won by a two-to-one margin. Widespread evidence of fraud existed, and the UNO candidate, Colonel Ernesto Claramount, and his supporters seized the Plaza Libertad in downtown San Salvador to protest the results. They were expelled from the square a week later. Supporters of Claramount declared that more than 200 demonstrators were killed. The government countered by declaring a state of siege and by charging that the demonstration was a bid by the PCES to seize power, a charge the PCES Central Committee branded "absolutely false" (*IB*, 15 April). General Romero was sworn into office on 1 July, and the state of siege was lifted soon thereafter.

International Activities and Contacts. A top-level delegation of the PCES met with Honduran Communist leaders in late 1976 in an "atmosphere of cordiality" to express their solidarity and deplore the longstanding border dispute between the two countries (*IB*, 15 November). Jorge Shafick Handal continues to be an indefatigable world traveler, having visited Bulgaria in May, where he was received by Todor Zhivkov. He went on to Romania in June and there conferred with Nicolae Ceaușescu, who pledged cooperation and friendship. Later the same month, Handal was in Moscow, where he was warmly greeted by members of the Central Committee of the Communist Party of the Soviet Union. Outlining the situation in El Salvador, he attacked the "gross tyranny and violence" of the country's ruling class (*FBIS*, 27 May, 28 June).

Publications. The PCES newspaper is *Voz Popular*. The party also publishes *La Verdad*.

Guerrillas. Marxist guerrilla movements continued in 1977 to operate in the country, the largest and the most widely publicized of which is the Popular Liberation Forces (Fuerzas Populares de Liberación; FPL), also known as the Farabundo Marti Brigade, after the leader of the 1932 revolt. The reputed head of the FPL is former FUSS leader Salvador Cayetano Carpio (*Latin American*

Political Report, 29 April). The much-splintered People's Revolutionary Army (Ejército Revolucionario del Pueblo; ERP) appears to be on the decline. Informed sources suggest that some of the alleged activities of ERP and the group known as the Armed Forces of the National Resistance (Fuerzas Armadas de Resistencia Nacional; FARN) are really the work of gangster elements linked to the Policía Nacional. Indeed, certain deeds attributed to the FPL may be the work of the right-wing terrorist organization known as the White Warrior Union (Unión Guerrera Blanca; UGB). The FPL and the ERP appear to have ties with the Sandinista National Liberation Front in Nicaragua and with the Guerrilla Army of the Poor in Guatemala (*FBIS,* 29 September; *NYT,* 2 June).

The election campaign was punctuated by kidnapings and killings. The greatest outrage of the FPL was the seizure of Mauricio Borgonovo Pohl, the foreign minister of El Salvador, on 22 April. The FPL demanded the release of thirty-seven political prisoners in exchange for the minister. Despite pleas from the archbishop of San Salvador and many others, the government refused to bargain and the body of Borgonovo was found at Santa Tecla on 11 May. The demand for the release of political prisoners underscored the fact that an estimated 800 persons had been detained incognito since the election (*Latin American Political Report,* 29 April). In retaliation, the UGB assassinated a priest prominent in the peasant movement and the government began a crackdown on the FPL, with President Molina again attacking "communist priests" for inciting terrorism (*FBIS,* 20 May). The ERP became active in August. In September, guerrilla groups seized several radio stations and killed the government-appointed rector of the University of El Salvador.

Eastern Connecticut State College   Thomas P. Anderson

Guadeloupe

Guadeloupe's Communist Party (Parti Communiste Guadeloupéen; PCG) was founded in 1944. In 1958, under pressure from nationalist movements to change Guadeloupe from a French Overseas Department to an autonomous or independent state, it transformed itself from a federation within the French Communist Party (PCF) to an autonomous party with close links to its former parent. Since the May 1968 general strike in France the PCG, like the PCF, has been challenged as too conservative and bureaucratic by an assortment of small groups of pro-Chinese, nationalists, Trotskyites, and others collectively called "gauchistes."

Unlike some of these far-left movements, however, the PCG is legal and is represented in the French legislature as well as in the local General Council. For example, Hégésippe Ibéné, PCG mayor of Sainte-Anne, is one of Guadeloupe's representatives in the National Assembly; Marcel Gargar and Georges Dagonier, allied with the party, represent Guadeloupe in the Senate. Out of thirty-six members of the General Council, seven are Communists. They have allied themselves with seven Socialists, five Progressives, and two unaffiliated councilors to control the Council. However, since the Council's main purpose is to approve the local budget submitted by the appointed prefect, its influence is mainly as a forum for discussion.

The PCG's reported 3,000 members account for less than one percent of Guadeloupe's population of 329,000. The party nonetheless succeeds in maintaining the above elected officials in office and also the mayors of major towns and cities such as Basse-Terre, the capital, and Pointe-à-Pitre, the major port and industrial center. In the municipal elections of 13 and 20 March 1977, five out of six incumbent Communist mayors were re-elected, including Dr. Henri Bangou, the influential mayor of Pointe-à-Pitre. The election of the sixth, deputy Hégésippe Ibéné, mayor of Sainte-Anne, was annulled by the sub-prefect because of brawling during the balloting which resulted in the apparent loss of important election documents. At a special election on 17 April, Ibéné won decisively. On 25 September the senatorial elections sent Marcel Gargar, the incumbent, back to the Palais de Luxembourg along with Georges Dagonier who was also supported by the unified left.

Leadership and Organization. Guy Daninthe was re-elected first secretary of the PCG at the Sixth Congress of the party held in December 1976.

At the base of party structure are very small cells named after prominent personalities in party history. The cells are linked together in fifty branches which are organized into eleven sections. Most party members are workers and professionals.

Tied with the PCG is Guadeloupe's largest trade union, the General Confederation of Labor of Guadeloupe (CGTG), which has bonds with the French General Confederation of Labor (CGT). The secretary general is Claude Morvan. Another ally, the Union of Guadeloupan Women, has been headed by Madame George Tarer. The Union of Communist Youth, which held its Second Congress in October 1977, is presided over by Jean-Claude Lombion.

The PCG followed the lead of the French Communist Party in allying itself with Socialists and Progressives on the island. The three parties form the Permanent Committee of the Guadeloupan Left (Comité Permanent de la Gauche Guadeloupéenne). The party also supports actions and meetings of the League for the Rights of Man.

The death of Paul Lecavé, former deputy and mayor of Capesterre, at the end of 1976, created a problem of discipline within the party. PCG member Alexis De Lacroix resigned from the party over the issue of succession and then overcame PCG opposition to win Lecavé's place as mayor and as general councilor. The party denounced him and other Communists and former Communists who supported his candidacy. By June the PCG opened a campaign against De Lacroix's handling of Capesterre affairs. An ideological school was opened in October to improve general party discipline and solidarity.

Domestic Attitudes and Activities. The party continued to call for recognition of Guadeloupe as an autonomous entity or nation within the French Republic. Goals were articulated along the lines of Eurocommunism, blending nationalism and Socialism. Party spokesmen rejected the idea of complete independence, however, as a trap, arguing that at present it would bring neo-colonialism in its wake. Concretely, autonomy would mean the establishment of an executive responsible to an elected assembly with significant powers, plus an organism for ensuring close ties with France.

The problems of departmentalization emphasized during the year by the PCG included the inability of Guadeloupan citizens to control their own cultural or economic affairs—including inflation, unemployment, emigration, decrease in sugar production, and a trade imbalance—and the failure of the French government to guarantee services and protections provided to French citizens in metropolitan France. Frequent visits by French government ministers were seen as empty gestures or as efforts to offset the growing importance of the united left in France. Strikes with PCG support continued in almost every sector of the economy, as they had done in years past. Delay in the promised expansion of Basse-Terre port facilities, particularly damaging to small-scale banana producers who depend on the port for their exports, inspired a Communist-supported walkout by members of the General Council at the end of June.

International Views and Policies. The PCG tended to eschew direct reference to the Sino-Soviet dispute although its support for the USSR was clear from its activities and statements. The party focused more explicitly on friendship with Cuba and the French Communist Party. Party member Eugéne Laventure, president of an agriculture union, visited Cuba at the end of 1976 and reported on his trip in January 1977, and first secretary Guy Daninthe followed the same route some months later. A delegation traveled to Cuba for May Day celebrations and joined other Caribbean Communist parties in a meeting with Fidel Castro. In April the PCF sent a delegation to Guadeloupe to show its solidarity with Ibéné in the disputed election and on 3 May the PCG met in Paris with the PCF and party leaders from Martinique and Réunion. On 10 May the three overseas parties met in Pointe-à-Pitre to underscore their joint support for self-determination. In September the PCG hosted an anti-colonial conference attended by Communist, Socialist, and Progressive parties from the four major French overseas departments—Guadeloupe, Martinique, Réunion, and Guyane. Official declarations called for autonomy for the departments and for solidarity of the left, the latter showing that they are not bound by Communist-Socialist disputes in France.

Publications. The PCG's positions are made known to the public through its newspaper, *L'Etincelle* (Spark), a source of news to many who are not in the PCG. The weekly is usually printed in 12,000 copies, though on special occasions the issues may run to 16,000. This year, for the first time, Daninthe spoke to the nation over the government radio.

Howard University   Brian Weinstein

Guatemala

The Communist party in Guatemala, which since 1952 has been called the Guatemalan Party of Labor (Partido Guatemalteco del Trabajo; PGT), originated in the predominantly Communist-controlled "Socialist Labor Unification" founded in 1921. This group became the Communist Party of Guatemala (Partido Comunista de Guatemala: PCG) in 1923 and joined the Communist International in 1924. Increasing Communist activities among workers during the mid-1920s were cut off by the end of the decade and were kept at a minimum throughout the dictatorship of Jorge Ubico (1931-44). In 1946-47 new Marxist groups appeared in the trade union and student movements, organized in the clandestine "Democratic Vanguard." At an underground congress in 1949 this group took the name PCG. A prominent Communist labor leader founded a second and parallel Communist party in 1950, called the "Revolutionary Workers' Party of Guatemala." The two groups merged into a single PCG in 1951. In 1952 the PCG adopted the name PGT, which it has continued to use.

The PGT operated legally between 1951 and 1954 and played an active role in the administration of Jacobo Arbenz. Outlawed in 1954 following the overthrow of Arbenz, it has operated underground since then. Although the party has some influence among students, intellectuals, and workers, it does not play any significant role in national affairs. In the most recent national election, March 1974, the conservative coalition candidate General Kjell Laugerud García won a disputed victory over his non-Communist left opponent. The next national elections are scheduled for March 1978.

According to U.S. intelligence sources, the PGT is estimated to have 750 members. The population of Guatemala is 6,183,000 (1977).

Guerrilla Violence. Various guerrilla groups have operated in Guatemala in recent years, including the Revolutionary Armed Forces, which is the military arm of the PGT, and the Rebel Armed Forces (Fuerzas Armadas Rebeldes; FAR), at least some of whose members have claimed affiliation with the PGT. The 13 November Revolutionary Movement (MR-13) has been inoperative for two years. The Revolutionary Armed Forces and the FAR are believed to have fewer than 100 members each, in addition to several hundred sympathizers.

The most active of the guerrilla organizations in 1977, and now the largest, was the self-styled Guerrilla Army of the Poor (Ejército Guerrillero de los Pobres; EGP). The EGP began its operations in late November 1975 when it assumed responsibility for the murder of an anti-Communist leader and proclaimed in bulletins to the news media "a war to the death on U.S. imperialism and its local representatives." Its membership is believed to contain remnants of leftist guerrilla groups who succumbed to the effective counterinsurgency tactics of the Guatemalan military during the late 1960s and the "law and order" administration of General Carlos Arana Osorio (1970-74). Although the EGP has not claimed any direct affiliation with the PGT, there is strong evidence on which to base such an inference (for this reason, the EGP's operations are discussed below in connection with the PGT's domestic activities). The guerrilla situation is complicated by the continued existence of non-ideological groups of common criminals who engage in kidnaping, extortion, robbery, and other acts of violence.

Although the presidency of General Laugerud has been relatively free of the extremist violence that convulsed Guatemala from 1966 to 1974, politically motivated killings involving leftist groups and right-wing paramilitary organizations were a common feature of Guatemalan daily life in 1977. The victims of terrorist acts have by no means been confined to politicians and members of the military. Persons with little influence in the nation's political or economic life, but with some standing in their local communities, were frequently the objects of torture and murder by "unidentified" elements. A study of 111 cases of political violence occurring in June, July, and August revealed that eighty-nine murder victims were peasants or workers, many of whom were apparently involved in local grass-roots organizations. Six were students or professionals, and the remainder were landowners, businessmen, right-wing politicians, bodyguards and policemen (*NYT,* 2 November).

On 22 March a government minister stated that a series of strikes involving high school students, state banks, several private industries, and the capital's municipal workers were "part of a subversive plot directed from abroad by politicians who are trying to take advantage of the situation" (*El Imparcial,* 23 March). On 1 April he again stated that worker and student strikes were "part of an unsuccessful subversive conspiracy to create chaos and anarchy" and added that the situation in the country could lead to the establishment of a state of siege (ibid., 2 April).

Although President Laugerud has attempted to dissociate his administration from right-wing violence, its inability to account for the "disappearance" of numerous persons with leftist sympathies has led to widespread criticism of the state of human rights in Guatemala. At a press conference for foreign newsmen, Laugerud stated his belief that since 1960 guerrilla activities in Guatemala have been supported, financed, and directed by Fidel Castro. He added that at one time there were guerrillas professing a Trotskyite ideology, "but today they have a Castroite ideology represented by the self-styled Poor Peoples Guerrilla Army" *(Diario de Centro America,* 6 May). The National Committee of Labor Unity (CNUS), which encompasses the largest labor confederations and peasant leagues, accused the government of "obvious inability to guarantee human rights" (*Prensa Libre,* 9 June).

Guatemalan high school and university student agitation escalated in August following the killing of the vice president of the Students Association at the Rafael Aqueche Institute, and the murder of another university leader. Demonstrations and protest rallies were held in Guatemala City and Quezaltenango, the country's second largest city, accusing national authorities of responsibility for the incidents. On 14 September hundreds of university and high school students staged a demonstration in Guatemala City demanding respect for human rights and political freedom. Disturbances erupted in the capital's Central Park, culminating in the stoning of the Government Palace and confrontations between police and demonstrators. Four persons were killed and at least fifty wounded. A police communiqué charged that the incident was "part of a plan by extremist groups to provoke police authorities and take advantage of student discontent" (*El Imparcial,* 16 September). President Laugerud condemned the violence and said that it was instigated by "professional agitators trained in Cuba and the Soviet Union." For its part, the Association of University Students (AEU) blamed "provocateurs paid by the fascist sectors" for the outburst (EFE, Madrid, 18 September).

On 10 November a university leader was kidnaped near the San Carlos campus. The University's Superior Council demanded that Mario Sandoval Alarcón, the acting president of the republic, undertake an immediate investigation (ACAN, Panama City, 10 November). On 16 November Sandoval stated that workers' strikes and demonstrations organized by CNUS were "part of a Communist plot to seize power" and would not be allowed to undermine public order (ibid., 17 November). As leader of the conservative National Liberation Movement (MLN) and the country's top anti-Communist leader, Sandoval has been accused of involvement with right-wing terrorism in recent years, going back as far as the Mano Blanca extermination squads of the late 1960s. However, there is no indication that he is connected with the emergence of the Secret Anticommunist Army (Ejército Secreto Anticomunista; ESA), whose first communiqué issued on 22 June announced its intention of "protecting social classes attacked by Communist gangs." The ESA warned that it will fight relentlessly against leftist organizations and that it has already begun to judge the most prominent Communists who promote terror in the country (*El Imparcial,* 23 June). The emergence of the ESA produced an announcement from the government that the group would be "vigorously combatted." In October the ESA issued "death sentences" against union leaders and members for their alleged Communist affiliation. Similar threats had been made previously against several newsmen.

On 20 July the National Directorate of the Christian Democratic Party was called to an emergency meeting to discuss protective measures for several of its leaders who had reportedly received death threats from the Mano Blanca organization. Anonymous notes were received indicating that "July will be the month for elimination of Communists." (Ibid., 21 July.) The threat to the Christian Democrats was the first clandestine activity of the Mano Blanca in several years. No further activities by this group were reported, nor is there any evidence that the threats were carried out. Just the same, in late July and August seven members of the MLN were assassinated in various parts of the country, presumably by leftist organizations.

In November a new clandestine group of the left called the Labor Self-Defense Committee (Comité de Autodefensa Obrero) took credit for the bombing of the Association of Urban Bus Companies of the capital's transportation system. According to a communiqué delivered to news media on 5 November, the attack was intended to be "a warning to the exploiting classes, their lackeys and the officials who repress the workers." The communiqué, which bore the seal of a sickle and hammer, appealed to the labor class to make use of every form of struggle to eliminate "man's exploitation by man" (ACAN, Panama City, 5 November).

The PGT: Leadership and Organization. Little information is available on the present leadership of the PGT or the party's structure. Since 1972, two general secretaries and nineteen ranking members of the Central Committee have "disappeared," apparently the victims of assassination. Following the murder of Humberto Alvarado Arrellano in December 1975, Isías de León became general secretary. Other prominent members of the Central Committee are Otto Sánchez, Jorge Muñoz, A. Bauer Pais, Antonio Fuentes, and Pedro González Torres.

The PGT has a youth auxiliary, the Patriotic Youth of Labor (Juventud Patriótica del Trabajo). Student agitators are active at the secondary and university levels, although direct affiliation with the PGT is disclaimed. Student leaders supported by the PGT have been unsuccessful in recent years in their efforts to gain control of the influential AEU, although the association's statements on domestic issues tend to be strongly critical of the government and its inability to control right-wing paramilitary violence.

The PGT also controls the clandestine Guatemalan Autonomous Federation of Trade Unions (Federación Autónoma Guatemalteca), a small and relatively unimportant labor organization. The federation became an affiliated member of the Communist-front World Federation of Trade Unions (WFTU) in October 1974. The National Committee of Labor Unity (CNUS), which includes some seventy unions, has become the most important voice for organized labor, and many observers feel that its militant activities in 1977 were the result of increasing PGT influence within its ranks.

Domestic Attitudes and Activities. It is difficult to determine whether the PGT's Central Committee met on a regular basis during 1977, or where it met. Likewise, there is little data to reveal the content of any political resolutions that may have been adopted. Thus, in order to characterize the PGT's attitudes on domestic and foreign issues, it is necessary to turn to the statements by party leaders who either publish abroad or grant interviews on an irregular basis.

Writing in the *World Marxist Review,* A. Bauer Pais stated that Guatemala is virtually an occupied country whose natural resources are either owned or controlled in one way or another by foreigners, above all, North Americans. He contended that oil and nickel, the country's key resources, have been put at the disposal of multinationals. He added that to bring these natural resources under national control, it would be necessary to carry out an agrarian reform; confiscate and nationalize all mineral, transportation, banking, and plant enterprises owned by foreign monopolies; annul the country's "shackling" foreign debt; establish trade relations with all countries on the basis of mutual benefit; and introduce economic planning (*WMR,* April).

Central Committee member Jorge Muñoz characterized the situation in Guatemala as one of further deterioration of living conditions for most of the nation; increased repression and terror; activization of the struggle of the masses, especially among working class sectors; and acute contradictions within the ruling classes. According to Muñoz, the PGT believes that under current conditions the working people can come to power only through armed struggle: "Confrontations between the oppressed and the oppressors, between the forces of revolution and counterrevolution, were, are, and will be more uncompromising with each passing day" (*Latinskaya Amerika,* Moscow, July-August). Muñoz does not rule out the necessity of using peaceful forms of struggle as a matter of tactics. Conditions in the country are viewed as favorable for the broadest possible popular struggle for "purposes of blocking fascism." The party has put forth a specific program consisting of five points: (1) against the high cost of living; (2) for higher wages and incomes for the working masses; (3) against government repression and terror; (4) in favor of giving the land to the peasants; and (5) in favor of the rights of the individual and democratic freedoms. With respect to the party's goal of achieving greater consolidation of the trade union movement, Muñoz expressed the belief that the Guatemalan working class has made substantial strides toward union unity. In addition, he feels the peasants' movement for land has become stronger and that student organizations are also being restored. (Ibid.)

The PGT has expressed its support for setting up a broad front involving urban and rural workers, peasants, and representatives of the middle segments: "Only in this way can conditions be created for the victory of the revolution and the election of a people's government responsible for implementing the structural changes the country needs" (ibid.). To achieve these goals, the party is prepared to use both legal and illegal means of struggle. Precisely to what extent the PGT was responsible for the instigation of violent acts in 1977 is difficult to ascertain. The traditional military arm of the party, the Revolutionary Armed Forces, was virtually inactive. However, an urban cell of the PGT claimed credit for the assassination of a former defense minister and two other persons on 29 September. The former minister, a retired military man, had actively fought Communist guerrilla activity in the late 1960s and was blamed for the disappearance of numerous leftist political leaders (*El Imparcial,* 30 September). On 11 October the PGT celebrated the anniversary of its founding by exploding bombs, painting walls with PGT slogans against the government, and inundating cities throughout the country with party propaganda (*Prensa Libre,* 12 October).

The most enigmatic aspect of the PGT's activities in 1977 continues to be the degree of its involvement with the self-styled Guerrilla Army of the Poor, which carried out a number of kidnapings and robberies during the year. Given the ideological orientation of the EGP and the targets of its rural and urban attacks, some degree of PGT influence, if not control, appears highly feasible. According to U.S. and Guatemalan sources the EGB descends directly from the Revolutionary Armed Forces. The guerrillas are believed to number about 300, divided into four independent commands, three in the countryside and one in Guatemala City. They have been most active in propaganda and organizing in El Quiché, a mountainous region in northern Guatemala; near Esquintla, along the tropical Pacific Coast; and to a lesser extent in the department of Zacapa, where the guerrillas had their strongest support ten years ago (*Washington Post,* 30 June). Guatemalan intelligence reported in late 1976 that the EGP's principal leader is César Montes, a member of the PGT in the 1960s and a leader of the Revolutionary Armed Forces until it was crushed with U.S. support in the late 1960s (*El Imparcial,* 4 December 1976). The influence of the PGT is believed to be greatest within the guerrilla unit operating in Guatemala City. U.S. and Guatemalan officials agree that the guerrillas are not under the direct command of the PGT, although many urban guerrillas are believed to be party members. President Laugerud told a group of foreign journalists in May that a PGT delegation had traveled to Cuba to ask Castro to withdraw his support of the EGP because of increased army pressure on the party as a result of guerrilla activity. In a communiqué issued in June, the PGT denied having made any such request and stressed that "such statements distort facts and only serve the purpose of an illegal government which lacks popular support and violates human rights daily" (Havana International Service, 24 June).

While much of the EGP's activity involved various acts of sabotage directed against large sugar cane and cotton plantations and arson attacks on factories in the capital, the movement's most spectacular act in 1977 was the kidnaping on 29 May of Salvador's ambassador to Guatemala on the eve of the opening session of the eighteenth assembly of governors of the Inter-American Development Bank (IDB). In a message prepared for news media, the EGP declared that Eduardo Casanova had been singled out as a kidnap victim because he had formerly served as the head of El Salvador's National Guard, during which time he was charged with the "assassination and disappearance of hundreds of Salvadoran patriots and revolutionaries." As a *quid pro quo* for Casanova's release, the EGP demanded that the president of the IDB order an extensive communiqué read at the assembly's opening session on 30 May. The statement accused officials of the various countries participating in the meeting of pursuing a financial policy "which is at the service of the dominant classes of the United States, the great monopolies, and the oligarchies of Latin America." The communiqué added that expansion of the IDB's activities would "sooner or later lead to the polarization of the struggle between the exploited and the exploiters, the dominant and the dependent" (*El Imparcial,* 31 May). While an embarrassed President Laugerud condemned the kidnaping as a "display of international terrorism," Casanova was released unharmed on 31 May, twenty-four hours after the EGP's proclamation had been read. Salvadoran guerrillas applauded the EGP's action as "a demonstration of Central American unity and proletarian internationalism" (ACAN, Panama City, 8 June).

On 23 August the EGP issued bulletins claiming credit for the murder of five persons it accused of being "allies of exploitative capitalism" (*El Imparcial,* 24 August). In October approximately twenty guerrillas attacked the town of El Ruedito, Chiquimula Province, and kidnaped the military commissioner and mayor. In November a group estimated at 100 guerrillas staged rallies and destroyed crops and equipment on two large plantations in Esquintla (ACAN, 10 November). At year's end, press correspondents reported increased military mobilization in the northwest and Pacific coastal regions of the country, presumably in search of guerrillas. Although the guerrillas are unlikely to threaten the government in the short run, the long-run potential for increasing instability exists. Guatemala's population remains overwhelmingly rural, Indian, and poor. The great majority of the Indian communities are separated both ethnically and economically from participation in national life.

International Positions and Contacts. The PGT's positions on international issues follow closely those of the USSR. In a joint declaration by Central American Communist parties marking the sixtieth anniversary of the October Revolution, Socialism was described as "stronger than ever." The document cited "the economic and military power of the states ruled by the working class and the great progress of the communist and workers parties in both dependent colonial and developed capitalist countries." The successful struggle of peoples in Vietnam, Laos, Angola, and Mozambique "underscores the possibility of establishing socialism throughout the entire world." The initiatives of the Soviet Union concerning detente, disarmament and international cooperation were listed as "decisive contributions in the development of Lenin's policy of peaceful coexistence" (*Horizon,* East Berlin, 29 August).

In his analysis of the failure of Trotskyism in Guatemala, Jorge Muñoz accused its supporters of attempting to split the revolutionary movement by belittling the prestige of the PGT, slandering the Soviet Union, and serving the interests of American imperialism (*Latinskaya Amerika,* July-August).

In a communiqué circulated in various capitals of Central America, the PGT charged that the Guatemalan government was stirring up the conflict with Great Britain over Belize in order to divert the people's attention from Guatemala's acute social and economic problems. The document accused the transnationals of putting pressure on President Laugerud's regime and charged the government with "exalting a false nationalism to divide the peoples of Guatemala and Belize and lead them to a bloodbath" (*Granma,* Spanish edition, 27 July).

Little information is available on the international contacts maintained by the PGT in 1977. Party delegations visited Hungary and Czechoslovakia in late 1976. Delegates attended an international symposium in Havana on the "Protection of Natural Resources," sponsored by the *WMR* in collaboration with the Cuban Communist Party (*WMR,* April). In September the PGT signed the "Declaration of Fraternal Latin American Communist Parties" in commemoration of the sixtieth anniversary of the October Socialist Revolution.

Publications. The PGT publishes a clandestine newspaper, *Verdad.*

Washington College   Daniel L. Premo

Guyana

The People's Progressive Party (PPP) of Guyana was founded in 1950. At its First Congress, in 1951, it declared itself a nationalist party, committed to Socialism, national independence, and Caribbean unity. During nearly two decades following, the leadership of the PPP was predominantly Marxist-Leninist, but the party followers in general were not knowledgeably so. In 1969 the leader of the party, Cheddi Jagan, moved for the first time to align the PPP unequivocally with the Soviet Union and, in turn, he PPP was recognized by Soviet leaders as a bona fide Communist party. Party leaders say that the process of transforming the PPP into a Leninist party began in 1969 (*Mirror,* 28 March 1976).

The PPP is a legal organization and represents the major opposition to the ruling People's National Congress (PNC), a party led by one-time PPP member, and present Guyanese prime minister, Forbes Burnham. Particularly since Burnham's break with the PPP in the mid-1950s, Guyanese politics has been heavily influenced, at times determined, by ethnic differences in the country—roughly 50 percent of the population is of East Indian descent (traditionally supporting the PPP), some 40 percent of African descent (generally supporting the PNC), and the remainder assorted Amerindians, Portuguese, Chinese, and racial mixtures. In 1973 Burnham was reelected for his third term while the PPP, still claiming to be the majority party in the country, received only 26 percent of the vote (and fourteen out of fifty-three seats in parliament). Jagan (with some justification) protested that fraud and illegal maneuvers had prevailed. The PPP boycotted parliament until May 1976.

The membership of the PPP is unknown, though the number of active and influential Marxist-Leninists is probably no more than several hundred. In the past few years a number of blacks have joined the PPP, while many East Indians have drifted into the PNC. The population of Guyana is approximately 850,000.

Leadership and Organization. At its Nineteenth Congress in 1976, the PPP returned Cheddi Jagan to his long-held position as secretary general and elected its thirty-two-member Central Committee.

Among the prominent party leaders, all of whom are among the fourteen PPP members of parliament, are Janet Jagan (PPP secretary for international affairs), Ram Karran (secretary for labor), Clinton Collymore (columnist for *Mirror*), Reepu Daman Persaud (chairman for auditing and control commission), Harry Persaud (organizing secretary), and Feroze Mohamed (secretary for youth affairs).

The Progressive Youth Organization (PYO), traditionally a source of strong personal support for Cheddi Jagan, celebrated its twenty-fifth anniversary in early September 1977. The PYO, torn by internal dissension in recent years, is headed by First Secretary Navin Chandarpaul. Founded as the Pioneer Youth League in 1952, the PPP daily organ described the PYO as the "longest functioning militant youth organization in Guyana" (*Mirror,* editorial, 4 September). The PYO had its celebration in a tent when the several hundred delegates were denied use of public school facilities. Resolutions of the meeting dealt with the need to reorient the national educational system as well as assorted other domestic and international issues (ibid., 11 September). In his keynote address on 3 September, Cheddi Jagan told the delegates that now that the PYO had passed through "hell's fire and come out more purified," it was "steeled with Marxist-Leninist ideology and consciousness which cannot be defeated" (ibid., 6 September). The PYO won none of the sixteen seats on the Executive Council of the University of Guyana Student Society in October, though the conduct of the elections was challenged.

The PPP-controlled Guyana Agricultural and General Workers' Union (GAWU), based in the sugar industry, claims to be the largest trade union in the country with some 20,000 members. Ram Karran is president and Pariag Sukhai is secretary general. The GAWU is a member of the Guyana Trade Union Congress (TUC), though it is frequently critical of TUC administration and policies. During 1977 the GAWU sought to negotiate a change in worker profit-sharing conditions with the state-owned Guyana Sugar Corporation (Guysuco), and later with the PNC government. When no satisfaction was forthcoming, a strike was called for 24 August. In the course of the strike, which dragged on for months, much of the sugar harvest was lost and the government accused the GAWU of having foreign backing in an attempt to overthrow President Burnham. Tough national security legislation was passed, giving the government broad powers of arrest, detention, and restriction of movement. The GAWU protested the powers, particularly when police seized relief food supplies destined for the families of striking workers, though the supplies were later released.

The PPP also sponsors the Women's Progressive Organization (WPO).

Party Internal Affairs. The core leadership of the PPP has been shaken on several occasions since Jagan's 1969 decision to become affiliated with the pro-Soviet Communist bloc. The most recent crisis, which began in 1975, and evidently tapered off in 1977, was caused by Jagan's adoption of a policy of "critical support" for the PNC government. Prime Minister Burnham has encouraged this dissension, in part by appointing several prominent PPP defectors—notably Ranji Chandisingh and Vincent Teekah, to important positions in the government and the PNC.

Domestic Attitudes and Activities. According to the PPP, Guyana is in a state of severe and mounting political, economic, and social crisis. The crisis of production, which is at the root of the problem, has led to budgetary and balance of payments deficits. A serious shortage of foreign exchange has led to important restrictions which, in turn, have caused a shortage of essential commodities for consumption and production. Domestically, an inflationary spiral and higher prices have meant a decline in living standards and cuts in social services. With the chronic high level of unemployment and underemployment aggravated by retrenchment, crime is increasing and the social fabric is breaking down. The PPP charges that "no serious attempt is being made to grapple with the crisis at its roots." (*Mirror,* 14 August.)

Jagan has described the PCN as a minority party with a "reactionary bureaucratic petty-bourgeois class being a dominant force in the leadership and in the state apparatus." The PNC's basic problem is that "it has built a strong wall between the Party with its bureaucratic representatives and the people." (Ibid., 25, 18 August.) The Burnham government is a "semi-dictatorship" which harasses leftists, obstructs the freedom of the press, and refuses to allow personal freedoms or free and fair elections (ibid., 9 January, 26 July; *Advocate-News,* Bridgetown, 22 February).

The PPP policy of "critical support" for the PNC, Jagan has written, "is above all intended to give a firm rebuff to enemy number one, imperialism, to join the PNC in creating national unity and national security in defense of the sovereignty and territorial integrity of Guyana." It must involve both unity and struggle—"unity and cooperation with the positive trends and the revolutionary democrats and socialists in the PNC; isolation of and struggle against the negative trends and the bureaucratic-capitalists of the PNC." (*IB,* No. 2, 1977.)

To pull Guyana out of its crisis, the PPP in August called for the establishment of a National Patriotic Front and for the formation of a front government including "all parties and groups which are progressive, anti-imperialist and wish to see Guyana take a socialist-oriented or non-capitalist path of development." This government would bring about a revolutionary alliance of the workers, peasant farmers, revolutionary intellectuals, progressive businessmen, and the middle strata generally. The national government should be based on political, economic, and social democracy; there should be free and fair elections with the full exercise of democratic freedoms; and workers should control economic management and decision-making. The people should have the right of free association, in trade unions, cultural, religious, or other groupings. (Ibid., 14 August.) Speaking to newsmen at Freedom House in Georgetown, Jagan presented the "minimum program" of the revolutionary national front government. As summarized in a *Mirror* editorial (21 August), the points were: state ownership of the commanding heights of the economy; central planning and planned proportional development of the economy with emphasis on industry and agriculture; expansion of the state and cooperative sectors; land reform aimed at ending rapacious landlordism; worker control and meaningful involvement of the people in all aspects of socio-economic reconstruction; firm measures to end corruption, nepotism, favoritism, racial and political discrimination; creation of a democratically-run and people-managed National People's Militia with branches in every city block, village and settlement; imbuing the people with a revolutionary scientific Socialist (Marxist-Leninist) ideology; and respect for, and observance of, the fundamental rights laid down in the constitution. (Also see ibid., 10, 14 August.)

The PNC immediately rejected the PPP call. The latter party responded by charging that the "anti-national and anti-patriotic" right wing of the PNC had its way (ibid., 21 August). The PNC frequently speaks of unity, according to a *Mirror* editorial, but "it is concerned with power." It is trying to create a one-party state, making the army its willing instrument of control. (Ibid., 23 August.) Indeed, "it is precisely because the constitutional formula proposed by the PPP for a national front government is based on a democratic foundation and free and fair elections that the minority PNC has rejected the proposal." The PPP then called on the Guyanese people to "fight for a political solution as the only way to solve the crisis and avert the danger facing Guyana." (Ibid., 28 August.)

International Views and Contacts. During 1977 the PPP repeatedly charged that the United States, upset by the leftward direction of events in Guyana, was trying to arrest and reverse trends in the country. In particular, the party warned that PNC efforts to secure foreign loans opened the door to American control. In May the PPP demanded the elimination of all U.S. military bases in Panama, Cuba, and Puerto Rico and called for cancellation of the agreement which allows the U.S. Air Force to overfly Guyana and use air installations in the country (AFP, 14 May). Jagan called the Soviet

October Revolution "the most important event of our times" and said that "the PPP has always guided its activities by the enormous experiences of the CPSU" (Havana Domestic Service, 13 April). The PPP leader travelled widely in Cuba, Eastern Europe, the Soviet Union, and countries of the non-Soviet bloc. The PPP position with respect to the Soviet-bloc countries was complicated to some extent by the very close relations Prime Minister Burnham also maintains with those countries. After attending May Day activities in Cuba, the PPP participated in a conference of the Communist parties of the Caribbean sub-region being held in Havana (see *Granma*, English ed., Havana, 15 May).

Publications. The PPP's newspaper, *Mirror,* is published in Georgetown and edited by Janet Jagan. The party's theoretical journal is *Thunder.*

Hoover Institution   William E. Ratliff
Stanford University

Haiti

The United Party of Haitian Communists (Parti Unifié des Communistes Haitiens; PUCH) was formed in November 1968 by the merging of several smaller leftist parties. The membership of the PUCH is unknown but presumed to be less than several hundred persons, most of whom are underground, in jail, or in exile. The population of Haiti in 1977 was approximately 5,000,000.

All political parties in Haiti have been outlawed since 1949. In April 1969 a law was passed declaring all forms of Communist activity crimes against the state, the penalty for which would be both confiscation of property and death. Most PUCH activities have been carried on outside of Haiti among exiles in Europe, the Soviet Union, and Cuba. Some PUCH members were among the political prisoners ceremoniously released and sent into exile during the year. The main party spokesman during the year was Jacques Dorcilien. The party says it is disseminating revolutionary ideas, starting more cells in industry and agriculture, and forging links between the party and the workers, peasants, and other sectors of the population.

Domestic and International Views. During 1977 the PUCH condemned the government of Jean-Claude Duvalier for blocking national unity and the development of class consciousness among the workers, denying democratic liberties, subordinating foreign policy to the dictates of foreign imperialists, and keeping the people in a state of abject poverty and cultural backwardness. The Communist parties of the Caribbean, including the PUCH, meeting in Havana after celebrations on May Day, agreed on the need to mobilize public opinion to demand that the crimes and tortures of the Haitian government be stopped, that prisoners be set free, and that democratic rights be restored. (*Granma*, English ed., Havana, 15 May.)

Publications. The PUCH publishes the irregular, clandestine *Boukan* for circulation in Haiti. Several PUCH press organs are published in Canada, Mexico, and France.

Hoover Institution   William E. Ratliff
Stanford University

Honduras

The Communist Party of Honduras (Partido Comunista de Honduras; PCH) was organized in 1927, destroyed in 1932 during the reign of Tiburcio Carías, and reorganized in April 1954. In 1967 a dispute over strategy and tactics led to the expulsion of one group and the division of the PCH into rival factions. A later division within the PCH led to the formation of the Honduran Workers' Party (Partido de los Trabajadores Hondureños; PTH), but this group has dissolved. Since 1971 a self-proclaimed pro-Chinese Communist Party of Honduras/Marxist-Leninist (PCH-ML) has functioned but little is known about its leadership and membership. The PCH has been illegal since 1957 but under different governments has carried out both clandestine and open activities.

In December 1972 the armed forces of Honduras overthrew the government of President Ramón Cruz in a non-violent coup. On 22 April 1975 General Oswaldo López was replaced as head of government by Colonel Juan Alberto Melgar Castro.

The membership of the PCH is estimated at 650. The PCH-ML probably has fewer than 100 members. The population of Honduras is 2,912,000 (estimated 1977).

Leadership and Organization. The secretary general of the PCH is Dionisio Ramos Bejarano. Other important leaders are Rigoberto Padilla Rush, Secretary of the Central Committee and member of the Political Commission; Milton Rene Paredes, a Central Committee member; Mario Sosa Navarro, a member of the Political Commission; and Rigoberto Luna, active in the party's work with labor unions. Longino Becerra, a propaganda spokesman in the 1960s, resurfaced in April 1977 after five years of unexplained absence.

Probably the most important event of the year for the PCH was its Third Congress, evidently held in early June in semi-secret fashion "somewhere on the national territory" (*La Tribuna*, Tegucigalpa, 15 June). At a public press conference held on 14 June by Ramos, Sosa, Padilla and Becerra, Ramos noted that the party's Congress approved several reforms in party statutes, elected a new Central Committee, and presented the party's position on various national issues.

The party has been active in recruitment and organizational work among university and secondary students, urban workers, banana workers on the North Coast plantations operated by United Brands (Tela Railroad Company) and Standard Fruit Company (a Castle and Cook subsidiary), and peasants, but has also lost members from these groups.

The PCH has claimed in the past that students make up 20 percent of its members but no figures were forthcoming on party membership at the June 1977 Congress. The PCH sponsors the Socialist Student Front (FES) and the Federation of Secondary Students (FESE). The FES is probably the second most important university student organization in Honduras and operates relatively freely on the campuses of the National Autonomous University of Honduras (UNAH) in Tegucigalpa, the capital, and San Pedro Sula, the most important city on the North Coast. The FESE, now in its seventh year, claims membership of more than 40,000—though this figure is probably exaggerated. Identity of the officers elected in its Seventh Congress on 5-7 June 1977, in Tegucigalpa, is not known.

The FESE was probably active in supporting candidates of two "progressive groups," the Revolutionary Action Front (FAR) and Struggle Committee of Secondary Students (CLES), whose efforts at distributing election literature at the Vicente Caceres Central Institute on 17 June were broken up by some thirty-five university students belonging to the right-wing United Democratic University Front (FUUD), which dominates the UNAH.

Although Monseñor Hector Enrique Santos, the archbishop of Tegucigalpa, charged on 6 August 1976 that the Communists were making efforts to "control" elementary schools in the same way as they do the university and secondary schools (*FBIS*, 9 August 1976), there was little evidence that this was occurring in late 1977.

The PCH has tried unsuccessfully to influence both the National Innovation and Unity Party (PINU) and the Christian Democratic Party (PDC), neither of which has been able to obtain legal recognition from the government though both participate in the Advisory Council to the Chief of State (CAJEDE), a body which began functioning in June 1976 as a channel of communication between the government and the people. Also participating in CAJEDE deliberations in 1976-1977 were representatives of the armed forces, labor and peasant organizations, cooperative and women's groups, and the National University—two of whose student and faculty representatives have been charged privately with being PCH members.

The leadership of different factions of the traditional Liberal and National parties, and the nation's principal newspapers, were divided on the question of legalizing the PCH in anticipation of elections which may be held in 1979-1980 to transfer power to a constitutional government. After a former foreign minister and Liberal Party leader, who was also a CAJEDE delegate, proposed that the party be legalized, national opinion on the matter surged back and forth. Shortly thereafter, the president of the Central Committee of the National Party indicated that "even though the [Communist] party is found in clandestinity, it is known that communists are found everywhere, that they have infiltrated the government, political, and even religious organizations." However, "it is better that they struggle in the open and not underwater." (*La Tribuna*, 10 June 1977.)

Although many people thought a 10,000 membership figure was too high for filing petitions for presidential candidate registration, Secretary General Ramos did not think that collection of 10,000 names nor the creation of a specific number of departmental and municipal committees would be a problem (*FBIS*, 12 October). Two members of the Supreme Council of the Armed Forces expressed their disapproval of PCH legalization.

On 21 December 1976 a retired colonel claimed seven Communists were filling high army positions (*Latin America*, London, 21 January 1977). When asked to substantiate his charges, the officer remained silent. On 15 January, Melgar Castro himself, and then on 12 March the head of Army intelligence, denied there was any Communist infiltration in the armed forces (*FBIS*, 18 January and 14 March).

PCH influence in the trade union movement was substantially reduced in 1977 when Andres Victor Artiles and Celeo Gonzalez led workers organized into a Democratic Front—which ousted President Napoleon Acevedo Granados and a coalition of PCH and Christian-Democratic-oriented leaders— from the banana workers' union of the Standard Fruit Company (SUTRASFCO) and the FESITRANH. The struggle for control between the PCH and the Democratic Front broke out in mid-February 1977 with the arrest of several officers of the Empresa Asociative de Isletas who were allied with Acevedo in the SUTRASFCO. The Acevedo group tried to lock out Democratic Front delegates from the Extraordinary Congress of SUTRASFCO in March, but failed, and public security forces maintained order as delegates elected a new leadership. Two and a half weeks later, PCH influence in FESITRANH was further reduced after Democratic Front delegates supported a ticket opposed to Acevedo. Subsequently, some 200 workers loyal to Acevedo conducted work stoppages on Standard Fruit plantations and were dismissed (*FBIS*, 2 May). In turn, the new FESITRANH leadership was roundly booed by a group of workers and university students—some of whom carried PCH banners—at a May Day Rally sponsored by opponents in La Lima, Cortes (*La Prensa*, San Pedro Sula, 2 May 1977). However, by 18 June 1977, the Democratic Front officially solidified its control of SUTRASFCO at a Congress in La Ceíba. Afterwards, Acevedo was dismissed by Standard Fruit Company for failure to return to his former job within the two-day period called for by his contract with the union for individuals given time off for union duties; Acevedo also lost his position on the CAJEDE council.

While there may have been some PCH influence in National Association of Honduras Peasants (ANACH) local organizations in 1975-1976, this influence appeared minimal in 1977, especially at the Department and national levels. PCH influence was also minimal in the Christian Democratic-oriented National Union of Peasants (UNC), though Marxist ideas appealed to many members and leaders.

Probably the most important PCH influence in the rural sector came through the Peasant Training Programs (PROCCARA) of the National Agrarian Institute which had signed an agreement for such programs some years ago with the Food and Agriculture Organization (FAO) of the United Nations. Although it is difficult to obtain specific details about the nature of many training programs and sessions, there is evidence of a strong Marxist content in printed materials distributed in late 1976 and early 1977. In late January 1977, Efraín Díaz Galeas, President of the Federation of Agrarian Reform Cooperatives of Honduras (FECORAH) charged that the PROCCARA program was infiltrated by Communists (*La Prensa*, 1 February). In June, I was informed by some INA officials that many PROCCARA instructors were not only "not Hondurans who knew nothing of Honduran traditions" but many "were also Communists." Díaz Galeas was also a participant in a bizarre set of events when he returned from an East European trip in late January 1977, ostensibly at the invitation of the Bulgarian government, and said that he had been put on a plane in San José, Costa Rica, and forced to go to Havana, Cuba, when he thought he was going to Europe. He reportedly was displeased when he was taken from the José Martí Airport in Havana to a hotel where he was interrogated for almost three days about agrarian activities in Honduras. One source indicated that at least two of the interrogators belonged to the Cuban intelligence service. Upon Díaz' return, he indicated he met with high officials of the Honduran Armed Forces to acquaint them with the events (*La Prensa*, and *FBIS*, 1 February).

Communist influence in PROCCARA was undoubtedly reduced when Rigoberto Sandoval Corea resigned on 14 March as Executive Director of the Agrarian Institute and a wholesale dismissal of Honduran and international employees followed under his former deputy and successor.

Domestic Views. Until 1976 the PCH supported the government of the Armed Forces, especially the five-year National Development Plan and the Agrarian Reform Law of 14 January 1975. On 3 March 1977, the Political Commission of the Central Committee charged that "opponents of all changes in Honduras began a campaign of political pressure on the lieutenant colonels who had assumed key posts in the government and the armed forces" in January 1974. The object of the recent campaign was "to set as many of them as possible against reform and isolate . . . those who showed greater firmness in implementing the reform plan announced on 1 January 1974." (*IB*, No. 6, 1977.) The re-shuffling of various senior Army officers to new posts between 1-5 January 1977 also concerned the PCH along with the replacement of the minister of labor.

What many observers considered a move to the center the PCH regarded as a swing to the right. The PCH Political Commission considered the January officer re-assignments and the February arrests of the Isletas leaders as encouraging to "forces interested in spreading fascist methods far and wide," including "the dictatorial regimes of Central America," especially Nicaragua's General Anastasio Somoza and the American Institute of Free Labor Development. However, the PCH did recognize that there was a "climate of peace in Honduras and that the government had not been as repressive" as those of Guatemala, El Salvador and Nicaragua. As a consequence, the PCH proposed that (1) "fascist-like tendencies" inside or outside the government should be exposed, (2) "unity of the more socially-conscious and progressive segments of the population should be supported," and (3) "paramilitary groups" similar to those operating in Guatemala, El Salvador and other parts of Latin America should be prevented from operating in Honduras. (*IB*, No. 6; *Tiempo*, Tegucigalpa, 9 March 1977). During the 14 March 1977 press conference that followed the party's Third Congress, Longino Becerra said that the government headed by General Melgar Castro had "entered into a regressive process of abandoning the social reforms that were outlined in 1972" (*El Día*, Tegucigalpa, 14 June). The PCH was further opposed to the constitutionalization of General Melgar Castro as president, especially after the general encountered considerable popular enthusiasm on several weekends in different parts of the country. By October, Secretary General Ramos declared that there was "no respect for human rights" in the country and that the electoral process announced for 1979 was not democratic because it left out groups like the Communist Party which could have easily met the legal requirements for registration (*FBIS*, 12 October).

International Activities and Contacts. While the four PCH leaders participating in the 14 June press conference said that their party was one of many Communist parties around the world, they claimed that they did not "receive directives from abroad since the world communist organization does not trace out directions for any particular party." The PCH said it was not a "pro-Soviet, pro-Cuban, nor pro-Chinese party," and concluded: "We are a national party, composed of Hondurans." (*La Tribuna*, 15 June.)

Just the same, Longino Becerra participated in an international symposium in Havana in early 1977 sponsored by the *World Marxist Review* in collaboration with the Communist Party of Cuba. In early June the Central Committee of the Communist Party of the Soviet Union sent its fraternal greetings along with wishes for "strengthening . . . the PCH's ranks on the basis of the principles of Marxism-Leninism and proletarian internationalism." (*FBIS*, 13 June.)

In July, the PCH may have strained relations with the Melgar Castro regime by extending the party's "sympathy and solidarity with the people of Belize" in their "struggle" to rid themselves "of the British colonialist yoke" and their repudiation of Guatemala's "annexationist aspirations." Interestingly, the PCH also said that it did not "criticize the Honduran . . . government's support of the Guatemalan cause because . . . it is a support devoid of any material commitments and does not oppose the principle of self-determination of peoples." (*FBIS*, 13 July.)

On 26 August 1977, the PCH joined with the Communist parties of El Salvador, Guatemala, Mexico, and Panama to issue a joint declaration of international solidarity on the sixtieth anniversary of the October Revolution in the Soviet Union (*FBIS*, 30 September).

In October, PCH Politburo member Milton Paredes and Ricardo Valladares, a member of the party's "international relations section," were reported by the French Communist newspaper *L'Humanité* to have met with French Communist Party Politburo members in what was probably an effort to extend the PCH's links with European Communist parties (*ibid.*, 19 October).

Publications. The PCH publishes *El Trabajo*, a theoretical, political, and informational journal, and two other publications, *Adelante* and *Patria*, all of which have been appearing sporadically in the past year. Party statements are often found in the *World Marxist Review* and that journal's *Information Bulletin*.

The PCH-ML. The pro-Chinese PCH-ML was reported by Chinese sources to be active in support of the election of Hua Kuo-feng as Chairman of the Central Committee of the Communist Party of China. The Chinese said the PCH-ML Political Bureau sent a letter on 31 October 1976 from Honduras in support of Hua in the struggle against the "Gang of Four" in China (*Peking Review*, 24 December 1976). In January 1977, the Chinese also said that Chairman Hua met a PCH-ML delegation "recently" and hosted a banquet in their honor (*FBIS*, 11 January; *Peking Review*, 21 January). While various Chinese officials are mentioned, no Hondurans are identified by name.

Texas Tech University   Neale J. Pearson

Martinique

The Martinique Communist Party (Parti Communiste Martiniquais; PCM) is one of the oldest Communist parties in the world, having been founded in July 1921. However, it has never fully recovered from the highly publicized defection in 1956 of its leader Aimé Césaire, a famous poet, deputy in the National Assembly, and mayor of Fort-de-France, the capital. Today membership is about 1,000 out of the island's total population of 327,000 (estimated 1977). The PCM now dates its founding to 1957.

In 1957 another change took place. Under continuing pressure from nationalist groups to change Martinique from a French Overseas Department to an autonomous or independent state, the party transformed itself from a federation when its ties to the French Communist Party (PCF) were loosened and the Martinique party became autonomous. Since the May 1968 general strike in France the PCM, like the PCF, has been challenged as too conservative and bureaucratic by an assortment of small groups of pro-Chinese, nationalists, Trotskyites, and others collectively called "gauchistes." In addition, the Martinique Progressive Party (Parti Progressiste Martiniquais; PPM), which Césaire founded after leaving the PCM, competes effectively for votes in Fort-de-France, the only important city, thus depriving the Communists of a potentially important political base.

The PCM is a legal party. Although it is not represented in the French National Assembly or Senate, it currently has three councilors in the local thirty-six-member General Council. Thus, a coalition of pro-government parties continued to dominate the General Council. The PCM, which lost one General Council seat in 1976, further declined in the municipal elections of 13 and 20 March 1977. Only 9,040 out of 116,879 votes cast went to the PCM. Georges Fitte-Duval, who had lost his General

Council seat in 1976, failed to gain re-election as mayor of Saint-Esprit, and Armand Nicolas lost his bid to enter the Basse-Pointe city hall. When the dust settled, the party had retained control of Lamentin, its strongest base, Morne Rouge, and Macouba. Before the elections the PCM asked Césaire's PPM to run joint lists of candidates, but the latter refused. After the elections, PCM leaders hinted Césaire may have sabotaged their efforts.

Leadership and Organization. Significant changes in leadership of the PCM came out of the Sixth Congress in December 1976. Armand Nicolas replaced Jean-Claude Nicolas as first secretary of the party. Nine new members were also elected to the thirty-six-member Central Committee, and four new persons were elected to the thirteen-member Politburo, in each case replacing considerably older individuals. Under the Politburo are sections and very small cells of one or two dozen members.

Martinique's largest trade union, the General Confederation of Labor of Martinique (CGTM), is closely linked to the PCM and to the Communist-dominated General Confederation of Labor (CGT) in France. Victor Lamon, secretary general of the CGTM, is a Communist member of the General Council. The party is also closely tied to the tiny Union of Communist Youth and the Union of Martiniquan Women, the latter headed by Solange Fitte-Duval, sister of the former Communist mayor of Saint-Esprit.

With respect to internal party programs the Central Committee adopted a report on 12 January to improve the ideological training of members, an issue discussed at the Sixth Congress. In addition, they announced the imminent reappearance of *Action*, a political magazine, the opening of party training schools, and the creation of a library. A party seminar was held on "the National Problem in Martinique," namely, the problem of autonomy for the island. (Autonomy within the French state is considered desirable because it would mean local control over the economy without losing French aid from a government of Socialists and Communists in France, if one should come to power. Autonomy would mean the establishment of an executive responsible to an elected assembly with significant powers, plus an organism to ensure close ties with France.)

Domestic Attitudes and Activities. The PCM hesitated to follow the lead of the PCF when the latter broke with Socialists and Progressives, trying instead to develop leftist unity. The PCM, the Socialist Party, and Césaire's PPM, maintained their "Permanent Committee of the Martiniquan Left." Trade unions, including the CGTM, and discussion groups, such as the Cercle Victor Schoelcher, were part of it even as Communists and Socialists in France traded ideological blows. The 29 September 1977 issue of *Justice* announced an article called "The Common Program in Difficulty," but it did not appear. Instead, throughout the year, the PCM supported greater unity efforts. On 1 May it joined with other parties in a joint appeal for self-determination for the island. Two days later the Communist parties of Martinique, Guadeloupe, Réunion, and France met in Paris to reaffirm their solidarity. On 8 June the PCM proposed a "National Martiniquan Front for Autonomy" and on 30 June the PPM, Socialists, and CGTM union agreed. Communists were asked to support the left's candidates for the two Senate seats—Georges Gratiant (PCM) and Rodolphe Désiré (PPM)—though both lost in the 25 September election. On 16 October a celebration at Lamentin marked the twentieth anniversary of the founding of the PCM, and other parties joined it.

During 1977 the PCM threw its support behind numerous local strikes, such as those of garage and construction workers, as well as the annual general strikes. They continued to denounce the partisanship of government-controlled local radio and television stations (F.R. 3 or France Région 3) and the failure of Paris to provide Martiniquans with the same rights and privileges as have been provided in metropolitan France.

In the General Council the three Communists presented a motion designed to redress the continuing very difficult economic situation. In it they proposed a rebuilding of the sugar industry, still in decline, a reopening of some hotels that had closed their doors, and other measures. They denounced the economic plan of the French prime minister. The party began to praise the Creole language, spoken by all native-born islanders but written by practically none. The PCM proposed that schools should actually be conducted in both Creole and French, asserting that Creole is a key element in Martiniquan national identity. Thus, the party wished to identify itself with nationalist sentiments without espousing complete nationalist goals of independence.

International Views and Policies. Strongly pro-Soviet, the PCM in 1977 sent missions to Russia, East Germany, and Cuba. First Secretary A. Nicolas traveled to Eastern Europe, including Romania. Ties with Cuba became even closer. Martiniquan physicians traveled to Havana; Cuban musicians arrived in Fort-de-France; in April, the Martinique-Cuba Friendship Association sent a delegation to Cuba to study education. In May the PCM delegation to the Conference of Caribbean Communist Parties met with Prime Minister Fidel Castro. The PCM joined Communists from the other three major French overseas departments in a meeting in Guadeloupe in September.

Publications. The PCM's weekly newspaper, *Justice*, is the party's only important organ for transmitting information to the general public. This year, under the direction of G. Thimotée, *Justice*, printed in 8,000 copies, expanded from eight to twelve pages. For the first time in memory, the newspaper published a short article in Creole. *Justice* and the PCM also published an *Essay on the Martiniquan Nation.*

Howard University   Brian Weinstein

Mexico

The Mexican Communist Party (Partido Comunista Mexicano; PCM) was founded in 1919 as the Communist Party of the Mexican Proletariat, but has held its present name since 1920. Although party membership has long been estimated at approximately 5,000, it has recently been placed at many times that figure, probably more nearly reflecting faulty estimates (then and/or now) than spectacular growth over the past year. Current estimates range from 60,000 (*NYT,* 27 December 1977) to 100,000 (*Granma,* Havana, English ed., 18 December). The population of Mexico is 64,487,000 (estimated 1977).

The PCM has been legal in recent years and a party delegation was received by the new president of Mexico, José López Portillo, at the beginning of the year. However, since the party has consistently failed to demonstrate the 60,000 membership necessary for official registration, it has not been entitled to have candidates' names printed on election ballots. (Valentín Campa, who ran as a PCM write-in candidate in the 1976 presidential election, unofficially claimed 500,000 of the 18.5 million votes cast.) Political reforms underway during 1977 are expected to improve the PCM's position in the future with respect to full-fledged legality and electoral participation. According to a proposed law sent to congress in late 1977, political parties can be legally recognized with a minimum of requirements, but they must win at least 1.5 percent of the vote in two consecutive elections or forfeit their registration. Furthermore, political associations and coalitions of parties will be able to present a united front in an election. Early in December the PCM, the Party of the Mexican People (see below), and the Revolutionary Socialist Party (see below) met in Mexico City to work out what they called an unprecedented political alliance for revolutionary purposes. In a public statement, the parties said: "The strategic objective of this new alliance is to build a single party capable of guiding the working class and the people to achieve their present and future demands" and "to lay the foundations for the revolutionary transformation of Mexican society." The immediate objective of the party will be to "struggle for the formation of an anti-imperialist, anti-monopolist, democratic government." Its leaders left open the possibility of merging with other parties that support the construction of a Socialist society in Mexico.

Prominent PCM members include Arnaldo Martínez Verdugo, who was re-elected secretary general at the eighteenth party congress, Arturo Martínez Nateras, Gilberto Rincón Gallardo, and Manuel Marcue Padinas.

Party Positions and Internal Affairs. From 23 to 25 May the PCM held its eighteenth national congress, the first convened openly and reported publicly since 1947. It was attended by fraternal delegates from Communist parties of Eastern Europe, Latin America, the United States, Western Europe, and Japan. Positions taken by the party leadership at the congress included support for the Soviet Union and condemnation of the Chinese Communist regime, the latter especially for its "pro-imperialist" position on Angola; criticism of the government of Mexico as representing the Mexican bourgeoisie in alliance with the forces of international capitalism and North American imperialism; support for the nationalization of industry and the raising of the standards of living of workers and peasants; amnesty for political prisoners, which PCM sources had previously estimated at 1,200; and a strategy of unity of the left in a broad front of democratic, anti-imperialist, and Socialist forces. In addition, party leaders announced a membership drive designed to make the PCM a mass party, and called for the implantation of political and civil freedoms in Mexico and an end to interference in union affairs. Previously, PCM leaders had condemned the use of violence in Mexican politics and had called for the extension of the vote to priests and soldiers, who are at present unenfranchised.

The PCM and Other Left-Wing Parties. Several parties have cooperated with the PCM in issuing public statements, and in May discussions were held among representatives of some of these parties looking toward unity of action and possibly eventual merger. The most important was the Popular Socialist Party (PPS), a legally registered party founded and led for many years by Vicente Lombardo Toledano, and after his death in November 1968, by Jorge Cruickshank García. PPS publications are *Viva México!* and *Avante!* Although a Marxist party staying close to the views of Moscow, the PPS has generally collaborated with Mexico's ruling party, the Institutional Revolutionary Party (Partido Revolucionario Institucional; PRI) and received in return various public posts and, reportedly, unannounced subsidies. After the 1976 election, Cruickshank became the first non-PRI senator since the government party's founding. However, a majority of PPS members abandoned Cruickshank, charging that his senate seat was a payoff for overlooking the PRI's alleged electoral theft of the gubernatorial seat in Nayarit state from a PPS candidate in 1975. In September this faction, which began collaborating with the PCM, became the Party of the Mexican People (PPM) under the leadership of Alejandro Gascón Mercado and Manuel Stephens García.

Other parties sometimes collaborating with the PCM were the Mexican Workers Party (PMT), founded in 1974 and headed by a leader of the 1968 student movement, Herberto Castillo; the

Socialist Workers Party (PST), led by Graco Ramírez, founded in 1975 by former members of the PMT; and the Revolutionary Socialist Party (PRS), led by Roberto Jaramillo. The PCM and several other parties issued a statement in January calling for modification of the party registration laws so that they could register legally, while supporting a minimum membership requirement so that many "miniscule" parties of Socialist orientation would not be legally registered and thus dissipate left-wing electoral support. The leading Trotskyist organizations are the International Communist Group (GCI) and the Socialist League (LS). Early in 1976 the LS split into two factions, the Militant Tendency (TM) and the Bolshevik Leninist Faction (FBL). In 1976 the TM supported Valentín Campa, the PCM presidential candidate; the FBL considered the TM too "reformist" and too willing to collaborate with bourgeois forces.

Foreign Travel. After visiting the Soviet Union in January, Martínez Verdugo, with other PCM members including Antonio Franco, met with Santiago Carrillo, secretary general of the Communist Party of Spain, and other Spanish party leaders, in Madrid in July, going on to Romania and the Soviet Union. Martínez Nateras was in Cuba in July before going on to Hungary and Poland. Three leaders of the Mexican Communist party, Arnaldo Martínez Verdugo, Antonio Franco, and Encarnacíon Pérez Gaytán, were given visas to visit the United States in response to an invitation from Gus Hall, leader of the U.S. Communist party. This was the first time in thirty years that leaders of the Mexican Communist party had been given visas to the United States. In October a delegation from the PCM headed by Gilberto Rincón Gallardo visited East Germany.

Publications. The main PCM publications are the weekly *Oposición* and the theoretical journal, *Socialismo.* The GCI issues *Bandera Roja;* the LS *El Socialista* is open to both factions. Various leftists also publish in *Politica* and *Siempre!*

Political Violence. In July an attempt was made to unify the two PCM-sponsored unions at the National Autonomous University (UNAM), one representing the professors and the other university workers. Ensuing violence led to police occupation of university buildings and the arrest of 531 unionized workers. In August a shoot-out took place between police and 23rd of September militants at UNAM; in May and December police occupied the Benito Juarez University campus in Oaxaca.

Political violence throughout the country was more prevalent during 1977 than it had been for a long time. The press frequently reported kidnappings, assassinations, bombings, holdups, shoot-outs, and hijackings. Responsibility for the actions was claimed by or attributed to a variety of old and new groups.

Most violence was associated with the 23rd of September Communist League, named after the date of an attack on a military garrison in Chihuahua State in 1965, the beginning of the current phase of organized guerrilla activity in Mexico. The group was early active in Guadalajara and Mexico City and today is reportedly headed by Marta Ofelia Contreras Ortiz, alias "Monica." The League, credited with the deaths in recent years of over eighty policemen, was involved in shoot-outs with police in Guadalajara and the Federal District, usually as a result of police raids. The persistence and widespread activities of the League were clearly an embarrassment to police and the army. The government on several occasions announced that the League had been disbanded or that all but a few of its surviving members had been apprehended, only for further incidents to show that the League was still active. However, some of the acts credited to the League, such as the assassination of the university lecturer Alfonso Peralta Reyes, a leader of the Trotskyite Workers' Revolutionary Party (Partido Revolucionario de los Trabajadores; PRT), were of such a character as to suggest that right-wing terrorists or even para-police government agents were using the 23rd of September League to settle scores of their own. The Socialist Workers Party, in fact, alleged that sectors of the League were sponsored by the CIA, adding the charge that the CIA maintained a gang of right-wing Cuban exiles in Mexico to use in terrorist acts against embassies of the Socialist countries. The League's underground magazine is *Madera*.

The previously unknown Union of the People (UP) took responsibility for a wave of bombings of government offices and American-owned businesses in Mexico City, Guadalajara, and Oaxaca in September, with UP leaflets signed by Eleazar Campos, Antonio Montano Torres, Cristóbal Domínguez, and Lidia González Luján. The United Revolutionary Party of America, apparently a peasant organization in Morelos state, made a brief and violent appearance in a September kidnapping. The People's Revolutionary Armed Forces (FRAP) hijacked a bus in August in a bloody and abortive attempt to secure the release of Ramón Cantana López, in jail since 1974 for his part in the kidnaping of the father-in-law of then President Luís Echeverria. The police announced the discovery of a FRAP camp at Punta de Mita in Nayarit state in the anti-FRAP drive that followed the hijacking. The Party of the Poor (PP), led until their deaths by Lucio Cabanas and Genero Vázquez Rojas, was dormant in 1977 due to a harsh counterinsurgency campaign by the army in the state of Guerrerro, where a virtual state of siege obtained and numerous civil rights were reportedly violated. PPS members were assassinated in the states of Morelos and Chihuahua; on both occasions the PPS blamed local political and business leaders. A special counterinsurgency force, the White Brigade (BB), whose existence is denied by the government, is reportedly responsible for dealing severe blows to several guerrilla organizations (*Los Angeles Times,* 1 January 1978).

University of New Mexico   Martin C. Needler

Nicaragua

The Socialist Party of Nicaragua (Partido Socialista de Nicaragua; PSN) was founded in 1937. It was declared illegal a year later and has been a clandestine organization ever since. The Sandinist Liberation Front (Frente Sandinista Liberación Nacional; FSLN) is a Castroite guerrilla organization founded in 1961.

The PSN is pro-Soviet. In 1967 an internal struggle resulted in the expulsion of some party leaders who then organized the Communist Party of Nicaragua (Partido Comunista de Nicaragua; PCN), which is anti-Soviet.

The PSN has only about 160 members; the PCN is probably smaller. The FSLN is now reported to have some 500 armed members and is thought to have increased its influence in city and countryside.

The population of Nicaragua is 2,224,000.

The PSN. The PSN has a negligible effect on the national political situation. This is due to its small, scattered membership and internal splintering, and the thorough suppression of the government of President Anastasio Somoza. The PSN believes that the independence of Nicaragua is nominal, being merely the façade of a semi-colonial and feudal regime fully devoted to imperialism. Tactically, the PSN calls for a united front of workers, students, peasants, the middle class, and other "progressives" against the Somoza government. While the PSN believes in armed struggle, it considers that the appropriate conditions in Nicaragua are still lacking. At this stage, it prefers building up its influence. The General Confederation of Labor operates under Communist leadership.

The FSLN. Founded in 1961 by Carlos Fonseca Amador, the Sandinist National Liberation Front has consistently maintained the necessity for direct action against the Somoza government, though there is currently a split between those who favor a more protracted struggle and the dominant wing which favors random violence. Suspected Sandinistas are tried in military courts. The FSLN, which is thought to include an increasing number of politically discontented Catholics, has received training and assistance from Cuba and other communist countries and utilizes sanctuaries in Costa Rica and Honduras.

The first half of the year 1977 was fairly quiet for the FSLN. The guerrilla war which had been going on sporadically since 1974 (*YICA, 1977*, p. 477) had come to a virtual halt. In October President Somoza lifted the national state of siege that had been in effect for nearly three years. The FSLN immediately struck in several parts of the country and pitched battles took place with the Guardia Nacional. FSLN guerrillas stormed Guardia posts at San Carlos, Masaya and on the outskirts of the capital city of Managua. Near the Costa Rican border Nicaraguan aircraft fired at suspected guerrillas, and in the process narrowly missed killing Costa Rican nationals, including a government minister who happened to be in the area. By the end of October twenty government troops and ten guerrillas had been reported killed and there were press rumors that the 41-year dynasty of the Somoza family was in serious trouble.

Hoover Institution   John J. Tierney, Jr.
Stanford University

Panama

The Communist Party of Panama was founded in 1930 but was dissolved in 1943 with the formation of the People's Party of Panama (Partido del Pueblo de Panama; PDP). All political activity in Panama focused on the canal issue, the signing of the new treaty in Washington, and the national plebiscite on 23 October. Because the PDP was actively involved in supporting General Omar Torrijos Herrera and his campaign for national sovereignty, the party enjoyed more freedom of political action than usual despite its continuing (since 1953) illegality. The size of the PDP is estimated at between 350 and 500. The population of Panama is 1,750,000 (estimated 1977).

The intense political activity surrounding the canal issue has served to squeeze out the consideration of other problems facing Panama and to cover over the usual shifts in political movements, nomenclatures, and personnel on the far left. The same organizations that operated on the left in 1976 continued their existence in 1977, including the Revolutionary Unity Movement (MUR), the National Action Vanguard (VAN), the Panamanian Revolutionary Union (URP), and the National Liberation Movement of 29 November (MLN-29-11). None of these groups has more than fifty members. All fell into line on the treaty issue. Only the student movement on the far left continued its opposition in coalition with some middle class professionals.

PDP: Leadership and Organization. Since 1951 the secretary general of the PDP has been Rubén Darío Sousa. Other leaders are Miguel Parcell and Luther Thomas. The PDP's organization exists mainly underground and is principally a cadre of some ten to fifteen individuals. The PDP's labor affiliate, the Trade Union Federation of Workers of the Republic of Panama (Federación Sindical de Trabajadores de la República de Panamá; FST) was disbanded in 1968 along with other labor unions. The PDP works with students through the University Reform Front (Frente Reformista Universitario; FRU), and the Federation of Students of Panama (Federación de Estudiantes de Panamá; FEP).

Domestic Views and Activities. The canal issue is a natural subject for any pro-Soviet "anti-imperialist" organization and the PDP predictably gave its full support to the Torrijos government, a government it otherwise considers pro-foreign investment, pro-private enterprise, and generally supportive of the private sector. Despite the clauses in the treaty which permit the continued existence of United States' military bases on the isthmus for some years and the right of the U.S. to intervene at any time to insure the continued neutrality of the waterway, the PDP has seen fit to stand with General Torrijos on the issue arguing that the new treaty opens the door to further change in the future. The economic situation in Panama continues to be difficult, in part because of the uncertainty surrounding the treaty. The ultra-left students attack the economic situation, the new treaty, and the cash settlement as part of an "imperialist plot."

International Views and Contacts. The PDP continues to be pro-Soviet in its policies, and as relations between the Carter administration and the USSR improved in 1977 there was no concern over General Torrijos's two visits to Washington or his public embrace of the United States chief executive.

Publications. The PDP publishes a monthly newspaper, *Unidad*.

National University   Charles F. Denton
Heredia, Costa Rica

Paraguay

Although the Paraguayan Communist Party (Partido Comunista Paraguayo; PCP) was founded on 19 February 1928, its first congress, which adopted the party's program, was not held until 1941. The party has been illegal throughout its existence except for the period between August 1946 and January 1947. The Communists participated in the short civil war against the government of President Higinio Morinigo early in 1947. At that time they had not only extensive trade union influence, but also a substantial number of party members among young army officers. With the collapse of the anti-Morinigo forces, the Communists were outlawed once again. The PCP held its Second Congress in August 1949, and in the early 1950s, before the seizure of power by General Alfredo Stroessner, was able to rebuild some influence in the organized labor movement. However, the Stroessner regime drove the party deeply underground. During the 1960s and early 1970s the traditionally pro-Soviet PCP was wracked by dissension. The Third Congress, in April 1971, adopted a program, a party constitution, and a political thesis, and chose a new Central Committee. It was not until December 1974 that an agreement was reached among some feuding factions, assuring the unity of the party.

After being ousted from the main body of the PCP, onetime secretary general Oscar Creydt formed a rival, pro-Chinese party of the same name in 1965.

The membership of the Paraguayan Communist movement, including factions and sympathizers, has been estimated at approximately 3,500. Many are exiles in various Latin American and European countries. The population of Paraguay was estimated in 1977 at 2,700,000.

Organization and Domestic Activity. The most important event for the Paraguayan Communists during 1977 was the release from prison in January of Antonio Maidana, PCP chairman, and Julio Rojas and Alfredo Alcorta, members of its Central Committee, all of whom had been in jail for more than eighteen years. After being given their freedom, they were kept under virtual house arrest. Although it was possible for some people to visit them, the underground party leaders could not do so. (*El Dia*, Mexico City, 18 February.) Early in April the three men took refuge in the Peruvian Embassy. The government refused to allow them to leave the country, on the grounds that they were not being persecuted and therefore were not legitimate political refugees (*FBIS*, 18 April).

The PCP held a clandestine conference somewhere in Paraguay late in 1976. Documents issued after this meeting claimed that over the previous eighteen months the party's membership had increased 600 percent and that the party had been able to carry out a successful fund-raising campaign for the first time in ten years (*IB*, 15 January).

The party strongly opposed Stroessner's effort, late in 1976, to be elected president for the sixth time. It claimed that he was sponsored by "the State Department, Pentagon, the CIA, the big North American monopolies, the oligarchies of Brazil and other countries of our continent." Calling for "joint or coordinated mass actions on the basis of a general democratic minimum program," it declared that "today, more than ever before, it is a patriotic duty to organize broad joint action of representatives of the Colorado, Liberal Radical, Febrerist, Liberal, Christian Democratic, and Communist parties and non-party people." (*WMR*, 15 February.) None of the other parties replied positively to the PCP's call for unity.

International Views and Contacts. The PCP's continuing association with pro-Moscow Communist parties was expressed in an article on the October Revolution by Pedro Vásquez, member of the Central Committee: "The significance of the October Revolution is that it provided the answer to such key questions of today as — how to overcome the ever-present contradictions between man and nature; how to achieve social progress and to distribute the material and spiritual values in society. It created the new Soviet man and the new, multinational state — the Union of Soviet Socialist Republics, progressing confidently toward communism." (*WMR*, September.)

The PCP was represented at a meeting of Latin American Communist parties in Cuba which discussed the question of "Protecting Natural Resources and Fighting for National Independence" (ibid., April). Pedro Vasquez was one of the authors of an article in *World Marxist Review* (August) entitled "Some Problems of the Ideological Struggle in Latin America."

The Maoists. The pro-Chinese faction of the Paraguayan Communists, headed by Oscar Creydt, maintained its alignment with Peking. In December 1976, Creydt sent a message to First Secretary Hua Kuo-feng, congratulating him and the Chinese people on Hua's victory over the Gang of Four, which Creydt said had "further strengthened our trust in China." He added: "Our conviction in the world-wide victory of the proletarian revolution has become firmer than ever." (*FBIS*, 29 December.) In March 1977, Creydt visited China. He was received by Politburo member Chi Teng-kuei, with whom he had a "cordial and friendly conversation" (*Peking Review*, 8 April).

Other Leftist Groups. Although there was no specific evidence to substantiate the idea, elements of the Stroessner government claimed that the Argentine Trotskyist People's Revolutionary Army (ERP) had been seeking to establish guerrilla contacts in Paraguay (*Manchester Guardian*, 20 February).

Rutgers University   Robert J. Alexander

Peru

The Peruvian Communist Party (Partido Communista Peruano; PCP) had its origins in the Peruvian Socialist Party founded by José Carlos Mariátegui on 7 October 1928. It took its present name in 1930 on orders from the Communist International. Since 1964 the movement has been divided into a pro-Soviet party and several pro-Chinese splinter groups, some of them using the PCP name.

There also exist in Peru various Marxist-Leninist organizations to the left of the PCP. These include the Castro-oriented Movement of the Revolutionary Left (Movimiento de Izquierda Revolucionaria; MIR), the Trotskyite Revolutionary Left Front (Frente de Izquierda Revolucionaria;

FIR), the Marxist Workers' Revolutionary Party (Partido Obrero Marxista Revolucionario; POMR), and the Revolutionary Vanguard (Vanguardia Revolucionaria; VR).

U.S. intelligence estimates place the current membership of the pro-Soviet PCP at 2,000 and that of the pro-Chinese PCP groups at 1,200. Other Marxist-Leninist groups are small, with the VR and the FIR having the largest memberships. The population of Peru is about 16,579,000 (estimated 1977).

A constitutional provision prohibits Communist parties from participating in Peruvian elections, which have not been held since the military assumed power in October 1968. The Communists have been allowed to engage in political activities subject to varying degrees of police surveillance and harassment. General Juan Velasco Alvarado, who was ousted from the presidency in August 1975 and died in December 1977, permitted the pro-Soviet PCP to function freely, but kept considerable control over other leftist groups. Several pro-Chinese and Trotskyist leaders were deported. The Velasco government also sought to co-opt leaders of various Marxist-Leninist groups, such as ex-guerrilla leader Héctor Bejar. During 1977 government policies toward the PCP and other Communist groups remained cautious under the conservative presidency of General Francisco Morales Bermúdez. In an attempt to quiet growing opposition to military rule, the government has said that it hopes to have a civilian president in office before the end of 1980. As the first step toward restoring civilian control, the military has scheduled an election for 4 June 1978 to choose members to a constituent assembly to re-draft Peru's constitution, presumably in accordance with what the military regards as its most significant social reforms.

The Pro-Soviet PCP. Leadership and Organization. The highest organ of the pro-Soviet PCP is officially the National Congress, which is supposed to meet every three years. Its Sixth Congress, the most recent, met in November 1973. The PCP is organized from cells upward through local and regional committees to its Central Committee. Regional committees exist in at least twenty-two cities. Lima has the largest number of local committees, concentrated in low-income neighborhoods and in the slum areas which the government now refers to as "new towns." The PCP employs around sixty paid officials, including leadership and rank and file cadres. The party's expenditures include subsidies for the General Confederation of Workers of Peru (Confederación General de Trabajadores del Perú; CGTP), the Peruvian Communist Youth (Juventud Comunista Peruana; JCP), and specific regional committees of the party. Jorge del Prado has served as general secretary of the party for seventeen years; Raúl Acosta Salas is under-secretary. Jaime Figueroa is head of the party's National Propaganda Committee and Mario Ugarte serves as head of the Finance Committee. Other prominent members of the Central Committee are Isidro Gamarra, Guillermo Herrera, José Ramírez, Julio Rodríguez, Alfonso Oblitas, Gustavo Espinosa, José Martínez, Vicente Ramírez, Adolfo Otiniano, José Reccio, and Florencia Chávez. According to del Prado the oldest members in terms of active membership in the party besides himself are Raúl Acosta and Isidro Gamarra. The other members of the Political Committee and the Central Committee have been active for "only twenty years or less." A good percentage of the young cadres reportedly entered the party leadership at the Sixth Congress (*Oiga,* 10 June).

The PCP's youth group, the Peruvian Communist Youth (JCP), is relatively small and operates mainly in the universities. Jorge Tapia is the group's general secretary. In an appeal circulated on the forty-seventh anniversary of the JCP, Peruvian youth were called upon to form a vast anti-imperialist front as a patriotic duty: "The JCP is determined to fight in common with the communists and all working people against the intrigues of the oligarchy and imperialism for establishment of a just society in Peru" (*IB,* 21 March). On 26 March three members of the JCP were elected to serve on the committee to coordinate Peru's participation in the Eleventh World Festival of Youth scheduled for Havana in July 1978 (*Unidad,* 31 March).

Several universities were closed in February as a result of agitation by students and professors (*La Crónica,* 22 February). Confrontations between "Marxist students" and police were reported near San Marcos National University in Lima and also in Cuzco following the government's announcement of austere economic measures on 10 June. The JCP consistently attributes such disturbances to the "adventurist tactics employed by the feeble leadership of Maoist and Trotskyist student groups" (*Unidad,* 10 March). In June the PCP expressed its concern about the competition between Maoism and other leftist groups in the universities. According to Jorge del Prado, "the students have always been allies of the worker movement, but in Latin America, Yankee imperialism has set in motion a strategy aimed at dividing the left, and it has succeeded in separating the student movement from the anti-imperialist struggle" (*Oiga,* 10 June). The JCP's attempts to reach agreement with the VR or the various Maoist and Trotskyist groups did not progress very far in 1977. Ideological differences were overcome only in their continued opposition to government initiatives to institute a system of general studies and departments patterned after the U.S. experience of separation of academic operations from university administration.

A major source of the PCP's influence lies in its control over the General Confederation of Workers of Peru (CGTP). The CGTP was organized three months before the military coup of 1968 and was given legal recognition a few months afterward. By the beginning of 1975 it had become the largest of Peru's trade union federations, largely as a result of the sympathetic treatment it received from the Velasco government. Citing Labor Ministry figures, CGTP press secretary Hernán Espinoza claimed that 600,000 out of a work force of 2.5 million are members of the Confederation (LATIN, Buenos Aires, 25 November). The CGTP's strongest opposition within the trade union movement comes from the government-sponsored Central Organization of Workers of the Peruvian Revolution (CTRP), and the Confederation of Workers of Peru (CNT), whose political involvement is with the Aprista (American Popular Revolutionary Alliance; APRA) party.

In April officials of the CGTP, headed by President Isidro Gamarra, were granted a meeting by General Morales to discuss the government's proposed Tupac Amaru plan for political and socioeconomic development. The CGTP requested the "intensification of structural changes in order to contribute to national and social liberation." The leaders said that labor policy should guarantee wage increases, labor union freedom, and annual wage reviews. The CGTP condemned management for taking advantage of the existing state of emergency to carry out "violent aggression" against the workers (*Unidad,* 7 April). On 10 June the government announced an emergency economic program calling for severe austerity measures. On 21 June the Interior Ministry charged the CGTP with promoting subversion among its members and with responsibility for demonstrations by workers and students on 16 June protesting the government's program. The ministry informed the Confederation's leadership that the government would not "submit to coercion in making its decision" and would "severely punish" anyone who encouraged acts intended to disrupt the public order (*La Crónica,* 22 June).

Following violent disturbances in cities throughout the nation on 13 July, rural and urban labor organizations of various political tendencies called for a twenty-four-hour general strike on 19 July to support demands put to the government. The strike was organized by the CGTP, the National Agrarian Confederation (CNA), the Christian National Workers Confederation, and the Lima Central Organization of the Workers of the Peruvian Revolution (CTRP). Observers found it significant that for the first time a general strike had been called by such ideologically divergent organizations, many of which have been in constant conflict in recent years. The groups approved a set of demands which included: (1) wage and salary increases based on the rising cost of living; (2) a price freeze on all staple goods; (3) reactivation of annual salary and social adjustments; (4) reinstatement of dismissed workers and release of those under arrest; (5) return of exiles; (6) lifting the state of emergency; (7) defending the peasants' right to land; and (8) better prices for agricultural products (AFP, Paris, 18 July). The government responded by issuing a decree authorizing the dismissal and arrest of strike leaders.

General Morales met with a delegation from the CGTP again in August to request that "antagonisms be overcome and quarrels forgotten." He explained that even before the 19 July strike that paralyzed Lima the government had drawn up measures intended to alleviate the country's serious economic situation (*El Comercio,* 11 August). On 12 August various labor leaders expressed their concern about the dismissal of personnel following the 19 July general strike. According to unofficial sources, the number dismissed ranged from 3,000 to 4,000 throughout the country. The CGTP subsequently condemned the plans of "ultra-leftwing" elements to organize anti-government demonstrations on 22-23 August, stating that their "subversive" goal was to "undermine the unity of the working class in defense of its rights and interests and the prestige of labor union leaders" (*Pravda,* 26 August). On 25 November the CGTP called for a national rally to demand that the government rehire its members who participated in the July strike. According to a union communiqué, rallies were to be staged in major cities throughout the country (LATIN, 25 November). There was no indication that the government was any less determined to control the activities of extremists within the trade union movement, or any more receptive toward criticism of the military's increasingly conservative policies.

The PCP continues to exert some influence in the peasant sector through its participation in the National Agrarian Confederation (Confederación Nacional de Agricultores; CNA) established on 3 October 1974. It claims to represent 3.5 million peasants with 20 departmental agrarian federations, 170 agrarian leagues, and more than 3,800 rank and file organizations such as agrarian cooperatives, Indian communities, small and medium landowners, and landless peasants. In a communiqué published on 18 June, the CNA outlined its position in response to the economic measures announced by the government. While recognizing the existence of an economic crisis, the statement concluded that the proposed economic measures would have an even more adverse effect on the economy, particularly by endangering the basic needs of workers in the lowest income brackets. Avelino Mar Arias, president of the CNA, stated that "all economic policies should guarantee the consolidation of structural reforms, including agrarian reform and labor stability." The document contains a reaffirmation of the CNA's "anti-oligarchical and anti-imperialist position" and its "irrevocable determination to struggle for the construction of Peruvian socialism" (*El Correo,* 20 June).

In a statement on the government's proposal to elect a constituent assembly in 1978, the CNA criticized "traditional elections which have never served the poor of the city or the countryside." After demanding the participation of rank and file organizations in the assembly, the document stressed that "the people's struggle is directed at deepening the country's structural changes because if the reforms are stopped modern capitalism would be consolidated, bringing new forms of exploitation" (AFP, 3 October). In a news conference held on 14 November, Mar Arias denied government charges that the CNA's leaders were conducting a dishonest policy of attacking the government and manipulating the peasants. He stated that agrarian reform has been one of the most valuable achievements of the Peruvian revolution, but that its advancement has been hindered by "the pro-imperialist and pro-oligarchic enemies of the peasants." (Ibid., 15 November.)

The PCP's principal opposition in the peasant sector comes from the pro-Chinese orientation of several parties belonging to the Confederation of Peruvian Peasants (Confederación de Campesinos Peruanos; CCP). According to Raúl Acosta Salas, one faction of the CCP is under the direction of "Bandera Roja" and the other follows the dictates of the Revolutionary Vanguard. The latter managed to achieve majority strength within the CCP at one point, but has since been weakened by internal divisions (*Unidad,* 4 February 1976). In October Andrés Luna Vargas, secretary general of the CCP, described the constituent assembly as "an alternative presented by the government to divert the masses from their revolutionary objectives." Luna stated that the agrarian reform established by the government goes against the interests of peasants, who, in effect, become employees of official agencies (AFP, Paris, 12 October). The CCP periodically protests that pressure continues to be exerted upon its leadership. Overall, the CCP maintains a class struggle policy and, in general, views the government as one of the main enemies of the people.

Domestic Attitudes and Activities. The PCP has been forced to redefine its domestic position by the gradual erosion of the image of revolutionary development in Peru. In a political statement issued by the Central Committee on 20 December 1976, the PCP called on all revolutionary and other progressive forces to support an emergency program aimed at safeguarding the achievements of the process begun in 1968. The statement cited growing disenchantment of the workers with the rising cost of living and the dangers connected with the counterrevolutionary activity of the ultra-right, Apristas, and the ultra-left. The Central Committee reaffirmed that "the Peruvian revolution would become futile if it abandoned its fundamental aims; genuine and definitive national liberation and social progress" (*IB*, 15 February). In a five-point political program, the party called for the strengthening of trade union organization and more active development of political consciousness among peasant and student groups. It also demanded the restoration of constitutional guarantees, renewal of the publication of revolutionary organs, and release of imprisoned trade union leaders. (Ibid.)

On 13 January the PCP protested the deportation of four retired military officers who had been instrumental in the organization of the Socialist Revolutionary Party (Partido Socialista Revolucionario; PSR) in November 1976. The PSR's organizational manifesto called for "the defense and consolidation of the reforms already begun and those still needed to take the country out of the capitalist system and build Peruvian socialism" (*Latin America,* 10 December 1976). The PCP welcomed the creation of the PSR as "a new political organization of revolutionary patriots whose members associate themselves with the first phase of the Peruvian revolution." The PCP continued to be supportive of the PSR in 1977. Jorge del Prado stated in April that "the PSR came into existence with a platform that is generally correct" (*Caretas,* 21 April). It is somewhat unusual for the PCP to greet the formation of an additonal left-wing party with some degree of enthusiasm, since in the past the party has expressed its concern over the tendency of the Marxist left to factionalize. Differences between the two groups appear to be more a matter of degree than kind. For example, according to its secretary general, Antonio Meza Cuadra, the PSR is in favor of socializing most, but not all, of the means of production. The PSR has also tended to be less critical of the government's Tupac Amaru plan.

In February the PCP repudiated the amended impresarial partnership law promulgated by the government. The new law, called the Law of Industrial Communities, replaced one that was seven years old. It annuls the workers' status as partners in private enterprises, but grants them continued representation at board meetings. The PCP charged that the new law constitutes a negative modification of one of the most important conquests of the revolutionary process begun in 1968 (*Unidad,* 4 February). Party leaders also supported the CGTP and other labor organizations in denouncing the "offensive being waged by management against job stability and workers' rights." An editorial in *Unidad* (31 March) claimed that "the new law on stability reflects an anti-labor union offensive by the Industries Association that is now intensely interested in destroying the principle of job stability."

On 13 May members of the PCP's Political Commission were invited by President Morales to discuss the government's Tupac Amaru plan for the political and socioeconomic development of Peru during the next four years. In presenting its analysis of the interview, the Political Commission reportedly told the president that the only solution for Peru was a return to the anti-imperialist and anti-oligarchical direction that determined the assumption of power by the military in 1968. Overall, the Commission assessed the interview as "a positive event," emphasizing the visit as recognition of the PCP's importance in the country's political life and "a blow to political sectors of the far right and the Maoist far left who have sought to isolate and divide the Peruvian Communist party" (*Unidad,* 19 May). In a subsequent assessment of the importance of the party's talks with Morales, del Prado stated that it was the first time the military government had officially recognized the PCP. While the PCP was not persecuted during the Velasco phase of the military government, like the other political parties, it was not officially recognized. In this respect, the PCP's leadership believes that a positive change has taken place. It considers the party's talks with Morales military recognition of the legal existence of the PCP. As del Prado stated during an interview in July: "The meeting with the president has strengthened the party's legality and confirmed its significance in the country's general political life" (*Rude Pravo,* Prague, 6 July).

While maintaining a moderate attitude toward the Tupac Amaru plan, the PCP has singled out certain features that it considers to be contradictory to the people's interest. For example, the plan considers the activity of trade union organizations and their leading representatives harmful to the country's economic and social development. The party also feels that the working people are unjustifiably blamed for the country's growing economic crisis. According to del Prado, the Tupac Amaru plan represents a program of "national, reformist capitalism with emphatic tendencies toward the so-called 'modern' capitalism." (Ibid.) In comparing the new plan with the former Inca government plan of the Velasco administration, the PCP perceives that "an obvious withdrawal from the general political concept of economic and social development of the country has taken place."

In June del Prado stated that the PCP would participate in the 1980 elections in order to look out for the people's gains in Congress: "We will demand that the gains be institutionalized and that things move forward. And if the government is reactionary, we will struggle in the streets" (*Oiga,* 10 June). In evaluating President Morales' message of 28 July—in which he announced the scheduling of elections—the PCP stated that the consolidation of the structural changes and social advances achieved since 1968 was "the most important objective at this crucial moment." The party added that neither the assembly nor the general elections would have positive results if the literacy requirement was not abolished and the voting age lowered from twenty-one to eighteen (*Unidad,* 4 August). The government subsequently granted the vote to eighteen-year-olds, but it continued to deny the vote to approximately four million illiterates, most of whom are non-Spanish speaking Indians in the Central Andean area.

In a statement issued by the Political Committee in October, the PCP strongly criticized the government's acceptance of economic measures recommended by the International Monetary Fund. The measures announced by the government were considered to be "one more step toward the adoption of capitalist decisions to solve the current economic crisis by making greater concessions to the demands of the IMF and by placing the effects of the crisis on the shoulders of the popular masses affected by inflation and unemployment" (*El Comercio,* 16 October). The party stressed that wages should be increased, industry restructured, and agrarian reform and state enterprises defended and developed. The PCP also believes that the government must nationalize commercial banks and the basic export sectors of those industrial enterprises that monopolize production essential for the supply of necessities.

Despite occasional criticisms, the PCP adopted a generally conciliatory approach toward the military and its development policies in 1977. In doing so, the party appears to be pursuing several aims. First, it hopes to keep certain of its members who are already a part of the regime's bureaucratic apparatus in their present positions. Second, it does not wish to provoke Peru into breaking off relations with the Soviet Union, since any diplomatic tension with Moscow works to the advantage of Peking. Third, the question of the PCP's "legal status" is a crucial one insofar as the party's political activities are concerned. One source reported in September that the PCP had been classified by the government as "international" in orientation and therefore "beyond the legal concepts for participation in the Peruvian system" (*Christian Science Monitor,* 9 September). However, the party's decision in October to reaffirm its support for the government's plan to hold elections for a constituent assembly next June suggests that the Morales government has done nothing yet to proscribe officially the PCP's participation.

International Views and Positions. The PCP continues to follow closely the Soviet line in its international positions. In response to conservative criticism that the PCP is simply a tool of international Communism, del Prado responded that "the PCP is in fact playing the role of the vanguard of the Peruvian working class and is a recognized detachment in the struggle against imperialism and the oligarchy and for socialism on Peruvian soil" (*Unidad,* 14 February). According to Moisés Arroyo, a member of the editorial staff of *Unidad,* "the process of anti-imperialist and anti-oligarchic changes has slowed down in Peru." Arroyo added that Peru cannot resolve its acute economic problems by granting economic and political concessions "to those who would like to nullify revolutionary gains and reestablish foreign control over our natural resources." He added that the PCP is opposed to seeking credits from international monetary organizations (see above), increasing private investment and assisting capitalist enterprises at what it considers to be the detriment of the state and at the cost of greater exploitation of the working people (*WMR,* April).

In discussing the most important achievements of the military government during its first seven years—the party considers that no substantial change has been made in the last two years—Jorge del Prado singled out the practice of a pluralist international policy "which has permitted the expansion of Peru's field of action as an independent nation and the preservation of its sovereignty" (*El Correo,* 1 September). Writing in the *World Marxist Review* (September), Carlos Nuñez, alternate member of the Central Committee, referred to the growing number of treaties between Peru and Socialist countries for economic, technical, and financial assistance. Trade agreements based on "mutual respect and equality" and "exempt from restrictive stipulations" have helped to accumulate resources needed for the social progress and economic independence of Peru. He added that Peruvian Communists take legitimate pride in the "universally recognized prestige of the Soviet Union."

A PCP delegation headed by Alfonso Oblitas attended the World Conference for the Independent and Peaceful Reunification of Korea held in Brussels on 21-22 February. Moisés Arroyo attended an international symposium in Havana on the topic of protecting natural resources. The PCP reaffirmed its solidarity with Cuba and Panama, and its support for the governments in Latin America which are struggling to recover their natural resources and defend their sovereignty (*WMR,* April). A study delegation led by César Alva visited Prague in May. Jorge del Prado headed a PCP delegation that visited Hungary, Poland, Romania, Czechoslovakia, Bulgaria, and the Soviet Union during June and July. While in Moscow, representatives of the CPSU and the PCP noted that the development of cooperation between the USSR and Peru is in accordance with the mutual interests of both peoples. Del Prado praised the Soviet leadership for its efforts to create a climate of international peace and achieve concrete measures of military disarmament. In a joint communiqué, party leaders called for strengthening the fraternal relations between the two countries on the basis of the principles of Marxism-Leninism and proletarian internationalism (Tass, 11 July).

Publications. The official organ of the PCP is the weekly newspaper *Unidad,* which claims a circulation of more than 10,000. The newspaper was allowed to resume publication in January after having been closed down by the government, along with other papers of the left and the right, in July 1976.

Other Parties. From their inception in the 1960s, the pro-Chinese groups have experienced continuous internal dissension and splits. As many as twenty Marxist political organizations have been identified in the past, many of which, strictly speaking, no longer exist.

In recent years there have been at least three major factions of the pro-Chinese PCP. The one which enjoys more or less official recognition from the Chinese Communist party is headed by Antonio Fernández Arce and is known as the Peruvian Communist Party, Marxist-Leninist (PCC-ML). Its members are affiliated with the Peru-China Cultural Institute. Fernández Arce headed delegations that visited Peking in May and Albania in October. In September the PCC-ML sent a letter to the Communist Party of China congratulating it on the "victorious" closing of the Eleventh National Congress of the CCP and on the election of Hua Kuo-feng as chairman of the party's Central Committee. The letter also noted the Congress' support for "the oppressed people and nations in Asia, Africa and Latin America . . . subjected in varying degrees to the aggression, intervention and control by imperialism and social-imperialism, represented by the United States and the Soviet Union" (NCNA, Peking, 16 September).

A second pro-Chinese faction is headed by Saturnino Paredes Macedo and, from its somewhat sporadic periodical, *Bandera Roja,* is generally known as the PCP-Bandera Roja. The Red Fatherland faction, so-called because of its periodical, *Patria Roja,* is believed to have the largest following of all pro-Chinese groups among students and labor. It reportedly exercises control over national labor organizations with memberships in excess of 100,000. The Bandera Roja faction, on the other hand, heads only local organizations with fewer than 100,000 affiliates (*Marka,* 8 January 1976). The Patria Roja group also controls one of the labor "unification organizations" (Comité de Coordinacíon y Unificación Sindical Clasista; CCUSC), which has engaged in fierce competition with a similar unifying organization controlled by the CGTP. The pro-Chinese groups have had relatively little success in acquiring influence within the peasant movement, although the Confederation of Peruvian Peasants (CCP) has a pro-Chinese orientation (see above).

In addition to the pro-Chinese groups, there are several Marxist-Leninist parties and movements of Castroite and Trotskyite orientation. Although these groups are now small compared to their size in the early 1960s, they retain some ideological influence, particularly among students. Among these is the Front of the Revolutionary Left (FIR), a sympathizing section of the Fourth International. The largest of the Trotskyist organizations is the Marxist Workers Revolutionary Party (POMR), headed by Ricardo Napuri. Like their Maoist counterparts, these Marxist groups operate underground and have remained steadfast in their opposition to both the military government and the pro-Soviet PCP. In a rare interview, Ricardo Napuri described the PCP as "a workers' party with a pro-bourgeois leadership . . . subordinated to the Kremlin bureaucracy. It maintains itself by carrying out its role as intermediary between imperialism and the proletariat" (*Equis,* Lima, 6 July).

Washington College   Daniel L. Premo

Puerto Rico

The Puerto Rican Communist Party (Partido Comunista Puertorriqueño; PCP) has long been closely associated with the Communist Party of the United States (CPUSA) and has continued to share its pro-Soviet views. The Armed Forces of Puerto Rican National Liberation (Fuerzas Armadas de Liberación Nacional Puertorriqueña; FALN) appears to have its origins in predecessor terrorist groups. The Independent Revolution Armed Command (CIRA) is a relatively new organization. The Puerto Rican Socialist Party (Partido Socialista Puertorriqueño; PSP), formerly the Pro-Independence Movement (Movimiento Pro-Independencia; MPI), maintains close ties with Cuba and appears to continue to maintain an independent stance in the Sino-Soviet dispute. The International Workers League (Liga Internacionalista de los Trabajadores; LIT) is reportedly associated with the Fourth (Trotskyist) International. Little is known of the Lolita Lebrón Puerto Rican Liberation Command.

Most of these organizations seem to have few members. Recent estimates of membership are: PCP, slightly over one hundred; FALN, twelve; PSP, several thousand. The PSP appears to have polled around 11,000 votes in the island's 1976 gubernatorial elections. With the exception of the PSP, none of these groups has ever participated in a gubernatorial election and, at least since 1948, none but the PSP has been represented in either legislative house.

The population of Puerto Rico is 3,200,000 (estimated 1977).

The PCP: Organization. The Puerto Rican Communist Party was founded in 1934, dissolved in 1944, and refounded in 1946. Party institutions include the National Party Congress, the Central Committee, the Politburo, and the General Secretariat, the latter headed by General Secretary Franklin Irizarry. A recent Czech study claims that three-fourths of party members are peasants and workers being paid wages and that forty percent are thirty years of age or older.

Domestic Views. In a 1976 article Irizarry denounced the U.S. imperialistic policy which has oppressed the Puerto Rican people and denied them the opportunity of true self-determination. He dismissed the 1952 Commonwealth status as a ploy of the imperialists to disguise increased colonialism and elections as a part of that deception. He attacked the policy of permitting mainland corporations to freely invest on the island, claiming that over 80 percent of Puerto Rico's economy is in mainland hands. He praised PCP organizational efforts, despite active opposition from the government and the Maoists. He reaffirmed the party's commitment to Marxism-Leninism and to winning economic and political independence for the island. (*WMR*, August, 1976.)

International Views and Policies. Irizarry led a PCP delegation to Cuba to join the May Day celebrations held on that island. While there, the delegation joined Communist delegations from other Caribbean lands in a special session on cooperation and development. They reaffirmed the principles of their 1975 Communist declaration and renewed their attacks on imperialism, making special reference to the sophisticated forms utilized by the USA. They then lauded the peaceful coexistence policies of the Socialist countries, especially the USSR. They also praised the revolutionary and anti-imperialist movements of their region and the anti-imperialist policies of Cuba and some other Caribbean nations. The evil effects of colonialism came under sharp attack, with particular attention devoted to the case of Puerto Rico and those regional governments which in the view of the delegates aided the imperialists and their oppression. (*Granma,* Havana, English ed., 15 May.)

Publications. The PCP publishes the newspapers *El Pueblo* and *El Proletario.*

The FALN. The Armed Forces of National Liberation is an underground revolutionary group advocating national independence for Puerto Rico. Little is known of its membership, organization, or ideology. As has been suggested in earlier volumes of this *Yearbook,* the FALN may have merged from several earlier revolutionary groups. FALN goals include independence for Puerto Rico and freedom for Puerto Rican nationalists imprisoned in the U.S. In 1976, the then governor of Puerto Rico, Rafael Hernández Colón, claimed the FALN might have no more than ten members, with up to three-person cells in Chicago, New York, and Washington (*NYT,* 13 July 1976). Recent estimates also suggest a maximum membership of ten (*NYT,* 22 February, 4 August 1977). During 1977, the FALN was suspected of or claimed credit for a number of bombings in the United States, as it has for the past several years. According to the FALN, large multinational corporations are primary targets for revolutionary bombings (*NYT,* 4 August).

In February the FALN claimed responsibility for two explosions in Manhattan buildings. In a message phoned to New York radio stations the FALN opposed former U.S. President Ford's support for Puerto Rican statehood, and chided President Carter for his failure to free five imprisoned Puerto Rican nationalists in the United States. The message demanded that the Federal Bureau of Investigation cease harrassing Puerto Ricans and the current federal grand jury investigation of the FALN be terminated. It warned of violent action if repression of Puerto Rican independence advocates was not halted. (*NYT,* 19 and 20 February.) Additional bombings occurred near an FBI office in New York City in March, at the Cook County Building in Chicago in June, and at other locations (*NYT,* 22 March, 5 and 6 June; *CSM,* 4 August; *New York Daily News,* 5 and 10 August). The *New York Times* reported that by October the FALN had claimed credit for over forty bombings in four U.S. mainland cities and *Time* magazine alleged that by October the number of FALN bombings had reached sixty-five (*NYT,* 12 October; *Time,* 24 October).

The CIRA. The Independent Revolution Armed Command appears to be a relatively new Puerto Rican independence and terrorist organization. Little is known of its political tenets beyond its calls for Puerto Rican independence and its assertions of unjust treatment of Puerto Ricans residing in the United States (*NYT,* 12, 13 March). CIRA has been suspected of mailing more than twenty letter bombs—most of which were discovered in Manhattan—addressed to various government agencies, including the Central Intelligence Agency, the Federal Bureau of Investigation, and the Department of Justice. Some have been addressed to leading political figures, including former President Ford, then President-elect Carter, and Senator Daniel P. Moynihan (D-N.Y.). Still others have been intended for Puerto Rican government offices in New York City. In some instances radio stations have received telephone messages which alleged that the bombs were CIRA devices. (*NYT,* 2 December 1976, 13 March 1977.)

The PSP. The Puerto Rican Socialist Party was founded in November 1971 at the Eighth Annual Assembly of the Pro-Independence Movement. It participated in the 1976 Puerto Rican insular elections, and its gubernatorial candidate, Lic. Juan Marí Bras, received approximately 11,000 votes.

Organization and Leadership. The PSP is guided by the Party Congress (the Second Congress met in late 1975), a Central Committee, and a Political Commission. The party's Central Committee recently undertook a self-study program, and at its conclusion, reelected Julio Vivres Vásquez its chairman and Lic. Juan Marí Bras as general secretary. Carlos Gallisá was elected first deputy general secretary, Pedro Biagés, second deputy general secretary, and Lucia Romero, organizing secretary (*Granma,* English ed., 27 February).

Domestic Attitudes and Activities. The PSP has traditionally supported Socialism and independence for Puerto Rico. It has maintained that the island is an oppressed colony of the United States. At a recent symposium held in Havana by the *World Marxist Review*, PSP Central Committee member Carlos Rivera noted that Puerto Rico is dominated economically and politically by the United States and that it serves as a strategic Caribbean base for the U.S. The PSP opposed outgoing President Ford's suggestion in late 1976 that Puerto Rico should be granted statehood. As reported by Tass, the party claimed that the president's statement was in opposition to the Puerto Ricans' right to determination of their own future, and was further evidence of colonialism. It reaffirmed its position that independence is the only viable solution to the island's current plight. (*FBIS,* 10 January.) While traveling through Latin American nations in search of support for Puerto Rican independence, Wilfredo Matus, director of the PSP political school, noted that the United States sought to secure control over Puerto Rico because of the island's potential mineral wealth and its value as a market for mainland production. Ismael Davila criticized U.S. economic policies that caused massive unemployment and inflation in Puerto Rico and compelled Puerto Ricans to seek employment on the U.S. mainlaind (*Granma,* English ed., 17 April).

Speaking at a symposium in Mexico City in May, Marí Bras maintained that the Carter administration's position on human rights was invalid as long as the federal government continued to imprison the five Puerto Rican nationalists (ibid., 8 May), one of whom was released by President Carter in October. The Cuban press reported that Marí Bras and other PSP leaders visited Cuba in June, where they were joined by Carlos Rivera, the PSP delegate to Cuba. While there the general secretary was interviewed by the Cuban Communist Party organ. He asserted that the United States government position with regard to Puerto Rico had become confused and that the U.S. is being forced to concede the failure of the Commonwealth (Estado Libre Asociado) as a means of terminating colonialism. He accused both major U.S. political parties of endeavoring to strengthen control over Puerto Rico by seeking to make it a permanent part of the U.S. Marí Bras added that the PSP would seek to enlighten the people of Puerto Rico concerning their current ills, including the worsening unemployment, rising prices, and increasing public debt. He noted that there was growing support for Puerto Rican self-determination, not only on the island but on the United States mainland and throughout the world. Later in the year, the general secretary also charged that the U.S. government was aiding the island's National Guard as part of a policy of curtailing efforts of university students and organized labor (*Granma,* English ed., 10 July).

International Attitudes and Activities. The PSP has always refused to take sides in the Sino-Soviet dispute; it has had a close relationship with the Cuban government and vocally supported several governments which have emerged victorious from national liberation struggles, such as those in Angola and Vietnam. During his visit to Havana in June, Marí Bras told Cuban newsmen (*Granma,* 8 June) that he considered the Cubans a primary source of support in Puerto Rico's struggle against the United States. He noted further that this Cuban assistance had led to additional support from individuals, political groups, and governments on all continents. He specifically referred to Fidel Castro's statement, supported by the First National Congress of the Cuban Communist Party, indicating that solidarity with the people of Puerto Rico is of primary importance in Cuba's foreign policy.

During the year, PSP representatives traveled to a number of nations and attended various international gatherings, among them the Eighteenth Congress of the Communist Party of México, where the PSP delegation was headed by Gallisá (*Granma,* English ed., 12 June) and the World Conference for the Independence and Peaceful Reunification of Korea in Brussels (*FBIS*, 9 March).

Publication. The PSP publishes the daily newspaper *Claridad.*

The LIT. During the 1976 election campaign, the International Workers League endorsed the platform and candidates of the Puerto Rican Socialist Party, finding these the only viable—if not ideal—alternative of the 1976 insular campaign. LIT claimed that despite their statements to the contrary, neither the incumbent Popular Democratic Party (Partido Popular Democrático; PPD) nor the challenging New Progressive Party (Partido Nuevo Progresista; PNP), whose members generally advocate statehood, truly represented the island's workers. Another contender, the Puerto Rican Independence Party (Partido Independentista Puertorriqueña; PIP) was criticized for being unclear with regard to certain aspects of its platform, failing to specify plans for assisting the workers, and for endeavoring to return Puerto Rico to a personalistic type of rule, reminiscent of that of former PPD Governor Luis Muñoz Marín. The LIT advocates elimination of capitalism and the participation of all workers in the struggles for the island's national liberation and the development of Socialism. (*Intercontinental Press,* New York, 15 November and 20 December 1976.)

Lolita Lebrón Puerto Rican Liberation Command. This apparently new terrorist group claimed that it had placed two bombs, which were dismantled at the Reserve Army Training Corps center of the University of Puerto Rico in January (*NYT,* 6 January). Little else is known about the Command or its efforts.

St. John's University   Frank Paul Le Veness
New York

United States of America

The Communist Party, U.S.A. (CPUSA) is the largest and most influential Marxist-Leninist organization in the United States. It is descended from the Communist Labor Party and the Communist Party, both formed in 1919. At various times the CPUSA has also been called the Workers Party and, for a brief period during World War II, the Communist Political Association.

The Socialist Workers Party (SWP) is the leading Trotskyite party. Organized in 1938, it traces its origin to 1928, when several CPUSA members were expelled for supporting Leon Trotsky. The SWP has spawned numerous other Trotskyite groups, including the Workers' World Party, the Spartacist League and the Revolutionary Marxist Organizing Committee.

The two most important Maoist sects are the Revolutionary Communist Party (RCP), formerly the Revolutionary Union, and the Communist Party (Marxist-Leninist)—CPCM-L—formerly the October League. A commitment to Marxism-Leninism is also proclaimed by such groups as the

Weather Underground Organization (WUO), Prairie Fire Organizing Committee (PFOC), the Marxist-Leninist Organizing Committee, the Communist Labor Party, the Revolutionary Student Brigade, the Revolutionary Workers' Congress, the August 29th Movement, the Revolutionary Socialist League, and the Proletarian Unity League. All of these emerged, at least in their Marxist-Leninist guise, in the early 1970s, usually under the direction of veterans of the now defunct Students for a Democratic Society (SDS). The Progressive Labor Party (PLP) came into existence in 1965 following the expulsion of several CPUSA members for ultra-leftism. The PLP strongly supported Maoism until 1971. Its present ideological posture is rigidly Stalinist.

The CPUSA is a legal party. Restrictive laws which hindered access to the ballot in some states have been removed or are under legal attack. In 1976 the party's presidential ticket of Gus Hall and Jarvis Tyner was on the ballot in nineteen states and the District of Columbia, receiving about 60,000 votes. At present it has no representation either in Congress or in any state legislature.

The CPUSA claims to have about 18,000 members; outside estimates give it only about 5,000 (*Nation,* New York, 25 September 1976). Membership is mainly concentrated in a few industrial states, and recruitment efforts are particularly aimed at minorities (blacks, Puerto Ricans, Chicanos) and young industrial workers. The population of the U.S.A. is almost 218 million.

The SWP, like the CPUSA, runs candidates for state, local, and national office. While none have been elected, the SWP has drawn more votes than the CPUSA. The SWP claims 2,500 members; other estimates are around 1,500. The SWP, although concentrated in the industrial states, has established strong local chapters in some areas of the South and Southwest where the CPUSA has made no headway. The other Communist groups are quite small, ranging from a few dozen to a thousand or so members.

The CPUSA and SWP are active in broad-scale left movements, such as support of school busing and black causes, attacks on the Chilean junta and support for the MPLA in Angola. The smaller sects, whose origins go back to the campus turmoil of the 1960s, no longer appear to wield much influence in the colleges and universities. In general, the continuing economic problems in the United States have not stimulated any noticeable growth in Marxist-Leninist influence, but an increasing attraction toward Marxism-Leninism is apparent among the remnants of the New Left.

The CPUSA: Leadership and Organization. The leadership of the CPUSA remained largely intact in 1977. Gus Hall continued as general secretary and Henry Winston as national chairman. Arnold Bechetti is organizational secretary, Betty Smith is national administrative secretary, and Sid Taylor is national treasurer. Other important party leaders incude: Helen Winter (international affairs secretary), James Jackson (national education director), Grace Mora (chairwoman, Puerto Rican Commission), Alva Buxenbaum (chairwoman, Commission for Women's Equality), George Meyers (chairman, National Labor Commission), Lorenzo Torres (chairman, National Chicano Commission), William Patterson and Roscoe Proctor (co-chairmen, Black Liberation Commission), Victor Perlo (chairman, Economics Commission), Alex Kolkin (chairman, Jewish Commission), Carl Bloice (editor, *People's World*), Danny Rubin (chairman, Commission on Unemployment and Inflation), and Si Gerson, Claude Lightfoot, Angela Davis, Charlene Mitchell, and Herbert Aptheker (Central Committee members).

Among the party leaders in important states are Jarvis Tyner (New York), Jim West (Ohio), Ishmael Flory and Jack Kling (Illinois), William Taylor and Al Lima (California), Tom Dennis (Michigan), Thomas Crenshaw (Missouri), Lee Dlugin (New Jersey), Ed Teixeira (New England), Rasheed Storey and Sondra Patrinos (Pennsylvania).

While the CPUSA does not officially have any affiliated organizations, the Young Workers Liberation League (YWLL) is, in fact, the party's youth arm. An independent estimate put YWLL membership at 3,000 in 1976. Some 800 people attended its fourth convention in New York in October. Jim Steele was reelected chairman. Other leaders include Jay Schaffner (organizational secretary), Richard Hoyen (student secretary), and Jill Furillo (editor, *Young Worker*). A sixty-three member National Council (formerly Central Committee) was selected. The convention took steps to make it easier for high school youth to join and reported that fifteen percent of the delegates were high school students. Steele called upon YWLL members to take the lead in organizing united fronts with youth groups seeking jobs. He also insisted the YWLL had to address itself to other concerns which affect young people's lives, including sports, art, music, and culture. (*Daily World,* 8 October.)

A number of other organizations, while not as directly tied to the CPUSA, are dominated by the party and largely led by party functionaries. They represent the CPUSA's united-front policies in different areas of American life. The most prominent and successful organization has been the National Alliance against Racist and Political Repression (NARPR). Charlene Mitchell, onetime CPUSA candidate for the U.S. Presidency is executive director. Co-chairmen include Bert Corona, Angela Davis, and Clyde Bellecourt (of the American Indian Movement). The NARPR has focussed its efforts on North Carolina, alleging that this state has instituted anti-labor and anti-black repression. Its fourth congress, held in St. Louis in November, focused on the "Wilmington 10," a group of North Carolina blacks allegedly imprisoned unjustly.

The National Coalition to Fight Inflation and Unemployment (NCFIU), of which Elizabeth Merkelson is executive secretary, held a meeting in January to draw up a "People's Economic Agenda" designed to deal with youth unemployment (ibid., 20 January). The National Co-ordinating Committee for Trade Union Action and Democracy (TUAD) was founded in 1970 to help increase party influence in the trade union movement. Rayfield Mooty and Fred Gaboury are TUAD leaders.

The CPUSA's principal front in the women's field is Women for Racial and Economic Equality (WREE), led by Georgia Henning and Sondra Patrinos. WREE's first national convention, held in Chicago in March, attracted 530 delegates. WREE opposes the Equal Rights Amendment to the U.S. constitution in its present form, but supports a "Women's Bill of Rights" which focuses on economic issues, educational opportunities, and availability of day care for children. Other party-dominated organizations include the Committee for a Just Peace in the Middle East, the National Council of American-Soviet Friendship, the Chile Solidarity Committee, the Metropolitan Council on Housing, and the National Anti-Imperialist Movement in Solidarity with African Liberation.

Party Internal Affairs. The dispute over the Jewish question (see *YICA, 1976,* p. 524, and *1977,* p. 496) became more acrimonious. In May the CPUSA published a bitter attack on the *Freiheit,* a Yiddish-language daily long identified with the party, edited by former long-time party functionary Paul Novick. Novick was expelled in 1972 for his position on Israel. The CPUSA called upon the *Freiheit's* readers to produce a new leadership, accusing the paper of being in the open service of imperialism. Novick, identifying the paper with the doctrines of Eurocommunism, accused the CPUSA of bordering on anti-Semitism and ridiculed it for its isolation stemming from its lockstep obedience to the USSR (*NYT,* 15 May).

Domestic Attitudes and Activities. The CPUSA found little to approve in the Carter administration's first year in office. It attacked the president's cabinet nominees as captives of big business and was particularly critical of Attorney-General Bell, labeling him a segregationist (*Daily World,* 6 January). The party also demanded that Budget Director Bert Lance be fired (ibid., 17 August). The president's programs were regarded just as unfavorably. The CPUSA claimed the fuel shortage in America was created by manufacturers to enable prices to rise, characterized the Carter energy program as a ripoff, and urged nationlization as the only solution (ibid., 14 April). A similar suggestion greeted the New York blackout when the party called the Consolidated Edison company the city's biggest looter (ibid., 16 July).

President Carter's human rights policy incurred hostility. The CPUSA suggested it was hypocritical to deny rights at home while seeking to discredit Socialism in Russia, Eastern Europe, and Southeast Asia (ibid., 16 June). There were frequent discussions of an upsurge of nazism in America and charges that the rights of blacks, Indians and Chicanos were being violated. The CPUSA strongly attacked Allan Bakke, a white student who claimed to be a victim of reverse discrimination, arguing that affirmative action programs for other races were necessary to make up for centuries of discrimination against them (ibid., 25 August). The party also denounced the execution of convicted murderer Gary Gilmore, charging that the death penalty gave the ruling class a weapon of repression (ibid., 18 January).

Administration military policy also came in for criticism. The increase in the military budget was decried as an obstacle to détente (ibid., 22 Febraury). the B-1 bomber program was seen as unnecessary and provocative; when Carter abandoned it, the CPUSA claimed that he had surrendered to popular pressure (ibid., 29 June). The party also opposed the cruise missile and the neutron bomb, claiming that they undermined détente (ibid., 6 August).

International Views and Policies. The CPUSA is one of the staunchest supporters of the USSR in the world Communist movement. Dissidence in Communist countries was frequently denounced. The dissidents' protests against denials of human rights in Russia were seen as efforts to derail détente and cover up Western violations of the Helsinki agreements (ibid., 2 February). The forced exile of Wolf Bierman from East Germany was held to be entirely justified (ibid., 20 January). The Charta 77 movement was interference in the internal affairs of Czechoslovakia (ibid., 28 January).

Gus Hall vigorously defended the USSR against the criticisms of Santiago Carrillo, charging that the Spanish party leader had lent himself to a slander campaign. Hall criticized "some parties" for not placing enough emphasis on struggle "against the imperialism of their countries," while admitting that some honest criticisms of specific practices in Socialist countries were permissible. (Ibid., 30 July, 6 September.) In response to Eurocommunist assertions of independence from Moscow, Hall insisted that all Communist parties were independent and there was no single road to Socialism, although "some parties tend to put such one-sided emphasis on the peacefulness of the transition that it leaves the doors wide-open for illusions" that force will not be needed to defeat counter-revolution (ibid., 3 September).

Believing that the world balance of power is shifting to the Socialist countries, the CPUSA supports American withdrawal from South Korea and reunification of Korea under Kim Il-song (ibid., 13 July.) The new regime in Ethiopia was applauded; U.S. meddling in the Horn of Africa was attacked. Also attacked was U.S. interference in Zaire to protect its monopoly interests (ibid., 23 March). American policy in the Middle East was condemned for its support of Israel and for trying to ignore the Soviet Union (ibid., 22 February). President Sadat's Mid-East initiatives were also criticized. Aid was urged for Vietnam, and independence for Puerto Rico, and the administration's SALT proposals were derided (ibid., 16 February, 17 August, 2 June). The party supported the Canal treaty with Panama but added that U.S. military rights should be further curtailed (ibid., 20 August).

International Activities and Contacts. In June 1977, Gus Hall met in Moscow with Brezhnev, Suslov, and Ponomarov. Hall also attended the 60th anniversary celebration of the October Revolution and received the Order of Lenin. Politburo member James West was in Bulgaria in July for talks. In June, Arnold Bechetti, Si Gerson, and Lorenzo Torres were in Cuba. In March, George Myers attended a trade union congress in Moscow, and Jack Kling and Joelle Fishman met with János Kádár. James Jackson was a visitor to Ethiopia. A joint meeting of the Communist parties of the U.S. and Mexico in October resulted in a denunciation of American interference in Latin America and a call for amnesty for illegal entrants from Latin America arrested in the U.S. (ibid., 26 October).

Publications. The *Daily World,* published five times a week in New York, is the CPUSA's major publication (claimed circulation, 30,000). *Political Affairs* is a theoretical journal. Other party-linked papers are *People's World,* a San Francisco weekly; *Freedomways,* a black quarterly; *New World Review,* a bimonthly journal on international affairs; *Jewish Affairs,* a bimonthly newsletter; *Cultural Reporter; African Agenda; Labor Today; Korea Forum;* and *Black Liberation Journal.* International Publishers has long been identified as the party's publishing outlet.

The SWP: Leadership and Organization. Jack Barnes is national secretary and Barry Shepard is organizational secretary of the Socialist Workers Party. Other party leaders include Malik Miah (black liberation director), Mary-Alice Waters (editor, *Militant*), Cindy Jaquith (women's liberation director), Olga Rodríguez (Chicano liberation director), Tony Thomas, Doug Jenness, Frank Lovell, Ed Shaw, George Breitman, Fred Halstead, Gus Horowitz, Lew Jones, and Catarino Garza.

The most important party auxiliary is the Young Socialist Alliance (YSA). Chuck Petrin, elected national organizational secretary at the group's national convention in January 1977, claimed 800 members. An internal party memorandum indicates, however, that in the last year YSA membership has dropped from 1150 to 556. The decline was a consequence of a decision to coopt nearly 600 YSA members into the SWP to bolster party membership for next year's World Congress of the Fourth International. The YSA, as a result, is suffering from organizational weakness, political inexperience, financial chaos and a failure to carry out party directives. Other officers are Rick Berman, national chairperson, and Cathy Sedwick, national secretary. Some 700 persons attended the conference. Most YSA members are students and nearly half are women. About one-fifth of the membership and one-half of the leadership is made up of minorities. The two central campaigns for 1977 were to be a defense of the South African struggle and a defense of women's rights (*Militant,* 21 January).

Other party organizations include the Political Rights Defense Fund and the National Student Coalition Against Racism (NSCAR). NSCAR met in October in New York to assess the struggle against racism. Other group activities include protests against U.S. policy in South Africa, defense of immigrant workers, support of affirmative action, and opposition to anti-busing actions. (Ibid., 22 April.)

Party Internal Affairs. The SWP's twenty-ninth national convention, in August, was attended by 1,685 party members, virtually the entire party. The party emphasized a need to raise money and reported on organizational difficulties stemming from an earlier decision to break down city-wide locals into smaller branches (see *YICA, 1977,* p. 499). The party emphasized the need for further expansion, both numerically and geographically. Most members are young and a large percentage are women. Blacks are not well represented.

The convention also admitted the forty-five members of the Revolutionary Marxist Committee (RMC) to the SWP. The RMC, a splinter Trotskyite group, was centered in Detroit but its members were scattered around the country. The SWP once again refused to admit members of the Revolutionary Marxist Organizing Committee, which supports the International Majority Tendency in the Fourth International, a faction supporting the use of terrorism in Latin America and closer ties with some Stalinist parties.

Domestic Attitudes and Activities. Active on varied issues in 1977, the SWP participated in protests against Alan Bakke and demanded continuation of affirmative-action programs (*Militant,* 30 September). It also supported full civil rights protection for homosexuals (ibid., 1 July). The SWP continued to support the Equal Rights Amendment for women and denounced the CPUSA for its opposition. At a national conference of the National Organization of Women (NOW), however, a resolution denouncing the SWP was passed. The party was charged with trying to exploit NOW for socialist rather than feminist aims. The SWP quickly charged NOW with red-baiting. (Ibid., 6, 13 May.)

Other party activities included support for the insurgent candidate for president of the Steelworkers' Union, Ed Sadlowski; opposition to the death penalty; support for Puerto Rican independence; and continuation of a major lawsuit against the U.S. government for illegal spying on SWP activities. In general, the SWP criticized the CPUSA for its brand of coalition politics and insisted that an independent Socialist movement is necessary. The party gave support to the Raza Unida political party, a Chicano group concentrated in Texas and Colorado.

International Views and Policies. While critical of both superpowers, the SWP directs most of its attack at the U.S. Attacks on the Soviet Union have become sharper in recent years. In 1977 the SWP voiced support for Soviet dissidents, and for Charta 77, and claimed that there is growing unrest and oppositon to Stalinism in Eastern Europe (ibid., 18 February). U.S. foreign policy was regularly denounced for serving the interests of world imperialism. The Chinese government was likewise a target. While supporting some polciies of such countries as Mozambique, Vietnam, and Cambodia, the SWP denounced them for repression. Eurocommunists were attacked as Stalinists. On the Middle East, the SWP was far more hostile to Israel than the CPUSA, and frequently called for its elimination.

The SWP publishes a weekly, *The Militant,* and the monthlies *Young Socialist* and *International Socialist Review.*

Maoist Groups. The Maoist movement in the U.S.A. is composed of a large number of small groups which disagree very strongly with each other. The recent upheavals in China have caused a great deal of uncertainty and confusion, leading to vitriolic debates about who is a real Maoist and whether the Chinese government has abandoned the revolutionary path. The two largest organized groups are the Revolutionary Communist Party and the Communist Party (Marxist-Leninist), formerly the October League. The *Guardian,* published in New York City, represents an independent Maoist line.

The CP(M-L) is led by Michael Klonsky, chairman, and Eileen Klehr, vice-chairman. Its founding congress was held in June 1977. Most of the party's activists are veterans of the student movement of the 1960s. The CP(M-L) has been recognized by the Chinese Communist leadership. Klonsky and Klehr were received in Peking in July by Hua Kuo-Feng and prominently displayed by the Chinese (*Guardian,* 27 July). In accord with Chinese policy, the group denounces both superpowers but labels the USSR the more dangerous. The U.S.A. is seen as falling behind Russia militarily, and hence the main attacks must be directed against Soviet social imperialism (ibid., 27 April, 1 June).

The CP(M-L) has revived much of the rhetoric of the 1930s, denouncing the CPUSA as the most dangerous of the bourgeois parties in America and as social fascist. It has also revived the theory of self-determination in the black belt, under the aegis of Harry Haywood, one of the authors of the theory almost fifty years ago. It argues that blacks have the right of self-determination in the South and regional autonomy elsewhere, a right also possessed by other minorities (ibid., 27 April). The party has taken over the U.S.-China People's Friendship Association and also controls the Fight Back organization.

The Revolutionary Communist Party, with nearly 2,000 members, is probably the largest Maoist group. Its youth organization is the Revolutionary Student Brigade. Party leaders include Bob Avakian, Nick Unger, Barry Romo, and Leibel Bergman. The RCP apparently has few black members but some Chicanos and Asian Americans. It controls the Vietnam Veterans Against the War and the National Workers Organization. In October the RCP established a youth group, Youth in Action, with its own paper, *The Young Red.* By not endorsing the purge of the Gang of Four in China the RCP has lost its Maoist franchise to the CP(M-L). It has attacked both superpowers, directed strong attacks at Cuba, and urged superpower withdrawal from Angola (ibid., 9 February). The group opposes school busing for desegregation in Boston and the Equal Rights Amendment (ibid., 1 June).

The *Guardian* has criticized all the other radical groups and enunciated "29 principles" as the basis for organizing Guardian Clubs around the country (ibid.).

Other Groups. The Weather Underground Organization (WUO) apparently split during 1977. A number of its members surfaced and surrendered to authorities to face trial on various pending charges. The most prominent was Mark Rudd, one-time leader of the Columbia University student uprising. Bernadine Dohrn has reportedly opposed this policy of "inversion" as an abandonment of the politics of armed struggle (*Guardian,* 27 April). Dohrn has attacked other WUO leaders Bill Ayers and Jeff Jones as white male chauvinists (*NYT,* 18 January). In November Clayton Van Lydegraf, a key leader in the Weather Underground, was arrested with several other people in Houston and charged with conspiracy to plant bombs in several locations (*San Francisco Examiner and Chronicle*, 20 November). The Prairie Fire Organizing Committee (PFOC), close to the WUO, issued a provisional political statement emphasizing the struggle for national liberation and published a journal, *Breakthrough* (*Guardian,* 27 July).

The Progressive Labor Party (PLP) has apparently been wracked with internal feuding. Its paper, *Challenge,* appeared irregularly.

Emory University   Harvey Klehr

Uruguay

The Communist Party of Uruguay (Partido Comunista del Uruguay; PCU) dates from September 1920, when a congress of the Socialist Party voted to join the Communist International. The present name was adopted in April 1921. In December 1973 the PCU was declared illegal for the first time in its history and remains so today.

Among the other Uruguayan Marxist-Leninist groups are the Revolutionary Communist Party of Uruguay (Partido Comunista Revolucionario del Uruguay; PCRU) and the National Liberation Movement (Movimiento de Liberación Nacional; MLN), the latter better known as the Tupamaros.

In August 1977 Uruguayan President Aparicio Méndez and his cabinet ministers had the Ministry of the Interior issue a communique stating that "traditional political parties" would be allowed to participate in elections to be held in 1981. Both Marxist and anti-Marxist commentators interpreted this to mean that the traditional Colorado and Blanco parties would be on the ballot but that the currently-outlawed PCU, the Socialist Party, and other groups which fielded candidates in 1971 under the coalition Broad Front (Frente Amplio; FA) banner would not. The population of Uruguay is 2,800,000.

The PCU: Organization and Leadership. PCU First Secretary Rodney Arismendi was exiled to Moscow in January 1975. The PCU Central Committee has 48 members and 27 alternates. The five-member Secretariat consists of Arismendi, Enrique Pastorino, Jaime Pérez, Enrique Rodríguez, and Alberto Suárez. Pastorino remains president of the pro-Soviet World Federation of Trade Unions (WFTU) and, through the International Labor Office in Geneva, has been given United Nations diplomatic immunity. PCU-member Julia Arévalo, in prison since 1976, is a vice-president of the Women's International Democratic Federation. Suárez was organizational secretary until deposed by the PCU Central Committee for not preparing the party to cope with being outlawed. However, on 28 February 1977 Suárez was publicly greeted as a PCU leader in the German Democratic Republic in the presence of Arismendi (ADN news service, East Berlin, 28 February).

The PCU's youth organization is the Union of Communist Youth (Unión de la Juventud Comunista; UJC). The PCU led the once-powerful, but now outlawed, National Convention of Workers (CNT), which still conducts international campaigns against the present government.

Domestic Attitudes and Activities. On 22 July the PCU issued a leaflet from an underground press denouncing the government's Institutional Act No. 7, which deprives certain civil servants of their job security. (Previously, public officials could not be fired without a formal charge and conviction of incompetence or malfeasance.)

During the last half of 1977 the PCU was concerned that the military-backed government of President Méndez would create a legislative-type junta of high-ranking military officers and leaders of the Colorado and Blanco parties in 1978, without any representatives from the FA, and thus avoid allowing Marxist-Leninists to participate in the scheduled elections of 1981 (*Latin America,* London, 13 May; AP, Montevideo, 10 November). PCU and Tupamaro agents trying to use old peso notes taken in bank robberies during the past decade have been frustrated by the government's printing of new currency.

International Views and Positions. During 1977 the exiled PCU first secretary issued statements on events inside Uruguay and on international affairs from various Communist nations he visited. On 12 March in a television interview in Moscow, Arismendi announced a propaganda campaign against the governments of Uruguay and Chile by Communist parties and sympathizers in Latin American republics and the United States (Tass, Moscow, 12 March). On 3 June in Havana, at a conference of the Cuban Institute for Friendship with Peoples (ICAP), Arismendi called on Cubans and Uruguayan Marxist exiles to work together to overthrow the Uruguayan government (Havana television, 3 June). In September, on the fifty-seventh anniversary of the founding of the PCU, he called upon PCU members and sympathizers with Communism in Uruguay to unite in a struggle to destroy the government of President Méndez, and to turn power over to the PCU, the unions of the CNT, and the groups of the FA. Arismendi demanded that all Uruguayan exiles be allowed to return to their country. (Ibid., 21 September.) On 29 September Communist Party of Italy secretary general Enrico Berlinguer met with Arismendi and Rodríguez in Rome. During that month the PCU received pledges of propaganda support from the Communist parties in Italy and Bulgaria.

On 15 July the Motevideo police arrested a reporter for the Mexican daily *Excelsior.* By 28 July Arismendi in Moscow had mounted an international campaign of protest, declaring that the Mexican newsman was merely an investigating reporter uncovering irregularities in Uruguay's ministries of defense, interior, and justice (*Excelsior,* Mexico City, 28 July). The PCU demanded that the Inter-American Press Association (SIP) condemn the arrest, but a SIP investigation revealed no clear violation of press freedom.

The PCRU. The Revolutionary Communist Party of Uruguay describes itself as a Marxist-Leninist political party aligned internationally to the People's Republic of China. In December 1976 it was revealed that the PCRU Central Committee members are all under arrest in Montevideo, among them political secretary Mario Echenique. Party members met in Albania at the end of 1976 and issued a joint policy statement with several other pro-Chinese Communist parties from Latin America (see *Chile*).

The MLN (Tupamaros). On 16 February the Uruguayan Supreme Court gave MLN leader Antonio Mas thirty years in prison for having murdered U. S. government official Dan Mitrione in 1970. Mas has been serving another sentence for attempted violent overthrow of the government. He also is charged with killing three police officers and having been one of the kidnappers of the British ambassador to Uruguay in 1970. (*TELAM* news service, Montevideo, 16 February.)

In mid-March the military justice court in Montevideo ordered the release of more than 1,200 MLN guerrillas and other extremists who have served most or part of their sentences (*Radio Carve,* Montevideo, 31 March). In July a military court in Montevideo charged twenty students of economics at the national university with forming a group plotting on behalf of the Tupamaros. The group carried the name "26th of March Independence Movement," an affiliate of the MLN. (*Agence France Presse,* Montevideo, 28 July.)

Arizona State University   Marvin Alisky

Venezuela

The Communist Party of Venezuela (Partido Comunista de Venezuela; PCV), the oldest of the extreme leftist groups in the country, was founded in 1931. After the death of dictator Juan Vicente Gómez in late 1935, the party gained considerable influence in the labor movement and in other parts of Venezuelan society. However, the PCV's participation in guerrilla activities in the early 1960s greatly undermined its strength and influence, as did two later splits in the party. The first took place in December 1970, when most of its youth organization and substantial elements of the adult party broke away to form the Movement Towards Socialism (Movimiento al Socialismo; MAS). The other occurred in mid-1974 when a group of party leaders split away to form the Vanguardia Comunista (VC).

Another Marxist-Leninist group, the Movement of the Revolutionary Left (Movimiento de Izquierda Revolucionario; MIR), originated in 1960 from a split in the Democratic Action Party

(Acción Democrática; AD), which controlled the government from 1959 to 1969 and returned to power early in 1974. Other elements on the far left, Maoists and Trotskyists, have appeared in recent years.

There remain some active remnants of the urban and rural guerrilla movement which had its high point in the early 1960s, when both the PCV and the MIR participated in it. The major elements of both parties withdrew from the guerrilla struggle in the 1965-66 period and since then the guerrillas have been of marginal importance in Venezuelan national politics.

The PCV may have about 3,000 members, the MAS perhaps considerably more; the strength of the other groups is not known.

The population of Venezuela is about 12.5 million.

The PCV: Organization, Leadership and Program. The top leadership of the PCV is its eighteen-member Politburo. This body includes Gustavo Machado, party chairman; Jesús Faría, secretary general, and Radamés Larrazábal, who in recent years has been the principal public spokesman for the party.

Until the December 1970 split, the PCV's Venezuelan Communist Youth (Juventud Comunista Venezolana; JCV) was the largest political group in the student movement. The split deprived the JCV of most of its leaders and members and threw it into much confusion. It reduced PCV influence in the student movement to minor proportions, the leading position being taken by the MAS youth group.

The principal center of PCV influence in the labor movement is the United Workers Confederation of Venezuela (Confederación Unitaria de Trabajadores de Venezuela; CUTV), established in the early 1960s when the PCV lost virtually all influence in the majority Confederation of Workers of Venezuela (Confederación de Trabajadores de Venezuela; CTV). Although most PCV trade union activities are concentrated on the CUTV, in a few isolated cases the Communists have apparently been able to regain some following in the CTV. Thus, in the steel workers union in the East, the PCV won two seats in union elections early in 1977. In recent years the CUTV has been further weakened by the withdrawal of elements associated with the MAS and the Vanguardia Comunista and their entry into the CTV. The last CUTV congress, its seventh, was held in March 1976. The agenda included discussion of wage increases, inflation, and unemployment, as well as the "struggle for full national independence against imperialism" and the specific problems of women workers. A new executive committee was chosen and Cruz Villegas was reelected president. Early in 1977, the CUTV issued an appeal to the country's other central labor groups to form a united front to fight the rising cost of living (*WMR,* May). This appeal went unanswered.

Domestic Attitudes and Activities. The PCV adopted its present program at its fifth congress in 1974. According to Jerónimo Carrera, member of the PCV Central Committee, in the preceding period, subsequent to their disengagement from guerrilla activities, internal problems had "prevented deeper analysis of the causes of the left deviations that had lost us those of our supporters among the masses . . . ." These problems also "hampered the conduct of research demanded of us by the changing realities of a country that was developing fast along capitalist lines but was seen by us as it had been twenty years earlier" (*WMR,* May 1977).

The Central Committee of the PCV held plenums in November 1976, and in February and July of 1977. The Party's Eighth National Conference met in September. Each of these meetings took actions of some significance.

The Seventh Plenum in November 1976 adopted a resolution commenting on the current world and national situations. After praising the Soviet Union's "policy of detente and peace," the resolution noted that "it is significant to us that the stand of the present government of Venezuela coincides, in part, with these aims. We also appreciate that Venezuelan diplomacy sides with the nations facing problems brought about by imperialist or colonialist oppression." It expressed approval for the nationalization of the oil and iron mining sectors, but added that "the Communists witness the accelerated process of capitalist concentration, which is confirmed by the Central Bank of Venezuela and other official bodies. State credits serve, directly or otherwise, the private economic sectors." It was also very critical of the inflation, and the agricultural situation, claiming that "now, sixteen years after its proclamation, the law on agrarian reform has yet to be implemented." The Seventh Plenum Resolution also expressed preoccupation with the country's growing environmental problems and urged the establishment of a national oil tanker fleet. Finally, it issued a call for leftist unity for the forthcoming 1978 presidential election (*IB*, 31 December 1976).

The Eighth Plenum, in February, drew up a program of events for the celebration during the year of the sixtieth anniversary of the Bolshevik Revolution. It was noted that the party "will strive to draw a broad mass of the country's people into these activities." (*FBIS*, 9 February).

The Ninth Plenum, held early in July, devoted most of its attention to the problems of the coming election campaign. It issued an appeal for unity of all of the leftist forces in the campaign and stressed the need to prevent the polarization of the electorate around the AD and Copei, such as had occurred in 1973. It urged that the far leftist groups agree not only on a presidential nominee but also on common slates for legislative offices as well (*El Nacional*, Caracas 7 July).

Throughout the first eight months of the year, the PCV continued to work for unity of the far left for the 1978 election. In April it sponsored a meeting, held in its national office, with a group of independent leftist politicians, at which it was agreed that unity of all the far left groups was desirable. The PCV representatives insisted on their willingness to support a united front if it could be formed. In early June, when it became clear that the MAS would not join any left grouping, Héctor Mujica announced that the PCV still hoped that all other left groups, including the PCV, the MIR, the MEP, the Trotskyist Socialist League and the Revolutionary Action Group (GAR) would be able to reach agreement on a common presidential candidate (*El Nacional*, 3 June).

However, when all efforts to bring the various far left groups together failed, the Eighth National Conference of the PCV named its own candidate for the presidency, Héctor Mujica, an alternate member of the PCV Central Committee and president of the National Journalists Association. In his acceptance speech, Mujica commented that his nomination would "serve, in the first place, to rebuild the party and to give Venezuelans a positive alternative to the traditional parties—Democratic Action (AD), the party in power, of a social democratic orientation, and Copei, a Christian Democratic party" (*FBIS*, 7 September).

From time to time during the year, the PCV leadership published statements concerning current events and problems. Thus, in January the party attacked the government's move to raise milk prices, calling it "social aggression" (*FBIS*, 12 January). In September, Mujica strongly attacked a demand of the Federation of Chambers of Commerce and Industry for changes in the government's economic program (*FBIS*, 16 September).

International Views and Positions. The PCV is a very orthodox pro-Moscow party. This fact was emphasized by the publication in *World Marxist Review* of an article by Jerónimo Carrerra entitled "The Sacred Flame of Internationalism. This article ended: "If we communists want the revolution predicted by the *Manifesto* and first materialized in the Red October of 1917 to spread ultimately to the whole world, we must keep up the sacred flame of internationalism and feed it day after day" (*WMR*, September).

The PCV was represented, with observer status, at a meeting of Caribbean Communist parties held in Havana early in May (*Granma*, Havana, 3 May). Subsequently, Faría and other members of the Venezuelan delegation met extensively with Carlos Rafael Rodríguez and other leading members of the Cuban party's Politburo and Secretariat. (*FBIS*, 12 May).

In March the PCV caused a considerable public stir when it accused eight Venezuelan newsmen of being CIA agents. Those accused presented a formal complaint to the Association of Venezuelan Journalists (*FBIS*, 6 March). The PCV accused them and a long list of other people of following CIA instructions "with a view to destabilizing the existing regime, to undermining the prestige of progressive circles and to conducting an anti-Soviet campaign on instructions from Washington" (*FBIS*, 7 March).

On one international issue the Communists acted with considerable caution. They were called in by President Carlos Andrés Pérez early in Juanuary to be briefed on the status of negotiations over a border dispute with Colombia. Subsequently, the Eighth Plenum issued a statement which thanked the president for his information, noted that the issue was "a question of a delicate state matter and therefore we have taken a prudent stand. . . ." The statement noted that "the attitude of Venezuela's Communists on border issues is clear. We are against the exacerbation of animosities and against an insincere display of patriotism" (*IB*, 28 February).

Publications. The PCV's principal organ is the newspaper *Tribuna Popular*. Its theoretical periodical, *Documentos Politicos*, has had some difficulty in coming out since the MAS split.

The VC. The launching of the Vanguardia Comunista in June 1974 was significant because it represented a split in the "old guard" of the Venezuelan Communist movement. Particularly interesting was the presence in its leadership of Eduardo Machado. In all previous divisions of the Communist Party, the Machado brothers, Gustavo and Eduardo, had always been aligned together. Another member of the PCV old guard who helped form Vanguardia Comunista was Guillermo García Ponce.

The VC's First Congress, held in November 1974, proclaimed the new group to be a "Marxist-Leninist party . . . faithful to the traditions of international solidarity." The Congress elected Machado president and García Ponce as secretary general (*El Nacional*, 4 November).

The VC's position remained an orthodox one. In September, when a Caracas paper alleged that the Vanguardia Comunista favored Eurocommunism, Machado and García Ponce issued a denial. Their statement said that the next congress of the VC, to be held in 1978, would consider a report on the world Communist movement. In preparation for this, several VC leaders would be going abroad to confer with Communist leaders in the USSR, Spain, Czechoslovakia, France, Bulgaria, Italy, Romania, Yugoslavia, the United States, and Cuba (*FBIS*, 21 September).

A Plenum of the Central Committee of the VC, meeting early in July, made several important decisions. One of these was not to run a candidate in the 1978 presidential election. An article written by García Ponce right after the plenum analyzed the electoral situation. It argued that "the answer to this situation is not to be found in the old schemes of the 'leftist front' nor in single party solutions. . . . What must be done, urgently and dramatically, is to defeat Democratic Action. . . ." Only two candidates, José Vicente Rangel and Luis Herrera Campins (of Copei) could possibly do this. These, García Ponce said, could "become candidacies of national convergence, as long as their backers are capable of assuming a course of conduct that is consistent with the needs and interests of the country's majorities. . . ." (*Ultimas Noticias*, Caracas, 3 July). The other significant decision was to withdraw its followers from the PCV-dominated CUTV, and have them join the CTV. A statement issued to explain this action argued: "We must be where the working masses and the workers in general are. . . ." (*El Nacional*, 30 June).

The MAS. The Movement Toward Socialism was formed late in 1970 and constituted the first major split in the PCV. Former PCV Politburo member Pompeyo Márquez is the MAS secretary general. The MAS took with it a large part of the intermediary leadership cadres of the PCV, a majority of the former PCV rank and file, and virtually all of the JCV.

The MAS youth organization is the Juventud Comunista-MAS (JC-MAS), which initially dominated most of the student bodies of Venezuelan universities. Although its influence has somewhat declined, the JC-MAS remains the largest political group in the student movement. The MAS at its inception had some influence in the CUTV trade union movement. Those who went with MAS first formed the "CUT Clasista" as a rival organization. In July 1974 the MAS Central Committee decided to have its supporters enter the CTV, the majority union group, and the MAS now has one seat on the CTV Executive Committee.

Internal Dissensions. Internal dissension, which had broken out in the MAS in 1976, continued throughout 1977. One source of dissension certainly was the question of the party's presidential nominee for the 1978 election, but behind this there seemed to be broader ideological and political issues. Teodoro Petkoff was widely felt to be the leader, although not the most open spokesman, for a group which was critical of the majority of the party's leadership. The internal struggle in the MAS gained publicity on various occasions. In June, a public controversy arose between the JC-MAS and the party leadership. The Youth had planned a "symposium on the situation in education," to which the MAS leadership objected. The party Planning Commission suspended the symposium, but the JC-MAS leadership unanimously voted to go ahead with it. At the meeting of the JC-MAS leaders, Freddy Muñoz stated the position of the party chiefs but apparently was unable to convince the youth of its correctness (*Ultimas Noticias,* 12 June). In August, a letter from four dissident leaders of the MAS to the delegates at the party's July convention was published. This document, signed by Germán Lairet, J.M. Blanco Ponce, Antonio José Urbina, and Alfredo Padilla, started out saying "it is evident that the MAS is facing an extremely delicate internal situation." It went on to argue that the national leadership had used "certain bad practices" in the conduct of local and regional meetings leading up to the national convention. It claimed that "the right to think and 'to let the mind wander' as well as the creative audacity which was previously an essential conquest of this movement, now face the danger of being replaced by dogmatism, a 'strait jacket,' a Stalinist stereotype. . . ," adding that "internal democracy is being strangled by ideological terrorism." The letter ended by exhorting the convention delegates to take steps to change the situation (*El Universal,* Caracas, 2 August).

Domestic Attitudes and Activities. Although in the beginning of the administration of President Pérez the MAS seemed to adopt a quite friendly attitude towards the president, this was not so during 1977. Thus on the occasion of Pérez's third annual message to congress in March, Rangel, the MAS presidential candidate, said in a press conference that "three years into this administration we can say responsibly that the illusions and expectations created by the decree and announcements made by the president of the republic on assuming his lofty post have become a widespread feeling of frustration." He asserted that "essentially the current administration's policy is designed to consolidate the dominant power of a business minority liberally helped by petroleum revenue through government expenditures and credit. The grip of runaway price increases for basic consumer items is holding the people down on the one hand, and on the other there is the repression of any labor or trade union attempt at demanding rights" (*Ultimas Noticias,* 16 March). Two months later, MAS Secretary General Pompeyo Márquez strongly attacked allegedly widespread corruption in the administration, and the Pérez government's failure to do anything about it. He also noted that "the government has been lacking in plans for coping with the serious problems involving shortage which are reflected most keenly in the scarcity of such items as meat, coffee, milk, eggs, sugar and other foods" (*El Nacional,* 23 May).

For its part, the governing Acción Democratica Party strongly attacked the MAS. In January, Luis Pinerua, then secretary general of AD, and later in the year named its presidential candidate, claimed that "the MAS is a disguised version of the Venezuelan Communist Party, from whose ranks the MAS leaders came. If today they appear under the guise of Socialism, it is because they are convinced that under their original image, they had no chance of obtaining political influence in Venezuela. If the MAS leaders were to succeed politically, we would soon see the Soviet Union give them its blessing" (*FBIS*, 18 January).

Much of the MAS's effort during 1977 was concentrated on the presidential campaign, which got in full swing during the year, although the election will not be until December 1978. As early as November 1976, in a MAS national convention, Teodoro Petkoff, who had nursed ambitions of being the 1978 presidential nominee, stepped aside in favor of José Vicente Rangel, the party's 1973 candidate. The official endorsement of Rangel took place at the MAS nominating convention at the end of July. This meeting was preceded by gatherings of 5,000 rank and file groups, 600 municipal conventions, 28 regional ones and 5 national sector conferences (*Ultimas Noticias*, 30 June). Although the MAS leadership claimed that it favored unity of the left against the two major parties in the 1978 campaign, it was clear that the purpose of the party in that campaign was going to be to establish itself as the third alternative in national politics. Pompeyo Márquez made this clear in a statement early in April. He commented that "to convert socialism into a force of the masses which will attract multitudes is no easy task, and it can hardly be accomplished through 'fronts' or a 'unity' of parties and factions which have differing views concerning the country today and its immediate future. This is the kind of 'unity' which detracts rather than adding. . . ." (*Ultimas Noticias*, 3 April). In July the MAS specifically rejected the offer of the MIR to support Rangel (*FBIS*, 6 July).

International Views. The MAS continued during 1977 to maintain an independent attitude on foreign issues and in its relations with foreign parties. However, it was reported that Teodoro Petkoff, in outlining MAS policies in March, "seemed to be identifying closely with the 'Euro-communism' of the Spanish, French and Italian Communist Parties" (*Latin America Political Report*, London, 8 April).

On foreign policy issues, MAS supported an agreement presumably reached for Venezuela to supply Cuba with oil, although insisting that President Pérez publish the details of the agreement. It also supported the official Venezuelan government policy of continuing to push up oil prices, although expressing skepticism as to whether the government wasn't offering under-the-counter rebates to foreign companies purchasing Venezuelan oil.

Publications. The principal MAS organ is the newspaper *Punto*, edited by Pompeyo Márquez.

The MIR. the MIR was established in 1960 by dissidents from the AD, including most of the party's youth movement. In 1962 the MIR joined in launching a guerrilla effort which lasted for several years. A large element in the party leadership and rank and file, headed by Domingo Alberto Rangel, withdrew from guerrilla activites in 1965-66, and later quit the party. However the MIR officially foreswore participation in the guerrilla only in 1969.

During 1977, the activities of the MIR received only modest public attention. However, its offer to support the presidential candidacy of MAS nominee Rangel, and MAS's rejection of that offer, were reported (*FBIS*, 8 July). So was the party's final decision in August to name its only member of the Chamber of Deputies, Américo Martín, a one-time guerrilla leader, as its presidential candidate (*FBIS*, 15 August). In July, two local leaders of the MIR in the eastern city of Maturin were arrested by the secret police for allegedly being implicated with guerrillas which were operating in the vicinity. Both of those arrested proclaimed their innocence (*El Nacional*, 11 July). The MIR made some progress in the labor movement for the first time in many years when it unexpectedly won the steel workers union election in June (*El Nacional*, 19 June).

The Maoists. There are at least four Maoist groups in Venezuela. These are the Patria Nueva movement; the Party of the Venezuelan Revolution (Partido de la Revolución Venezolana; PRV), reportedly led by Douglas Bravo, one-time PCV Politburo member; the Ruptura movement; and the Popular Struggle Committees (CLP). The last two were established in 1976. None of them has any influence in the labor movement, although the CLP has some marginal following among students in the Central University. The PRV has participated at times in the continuing guerrilla activity.

The Trotskyists. The first evidence of a Trotskyist movement in Venezuela was the appearance on 1 May 1972 of *Voz Marxista,* organ of the Venezuelan Trotskyist Group (Grupo Trotskista Venezolano). In 1973 this group took the name Socialist Workers Party (Partido Socialista de Trabajadores). It supported the candidacy of Rangel in the 1973 election, but appears to have merged late in 1974 with a number of groups which had advocated abstention or a blank vote. These formed the Socialist League (Liga Socialista; LS). The LS is the Venezuelan section of the United Secretariat of the Fourth International. It publishes a fortnightly, *Voz Socialista.* Little publicity was given to LS activities during 1977, However, it is known that they participated in some of the fruitless negotiations to work out a joint candidacy of the far left for the 1978 election.

The Guerrillas. There was some resurgence during the year of guerrilla activity, particularly in the mountainous eastern part of the country. Armed bands carried out several spectacular operations during the year. In June fifteen men armed with machine guns attacked the police station of Urica (*FBIS,* 1 July). In September thirty-four guerrillas seized the village of Caigua and forced its inhabitants to come into the public square to hear the leader of the guerrilla group exhort them to overthrow the government by force (*NYT,* 7 September). On 14 August, thirteen guerrilla prisoners escaped from the jail of De la Pica in Monagas State (*FBIS*, 16 August). There was one outbreak of guerrilla violence in Caracas. In August pipe-bombs were exploded in several places in the central part of the city. The bombs released sheets of paper proclaiming that the bombs had been placed by the César Sánchez Brigade of the Party of the Venezuelan Revolution (*Ultimas Noticias,* 23 August).

Most of the guerrilla activity was apparently carried out by the so-called Red Flag (Bandera Roja). At various times during the year, police and military men succeeded in arresting leaders and members of the group. Early in October one of the principal figures in Bandera Roja, Argenio Betancourt, was arrested in Monagas State (*FBIS,* 17 October).

The guerrilla activities represented no significant threat to the regime or to the general political situation. However, on a local basis the guerrillas did succeed in generating a degree of instability which had negative economic and political effects.

Rutgers University Robert J. Alexander

MIDDLE EAST AND AFRICA

Egypt

The year 1977 was one of failure and setback for the Communist movement in Egypt. It started with violent riots in January which the government accused Communists of instigating. In the course of the year, with the deterioration of Egyptian-Soviet relations, police arrested a number of members of clandestine Communist groups, and the legitimate left-wing National Progressive Unionist Party (NPUP) came under continuous and heavy attack. The only two leftist publications faced setbacks: the monthly *alTali'ah* (Vanguard), edited by Lufti al-Khouli, was shut down, and the weekly *Roz el-Youssef* underwent a change of its chief editor and in its political orientation.

In January, Egypt's major cities witnessed massive and violent riots after a government decision to discontinue subsidies for a number of basic commodities. The riots—the most widespread and violent since Black Saturday, January 26, a quarter of a century ago—left an official death toll of about seventy. Economic decisions were shelved, curfew was imposed, and the army was called in to maintain law and order. The government accused extreme-leftist elements and the NPUP of inciting the riots. Both President Anwar Sadat and Prime Minister Mamduh Salem identified the Communists as being responsible for the riots.

Political observers have been skeptical of this interpretation and see the events as expression of popular social discontent and an outburst of the long-suffering masses against unexpected price increases which were imposed without any preparations or psychological build-up. Whether clandestine Communist groups, or others, played a role in the riots or not, is yet to be factually and legally ascertained. (*Africa Confidential*, London, 4 February.)

In the light of these developments, the government found it in its best interest to intensify the campaign against the Communists. The interior minister announced the uncovering of a plot to burn Cairo (*al-Ahram*, 21 January). In his speech to the People's Assembly, the prime minister laid the blame on subversive Communist groups and expressed deep regret that the NPUP "had involved itself shamefully" in this national crime. The objective of the riots, he added, was the seizure of power by the Communists (ibid., 30 January). Government officials placed responsibility for the riots on the NPUP and also on the four clandestine Communist groups which the public prosecutor identified on 20 January as the Egyptian Communist Party, the Egyptian Communist Labor Party, the Revolutionary Current (Maoist), and the 8th of January Organization.

Mass trials were announced for those alleged Communist plotters who were arrested and for other rioters. A number of leading NPUP members were among those to be tried: Dr. Rifaat al-Said, Husein Abdel Razek, and other known Communists such as journalists Abdel Moniem al-Ghazzali and Philip Gallab, and the lawyer Zaki Murad. However, most of the 1,200 to 1,600 persons arrested were released four to eight weeks later. None of the NPUP leaders were implicated or tried. The charge against the party was quietly dropped.

Relations between the NPUP and the government continued to be strained. It was reported that some leading left-wing politicians were prohibited from traveling abroad without a special permit (*Roz el-Youssef*, 11 April). The government denied this report immediately and was quick to confirm its liberal travel policy. When NPUP general secretary Khaled Mohi el-Din, in Rome, made a number of criticisms of the regime, he was heavily attacked and his comments were described by the spokesman of the ruling party as "unpatriotic and immoral" (*al-Ahram*, 3 May).

President Anwar Sadat persisted in attacking the NPUP and the Communists in his speeches and press conferences. He described Egyptian Communists as "traitors and stooges of the Soviet Union," attacked the NPUP leadership, and vowed that he would not allow an atheist (i.e., Communist) to occupy any important position in the area of the media and culture (ibid., 26 June). In his 26 July speech at Alexandria University, he repudiated the atheist left and associated leftists with Moscow.

In October, the police arrested more members of both the Egyptian Communist Party and the Egyptian Communist Labor Party, confiscating leaflets which attacked the regime. According to newspaper stories, police also found plans to sabotage certain factories and infiltrate worker and student groups in order to arouse the people against the government.

The NPUP continues to be the focal opposition in Egyptian politics. It has denounced the government emergency measures which followed the January riots and described the referendum which was held as "unconstitutional." It opposed and continued to criticize the mainstream of presidential and government policies, the most recent of which was the president's visit to Jerusalem on 19 November.

Given the turbulent events of 1977 and assuming a continuation of existing political tendencies in the country, further confrontation between the government and Communist movement in Egypt seems inevitable.

Cairo University and
  American University in Cairo

Ali E. Hillal Dessouki

Iran

Precursors of Communist activity in Iran were organized in Tiflis and Baku early in the century, the Persian Social Democratic Party in 1904, and the Hezb-e 'Adalat (Justice Party) in 1917. At its first major party congress, convened in June 1920 at Pahlevi (Enzeli), on the Caspian Sea, the Justice Party changed its name to the Communist Party of Iran. In 1931 the government banned Communist activities. In October 1941 a group of German-educated Marxist intellectuals formed the present Tudeh Party (Party of the Masses). During the 1941-53 period of relative political freedom, it grew in size and influence to become the largest party in the country. In 1945-46, however, a split developed and in 1949 the party was outlawed. Even so, the Tudeh Party expanded during the Mosaddeq period of the early 1950s. Then after the return of the Shah to power in late 1953, the Communists were effectively suppressed. A number of leaders managed to escape and reorganized the Tudeh Party in East Germany.

Today, Iranian Communist activity is confined almost entirely to groups operating outside the country. Within Iran, whose population is about 35 million, Tudeh membership probably does not exceed 1,500. Perhaps 15,000 to 20,000 Iranians are associated with other Marxist-Leninist groups and engaged in opposition activities of various kinds. Among them are the following four, all formed since 1960 and all claiming a presence both within and outside the country:

— Revolutionary Tudeh Party (Hezb-e Tudeh-e Iran), formed in 1965 by a Maoist group that had been expelled from the Tudeh Party. It publishes *Setareh-i Sorkh* (Red Star).

— Organization of Marxist-Leninists (Sazman-e Marxist-Leninist), organized in 1967 by two Maoist members from the Central Committee of the Tudeh Party. It publishes *Tufan* (Storm).

— Guerrilla Organization of the Devotees for the People (Cheraki Feda-ye Khalq), established in Iran during 1971. A number of founders had been members of the Tudeh youth organization. They left the party because of its opposition to guerrilla warfare. This group is well organized and has been responsible for a number of violent acts directed against the government. Approximately 200 members have been either killed in action or executed. The group tends to identify more with Latin American revolutionaries than with either the USSR or China.

— A section of the National Front (Jebheh-e Melli) which supported Mosaddeq has become Marxist since 1972. It publishes *Bakhtar-Emruz* (Today's West).

In 1977 domestic Marxist guerrilla groups somewhat diminished their violent activities, which had culminated in numerous acts of sabotage and assassinations during 1976. Although sporadic violence occurred throughout the year, the general slowdown coincided with a series of noticeable liberalizing acts undertaken by the regime. Apparently 1977 was a year for tactical reassessment by the guerrilla groups. A number of members temporarily left the country.

Tudeh Party Leadership and Domestic Issues. Iradj Eskandari has been first secretary of the movement since 1971. Becaue of the government's repressive policy, the party seldom publishes names of members. Most pronouncements are issued in the name of the Central Committee.

The leadership of the Tudeh Party places great stress on the need to turn the Iranian masses against the government. It consistently attacks the leadership of the Shah and his government's alleged oppression, injustice, backwardness and corruption. The major goal continues to be overthrow of the Shah and, with him, of the Pahlavi dynasty.

Yet, in 1977 the government dramatically changed its policy toward political dissent. A policy of liberalization was instituted which coincided with the accession to power of the Carter administration in the United States. Early in the year, for instance, the Iranian press carried a series of articles discussing political opposition movements both within and outside Iran. Then, during April, the government conducted an open and highly publicized trial of eleven persons accused of associating with the revolutionary wing of the Tudeh Party. Western observers were permitted to attend. Also, in 1977 the Shah received representatives of Amnesty International, the International Red Cross, and the International Commission of Jurists which is located in Geneva.

Iradj Eskandari's statement on "Illusions of Bourgeois Reformism in Developing Countries" (*WMR,* May 1977) was designed to deal with the Shah's new policy. He wrote that "reformism is a key ideological weapon" in attempts to "prevent the developing countries from choosing the correct path," and further, that the governmental machinery in Third World countries "sometimes serves as the conduit of reformist conceptions." Eskandari specifically criticized Iran's "revolution from the top" as a "neocolonialist" tactic designed to ensure long-term oppression and imperialism.

Tudeh International Policy. The Tudeh Party has been a consistent and strong supporter of the Soviet Union. The United States and the People's Republic of China are considered implacable enemies of both the Iranian people and the Tudeh Party itself. Although in past years China had been the major target of Communist attacks, in 1977 relatively more emphasis was placed on criticism of the U.S. Part of the reason for this shift in emphasis may be found in the growing sympathy for the Chinese within the party itself. Two of the defendants in the spring "trial of the eleven" claimed that they had undergone guerrilla training in China.

Publications. The two publications of the Tudeh Party are *Mardom* (People) and *Donya* (World). These newspapers, published in Eastern Europe, contain articles dealing with Marxist-Leninist theory, international politics and economics, and the Iranian social and political scene.

University of Texas, Austin   James A. Bill

Iraq

The Iraqi Communist Party (ICP) was founded in 1934. Illegal until 1973, in that year it established an alliance with the ruling Ba'th Socialist Party (BSP) called the Progressive National Front. Cooperation between the ICP and the BSP, however, has since become difficult because of the growing conflict between the Ba'th governments in Iraq and Syria. Matters came to a head in December 1976 when Iraq accused Syria of having planted a bomb at Baghdad's international airport. The ICP apparently did not share the official view concerning Syrian complicity and has continued to cooperate with the ruling BSP, but friction apparently exists between some BSP leaders and the Iraqi Communists.

The party's first secretary is 'Aziz Muhammad. There are no reliable figures concerning the strength of the ICP membership, which is estimated to number about 2,000. The population of Iraq is about 10 million.

Domestic Attitudes and Activities. During 1977 the ICP operated with a fair degree of freedom, as heretofore, yet there seemed to be a feeling of increasing restriction, although Communist literature continued to circulate and official relations between the ICP and the BSP were friendly. Despite their cooperation with the ruling party, the Communists have made relatively little progress in Iraq. According to some ICP sources, their work has been impeded by that very cooperation, which is said to have discouraged opponents of the BSP from taking a more active role. Other obstacles are supposedly found in the growth of Arab nationalism, to which the BSP has contributed, and in the strength of Islam among the "illiterate masses."

Arab Policy. In its circulars and public statements, the ICP always has called for unity among all Arab progressive and liberation movements in the struggle against "reactionary anti-imperialist and Zionist forces" on both regional and international levels.

The ICP calls for the liberation of all occupied Arab land in Palestine. It stands for the Palestinian Arabs' right to self-determination, an independent Palestinian national state, repulse of Israeli "aggressions," and defense of "progressive Arab regimes." ICP opposed Syria's intervention in the Lebanese civil war, a subject on which Syrian Communists have remained quiet.

International Activities and Contacts. The ICP is pro-Soviet in orientation and regards support by "Socialist" states as crucial for the progress of national liberation movements in Asia and Africa ('Aziz Muhammad, "Key Trends in the Liberation Process," *WMR*, February 1977). The vice-president of Iraq, early in 1977, led a delegation to the USSR which confirmed cooperation between the two countries. On 8 February the ICP Central Committee expressed satisfaction with both the visit and the steady development of friendship between Iraq and the Soviet Union.

A month later, 'Aziz Muhammad, in an interview with a Tass correspondent, lauded the impact of the Soviet party congresses, and especially the Twenty-fifth Congress, on world events. In mid-April a Soviet party delegation visited Baghdad and held discussions with ICP leaders.

Close relations continued between the ICP and the ruling parties of Eastern Europe. In May a delegation from East Germany held conversations with the ICP, and in June the Czechoslovak party chief, Gustav Husák, paid a similar visit. In August, 'Aziz Muhammad visited Bulgaria, where he held discussions with Bulgarian party chief Todor Zhivkov.

Publications. The principal ICP media are the daily *Tariq al-Sha'b* (People's Way), the weekly *al-Fikr al-Jadid* (New Thought), and the monthly *al-Thaqafa al-Jadida* (New Culture). A number of booklets and pamphlets are also published on current questions.

The Johns Hopkins University   Majid Khadduri

Israel

The Communist movement in Palestine dates back to 1920. Two years later, a Palestine Communist Party (Palestinische Kommunistische Partei; PKP) was established and it joined the Comintern in 1924. Following periodic appearance of factional divisions, the PKP split along ethnic lines in 1943. While the Jewish group retained the original name, the Arab faction called itself the League for National Liberation ('Usbah al-Tahrir al-Watani). In October 1948, with the new state of Israel in control over most of Palestine, both groups reunited to form the Israeli Communist Party (Miflaga Kommunistit Isra'elit; MAKI).

The movement split again in 1965, partly along ethnic lines. The "New Communist List" (Reshima Kommunistit Hadasha; RAKAH)—pro-Moscow, strongly anti-Zionist, and drawing a majority of its members from the Arab population—emerged as the main party and increasingly gained international recognition as the Communist Party of Israel (CPI). MAKI, which became an almost completely Jewish organization and moderate in its opposition to government policies, was eclipsed. In 1975, MAKI disappeared as a separate organization after merger with MOKED ("Focus"), a Zionist socialist organization moderate in attitude toward the Arabs. In 1977, MOKED united with other non-Communist groups in the "peace camp" to form Peace for Israel (Shalom le-Israel, SHELLI). By this time, some former (post 1965) MAKI members had joined or at least supported RAKAH as the country's only Communist party.

In keeping with Israel's competitive political party system, Communists have been free to organize and participate in public life. The prevailing system of proportional representation has facilitated election of candidates from small parties, including the Communists, to the Knesset (parliament).

From the beginning of the state, MAKI (and later RAKAH) found its main support among the Arab minority. This resulted from the absence of an Arab nationalist party in Israel, which left the Communists as the only alternative to Zionist parties. Communists also gained Arab support by their strong stand against official policies toward the Arab minority and toward the Arab world and not from any espousal of Marxism-Leninism by a large number of Arab voters. Increasingly they have gained support of young, educated Arabs. Although RAKAH's membership is about 80 percent Arab, many of its leaders (including a majority on top party organs) are Jews. The party presents itself as a model for Arab-Jewish cooperation.

In recent years, RAKAH has gained unprecedented electoral strength among the Israeli Arabs, who now form about 15 percent of the population and are concentrated mainly in the northern province of Galilee. This has resulted from resentment against the gradual expropriation of Arab land, as well as from a growing general estrangement from the state and identification with Arab Palestinian nationalism. In the general election of December 1973, RAKAH received 37.5 percent of the total Arab vote. Two years later the RAKAH-led "Democratic Front," which incuded non-Communist Arab intellectuals and merchants, won 67.3 percent of the vote and eleven out of seventeen council seats in the municipal elections at Nazareth (Israel's largest Arab city; population ca. 40,000). One of RAKAH's leaders, Tawfiq Zayyad, was elected mayor by a large majority. Further gains were made at local elections in smaller Arab towns during 1976, giving RAKAH and its allies a total of fifty-seven seats on twenty-five local councils.

RAKAH's membership is estimated at about 1,500. Israel's population in September 1977 (not including occupied territories) was 3,628,000.

RAKAH is isolated from the mainstream of Israeli politics. No Communist party has ever participated in the cabinet. Between 1973 and 1977 RAKAH had four members out of a total of 120 in the Knesset. A RAKAH-led coalition, the Democratic Front for Peace and Equality (DFPE), established following the Eighteenth Party Congress' call in December 1976 for unity with groups that stand for "peace and democracy," won 4.6 percent of the vote in 1977. This entitled the DFPE to five seats in the Knesset, one of which went to each of the non-Communist coalition partners: Black Panthers (an Afro-Asian Jewish group protesting against the alleged discrimination by the Jews of European origin) and Arab Local Council Heads. The less radical SHELLI, which won two seats, sometimes votes with DFPE.

Leadership and Organization. The RAKAH Congress meets at four-year intervals. The Eighteenth Congress (actually the fourth Congress of RAKAH, which sees itself as the direct successor to the 1920 organization, the PKP, and the pre-1965 MAKI as the Communist Party of Israel), made up of 48 delegates, met in December 1976 at Haifa. Representatives of the eighteen foreign Communist parties, including one from the Soviet Union, were present. The Congress elected a Central Committee of thirty-one members and five candidates as well as a Central Control Commission. ("Theses of the 18th Congress of the C.P.I.," *Information Bulletin*, No. 9-10/76.)

Meeting in plenary session on 25 December 1976, the Central Committee elected a Political Bureau of nine members and a Secretariat of seven. The Political Bureau includes David (Uzi) Burnstein, Benjamin Gonen, Emile Habibi, David (Sasha) Khenin, Ruth Lubitz, Salim al-Qasim, Tawfiq Tubi, Emile

Tuma, and Meir Vilner. Secretaries are Yehoshua Irge, Zahi Karkabi, Saliba Khamis, Khenin, Jamal Musa, Tubi, and Vilner. Vilner was re-elected general secretary, while Tubi became the new deputy general secretary. The four RAKAH members in the Knesset before the 17 May general elections were Vilner, Tubi, Avraham Levenbraun, and Zayyad; the three since the 17 May elections are Tubi, Zayyad, and Vilner, along with their two DFPE allies: Hanna Moiss of the Arab Local Council Heads and Charlie Biton of the Black Panthers. Organized on the basis of "democratic centralism," RAKAH's structure includes regional committees, seventy-nine local branches, and cells based on both residence and place of work.

Auxiliary and Mass Organizations. RAKAH provides the dominant core of the Nazareth Democratic Front and other anti-establishment electoral lists in smaller Arab towns, as well as the DFPE (see above). RAKAH sponsors an active children's Young Pioneer movement and a youth organization, the Young Communist League, 272 members of which joined the party at the Eighteenth Congress. RAKAH also participates in the Democratic Women's Movement, the Israeli Association of Anti-Fascist Fighters and Victims of Nazism, and the Israel-USSR Friendship movement.

Party Internal Affairs. Several plenary meetings of the Central Committee were held during 1977. One session in Tel Aviv concerned itself with preparations for the general election and decided on a fund-raising campaign to cover expenses. Resolutions were passed on numerous substantive matters.

Domestic Attitudes and Activities. RAKAH leaders continued to stress the adverse economic consequences of government military spending. Writing in the *WMR* (August 1977, p. 76), Tuma pointed out that "60 percent of the state budget of 1976-77 was spent on 'security' and this represents 40 percent of the gross national product (GNP)." He criticized the increasing profits of the "big capitalists" at a time when an inflation rate of 30 percent was causing "deprivation for the working people." Rejecting the government's proposed budget, Vilner told the Knesset that the main burden was being imposed on the poor. The Central Committee called for higher wages and improved working conditions. RAKAH leaders also repeatedly pointed to revelations of corruption in the Labor Party.

While RAKAH condemned discrimination against the Jews of Afro-Asian origin, most domestic emphasis continued to focus on the condition of the Israeli Arabs. In his article, Tuma condemned "the process of expropriating Arab land in Galilee for the purpose of 'judaizing' the area." (Ibid., pp. 77-78.) He referred to this as "an aggressive racist measure." The views of Yisrael Koenig, the interior ministry's northern district representative, whose memorandum proposing discriminatory measures to prevent the emergence of an Arab majority in Galilee was leaked in 1976, remained one of RAKAH's primary targets. Speaking before the Knesset, Zayyad condemned Keonig's "racist attitudes" and the government that kept him in office (*Jerusalem Post*, 5 July).

The 17 May elections were a limited success for RAKAH. With 79,733 votes (4.6 percent of the total), in comparison to 3.4 percent in 1973, the RAKAH-led DFPE won only five seats instead of the seven or more that observers had predicted. The percentage of the Arab vote going for RAKAH (and its coalition partners) rose from 37.5 in 1973 to about 50 in 1977. But a disproportionate percentage of these citizens are too young to vote, and an unusually low Arab voting turnout (about 70 percent) in this election minimized RAKAH's success. According to some analyses, RAKAH's support for the existence of Israel deprived it of support from many Arabs, whose Palestinian Arab nationalism was represented by a new movement, the "Sons of the Village." On the other hand, the reluctance of some Arabs to vote Communist, even as the only alternative to Zionist parties, may also explain the low turnout. RAKAH gained in virtually all sectors of the Arab population (and also doubled its minuscule support among Jews), but achieved its highest proportion of the vote in Arab towns, 62 percent in Nazareth and 90 percent in Shafaram. Muslim and Christian Arabs voted for the party in about equal proportions.

Smaller gains were made among Bedouins and among the Druze sect, both of which had previously provided the party virtually no votes. RAKAH leaders expressed satisfaction with their party's gains but described the Likud victory as a "catastrophe" (Vilner, quoted in the *Jerusalem Post*, 28 June) and as a victory for the "big bourgeoisie."

Shots fired at Zayyad's home on 12 May led to speculation about attempts to intimidate Arab voters. In a complaint to the Central Elections Committee, RAKAH accused ministers in the government of warning Arabs not to vote for the DFPE. Several arrests followed clashes between RAKAH supporters and members of the Jewish Defense League during a 1 May rally in Nazareth.

RAKAH's performance in the Histadrut (Trade Union Federation) elections of 21 June was unexpectedly poor. It received only 31 percent of the Arab vote, 59 percent of which went to the Labor Alignment. Contrary to expectations, RAKAH failed to win control of local labor councils in Shafaram and Nazareth.

International Activity and Contacts. A delegation, composed of Tuma and Burnstein, met with Czechoslovak leaders in Prague during May. The visit also included a meeting between RAKAH and representatives of the Palestine Liberation Organization (PLO), the first such one to be officially announced. Khenin traveled to Budapest in August as the invited guest of the Hungarian Socialist Workers' [Communist] Party. Burnstein also visited Bulgaria that same month. RAKAH was represented at the World Assembly of Peace, held in Warsaw during May, and a delegation attended the sixtieth anniversary of the October Revolution in Moscow during early November.

International Views and Policies. A RAKAH statement published in the *Jerusalem Post* on 3 February (*FBIS*, 4 February) asserted that "all the neighboring Arab states and the great majority of the PLO are willing to conclude a just and realistic peace with the State of Israel." Blame was laid on "the policy of the [Labor] government and the extreme rightist bloc—Likud—demanding measures of territorial annexation, and denying the Palestine Arab people's right to establish an independent state alongside of the State of Israel." It "prevents peace and is liable to lead to a fifth Israeli-Arab war, bloodier than all the previous ones." A peace plan, which had originated in the Eighteenth Party Congress, reads as follows:

   — The June 4,1967 lines will constitute the peace borders. Israel will withdraw all her forces from all the Arab territories seized in the June 1967 war.
   — Respect for the right of the Palestine Arab people to self-determination and to establish an independent state, alongside the State of Israel.
   — Implementation of a just solution to the problem of the Palestine refugees, in accordance with the UN decisions, recognizing their right to choose between return to their homeland and receiving compensation.
   — Respect for the right of the State of Israel and the Arab states to sovereign existence and development in conditions of peace and security.
   — Guarantee of Israel's freedom of navigation through the Suez Canal and the Tiran Strait, as to all other states.
   — All sides will renounce a state of belligerency and will respect the sovereignty and territorial integrity of all the states in the region, as well as their right to live in peace within recognized and secure borders, free from the threat or use of force.

As safeguards for the peace settlement, the statement called for "international guarantees under UN auspices, with the participation of the Soviet Union, the United States, and other states," and for "agreements taking the form of treaties."

Other statements asserted that the PLO is the sole spokesman of the Palestinian Arab people and must participate in all negotiations relating to the Arab-Israeli conflict. A statement by the Political

Bureau (Tass; *FBIS*, 6 September) condemned agriculture minister Ariel Sharon's plan for "mass colonization of the occupied territories." The government's allegedly inhumane treatment of Arab political prisoners and eviction of Arabs from Jerusalem were condemned by the Central Committee in January. Vilner subsequently attacked the government's extension of certain Israeli laws to the occupied West Bank and Gaza Strip as a step toward annexation. The Political Bureau warned that "Israel's military and political intervention in the south of Lebanon may escalate into a direct attack on that country by the Israeli army" (Tass; *FBIS*, 25 August).

RAKAH statements condemned U.S. support for Israeli policies and accused it of hindering a reconvening of the Geneva conference and "trying to debar the Soviet Union from the process of establishing a just and lasting peace" (ibid., 6 September). Other statements condemned the "anti-Soviet campaign of Israel and the U.S. as attempts to divert attention from Israeli violations of human rights and as threatening to renew the cold war."

RAKAH described USSR policy as lacking any selfish concern and as being "based upon the principles of Leninism, of supporting all peoples struggling against imperialism, colonialism and for their national and social liberation" (quoted by Jack Kling, "Some Reflections on the 18th Congress, Communist Party of Israel," *Political Affairs*, April, p. 25).

Publications. The RAKAH newspaper *al-Ittihad* (Union) is an Arab biweekly published at Haifa, edited by Tubi and Habibi. A Hebrew weekly, *Zo Ha-Derekh* (This is the Way), is edited by Vilner in Tel Aviv. Other party publications are: *al-Darb* (The Way), an Arabic theoretical magazine edited by *Arakim: Be'ayot ha-Shalom ve-ha-Sotziyalism* (Values: Problems of Peace and Socialism), published Haifa; *al-Ghad* (Tomorrow), a magazine for youth; the Yiddish *Der Weg* (The Way), published by Vilner at Tel Aviv; the Bulgarian *Tovaye Putnam* (This is the Way), appearing biweekly in Jaffa; *Arakim: Be'ayot ha-Shalom ve-ha-Sotziyalizm* (Values: Problems of Peace and Socialism), published irregularly in Tel Aviv; and a sporadic English *Information Bulletin of the Communist Party of Israel.*

*   *   *

Other Marxist Organizations. Several other Marxist groups exist in Israel, but none of them compares to RAKAH as a political force. Each consists of a handful of members, mostly young Jews, but none offers its own list of electoral candidates.

The most radical trend is represented by the Israeli Socialist Organization (Irgun Sotziyalisti Isra'eli; ISO; formed by a group expelled from MAKI in 1962. Widely known by the name of its monthly publication *Matzpen* (Compass) issued at Tel Aviv, the ISO condemns the establishment of Israel at the expense of Palestinian Arabs and its "open alliance with . . . imperialism, and collusion with the most reactionary forces in the Arab world." The ISO recognizes the continued existence of a Hebrew nation in Palestine, but calls for "de-Zionification," "a socialist revolution," and "integration into a unified, socialist Middle East." It criticizes the USSR's policy of "peaceful coexistence," Soviet "bureaucracy," and RAKAH's acceptance of the Soviet party line. It has also censured Peking's policies. (Arie Bober, *The Other Israel: The Radical Case Against Zionism*, New York, 1972, is a collection of official ISO statements.) The *Matzpen* viewpoint has received most attention outside Israel. Several splits in the organization occurred during the early 1970s. Breakaway groups include the Revolutionary Communist League (Brit Kommunistit Mahapkhanit), which is associated with the Fourth (Trotskyite) International; the Workers' League (Brit ha-Po'alim), also Trotskyite; and the Maoist-oriented Revolutionary Communist Alliance-Struggle (Brit Kommunistit Mahapkhanit-Ma'-avak).

The Israeli New Left (Smol Yisrael Chadash; SIAH) was created in 1968. It consists of a few members, mainly students, previously associated with MAKI and MAPAM (The United Workers' Party, formerly a far-left movement but now part of the Labor Alignment). SIAH, which identifies with the radical student movement in Europe, professes devotion to a combination of Zionism and Marxism and calls for creation of an independent Palestinian state to exist alongside Israel. Its publications include *Siah* (published irregularly in Hebrew) and *Israleft*, a biweekly English newsletter that disseminates statements by various leftist and peace groups.

Indiana State University   Glenn E. Perry
Terre Haute

Jordan

The Communist Party of Jordan (al-Hizb al-Shuyu 'i al-Urdunni; CPJ) was officially established in June 1951 and has operated under the guise of various popular front organizations since that time. Its center of activity has been the West Bank, where it has drawn support from students, teachers, professional workers, and the "lower middle class."

The CPJ has been illegal since 1957, although the government's normally repressive measures on occasion have been relaxed. At present, Communist party membership is punishable by jail sentences from three to fifteen years. Few other radical organizations are active in Jordan; however, various Palestinian groups, such as the Marxist-oriented Popular Front for the Liberation of Palestine (embittered by "repression" of the Palestinians during 1970-71), urge the overthrow of King Hussein. They appear to have little overt influence in Jordan.

The CPJ has perhaps no more than 500 members, mostly Palestinians. Jordan's population of about 2,899,000 includes more than 700,000 in Israeli-occupied East Jerusalem and the West Bank.

Leadership and Organization. The CPJ is said to be a tightly organized, well-disciplined network of small cells. Due to secrecy, little information is available on the party leadership. Fu'ad Nassar, who died in late 1976, was the party's first secretary general. Faiq Muhammad Warrad then succeeded to that post. Other prominent party members reportedly include 'Abd al-Muhsin Abu Maizar, also of the Palestine National Front (PNF), and Ishaq al-Khatib. 'Arabi 'Awad, CPJ Central Committee member and PNF leader, reportedly heads the CPJ West Bank branch, and has spent more than ten years in Jordanian or Israeli jails. Other members of the Central Committee include 'Isa Madanat, Na'im Ashhab, and Ya'qub Diya' al-Din. Jiryas Qawwas, is an associate of 'Awad and also a prominent West Bank Communist PNF official; a former teacher, he claims to have spent more than thirteen years in Jordanian and Israeli jails.

Auxiliary and Mass Organizations. The Palestine National Front is composed of professional and labor union representatives and "patriotic personalities." It was established in August 1973 on the West Bank, evidently on CPJ initiative. The PNF generally follows the Palestine Liberation Organization (PLO) line, advocating an independent Palestinian state on the West Bank together with the Gaza Strip, and urging Palestinian participation in the Geneva peace talks. Its program includes mass political struggle and armed resistance in the occupied territories.

The PNF's precise relationship to the CPJ is unknown. According to Israeli officials, the CPJ forms the core of the PNF. The PNF is a member of the PLO, and its Central Committee includes representatives of most Palestinian factions and commando organizations. At least some of its leadership comes from the CPJ. West Bank Communists have thus become closely associated with Palestinian nationalist forces.

Party Internal Affairs. The CPJ has been described officially as the working-class party of two fraternal peoples—Jordanian and Palestinian. Despite its support of Palestinian statehood, the CPJ remains somewhat suspicious of the PLO, an attitude that is reciprocated. In 1975, West Bank Communists began signing official statements "Communist Party of the West Bank," as did affiliated student, labor, and women's associations. The CPJ's West Bank newspaper *al-Watan* appeared under the auspices of the "Palestine Communist Party," a name apparently adopted by West Bank cells without prior approval by the CPJ Central Committee.

Domestic Attitudes and Activities. The CPJ seemingly has devoted little attention to purely domestic issues. Like other Palestinians of whatever ideological persuasion who are anti-Hussein, party leaders denounce the "reactionary regime" in Amman and its links to "imperialism." They advocate establishment in Jordan of a "democratic independent state" whose goal is social development. The CPJ considers its efforts to establish a national front in Jordan a precondition for establishment of a national liberation regime. These activities are designed, among other things, to eliminate "imperialism" on the East Bank.

The Palestine issue has vexed the party since its inception. As a generally pro-Soviet organization, CPJ evidently has not been entirely free to take an independent stand. Consequently, it has lost support to more committed and radical Palestinian liberation movements. In fact, the CPJ's basic position on Palestine is similar to that of the main Palestinian groups. The party recognizes the PLO as the sole representative of the Palestinian people.

International Activities and Attitudes. Secretary General Warrad met with Czechoslovak and Romanian party leaders in April 1977, discussing the Middle East and interparty relations. An article by Na'im Ashhab compared Eastern and Western compliance with the Helsinki accords. Ashhab accused the United States of supporting Israeli "aggression," delivering arms to "reactionary" Persian Gulf regimes, contributing to the Lebanese civil war, and furthering nuclear proliferation. He praised the USSR for its support of a "new international economic order," protecting the sovereignty of the Middle Eastern countries, and supporting the "legitimate rights" of the Palestinian people (*WMR,* June).

Publications. The CPJ publishes *al-Jamahir* (Masses), and an underground newspaper, *al-Watan* (Homeland), both appearing once or twice a month, the former in Jordan and the latter on the West Bank. The party also issues a political and theoretical magazine *al-Haqiqah* (Truth), distributed in Jordan and the West Bank, as well as pamphlets. These publications are distributed clandestinely on both sides of the Jordan River, except for *al-Watan,* which is restricted mainly to the West Bank. The PNF publishes its own newspaper, *Filastin* (Palestine). News of CPJ activities also appears in the organs of the Lebanese Communist Party, *al-Akhbar* and *al-Nida.*

U.S. Department of State   Norman F. Howard
Washington, D.C.

(Note: Views expressed in this article are the author's own and do not represent those of the State Department.)

Lebanon

The Lebanese Communist Party (al-Hizb al-Shuyu'i al-Lubnani; LCP) was established in 1924. During the period of the French mandates it accepted members from both Lebanon and Syria. In 1944 a party congress established separate movements for Lebanon and Syria, respectively. In 1965 the LCP decided to end its previous policy of working independently of other Lebanese political groups. Since then it has become a member of the Front of Progressive Parties and National Forces (FPPNF), under the leadershp of the Progressive Socialists. The front was headed by Kamal Jumblat until his assassination on 16 March 1977. It is now led by his son, Walid Jumblat.

The government ban on the LCP and other controversial parties was lifted 13 August 1970. The LCP has been an active participant in the civil war which began in 1975.

The LCP is estimated to have about 2,500 members and sympathizers. The population of Lebanon is about 2.5 million.

Leadership and Organization. The Congress, which is supposed to be convened every four years, is the supreme LCP organ. The Fourth Congress was to be held in 1976, but continuing instability in Lebanon has made such a meeting impossible. Until the next congress, authority is vested in the twenty-four member Central Committee, which in turn elects the eleven-member Political Bureau, five secretaries, Central Control Commission, and Financial Commission. The primary structure of the LCP is based on the employment or residential principle. Local, city, and industrial party organizations are formed into districts and regions. Niqula al-Shawi is secretary general; George Hawi is his deputy and heads the Secretariat. Both are Greek Orthodox by birth. Other secretaries are Nadim 'Abd al-Samad (in charge of the Foreign Department), Karim Muruwwah, and Khalil al-Dibs. Other members of the Political Bureau include Ghassan al-Rifa 'i, Georges Batal, and 'Ali al-'Abd.

Domestic Views and Activities. Throughout the Lebanese civil war and its aftermath, LCP leaders affirmed their solidarity with "other progressive forces," the Progressive Socialist Party, and Palestinian resistance. They called for a political solution to the crisis, holding that no peace could be achieved through military conflict. They have strongly opposed the presence of Syrian peace-keeping forces. At a meeting in Moscow during June 1977, members of the LCP delegation avowed support for efforts of legitimate authorities in Lebanon who, they explained, were seeking to insure Lebanese national independence, sovereignty, and territorial unity. They condemned Israeli hostilities in southern Lebanon as jeopardizing these objectives.

The LCP reacted strongly to the assassination of Kamal Jumblat. In an interview with the Hungarian MTI news agency two days later, Niqula al-Shawi stated: "With a feeling of profound indignation and pain I have learned about the murder of the leader of the Lebanese national movement, an outstanding leader of the Arab liberation movement, Kamal Jumblat, who is known in the entire world as a fighter for peace, democracy, and social progress" (Tass, 18 March). LCP joined with other Lebanese and Arab leftists and Communists on 1 May in a mass rally at Beirut to honor

Kamal Jumblat. "Jumblat Day" was described by various international newspapers as the largest leftist gathering held in Beirut since LCP's Third Congress. The slain man's son, Walid Jumblat, succeeded his father as leader of both the Progressive Socialist Party and the FPPNF. (The FPPNF comprises thirteen parties and groups.) An "emergency committee" was established to lead the movement. It has representatives of six parties, including the LCP.

International Views and Activities. The LCP maintains that imperialism, Israel, and Arab reaction are responsible for obstructing peace in the Middle East. A just and lasting peace must be based on "insuring the legitimate rights and interests of all countries and peoples of the region, including the Palestinian Arab people struggling to secure the right to establish their own homeland" (*FBIS*, 13 June 1977). During the year, the LCP reaffirmed its support for the general policy of the Soviet Union in the Middle East conflict. The party was strongly critical of Sudan, which was seen as playing a reactionary role in Africa and being close to Peking's position. According to *al-Nida'*, "In the context of coordinating its policy primarily with Saudi Arabia and Egypt [Sudan is] striving to strengthen its relations with the countries of the West and to obtain additional financial and military aid from them" (*FBIS*, 2 June).

During a visit to the USSR in June, an LCP delegation expressed respect for the achievements of the Soviet Communist party and support for the new draft Soviet constitution, which it called "a gigantic weapon in the struggle for peace and democracy and socialism." The LCP noted also "the continuing development and deepening of socialist democracy in the Soviet Union." (*FBIS*, 10 June). During 20-23 June, Niqula al-Shawi visited South Yemen and had talks with its premier. In July, a high-level LCP delegation spent three days in Ethiopia and another delegation visited East Germany. In late October, an LCP delegation visited Algeria to discuss the situation in Lebanon with officials of the National Liberation Front.

Publications. The LCP publishes a daily newspaper, *al-Nida'* (Call); a weekly magazine, *al-Akhbar* (News); and a literary and ideological monthly, *al-Tariq* (Road). These organs also serve as general information media for illegal Communist parties in the Middle East. Since the outbreak of the Lebanese civil war in 1975, publication and distribution of these periodicals have been disrupted to varying degrees.

Other Communist Organizations. The Organization of Communist Action in Lebanon (OCAL) is led by Muhsin Ibrahim as secretary general. Like the LCP, OCAL is in the FPPNF. It has been designated one of the six movements in the FPNF forming an emergency committee to make the front more "collective" than before. OCAL was actively involved in the Lebanese war, fighting alongside the Progressive Socialists, the Independent Nasserite Movement, and the Communist Party of Iraq.

Three other Lebanese Communist organizations have been mentioned in the news media: the Communist Labor Organization, the Revolutionary Communist Organization, and the Lebanese Communist Union.

Stanford University   Michel Nabti

Réunion

The Réunion Communist Party (Parti Communiste Réunionnais; PCR) was founded in May 1959 after the Réunion federation of the French Communist party was transformed into an autonomous organization. Réunion is a French overseas department, and the PCR is a legal party. The population of Réunion is approximately 504,000. Estimates of PCR membership differ considerably. Membership attendance figures for section assemblies held in January 1977 suggest total strength of about 2,000 members (*Témoignages,* 29-30 January, 2 February).

Despite the PCR's strong party organization and Réunion's general leftist orientation, leftist opposition has not been able to overcome the Giscardian-Gaullist domination of elected offices on the island. The PCR won only 28.5 percent of the votes in the cantonal elections of March 1976, and in the municipal elections of March 1977 the party received 28.5 percent of the first-round vote in large towns. It drew ahead of majority-party lists in only one large town, and even here it lost in the second round.

The PCR and other leftist organizations have protested against fraudulent electoral practices supposedly indulged in by the majority both before and after all recent elections in Réunion. The party's daily, *Témoignages,* thus carried frequent stories of improper registration tactics throughout the months preceding the 1977 municipal elections.

Party Organization and Internal Affairs. The secretary general of the PCR, Paul Vergès, mayor of Le Port and a former deputy, was reelected at the party's Fourth Congress in August 1976. The PCR has a thirty-four-member Central Committee, an eleven-member Political Bureau, and a Secretariat, whose members were elected at the 1976 congress (*IB,* no. 17, 1976). Sectional general assemblies are held periodically to rally party militants for political activities (*Témoignages,* 29-30 January, 2 February 1977). Support for the PCR comes from the Réunion General Confederation of Labor (Confédération Générale des Travailleurs Réunionnais; CGTR) headed by Bruny Payet, and from the party's Women's League and the Youth Front for Autonomy, directed by Elie Hoarau. The PCR draws its membership from Réunion's urban and rural working-class populations. Vergès explained the party's strategy for increasing its support in March 1977: "We're trying to draw together the victims of the [economic] crisis and the different tendencies manifesting a desire for change" (ibid., 5-6 March).

Domestic Policies and Activities. In 1977 the PCR was preoccupied with preparations for the 1978 legislative elections and with propaganda for Réunion's autonomy. The party expects to play the strongest role in a Réunion united leftist front in March 1978; to further this objective, the PCR held meetings with Socialists and radicals throughout the year. The failure of a Socialist party leader to stand aside in favor of the leading Communist list cost the PCR a victory in the municipal elections in March 1977.

Vergès has made autonomy for Réunion the central focus of his party's policies for several years. He considers that Réunion's present status as a French department is a holdover of colonialism. On a more practical level, the PCR has emphasized that the price of rice would be lower and that the Réunion economy would not be tied to the anti-inflationary Barre Plan if the island could attain autonomy and become an associate member of the EEC (*Témoignages,* 28 January, 25, 28 February, 14 April). The PCR has obtained support from the island's left-wing radical group on the autonomy question (ibid., 22 September).

Other political issues raised by the PCR in 1977 include improvement of government housing programs, relief for the 50,000 to 60,000 unemployed on the island, and creation of free breakfast programs for school children. Longer-range party goals involve nationalization of the sugar industry, agarian reform, and control over foreign trade.

International Activities. Representatives of the PCR have attended international Communist meetings such as the one held by the *World Marxist Review* in Prague in April 1977. The party's major forum for international activities, however, is its periodic meetings with Communist representatives from France, Guadeloupe, and Martinique. The 3 May 1977 meeting of these parties in Paris called upon the Union of the Left to place self-rule for the overseas territories and departments in high priority for the 1978 election campaign (*IB,* no. 10). Twelve leftist parties and organizations from the overseas departments and territories met in Guadeloupe on 10-11 September to prepare a manifesto addressed to the parties that had subscribed to the Common Program for the 1978 elections. The PCR and its support organizations played a major role in these meetings. (*Témoignages,* 13, 20 September).

In its daily newspaper and its meetings, the party devotes minimal attention to international Communist issues and major foreign policy questions.

Publications. The PCR publishes a daily newspaper, *Témoignages,* which has an estimated circulation of 5,000. The CGTR publishes the *Travailleur réunionnais* twice a month.

Stanford University   Peter S. Stern

Senegal

The African Independence Party (Parti Africain de l'Indépendance; PAI) of Senegal was founded in 1957 and banned by the government in 1960, shortly after that country became independent. The party operated clandestinely in the former French colonies of western Africa during its early years, but since 1962 has restricted its activities to Senegal. When the ban was lifted in August 1976, exiled leader Majmout Diop received a pardon. He returned and took over the movement at that time.

The PAI membership seems small, but there is no current estimate of its strength. The population of Senegal is approximately 5,301,000.

The PAI is the only legal Communist party under President Léopold Senghor's new multiparty system in which Marxist-Leninist, Socialist, liberal democratic, and conservative ideologies are each represented by a single organization. Nevertheless, there is at least one other Communist party in Senegal, a clandestine PAI which calls itself the sole legitimate representative of Marxism-Leninism. Yet another political movement, tolerated but without official recognition, enjoys strong Communist support: the National Democratic Rally (Rassemblement National Démocratique; RND), headed by Sheikh Anta Diop.

The emerging multiparty system in Senegal is the product of Senghor's desire to create a democratic political system and to move away from a one-party state. Under the new dispensation, Senghor attached the Socialist label to his own party. He offered the Marxist-Leninist designation to the RND, but Sheikh Anta Diop refused it, considering it a liability in a predominantly Islamic country. Diop claimed that the government purposely imposed the label after his party had filed for official registration (*Washington Post,* 11 June 1976). The RND is widely regarded as the most important opposition political force in Senegal. Its strength comes from a combination of leftist intellectuals, former Communists, nationalists, and supporters of traditional African and Islamic traditions in a country whose culture has been dominated by the French-oriented Négritude of Senghor (*Africa,* London, July 1977). Although rejecting formal designation as Marxist-Leninist, the RND receives support from Communists and former Communists.

The other Communist party, this one clandestine, claims to be the legitimate PAI. According to the *Revue française d'études politiques africaines* (Paris) for April 1977, this underground PAI attempted to gain official recognition from the government two years ago. On 7 March it renewed the request for recognition, but without success. A declaration signed "Central Committee of the PAI" appeared in a clandestine issue of *Monsarev* (Independence), which is the official organ of the legal PAI, claiming that recognition of Majmout Diop's group was "completely unrealistic" and could in no way "impede the action of the real PAI" (*Africa,* Dakar, April). An unattributed article in *African Communist* (London, no. 68, 1977) asserted that Majmout Diop's party "was in fact set up by Senghor himself" and that "Diop was given 600,000 French francs for his party for personal use."

Senghor's multiparty system should face a major test in February 1978, when elections take place to select 100 members of the National Assembly. Two months later, Senghor himself will stand for reelection as president. Although the PAI has announced that it will run candidates in the 1978 elections, neither the party nor the government expects the Communist presence to have any substantial impact on the outcome (*Le Soleil,* 6 March).

Party Organization and Internal Affairs. No information is available about the leadership, organization, and strength of the clandestine PAI. The official PAI held its most recent national conference at Dakar and elected a five-member provisional secretariat comprised of Majmout Diop, president; Bara Goudiaby, secretary general; Malick Sow, financial affairs; Balla Ndiaye, mass movements; and Nguirane Ndiaye, press (*Le Soleil,* 19 August 1976). The PAI also has a Central Committee and a Political Bureau.

According to Majmout Diop, urban intellectuals constitute most of the PAI membership. In the course of an interview, Diop acknowledged that after sixteen years of exile and underground activity, the party structure would have to undergo a housecleaning process, after which "we will carry out recruitment and propaganda in the working class and peasantry." (Ibid., 1 September.) The PAI sat out regional elections in 1976 (ibid., 12 November). While it expects to offer candidates for the legislature in 1978, the party is still in the rebuilding process (*Voix d'Afrique*, Dakar, 17 October-6 November 1977). A "Manifesto of Senegalese Workers," released during the summer, emphasized the general outlines of PAI recruitment objectives and its minimal policy goals: "Building an increasingly strong working-class basis for the PAI; mobilizing workers, revolutionary intellectuals, and peasants in the PAI . . . ; and the systematic but unhurried execution of the party's strategy based upon the realization of its minimal program—economic independence" (*Africa*, Dakar, August-September 1977).

Domestic Policies and Activities. The PAI official program calls for "application of the principles of scientific socialism in order to consolidate the independence of Senegal and to construct a Senegalese socialist society based upon the respect for the principles of national sovereignty and democracy" (*Le Soleil*, Dakar, 1 September 1976). Majmout Diop has ceased his attacks against the Senghor government, choosing instead to emphasize the "democratic way" toward conquest and exercise of power, and to affirm the "national" dimension in which the party will carry out its "patriotic tasks" (ibid.). The PAI practices a two-tier policy of working for a minimalist program of political and economic independence for Senegal in the short run and socialization of Senagalese society as the long-term objective.

As *L'Année politique africaine* (Dakar) for 1976 observed, "Majmout Diop and his friends, as Marxist-Leninists, know full well that at the actual level of economic and social development in Senegal, characterized by a weak urban proletariat, any attempt, or even the desire, on the part of a Communist party to seize power would be nothing more than adventurism." It remains to be seen whether it is the legal or the clandestine PAI that commands the following of the party's old underground organization and support.

International Activities. The PAI sends representatives to international Communist gatherings. Amath Dansoko, a member of the Political Bureau, is on the editorial board of the *World Marxist Review* and occasionally contributes to that publication.

Publications. The PAI publishes a monthly, *La Lutte* (Struggle), and also a weekly, *Monsarev* (Independence). The clandestine PAI also publishes irregularly its own version of *Monsarev*.

Stanford University   Peter S. Stern

South Africa

During 1977 the South African Communist Party (SACP) will celebrate its twenty-fifth anniversary as a clandestine organization. Constituted in 1953 as a successor to the Communist Party of South Africa, outlawed and disbanded in 1950, the SACP has operated underground within the country and from exile. In the tradition of its predecessor as South Africa's first non-racial party, the SACP draws its membership from all racial groups, but black Africans comprise the "overwhelming majority of the leadership and membership" (*African Communist*, no. 65, p. 28). Under threat of arrest and imprisonment, cadres continue to work within the Republic of South Africa. Prominent party officials, including almost certainly the majority of the Central Committee, live outside the country. It is impossible to estimate the numerical strength of the SACP (out of a total South African population of 27,188,000), but its membership is extremely small.

Leadership and Organization. Dr. Yusef M. Dadoo, a sixty-eight-year-old Indian leader prominent in the party since the 1940s and in exile since 1960, has been SACP chairman since December 1972. The party secretary continues to be Moses Kotane, a seventy-two-year-old African elected in 1939 when the Communist party was legal. Having gone into exile under party directive in 1963, Kotane has been resident since 1968 in Moscow where he is under medical treatment for a heart ailment. Other leaders maintain anonymity, writing under pseudonyms in the party press.

The SACP continues to regard itself as "an integral part of the national liberation movement" (*African Communist,* no. 68, p. 46), an alliance operating both inside and outside South Africa. The recognized leading element of the movement is the African Nationalist Congress (ANC), the country's oldest such organization, under government ban since 1960. Acting ANC president Oliver Tambo and other leaders direct external activities and clandestine internal operations from headquarters in sympathetic black African states. The national liberation movement also includes the South African Indian Congress (SAIC) and the multiracial South African Congress of Trade Unions (SACTU), both of which lead a harassed semilegal existence under regular police surveillance within the country.

The SACP rejects charges that it has attemped to control other components of the national liberation movement: "We have always fought, and shall continue to fight for the complete independence and organizational integrity of the mass movements. Those of our members who have earned positions as mass leaders of the national movement have proved over and again their devotion to, and respect for, the decisions of the democratically elected collectives of which they have been part." (Ibid., no. 70, p. 44.)

At the same time, the SACP vigorously defends the "absolute right of our Party to exist as an independent organization and to continue to exercise its public role as the advance vanguard of the working class" (ibid.). It "must spare no effort in the work of strengthening our party underground, safeguarding our party's independence and maintaining its important role as part of the liberation alliance" (ibid., no. 7, p. 47). Major policy decisions apparently are taken by the upper echelons of the leadership at meetings outside the country, such as the plenary session of the Central Committee held at an unnamed site in April.

Domestic Activities and Attitudes. The SACP asserts that it has "no immediate political aims separate from the aims of the national liberation movement headed by the ANC"; the party allegedly stands "united by the immediate and foremost task—the destruction of racist domination and the achievement of the aims of the National Democratic revolution whose main content is the liberation of the African majority and other oppressed black groups" (*African Communist,* no. 70, p. 43).

Recent events in South Africa and neighboring states, in particular the upsurge in black militancy in Soweto during June 1976 and thereafter, as well as the continuing evolution of the Angola and Mozambique regimes in an explicitly Marxist-Leninist direction, have encouraged the SACP about prospects for change in the region.

According to the Central Committee, "the Soweto events have opened a new chapter in the history of the revolutionary struggle. . . . [T]hey raised the level of the people's preparedness and willingness to sacrifice to a higher level, enhancing enormously the striking power of the liberation movement. . . . Soweto closed the debate about the legitimacy of resorting to the armed struggle." (Ibid., no. 70, pp. 30-31.)

SACP had high praise for the youthful black militants who initiated and sustained the confrontations with white power. Their "inventiveness and ingenuity . . . in particular showed boundless revolutionary imagination" (ibid., no. 70, p. 30). The party recognized the important mobilizing role of Black Consciousness in organizational and ideological terms, yet it warned that "an ideology which proclaims colour as its sole foundation can more easily obscure the real issues because of its highly charged emotional content." It further stated that "used in place of genuine revolutionary doctrine, Black Consciousness is a misleading ideology of national liberation." (Ibid., no 70, p. 37.)

The SACP is sensitive to criticism from within and outside the national liberation movement that a party dedicated to armed struggle for sixteen years should have failed to transform the Soweto demonstration into an effective insurrection. It argues that the "people's armed conflict is a protracted process," requiring more than merely logistics and organization; hence revolutions "must not be tempted by the passion and excitement of the moment to spread a dangerous and damaging illusion that it will be short and swift" (ibid., no. 70. p. 34).

The SACP finds promise in Soweto events for a rapid expansion of revolutionary opposition to the point where "the new situation has brought closer than ever before the possibility of an effective beginning to the armed struggle" (ibid.). Acknowledging the spontaneous and independent nature of the initial Soweto demonstrations, SACP asserts that key student leaders have since turned to known ANC activists for advice and coordination. Many of them have already joined the ranks of the liberation movement and its armed wing, Umkhonto we Sizwe.

To capitalize upon the heightened mood of black defiance, especially among radicalized students and working youth, the SACP has given new emphasis to the strengthening of underground organizations and local leadership of both the party and its allies in the national liberation movement. In the SACP's view, it is the duty of the "liberation movement as a whole to give the mass movements which have arisen among the youth, and which played such a key role in sparking off the mass upsurge, a clear revolutionary political and organizational content." Simultaneously, "one of the supreme tasks of our revolutionary alliance is to ensure that the armed struggle establishes firm roots in every part of the country." (Ibid., no. 70, pp. 47, 49.) Yet the legal organizations and semilegal activity are still regarded as important; given the central role of the working class, the party calls for flexible tactics on the part of the legal trade unions. The SACP is also willing to consider the potential of the factory and liaison committees permitted Africans by the government. Although the party is uncompromisingly opposed to Bantustan leaders, including Chief Gatsha Buthelezi of Kwazulu, it continues to regard the bulk of the black middle class, especially in urban areas, as an important group whose support can and must be won. Equally, the SACP calls for mobilization and organization of the rural population within the national liberation front.

Looking beyond the overthrow of the present system, the SACP invokes the example of the regimes in Angola (MPLA) and Mozambique (FRELIMO) to establish Marxist-Leninist vanguard parties. Both the MPLA and FRELIMO "recognize two universal historical truths: that the motive force of history is class struggle; and that the working people need a vanguard party based on the ideology of Marxism-Leninism to ensure that state power in the post-liberation era becomes an instrument for eventually achieving full emancipation within a framework of Socialism." (Ibid., no. 70, p. 26.)

International Views and Activities. The SACP continues its loyalty to the Soviet Union within the international Communist movement. It condemns the policies of the "clique" on the mainland of China and has called for another international conference of Communist and workers' parties. The SACP has also rallied to the Soviets in their disputes with West European Communist movements. It notes, with seeming regret, that "unfortunately a few fraternal parties in Western Europe" have also joined the "orchestrated campaign of vilification" that condemns the Soviet Union and some of its East European allies for violation of human rights and democracy. It also rejects the contention of similarly unnamed West European Communist parties that "proletarian internationalism as we have understood it is obsolete," and continues to assert that there is "no theoretical or practical justification for 'Afro-Communism,' 'Arab-Communism' or 'Euro-Communism' " (*African Communist,* no. 70, pp. 61, 64, 66).

Publications. The SACP puts out an underground publication in South Africa called *Inkululeko-Freedom,* organ of its Central Committee. At least nineteen issues of this journal have appeared since July 1971. SACP also distributes a clandestine version of *African Communist,* its overseas quarterly printed in the German Democratic Republic and distributed externally from London. Other SACP publications include proclamations and pocket-sized Marxist-Leninist classics. The ANC's official publication, *Sechaba,* is published quarterly in London. ANC clandestine publications are *Vukani-Awake* and *Amandla-Maatla.*

Duke University   Sheridan Johns

Sudan

The Sudanese Communist Party (al-Hizb al-Shuyu 'i al-Sudani; SCP) traces its origins to 1946. It gradually became a focal point of opposition, successfully infiltrating a number of professional, student, and labor groups. Implication in the coup attempt of 19 July 1971 led to severe repression of the party (see *YICA, 1972,* pp. 290-92). Numerous SCP leaders were executed, including former Secretary General 'Abd al-Khaliq Mahjub. Thousands of party members were arrested and held without trial. The SCP has also been accused of participating in more recent plots against the government, namely in September 1975 and July 1976.

No reliable figures exist on present SCP membership. Before the 1971 coup attempt, the party was estimated to have from 5,000 to 10,000 active members. An unknown number are continuing party activities in exile or clandestinely within Sudan.

Leadership and Organization. Names of party leaders generally have been absent from party statements and international press reports on the SCP. Muhammad Ibrahim Nuqud is secretary general. Ibrahim Zakariya, an occasional contributor to *World Marxist Review,* is a member of the SCP Central Committee. A report on political prisoners printed by the Organization of the SCP in the United Kingdom during March mentioned three additional members of the Central Committee: Suleiman Hamid, Suoodi Darag, and 'Abd al-Magid Shakak. Dr. 'Izz al-Din 'Ali 'Amir, is known as a spokesman for the SCP in Great Britain. Other leading members include Ibrahim Zakariya, Mahjub 'Uthman, and al-Fajjani al-Tayyib; the last two were arrested in October 1974 after returning from exile.

The SCP has always been active in mass organizations—trade unions, youth, women's, and other associations. The party operates through local branches which are set up at places of residence and work. On the next higher level are the regional organizations. The party has held four congresses: 1950, 1951, 1956, and 1967. It has also convened conferences in 1949, 1966, and 1970.

Domestic Views and Activities. During 1977 the SCP placed stress on its campaign to free political prisoners in Sudan. Party members residing in the United Kingdom published a pamphlet in March accusing the Ja'far Numayri government of detaining prisoners without legal recourse; providing substandard medical services; depriving prisoners of adequate food, reading and writing materials, and blankets; and almost totally restricting visits from relatives and friends. Above all, the SCP charged the regime with torturing detainees to obtain confessions and information. The pamphlet called on the UN Human Rights Committee and such organizations as Amnesty International to assist. According to this report, seventeen Communists were incarcerated at Kobar prison, eighty-four students at Dabak detention camp (the majority being Communists and progressives), fifty Communists at Shala prison, and an unknown number at al-Ubayd, Damar, and Atbara prisons. Another SCP appeal to world public opinion called for release of all political prisoners (*Morning Star,* London, from Tass, 5 July).

These appeals were made against a background of continued arrests of SCP members. According to the Sudanese News Agency, six Communists sought by police since the attempted coup of July 1976 had been arrested while holding a meeting to discuss sending militant Communists to study in a Communist capital city (*Arab Report and Record,* London, 16-31 January 1977). On 15 June security forces raided an alleged cell of Communist activists at a house in Port Sudan. They locked up the leader of the local organization, who had been in hiding since 1971, as well as fifteen others. The following month a large number of Communists were imprisoned in the Red Sea Province. Authorities reported the seizing of "documents, printing equipment and papers [that] revealed the nature of their secret plans, their activities . . . and the way in which they coordinated their infiltration into student and workers groups and various residential areas of the Red Sea Province (Omdurman domestic service, in *FBIS,* 11 July).

On 7 August Sudanese President Ja'far Numayri proclaimed a general amnesty for all those convicted of political crimes since he took power in May 1969, provided that they would pledge their loyalty to the existing constitution and, if in exile, would return to Sudan. A subsequent decree issued by Numayri pardoned twenty-eight prominent opposition leaders, the most notable being Sadiq al-Mahdi, leader of the opposition Umma Party and former Sudanese prime minister, and Ibrahim Nuqud. The SCP, however, was not appeased. In September its spokesmen at Beirut pointed out that the SCP had not been a direct party to reconciliation, and that many Communists and trade unionists were still in jail. Nevertheless, the government's new course was of significance to the SCP, especially insofar as it bore on the pardon of al-Mahdi. As prime minister, al-Mahdi had been known for his fierce opposition to the Communists. Now he included the Communists among those to whom fundamental freedoms should be restored as a precondition for national reconciliation. According to al-Mahdi, "We must take the myths out of Marxism, integrate the communists into the national community so that our country may leave underdevelopment behind" (*An-Nahar Arab Report and MEMO,* Beirut, 19 September). He called for transformation of the single ruling party into "a true national alliance, freely entered into, which would even include the communists, provided they, like the Eurocommunists, abandoned outmoded notions such as the dictatorship of the proletariat and unconditional loyalty to the USSR" (*Le Monde,* Paris, 13 September). SCP spokesman Ibraham Zakariya, whereabouts still unknown, had made a similar proposal five months earlier when he suggested that "to begin solving [Sudan's problems] effectively, it is indispensable that all progressive social forces should cooperate. This, in turn, makes it necessary to discard authoritarian forms and methods of government and pursue a policy based on the principles of the national democratic front" (*WMR,* April). Zakariya did not indicate, however, the names of the members of this national democratic front.

The SCP was also much concerned with the so-called "Southern problem." A pro-SCP article castigated government repression in the South, called for the removal of Numayri, and argued that the 1972 Addis Ababa agreement had failed to solve the southern problem. Its roots were to be found in "the uneven economic and cultural development as between south and north." A solution should be sought in terms of the 9 June 1969 declaration calling for "regional self-rule within a united Sudan." The Numayri government was said to have placed "power in the hands of pro-capitalists, of imperialist agents and of persons seconded to Numayri by imperialist powers." Hence, the article concluded, "progress in the Sudan and the solution of the country's problems, including the Southern problem . . . can only be achieved by the defeat of the whole regime and its system" (*African Communist,* first quarter, 1977).

Publications. The SCP publishes the clandestine newspaper *al-Maydan* (Forum). In addition, an English-language paper, *Advance,* appears sporadically for the people of southern Sudan. News of the party has also been printed in the Lebanese Communist Party publications *al-Nida'* and *al-Akhbar* when conditions in Lebanon have allowed.

Stanford University   Patricia Mihaly

Syria

The Syrian Communist Party (al-Hizb al-Shuyu'i al Suri; SCP) is an offshoot of the Lebanese Communist Party (LCP). In 1944, the first congress of the LCP decided to form a separate movement under the leadership of Khalid Bakdash. The SCP gained de facto legality in March 1972 through participation in the National Front formed by al-Asad. SCP membership is estimated at between 3,000 and 4,000, with perhaps another 10,000 sympathizers. Estimates of the party's strength, however, differ considerably. Another one speaks of 30,000 card-carrying members. The population of Syria is almost eight million.

Leadership and Organization. The SCP leader continues to be Khalid Bakdash, a Syrian Kurd. At the party's fourth congress in 1974, Yusuf Faisal was elected to the newly established post of deputy secretary-general. The following comprised the new Politburo: Bakdash, Ibrahim Bakri, Khalid Hammami, Daniel Ni'mah, Maurice Salibi, Dhahir'Abd al-Samad, Ramu Shaikhu, 'Umar Siba'i, and Murad Yusuf. Siba'i is minister of communications and 'Abd al-Samad minister of state in the Syrian cabinet. Bakdash and Ni'mah are SCP representatives in the National Progressive Front.

In 1973 a faction that also identifies itself as the SCP split away from the party. This faction still operates in a clandestine fashion under the leadership of Riyad al-Turk, its first secretary. It has no members in either the Syrian cabinet or the National Progressive Front (a coalition of the Ba'ath Party, the SCP, and other "progressive" and nationalist forces, formed in 1971).

Domestic Views and Activities. At a plenary session of the SCP Central Committee in April 1977 the party reaffirmed its approval of participation by Syrian Communists in the National Front. On August 1-2, elections to the 195-member Syrian People's Council were held. Khalid Bakdash did not stand as a candidate, but six Communists were elected to the legislature. The clandestine breakaway SCP boycotted the election.

According to an article by Khalid Bakdash, the SCP stands for:

—strengthening and enlargement of the state sector of the national economy . . .

—protection of the oil industry and other natural riches from imperialist capital . . .

—protection of national industry, enterprises in the state and private sectors and small industry from competition from imperialist monopolies . . .

—full implementation of agrarian reform

—distribution of all confiscated landowners' lands among peasants and

—use of irrigated lands, particularly in the Euphrates valley, by creating state farms and cooperatives there.

Bakdash also noted SCP involvement in the struggle against rising prices of essential goods and for solution of the housing and transport crises (*Pravda,* 6 August).

International Views and Activities. According to the SCP, "the Geneva conference is the only international mechanism by which a just and lasting solution to the Middle East conflict can be found." The party stresses the necessity of participation by both the Palestine Liberation Organization and the Soviet Union in any peace effort. The SCP condemns "American imperialism, Zionism and Arab reaction" for obstructing progressive Arab regimes and the Palestine resistance movement (*FBIS,* 16 August). It continues to support the Syrian government in its demand for the liberation of all lands occupied by Israel since 1967. The party also defends the Palestinians' right to "return to their homeland and to create their own independent national state" (*Pravda,* 10 August).

The SCP has been outspoken in its criticism of Egypt which, allegedly, is opening the door to imperialist forces and to internal and external reaction. Egypt, moreover, is accused of obstructing the relationship between the progressive Arab movement and its "true ally, the Soviet Union," while deepening cooperation with the Saudi reaction. The SCP expressed its solidarity with the Egyptian people, Egyptian Communists, Nasir's supporters, and leaders of trade unions and student organizations. It demanded that prisoners should be released, protested repression and anti-popular legislation (Tass, 19 February). In May, the SCP strongly supported Libya during the border crisis with Egypt. According to the SCP, Egypt's present policy sustains American imperialism in its efforts to obstruct Libya's socialist program. Egypt supposedly undermines Arab solidarity and diverts Arab attention from the struggle against Israeli occupation and the denial of Palestinian national rights (Tass, 3 May).

The SCP has likewise expressed concern over tensions in the Horn of Africa involving Somalia, the Sudan, and Ethiopia. It supposedly fears an imperialist-reactionary plot to weaken African unity and undermine those African states which have chosen the socialist road to development.

The SCP consistently accuses the United States of attempting to undermine Soviet-Arab and particularly Soviet-Syrian friendship. The SCP also condemns Saudi Arabia for encouraging the Arab states to abandon Soviet friendship and aid in return for securing U.S. assistance. According to the SCP, this policy is bound to isolate the Arab states from the Soviet Union, without providing an alternative source of military and economic support.

The SCP has declared its opposition to U.S. production of the neutron bomb as "an enormous danger to the cause of peace" (Tass, 24 October).

Publications. The official organ of the SCP is the fortnightly newspaper *Nidal al-Sha'b* (People's Struggle), which is banned but has been circulated freely since the party joined the National Progressive Front. The SCP also disseminates its news through the two legal publications of the Lebanese Communist Party in Beirut, *al-Nida'* and *al-Akhbar,* as the situation in Lebanon permits.

Stanford University   Patricia Mihaly

INTERNATIONAL COMMUNIST FRONT ORGANIZATIONS

A network of international organizations, while allegedly democratic and non-governmental in uniting people, provides, in fact, fronts for Soviet policies. It dates back to 1921, when Lenin conceived of the idea to propagate Communism through trade unions, youth movements, cooperatives, and other bodies as "transmission belts." Most present-day organizations were started during the late 1940s, when the USSR launched them or secured control of existing ones.

The following twelve have been selected for this annual review of international Communist front organization activities: Afro-Asian People's Solidarity Organization (AAPSO), Afro-Asian Writers' Permanent Bureau (AAWPB), International Association of Democratic Lawyers (IADL), International Federation of Resistance Fighters (FIR), International Organization of Journalists (IOJ), International Union of Students (IUS), Women's International Democratic Federation (WIDF), World Federation of Democratic Youth (WFDY), World Federation of Scientific Workers (WFSW), World Federation of Trade Unions (WFTU), World Peace Council (WPC), and Christian Peace Conference (CPC).

Afro-Asian Peoples' Solidarity Organization. Set up at Cairo in 1958 as an anti-colonialist offshoot from the World Peace Council, the Afro-Asian Peoples' Solidarity Organization during its first few years was jointly controlled by the USSR, China, and the United Arab Republic. The Sino-Soviet dispute led to disruption of the AAPSO conferences in 1963 and 1965, and finally to a split following the WPC meeting at Nicosia, Cyprus, in February 1967. The Chinese boycotted that meeting, which decided to hold the next AAPSO conference in Algiers rather than in Peking as planned. Since then, Soviet domination of AAPSO has continued.

Structure and Leadership. AAPSO's organizational structure has been and is relatively loose. Although meetings of its Congress and Council have been held, in a practical sense the Secretariat has been the key organizational unit. The eleventh Council meeting, in March 1974, established the Presidium, which apparently will bear primary responsibility, along with the Secretariat, for the development and execution of policy.

Yusuf el-Sebai, the AAPSO's secretary general since its foundation, was reelected at the eleventh Council and was also elected chairman of the Presidium. Since he is secretary general also of the AAWPB-Cairo (see below), these two organizations have in effect an "overlapping directorate." Both are headquartered in Cairo and both focus on problems of the same geographical area. The AAPSO at present appears to be the more active and important.

Views and Activities. On 10 December 1976, in Athens, the AAPSO sponsored a conference on Cyprus and Palestine, reportedly attended by 200 delegates representing sixty-eight organizations. A resolution of support for Cyprus backed the USSR's proposal for a conference within the U.N. framework; also an appeal was issued asking that Turkey be pressured into observing the U.N. resolutions on Cyprus. The final statement on Palestine said that the Palestinian revolution was an "important part of the Arab national liberation movement" and that the Palestine Liberation

Organization was "the only legitimate representative of the Palestinian people." The situation in Lebanon was said to be the result of an imperialist-Zionist reactionary plot. According to the statement, there could be no just peace in the Middle East without the complete evacuation of Israeli troops from all occupied Arab territories. (*Cyprus Mail,* 11-12 December 1976; *L'Humanité,* Paris, 13-15 December.)

More than fifty organizations and liberation movements sent delegates to the AAPSO Presidium session in March 1977 at Cotonou, in the People's Republic of Benin. The session praised the USSR's support of peoples fighting for their freedom, condemned the alleged collaboration of certain reactionary Arab countries with imperialists in efforts to subvert the Ethiopian revolution, and hailed the sixtieth anniversary of the October Revolution. The participants also supported the Secretariat's decision to hold the AAPSO Sixth Congress and the twentieth anniversary celebration at Baghdad in 1978. (*Ehuzu,* Cotonou, 28-29 March; Addis Ababa Radio, 30 March.)

At the consultative meeting of the Afro-Asian Solidarity Committee of Arab states in Cyprus on 17 September, Yusef el-Sebai stressed that Israel's policy is based on the direct political, military, and economic backing of the United States. He claimed that U.S.-Israeli plans for the Middle East seek to prevent a resumption of the Geneva peace conference and to keep the Soviet Union and the PLO from participating in a settlement. In his closing remarks, el-Sebai argued that all progressive and anti-imperialist forces should oppose the "intrigues" of imperialism and Zionism, and should recognize the importance of a close alliance with the Socialist countries, "above all with the Soviet Union." He added that the military presence of the United States, Britain, and Iran in the Persian Gulf threatened the national interests of the Arab peoples (Tass, 17 September).

Afro-Asian Writers' Permanent Bureau. The AAWPB originated from a Soviet-sponsored "Afro-Asian Writers Conference" in Tashkent in 1958. Following a second such conference, at Cairo in February 1962, a "Permanent Bureau" was established, with headquarters in Colombo, Ceylon (now Sri Lanka). The Chinese Communists gained control of the organization at a meeting of its executive committee in Bali, Indonesia, July 1963, and established a new Executive Secretariat in Peking, 15 August 1966. Officially still based in Colombo, the AAWPB operates exclusively from Peking. A pro-Soviet faction—the AAWPB-Cairo—broke away after the Chinese began to dominate the organization. The AAWPB-Peking, which has not yet held a third conference, appears to have no activities outside its irregular publication, *The Call,* and occasional statements carried by the New China News Agency.

The AAWPB-Cairo. The pro-Soviet AAWPB, founded 19 June 1966 by delegations from Cameroon, Sri Lanka, India, Sudan, the USSR, and the United Arab Republic, held a relatively successful "Third Afro-Asian Writers' Conference" at Beirut in 1967 which was attended by some 150 delegates from forty-two countries. This was the first serious blow to the pro-Chinese AAWPB. Since then the pro-Soviet AAWPB appears to have consolidated and augmented its base of support.

Yusef el-Sebai is secretary general of the AAWPB-Cairo (also secretary general of the AAPSO and a member of the Presidential Committee of the WPC). The assistant secretary general is Edward el-Kharat. Both are from Egypt. The ten members of the Permanent Bureau are from India, Japan, Lebanon, Mongolia, the former Portuguese colonies, Senegal, South Africa, the USSR, Sudan, and Egypt. There is also a thirty-member Executive Committee. The group's organ, *Lotus,* is a "literature, arts and sociopolitical quarterly," and appears in English, French, and Arabic editions. Books by various Afro-Asian men of letters have been published in the USSR by the AAWPB-Cairo.

The AAWPB-Peking. The pro-Chinese AAWPB, as already noted, is a continuation of the original body. Frederik L. Risakotta, of the Peking-based "Delegation of the Central Committee" of the Communist Party of Indonesia, is "acting head ad interim" of the group's Secretariat. Relatively inactive, it has issued *The Call* at irregular intervals.

International Association of Democratic Lawyers. An "International Congress of Jurists," meeting in Paris in October 1946 under the auspices of a para-Communist organization (the Mouvement National Judiciaire) and attended by lawyers from twenty-five countries, founded the International Association of Democratic Lawyers. The leading role in the IADL was played by leftist French lawyers, and by 1949 most non-Communists had resigned. In 1950 the French government expelled the IADL from its base in Paris. It then moved to Brussels, where it remains, although some organization work has been carried out from Warsaw.

Membership is open to lawyers' organizations or groups, and to individual lawyers, and may be on a "corresponding," "donation," or "permanent" basis. Lawyers holding membership through organizations or individually are estimated to number about 25,000. While publishing no details of its finances, the IADL claims to be supported by membership fees and donations. It holds consultative status, Category C, with the U.N. Economic and Social Council.

Structure and Leadership. The highest organ of the IADL is the Congress, in which each member organization is represented. The latest Congress met in Algiers in April 1975. The Congress elects the Council, which is supposed to meet yearly and consists of the Bureau, the Secretariat, and a representative of each member organization. Robert Dachet (Belgium), secretary general, died on 26 November 1976 (WFTU *Flashes,* no. 1, 1977) and Pierre Cot (France), IADL president since 1960 and a founding member of the WPC, died in the fall of 1977 (*L'Humanité,* 22 August). At present both positions are vacant.

Views and Activities. Pierre Cot and Joe Nordmann (France), deputy president, met with representatives of all the IADL affiliates in December 1976 at the UNESCO building in Paris. Messages were received from various international organizations and from USSR President Podgorny, Pham Van Dong of Vietnam, and Algerian President Boumedienne. Three workshops discussed detente, people's rights in the face of multinational corporations, and the rights of workers in their firms. The IADL's aim, it was stated, was to put law at the service of men, democracy, freedom, and the new international economic order (*L'Humanité,* 13 December).

Throughout the year, the IADL issued a series of protests. In April, it cited Israel's refusal to allow Mrs. Felicia Langer to plead before military tribunals there in the trial of Palestinian patriots (ibid., 6 April). It also pointed to imperialist interventions in Zaire and the jailing of hundreds of people in South Africa (*Neues Deutschland,* East Berlin, 16 April; *L'Humanité,* 13 May).

In the summer of 1977, IADL representatives visited the Middle East. The leader of the delegation, a member of the Paris Bar, announced after the trip that the Iranian authorities had prevented him from meeting with political prisoners, despite a previous promise (*L'Humanité,* 23 July).

Publications. The principal IADL publications, *Review of Contemporary Laws* and *Information Bulletin,* appear irregularly in English and French.

International Federation of Resistance Fighters. The FIR (Fédération Internationale des Résistants) was founded in 1951 in Vienna as the successor to the International Federation of Former Political Prisoners (Fédération Internationale des Anciens Prisonniers Politiques). With the name change; membership eligibility was widened to include former partisans and resistance fighters, and all victims of Nazism and fascism and their descendants.

The FIR claims three million full members. In 1971 it claimed affiliated groups and representation in every country of Europe (*Résistance Unie,* no. 14). The headquarters is in Vienna, and a small secretariat is maintained in Paris. In 1972 the FIR was granted Status B with the U.N. Economic and Social Council.

Structure and Leadership. The organs of the FIR are the Congress, General Council, Bureau, and Secretariat. The Congress, which is supposed to meet every four years, elects the president, vice-president, and members of the Bureau, and determines and ratifies members of the General Council after they have been nominated by national associations. The General Council is supposed to meet at least once a year. The Bureau supervises the implementation of the decisions reached by the Congress and the General Council, and is responsible for the budget; from among its members it elects the Secretariat. Arialdo Banfi (Italy) is president and Alex Lhote (France) is secretary general.

Views and Activities. The single important organizational meeting of the FIR in 1977 took place on 27 March in Athens, where the Bureau discussed strengthening FIR activities in the struggle for peace and disarmament, and the "disturbing" rise of neo-fascism, particularly in Federal Germany (*Rizospastis,* Athens, 29 March; *Neues Deutschland,* 29 March).

Informal gatherings during the remainder of the year discussed various issues touching on FIR interests. The FIR called for an end to the arms race and petitioned ECOSOC to investigate the fate of political prisoners in Greece and the rise of neo-fascism (*Résistance Unie,* no. 7).

Publications. As of 1977, the FIR had a single publication, *Résistance Unie/Service d'Information.*

International Organization of Journalists. The IOJ was founded in June 1946 in Copenhagen. Merging with it at the time were the International Federation of Journalists (IFJ) and the International Federation of Journalists of Allied and Free Countries. The IOJ headquarters, originally in London, was moved to Prague in 1947. By 1952 the participating non-Communist unions had withdrawn in order to refound the IFJ. Since 1955 the IOJ has made unsuccessful overtures to the IFJ for forming a new world organization of journalists. It was for the purpose of bridging differences with the IFJ that the IOJ had founded in 1955 the International Committee for Cooperation of Journalists (ICCJ). No IFJ member is known to have become affiliated with the ICCJ, perhaps because most ICCJ officers are also leading members of the parent IOJ.

A rival organization, the Afro-Asian Journalists' Association, established in 1963 by pro-Chinese journalists, appears to have drawn little other support (see *YICA, 1976,* p. 580).

The IOJ claims 150,000 members, in 110 countries. It was awarded consultative status, Category II, with the U.N. Economic and Social Council.

Structure and Leadership. The highest IOJ body, the Congress, meets approximately every four years. It elects the Executive Committee, made up of the Presidium (president, vice-presidents, secretary general), other officers (secretaries and treasurer), and ordinary members. At the Eighth Congress, in Helsinki on 21-23 September 1976, Kaarle Nordenstreng (Finland), professor of journalism, was elected president. Jiří Kubka (Czechoslovakia), remained as secretary general. Jean-Maurice Herman (France), the outgoing president, was named as honorary president. Also elected to the Presidium, all with the title of vice-president, were the chairman of the Leadership of the Union of Journalists of the USSR, the secretary general of the Somali Journalists' Association, a representative of the Puerto Rican Committee of the IOJ, the secretary general of the National Syndicate of Press Workers in Venezuela, the chairman of the National Union of Journalists of Mali, the assistant director of *Horoya* (in Guinea), the secretary general of the National Syndicate of Journalists (France), the chairman of the Iraqi Journalists' Union, a representative of the Chilean Committee of the IOJ, and a representative of the Union of Democratic Journalists (Mexico). (*Democratic Journalist,* no. 12, 1976.)

Views and Activities. Throughout 1977 the IOJ sought to inform the public on the Helsinki Agreements. In general this meant strong support for the Accords coupled with criticism of the West for its "unwillingness" to follow completely the spirit and letter of the understanding reached at Helsinki. Writing in *Pravda,* Kaarle Nordenstreng noted that "the mass media bear a good deal of responsibility for maintaining the Helsinki spirit both nationally and internationally," and said that "in the journalistic circles of Socialist countries, this responsibility is universally recognized." Analysis of "material published by so-called respectable Western newspapers," he went on, "from the start of preparatory consultations in 1972 up to the signing of the Final Act in 1975," showed "the publications which shape public opinion at any rate did not act as objective observers, thoroughly informing their audiences and explaining in depth the essence of complex social problems. Those newspapers took up a quite reserved attitude towards the European Conference and often even an overtly negative one . . ." (Tass, 14 May).

The twenty-third course at the IOJ school in Budapest began on 7 January. It was attended by sixteen participants from Bangladesh, Egypt, Ghana, Iraq, Nigeria, Syria, Tanzania, Zambia, and Zimbabwe (Rhodesia). Two Chilean journalists living in exile and four reporters from India spent most of the winter and spring in Budapest as guests of the IOJ. On 13 January a special "qualification" course for journalists from Africa and Asia began at the International Solidarity School in Berlin. There were twenty-three participants from thirteen countries, including members of the liberation movements in Namibia (Southwest Africa) and Zimbabwe. Several journalists also attended this course who had been nominated by UNESCO. (ADN, 13 January; *Neues Deutschland,* 14 January). IOJ secretary general Kubka and representatives of journalist federations of six East European countries attending a meeting of the Social Commission in Budapest on 11 January, focused on joint recreation projects and the further development of friendly ties (MTI, 11 January). The following week, in Prague, Nordenstreng chaired a meeting of the IOJ Secretariat and had a series of talks with the Czechoslovak deputy prime minister, who assured him that his government would continue to provide support for the work of the IOJ (CTK, 19 January).

It was announced in late summer that Kubka had been elected a member of the WPC Presidential Committee (*Journalists' Affairs,* no. 9/10).

Publications. The IOJ's fortnightly *Journalists' Affairs* and monthly *Democratic Journalist* appear in English, French, Spanish, and Russian editions.

International Union of Students. A congress in Prague in August 1946, attended by students of varying political persuasions, saw the founding of the International Union of Students. In 1951 most of the non-Communist student unions withdrew because of domination of the IUS by pro-Soviet groups. The 1960s were marked by bitter debates between pro-Soviet and pro-Chinese students. In the middle 1960s the Chinese withdrew from active participation.

The IUS claims to have ninety-nine member organizations with members totaling ten million, mostly in Communist ruled countries. It has consultative Category C status with UNESCO. Applications for Category B status have been repeatedly deferred.

Structure and Leadership. The IUS has headquarters in Prague. Its highest governing body, the Congress, is supposed to meet every three years. Each affiliated and associated organization is permitted to send delegates. The Congress elects the national unions to be represented on the Executive Committee; the national unions then determine which individual(s) will represent them. The Executive Committee meets once a year.

The Twelfth Congress, held in Sofia on 1 November 1977, elected Miroslav Stepan, representative of the Czech Student Center, as president. Fathi al-Fadl, representative of the Sudanese Federation of Students, was reelected secretary general. The vice-presidents are representatives from the following organizations: Organization of Students of Dakar University; Council of Presidents of the Federation of Chilean Universities; University Students Federation, Cuba; All-Indian Federation of

Students; (North) Korean Committee of Students; National Union of Students, Mozambique; General Union of Palestinian Students; Federation of Students, Panama; Socialist Union of Polish Students; Council of Students of the Soviet Union; National Union of Vietnamese Students; and National Student Council, Bulgaria. The new secretaries represent organizations in Cyprus, Ghana, Hungary, Ireland, Namibia, Puerto Rico, Romania, Somalia, Uruguay, and the People's Republic of Yemen. (BTA, 2 November.)

Views and Activities. On 8 November 1976 over sixty student associations including both IUS affiliates and friendly organizations from Arab and African countries, as well as observers from five international organizations, discussed IUS activities on anti-imperialist solidarity, the democratization of education, the struggle for a new and just system of economic relations, and the strengthening of cooperation with regional and non-governmental organizations. Recommendations for nine new affiliations were confirmed at this meeting—from Angola, Barbados, Benin, Gambia, Libya, Rwanda, Saudi Arabia, Trinidad and Tobago, and the youth section of the South-West African People's Organization SWAPO). (*World Student News,* no. 2, 1977.)

Suleiman Nur (Somalia), secretary, wrote in an article in *World Student News* (no. 3) on the growing importance of Accra as a center of student activities. The Ghanaian capital has been the site of the congress of the All-African Students' Union (AASU), the IUS Executive Committee meeting, and several other gatherings. Nur remarked that the AASU congress was satisfied with the cooperation between it, the IUS, and the Continental Organization of Latin American Students (OCLAE). Indeed, cooperation between the IUS and the AASU has risen rapidly in the past five years, with five joint seminars held in 1976. Nur finished his comments by saying that, thanks to the IUS, the AASU had "lifted the African struggle against imperialism and reaction to new heights of political awareness and militancy."

Throughout 1977 various groups associated with the IUS met to prepare for its Twelfth Congress, which opened on 25 October in Sofia with representatives attending from fifty-nine member-organizations, twelve organizations not officially associated with the IUS, and fifteen international and regional organizations. Greetings were received from high political figures, among whom were Kurt Waldheim, Yasir Arafat, and Erich Honecker. There were also messages from various "progressive" student movements, the IOJ, WPC, WFDY, and other international groups. (Tass, 21 October; BTA, 25/27 October.)

The main report, delivered by Dusan Ulcak, touched on "the Role and Tasks of the IUS in the Common Anti-Imperialist Struggle for Peace and Security, for International Cooperation, National Independence, Social Progress, and Student Rights" (BTA, 27 October). During the Congress considerable attention was devoted to the IUS-launched anti-imperialist campaigns. The Congress charged the Executive Committee and Secretariat with the tasks of strengthening solidarity with other international and regional democratic and progressive organizations in the general anti-imperialist struggle. At the same time the Congress called upon the progressive-minded students to step up their struggle for general and full disarmament, against the quantitative and qualitative arms race, and against the manufacture of new mass destruction weapons, having in mind above all the neutron bomb.

A rather lengthy discussion took place over the situation in the Middle East. The Congress called for the reconvening of the Geneva conference with the participation of the PLO as a full-fledged member. The same resolution condemned the "reactionary and racist essence" of Zionism and expressed full support for the PLO as the sole legitimate representative of the people of Palestine. Regarding South Africa, Namibia, and Zimbabwe, the delegates affirmed unswerving solidarity with the struggle of the people and students of that area. Plans were laid for a conference of students to promote the struggle against racism and apartheid. Another resolution asked all states to impose a full diplomatic, political, military, and economic boycott on South Africa and Rhodesia.

Problems relating to Northern Ireland and Latin America occupied a number of delegates. The Irish Republican Army was strongly condemned, and plans were laid for a center for solidarity with Chile in "every university" in Latin America. For the first time at a major IUS gathering, a position was taken toward the establishment of "fairer international economic relations." In this context, the delegates praised the decision of some oil-producing countries to aid in the economic development of the Third World.

The Congress called on all friendly international organizations to promote the granting of status "A" in UNESCO and Category "1" at the U.N. to the IUS. A unanimously adopted resolution congratulated the people and the students of the Soviet Union on the sixtieth anniversary of the October Revolution. (BTA, 1 November.)

Not all the delegates agreed with the proceedings or outcome of the Congress. Specifically, some criticized the IUS for following initiatives laid down by Soviet foreign policy. In response, the leadership suggested tongue-in-cheek that perhaps the IUS should "have supported war, the arms race, racism, interference in home affairs, in order to be qualified as a free-minded and independent organization." Apparently the criticism was of little effect, for "attempts at using the Congress for anti-Soviet and anti-Sovietist attacks were spontaneously and firmly rebuffed by the majority of student organizations represented." (BTA, 2 November.)

At an "International Student Forum" jointly organized by the IUS, AASU, and OCLAE, in Tripoli on 11 January, the main topic was "The Tasks and Contribution of the Students and their Organizations in the Struggle for a New International Economic Order in the Interest of Development and Progress." The same topic was later to appear on the agenda of the IUS congress. The participants cited imperialist and neo-colonialist domination and exploitation of the peoples of the developing countries, an international division of labor which runs counter to the interests of the peoples of the developing countries, and attempts by multinational corporations to exploit the developing world as primary causes of the present inequity within the international economic order.

The forum put forward a number of "concrete proposals," including a call for a general intensification of the anti-imperialist, anti-Zionist struggle, and a greater effort to promote the role of intergovernmental organizations in economic development. In this latter respect, it was stated that the IUS, AASU, and OCLAE should strive to increase their participation in all international national, and regional intergovernmental organizations such as UNESCO, ECOSOC, FAO, and UNCTAD in order to involve more effectively these groups in the transformation process. (*World Student News,* no. 5/6.)

Publications. The IUS issues a monthly magazine, *World Student News,* in English, French, German, and Spanish and a fortnightly bulletin, *IUS News Service* in English, French, and Spanish.

Women's International Democratic Federation. The WIDF was founded in Paris in December 1945 at a "Congress of Women" organized by the Communist-dominated Union des Femmes Françaises. The WIDF headquarters was in Paris until 1951, when it was expelled by the French government. It was then moved to East Berlin.

The WIDF holds Category A status with the UN Economic and Social Council, and Category B with UNESCO. It is also on the Special List of the International Labor Organization (ILO) and chairs the Non-Governmental Organization (NGO) subcommittee on the Status of Women in the framework of the NGO's Human Rights Commission. The WIDF has 123 national affiliated organizations in 109 countries, but has not published membership figures since 1966, when it claimed "over 200 million."

Structure and Leadership. The WIDF's highest governing body is the Congress, which meets every four years. Next in authority is the Council, which meets annually and is in control between congresses; it elects the Bureau and the Secretariat. The Bureau meets at least twice a year and implements decisions taken by the Congress and the Council, and is assisted by the Secretariat. Fanny Edelman (Argentina) remains as secretary general, and Freda Brown (Australia) stays as president.

WIDF membership is open to all women's organizations and groups, and in exceptional cases to individuals. The WIDF seeks to maintain contact with nonaffiliated women's groups through its International Liaison Bureau, which has a general headquarters in Copenhagen and a secretariat in Brussels.

Views and Activities. Early in 1977, Brown outlined some of the activities the WIDF would be undertaking. In particular, three seminars were planned, dealing with the role of women in the developing world; the experiences of women in the young African nation-states and the problems they face in overcoming the colonial heritage; the role and tasks of women and their organizations in the struggle against colonialism, neo-colonialism, and apartheid; and women and development. She also described plans for WIDF regional centers in Cuba and Somalia, and national literacy centers in India, Angola, and Portugal. (*Women of the Whole World,* no. 1.)

The Bureau meeting at Lisbon in November 1976 admitted four new members: the Women's Organization of the Bahrain National Liberation Front; the Women's Movement of Guyana; the Progressive Union of Women, Surinam; and the Women's Organization of the Party of Progress and Socialism, Morocco (ibid.). It was decided at the Bureau meeting to hold a seminar on "multinationals" in the latter part of January 1977. On 27 January delegates from thirty-one countries attended the "Latin American Women's Seminar against Multinationals" in Panama. All representatives from Latin America expressed their solidarity with the peoples of Chile and Panama and denounced multinational companies for being the main cause of underdevelopment in their area. (Havana radio, 28 January.)

On 12 February, in East Berlin, over 100 representatives of international, regional, and national organizations attended a meeting of the Women's Congress Continuation Committee. This committee had been set up by the WIDF's World Congress for International Women's Year. Under the slogan "equal rights, development, and peace" the committee evaluated the results of International Women's Year. Looking ahead, four commissions considered proposals for action on peace and disarmament, elimination of illiteracy, preparations for International Children's Year in 1979, and problems of working women. It was decided to continue working as an international committee for the UN's "Women's Decade 1976-1985." (*Neues Deutschland,* 12-17 February.)

Over 200 representatives of women's organizations from Africa, Asia, Europe and America, as well as delegates from UNESCO and other international organizations, participated in the WIDF-sponsored "International Women's Seminar on Colonialism," conducted at Conakry on 6 February. Brown accused the U.S. of being the main instigator of conspiracies against the progressive African countries. The final document pointed to the danger of international imperialism's subversive activities against independent Africa and called on women to deepen the process of relaxing tension. It also emphasized the importance of solidarity between the African women's movement and its counterpart in the Communist countries if a successful struggle against imperialism is to be carried out. (Tass, 10-11 February.)

A member of the WIDF Secretariat spoke about Chile at a press conference in Berlin given by the WIDF and the International Federation of Women in Legal Careers. At the same time, reports were distributed on a fact-finding mission to Brazil, Chile, Argentina, Paraguay, and Uruguay, and an appeal was issued demanding amnesty for political prisoners in Brazil. (*Neues Deutschland,* 28 April; ADN, 1 April.) A few weeks before, the wife of the secretary general of the Chilean Communist party, Luis Corvalán, met Brown and other members of the Secretariat and staff at the WIDF headquarters in East Berlin. She thanked the Federation for its work toward the release of her husband and other political prisoners. Brown indicated that the women's movement would strengthen its solidarity with all political prisoners in Chile and that a Spanish lawyer who was in Chile on the WIDF's behalf would speak about her experiences before the UN Human Rights Commission. (Ibid., 1 February.)

Two WIDF representatives from Finland spoke at a press conference in East Berlin on 17 August after visiting South Africa and Namibia. A report on their visit was given to the UN International Conference for Action against Apartheid. (ADN, 17/20 August.)

Publications. The WIDF publishes a quarterly, *Women of the Whole World,* in English, French, Spanish, German, and Russian, and issues various pamphlets and bulletins.

World Federation of Democratic Youth. Founded in November 1945 at a "World Youth Conference" convened in London by the World Youth Council, the WFDY appeared to represent varying shades of political opinion, but key offices were fast taken by Communists. By 1950 most non-Communists had withdrawn and established their own organization, the World Assembly of Youth. Originally based in Paris, the WFDY was expelled by the French government in 1951. Its headquarters has since been in Budapest.

All youth organizations that contribute to the safeguarding of the activities of young persons are eligible for membership in the WFDY, which claims to enroll 150 million persons from 210 organizations in 104 countries. Most members live in Communist-ruled countries.

Structure and Leadership. The highest governing body of the WFDY is the Assembly, which convenes every three years and to which all affiliated organizations send representatives. The Assembly elects the Executive Committee, which meets at least twice a year. Day-to-day work is conducted by the Bureau and the Secretariat. Piero Lapiccirella (Italy) is president. Early in 1977 it was announced that Jean-Charles Negre (France) had resigned as secretary general (*WFDY News,* no. 1, 1977).

Views and Activities. The final 1976 issue of the WFDY journal noted acceptance of a proposal by the Hungarian Communist Youth League (KISZ) for a "European Youth and Student Conference on Disarmament." This had been first suggested by a Hungarian delegate to the WPC-organized "World Conference to End the Arms Race," Helsinki, September 1976. The new conference was tentatively set for Budapest in the fall of 1977. (Ibid., no. 11-12.)

The WFDY announced at the same time a number of new affiliates: Organization of Austrian Communist Students, Organization of Danish Communist Students, Dominican Revolutionary Youth, General Union of the Iraqi Youth, Progressive Youth League of Malta, Youth of the Progress and Socialism Party of Morocco, Youth of the Union of Popular Forces of Morocco, Norwegian Socialist Youth Union, Philippine National Youth Council, and Communist Youth of Salvador (ibid.).

Discussions on the disarmament conference began early in 1977, when representatives of European member organizations of the WFDY met in Budapest on 5 February (ibid., no. 4, 1977). In March, at Keszthely, Hungary, representatives of twenty-one international and regional organizations and twenty-nine national groups continued the preparations for the conference. The proposals put forward at Keszthely by P. Lapiccirella elicited a "broad exchange of opinions"; that is, there apparently were difficulties at this meeting. Nonetheless, it was decided that two preparatory seminars should be held in Czechoslovakia, one in June and the other in September (ibid., no. 7). In June, representatives of the WFDY, the IUS, the International Union of Socialist Youth, the Council of European National Youth Committees, the European Federation of Liberal and Radical Youth, and the European Union of Young Christian Democrats attended the seminar at the IUS headquarters in Prague (CTK, 23 June). The conference, however, appeared to be pushed back from September to November, and even the latter date was only tentative.

The WFDY Executive Committee, meeting in Havana on 10 April, discussed preparations for the Eleventh World Youth Festival, finances, and elections to the WFDY's executive bodies. The next Executive Committee meeting was scheduled for East Berlin in February 1978 (*WFDY News,* no. 7).

At Budapest in February, WFDY representatives attended a meeting of the International Voluntary Service for Friendship and Solidarity of Youth (SIVSAJ), a WFDY subsidiary. A number of "activities" were reviewed, including a solidarity train for Vietnam, a campaign to equip a school in Guinea-Bissau, and the establishment of a youth center in South Yemen. It was decided that SIVSAJ would introduce Julio Antonio Mella brigades (voluntary work groups) into Mozambique, Somalia, and Guinea-Bissau (ibid., no. 5).

On 13 July the WFDY sent messages of protest to U.S. President Carter and Japanese Prime Minister Fukuda bitterly denouncing "their maneuvers to split Korea and start a war." The protest to Carter stated that the WFDY demands "that you immediately withdraw all U.S. troups and atomic weapons from South Korea in conformity with your campaign commitments." The message to Fukuda stated: ". . . we bitterly denounce the Japanese Government's obstruction to the reunification of Korea and its reinvasion of South Korea." (KCNA, Pyongyang, 13 July.)

Acting along with other front organizations, the WFDY issued a statement of protest regarding the neutron bomb and the arms race. This statement condemned the alleged fresh attack against detente and disarmament by the militaristic circles in the U.S., and particularly criticized propaganda efforts within the U.S. to fill the general public with fear by spreading the myth of the so-called Soviet threat. (MTI, 30 July.)

Eleventh World Youth Festival. According to the WFDY, national committees for the Eleventh World Youth Festival, scheduled for Havana in 1978, had been set up in Cuba, East Germany, USSR, Hungary, Finland, Cyprus, Greece, Sweden, Jamaica, Guyana, France, Poland, Britain, Norway, Czechoslovakia, Somalia, and Mongolia (*WFDY News,* no. 1). On 7 February a consultative meeting of international organizations to prepare for the festival was held in Prague. On 6 April the third meeting of the International Preparatory Committee (IPC) for the festival met in Havana, attended by two hundred representatives from seventy-nine youth organizations in sixty-nine countries and from fifteen international and regional organizations. The head of the Czechoslovak delegation stated: "It is a great victory that the host will be revolutionary Cuba, where Socialism has taken roots in spite of the attacks and intrigues of world imperialism. This fact will be a great support for the revolutionary and democratic forces in Latin America in their struggle for the victory of the revolution." (CTK, 1 April.) The final communiqué stated that a Permanent Commission had been elected, comprising representatives from twenty-nine countries as well as from international organizations; it also indicated that an international solidarity fund had been established. The festival's venue (Havana) and slogan—"For Anti-Imperialist Solidarity, Peace and Friendship"—was confirmed (*Granma,* Havana, 6-9 April; Havana radio, 6 April). Indications of internal difficulties surfaced in an article in the *Guardian* (London, 9 May) which reported that differences had broken out between the delegations from East and West Europe.

Cuban president Castro expressed the hope that 50 million pesos would be collected for the festival. Students working in the sugar cane fields were giving their wages to the fund and donations were expected from other countries, in particular "Socialist ones," he said. In order to allay any fears that the Cuban people would have to sacrifice on behalf of the festival, Castro pointed out that Cuba expected to receive "thousands of tons of food," and so "a minimum of economic sacrifice would be necessary." (Havana radio, 26 July.)

Publications. The WDFY publishes a bimonthly magazine, *World Youth,* in English, French, German, and Arabic. The monthly *WFDY News* appears in English, French, and Spanish.

World Federation of Scientific Workers. The World Federation of Scientific Workers was founded in London in 1946 at the initiative of the British Association of Scientific Workers, with eighteeen organizations of scientists from fourteen countries taking part. Although it purported to be a scientific rather than a political organization, Communists obtained most official posts at the start and have kept control since. The headquarters is in London, but the secretary general's office is in Paris.

WFSW membership is open to organizations of scientific workers everywhere and to individual scientists in countries where no affiliated groups are active. The WFSW claims to represent 300,000 scientists in 28 countries, most of the membership deriving from 14 groups in Communist-ruled countries. The only large non-Communist affiliate, the British Association of Scientific Workers, has 21,000 members. Scientists of distinction who do not belong to an affiliated organization may be nominated for "corresponding membership." The WFSW has a constitution and a "Charter for Scientific Workers" to which affiliates must subscribe.

Structure and Leadership. The governing body of the WFSW is the General Assembly, in which all affiliated organizations are represented. Eleven Assembly meetings have been held, the most recent being in September 1976 in London. Between Assemblies, the Executive Council and its Bureau are responsible for operations. There are three standing committees: the Science Policy Committee, the Socio-Economic Committee, and the Comittee on Peace and Disarmament. Eric Burhop (U.K.) is president and chairman of the Executive Council; J. M. Legay (France) is secretary general, having been elected to this position at the Eleventh Assembly (*Scientific World,* no. 4, 1976).

Views and Activities. The Eleventh Assembly, London, 21 September 1976, heard reports on the strengthening of the WFSW's influence and the usefulness of its cooperation with such organizations as UNESCO, ILO, WFTU, and the Pugwash Movement.

The Assembly adopted resolutions prepared by working groups, including one calling on scientific workers to participate actively in the struggle for disarmament and a special resolution protesting against job discrimination in West Germany. The Union of Democratic Scientists of Federal Germany, the Scientists' Organization of Spain, and organizations from Colombia and Finland were accepted as new affiliates. (*Neues Deutschland,* 24 September; 20-22 September.)

Several delegates from the USSR encountered difficulties in entering the U.K., which caused the meeting to be postponed from 17 to 21 September. Those who received visas on time held a symposium during which they passed a resolution criticizing the delay and describing it as a "violation of the spirit of the decisions of the Conference for Security and Cooperation in Europe" (Tass, 20 September).

A meeting on 4 January at the Moscow House of Scientific and Technical Propaganda celebrated the thirtieth anniversary of the WFSW. President Burhop pointed out to the participants that it was necessary to examine the question of the rights of scientists, whose situation in a number of countries was becoming extremely grave. In some American countries, he said, they were put into concentration camps and tortured, while in contrast, the USSR had created a businesslike atmosphere for scientists which allowed them everything necessary for fruitful endeavors. (Tass, 4 January.)

The Bureau meeting in Morainvilliers, France, on 29-30 January, decided to convene in 1978 an "International Symposium on Multinational Companies" and a "West European Conference on the Implementation of the UNESCO Recommendation on the Status of Scientific Researchers" (*Scientific World,* no. 2, 1977). In the summer, the WFSW issued a brochure criticizing the "U.S. decision" to produce the neutron bomb (*Neues Deutschland,* 30-31 July).

Publications. The official publicaton of the WFSW is the quarterly *Scientific World,* issued in English, French, German, Spanish, Russian, and Czech. The *WFSW Bulletin* is issued irregularly and only to members.

World Federation of Trade Unions. The WFTU, set up at the initiative of the British Trade Union Congress, held its founding Congress in October 1945 in Paris, where its first headquarters was established. Expelled from Paris and next from Vienna for subversive activities, the headquarters has been in Prague since 1956. Some non-Communist affiliates gave up their membership in 1949 to found an alternative organization, the International Conference of Free Trade Unions (ICFTU). The WFTU claims to have about 150 million members in 68 countries, but some 90 percent are from Communist-ruled countries, including over 107 million in the Soviet Union.

Structure and Leadership. The highest WFTU authority, the Congress, meets every four years and is composed of delegates from affiliates in proportion to the number of their members. The Congress, which has no policy-making function and is too large to transact much specific business, elects the General Council, Executive Bureau, and Secretariat. The General Council has about sixty-six regular and sixty-eight deputy members representing the national affiliates and eleven Trade Union Internationals (TUIs). The latest Congress, held in Varna, Bulgaria, in 1973, reelected Enrique Pastorino (Uruguay) as president and Pierre Gensous (France) as secretary general. At the December 1976 Bureau meeting, A.I. Shibaev the new chairman of the All-Union Central Council of Trade Unions of the USSR, replaced Alexander Shelepin (USSR) on the WFTU's Bureau and General Council (*Trud,* Moscow, 5 December). The Executive Bureau is the most powerful body of the WFTU, having assumed much of the authority which, before 1969, was enjoyed by the Secretariat that was revamped by the 1969 Congress and reduced to six members, including the secretary general.

The TUIs represent workers of particular trades and crafts. One of their main purposes is to recruit local unions which do not, through their national centers, belong to the WFTU. Though the TUIs are in theory independent, their policies and finances are controlled by the WFTU department having supervision over their particular areas. The WFTU General Council in December 1966 decided that each TUI should have its own constitution; this move, taken to bolster the appearance of independence, had the purpose of allowing the TUIs to join international bodies as individual organizations.

In recent years the WFTU has moved vigorously to establish working relationships with non-Communist trade unions and intergovernmental organizations. In this area of operation one of the most important structural linkages is the WFTU's "Special Commission on UN Agencies," created in 1967 to facilitate WFTU activities in the UN. The WFTU enjoys Category A Status with a number of UN agencies, and has permanent representatives at the UN in New York and at the International Labor Organization (ILO), the Food and Agriculture Agency (FAO), and UNESCO.

Views and Activities. Shortly before the opening of the Fifteenth WFTU Bureau meeting, in New Delhi, December 1976, Pastorino and Gensous held a press conference at which they spoke of the important issues facing their organization. High on the agenda was the task of "strengthening solidarity" and "unity of action of world trade union centers at different levels." (Tass, 9 December). Indeed this theme of trade union cooperation was to underlie most of the WFTU activity throughout 1977. In line with this call for greater unity, the Asian affiliates of the WFTU met in New Delhi on 1 December 1976 and pledged themselves to a common struggle for independent economic development (*Patriot,* New Delhi, 2-3 December). On 3 December the Bureau opened its session, with representatives from twenty-nine countries. Among appeals issued at the end of the session were those dealing with the formation of a "United Asian Trade Union Conference," the drive for a "new economic order," and the initial call for the Ninth WFTU Congress, to be held in Prague in April 1978 (ibid., 3-5 December; *Trud,* 5 December). Gensous announced that he anticipated well over 200 million workers to be represented at the Congress; the main themes, he indicated, would be "workers' unity," the role of the working class in the struggle for a new international economic order, and economic development (*New Age,* New Delhi, 12 December).

In January 1977 the WFTU Secretariat met to discuss preparations for a week of solidarity with the workers and peoples of South Africa, 17-22 January. The WFTU noted that other trade union organizations, such as the International Confederation of Free Trade Unions and the World Confederation of Labor, had joined in these preparations (CTK, 7 January). The conference for solidarity with South Africa opened in Luanda on 31 January, officially entitled the "First Pan-African Trade Union Conference for Solidarity with the Workers and People of South Africa," with delegates from African countries and countries in Europe and Latin America. The Communist states' support for the anti-imperialist fight in Africa was praised by the delegates, and an appeal was issued for the formation of an international trade union committee for solidarity with the people of South Africa. (*Neues Deutschland,* 1-3 February.)

Early in December 1976, members of the WFTU's Education Department met with representatives of affiliated unions in Bulgaria, Cuba, Czechoslovakia, France, East Germany, Hungary, Syria, and the USSR to review training procedures for trade union officers in developing countries. During 1976 some 600 trade unionists attended courses offered by the Department, and more than 1,200 persons from the developing countries participated in other training activities sponsored by the WFTU. Nonetheless, it was decided that more effort should be placed in training trade unionists from the developing world. Also stressed was the need for further cooperation with the ILO, especially its Workers' Education Department (*Flashes,* no. 45, 7 December). Ibrahim Zacharia represented the WFTU at a consultation between the three international trade union organizations (WFTU, ICFTU, and WCL) and the FAO, at the FAO's headquarters in Rome in November 1976. Delegations from the Agricultural and Food Workers' TUIs were also present. It was agreed that a regional consultation between FAO member countries and the international trade union organizations on the subject of Asia and the Far East should be convened in October 1977 (ibid.). On 30 June 1977, Gensous led a WFTU delegation to the ILO's "Second International Trade Union Conference against Aparthied" (ibid., no. 25).

Late in 1976 a preparatory committee was set up for a "World Trade Union Conference of Working Youth," with participating representatives from the WFTU and trade unons in Algeria, Cyprus, Cuba, France, Iraq, Japan, East Germany, and the USSR (ibid., no. 2 , 1977). Representatives from ninety-nine organizations from seventy-six countries, the ILO, and UNESCO attended the subsequent conference in Nicosia, Cyprus, on 20 March. (*Neues Deutschland,* 9 March; *Flashes,* no. 9.)

Representatives from the WFTU, the Arab Labor Organization, the Organization of African Trade Union Unity (OATUU), and twenty-one countries attended on 7 February a meeting of the WFTU's Economic and Social Affairs Committee. Enrique Pastorino opened the meeting by pointing out that even during "the short period of little more than two years since its foundation, the committee had proven capable of providing efficient help in solving many social problems faced by workers." He went on to say that the scope and activity of the committee would expand, and that representatives from other trade unions would be welcome in the committee regardless of their political views or the social systems they represent. The secretary of the committee said that three international seminars would take place in 1977: the economic crisis in the West, the social welfare position of the working class, and the workers' participation in company planning and management. (MTI, 7-9 February.)

The Bureau and General Council met on 13-16 April in Warsaw. Gensous delivered the major address, calling for new economic relations between capitalist and Socialist countries and capitalist and developing countries. He also spoke in support of the Helsinki Agreement and against the arms race. In closing, he warned the delegates of those forces seeking to "hamper" the implementation of the Helsinki Agreement. In line with its desire for diversity, the WFTU sought to include the ICFTU and the WCL in its Ninth Congress, in 1978. Acting on the basis of this position, the WFTU invited non-WFTU members to join the committee drawing up the principal documents for the congress; it proposed as well to invite non-members to participate in future Council sessions. (PAP, 13 April;

Flashes, no. 14.) During the council session, six new affiliates joined the WFTU, from the developing world. A representative of the Italian General Confederation of Labor (CGIL) criticized the economic and social sections of the Council report given by Gensous, which he said dealt in a generalized, inadequate, and propagandistic manner with the situation in capitalist countries and paid no attention to problems in the Socialist states. He indicated that the Italians would be looking closely at the preparations for the congress to see if diversity actually was allowed. [It should be noted that the CGIL is no longer a full member of the WFTU. It is an associate member, and as such attends meetings in a consultative capacity.] (*L'Unitá,* Rome, 23 April.)

The dialogue between the WFTU and the CGIL continued at the latter's congress at Rimini, 6 June. At this congress, Gensous once again turned to the topic of trade union unity, warning against complacency about the state of relations between the three international trade union organizations and particularly about the virtual non-existence of relations between the WFTU and the ICFTU. He asked if unity must wait until an agreement was reached on all objectives, or whether there could not be cooperation now on common critical issues such as a new international economic order, the struggle against multinational corporations, and the arms race.

Publications. The most important publication of the WFTU is an illustrated magazine, *World Trade Union Movement,* circulated in some seventy countries in English, French, Spanish, German, Russian, and other languages. *Flashes,* published several times a month in four languages, is an information bulletin of four to five pages.

World Peace Council. The "world peace movement" headed by the WPC dates from August 1948, when a "World Congress of Intellectuals for Peace" in Wroclaw, Poland, set up an organization called the International Liaison Committee of Intellectuals. This committee in April 1949 convened a "First World Peace Congress" in Paris. The congress launched a "World Committee of Partisans of Peace" which in November 1950 was renamed the World Peace Council. Originally based in Paris, the WPC was expelled in 1951 by the French government. It moved first to Prague and then in 1954 to Vienna, where it adopted the name "World Council of Peace." Although outlawed in Austria in 1957, it continued its operations in Vienna under the cover of a new organization, the International Institute of Peace (IIP), subsequently referred to by WPC members as the "Scientific-Theoretical Workshop of the WPC" (CTK, 16 December 1971). In September 1968 the World Council of Peace transferred its headquarters to Helsinki, while the IIP remained in Vienna. Although no formal announcement was made, the World Council of Peace has reverted to its earlier name, the World Peace Council.

Structure and Leadership. The WPC is organized on a national basis with Peace Committees and other affiliated groups claimed in 120 countries. No precise figure is available on the total individual membership. The highest authority is the 600-member Council, which elects the 101-member Presidential Committee, which in turn elects the 24-member Bureau and 18-member Secretariat. Memberships of these groups is divided among representatives from various countries. Communist-front organizations such as the IUS, WFDY, WFSW, WFTU, and WIDF are represented on the Presidential Committee.

Amendments adopted at the February 1974 meeting of the Council require it to meet every three years, instead of every two, and urge the national peace movements—Peace Committees—to meet annually. The Presidential Committee meets once a year, while the Bureau normally meets three or four times a year to review international events and the Council's work and to execute decisions of the Presidential Committee. It appears, however, that the Bureau has authority to act independently on a wide range of matters. The executive bodies of the IIP—ostensibly independent of those of the WPC, but in fact elected by the Council—are the seven-member Presidium and thirty-member Executive Committee. At the May 1977 Council session, in Warsaw, a new Council was elected, with Romesh Chandra, formerly secretary general, elected as president. Twenty vice-presidents, a Bureau, and a Presidential Committee were also chosen. (*New Perspectives,* no. 6, 1976, and no. 1, 1977.)

The WPC has "Consultation and Association, Category A Status" with UNESCO.

Views and Activities. At its Bureau meeting in Caracas, December 1976, the WPC set forth its "Action Program" for 1977. This Program can be broken down into geographical and functional activities and conferences.

    —*Europe:* Campaign to implement the decisions reached at the CSCE Conference.

    —*Asia:* National seminars on peace and security; Asia Week, 5-12 April; and campaigns against military pacts and bases.

    —*Africa:* Increased cooperation with the Organization of African Unity; visits by WPC delegations; and African Liberation Week, 18-25 May.

    —*Middle East:* Campaigns for peace and justice.

    —*Mediterranean:* Campaigns on behalf of peace, security, and cooperation; and an international conference on these topics in Athens, 25-27 November.

    —*Latin America:* National seminars opposing foreign military bases; and campaigns for ending colonialism, with special emphasis on Puerto Rico and Panama.

    —*Actions for development, economic independence, and against neo-colonialism:* Campaigns to rally public opinion for the implementation of the UN Declaration on a new international economic order and its Program of Action, and of other UN, UNCTAD and "non-aligned" decisions on development which have been supported by the WPC; the exposure of imperialist distortions on the Third World; and an "International Week of Mass Mobilization against Multinational Corporations."

    —*Racism:* Preparations for a "World Conference Against Racism," 1978; support for national campaigns against racism; and solidarity with African liberation movements.

    —*Human Rights:* Meetings of the WPC International Commission of Inquiry into the Violations of Human Rights, including a session on "job denial" in Federal Germany; campaigns against the violations of human rights, and for the release of political prisoners in many countries.

    —*Cooperation with the UN and its Specialized Agencies, with the OAU, and with other intergovernmental organizations:* Strengthening the work of the WPC representative's office in Geneva and setting up offices in New York (UN) and Paris (UNESCO).

    —*Mobilization of public opinion agianst the policy of destabilization:* "World Conference against the Destabilization Conspiracies by Imperialism."

The first major 1977 conference sponsored by the WPC was the World Forum of Peace Forces, Moscow, 11-14 January. Romesh Chandra, speaking both as president of the International Continuing Liaison Council (CLC), established by the World Congress of Peace Forces in 1973, and as secretary general of the WPC, stated that the Forum would consider questions related to the relaxation of international tensions. More specifically, Sean MacBride, chairman of the International Peace Bureau, stressed the importance of mobilizing public opinion against the arms race and the large industrial and financial complexes that benefit from it. (Tass, 13 January.) The Conference opened with 500 delegates from 220 national organizations in 115 countries and from 70 international organizations (Moscow radio, 19 January). The discussions at the Forum were concentrated within thirteen working groups, each of which dealt with aspects of detente: "The concept of detente, ways of strengthening it, overcoming obstacles to it, as well as the relationship of detente to the most essential international issues of our time—disarmament, national independence and liberation, the new international economic order, democratic freedoms, and human rights." Overall, the talks focused on the new role of world public opinion and on the problems of cooperation among the peace forces of the world. (Tass, 16 January.) Prior to the ending of the Forum, a permanent body entitled "International Forum for Liaison among Peace Forces" [this appears to be an enlargement of the CLC] was created with Romesh Chandra as president. Among the several vice-presidents elected were representatives of the WPC's Presidential Committee, the IIP, the International Peace Bureau, the Women's International League for Peace and Freedom, and individuals from various countries. Oleg Kharkhardin (USSR) was selected as executive secretary. (*Neues Deutschland,* 14-17 January.) In his closing address Chandra called the Forum an unprecedented event in the history of non-governmental action for it had succeeded in bringing together representatives of very different political parties and in creating a new permanent body to carry on the struggle for peace (*New Age,* 23 January). As the Forum ended, the Japanese delegation publicly expressed reservations about the procedures taken to release the final statement and the emphasis placed in the statement on "detente" as the "sole and supreme road to peace" (KYODO, Tokyo, 17 January).

Within weeks of the Moscow Forum, several important WPC meetings were held in Sofia. On 9 February, Chandra opened a gathering of representatives of European peace movements. In his address, he stressed the continued importance of public opinion in the implementation of the Final Act of Helsinki. He reminded the delegates that certain elements were trying "to minimize its significance and to distort its principles. They say they support Helsinki but they continue to arm themselves." (BTA, 9 February.) Several proposals were adopted in response to Chandra's call for increased public pressure behind the Helsinki Accords: mass meetings would be held in every large European city in order that the peace movements could make public their programs for detente and disarmament, and the WPC would send its own delegation to the Belgrade meeting to report on the activities of the national peace movements and to record the number of signatories to the Second Stockholm appeal. (*MTI,* 10 February.)

Immediately after that the Presidential Committee gathered in Sofia to discuss the role of public opinion in implementing the conclusions of the Helsinki Conference, the campaign for signatures to the New Stockholm Appeal (see *YICA, 1976,* p. 597) and preparations for the WPC's thirtieth anniversary (Sofia radio, 11 February). The role of public opinion appeared to dominate the discussions. Following the meeting of the Presidential Committe, an International Preparatory Committee met in Sofia to begin preparations for the World Assembly of the Builders of Peace. Again stressing the role of public opinion, the Committee asked national peace groups, political parties, TU organizations, women's and youth organizations, religious, social, and cultural groups to gather in Warsaw on 6 May to discuss the "consolidation of detente and the furthering of disarmament." (Ibid., 14 February.)

Throughout the spring, most of the WPC's efforts were centered on the upcoming World Assembly. In early March delegations from the WPC toured Africa, Latin America, Western Europe, and the Caribbean to rally support for the Assembly. Round tables, forums, and seminars were held in a variety of locales. In April Chandra stated that the Assembly would be a "Parliament of the Peoples," and would be open to all political parties and organizations. It would focus, he said, on a wide range of issues (the list he submitted corresponded closely to the WPC's Action Program for 1977). (PAP, 19 March, 1 April.)

The Assembly opened in Warsaw on 6 May. In attendance were 1,500 delegates from 125 countries and 50 international organizations. Twenty working groups dealt with various issues set before the Assembly. Although the list was lengthy, covering matters from the Middle East to Human Rights, the key items were detente (more often than not phrased as "military détente") and disarmament. The stress on disarmament was particularly notable in the reports found in the Soviet press: Tass stated (6 May) that special significance should be given to ending the dangerous arms race. *Pravda* (9 May) noted that the delegates had concluded that those peoples commited to disarmament should increase their "vigilance in the face of the imperialists' intrigues and to be more active in exposing attempts to deceive the peoples by means of propaganda campaigns calculated to conceal the real culprits of the arms race."

During the debates in the Assembly on Human Rights, the delegates voiced condemnation of the reactionary regimes in capitalist countries where basic human rights were violated. It was stated repeatedly in these discussions that the "campaign currently developing in the West with respect to the Socialist countries" was "a hypocritical, futile attempt to undermine the efforts of the supporters of peace and to discredit the Socialist countries in their eyes." Linking the issues of human rights to the Helsinki Agreements, "all speakers condemned the attempts by the opponents of détente to poison the atmosphere of the upcoming Belgrade Conference" by improperly inserting the charge that "basket three" of Helsinki had been violated by the Socialist camp. (*Pravda*, 9 May.)

Attending the Assembly were representatives from several inter-governmental and non-governmental agencies, including the UN, UNESCO, and UNCTAD. The delegates stated that greater cooperation between the WPC and these organizations would help consolidate peace and understanding between nations (PAP, 9 May). Shortly before, the Chinese spokesman at the UN Special Committee on Decolonization, which accepted an invitation to send a representative to the Assembly, expressed disapproval of the "committee's representation at conferences of the WPC—the highest tool of a certain super-power" (*Documents of the Special Committee Session,* 2 May).

During a meeting of religious "personalities" at the World Congress of Peace Forces in Moscow in October 1973, the idea emerged for an international conference of religious leaders. Later it was stated that the initiative for this conference came from the Russian Orthodox church (Tass, 28 September 1976). A preparatory committee was established in 1973; in the spring of 1976 several seminars and meetings were held by this committee, one of which was organized by the Christian Peace Conference (ADN, 1 March 1976). (For additional information on the CPC, see *YICA, 1976* and *1977.*) The "World Conference of Religious Workers for Lasting Peace, Disarmament, and Just Relations between Peoples" met in Moscow on 6-10 June 1977. Attending were 700 "Christians, Buddhists, Hindus, Jews, Moslems, Shintoists and Sikhs from 107 countries, including representatives or observers from the World Council of Churches, the Roman Catholic Church, the Lutheran World Federation, the Baptist World Alliance, the World Muslim Congress, the Asian Buddhist Conference for Peace, and the All-Africa Conference of Churches" (*New Times,* Moscow, no. 25). Patriarch Pimen of Moscow and All-Russia and Romesh Chandra delivered the major speeches. The Conference was divided into three working groups, focusing respectively on "lasting peace, disarmament, and just relations between peoples." The final appeals of the Conference called for the continuation of detente, a world disarmament conference, and the mobilization by religious leaders of public opinion in favor of general and complete disarmament. (Ibid.)

Representatives of the WPC and the AAPSO gathered in Lisbon on 20 January to begin preparations for a world conference against apartheid (*Neues Deutschland,* 25 January). Within weeks, a delegation from the Portuguese preparatory commmmittee visited the AAPSO headquarters in Cairo. It was at this occasion that the agenda for a second preparatory meeting was set forth (*Diario de Noticias,* Lisbon, 19 March). This second preparatory meeting took place in Lisbon on 23 April and was attended by representatives from twenty-three countries. At this meeting strong criticism was expressed of Western support for the South African regime (*Neues Deutschland,* 26 April). The conference itself convened in Lisbon on 16 June, entitled "World Conference against Apartheid, Racism and Colonialism in South Africa," with 400 representatives from twenty countries, fifteen international organizations, and five UN agencies present, along with a number of individuals from various liberation movements. The final declaration demanded that the UN Security Council prevent foreign investment in South Africa and called for the withdrawal of all multinational companies from South Africa, for an arms embargo on that country, and for condemnation of the U.S., France, West Germany, and Israel for complicity in the alleged South African nuclear program. Finally the declaration strongly supported the armed struggles of the people against the governments of Rhodesia, Namibia, and South Africa, and urged the Arab and non-aligned countries to consider an economic boycott of the Western countries maintaining trade relations with Rhodesia and South Africa, (Lisbon radio, 20 June.)

In November 1976 a preparatory meeting for an "International Conference for Peace, Security and Cooperation in the Mediterranean" was held in Athens. In July 1977 the preparatory commission gathered in Athens to continue planning for the conference, which was scheduled for 25-26 November. Key items discussed at this meeting were the Middle East, Cyprus, disarmament, and economic cooperation within the Mediterranean area. Chandra, during an address to the commission, claimed that there was an "imperialist conspiracy" to partition Cyprus and turn it into a NATO military base. (*Rizospastis,* Athens, 22-23 July.)

The International Liaison Forum of Peace Forces, which had been established at the January gathering of the World Forum of Peace Forces and which subsequently acted as the operational arm of the WPC on matters of disarmament, met several times during 1977. At its June meeting, Chandra, V. Shaposhnikov, deputy head of the International Department of the Soviet Communist party's Central Committee and Risto Hyvarinen, special representative of the UN Secretary General at the Geneva Conference of the Disarmament Committee, discussed ways that various political forces and public opinion could be marshaled on behalf of the upcoming UN session on disarmament. More specifically, they discussed the possibility of a major international conference linked with the UN session on disarmament. (*Neues Deutschland,* 14 June.)

Christian Peace Conference. The Christian Peace Conference (CPC), which has been under Soviet domination since 1968, is noted here because it operates in tandem with the WPC and claims to have members in forty-eight countries. Early in 1977 Dr. K. Toth (Hungary), secretary general, three vice-presidents and the international secretaries from fifteen countries attended the CPC's International Secretariat meeting in Prague, 11 January. The final communiqué expressed support for the disarmament proposals contained in the declaration of the meeting of the Political Consultative Committee of the Warsaw Treaty in Bucharest the previous November and welcomed the convening of a special UN session on disarmament in 1978. It pledged as well support for UN proposals for a conference against apartheid in Africa and for economic sanctions against Chile. In the area of human rights, the delegates expressed their determination to defend these rights, and to oppose any attempts by reactionary forces to use this issue of human rights as a "pretext for reviving the cold war spirit and impeding detente." (CTK, 7, 13, 17 January; *CPC Information,* no. 209.)

Late in January, Toth attended a meeting in Dar-es-Salaam to prepare for an "African Christian Peace Conference" in Freetown, Sierra Leone. In early February, the CPC's president, Metropolitan Nikodim (USSR), invited the vice-presidents and secretary general to Leningrad for talks. The health of the CPC's president—he has suffered five heart attacks—was discussed and suggestions were made to lighten his duties. Also reviewed were the preparations for the All-Christian Peace Assembly (*CPC Information,* no. 210-211).

The Working Committee Meeting, Limuru, Kenya, 22 April, brought together delegates from twenty-two countries and five continents. The main topics discussed were Christians' contribution to peace, justice, and freedom in Africa; the "oppression of progressive forces" in Latin America; preparations for the All-Africa Christian Peace Assembly in Sierra Leone, 14 December 1977; and the All-Christian Peace Assembly in Prague, 22 June, 1978. Metropolitan Nikodim indicated in a letter that for health reasons he was unable to bear the whole burden of the presidency and wished Metropolitan Philaret to be "co-opted" to the Working Committee and elected a vice-president as a representative of the Russian Orthodox church. This proposal was agreed to by the Working Committee. Prior to the end of the session, resolutions were adopted on South Africa, the Indian Ocean, and the Middle East. It was agreed that a session of the Working Committee would be held in Federal Germany on 11 November. (Ibid., no. 215.)

Throughout the spring there were various CPC gatherings. A CPC-sponsored meeting in Mexico, 7 March, agreed to set up a regional CPC committee for Latin America and the Caribbean. The CPC Working Committee meeting in Limuru in April accepted the recommendations of the Mexican session (ibid., no. 216). In Prague, 16 May, a meeting with the Berlin Conference of Catholic Christians discussed the need to counter attempts to revive the Cold War. A communiqué indicated that the Helsinki provisions had also been reviewed (CTK, 18 May). A CPC delegation visited Ulan Bator on 5 April for talks on cooperation with representatives of the Asian Buddhist Peace Conference (*CPC Information,* no. 214).

The International Secretariat met in Bucharest, 16 June, and in Vogelenzang, Holland, 9 September. At this latter session, discussions dealt with "Christian Solidarity with the Third World," and preparations for the Secretariat meeting in Federal Germany, 11 November (ibid., nos. 218-220).

Publications. The WPC issues a semimonthly bulletin, *Peace Courier,* in English, French, Spanish, and German; a quarterly journal, *New Perspectives,* in English and French; an occasional *Letter to National Committees;* and a *Letter* to members. Several booklets were published in 1977: *Latin America: For Economic Independence, Against Fascism and Neo-Fascism,* an account of the Bureau meeting in Caracas in December 1976; and *International Public Opinion and the Helsinki Final Act,* an account of the Presidential Committee meeting in Sofia in February 1977.

California State University, Stanislaus   Paul F. Magnelia

SELECT BIBLIOGRAPHY 1976-77

GENERAL ON COMMUNISM

Ahlberg, Rene. *Die sozialistische Buerokratie.* Stuttgart: Kohlhammer, 1976. 120 pp.

Bauman, Zygmunt. *Socialism: the Active Utopia.* London: Allen & Unwin, 1976. 150 pp.

Besançon, Alain. *Court traité de soviétologie.* Paris: Hachette, 1976. 125 pp.

Broué, Pierre. *La question chinoise dans l'internationale communiste: 1926-1927.* Paris: Etudes et documentation internationales, 1976. 539 pp.

Brown, Archie, and Jack Gray, eds. *Political Culture and Political Change in Communist States.* New York: Holmes & Meier, 1977. 286 pp.

Byrnes, Robert F. *Soviet-American Academic Exchanges, 1958-1975.* Bloomington; Indiana University Press, 1976. 275 pp.

Cell, Charles P. *Revolution at Work.* New York: Academic Press, 1977. 240 pp.

Compton, P.A. and M. Pesci, eds. *Regional Development and Planning: British and Hungarian Case Studies.* Budapest: Akademiai Kiado, 1976. 233 pp.

Fetscher, Irving, ed. *Grundebegriffe des Marxismus.* Hamburg: Hoffmann & Campe, 1976. 303 pp.

Flechtheim, Osip K. *Weltkommunismus im Wandel.* Berlin: Europäische Ideen, 1977. 276 pp.

Geschwender, James. *Class, Race and Worker Insurgency.* New York: Cambridge University Press, 1977. 240 pp.

Gosztony, Peter. *Hitlers fremde Heere.* Duesseldorf: Econ Verlag, 1976. 548 pp.

Gurley, John G. *Challengers to Capitalism: Marx, Lenin, and Mao.* San Francisco: San Francisco Book Co., 1976. 175 pp.

Hansen, Emmanuel. *Frantz Fanon: Social and Political Thought.* Columbus: Ohio State University Press, 1977. 232 pp.

Hegedüs, Andrās. *The Structure of Socialist Society.* New York: St. Martin's, 1977. 230 pp.

Khamei, Anvar. *Le revisionnisme de Marx à Mao-Tse-Toung.* Paris: Anthropos, 1976. 423 pp.

Kolakowski, Leszek et al. *Radical Visions of the Future.* Boulder: Westview Press, 1977. 197 pp.

Labrande, Christian. *La Première Internationale.* Paris: Union Générale d' Editions, 1976. 445 pp.

Lane, David. *The Socialist Industrial State.* Boulder: Westview, 1976. 230 pp.

Lévy, Bernard-Henri. *La barbarie à visage humain.* Paris: Grasset, 1977. 240 pp.

Loeber, Dietrich Andre, ed. *East-West Trade: A Sourcebook on the International Economic Relations of Socialist Countries and their Legal Aspects.* Dobbs Ferry, N.Y.: Oceana Publications, 1976-77. 4 vols. 3,196 pp.

Lowenthal, Richard, *Model or Ally? The Communist Powers and the Developing Countries.* New York: Oxford University Press, 1977. 400 pp.

McCauley, Martin, ed. *Communist Power in Europe, 1944-1949.* New York: Harper & Row, 1977. 256 pp.

Meissner, Boris, ed. *Jahrbuch fuer Ost-West-Fragen 1976: Elemente des Wandels in der oestlichen Welt.* Cologne: Markus, 1976. 404 pp.

Moeller, Dietrich. *Karl Radek in Deutschland.* Cologne: Wissenschaft & Politik, 1976. 303 pp.

Pearce, Frank. *Crimes of the Powerful: Marxism, Crime and Deviance.* London: Pluto, 1976. 172 pp.

Pimlott, Ben. *Labour and the Left in the 1930s.* New York: Cambridge University Press, 1977. 270 pp.

Revel, Jean-François. *The Totalitarian Temptation.* New York: Doubleday, 1977. 311 pp.

Rice, Edward E. *Marx, Engels, and the Workers of the World.* New York: Four Winds, 1977. 184 pp.

Rothenberg, Morris. *Whither China: The View from the Kremlin.* Washington, D.C.: Center for Advanced International Studies, University of Miami, 1977. 310 pp.

Schulz, Eberhard, ed. *Die Ostbeziehungen der Europäischen Gemeinschaft.* Munich: Oldenbourg, 1977. 272 pp.

Sen Gupta, Bhabani. *Soviet-Asian Relations in the 1970s and Beyond.* New York: Praeger, 1976. 368 pp.

Sïk, Ota. *The Third Way: Marxist-Leninist Theory and Modern Industrial Society.* White Plains, N.Y.: International Arts & Sciences Press, 1977. 512 pp.

Staar, Richard F., ed. *1977 Yearbook on International Communist Affairs.* Stanford: Hoover Institution Press, 1977. 612 pp.

Ulam, Adam B. *Ideologies and Illusions: Revolutionary Thought from Herzen to Solzhenitsyn.* Cambridge: Harvard University Press, 1976. 335 pp.

Vree, Dale. *On Synthesizing Marxism and Christianity.* New York: Wiley, 1976. 206 pp.

Weeks, Albert L. *The Troubled Détente.* New York: New York University Press, 1976. 190 pp.

Wilhelm, Donald, *Creative Alternatives to Communism.* London: Macmillan, 1977. 173 pp.

Zarodov, K. I., ed. *Kommunisty mira—o svoikh partiiakh.* Prague: 1976. 199 pp.

SOVIET UNION

Allworth, Edward, ed. *Nationality Group Survival in Multi-Ethnic States: Shifting Support Patterns in the Soviet-Baltic Region.* New York: Praeger, 1977. 299 pp.

Anin, David, ed. *Die russische Revolution von 1917 in Berichten ihrer Akteure.* Munich: Berchmanns, 1976. 429 pp.

Avtorkhanov, Abdurakhman, *Tekhnologiia vlasti.* Frankfurt: Possev, 1976. 809 pp.

Baschanov, Boris. *Ich war Stalins Sekretaer.* Berlin: Ullstein, 1977. 269 pp.

Beckmann, Oda, and Sven H. Koch. *Freund und Fiend im Spiegel der sowjetischen Karikatur.* Bonn: Hochwacht, 1977. 168 pp.

Berner, Wolfgang et al. eds. *Sowjetunion 1975/76.* Munich: Hanser, 1976. 308 pp.

Bettelheim, Charles. *Class Struggles in the U.S.S.R., The First Period: 1917-1923.* New York: Monthly Review, 1976. 567 pp.

Bloch, Sidney, and Peter Reddaway. *Psychiatric Terror: How Soviet Psychiatry is Used to Suppress Dissent.* New York: Basic Books, 1977. 510 pp.

Borcke, Astrid von. *Die Urspruenge des Bolschewismus.* Munich: Berchmanns, 1977. 646 pp.

Boffa, Guiseppe. *Storia dell'Unione Sovietica.* Rome: Mondadori, 1976. 779 pp.

Chalidze, Valery. *Criminal Russia.* New York: Random House, 1977. 240 pp.

Dallin, Alexander, ed. *The Twenty-fifth Congress of the CPSU: Assessment and Context.* Stanford: Hoover Institution Press, 1977. 127 pp.

Deane, Michael J. *Political Control of the Soviet Armed Forces.* New York: Crane & Russak, 1977. 270 pp.

Deutscher, Tamara, ed. *Not by Politics Alone: the Other Lenin.* Westport: Lawrence Hill, 1976. 256 pp.

Dmytryshyn, Basil. *A History of Russia.* Englewood Cliffs, N.J.: Prentice Hall, 1977. 645 pp.

Douglass, Joseph D., Jr. *The Soviet Theater Nuclear Offensive.* Washington, D.C.: U.S. Government Printing Office, 1976. 248 pp.

Dunham, Vera. *In Stalin's Time.* Cambridge: Cambridge University Press, 1976. 283 pp.

Dunlop, John B. *The New Russian Revolutionaries.* Belmont, Ma.: Nordland, 1976. 344 pp.

Dunn, Dennis J., ed. *Religion and Modernization in the Soviet Union.* Boulder: Westview Press, 1977. 442 pp.

Dyomin, Mikhail. *The Day is Born of Darkness.* New York: Knopf, 1976. 368 pp.

Ferro, Marc. *La Révolution de 1917: Octobre.* Paris: Aubier Montaigne, 1977. 517 pp.

Fitzpatrick, Sheila, ed. *Cultural Revolution in Russia, 1928-1931.* Bloomington: Indiana University Press, 1977. 352 pp.

Geierhos, Wolfgang. *Vera Zasulic und die russische revolutionäre Bewegung.* Munich: Oldenbourg, 1977. 314 pp.

Gerson, Lennard D. *The Secret Police in Lenin's Russia.* Philadelphia: Temple Univeristy Press, 1976. 322 pp.

Geyer, Dietrich, ed. *Sowjetunion: Aussenpolitik, 1955-1973, Osteuropa-Handbuch.* Cologne, Boehlau, 1976. 878 pp.

Gilbert, Stephen P. *Soviet Images of America.* New York: Crane & Russak, 1977. 167 pp.

Golub, P.A. et al., comps. *Bor'ba partii bol'shevikov za armiiu v sotsialisticheskoi revoliutsii: sbornik dokumentov.* Moscow: Politizdat, 1977. 518 pp.

Halevy, Zvi. *Jewish Schools under Czarism and Communism.* New York: Springer, 1976. 298 pp.

Hill, Roland J. *Soviet Political Elites: The Case of Tiraspol.* New York: St. Martin's, 1977. 226 pp.

Hingley, Ronald. *The Russian Mind.* New York: Scribner's, 1977. 307 pp.

Juviler, Peter H. *Revolutionary Law and Order: Politics and Social Change in the USSR.* New York: Free Press, 1976. 274 pp.

Kemp, John L.H. *The Russian Revolution: A Study in Mass Mobilization.* London: Weidenfeld & Nicolson, 1977. 640 pp.

Kennan, G.F. *The Cloud of Danger.* Boston: Atlantic-Little Brown, 1977. 234 pp.

Klinghoffer, Arthur Jay. *The Soviet Union and International Oil Politics.* New York: Columbia University Press, 1977. 389 pp.

Kochan, Miriam. *The Last Days of Imperial Russia.* New York: Macmillan, 1976. 224 pp.

Kopelev, Lev. *To Be Preserved Forever.* Philadelphia: Lippincott, 1977. 268 pp.

Laird, Roy D., Joseph Hajda, and Betty A. Laird, eds. *The Future of Agriculture in the Soviet Union and Eastern Europe. The 1976-1980 Five-Year Plans.* Boulder: Westview, 1977. 242 pp.

Liebman, Marcel. *Connaitre Lénine.* Vervillers, Belgium: Marabout, 1976. 254 pp.

Linhart, Robert. *Lénine, les paysans.* Paris: Editions du Seuil, 1976, 171 pp.

Loewenthal, Richard, ed. *Die Sowjetunion als Weltmacht.* Berlin: Duncker & Humblot, 1976. 144 pp.

Luchterhandt, Otto. *Der Sowjetstaat und die Russisch-Orthodox Kirche.* Cologne: Wissenschaft & Politik, 1976. 320 pp.

McCauley, Martin. *Khrushchev and the Development of Soviet Agriculture: The Virgin Lands Programme, 1953-1964.* New York: Holmes & Meier, 1976. 232 pp.

Maddox, Robert J. *The Unknown War with Russia.* San Rafael, Ca.: Presidio Press, 1977. 156 pp.

Maximov, Vladimir E., ed. *Kontinent 2.* Garden City, N.Y.: Doubleday, 1977. 247 pp.

Medvedev, Roy A. ed. *The Samizdat Register.* New York: Norton, 1977. 320 pp.

Mikulinsky, S.R. et al., eds. *The Scientific Intelligentsia in the USSR.* Moscow: Progress, 1976. 247 pp.

Mrazkova, Daniela, and Vladimir Remes, eds. *The Russian War, 1941-1945.* New York: Dutton, 1977. 152 pp.

Myagkov, Aleksei. *Inside the KGB.* London: Foreign Affairs Publishing Co., 1976. 131 pp.

Parming, Tonö, and Elmar Järvesoo. *A Case Study of a Soviet Republic: The Estonian SSR.* Boulder: Westview, 1977. 320 pp.

Payne, Robert. *The Life and Death of Trotsky.* New York: McGraw-Hill, 1977. 498 pp.

Ponomarev, B.N. et al. *Istoriia Kommunisticheskoi Partii Sovetskogo Soiuza.* Moscow: Politizdat, 1976. 5th exp. ed. 782 pp.

Remnek, Richard B. ed. *Social Scientists and Policy Making in the USSR.* New York: Praeger, 1977. 175 pp.

Rothman, Stanley, and George W. Breslauer. *Soviet Politics and Society.* St. Paul: West Publ. Co., 1978. 341 pp.

Shtemenko, Sergei. *The Last Six Months.* New York: Doubleday, 1977. 436 pp.

Simmonds, George W., ed. *Nationalism in the USSR and Eastern Europe in the Era of Brezhnev and Kosygin.* Detroit: Univeristy of Detroit Press, 1977. 534 pp.

Snow, Russell E. *Bolsheviks in Siberia, 1917-1918.* Rutherford, N.J.: Fairleigh Dickinson University Press, 1977. 269 pp.

Stites, Richard. *The Women's Liberation Movement in Russia.* Princeton: Princeton University Press, 1977. 504 pp.

Suslov, Ilya. *Here's to Your Health, Comrade Shifrin!* Bloomington: Indiana University Press, 1977. 224 pp.

Stupperich, Robert, ed. *Kirche im Osten.* Goettingen: Vandenhoeck & Ruprecht, 1976. 192 pp.

Szajkowski, Zosa. *Kolchak, Jews, and the American Intervention in Northern Russia and Siberia, 1918-20.* New York: privately published, 1977. 218 pp.

Szporluk, Roman, ed. *The Influence of East Europe and the Soviet West on the USSR.* New York: Praeger, 1976. 272 pp.

Tucker, Robert C., ed. *Stalinism: Essays in Historical Interpretation.* New York: Norton, 1977. 331 pp.

Ulam, Adam B. *In the Name of the People: Prophets and Conspirators in Pre-revolutionary Russia.* New York: Viking, 1977. 418 pp.

Vanneman, Peter. *The Supreme Soviet.* Durham, N.C.: Duke University Press, 1977. 256 pp.

Voinovich, Vladimir. *The Ivankiad.* New York: Farrar, Straus & Giroux, 1977. 132 pp.

Whetten, Lawrence L., ed. *The Political Implications of Soviet Military Power.* New York: Crane & Russak, 1976. 183 pp.

Yanowitch, Murray. *Social and Economic Inequality in the Soviet Union.* White Plains, N.Y.: Sharpe, 1977. 200 pp.

Yanowitch, Murray, and Wesley A. Fisher, eds. *Social Stratification and Mobility in the USSR.* White Plains. N.Y.: Sharpe, 1977. 402 pp.

Zemtsof, Ilja. *La corruption en Union Soviétique.* Paris: Hachette, 1976. 189 pp.

EASTERN EUROPE

Antal, Endre. *Das Wirtschaftslenkungssystem des ungarischen Sozialismus.* Munich: Oldenbourg, 1976. 179 pp.

Arsintescu, Mihai et al. *National Defense: the Romanian View.* Bucharest: Military Publ. House, 1976. 266 pp.

Ash, William. *Pickaxe and Rifle: The Story of the Albanian People.* London: Howard Baker, 1974. 271 pp.

Bahro, Rudolf. *Die Alternative: zur Kritik des real existierenden Sozialismus.* Cologne: Europeische Verlagsanstalt, 1977. 548 pp.

Borowiec, Andrew. *Yugoslavia after Tito.* New York: Praeger, 1977. 128 pp.

Bracewell-Milnes, Barry. *Eastern and Western European Economic Integration.* New York: St. Martin's, 1976. 218 pp.

Butler, Thomas, ed. *Bulgaria, Past and Present.* Columbus, Ohio: AAASS, 1976. 397 pp.

Castellan, Georges, and Nicolaj Todorov. *La Bulgarie.* Paris: Presse Universitaires, 1976. 128 pp.

Chukanov, O.A. et al. *Sotsialisticheskaia ekonomicheskaia integratsiia.* Moscow: Mysl'., 1977. 335 pp.

Djilas, Milovan. *Wartime.* New York: Harcourt Brace Jovanovitch, 1977. 469 pp.

Doerrer, H., ed. *Arbeiterklasse-Intelligenz-Studenten.* East Berlin: Dietz, 1977. 400 pp.

Dreisziger, Nandor, ed. *The Hungarian Revolution Twenty Years After.* Ottawa: Hungarian Readers' Service, 1976. 219 pp.

Dziewanowski, M.K. *Poland in the 20th Century.* New York: Columbia University Press, 1977. 309 pp.

Enyedi, György. *Hungary: an Economic Geography.* Boulder: Westview, 1976. 289 pp.

Esti, Bela, ed. *The Liberation of Hungary, 1944-1945.* Budapest: Corvina, 1975. 231 pp.

Feiwel, George R. *Growth and Reforms in Centrally Planned Economies: The Lessons of the Bulgarian Experience.* New York: Praeger, 1977. 382 pp.

Fejtö, François. *Le coup de Prague 1948.* Paris: Editions du Seuil, 1976. 282 pp.

Guenther, Reinhard. *Feindbild Bundesrepublik aus der Sicht der DDR.* Bonn: Hochwacht, 1976. 206 pp.

Hacker, Jens. *Deutsche unter sich: Politik mit dem Grundvertrag.* Stuttgart: Seewald, 1977. 192 pp.

Hamel, Hannelore, ed. *BRD-DDR: Die Wirtschaftssysteme.* Munich: Beck, 1977. 220 pp.

Hanak, Tibor. *Die marxistische Philosophie und Soziologie in Ungarn.* Stuttgart: Enke, 1976. 231 pp.

Havemann, Robert. *Berliner Schriften, 1968-1976.* Berlin: Europeische Ideen, 1976. 100 pp.

Hegedüs, András et al. *The Humanization of Socialism: Writings of the Budapest School.* London: Allison & Busby, 1976. 177 pp.

Hejzlar, Zdenek, *Reformkommunismus: Zur Geschichte der Kommunistischen Partei der Tschechoslovakai.* Cologne: Europeische Verlagsanstalt, 1976. 497 pp.

Hergt, Siegfried. *DDR heute.* Leverkusen: Hegen, 1976. 360 pp.

Honecker, Erich. *Ausgewaehlte Reden und Schriften zur Militaerpolitik der SED.* East Berlin: Militaerverlag, 1977. 272 pp.

Horvat, Branko, *The Yugoslav Economic System.* White Plains, N.Y.: International Arts & Sciences, 1976. 400 pp.

Hoxha, Enver. *La grande divergence, 1960.* Paris: Nouveau bureau d'edition, 1976. 309 pp.

———. *Resistenza e Rivoluzione (Scritti Scelti, 1941-1944).* Milan: Mazzotta, 1977. 319 pp.

———. *Speeches and Articles, 1963-1964.* Tirana: The "8 Nëntori" Publishing House, 1977. 394 pp.

Ivanovic, Vane. *Memoirs of a Yugoslav.* New York: Harcourt Brace Jovanovich, 1977. 435 pp.

Janos, Andrew C., ed. *Authoritarian Politics in Communist Europe.* Berkeley: Institute of International Studies, 1976. 196 pp.

Korbel, Josef. *Twentieth Century Czechoslovakia.* New York: Columbia University Press, 1977. 346 pp.

Lasic-Vasojevic, Milija M. *Enemies on All Sides. The Fall of Yugoslavia.* Washington, D.C.: North American International, 1976. 290 pp.

Legters, Lyman H., ed. *The German Democratic Republic.* Boulder: Westview, 1977. 300 pp.

Logoreci, Anton. *The Albanians: Europe's Forgotten Survivors.* London: Gollancz, 1977. 230 pp.

Lippman, Heinz. *Honecker and the New Politics of Europe.* New York: Macmillan, 1977. 272 pp.

Ludz, Peter C. *Die DDR zwischen Ost und West, von 1961 bis 1976.* Munich: Beck, 1977. 367 pp.

Mlynar, Zdenek. *Praga, questione aperta.* Bari: De Donato, 1976. 284 pp.

Pastor, Peter. *Hungary Between Wilson and Lenin.* New York: Columbia University Press, 1976. 191 pp.

Pelikan, Jiri. *Socialist Oppositon in Eastern Europe: The Czechoslovak Example.* New York: St. Martin's, 1977. 221 pp.

Ra'anan, Gavriel D. *Yugoslavia after Tito.* Boulder: Westview, 1977. 125 pp.

Rakowska-Harmstone, Teresa, ed. *Perspectives for Change in Communist Societies.* Boulder: Westview, 1977. 200 pp.

Reuter-Hendrichs, Irena. *Jugoslawische Aussenpolitik, 1948-1968.* Cologne: Heyman, 1976. 363 pp.

Robinson, Gertrude Joch. *Tito's Maverick Media.* Urbana: University of Illinois Press, 1977. 263 pp.

Rusinow, Dennison. *The Yugoslav Experiment 1948-1976.* Berkeley: University of California Press, 1977. 431 pp.

Schwarzenbach, Rudolf. *Die Kaderpolitik der SED in der Staatsverwaltung.* Cologne: Wissenschaft & Politik, 1976. 243 pp.

Sher, Gerson S. *Praxis: Marxist Criticism and Dissent in Yugoslavia.* Bloomington: Indiana University Press. 1977. 383 pp.

Sïk, Ota. *Czechoslovakia: The Bureaucratic Economy.* White Plains, N.Y.: International Arts & Sciences Press, 1977. 138 pp.

Sozialistische Einheitspartei Deutschland. *Protokoll der Verhandlungen des IX. Parteitages.* East Berlin: Dietz, 1976. 2 vols.

Staar, Richard F. *Communist Regimes in Eastern Europe.* Stanford: Hoover Institution Press, 1977. 3rd rev. ed. 302 pp.

Staritz, Dietrich. *Sozialismus in einem halben Lande.* East Berlin: Wagenbach, 1976. 196 pp.

Steele, Jonathan. *Inside East Germany.* New York: Urizen, 1977. 256 pp.

Stroehm, Carl G. *Ohne Tito, kann Jugoslawien ueberleben?* Graz: Styria, 1976. 304 pp.

Triska, Jan F., and Paul M. Cocks, eds. *Political Development in Eastern Europe.* New York: Praeger, 1977. 374 pp.

Tökei, Ferenc. *Zur Theorie der Gesellschaftsformen.* Budapest: Akademiai Kiado, 1977. 150 pp.

Toma, Peter A., and Ivan Völgyes. *Politics in Hungary.* San Francisco: Freeman, 1977. 188 pp.

Van Brabant, Jozef M. *East European Cooperation: The Role of Money and Finance.* New York: Praeger, 1976. 426 pp.

Vanek, Jaroslav. *The Labour-Managed Economy.* Ithaca: Cornell University Press, 1977. 287 pp.

Völgyes, Ivan, and Nancy Völgyes. *The Liberated Female: Life, Work, and Sex in Socialist Hungary.* Boulder: Westview, 1977. 175 pp.

WESTERN EUROPE

Albright, David E., ed. *Communism and Political Systems in Western Europe.* Boulder: Westview, 1977. 320 pp.

Alvarez, Santiago. *El Partido comunista y el campo.* Madrid: Ediciones de la Torre, 1977. 258 pp.

Amendola, Giorgio. *Gli anni della repubblica.* Rome: Riuniti, 1976. 356 pp.

Becker, Jillian. *Hitler's Children.* New York: Lippincott, 1977. 322 pp.

Berlinguer, Enrico. *La politica internazionale dei comunisti italiani, 1975-1976.* Rome: Riuniti, 1976. 226 pp.

Berlinguer, Enrico et al. *Il ruolo dei giovani comunisti: breve storia della FGCI.* Florence: Guaraldi, 1976. 165 pp.

Blackmer, Donald M.L., and Sidney Tarrow. *Communism in Italy and France.* Princeton, N.J.: Princeton University Press, 1977. 664 pp.

Boldrini, Arrigo et al. *La politica militare dei comunisti.* Rome: Riuniti, 1976. 233 pp.

Calhoun, Daniel F. *The United Front: The TUC and the Russians, 1923-1928.* New York: Cambridge University Press, 1976. 450 pp.

Carrillo, Santiago. *Eurocomunismo y estado.* Barcelona: Editorial Critica, 1977. 218 pp.

———. *Partido Comunista de Espana.* Barcelona. Avance-Manana, 1976. 108 pp.

Cerny, Karl H., ed. *Scandinavia at the Polls: Recent Political Trends in Denmark, Norway, and Sweden.* Washington, D.C.: American Enterprise Institute, 1977. 304 pp.

Clark, Martin. *Antoniò Gramsci and the Revolution that Failed.* New Haven: Yale University Press, 1977. 256 pp.

Claudin, Fernando. *L'Eurocommunisme.* Paris: Maspero, 1977. 192 pp.

Comin, Alfonso C. *Cristianos en el partido, comunistas en la iglesia.* Barcelona: Iaia, 1977. 211 pp.

Communist Party of Great Britain. *The Little Red Struggler: A Handbook for Student Militants.* London: The Committee, 1976. 56 pp.

Cunhal, Alvaro. *A questao do estado questao central de cada revolução.* Lisbon: Avante, 1977. 39 pp.

Couloumbis, Theodore A. et al. *Foreign Interference in Greek Politics.* New York: Pella, 1976. 171 pp.

Dalma, Alfons. *Eurokommunismus: Italien, Frankreich, Jugoslawien, Spanien, Portugal.* Zurich: Interform, 1977. 110 pp.

Di Palma, Giuseppe. *Surviving without Governing.* Berkeley: University of California Press, 1977. 315 pp.

Ellenstein, Jean. *Le P.C.* Paris: Grasset, 1976. 224 pp.

Fabre, Jean et al. *Les communistes et l'état.* Paris: Editions Sociales, 1977. 253 pp.

Faller, Ugo. *Berlinguer: Il marxismo in doppiopetto.* Milan: Everest, 1976. 221 pp.

Ferreira, Francisco. *Alvaro Cunhal, heroi Sovietico: subsidios para uma biografia.* Lisbon: "O Seculo," 1976. 136 pp.

Fonveille-Alquier, François, *L'Eurocommunisme.* Paris: Fayard, 1977. 290 pp.

Fougermollas, Pierre. *La révolution prolétarienne et les impasses petites-bourgeoises.* Paris: Anthropos, 1976. 294 pp.

Garcia, Angel. *El Eurocomunismo.* Barcelona: Acerbo, 1977. 208 pp.

Glucksmann, André. *Les maîtres penseurs.* Paris: Grasset, 1977. 321 pp.

Gruppi, Luciano. *Il compromesso storico.* Rome: Riuniti, 1977. 345 pp.

Hobsbawm, Eric. *The Italian Road to Socialism.* Westport: Lawrence Hill, 1977. 118 pp.

Keefe, Eugene K. et al. *Area Handbook for Italy.* Washington, D.C.: Government Printing Office, 1977. 296 pp.

Kimmel, Adolf, ed. *Eurokommunismus: Die kommunistischen Parteien Frankreichs, Italien, Spaniens und Portugals.* Vienna: Boehlau, 1977. 320 pp.

Kommunistischer Arbeiterbund Deutschlands. *Was ist die KPD Fuehrung?* Stuttgart: Neuer Weg, 1977. 90 pp.

Kommunistische Partei Deutschlands. *Programm der KPD.* Cologne: Rote Fahne, 1977. 70 pp.

Kommunistische Partei Deutschlands (M/L). *III. Parteitag.* Ludwigshafen: Roter Morgen, 1977. 127 pp.

Kommunistische Partei Oesterreichs. *Beitraege zur Geschichte der KPOe.* Vienna: KPOe, 1976. 112 pp.

Kriegel, Annie. *Un autre communisme?* Paris: Hachette, 1977. 183 pp.

Lecoeur, Auguste. *Le P.C.F., continuité dans le changement.* Paris: Laffont, 1977. 312 pp.

Luciano, Giacomo. *Il PCI e il capitalismo occidentale.* Milan: Longanesi, 1977. 184 pp.

Mailer, Phil. *Portugal: The Impossible Revolution?* New York: Free Life, 1977. 399 pp.

Maude, George. *The Finnish Dilemma: Neutrality in the Shadow of Power.* New York: Oxford University Press, 1976. 153 pp.

Meney, Patrick. *L'Italie de Berlinguer.* Paris: Lattés, 1976. 314 pp.

Mer, Jacqueline. *Le Parti de Maurice Thorez ou le bonheur communiste français.* Paris: Payot, 1977. 248 pp.

Montaldo, Jean. *Les finances du P.C.F.* Paris: Albin Michel, 1977. 236 pp.

El PC español, italiano, y françes cara el poder. Madrid: Editorial Cambio 16, 1977. 201 pp.

Padovani, Marcelle. *La longue marche; le Parti Communiste Italien.* Paris: Calmann-Levy, 1976. 207 pp.

Pinto, Jaime Nogueira. *Portugal os anos do fim: a revolução que veio de dentro.* Lisbon: Sociedade de Publicações Economia e Financas, 1976. 276 pp.

Revesz, Laszlo. *A imprensa comunista e o avanço do P.C.P.* Lisbon: Selecta, 1976. 132 pp.

Salisbury, William T. *Spain in the 1970s.* New York: Praeger, 1976. 208 pp.

Spallone, Mario. *Vent'anni con Togliatti.* Milan: Teti, 1976. 164pp.

Tarrow, Sidney, *Between Center and Periphery.* New Haven: Yale University Press, 1977. 272 pp.

Tigrid, Pavel. *Amère Révolution.* Paris: Albin Michel, 1977. 288 pp.

Tato, Antonio. *Enrico Berlinguer: La Politica internazionale dei comunisti italiani, 1975-1976.* Rome: Riuniti, 1976. 226 pp.

Tavares-Teles, Antonio. *Otelo.* Lisbon: Boa Nova, 1976. 318 pp.

Togliatti, Palmiro. *I corsivi di Roderigo: interventi politico-culturali dal 1944 al 1964.* Bari: De Donato, 1976. 420 pp.

U.S. Library of Congress. Foreign Affairs and National Defense Division. *West European Communist Parties.* Washington, D.C.: Government Printing Office, 1977. 326 pp.

Valli, Bernardo, ed. *Gli eurocomunisti.* Milan: Bompiani, 1976. 256 pp.

ASIA AND THE PACIFIC

Ahn, Byung-joon. *Chinese Politics and the Cultural Revolution.* Seattle: University of Washington Press, 1977. 406 pp.

Barron, John. *Murder of a Gentle Land.* New York: Crowell, 1977. 240 pp.

Bernstein, Thomas P. *Up to the Mountains and Down to the Villages.* New Haven: Yale University Press, 1977. 432 pp.

Brugger, Bill. *Contemporary China.* New York: Barnes & Noble, 1977. 451 pp.

Carney, Timothy M., comp. *Communist Party Power in Kampuchea (Cambodia): Documents and Discussion.* Ithaca: Cornell University, 1977. 76 pp.

Choudhury, G.W. *Chinese Perception of the World.* Washington, D.C.: University Press of America, 1977. 105 pp.

Chu, Godwin C. *Radical Change through Communication in Mao's China.* Honolulu: University Press of Hawaii, 1977. 340 pp.

Domes, Juergen. *China after the Cultural Revolution.* Berkeley: University of California Press, 1977. 350 pp.

Dreyer, June T. *China's Forty Millions: Minority Nationalities and National Integration in the People's Republic of China.* Cambridge: Harvard University Press, 1976. 337 pp.

Dung, Van Tien. *Our Great Spring Victory: An Account of the Liberation of South Vietnam.* New York: Monthly Review, 1977. 275 pp.

Graebner, Norman A., ed. *Nationalism and Communism in Asia: The American Response.* Lexington: Heath, 1977. 204 pp.

Gurley, John G. *China's Economy and the Maoist Strategy.* New York: Monthly Review, 1976. 325 pp.

Hiniker, Paul J. *Revolutionary Ideology and Chinese Reality: Dissonance under Mao.* Beverly Hills: Sage, 1977. 320 pp.

Hofheinz, Roy, Jr. *The Broken Wave: The Chinese Communist Peasant Movement, 1922-1928.* Cambridge: Harvard University Press, 1977. 355 pp.

Hsüeh, Chun-tu. *Dimensions of China's Foreign Relations.* New York: Praeger, 1977. 310 pp.

Jain, Jagdish P. *China, Pakistan and Bangladesh.* New Delhi: Radiant, 1976. 264 pp.

Kim, Se-jin, ed. *Korean Unification.* Seoul: Research Center for Peace & Unification, 1977. 420 pp.

Lee, Chong-Sik, ed. *Materials on Korean Communism, 1945-1947.* Honolulu: University of Hawaii Press, 1977. 251 pp.

Leys, Simon. *Chinese Shadows.* New York: Viking, 1977. 220 pp.

Lindsay, Michael, ed. *The New Constitution of Communist China: Comparative Analyses.* Taipei: Institute of International Relations, 1976. 348 pp.

Mackerras, C., ed. *China: The Impact of Revolution.* New York: Longman, 1976. 256 pp.

Maitan, Livio. *Party, Army and Masses in China.* Atlantic Highlands, N.J.: Humanities Press, 1976. 373 pp.

Marxism on Vedanta: Papers of the Conference on the Communist Party of India, 6-7 May 1975. New Delhi: People's Publishing House, 1976. 293 pp.

Meisner, Maurice. *Mao's China.* New York: Free Press. 1977. 480 pp.

Mongol'skaia narodno-revoliutsionnaia partiia. Moscow: Politizdat, 1977. 174 pp.

Namboodiripad, E.M.S. *How I Became a Communist.* Trivandrum: Chinta, 1976. 211 pp.

Nelsen, Harvey W. *The Chinese Military System.* Boulder: Westview, 1977. 267 pp.

Penniman, Howard R., ed. *Australia at the Polls: National Elections of 1975.* Washington, D.C.: American Enterprise Institute, 1977. 373 pp.

Peyrefitte, Alain. *The Chinese.* Indianapolis: Bobbs-Merrill, 1977. 419 pp.

Pohl, Manfred. *Die Bauernpolitik der kommunistischen Partei Japans, 1922-1928.* Hamburg: Gesellschaft fuer Natur- und Voelkerkunde Ostasiens, 1976. 297 pp.

———. *Die Kommunistische Partei Japans.* Hamburg: Institut fuer Asienkunde, 1976. 341 pp.

Ponchaud, François. *Cambodge, année zéro.* Paris: Julliard, 1977. 250 pp.

Printz, Peggy, and Paul Steinle. *Commune Life in Rural China.* New York: Dodd Mead, 1977. 192 pp.

Rai Chowdhuri, Satyabrata. *Leftist Movements in India, 1917-1947.* Columbia, Mo.: South Asia Books, 1977. 313 pp.

Ro, Kwang H., and Tomas D. Wu. *China: Rise of Communism, and Foreign Relations since 1949.* Washington, D.C.: University Press of America, 1977. 239 pp.

Roy, Asish Kumer. *Communism in Asia: A Study in Strategy and Tactics.* Calcutta: Progressive, 1976. 144 pp.

Roy, Subodh, ed. *Communism in India; Unpublished Documents, 1935-1945.* Calcutta: National Book Agency, 1976. 419 pp.

Schell, Orville. *In the People's Republic.* New York: Random House, 1977. 271 pp.

Schran, Peter. *Guerrilla Economy: The Development of the Shensi-Kansu-Ninghsia Border Region, 1937-1945.* Albany: State University of New York Press, 1976. 323 pp.

Souvannaphouma, Prince Mangkra. *L'Agonie du Laos.* Paris: Plon, 1976. 221 pp.

Sutter, Robert G. *Chinese Foreign Policy after the Cultural Revolution.* Boulder: Westview, 1977. 150 pp.

Vladimirov, Oleg E., and V. Ryazantsev. *Mao Tse-Tung: A Political Portrait.* Moscow: Progress, 1976. 152 pp.

Vreeland, Nina et al. *Area Handbook for Singapore.* Washington, D.C.: Government Printing Office, 1977. 216 pp.

Weggel, Oskar. *Die Aussenpolitik der Volksrepublik China.* Stuttgart: Kohlhammer, 1977. 172 pp.

Williams, Justina. *The First Furrow.* Willagee: Lone Hand Press, 1976. 184 pp.

Wilson, Amy A. et al., eds. *Deviance and Social Control in Chinese Society.* New York: Præger, 1977. 250 pp.

Wilson, Dick, ed. *Mao Tse-Tung in the Scales of History.* New York: Cambridge University Press, 1977. 256 pp.

Witke, Roxane. *Comrade Chiang Ch'ing.* Boston: Little, Brown, 1977. 549 pp.

Wong, Paul. *China's Higher Leadership in the Socialist Tradition.* New York: Free Press, 1976. 310 pp.

THE AMERICAS

Artola Azcarate, Armando. *¡Subversion!* Lima, 1976. 207 pp.

Black, Jan Knippers, ed. *Area Handbook for Cuba.* Washington, D.C.: Government Printing Office, 1976. 550 pp.

Boorstein, Edward. *Allende's Chile: An Inside View.* New York: International Publ., 1977. 277 pp.

Castro, Fidel, *La experiencia cubana.* Barcelona: Blume, 1976. 317 pp.

Cochran, Bert. *Labor and Communism: The Conflict that Shaped American Unions.* Princeton: Princeton University Press, 1977. 440 pp.

De Vylder, Stefan. *Allende's Chile.* New York: Cambridge University Press, 1976. 251 pp.

Dennis, Peggy. *Autobiography of an American Communist.* Berkeley: Creative Arts, 1977. 300 pp.

Fontaine, Arturo A. et al. *Nuestro camino.* Santiago: Encina, 1976. 259 pp.

Franqui, Carlos. *Diario de la revolucion cubana.* Paris: Ruedo Iberico, 1976. 753 pp.

Gari, Juan José. *Orientalidad y nacionalismo.* Montevideo: Barreiro y Ramos, 1976. 98 pp.

Gonzalez Ruiz, José Maria. *The New Creation: Marxist and Christian?* Maryknoll, N.Y.: Orbis, 1976. 150 pp.

Henfrey, Colin, and Bernardo Sorj, comps. *Chilean Voices.* London: Harvester Press, 1977. 196 pp.

Hodges, Donald C. *Argentina, 1943-1976: The National Revolution and Resistance.* Albuquerque: University of New Mexico Press, 1976. 208 pp.

Izquierdo Quintana, Francisco. *Democracia sin comunismo.* Miami: Filocuba, 1976. 108 pp.

Labarca Goddard, Eduardo. *Vida y lucha de Luis Corvalan.* Mexico City: Cultura popular, 1976. 153 pp.

Lewis, Oscar et al. *Four Men Living the Revolution. An Oral History of Contemporary Cuba.* Urbana: University of Illinois Press, 1977. 538 pp.

Loveman, Brian. *Struggle in the Countryside.* Bloomington: Indiana University Press, 1976. 439 pp.

Mitford, Jessica. *A Fine Old Conflict.* New York: Knopf, 1977. 333 pp.

Myers, Constance Ashton. *The Prophet's Army: Trotskyists in America, 1928-1941.* Westport: Greenwood Press, 1977. 281 pp.

Needler, Martin C. *An Introduction to Latin American Politics: The Structure of Conflict.* Englewood Cliffs, N.J.: Prentice-Hall, 1977. 358 pp.

Partido Comunista Brasileiro. *Documentos de Partido Comunista Brasileiro, 1960-1975.* Lisbon: Avante, 1976. 234 pp.

Partido Comunista de Cuba. *The First Congress of the Communist Party of Cuba (December 17-22, 1975).* Moscow: Novosti, 1976.

El Partido Comunista Mexicano y el movimiento sindical. Mexico City: Cultura Popular, 1976. 184 pp.

Partido Comunista Peruano (M/L). *Documentos de la VII Conferencia Nacional.* Lima: Lucha de Clases, 1976. 99 pp.

Ravines, Eudocio. *Derrota mundial del comunismo.* Mexico City: G. de Anda, 1977. 337 pp.

Vekemans, Roger. *Teologia de la liberacion y cristianos por el socialismo.* Bogota: CEDIAL, 1976. 592 pp.

Weisbord, Vera B. *A Radical Life.* Bloomington: Indiana University Press, 1977. 330 pp.

Winston, Henry. *Class, Race and Black Liberation.* New York: International Publ., 1977. 242 pp.

Wright, Richard. *American Hunger.* New York: Harper & Row, 1977. 146 pp.

Young, Nigel. *An Infantile Disorder? The Crisis and Decline of the New Left.* Boulder: Westview, 1977. 484 pp.

Zhuchkova, Galina E. *Kolumbiia: kommunisty v bor'be za edinstvo narodnykh mass, 1958-1974.* Moscow: Nauka, 1976. 137 pp.

MIDDLE EAST AND AFRICA

Amirsadeghi, Hossein, ed. *Twentieth-Century Iran.* London: Heinemann, 1977. 299 pp.

Batatu, John. *The Old Social Classes and the Revolutionary Movements of Iraq.* Princeton: Princeton University Press, 1977. 1,184 pp.

Bechtold, Peter K. *Politics in the Sudan.* New York: Praeger, 1976. 359 pp.

Carter, Gwendolen M., and Patrick O'Meara, eds. *Southern Africa in Crisis.* Bloomington: Indiana University Press, 1977. 279 pp.

Farer, Tom J. *War Clouds on the Horn of Africa.* New York: Carnegie Endowment, 1976. 157 pp.

Gjerstad, Ole. *The People in Power: An Account from Angola's Second War of National Liberation.* Richmond, Canada: LSM Information Center, 1977. 108 pp.

Ismael, Tareq Y. *The Arab Left.* Syracuse: Syracuse University Press, 1977. 204 pp.

Johnson, R.W. *How Long Will South Africa Survive?* New York: Oxford University Press, 1977. 328 pp.

Kaplan, Irving et al., eds. *Area Handbook for Somalia.* Washington, D.C.: Government Printing Office, 1977. 392 pp.

Lee, Franz J.T. *Suedafrika am Vorabend der Revolution.* Frankfurt/Main: ISP Verlag, 1976. 231 pp.

Mamdani, Mahmood. *Politics and Class Formation in Uganda.* New York: Monthly Review, 1976. 339 pp.

Olorunsola, Victor A. *Soldiers and Power: The Development Performance of the Nigerian Military Regime.* Stanford: Hoover Institution Press, 1977. 169 pp.

Pearson, Roger, ed. *Sino-Soviet Intervention in Africa.* Washington, D.C.: Council on American Affairs, 1977. 103 pp.

Rubinstein, Alvin Z., ed. *Soviet and Chinese Influence in the Third World.* New York: Praeger, 1976. 232 pp.

Steenkamp, Willem. *Adeus Angola.* Cape Town: Howard Timmins, 1976. 145 pp.

U.S. Congress, House of Representatives Committee on International Relations. *The Soviet Union and the Third World: A Watershed in Great Power Policy?* Washington, D.C.: Government Printing Office, 1977. 186 pp.

Wassenaar, Andrea D. *Assault on Private Enterprise: The Freeway to Communism.* Cape Town: Tafelberg, 1977. 159 pp.

Zarodov, K.I., ed. *The National Liberation Movement: A Component of the Alliance of the World Revolutionary Forces.* Prague: Peace and Socialism, 1976. 117 pp.

INDEX OF NAMES